Praise for the First Edition of
Hadoop in Practice

A new book from Manning, Hadoop in Practice, *is definitely the most modern book on the topic. Important subjects, like what commercial variants such as MapR offer, and the many different releases and APIs get uniquely good coverage in this book.*

—Ted Dunning, Chief Application Architect, MapR Technologies

Comprehensive coverage of advanced Hadoop usage, including high-quality code samples.

—Chris Nauroth, Senior Staff Software Engineer
The Walt Disney Company

A very pragmatic and broad overview of Hadoop and the Hadoop tools ecosystem, with a wide set of interesting topics that tickle the creative brain.

—Mark Kemna, Chief Technology Officer, Brilig

A practical introduction to the Hadoop ecosystem.

—Philipp K. Janert, Principal Value, LLC

This book is the horizontal roof that each of the pillars of individual Hadoop technology books hold. It expertly ties together all the Hadoop ecosystem technologies.

—Ayon Sinha, Big Data Architect, Britely

I would take this book on my path to the future.

—Alexey Gayduk, Senior Software Engineer, Grid Dynamics

A high-quality and well-written book that is packed with useful examples. The breadth and detail of the material is by far superior to any other Hadoop reference guide. It is perfect for anyone who likes to learn new tools/technologies while following pragmatic, real-world examples.

—Amazon reviewer

Hadoop in Practice
Second Edition

ALEX HOLMES

MANNING

Shelter Island

For online information and ordering of this and other Manning books, please visit www.manning.com. The publisher offers discounts on this book when ordered in quantity. For more information, please contact

Special Sales Department
Manning Publications Co.
20 Baldwin Road
PO Box 761
Shelter Island, NY 11964
Email: orders@manning.com

Manning Publications Co.
20 Baldwin Road
Shelter Island, NY 11964

Development editor: Cynthia Kane
Copyeditor: Andy Carroll
Proofreader: Melody Dolab
Typesetter: Gordan Salinovic
Cover designer: Marija Tudor

ISBN 9781617292224
Printed in the United States of America
1 2 3 4 5 6 7 8 9 10 – EBM – 19 18 17 16 15 14

brief contents

contents

5 *Moving data into and out of Hadoop   174*

PART 3 BIG DATA PATTERNS.....................................253

preface

I first encountered Hadoop in the fall of 2008 when I was working on an internet crawl-and-analysis project at Verisign. We were making discoveries similar to those that Doug Cutting and others at Nutch had made several years earlier about how to efficiently store and manage terabytes of crawl-and-analyzed data. At the time, we were getting by with our homegrown distributed system, but the influx of a new data stream and requirements to join that stream with our crawl data couldn't be supported by our existing system in the required timeline.

After some research, we came across the Hadoop project, which seemed to be a perfect fit for our needs—it supported storing large volumes of data and provided a compute mechanism to combine them. Within a few months, we built and deployed a MapReduce application encompassing a number of MapReduce jobs, woven together with our own MapReduce workflow management system, onto a small cluster of 18 nodes. It was a revelation to observe our MapReduce jobs crunching through our data in minutes. Of course, what we weren't expecting was the amount of time that we would spend debugging and performance-tuning our MapReduce jobs. Not to mention the new roles we took on as production administrators—the biggest surprise in this role was the number of disk failures we encountered during those first few months supporting production.

As our experience and comfort level with Hadoop grew, we continued to build more of our functionality using Hadoop to help with our scaling challenges. We also started to evangelize the use of Hadoop within our organization and helped kick-start other projects that were also facing big data challenges.

The greatest challenge we faced when working with Hadoop, and specifically MapReduce, was relearning how to solve problems with it. MapReduce is its own flavor of parallel programming, and it's quite different from the in-JVM programming that we were accustomed to. The first big hurdle was training our brains to think MapReduce, a topic which the book *Hadoop in Action* by Chuck Lam (Manning Publications, 2010) covers well.

After one is used to thinking in MapReduce, the next challenge is typically related to the logistics of working with Hadoop, such as how to move data in and out of HDFS and effective and efficient ways to work with data in Hadoop. These areas of Hadoop haven't received much coverage, and that's what attracted me to the potential of this book—the chance to go beyond the fundamental word-count Hadoop uses and covering some of the trickier and dirtier aspects of Hadoop.

As I'm sure many authors have experienced, I went into this project confidently believing that writing this book was just a matter of transferring my experiences onto paper. Boy, did I get a reality check, but not altogether an unpleasant one, because writing introduced me to new approaches and tools that ultimately helped better my own Hadoop abilities. I hope that you get as much out of reading this book as I did writing it.

acknowledgments

First and foremost, I want to thank Michael Noll, who pushed me to write this book. He provided invaluable insights into how to structure the content of the book, reviewed my early chapter drafts, and helped mold the book. I can't express how much his support and encouragement has helped me throughout the process.

I'm also indebted to Cynthia Kane, my development editor at Manning, who coached me through writing this book and provided invaluable feedback on my work. Among the many notable "aha!" moments I had when working with Cynthia, the biggest one was when she steered me into using visual aids to help explain some of the complex concepts in this book.

All of the Manning staff were a pleasure to work with, and a special shout out goes to Troy Mott, Nick Chase, Tara Walsh, Bob Herbstman, Michael Stephens, Marjan Bace, Maureen Spencer, and Kevin Sullivan.

I also want to say a big thank you to all the reviewers of this book: Adam Kawa, Andrea Tarocchi, Anna Lahoud, Arthur Zubarev, Edward Ribeiro, Fillipe Massuda, Gerd Koenig, Jeet Marwah, Leon Portman, Mohamed Diouf, Muthuswamy Manigandan, Rodrigo Abreu, and Serega Sheypack. Jonathan Siedman, the primary technical reviewer, did a great job of reviewing the entire book.

Many thanks to Josh Wills, the creator of Crunch, who kindly looked over the chapter that covered that topic. And more thanks go to Josh Patterson, who reviewed my Mahout chapter.

Finally, a special thanks to my wife, Michal, who had to put up with a cranky husband working crazy hours. She was a source of encouragement throughout the entire process.

about this book

Doug Cutting, the creator of Hadoop, likes to call Hadoop the kernel for big data, and I would tend to agree. With its distributed storage and compute capabilities, Hadoop is fundamentally an enabling technology for working with huge datasets. Hadoop provides a bridge between structured (RDBMS) and unstructured (log files, XML, text) data and allows these datasets to be easily joined together. This has evolved from traditional use cases, such as combining OLTP and log files, to more sophisticated uses, such as using Hadoop for data warehousing (exemplified by Facebook) and the field of data science, which studies and makes new discoveries about data.

This book collects a number of intermediary and advanced Hadoop examples and presents them in a problem/solution format. Each technique addresses a specific task you'll face, like using Flume to move log files into Hadoop or using Mahout for predictive analysis. Each problem is explored step by step, and as you work through them, you'll find yourself growing more comfortable with Hadoop and at home in the world of big data.

This hands-on book targets users who have some practical experience with Hadoop and understand the basic concepts of MapReduce and HDFS. Manning's *Hadoop in Action* by Chuck Lam contains the necessary prerequisites to understand and apply the techniques covered in this book.

Many techniques in this book are Java-based, which means readers are expected to possess an intermediate-level knowledge of Java. An excellent text for all levels of Java users is *Effective Java*, Second Edition by Joshua Bloch (Addison-Wesley, 2008).

Roadmap

This book has 10 chapters divided into four parts.

Part 1 contains two chapters that form the introduction to this book. They review Hadoop basics and look at how to get Hadoop up and running on a single host. YARN, which is new in Hadoop version 2, is also examined, and some operational tips are provided for performing basic functions in YARN.

Part 2, "Data logistics," consists of three chapters that cover the techniques and tools required to deal with data fundamentals, how to work with various data formats, how to organize and optimize your data, and getting data into and out of Hadoop. Picking the right format for your data and determining how to organize data in HDFS are the first items you'll need to address when working with Hadoop, and they're covered in chapters 3 and 4 respectively. Getting data into Hadoop is one of the bigger hurdles commonly encountered when working with Hadoop, and chapter 5 is dedicated to looking at a variety of tools that work with common enterprise data sources.

Part 3 is called "Big data patterns," and it looks at techniques to help you work effectively with large volumes of data. Chapter 6 covers how to represent data such as graphs for use with MapReduce, and it looks at several algorithms that operate on graph data. Chapter 7 looks at more advanced data structures and algorithms such as graph processing and using HyperLogLog for working with large datasets. Chapter 8 looks at how to tune, debug, and test MapReduce performance issues, and it also covers a number of techniques to help make your jobs run faster.

Part 4 is titled "Beyond MapReduce," and it examines a number of technologies that make it easier to work with Hadoop. Chapter 9 covers the most prevalent and promising SQL technologies for data processing on Hadoop, and Hive, Impala, and Spark SQL are examined. The final chapter looks at how to write your own YARN application, and it provides some insights into some of the more advanced features you can use in your applications.

The appendix covers instructions for the source code that accompanies this book, as well as installation instructions for Hadoop and all the other related technologies covered in the book.

Finally, there are two bonus chapters available from the publisher's website at www.manning.com/HadoopinPracticeSecondEdition: chapter 11 "Integrating R and Hadoop for statistics and more" and chapter 12 "Predictive analytics with Mahout."

What's new in the second edition?

This second edition covers Hadoop 2, which at the time of writing is the current production-ready version of Hadoop. The first edition of the book covered Hadoop 0.22 (Hadoop 1 wasn't yet out), and Hadoop 2 has turned the world upside-down and opened up the Hadoop platform to processing paradigms beyond MapReduce. YARN, the new scheduler and application manager in Hadoop 2, is complex and new to the community, which prompted me to dedicate a new chapter 2 to covering YARN basics and to discussing how MapReduce now functions as a YARN application.

Parquet has also recently emerged as a new way to store data in HDFS—its columnar format can yield both space and time efficiencies in your data pipelines, and it's quickly becoming the ubiquitous way to store data. Chapter 4 includes extensive coverage of Parquet, which includes how Parquet supports sophisticated object models such as Avro and how various Hadoop tools can use Parquet.

How data is being ingested into Hadoop has also evolved since the first edition, and Kafka has emerged as the new data pipeline, which serves as the transport tier between your data producers and data consumers, where a consumer would be a system such as Camus that can pull data from Kafka into HDFS. Chapter 5, which covers moving data into and out of Hadoop, now includes coverage of Kafka and Camus.

There are many new technologies that YARN now can support side by side in the same cluster, and some of the more exciting and promising technologies are covered in the new part 4, titled "Beyond MapReduce," where I cover some compelling new SQL technologies such as Impala and Spark SQL. The last chapter, also new for this edition, looks at how you can write your own YARN application, and it's packed with information about important features to support your YARN application.

Getting help

You'll no doubt have many questions when working with Hadoop. Luckily, between the wikis and a vibrant user community, your needs should be well covered:

- The main wiki is located at http://wiki.apache.org/hadoop/, and it contains useful presentations, setup instructions, and troubleshooting instructions.
- The Hadoop Common, HDFS, and MapReduce mailing lists can all be found at http://hadoop.apache.org/mailing_lists.html.
- "Search Hadoop" is a useful website that indexes all of Hadoop and its ecosystem projects, and it provides full-text search capabilities: http://search-hadoop.com/.
- You'll find many useful blogs you should subscribe to in order to keep on top of current events in Hadoop. This preface includes a selection of my favorites:

  - Cloudera and Hortonworks are both prolific writers of practical applications on Hadoop—reading their blogs is always educational: http://www.cloudera.com/blog/ and http://hortonworks.com/blog/.

  - Michael Noll is one of the first bloggers to provide detailed setup instructions for Hadoop, and he continues to write about real-life challenges: www.michael-noll.com/.

  - There's a plethora of active Hadoop Twitter users that you may want to follow, including Arun Murthy (@acmurthy), Tom White (@tom_e_white), Eric Sammer (@esammer), Doug Cutting (@cutting), and Todd Lipcon (@tlipcon). The Hadoop project tweets on @hadoop.

Code conventions and downloads

All source code in listings or in text is presented in a fixed-width font like this to separate it from ordinary text. Code annotations accompany many of the listings, highlighting important concepts.

All of the text and examples in this book work with Hadoop 2.x, and most of the MapReduce code is written using the newer org.apache.hadoop.mapreduce Map-Reduce APIs. The few examples that use the older org.apache.hadoop.mapred package are usually the result of working with a third-party library or a utility that only works with the old API.

All of the code used in this book is available on GitHub at https://github.com/alexholmes/hiped2 and also from the publisher's website at www.manning.com/HadoopinPracticeSecondEdition. The first section in the appendix shows you how to download, install, and get up and running with the code.

Third-party libraries

I use a number of third-party libraries for convenience purposes. They're included in the Maven-built JAR, so there's no extra work required to work with these libraries.

Datasets

Throughout this book, you'll work with three datasets to provide some variety in the examples. All the datasets are small to make them easy to work with. Copies of the exact data used are available in the GitHub repository in the https://github.com/alexholmes/hiped2/tree/master/test-data directory. I also sometimes use data that's specific to a chapter, and it's available within chapter-specific subdirectories under the same GitHub location.

NASDAQ financial stocks

I downloaded the NASDAQ daily exchange data from InfoChimps (www.infochimps.com). I filtered this huge dataset down to just five stocks and their start-of-year values from 2000 through 2009. The data used for this book is available on GitHub at https://github.com/alexholmes/hiped2/blob/master/test-data/stocks.txt.

The data is in CSV form, and the fields are in the following order:

```
Symbol,Date,Open,High,Low,Close,Volume,Adj Close
```

Apache log data

I created a sample log file in Apache Common Log Format[1] with some fake Class E IP addresses and some dummy resources and response codes. The file is available on GitHub at https://github.com/alexholmes/hiped2/blob/master/test-data/apachelog.txt.

---

[1] See http://httpd.apache.org/docs/1.3/logs.html#common.

Names

Names were retrieved from the U.S. government census at www.census.gov/genealogy/www/data/1990surnames/dist.all.last, and this data is available at https://github.com/alexholmes/hiped2/blob/master/test-data/names.txt.

Author Online

Purchase of *Hadoop in Practice, Second Edition* includes free access to a private web forum run by Manning Publications where you can make comments about the book, ask technical questions, and receive help from the authors and from other users. To access the forum and subscribe to it, point your web browser to www.manning.com/HadoopinPractice, SecondEdition. This page provides information on how to get on the forum once you are registered, what kind of help is available, and the rules of conduct on the forum. It also provides links to the source code for the examples in the book, errata, and other downloads.

Manning's commitment to our readers is to provide a venue where a meaningful dialog between individual readers and between readers and the author can take place. It is not a commitment to any specific amount of participation on the part of the author, whose contribution to the Author Online forum remains voluntary (and unpaid). We suggest you try asking the author challenging questions lest his interest strays!

The Author Online forum and the archives of previous discussions will be accessible from the publisher's website as long as the book is in print.

about the cover illustration

The figure on the cover of *Hadoop in Practice, Second Edition* is captioned "Momak from Kistanja, Dalmatia." The illustration is taken from a reproduction of an album of traditional Croatian costumes from the mid-nineteenth century by Nikola Arsenovic, published by the Ethnographic Museum in Split, Croatia, in 2003. The illustrations were obtained from a helpful librarian at the Ethnographic Museum in Split, itself situated in the Roman core of the medieval center of the town: the ruins of Emperor Diocletian's retirement palace from around AD 304. The book includes finely colored illustrations of figures from different regions of Croatia, accompanied by descriptions of the costumes and of everyday life.

Kistanja is a small town located in Bukovica, a geographical region in Croatia. It is situated in northern Dalmatia, an area rich in Roman and Venetian history. The word "momak" in Croatian means a bachelor, beau, or suitor—a single young man who is of courting age—and the young man on the cover, looking dapper in a crisp, white linen shirt and a colorful, embroidered vest, is clearly dressed in his finest clothes, which would be worn to church and for festive occasions—or to go calling on a young lady.

Dress codes and lifestyles have changed over the last 200 years, and the diversity by region, so rich at the time, has faded away. It is now hard to tell apart the inhabitants of different continents, let alone of different hamlets or towns separated by only a few miles. Perhaps we have traded cultural diversity for a more varied personal life—certainly for a more varied and fast-paced technological life.

Manning celebrates the inventiveness and initiative of the computer business with book covers based on the rich diversity of regional life of two centuries ago, brought back to life by illustrations from old books and collections like this one.

Part 1

Background and fundamentals

Part 1 of this book consists of chapters 1 and 2, which cover the important Hadoop fundamentals.

Chapter 1 covers Hadoop's components and its ecosystem and provides instructions for installing a pseudo-distributed Hadoop setup on a single host, along with a system that will enable you to run all of the examples in the book. Chapter 1 also covers the basics of Hadoop configuration, and walks you through how to write and run a MapReduce job on your new setup.

Chapter 2 introduces YARN, which is a new and exciting development in Hadoop version 2, transitioning Hadoop from being a MapReduce-only system to one that can support many execution engines. Given that YARN is new to the community, the goal of this chapter is to look at some basics such as its components, how configuration works, and also how MapReduce works as a YARN application. Chapter 2 also provides an overview of some applications that YARN has enabled to execute on Hadoop, such as Spark and Storm.

Hadoop in a heartbeat

This chapter covers

- Examining how the core Hadoop system works
- Understanding the Hadoop ecosystem
- Running a MapReduce job

We live in the age of big data, where the data volumes we need to work with on a day-to-day basis have outgrown the storage and processing capabilities of a single host. Big data brings with it two fundamental challenges: how to store and work with voluminous data sizes, and more important, how to understand data and turn it into a competitive advantage.

Hadoop fills a gap in the market by effectively storing and providing computational capabilities for substantial amounts of data. It's a distributed system made up of a distributed filesystem, and it offers a way to parallelize and execute programs on a cluster of machines (see figure 1.1). You've most likely come across Hadoop because it's been adopted by technology giants like Yahoo!, Facebook, and Twitter to address their big data needs, and it's making inroads across all industrial sectors.

Because you've come to this book to get some practical experience with Hadoop and Java,[1] I'll start with a brief overview and then show you how to install

---

[1] To benefit from this book, you should have some practical experience with Hadoop and understand the basic concepts of MapReduce and HDFS (covered in Manning's *Hadoop in Action* by Chuck Lam, 2010). Further, you should have an intermediate-level knowledge of Java—*Effective Java*, 2nd Edition by Joshua Bloch (Addison-Wesley, 2008) is an excellent resource on this topic.

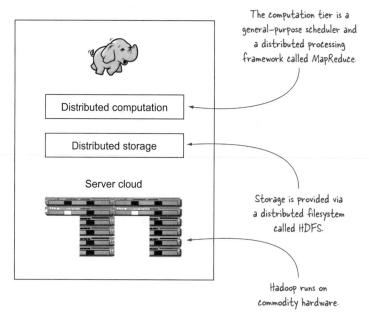

The computation tier is a general-purpose scheduler and a distributed processing framework called MapReduce.

Distributed computation

Distributed storage

Server cloud

Storage is provided via a distributed filesystem called HDFS.

Hadoop runs on commodity hardware.

Figure 1.1   The Hadoop environment is a distributed system that runs on commodity hardware.

Hadoop and run a MapReduce job. By the end of this chapter, you'll have had a basic refresher on the nuts and bolts of Hadoop, which will allow you to move on to the more challenging aspects of working with it.

Let's get started with a detailed overview.

1.1   *What is Hadoop?*

Hadoop is a platform that provides both distributed storage and computational capabilities. Hadoop was first conceived to fix a scalability issue that existed in Nutch,[2] an open source crawler and search engine. At the time, Google had published papers that described its novel distributed filesystem, the Google File System (GFS), and MapReduce, a computational framework for parallel processing. The successful implementation of these papers' concepts in Nutch resulted in it being split into two separate projects, the second of which became Hadoop, a first-class Apache project.

In this section we'll look at Hadoop from an architectural perspective, examine how industry uses it, and consider some of its weaknesses. Once we've covered this background, we'll look at how to install Hadoop and run a MapReduce job.

Hadoop proper, as shown in figure 1.2, is a distributed master-slave architecture[3] that consists of the following primary components:

---

[2]   The Nutch project, and by extension Hadoop, was led by Doug Cutting and Mike Cafarella.

[3]   A model of communication where one process, called the *master*, has control over one or more other processes, called *slaves*.

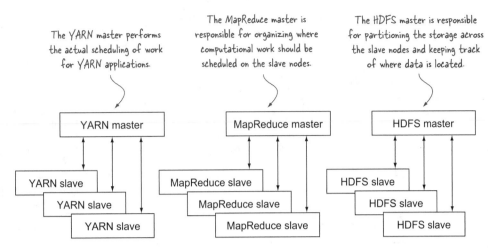

Figure 1.2 High-level Hadoop 2 master-slave architecture

- Hadoop Distributed File System (HDFS) for data storage.
- Yet Another Resource Negotiator (YARN), introduced in Hadoop 2, a general-purpose scheduler and resource manager. Any YARN application can run on a Hadoop cluster.
- MapReduce, a batch-based computational engine. In Hadoop 2, MapReduce is implemented as a YARN application.

Traits intrinsic to Hadoop are data partitioning and parallel computation of large datasets. Its storage and computational capabilities scale with the addition of hosts to a Hadoop cluster; clusters with hundreds of hosts can easily reach data volumes in the petabytes.

In the first step in this section, we'll examine the HDFS, YARN, and MapReduce architectures.

1.1.1 *Core Hadoop components*

To understand Hadoop's architecture we'll start by looking at the basics of HDFS.

HDFS

HDFS is the storage component of Hadoop. It's a distributed filesystem that's modeled after the Google File System (GFS) paper.[4] HDFS is optimized for high throughput and works best when reading and writing large files (gigabytes and larger). To support this throughput, HDFS uses unusually large (for a filesystem) block sizes and data locality optimizations to reduce network input/output (I/O).

Scalability and availability are also key traits of HDFS, achieved in part due to data replication and fault tolerance. HDFS replicates files for a configured number of times, is tolerant of both software and hardware failure, and automatically re-replicates data blocks on nodes that have failed.

---

[4] See "The Google File System," http://research.google.com/archive/gfs.html.

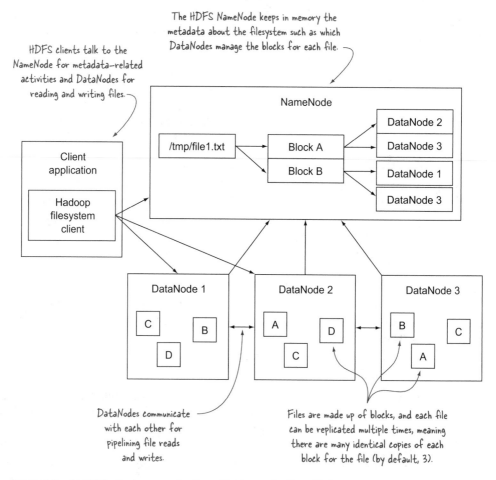

Figure 1.3 An HDFS client communicating with the master NameNode and slave DataNodes

Figure 1.3 shows a logical representation of the components in HDFS: the NameNode and the DataNode. It also shows an application that's using the Hadoop filesystem library to access HDFS.

Hadoop 2 introduced two significant new features for HDFS—Federation and High Availability (HA):

- Federation allows HDFS metadata to be shared across multiple NameNode hosts, which aides with HDFS scalability and also provides data isolation, allowing different applications or teams to run their own NameNodes without fear of impacting other NameNodes on the same cluster.
- High Availability in HDFS removes the single point of failure that existed in Hadoop 1, wherein a NameNode disaster would result in a cluster outage. HDFS HA also offers the ability for failover (the process by which a standby Name-Node takes over work from a failed primary NameNode) to be automated.

Now that you have a bit of HDFS knowledge, it's time to look at YARN, Hadoop's scheduler.

YARN

YARN is Hadoop's distributed resource scheduler. YARN is new to Hadoop version 2 and was created to address challenges with the Hadoop 1 architecture:

- Deployments larger than 4,000 nodes encountered scalability issues, and adding additional nodes didn't yield the expected linear scalability improvements.
- Only MapReduce workloads were supported, which meant it wasn't suited to run execution models such as machine learning algorithms that often require iterative computations.

For Hadoop 2 these problems were solved by extracting the scheduling function from MapReduce and reworking it into a generic application scheduler, called YARN. With this change, Hadoop clusters are no longer limited to running MapReduce workloads; YARN enables a new set of workloads to be natively supported on Hadoop, and it allows alternative processing models, such as graph processing and stream processing, to coexist with MapReduce. Chapters 2 and 10 cover YARN and how to write YARN applications.

YARN's architecture is simple because its primary role is to schedule and manage resources in a Hadoop cluster. Figure 1.4 shows a logical representation of the core components in YARN: the ResourceManager and the NodeManager. Also shown are the components specific to YARN applications, namely, the YARN application client, the ApplicationMaster, and the container.

To fully realize the dream of a generalized distributed platform, Hadoop 2 introduced another change—the ability to allocate containers in various configurations.

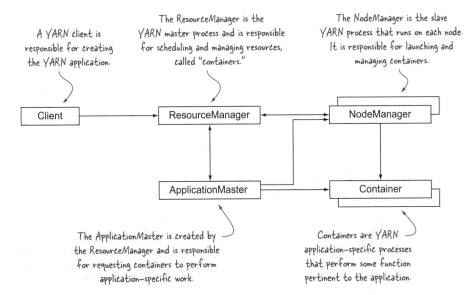

Figure 1.4 The logical YARN architecture showing typical communication between the core YARN components and YARN application components

Hadoop 1 had the notion of "slots," which were a fixed number of map and reduce processes that were allowed to run on a single node. This was wasteful in terms of cluster utilization and resulted in underutilized resources during MapReduce operations, and it also imposed memory limits for map and reduce tasks. With YARN, each container requested by an ApplicationMaster can have disparate memory and CPU traits, and this gives YARN applications full control over the resources they need to fulfill their work.

You'll work with YARN in more detail in chapters 2 and 10, where you'll learn how YARN works and how to write a YARN application. Next up is an examination of MapReduce, Hadoop's computation engine.

MAPREDUCE

MapReduce is a batch-based, distributed computing framework modeled after Google's paper on MapReduce.[5] It allows you to parallelize work over a large amount of raw data, such as combining web logs with relational data from an OLTP database to model how users interact with your website. This type of work, which could take days or longer using conventional serial programming techniques, can be reduced to minutes using MapReduce on a Hadoop cluster.

The MapReduce model simplifies parallel processing by abstracting away the complexities involved in working with distributed systems, such as computational parallelization, work distribution, and dealing with unreliable hardware and software. With this abstraction, MapReduce allows the programmer to focus on addressing business needs rather than getting tangled up in distributed system complications.

MapReduce decomposes work submitted by a client into small parallelized map and reduce tasks, as shown in figure 1.5. The map and reduce constructs used in

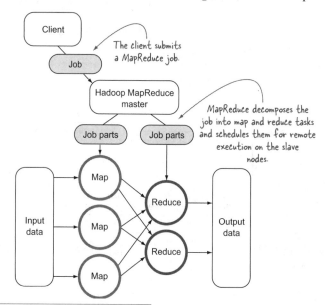

Figure 1.5   A client submitting a job to MapReduce, breaking the work into small map and reduce tasks

---

[5] See "MapReduce: Simplified Data Processing on Large Clusters," http://research.google.com/archive/mapreduce.html.

The map function takes as input a key/value pair, which
represents a logical record from the input data source.
In the case of a file, this could be a line, or if the
input source is a table in a database, it could be a row.

map(key1, value1) ⟶ list(key2, value2)

The map function produces zero or more output key/value pairs for
one input pair. For example, if the map function is a filtering
map function, it may only produce output if a certain condition is
met. Or it could be performing a demultiplexing operation, where
a single key/value yields multiple key/value output pairs.

**Figure 1.6   A
logical view of the
map function that
takes a key/value
pair as input**

MapReduce are borrowed from those found in the Lisp functional programming language, and they use a shared-nothing model to remove any parallel execution interdependencies that could add unwanted synchronization points or state sharing.[6]

The role of the programmer is to define map and reduce functions where the map function outputs key/value tuples, which are processed by reduce functions to produce the final output. Figure 1.6 shows a pseudocode definition of a map function with regard to its input and output.

The power of MapReduce occurs between the map output and the reduce input in the shuffle and sort phases, as shown in figure 1.7.

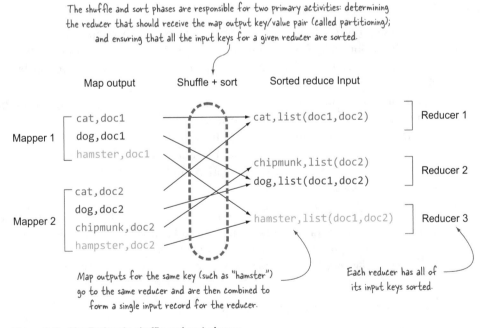

The shuffle and sort phases are responsible for two primary activities: determining
the reducer that should receive the map output key/value pair (called partitioning);
and ensuring that all the input keys for a given reducer are sorted.

Map outputs for the same key (such as "hamster")
go to the same reducer and are then combined to
form a single input record for the reducer.

Each reducer has all of
its input keys sorted.

Figure 1.7   MapReduce's shuffle and sort phases

---

[6]   A shared-nothing architecture is a distributed computing concept that represents the notion that each node
is independent and self-sufficient.

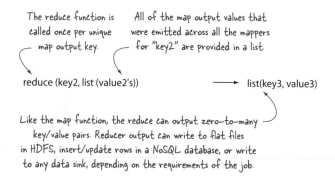

The reduce function is   All of the map output values that
called once per unique   were emitted across all the mappers
map output key.   for "key2" are provided in a list.

reduce (key2, list (value2's))   ⟶   list(key3, value3)

Like the map function, the reduce can output zero-to-many
key/value pairs. Reducer output can write to flat files
in HDFS, insert/update rows in a NoSQL database, or write
to any data sink, depending on the requirements of the job.

Figure 1.8   A logical view of the reduce function that produces output for flat files, NoSQL rows, or any data sink

Figure 1.8 shows a pseudocode definition of a reduce function.

With the advent of YARN in Hadoop 2, MapReduce has been rewritten as a YARN application and is now referred to as MapReduce 2 (or MRv2). From a developer's perspective, MapReduce in Hadoop 2 works in much the same way it did in Hadoop 1, and code written for Hadoop 1 will execute without code changes on version 2.[7] There are changes to the physical architecture and internal plumbing in MRv2 that are examined in more detail in chapter 2.

With some Hadoop basics under your belt, it's time to take a look at the Hadoop ecosystem and the projects that are covered in this book.

1.1.2   The Hadoop ecosystem

The Hadoop ecosystem is diverse and grows by the day. It's impossible to keep track of all of the various projects that interact with Hadoop in some form. In this book the focus is on the tools that are currently receiving the greatest adoption by users, as shown in figure 1.9.

MapReduce and YARN are not for the faint of heart, which means the goal for many of these Hadoop-related projects is to increase the accessibility of Hadoop to programmers and nonprogrammers. I'll cover many of the technologies listed in figure 1.9 in this book and describe them in detail within their respective chapters. In addition, the appendix includes descriptions and installation instructions for technologies that are covered in this book.

> **Coverage of the Hadoop ecosystem in this book**   The Hadoop ecosystem grows by the day, and there are often multiple tools with overlapping features and benefits. The goal of this book is to provide practical techniques that cover the core Hadoop technologies, as well as select ecosystem technologies that are ubiquitous and essential to Hadoop.

Let's look at the hardware requirements for your cluster.

---

[7] Some code may require recompilation against Hadoop 2 binaries to work with MRv2; see chapter 2 for more details.

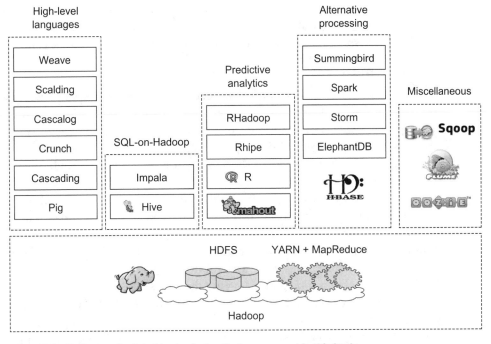

Figure 1.9 Hadoop and related technologies that are covered in this book

1.1.3 Hardware requirements

The term *commodity hardware* is often used to describe Hadoop hardware require-ments. It's true that Hadoop can run on any old servers you can dig up, but you'll still want your cluster to perform well, and you don't want to swamp your operations department with diagnosing and fixing hardware issues. Therefore, *commodity* refers to mid-level rack servers with dual sockets, as much error-correcting RAM as is affordable, and SATA drives optimized for RAID storage. Using RAID on the DataNode filesystems used to store HDFS content is strongly discouraged because HDFS already has replica-tion and error-checking built in; on the NameNode, RAID is strongly recommended for additional security.[8]

From a network topology perspective with regard to switches and firewalls, all of the master and slave nodes must be able to open connections to each other. For small clusters, all the hosts would run 1 GB network cards connected to a single, good-quality switch. For larger clusters, look at 10 GB top-of-rack switches that have at least multiple 1 GB uplinks to dual-central switches. Client nodes also need to be able to talk to all of the master and slave nodes, but if necessary, that access can be from behind a firewall that permits connection establishment only from the client side.

---

[8] HDFS uses disks to durably store metadata about the filesystem.

After reviewing Hadoop from a software and hardware perspective, you've likely developed a good idea of who might benefit from using it. Once you start working with Hadoop, you'll need to pick a distribution to use, which is the next topic.

1.1.4   *Hadoop distributions*

Hadoop is an Apache open source project, and regular releases of the software are available for download directly from the Apache project's website (http://hadoop.apache.org/releases.html#Download). You can either download and install Hadoop from the website or use a quickstart virtual machine from a commercial distribution, which is usually a great starting point if you're new to Hadoop and want to quickly get it up and running.

After you've whet your appetite with Hadoop and have committed to using it in production, the next question that you'll need to answer is which distribution to use. You can continue to use the vanilla Hadoop distribution, but you'll have to build the in-house expertise to manage your clusters. This is not a trivial task and is usually only successful in organizations that are comfortable with having dedicated Hadoop DevOps engineers running and managing their clusters.

Alternatively, you can turn to a commercial distribution of Hadoop, which will give you the added benefits of enterprise administration software, a support team to consult when planning your clusters or to help you out when things go bump in the night, and the possibility of a rapid fix for software issues that you encounter. Of course, none of this comes for free (or for cheap!), but if you're running mission-critical services on Hadoop and don't have a dedicated team to support your infrastructure and services, then going with a commercial Hadoop distribution is prudent.

> **Picking the distribution that's right for you**   It's highly recommended that you engage with the major vendors to gain an understanding of which distribution suits your needs from a feature, support, and cost perspective. Remember that each vendor will highlight their advantages and at the same time expose the disadvantages of their competitors, so talking to two or more vendors will give you a more realistic sense of what the distributions offer. Make sure you download and test the distributions and validate that they integrate and work within your existing software and hardware stacks.

There are a number of distributions to choose from, and in this section I'll briefly summarize each distribution and highlight some of its advantages.

APACHE

Apache is the organization that maintains the core Hadoop code and distribution, and because all the code is open source, you can crack open your favorite IDE and browse the source code to understand how things work under the hood. Historically the challenge with the Apache distributions has been that support is limited to the goodwill of the open source community, and there's no guarantee that your issue will be investigated and fixed. Having said that, the Hadoop community is a very supportive one, and responses to problems are usually rapid, even if the actual fixes will likely take longer than you may be able to afford.

The Apache Hadoop distribution has become more compelling now that administration has been simplified with the advent of Apache Ambari, which provides a GUI to help with provisioning and managing your cluster. As useful as Ambari is, though, it's worth comparing it against offerings from the commercial vendors, as the commercial tooling is typically more sophisticated.

CLOUDERA

Cloudera is the most tenured Hadoop distribution, and it employs a large number of Hadoop (and Hadoop ecosystem) committers. Doug Cutting, who along with Mike Caferella originally created Hadoop, is the chief architect at Cloudera. In aggregate, this means that bug fixes and feature requests have a better chance of being addressed in Cloudera compared to Hadoop distributions with fewer committers.

Beyond maintaining and supporting Hadoop, Cloudera has been innovating in the Hadoop space by developing projects that address areas where Hadoop has been weak. A prime example of this is Impala, which offers a SQL-on-Hadoop system, similar to Hive but focusing on a near-real-time user experience, as opposed to Hive, which has traditionally been a high-latency system. There are numerous other projects that Cloudera has been working on: highlights include Flume, a log collection and distribution system; Sqoop, for moving relational data in and out of Hadoop; and Cloudera Search, which offers near-real-time search indexing.

HORTONWORKS

Hortonworks is also made up of a large number of Hadoop committers, and it offers the same advantages as Cloudera in terms of the ability to quickly address problems and feature requests in core Hadoop and its ecosystem projects.

From an innovation perspective, Hortonworks has taken a slightly different approach than Cloudera. An example is Hive: Cloudera's approach was to develop a whole new SQL-on-Hadoop system, but Hortonworks has instead looked at innovating inside of Hive to remove its high-latency shackles and add new capabilities such as support for ACID. Hortonworks is also the main driver behind the next-generation YARN platform, which is a key strategic piece keeping Hadoop relevant. Similarly, Hortonworks has used Apache Ambari for its administration tooling rather than developing an in-house proprietary administration tool, which is the path taken by the other distributions. Hortonworks' focus on developing and expanding the Apache ecosystem tooling has a direct benefit to the community, as it makes its tools available to all users without the need for support contracts.

MAPR

MapR has fewer Hadoop committers on its team than the other distributions discussed here, so its ability to fix and shape Hadoop's future is potentially more bounded than its peers.

From an innovation perspective, MapR has taken a decidedly different approach to Hadoop support compared to its peers. From the start it decided that HDFS wasn't an enterprise-ready filesystem, and instead developed its own proprietary filesystem, which offers compelling features such as POSIX compliance (offering random-write support and atomic operations), High Availability, NFS mounting, data mirroring, and snapshots. Some of these features have been introduced into Hadoop 2, but MapR has offered them from the start, and, as a result, one can expect that these features are robust.

As part of the evaluation criteria, it should be noted that parts of the MapR stack, such as its filesystem and its HBase offering, are closed source and proprietary. This affects the ability of your engineers to browse, fix, and contribute patches back to the community. In contrast, most of Cloudera's and Hortonworks' stacks are open source, especially Hortonworks', which is unique in that the entire stack, including the management platform, is open source.

MapR's notable highlights include being made available in Amazon's cloud as an alternative to Amazon's own Elastic MapReduce and being integrated with Google's Compute Cloud.

I've just scratched the surface of the advantages that the various Hadoop distributions offer; your next steps will likely be to contact the vendors and start playing with the distributions yourself.

Next, let's take a look at companies currently using Hadoop, and in what capacity they're using it.

1.1.5 *Who's using Hadoop?*

Hadoop has a high level of penetration in high-tech companies, and it's starting to make inroads in a broad range of sectors, including the enterprise (Booz Allen Hamilton, J.P. Morgan), government (NSA), and health care.

Facebook uses Hadoop, Hive, and HBase for data warehousing and real-time application serving.[9] Facebook's data warehousing clusters are petabytes in size with thousands of nodes, and they use separate HBase-driven, real-time clusters for messaging and real-time analytics.

Yahoo! uses Hadoop for data analytics, machine learning, search ranking, email antispam, ad optimization, ETL,[10] and more. Combined, it has over 40,000 servers running Hadoop with 170 PB of storage. Yahoo! is also running the first large-scale YARN deployments with clusters of up to 4,000 nodes.[11]

Twitter is a major big data innovator, and it has made notable contributions to Hadoop with projects such as Scalding, a Scala API for Cascading; Summingbird, a

---

[9] See Dhruba Borthakur, "Looking at the code behind our three uses of Apache Hadoop" on Facebook at http://mng.bz/4cMc. Facebook has also developed its own SQL-on-Hadoop tool called Presto and is migrating away from Hive (see Martin Traverso, "Presto: Interacting with petabytes of data at Facebook," http://mng.bz/p0Xz).

[10] Extract, transform, and load (ETL) is the process by which data is extracted from outside sources, transformed to fit the project's needs, and loaded into the target data sink. ETL is a common process in data warehousing.

[11] There are more details on YARN and its use at Yahoo! in "Apache Hadoop YARN: Yet Another Resource Negotiator" by Vinod Kumar Vavilapalli et al., www.cs.cmu.edu/~garth/15719/papers/yarn.pdf.

component that can be used to implement parts of Nathan Marz's lambda architecture; and various other gems such as Bijection, Algebird, and Elephant Bird.

eBay, Samsung, Rackspace, J.P. Morgan, Groupon, LinkedIn, AOL, Spotify, and StumbleUpon are some other organizations that are also heavily invested in Hadoop. Microsoft has collaborated with Hortonworks to ensure that Hadoop works on its platform.

Google, in its MapReduce paper, indicated that it uses Caffeine,[12] its version of MapReduce, to create its web index from crawl data. Google also highlights applications of MapReduce to include activities such as a distributed grep, URL access frequency (from log data), and a term-vector algorithm, which determines popular keywords for a host.

The number of organizations that use Hadoop grows by the day, and if you work at a Fortune 500 company you almost certainly use a Hadoop cluster in some capacity. It's clear that as Hadoop continues to mature, its adoption will continue to grow.

As with all technologies, a key part to being able to work effectively with Hadoop is to understand its shortcomings and design and architect your solutions to mitigate these as much as possible.

1.1.6 *Hadoop limitations*

High availability and security often rank among the top concerns cited with Hadoop. Many of these concerns have been addressed in Hadoop 2; let's take a closer look at some of its weaknesses as of release 2.2.0.

Enterprise organizations using Hadoop 1 and earlier had concerns with the lack of high availability and security. In Hadoop 1, all of the master processes are single points of failure, which means that a failure in the master process causes an outage. In Hadoop 2, HDFS now has high availability support, and the re-architecture of MapReduce with YARN has removed the single point of failure. Security is another area that has had its wrinkles, and it's receiving focus.

HIGH AVAILABILITY

High availability is often mandated in enterprise organizations that have high uptime SLA requirements to ensure that systems are always on, even in the event of a node going down due to planned or unplanned circumstances. Prior to Hadoop 2, the master HDFS process could only run on a single node, resulting in single points of failure.[13] Hadoop 2 brings NameNode High Availability (HA) support, which means that multiple NameNodes for the same Hadoop cluster can be running. With the current design, one of the NameNodes is active and the other NameNode is designated as a standby process. In the event that the active NameNode experiences a planned or

---

[12] In 2010 Google moved to a real-time indexing system called Caffeine; see "Our new search index: Caffeine" on the Google blog (June 8, 2010), http://googleblog.blogspot.com/2010/06/our-new-search-index-caffeine.html.

[13] In reality, the HDFS single point of failure may not be terribly significant; see "NameNode HA" by Suresh Srinivas and Aaron T. Myers, http://goo.gl/1iSab.

unplanned outage, the standby NameNode will take over as the active NameNode, which is a process called *failover*. This failover can be configured to be automatic, negating the need for human intervention. The fact that a NameNode failover occurred is transparent to Hadoop clients.

The MapReduce master process (the JobTracker) doesn't have HA support in Hadoop 2, but now that each MapReduce job has its own JobTracker process (a separate YARN ApplicationMaster), HA support is arguably less important.

HA support in the YARN master process (the ResourceManager) is important, however, and development is currently underway to add this feature to Hadoop.[14]

MULTIPLE DATACENTERS

Multiple datacenter support is another key feature that's increasingly expected in enterprise software, as it offers strong data protection and locality properties due to data being replicated across multiple datacenters. Apache Hadoop, and most of its commercial distributions, has never had support for multiple datacenters, which poses challenges for organizations that have software running in multiple datacenters. WAN-disco is currently the only solution available for Hadoop multidatacenter support.

SECURITY

Hadoop does offer a security model, but by default it's disabled. With the security model disabled, the only security feature that exists in Hadoop is HDFS file- and directory-level ownership and permissions. But it's easy for malicious users to subvert and assume other users' identities. By default, all other Hadoop services are wide open, allowing any user to perform any kind of operation, such as killing another user's MapReduce jobs.

Hadoop can be configured to run with Kerberos, a network authentication protocol, which requires Hadoop daemons to authenticate clients, both users and other Hadoop components. Kerberos can be integrated with an organization's existing Active Directory and therefore offers a single-sign-on experience for users. Care needs to be taken when enabling Kerberos, as any Hadoop tool that wishes to interact with your cluster will need to support Kerberos.

Wire-level encryption can be configured in Hadoop 2 and allows data crossing the network (both HDFS transport[15] and MapReduce shuffle data[16]) to be encrypted. Encryption of data at rest (data stored by HDFS on disk) is currently missing in Hadoop.

Let's examine the limitations of some of the individual systems.

---

[14] For additional details on YARN HA support, see the JIRA ticket titled "ResourceManager (RM) High-Availability (HA)," https://issues.apache.org/jira/browse/YARN-149.

[15] See the JIRA ticket titled "Add support for encrypting the DataTransferProtocol" at https://issues.apache.org/jira/browse/HDFS-3637.

[16] See the JIRA ticket titled "Add support for encrypted shuffle" at https://issues.apache.org/jira/browse/MAPREDUCE-4417.

HDFS

The weakness of HDFS is mainly its lack of high availability (in Hadoop 1.x and earlier), its inefficient handling of small files,[17] and its lack of transparent compression. HDFS doesn't support random writes into files (only appends are supported), and it's generally designed to support high-throughput sequential reads and writes over large files.

MAPREDUCE

MapReduce is a batch-based architecture, which means it doesn't lend itself to use cases that need real-time data access. Tasks that require global synchronization or sharing of mutable data aren't a good fit for MapReduce, because it's a shared-nothing architecture, which can pose challenges for some algorithms.

VERSION INCOMPATIBILITIES

The Hadoop 2 release brought with it some headaches with regard to MapReduce API runtime compatibility, especially in the org.hadoop.mapreduce package. These problems often result in runtime issues with code that's compiled against Hadoop 1 (and earlier). The solution is usually to recompile against Hadoop 2, or to consider a technique outlined in chapter 2 that introduces a compatibility library to target both Hadoop versions without the need to recompile code.

Other challenges with Hive and Hadoop also exist, where Hive may need to be recompiled to work with versions of Hadoop other than the one it was built against. Pig has had compatibility issues, too. For example, the Pig 0.8 release didn't work with Hadoop 0.20.203, and manual intervention was required to work around this problem. This is one of the advantages of using a Hadoop distribution other than Apache, as these compatibility problems have been fixed. If using the vanilla Apache distributions is desired, it's worth taking a look at Bigtop (http://bigtop.apache.org/), an Apache open source automated build and compliance system. It includes all of the major Hadoop ecosystem components and runs a number of integration tests to ensure they all work in conjunction with each other.

After tackling Hadoop's architecture and its weaknesses, you're probably ready to roll up your sleeves and get hands-on with Hadoop, so let's look at running the first example in this book.

1.2   *Getting your hands dirty with MapReduce*

This section shows you how to run a MapReduce job on your host.

> **Installing Hadoop and building the examples** To run the code example in this section, you'll need to follow the instructions in the appendix, which explain how to install Hadoop and download and run the examples bundled with this book.

---

[17] Although HDFS Federation in Hadoop 2 has introduced a way for multiple NameNodes to share file metadata, the fact remains that metadata is stored in memory.

Let's say you want to build an inverted index. MapReduce would be a good choice for this task because it can create indexes in parallel (a common MapReduce use case). Your input is a number of text files, and your output is a list of tuples, where each tuple is a word and a list of files that contain the word. Using standard processing techniques, this would require you to find a mechanism to join all the words together. A naive approach would be to perform this join in memory, but you might run out of memory if you have large numbers of unique keys. You could use an intermediary datastore, such as a database, but that would be inefficient.

A better approach would be to tokenize each line and produce an intermediary file containing a word per line. Each of these intermediary files could then be sorted. The final step would be to open all the sorted intermediary files and call a function for each unique word. This is what MapReduce does, albeit in a distributed fashion.

Figure 1.10 walks you through an example of a simple inverted index in MapReduce. Let's start by defining your mapper. Your reducers need to be able to generate a line for each word in your input, so your map output key should be each word in the input files so that MapReduce can join them all together. The value for each key will be the containing filename, which is your document ID.

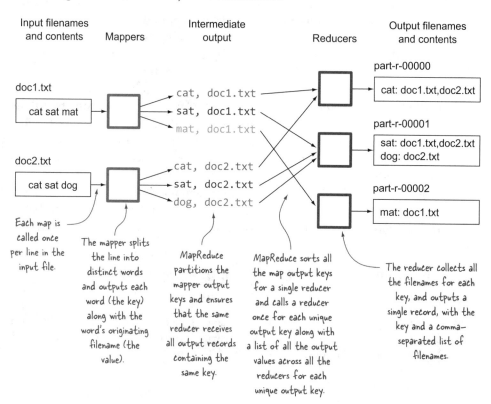

Figure 1.10 An example of an inverted index being created in MapReduce

This is the mapper code:

Extend the MapReduce Mapper class and specify key/value types for inputs and outputs. Use the MapReduce default InputFormat, which supplies keys as byte offsets into the input file and values as each line in the file. The map emits Text key/value pairs.

A Text object to store the document ID (filename) for the input.

MapReduce calls the setup method prior to feeding a map (or reduce) class records. In this example you'll store the input filename for this map.

Create a single Text object, which you'll reuse to cut down on object creation.

Extract the filename from the context.

Call this map method once per input line; map tasks are run in parallel over subsets of the input files.

The value contains an entire line from the file. The line is tokenized using StringUtils (which is far faster than using String.split).

For each word, the map outputs the word as the key and the document ID as the value.

```java
public static class Map
    extends Mapper<LongWritable, Text, Text, Text> {

  private Text documentId;
  private Text word = new Text();

  @Override
  protected void setup(Context context) {
    String filename =
        ((FileSplit) context.getInputSplit()).getPath().getName();
    documentId = new Text(filename);
  }

  @Override
  protected void map(LongWritable key, Text value,
                     Context context)
      throws IOException, InterruptedException {
    for (String token :
             StringUtils.split(value.toString())) {
      word.set(token);
      context.write(word, documentId);
    }
  }
}
```

The goal of this reducer is to create an output line for each word and a list of the document IDs in which the word appears. The MapReduce framework will take care of calling the reducer once per unique key outputted by the mappers, along with a list of document IDs. All you need to do in the reducer is combine all the document IDs together and output them once in the reducer, as you can see in the following code:

Much like in the Map class, you need to specify both the input and output key/value classes when you define the reducer.

The reduce method is called once per unique map output key. The Iterable allows you to iterate over all the values that were emitted for the given key.

Keep a set of all the document IDs that are encountered for the key.

Iterate over all the document IDs for the key.

Add the document ID to the set. You create a new Text object because MapReduce reuses the Text object when iterating over the values, which means you want to create a new copy.

The reduce outputs the word and a CSV list of document IDs that contained the word.

```java
public static class Reduce
    extends Reducer<Text, Text, Text, Text> {

  private Text docIds = new Text();
  public void reduce(Text key, Iterable<Text> values,
                     Context context)
      throws IOException, InterruptedException {

    HashSet<Text> uniqueDocIds = new HashSet<Text>();
    for (Text docId : values) {
      uniqueDocIds.add(docId.toString());
    }
    docIds.set(new Text(StringUtils.join(uniqueDocIds, ",")));
    context.write(key, docIds);
  }
}
```

The last step is to write the driver code that will set all the necessary properties to configure the MapReduce job to run. You need to let the framework know what classes should be used for the map and reduce functions, and also let it know where the input and output data is located. By default, MapReduce assumes you're working with text; if you're working with more complex text structures, or altogether different data-storage technologies, you'll need to tell MapReduce how it should read and write from these data sources and sinks. The following source shows the full driver code:[18]

```java
public int run(final String[] args) throws Exception {

    Cli cli = Cli.builder().setArgs(args)
                     .addOptions(IOOptions.values()).build();
    cli.runCmd();

    Path input = new Path(cli.getArgValueAsString(IOOptions.INPUT));
    Path output = new Path(cli.getArgValueAsString(IOOptions.OUTPUT));

    Configuration conf = super.getConf();

    Job job = new Job(conf);
    job.setJarByClass(InvertedIndexJob.class);
    job.setMapperClass(Map.class);
    job.setReducerClass(Reduce.class);
    job.setMapOutputKeyClass(Text.class);
    job.setMapOutputValueClass(Text.class);

    FileInputFormat.setInputPaths(job, input);
    FileOutputFormat.setOutputPath(job, output);

    if (job.waitForCompletion(true)) {
        System.out.println("Job completed successfully.");

        return 0;
    }
    return 1;
}
```

Annotations:
- Extract the input and output directories from the arguments.
- Get a handle for the Configuration instance for the job.
- The Job class's setJarByClass informs MapReduce that the supplied class should be used to determine the encapsulating JAR, which in turn is added to the classpath of all your map and reduce tasks.
- Set the Map class that should be used for the job.
- Set the Reduce class that should be used for the job.
- If the map output key/value types differ from the input types, you must tell Hadoop what they are. Here, the map will output each word and file as key/value pairs, and both are Text objects.
- Set the map output value class.
- Set the HDFS input directory for the job.
- Set the HDFS output directory for the job.
- Tell the framework to run the job and block until the job has completed.

Let's see how this code works. First, you need to create two simple input files in HDFS:

```
$ hadoop fs -mkdir -p hip1/input
$ echo "cat sat mat" | hadoop fs -put - hip1/input/1.txt
$ echo "dog lay mat" | hadoop fs -put - hip1/input/2.txt
```

Create two files in HDFS to serve as inputs for the job.

Next, run the MapReduce code. You'll use a shell script to run it, supplying the two input files as arguments, along with the job output directory:

```
$ hip hip.ch1.InvertedIndexJob --input hip1/input --output hip1/output
```

---

[18] GitHub source: https://github.com/alexholmes/hiped2/blob/master/src/main/java/hip/ch1/InvertedIndexJob.java.

> **Executing code examples in the book** The appendix contains instructions for downloading and installing the binaries and code that accompany this book. Most of the examples are launched via the hip script, which is located inside the bin directory. For convenience, it's recommended that you add the book's bin directory to your path so that you can copy-paste all the example commands as is. The appendix has instructions on how to set up your environment.

When your job completes, you can examine HDFS for the job output files and view their contents:

```
$ hadoop fs -ls output/
Found 3 items
output/_SUCCESS
output/_logs
output/part-r-00000

$ hadoop fs -cat output/part*
cat     1.txt
dog     2.txt
lay     2.txt
mat     2.txt,1.txt
sat     1.txt
```

This completes your whirlwind tour of how to run Hadoop.

1.3   *Chapter summary*

Hadoop is a distributed system designed to process, generate, and store large datasets. Its MapReduce implementation provides you with a fault-tolerant mechanism for large-scale data analysis of heterogeneous structured and unstructured data sources, and YARN now supports multi-tenant disparate applications on the same Hadoop cluster.

In this chapter, we examined Hadoop from both functional and physical architectural standpoints. You also installed Hadoop and ran a MapReduce job.

The remainder of this book is dedicated to presenting real-world techniques for solving common problems you'll encounter when working with Hadoop. You'll be introduced to a broad spectrum of subject areas, starting with YARN, HDFS and MapReduce, and Hive. You'll also look at data-analysis techniques and explore technologies such as Mahout and Rhipe.

In chapter 2, the first stop on your journey, you'll discover YARN, which heralds a new era for Hadoop, one that transforms Hadoop into a distributed processing kernel. Without further ado, let's get started.

Introduction to YARN

Imagine buying your first car, which upon delivery has a steering wheel that doesn't function and brakes that don't work. Oh, and it only drives in first gear. No speeding on winding back roads for you! That empty, sad feeling is familiar to those of us who want to run some cool new tech such as graph or real-time data processing with Hadoop 1,[1] only to be reminded that our powerful Hadoop clusters were good for one thing, and one thing only: MapReduce.

Luckily for us the Hadoop committers took these and other constraints to heart and dreamt up a vision that would metamorphose Hadoop above and beyond MapReduce. YARN is the realization of this dream, and it's an exciting new development that transitions Hadoop into a distributed computing kernel that can support

---

[1] While you can do graph processing in Hadoop 1, it's not a native fit, which means you're either incurring the inefficiencies of multiple disk barriers between each iteration on your graph, or hacking around in MapReduce to avoid such barriers.

any type of workload.[2] This opens up the types of applications that can be run on Hadoop to efficiently support computing models for machine learning, graph processing, and other generalized computing projects (such as Tez), which are discussed later in this chapter

The upshot of all this is that you can now run MapReduce, Storm, and HBase all on a single Hadoop cluster. This allows for exciting new possibilities, not only in computational multi-tenancy, but also in the ability to efficiently share data between applications.

Because YARN is a new technology, we'll kick off this chapter with a look at how YARN works, followed by a section that covers how to interact with YARN from the command line and the UI. Combined, these sections will give you a good grasp of what YARN is and how to use it.

Once you have a good handle on how YARN works, you'll see how MapReduce has been rewritten to be a YARN application (titled MapReduce 2, or MRv2), and look at some of the architectural and systems changes that occurred in MapReduce to make this happen. This will help you better understand how to work with MapReduce in Hadoop 2 and give you some background into why some aspects of MapReduce changed in version 2.

> **YARN development** If you're looking for details on how to write YARN applications, feel free to skip to chapter 10. But if you're new to YARN, I recommend you read this chapter before you move on to chapter 10.

In the final section of this chapter, you'll examine several YARN applications and their practical uses.

Let's get things started with an overview of YARN.

2.1 YARN overview

With Hadoop 1 and older versions, you were limited to only running MapReduce jobs. This was great if the type of work you were performing fit well into the MapReduce processing model, but it was restrictive for those wanting to perform graph processing, iterative computing, or any other type of work.

In Hadoop 2 the scheduling pieces of MapReduce were externalized and reworked into a new component called YARN, which is short for *Yet Another Resource Negotiator.* YARN is agnostic to the type of work you do on Hadoop—all that it requires is that applications that wish to operate on Hadoop are implemented as YARN applications. As a result, MapReduce is now a YARN application. The old and new Hadoop stacks can be seen in figure 2.1.

There are multiple benefits to this architectural change, which you'll examine in the next section.

---

[2] Prior to YARN, Hadoop only supported MapReduce for computational work.

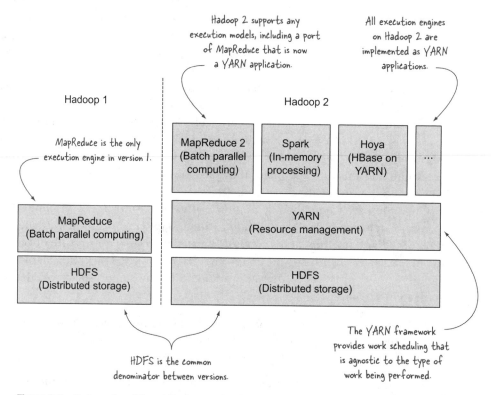

Figure 2.1 Hadoop 1 and 2 architectures, showing YARN as a generalized scheduler and various YARN applications

2.1.1   *Why YARN?*

We've touched on how YARN enables work other than MapReduce to be performed on Hadoop, but let's expand on that and also look at additional advantages that YARN brings to the table.

MapReduce is a powerful distributed framework and programming model that allows batch-based parallelized work to be performed on a cluster of multiple nodes. Despite being very efficient at what it does, though, MapReduce has some disadvantages; principally that it's batch-based, and as a result isn't suited to real-time or even near-real-time data processing. Historically this has meant that processing models such as graph, iterative, and real-time data processing are not a natural fit for MapReduce.[3]

The bottom line is that Hadoop version 1 restricts you from running exciting new processing frameworks.

YARN changes all of this by taking over the scheduling portions of MapReduce, and nothing else. At its core, YARN is a distributed scheduler and is responsible for two activities:

---

[3] HBase is an exception; it uses HDFS for storage but doesn't use MapReduce for the processing engine.

- *Responding to a client's request to create a container*—A container is in essence a process, with a contract governing the physical resources that it's permitted to use.
- *Monitoring containers that are running, and terminating them if needed*—Containers can be terminated if a YARN scheduler wants to free up resources so that containers from other applications can run, or if a container is using more than its allocated resources.

Table 2.1 compares MapReduce 1 and YARN (in Hadoop versions 1 and 2) to show why YARN is such a revolutionary jump.

Table 2.1 Comparison of MapReduce 1 and YARN

Capability	MapReduce 1	YARN
Execution model	Only MapReduce is supported on Hadoop 1, limiting the types of activities you can perform to batch-based flows that fit within the confines of the MapReduce processing model.	YARN places no restrictions on the type of work that can be executed in Hadoop; you pick which execution engines you need (whether it's real-time processing with Spark, graph processing with Giraph, or MapReduce batch processing), and they can all be executing in parallel on the same cluster.
Concurrent processes	MapReduce had the notion of "slots," which were node-specific static configurations that determined the maximum number of map and reduce processes that could run concurrently on each node. Based on where in the lifecycle a MapReduce application was, this would often lead to underutilized clusters.	YARN allows for more fluid resource allocation, and the number of processes is limited only by the configured maximum amount of memory and CPU for each node.
Memory limits	Slots in Hadoop 1 also had a maximum limit, so typically Hadoop 1 clusters were provisioned such that the number of slots multiplied by the maximum configured memory for each slot was less than the available RAM. This often resulted in smaller than desired maximum slot memory sizes, which impeded your ability to run memory-intensive jobs.[a] Another drawback of MRv1 was that it was more difficult for memory-intensive and IO-intensive jobs to coexist on the same cluster or machines. Either you had more slots to boost the I/O jobs, or fewer slots but more RAM for RAM jobs. Once again, the static nature of these slots made it a challenge to tune clusters for mixed workloads.	YARN allows applications to request resources of varying memory sizes. YARN has minimum and maximum memory limits, but because the number of slots is no longer fixed, the maximum values can be much larger to support memory-intensive workloads. YARN therefore provides a much more dynamic scheduling model that doesn't limit the number of processes or the amount of RAM requested by a process.
Scalability	There were concurrency issues with the JobTracker, which limited the number of nodes in a Hadoop cluster to 3,000–4,000 nodes.	By separating out the scheduling parts of MapReduce into YARN and making it lightweight by delegating fault tolerance to YARN applications, YARN can scale to much larger numbers than prior versions of Hadoop.[b]

Table 2.1 Comparison of MapReduce 1 and YARN *(continued)*

Capability	MapReduce 1	YARN
Execution	Only a single version of MapReduce could be supported on a cluster at a time. This was problematic in large multi-tenant environments where product teams that wanted to upgrade to newer versions of MapReduce had to convince all the other users. This typically resulted in huge coordination and integration efforts and made such upgrades huge infrastructure projects.	MapReduce is no longer at the core of Hadoop, and is now a YARN application running in user space. This means that you can now run different versions of MapReduce on the same cluster at the same time. This is a huge productivity gain in large multi-tenant environments, and it allows you to organizationally decouple product teams and roadmaps.

[a] This limitation in MapReduce was especially painful for those running machine-learning tasks using tools such as Mahout, as they often required large amounts of RAM for processing—amounts often larger than the maximum configured slot size in MapReduce.

[b] The goal of YARN is to be able to scale to 10,000 nodes; scaling beyond that number could result in the ResourceManager becoming a bottleneck, as it's a single process.

Now that you know about the key benefits of YARN, it's time to look at the main components in YARN and examine their roles.

2.1.2 YARN concepts and components

YARN comprises a framework that's responsible for resource scheduling and monitoring, and applications that execute application-specific logic in a cluster. Let's examine YARN concepts and components in more detail, starting with the YARN framework components.

YARN FRAMEWORK

The YARN framework performs one primary function, which is to schedule resources (*containers* in YARN parlance) in a cluster. Applications in a cluster talk to the YARN framework, asking for application-specific containers to be allocated, and the YARN framework evaluates these requests and attempts to fulfill them. An important part of the YARN scheduling also includes monitoring currently executing containers. There are two reasons that container monitoring is important: Once a container has completed, the scheduler can then use freed-up capacity to schedule more work. Additionally, each container has a contract that specifies the system resources that it's allowed to use, and in cases where containers overstep these bounds, the scheduler can terminate the container to avoid rogue containers impacting other applications.

The YARN framework was intentionally designed to be as simple as possible; as such, it doesn't know or care about the type of applications that are running. Nor does it care about keeping any historical information about what has executed on the cluster. These design decisions are the primary reasons that YARN can scale beyond the levels of MapReduce.

There are two primary components that comprise the YARN framework—the ResourceManager and the NodeManager—which are seen in figure 2.2.

- *ResourceManager*—A Hadoop cluster has a single *ResourceManager* (RM) for the entire cluster. The ResourceManager is the YARN master process, and its sole function is to arbitrate resources on a Hadoop cluster. It responds to client requests to create containers, and a scheduler determines when and where a container can be created according to scheduler-specific multi-tenancy rules that govern who can create containers where and when. Just like with Hadoop 1, the scheduler part of the ResourceManager is pluggable, which means that you can pick the scheduler that works best for your environment. The actual creation of containers is delegated to the NodeManager.

- *NodeManager*—The *NodeManager* is the slave process that runs on every node in a cluster. Its job is to create, monitor, and kill containers. It services requests from the ResourceManager and ApplicationMaster to create containers, and it reports on the status of the containers to the ResourceManager. The ResourceManager uses the data contained in these status messages to make scheduling decisions for new container requests.

In non-HA mode, only a single instance of the ResourceManager exists.[4]

The YARN framework exists to manage applications, so let's take a look at what components a YARN application is composed of.

YARN APPLICATIONS

A YARN application implements a specific function that runs on Hadoop. MapReduce is an example of a YARN application, as are projects such as Hoya, which allows multiple HBase instances to run on a single cluster, and storm-yarn, which allows Storm to run inside a Hadoop cluster. You'll see more details on these projects and other YARN applications later in this chapter.

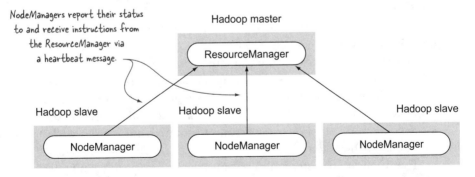

Figure 2.2 YARN framework components and their interactions. Application-specific components, such as the YARN client, ApplicationMaster, and containers are not shown.

---

[4] As of the time of writing, YARN ResourceManager HA is still actively being developed, and its progress can be followed on a JIRA ticket titled "ResourceManager (RM) High-Availability (HA)," https://issues.apache.org/jira/browse/YARN-149.

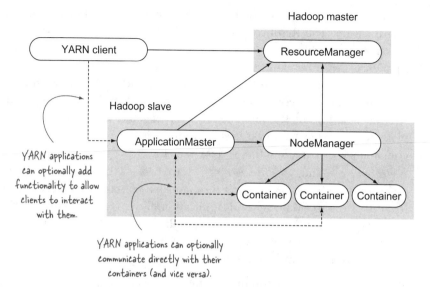

Figure 2.3   Typical interactions of a YARN application

A YARN application involves three components—the client, the ApplicationMaster (AM), and the container, which can be seen in figure 2.3.

Launching a new YARN application starts with a YARN client communicating with the ResourceManager to create a new YARN ApplicationMaster instance. Part of this process involves the YARN client informing the ResourceManager of the Application-Master's physical resource requirements.

The *ApplicationMaster* is the master process of a YARN application. It doesn't perform any application-specific work, as these functions are delegated to the containers. Instead, it's responsible for managing the application-specific containers: asking the ResourceManager of its intent to create containers and then liaising with the Node-Manager to actually perform the container creation.

As part of this process, the ApplicationMaster must specify the resources that each container requires in terms of which host should launch the container and what the container's memory and CPU requirements are.[5] The ability of the ResourceManager to schedule work based on exact resource requirements is a key to YARN's flexibility, and it enables hosts to run a mix of containers, as highlighted in figure 2.4.

The ApplicationMaster is also responsible for the specific fault-tolerance behavior of the application. It receives status messages from the ResourceManager when its containers fail, and it can decide to take action based on these events (by asking the ResourceManager to create a new container), or to ignore these events.[6]

---

[5]   Future versions of Hadoop may allow network, disk, and GPU requirements to be specified.

[6]   Containers can fail for a variety of reasons, including a node going down, a container being killed by YARN to allow another application's container to be launched, or YARN killing a container when the container exceeds its configured physical/virtual memory.

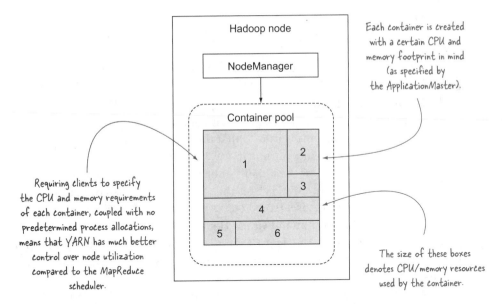

Figure 2.4   Various container configurations running on a single YARN-managed Hadoop node

A *container* is an application-specific process that's created by a NodeManager on behalf of an ApplicationMaster. The ApplicationManager itself is also a container, created by the ResourceManager. A container created by an ApplicationManager can be an arbitrary process—for example, a container process could simply be a Linux command such as awk, a Python application, or any process that can be launched by the operating system. This is the power of YARN—the ability to launch and manage any process across any node in a Hadoop cluster.

By this point, you should have a high-level understanding of the YARN components and what they do. Next we'll look at common YARN configurables.

2.1.3   YARN configuration

YARN brings with it a whole slew of configurations for various components, such as the UI, remote procedure calls (RPCs), the scheduler, and more.[7] In this section, you'll learn how you can quickly access your running cluster's configuration.

TECHNIQUE 1   Determining the configuration of your cluster

Figuring out the configuration for a running Hadoop cluster can be a nuisance—it often requires looking at several configuration files, including the default configuration files, to determine the value for the property you're interested in. In this technique, you'll see how to sidestep the hoops you normally need to jump through, and instead focus on how to expediently get at the configuration of a running Hadoop cluster.

---

[7] Details on the default YARN configurations can be seen at http://hadoop.apache.org/docs/r2.2.0/hadoop-yarn/hadoop-yarn-common/yarn-default.xml.

■ **Problem**

You want to access the configuration of a running Hadoop cluster.

■ **Solution**

View the configuration using the ResourceManager UI.

■ **Discussion**

The ResourceManager UI shows the configuration for your Hadoop cluster; figure 2.5 shows how you can navigate to this information.

What's useful about this feature is that the UI shows not only a property value, but also which file it originated from. If the value wasn't defined in a <component>-site.xml file, then it'll show the default value and the default filename.

Another useful feature of this UI is that it'll show you the configuration from multiple files, including the core, HDFS, YARN, and MapReduce files.

The configuration for an individual Hadoop slave node can be navigated to in the same way from the NodeManager UI. This is most helpful when working with Hadoop clusters that consist of heterogeneous nodes, where you often have varying configurations that cater to differing hardware resources.

By this point, you should have a high-level understanding of the YARN components, what they do, and how to configure them for your cluster. The next step is to actually see YARN in action by using the command line and the UI.

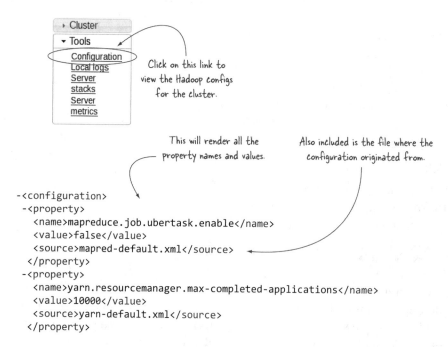

Figure 2.5   The YARN ResourceManager UI showing the cluster's configuration

2.1.4 Interacting with YARN

Out of the box, Hadoop 2 is bundled with two YARN applications—MapReduce 2 and DistributedShell. You'll learn more about MapReduce 2 later in this chapter, but for now, you can get your toes wet by taking a look at a simpler example of a YARN application: the DistributedShell. You'll see how to run your first YARN application and where to go to examine the logs.

If you don't know the configured values for your cluster, you have two options:

- Examine the contents of yarn-site.xml to view the property values. If an entry doesn't exist, the default value will be in effect.[8]
- Even better, use the ResourceManager UI, which gives you more detailed information on the running configuration, including what the default values are and if they're in effect.

Let's now take a look at how to quickly view the YARN configuration for a running Hadoop cluster.

TECHNIQUE 2 **Running a command on your YARN cluster**

Running a command on your cluster is a good first step when you start working with a new YARN cluster. It's the "hello world" in YARN, if you will.

■ **Problem**

You want to run a Linux command on a node in your Hadoop cluster.

■ **Solution**

Use the DistributedShell example application bundled with Hadoop.

■ **Discussion**

YARN is bundled with the DistributedShell application, which serves two primary purposes—it's a reference YARN application that's also a handy utility for running a command in parallel across your Hadoop cluster. Start by issuing a Linux find command in a single container:

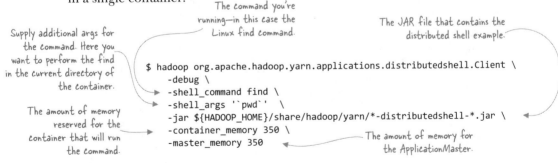

```
$ hadoop org.apache.hadoop.yarn.applications.distributedshell.Client \
    -debug \
    -shell_command find \
    -shell_args '`pwd`' \
    -jar ${HADOOP_HOME}/share/hadoop/yarn/*-distributedshell-*.jar \
    -container_memory 350 \
    -master_memory 350
```

The command you're running—in this case the Linux find command.

The JAR file that contains the distributed shell example.

Supply additional args for the command. Here you want to perform the find in the current directory of the container.

The amount of memory reserved for the container that will run the command.

The amount of memory for the ApplicationMaster.

If all is well with your cluster, then executing the preceding command will result in the following log message:

```
INFO distributedshell.Client: Application completed successfully
```

---

[8] Visit the following URL for YARN default values: http://hadoop.apache.org/docs/r2.2.0/hadoop-yarn/hadoop-yarn-common/yarn-default.xml.

There are various other logging statements that you'll see in the command's output prior to this line, but you'll notice that none of them contain the actual results of your find command. This is because the DistributedShell ApplicationMaster launches the find command in a separate container, and the standard output (and standard error) of the find command is redirected to the log output directory of the container. To see the output of your command, you need to get access to that directory. That, as it happens, is covered in the next technique!

TECHNIQUE 3   Accessing container logs

Turning to the log files is the most common first step one takes when trying to diagnose an application that behaved in an unexpected way, or to simply understand more about the application. In this technique, you'll learn how to access these application log files.

■ **Problem**

You want to access container log files.

■ **Solution**

Use YARN's UI and the command line to access the logs.

■ **Discussion**

Each container that runs in YARN has its own output directory, where the standard output, standard error, and any other output files are written. Figure 2.6 shows the location of the output directory on a slave node, including the data retention details for the logs.

Access to container logs is not as simple as it should be—let's take a look at how you can use the CLI and the UIs to access logs.

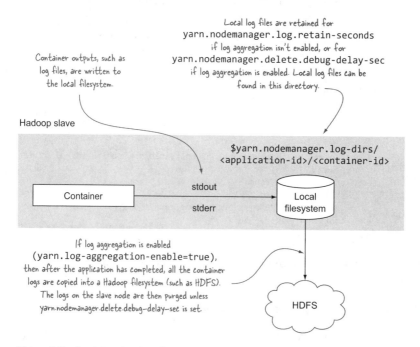

Figure 2.6   Container log locations and retention

Accessing container logs using the YARN command line

YARN comes with a command-line interface (CLI) for accessing YARN application logs. To use the CLI, you need to know the ID of your application.

> **How do I find the application ID?** Most YARN clients will display the application ID in their output and logs. For example, the DistributedShell command that you executed in the previous technique echoed the application ID to standard output:
>
> ```
> $ hadoop o.a.h.y.a.d.Client ...
> ...
> INFO impl.YarnClientImpl:
>     Submitted application application_1388257115348_0008 to
>     ResourceManager at /0.0.0.0:8032
> ...
> ```
>
> Alternatively, you can use the CLI (using yarn application -list) or the ResourceManager UI to browse and find your application ID.

If you attempt to use the CLI when the application is still running, you'll be presented with the following error message:

```
$ yarn logs -applicationId application_1398974791337_0070
Application has not completed. Logs are only available after
an application completes
```

The message tells it all—the CLI is only useful once an application has completed. You'll need to use the UI to access the container logs when the application is running, which we'll cover shortly.

Once the application has completed, you may see the following output if you attempt to run the command again:

```
$ yarn logs -applicationId application_1400286711208_0001
Logs not available at /tmp/.../application_1400286711208_0001
Log aggregation has not completed or is not enabled.
```

Basically, the YARN CLI only works if the application has completed and log aggregation is enabled. Log aggregation is covered in the next technique. If you enable log aggregation, the CLI will give you the logs for all the containers in your application, as you can see in the next example:

```
$ yarn logs -applicationId application_1400287920505_0002
client.RMProxy: Connecting to ResourceManager at /0.0.0.0:8032

Container: container_1400287920505_0002_01_000002
        on localhost.localdomain_57276
==================================================
LogType: stderr
LogLength: 0
Log Contents:

LogType: stdout
```

```
LogLength: 1355
Log Contents:
/tmp
default_container_executor.sh
/launch_container.sh
/.launch_container.sh.crc
/.default_container_executor.sh.crc
/.container_tokens.crc
/AppMaster.jar
/container_tokens


Container: container_1400287920505_0002_01_000001
           on localhost.localdomain_57276
======================================================
LogType: AppMaster.stderr
LogLength: 17170
Log Contents:
distributedshell.ApplicationMaster: Initializing ApplicationMaster
...

LogType: AppMaster.stdout
LogLength: 8458
Log Contents:
System env: key=TERM, val=xterm-256color
...
```

The preceding output shows the contents of the logs of the DistributedShell example that you ran in the previous technique. There are two containers in the output—one for the find command that was executed, and the other for the ApplicationMaster, which is also executed within a container.

Accessing logs using the YARN UIs

YARN provides access to the ApplicationMaster logs via the ResourceManager UI. On a pseudo-distributed setup, point your browser at http://localhost:8088/cluster. If you're working with a multi-node Hadoop cluster, point your browser at http:// $yarn.resourcemanager.webapp.address/cluster. Click on the application you're interested in, and then select the Logs link as shown in figure 2.7.

Great, but how do you access the logs for containers other than the Application-Master? Unfortunately, things get a little murky here. The ResourceManager doesn't keep track of a YARN application's containers, so it can't provide you with a way to list and navigate to the container logs. Therefore, the onus is on individual YARN applications to provide their users with a way to access container logs.

> **Hey, ResourceManager, what are my container IDs?** In order to keep the ResourceManager lightweight, it doesn't keep track of the container IDs for an application. As a result, the ResourceManager UI only provides a way to access the ApplicationMaster logs for an application.

Case in point is the DistributedShell application. It's a simple application that doesn't provide an ApplicationMaster UI or keep track of the containers that it's launched.

Figure 2.7   The YARN ResourceManager UI showing the ApplicationMaster container

Therefore, there's no easy way to view the container logs other than by using the approach presented earlier: using the CLI.

Luckily, the MapReduce YARN application provides an ApplicationMaster UI that you can use to access the container (the map and reduce task) logs, as well as a Job-History UI that can be used to access logs after a MapReduce job has completed. When you run a MapReduce job, the ResourceManager UI gives you a link to the MapReduce ApplicationMaster UI, as shown in figure 2.8, which you can use to access the map and reduce logs (much like the JobTracker in MapReduce 1).

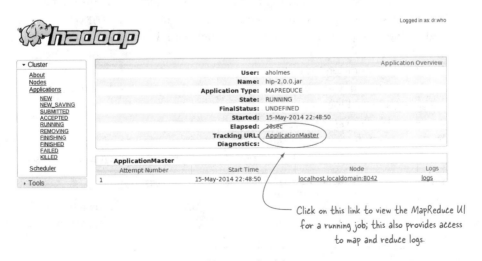

Figure 2.8   Accessing the MapReduce UI for a running job

If your YARN application provides some way for you to identify container IDs and the hosts that they execute on, you can either access the container logs using the Node-Manager UI or you can use a shell to ssh to the slave node that executed a container.

The NodeManager URL for accessing a container's logs is http://<nodemanager-host>:8042/node/containerlogs/<container-id>/<username>. Alternatively, you can ssh to the NodeManager host and access the container logs directory at $yarn .nodemanager.log-dirs/<application-id>/<container-id>.

Really, the best advice I can give here is that you should enable log aggregation, which will allow you to use the CLI, HDFS, and UIs, such as the MapReduce ApplicationMaster and JobHistory, to access application logs. Keep reading for details on how to do this.

TECHNIQUE 4   Aggregating container log files

Log aggregation is a feature that was missing from Hadoop 1, making it challenging to archive and access task logs. Luckily Hadoop 2 has this feature baked-in, and you have a number of ways to access aggregated log files. In this technique you'll learn how to configure your cluster to archive log files for long-term storage and access.

■ **Problem**

You want to aggregate container log files to HDFS and manage their retention policies.

■ **Solution**

Use YARN's built-in log aggregation capabilities.

■ **Discussion**

In Hadoop 1 your logs were stowed locally on each slave node, with the JobTracker and TaskTracker being the only mechanisms for getting access to these logs. This was cumbersome and didn't easily support programmatic access to them. In addition, log files would often disappear due to aggressive log-retention policies that existed to prevent local disks on slave nodes from filling up.

Log aggregation in Hadoop 2 is therefore a welcome feature, and if enabled, it copies container log files into a Hadoop filesystem (such as HDFS) after a YARN application has completed. By default, this behavior is disabled, and you need to set yarn.log-aggregation-enable to true to enable this feature. Figure 2.9 shows the data flow for container log files.

Now that you know how log aggregation works, let's take a look at how you can access aggregated logs.

Accessing log files using the CLI

With your application ID in hand (see technique 3 for details on how to get it), you can use the command line to fetch all the logs and write them to the console:

```
$ yarn logs -applicationId application_1388248867335_0003
```

Enabling log aggregation If the preceding yarn logs command yields the following output, then it's likely that you don't have YARN log aggregation enabled:

```
Log aggregation has not completed or is not enabled.
```

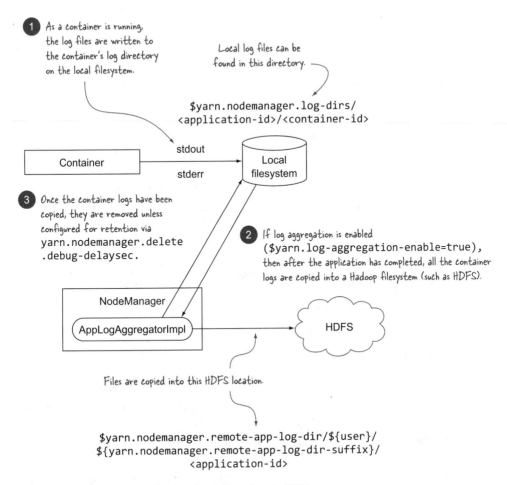

Figure 2.9 Log file aggregation from local filesystem to HDFS

This will dump out all the logs for all the containers for the YARN application. The output for each container is delimited with a header indicating the container ID, followed by details on each file in the container's output directory. For example, if you ran a DistributedShell command that executed ls -l, then the output of the yarn logs command would yield something like the following:

```
Container: container_1388248867335_0003_01_000002 on localhost
================================================================
LogType: stderr
LogLength: 0
Log Contents:

LogType: stdoutLogLength: 268
Log Contents:
total 32
-rw-r--r-- 1 aholmes 12:29 container_tokens
```

```
-rwx------ 1 aholmes 12:29 default_container_executor.sh
-rwx------ 1 aholmes launch_container.sh
drwx--x--- 2 aholmes tmp

Container: container_1388248867335_0003_01_000001 on localhost
================================================================
LogType: AppMaster.stderr
(the remainder of the ApplicationMaster logs removed for brevity)
```

The stdout file contains the directory listing of the ls process's current directory, which is a container-specific working directory.

Accessing aggregated logs via the UI

Fully featured YARN applications such as MapReduce provide an ApplicationMaster UI that can be used to access container logs. Similarly, the JobHistory UI can also access aggregated logs.

> **UI aggregated log rendering** If log aggregation is enabled, you'll need to update yarn-site.xml and set yarn.log.server.url to point at the job history server so that the ResourceManager UI can render the logs.

Accessing log files in HDFS

By default, aggregated log files go into the following directory in HDFS:

```
/tmp/logs/${user}/logs/application_<appid>
```

The directory prefix can be configured via the yarn.nodemanager.remote-app-log-dir property; similarly, the path name after the username ("logs" in the previous example, which is the default) can be customized via yarn.nodemanager.remote-app-log-dir-suffix.

Differences between log files in local filesystem and HDFS

As you saw earlier, each container results in two log files in the local filesystem: one for standard output and another for standard error. As part of the aggregation process, all the files for a given node are concatenated together into a node-specific log. For example, if you had five containers running across three nodes, you'd end up with three log files in HDFS.

Compression

Compression of aggregated logs is disabled by default, but you can enable it by setting the value of yarn.nodemanager.log-aggregation.compression-type to either lzo or gzip depending on your compression requirements. As of Hadoop 2.2, these are the only two compression codecs supported.

Log retention

When log aggregation is turned off, the container log files on the local host are retained for yarn.nodemanager.log.retain-seconds seconds, the default being 10,800 (3 hours).

When log aggregation is turned on, the yarn.nodemanager.log.retain-seconds configurable is ignored, and instead the local container log files are deleted as soon as they are copied into HDFS. But all is not lost if you want to retain them on the local filesystem—simply set `yarn.nodemanager.delete.debug-delay-sec` to a value that you want to keep the files around for. Note that this applies not only to the log files but also to all other metadata associated with the container (such as JAR files).

The data retention for the files in HDFS is configured via a different setting, `yarn.log-aggregation.retain-seconds`.

NameNode considerations

At scale, you may want to consider an aggressive log retention setting so that you don't overwhelm the NameNode with all the log file metadata. The NameNode keeps the metadata in memory, and on a large active cluster, the number of log files can quickly overwhelm the NameNode.

> **Real-life example of NameNode impact**   Take a look at Bobby Evans' "Our Experience Running YARN at Scale" (http://www.slideshare.net/Hadoop _Summit/ evans-june27-230pmroom210c) for a real-life example of how Yahoo! utilized 30% of their NameNode with seven days' worth of aggregated logs.

Alternative solutions

The solution highlighted in this technique is useful for getting your logs into HDFS, but if you will need to organize any log mining or visualization activities yourself, there are other options available such as Hunk, which supports aggregating logs from both Hadoop 1 and 2 and providing first-class query, visualization, and monitoring features, just like regular Splunk. You could also set up a query and visualization pipeline using tools such as Logstash, ElasticSearch, and Kibana if you want to own the log management process. Other tools such as Loggly are worth investigating.

For now, this concludes our hands-on look at YARN. That's not the end of the story, however. Section 2.2 looks at how MapReduce works as a YARN application, and later in chapter 10, you'll learn how to write your own YARN applications.

2.1.5   YARN challenges

There are some gotchas to be aware of with YARN:

- *YARN currently isn't designed to work well with long-running processes.* This has created challenges for projects such as Impala and Tez that would benefit from such a feature. Work is currently underway to bring this feature to YARN, and it's being tracked in a JIRA ticket titled "Roll up for long-lived services in YARN," https://issues.apache.org/jira/browse/YARN-896.
- *Writing YARN applications is quite complex, as you're required to implement container management and fault tolerance.* This may require some complex Application-Master and container-state management so that upon failure the work can continue from some previous well-known state. There are several frameworks whose goal is to simplify development—refer to chapter 10 for more details.
- *Gang scheduling, which is the ability to rapidly launch a large number of containers in parallel, is currently not supported.* This is another feature that projects such as Impala and Hamster (OpenMPI) would require for native YARN integration. The

Hadoop committers are currently working on adding support for gang scheduling, which is being tracked in the JIRA ticket titled "Support gang scheduling in the AM RM protocol," https://issues.apache.org/jira/browse/YARN-624.

So far we've focused on the capabilities of the core YARN system. Let's move on to look at how MapReduce works as a YARN application.

2.2   YARN and MapReduce

In Hadoop 1, MapReduce was the only way to process your data natively in Hadoop. YARN was created so that Hadoop clusters could run any type of work, and its only requirement was that applications adhere to the YARN specification. This meant MapReduce had to become a YARN application and required the Hadoop developers to rewrite key parts of MapReduce.

Given that MapReduce had to go through some open-heart surgery to get it working as a YARN application, the goal of this section is to demystify how MapReduce works in Hadoop 2. You'll see how MapReduce 2 executes in a Hadoop cluster, and you'll also get to look at configuration changes and backward compatibility with MapReduce 1. Toward the end of this section, you'll learn how to run and monitor jobs, and you'll see how small jobs can be quickly executed.

There's a lot to go over, so let's take MapReduce into the lab and see what's going on under the covers.

2.2.1   Dissecting a YARN MapReduce application

Architectural changes had to be made to MapReduce to port it to YARN. Figure 2.10 shows the processes involved in MRv2 and some of the interactions between them.

Each MapReduce job is executed as a separate YARN application. When you launch a new MapReduce job, the client calculates the input splits and writes them along with other job resources into HDFS (step 1). The client then communicates with the ResourceManager to create the ApplicationMaster for the MapReduce job (step 2). The ApplicationMaster is actually a container, so the ResourceManager will allocate the container when resources become available on the cluster and then communicate with a NodeManager to create the ApplicationMaster container (steps 3–4).[9]

The MapReduce ApplicationMaster (MRAM) is responsible for creating map and reduce containers and monitoring their status. The MRAM pulls the input splits from HDFS (step 5) so that when it communicates with the ResourceManager (step 6) it can request that map containers are launched on nodes local to their input data.

Container allocation requests to the ResourceManager are piggybacked on regular heartbeat messages that flow between the ApplicationMaster and the ResourceManager. The heartbeat responses may contain details on containers that are allocated for the application. Data locality is maintained as an important part of the architecture—when it requests map containers, the MapReduce ApplicationManager will use the input splits' location details to request that the containers are assigned to

---

[9] If there aren't any available resources for creating the container, the ResourceManager may choose to kill one or more existing containers to free up space.

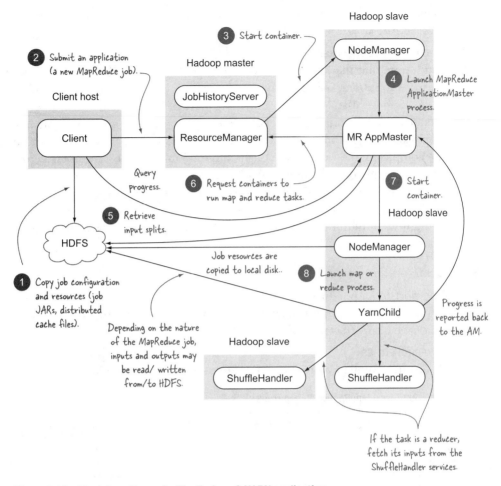

Figure 2.10   The interactions of a MapReduce 2 YARN application

one of the nodes that contains the input splits, and the ResourceManager will make a
best attempt at container allocation on these input split nodes.

Once the MapReduce ApplicationManager is allocated a container, it talks to the
NodeManager to launch the map or reduce task (steps 7–8). At this point, the map/
reduce process acts very similarly to the way it worked in MRv1.

THE SHUFFLE

The shuffle phase in MapReduce, which is responsible for sorting mapper outputs
and distributing them to the reducers, didn't fundamentally change in MapReduce 2.
The main difference is that the map outputs are fetched via ShuffleHandlers, which
are auxiliary YARN services that run on each slave node.[10] Some minor memory

---

[10] The ShuffleHandler must be configured in your yarn-site.xml; the property name is yarn.nodemanager.aux-
services and the value is mapreduce_shuffle.

management tweaks were made to the shuffle implementation; for example, io.sort.record.percent is no longer used.

WHERE'S THE JOBTRACKER?

You'll note that the JobTracker no longer exists in this architecture. The scheduling part of the JobTracker was moved as a general-purpose resource scheduler into the YARN ResourceManager. The remaining part of JobTracker, which is primarily the metadata about running and completed jobs, was split in two. Each MapReduce ApplicationMaster hosts a UI that renders details on the current job, and once jobs are completed, their details are pushed to the JobHistoryServer, which aggregates and renders details on all completed jobs. Refer to section 2.2.5 for additional details, including how to access the MapReduce ApplicationMaster UI.

Hopefully, you now have a better sense of how MapReduce 2 works. MapReduce configuration didn't go untouched in the move to YARN, so let's take a look at what's hot and what's not.

2.2.2   *Configuration*

The port of MapReduce 2 to YARN brought with it some major changes in the Map-Reduce properties. In this section, we'll cover some of the frequently used properties that have been affected.

NEW PROPERTIES

There are several new properties in MapReduce 2, identified in table 2.2.

Table 2.2   New MapReduce 2 properties

Property name	Default value	Description
mapreduce.framework .name	local	Determines which framework should be used to run MapReduce jobs. There are three possible values: ■ local, which means the LocalJobRunner is used (the entire MapReduce job is run in a single JVM). ■ classic, which means that the job will be launched on a MapReduce 1 cluster. In this case, the mapreduce.jobtracker .address property will be used to retrieve the JobTracker that the job will be submitted to. ■ yarn, which runs the MapReduce job in YARN. This can either be in a pseudo-distributed or full-blown YARN cluster.
mapreduce.job.ubertask .enable	false	Uber jobs are small jobs that can be run inside the MapReduce ApplicationMaster process to avoid the overhead of spawning map and reduce containers. Uber jobs are covered in more detail in section 2.2.6.

Table 2.2 New MapReduce 2 properties *(continued)*

Property name	Default value	Description
`mapreduce.shuffle` `.max.connections`	0	The maximum allowed connections for the shuffle. Set to 0 (zero) to indicate no limit on the number of connections. This is similar to the old (now unused) MapReduce 1 property `tasktracker.http` `.threads`, which defined the number of TaskTracker threads that would be used to service reducer requests for map outputs.
`yarn.resourcemanager` `.am.max-attempts`	2	The maximum number of application attempts. It's a global setting for all ApplicationMasters. Each application master can specify its individual maximum number of application attempts via the API, but the individual number can't be more than the global upper bound. If it is, the Resource-Manager will override it. The default value is 2, to allow at least one retry for AM.
`yarn.resourcemanager` `.recovery.enabled`	false	Enable RM to recover state after starting. If true, then `yarn.resourcemanager` `.store.class` must be specified. Hadoop 2.4.0 also brings in a ZooKeeper-based mechanism to store the RM state (class `org.apache.hadoop.yarn.server` `.resourcemanager.recovery.ZKRMState` `Store`).

`yarn.resourcemanager`
`.store.class`
	`org.apache.hadoop.yarn.`
	`server.resourcemanager`
	`.recovery.FileSystem-`
	`RMStateStore`
		Writes ResourceManager state into a file-system for recovery purposes.

CONTAINER PROPERTIES

Table 2.3 shows the MapReduce properties that are related to the map and reduce processes that run the tasks.

Table 2.3 MapReduce 2 properties that impact containers (map/reduce tasks)

Property name	Default value	Description
`mapreduce.map.memory.mb`	1024	The amount of memory to be allocated to containers (processes) that run mappers, in megabytes. The YARN scheduler uses this information to determine whether there's available capacity on nodes in a cluster. The old property name, `mapred.job.map.memory.mb`, has been deprecated.

Table 2.3 MapReduce 2 properties that impact containers (map/reduce tasks)

Property name	Default value	Description
`mapreduce.reduce.memory.mb`	1024	The amount of memory to be allocated to containers (processes) that run reducers, in megabytes. The YARN scheduler uses this information to determine whether there's available capacity on nodes in a cluster. The old property name, `mapreduce.reduce.memory .mb`, has been deprecated.
`mapreduce.map.cpu.vcores`	1	The number of virtual cores to be allocated to the map processes.
`mapreduce.reduce.cpu.vcores`	1	The number of virtual cores to be allocated to the reduce processes.
`mapred.child.java.opts`	`-Xmx200m`	Java options for the map and reduce processes. The `@taskid@` symbol, if present, will be replaced by the current TaskID. Any other occurrences of @ will go unchanged. For example, to enable verbose garbage collection logging to a file named for the TaskID in /tmp and to set the heap maximum to be a gigabyte, pass a value of `-Xmx1024m -verbose:gc -Xloggc:/tmp/@taskid@.gc`. Usage of `-Djava.library.path` can cause programs to no longer function if Hadoop-native libraries are used. These values should instead be set as part of `LD_LIBRARY_PATH` in the map/reduce JVM environment using the `mapreduce.map.env` and `mapreduce.reduce.env` configuration settings.
`mapred.map.child.java.opts`	None	Map process–specific JVM arguments. The old property name, `mapred.map.child.java .opts`, has been deprecated.
`mapreduce.reduce.java.opts`	None	Reduce process–specific JVM arguments. The old property name, `mapred.reduce.child.java .opts`, has been deprecated.

CONFIGURATION NO LONGER IN EFFECT

Common properties in MapReduce 1 that are no longer in effect in MapReduce 2 are shown in table 2.4, along with explanations as to why they no longer exist.

Table 2.4 Old MapReduce 1 properties that are no longer in use

Property name	Description
`mapred.job.tracker` `mapred.job.tracker.http.address`	The JobTracker no longer exists in YARN; it's been replaced by the ApplicationMaster UI and the Job-History UI.
`mapred.task.tracker.http.address` `mapred.task.tracker.report.address`	The TaskTracker also doesn't exist in YARN—it's been replaced by the YARN NodeManager.

Table 2.4   Old MapReduce 1 properties that are no longer in use *(continued)*

Property name	Description
`mapred.local.dir`	This used to be the local directory where intermediary data for MapReduce jobs was stored. This has been deprecated, and the new property name is `mapreduce.jobtracker.system.dir`. Its use has also been relegated to use only in the LocalJobRunner, which comes into play if you're running a local job (not on a YARN cluster).
`mapred.system.dir`	Much like `mapred.local.dir`, this is relegated to duty when running the LocalJobRunner.
`mapred.tasktracker.map.tasks.maximum` `mapred.tasktracker.reduce.tasks.maximum`	This was used to control the maximum number of map and reduce task processes that could run on a node. These were called "slots," and they were static in Hadoop 1. In Hadoop 2, YARN doesn't impose a static limit on the number of concurrent containers on a node, so these properties are no longer needed.
`mapred.job.reuse.jvm.num.tasks`	You used to be able to sequentially run multiple tasks in the same JVM, which was useful for tasks that were short-lived (and to diminish the overhead of creating a separate process per task). This is no longer supported in YARN.
`tasktracker.http.threads`	This is no longer used in MRv2. Map outputs are now fetched from a new ShuffleHandler service, which is NIO-based and is by default configured with no cap in the number of open connections (configured via `mapreduce.shuffle.max.connections`).
`io.sort.record.percent`	This shuffle property used to control how much accounting space was used in the map-side sort buffer (`io.sort.mb`). MapReduce 2 is smarter about how to fill up `io.sort.mb`.[a]

[a] "Map-side sort is hampered by io.sort.record.percent" and details can be seen at https://issues.apache.org/jira/browse/MAPREDUCE-64.

DEPRECATED PROPERTIES

Most of the MapReduce 1 (and many HDFS) properties have been deprecated in favor of property names that are better organized.[11] Currently Hadoop 2 supports both the deprecated and new property names, but it would be prudent for you to update your properties, as there's no guarantee that Hadoop 3 and later will support deprecated properties. Luckily, you get a dump of all the deprecated configuration properties on standard output when you run a MapReduce job, an example of which is shown here:

```
Configuration.deprecation: mapred.cache.files is deprecated.
Instead, use mapreduce.job.cache.files
```

---

[11] See the web page "Deprecated properties" at http://hadoop.apache.org/docs/stable/hadoop-project-dist/hadoop-common/DeprecatedProperties.html for the properties that have been deprecated and their new names.

It's clear that there were quite a few changes to MapReduce properties. You may be curious to know how the rest of MapReduce changed and what parts managed to retain strong backward compatibility. Did the MapReduce APIs and binaries escape unscathed with the major version bump in Hadoop?[12]

2.2.3 *Backward compatibility*

Backward compatibility is an important consideration for systems with large, established user bases, as it ensures that they can rapidly move to a new version of a system with little or no change. This section covers various parts of the MapReduce system and help you determine whether you need to change your systems to be able to function on MapReduce 2.

SCRIPT COMPATIBILITY

The scripts that are bundled with Hadoop remain unchanged. This means that you can continue to use hadoop jar ... to launch jobs, and all other uses of the main hadoop script continue to work, as do the other scripts bundled with Hadoop.

CONFIGURATION

With the introduction of YARN, and MapReduce becoming an application, many MapReduce 1 property names are now deprecated in MapReduce 2, and some are no longer in effect. Section 2.2.2 covers changes to some of the more commonly used properties.

API BACKWARD COMPATIBILITY

In porting MapReduce to YARN, the developers did their best to maintain backward compatibility for existing MapReduce applications. They were able to achieve code compatibility, but in some cases weren't able to preserve binary compatibility:

- *Code compatibility* means that any MapReduce code that exists today will run fine on YARN as long as the code is recompiled. This is great, as it means that you don't need to modify your code to get it working on YARN.
- *Binary compatibility* means that MapReduce bytecode will run unchanged on YARN. In other words, you don't have to recompile your code—you can use the same classes and JARs that worked on Hadoop 1, and they'll work just fine on YARN.

Code that uses the "old" MapReduce API (org.apache.hadoop.mapreduce package) is binary compatible, so if your existing MapReduce code only uses the old API, you're all set—no recompilation of your code is required.

This isn't the case for certain uses of the "new" MapReduce API (org.apache.hadoop.mapreduce). If you use the new API, it's possible that you are using some features of the API that changed; namely, some classes were changed to interfaces. A few of these classes are as follows:

---

[12] Semantic versioning (http://semver.org/) permits APIs to change in ways that break backward compatibility when the major version number is incremented.

- JobContext
- TaskAttemptContext
- Counter

This begs the question of what to do if you're using the new MapReduce API and have code that needs to run on both versions of Hadoop.

TECHNIQUE 5 Writing code that works on Hadoop versions 1 and 2

If you're using the "new" MapReduce API and have your own Input/OutputFormat classes or use counters (to name a few operations that are not code-compatible across MapReduce versions), then you have JARs that will likely need to be recompiled to work with MapReduce 2. This is a nuisance if you have to support both MapReduce 1 and 2. You could create two sets of JARs targeting each version of MapReduce, but you would likely owe your build team several beers and end up with more complicated build and deployment systems. Or you can use the tip in this technique and continue to distribute a single JAR.

■ Problem

You're using MapReduce code that isn't binary compatible with MapReduce 2, and you want to be able to update your code in a way that will be compatible with both MapReduce versions.

■ Solution

Use a Hadoop compatibility library that works around the API differences.

■ Discussion

The Elephant Bird project includes a HadoopCompat class, which dynamically figures out which version of Hadoop you're running on and uses Java reflection to invoke the appropriate method calls to work with your version of Hadoop. The following code shows an example of its usage, where inside an InputFormat implementation, the TaskAttemptContext changed from a class to an interface, and the HadoopCompat class is being used to extract the Configuration object:

```
import com.alexholmes.hadooputils.util.HadoopCompat;
  import org.apache.hadoop.mapreduce.InputSplit;
import org.apache.hadoop.mapreduce.RecordReader;
import org.apache.hadoop.mapreduce.TaskAttemptContext;

public class MyInputFormat implements InputFormat {
  @Override
  public RecordReader createRecordReader(InputSplit split,
                                    TaskAttemptContext context)
       throws IOException {
    final Configuration conf = HadoopCompat.getConfiguration(context);
      ...
  }
}
```

Which classes changed to interfaces in Hadoop 2? Some of the notable ones are `TaskAttemptContext`, `JobContext`, and `MapContext`. Table 2.5 shows a selection of some of the methods available in the `HadoopCompat` class.

Table 2.5   Common classes and methods that are not binary compatible across MapReduce versions

Hadoop class and method	HadoopCompat call	Where you'd encounter the interface
`JobContext` `.getConfiguration`	`HadoopCompat` `.getConfiguration`	This is probably the most commonly used class (now an interface). You'll likely bump into this interface as it's how you get to a map or reduce task's configuration.
`TaskAttemptContext` `.setStatus`	`HadoopCompat` `.setStatus`	You'll encounter this interface if you have a custom `InputFormat`, `OutputFormat`, `RecordReader`, or `RecordWriter`.
`TaskAttemptContext` `.getTaskAttemptID`	`HadoopCompat` `.getTaskAttemptID`	You'll use this interface if you have a custom `InputFormat`, `OutputFormat`, `RecordReader`, or `RecordWriter`.
`TaskAttemptContext` `.getCounter`	`HadoopCompat` `.getCounter`	You'll bump into this interface if you have a custom `InputFormat`, `OutputFormat`, `RecordReader`, or `RecordWriter`.
`Counter` `.incrementCounter`	`HadoopCompat` `.incrementCounter`	If you use counters in your jobs, you'll need to use the HadoopCompat call.

The `HadoopCompat` class also has a handy method called `isVersion2x`, which returns a Boolean if the class has determined that your runtime is running against version 2 of Hadoop.

This is just a sample of the methods on this class—for complete details, see the Elephant Bird project's HadoopCompat page on GitHub: https://github.com/kevinweil/elephant-bird/blob/master/hadoop-compat/src/main/java/com/twitter/elephantbird/util/HadoopCompat.java.

Maven Central contains a package with this library in it, and you can take a look at the Maven repository's page on "Elephant Bird Hadoop Compatibility" at http://mvnrepository.com/artifact/com.twitter.elephantbird/elephant-bird-hadoop-compat for an example entry you can add to your Maven file.

As you saw earlier, the main script in Hadoop 1, `hadoop`, continues to exist unchanged in Hadoop 2. In the next section you'll see how a newer version of the script should be used to run not only MapReduce jobs but also issue YARN commands.

2.2.4   Running a job

It's time to run a MapReduce 2 job. Don't worry, doing so is pretty much identical to how you did it in MapReduce 1.

TECHNIQUE 6   **Using the command line to run a job**

In this technique you'll learn how to use the command line to run a MapReduce job.

■ **Problem**

You want to use the YARN command line to run a MapReduce job.

■ **Solution**

Use the yarn command.

■ **Discussion**

In Hadoop 1, the hadoop command was the one used to launch jobs. This command still works for backward compatibility reasons, but the YARN form of this command is the yarn script, which works much like the old hadoop script works. As an example, this is how you'd run the pi job bundled in the Hadoop examples JAR:[13]

```
$ yarn jar ${HADOOP_HOME}/share/hadoop/mapreduce/*-examples-*.jar pi 2 10

Estimated value of Pi is 3.1428000
```

If you're in the habit of using hadoop to run your jobs, give some thought to replacing it with the yarn command. It's unclear whether there are plans to deprecate and remove the hadoop command, but you can be sure that the yarn equivalent is here to stay.

The ways you can launch MapReduce jobs have changed in version 2, and so has the mechanism by which you view the status and details of running and completed jobs.

2.2.5   *Monitoring running jobs and viewing archived jobs*

When running MapReduce jobs, it's important for monitoring and debugging purposes to be able to view the status of a job and its tasks and to gain access to the task logs. In MapReduce 1 this would have all been carried out using the JobTracker UI, which could be used to view details on running and completed or archived jobs.

As highlighted in section 2.2.1, the JobTracker no longer exists in MapReduce 2; it has been replaced with an ApplicationMaster-specific UI, and the JobHistoryServer for completed jobs. The ApplicationMaster UI can be seen in figure 2.11. For fetching map and reduce task logs, the UI redirects to the NodeManager.

> **Figuring out where your ResourceManager UI is running** You can retrieve the host and port of the ResourceManager by examining the value of yarn.resourcemanager.webapp.address (or yarn.resourcemanager.webapp.https .address if HTTPS access is required). In the case of a pseudo-distributed installation, this will be http://localhost:8088 (or port 8090 for HTTPS). Copying the host and port into your browser is sufficient to access the UI as a URL path isn't required.

---

[13] This example calculates the value of pi using the quasi-Monte Carlo method.

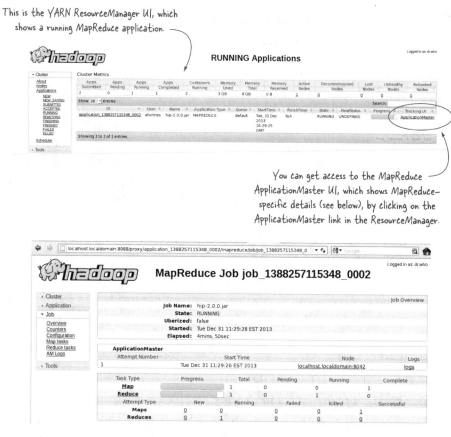

Figure 2.11   The YARN ResourceManager UI, showing applications that are currently executing

The JobHistoryServer can be seen in figure 2.12.

MapReduce 2 has changed how jobs are executed, configured, and monitored. It has also introduced new features, such as uber jobs, which are up next.

2.2.6   *Uber jobs*

When running small MapReduce jobs, the time taken for resource scheduling and process forking is often a large percentage of the overall runtime. In MapReduce 1 you didn't have any choice about this overhead, but MapReduce 2 has become smarter and can now cater to your needs to run lightweight jobs as quickly as possible.

TECHNIQUE 7   Running small MapReduce jobs

This technique looks at how you can run MapReduce jobs within the MapReduce ApplicationMaster. This is useful when you're working with a small amount of data, as you remove the additional time that MapReduce normally spends spinning up and bringing down map and reduce processes.

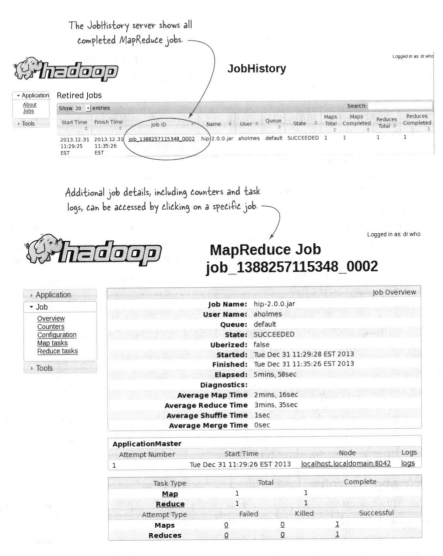

Figure 2.12   The JobHistory UI, showing MapReduce applications that have completed

■ **Problem**

You have a MapReduce job that operates on a small dataset, and you want to avoid the overhead of scheduling and creating map and reduce processes.

■ **Solution**

Configure your job to enable uber jobs; this will run the mappers and reducers in the same process as the ApplicationMaster.

■ **Discussion**

Uber jobs are jobs that are executed within the MapReduce ApplicationMaster. Rather than liaise with the ResourceManager to create the map and reduce containers, the

ApplicationMaster runs the map and reduce tasks within its own process and avoids the overhead of launching and communicating with remote containers.

To enable uber jobs, you need to set the following property:

```
mapreduce.job.ubertask.enable=true
```

Table 2.6 lists some additional properties that control whether a job qualities for uberization.

Table 2.6   Properties for customizing uber jobs

Property	Default value	Description
mapreduce.job .ubertask.maxmaps	9	The number of mappers for a job must be less than or equal to this value for the job to be uberized.
mapreduce.job .ubertask.maxreduces	1	The number of reducers for a job must be less than or equal to this value for the job to be uberized.
mapreduce.job .ubertask.maxbytes	Default block size	The total input size of a job must be less than or equal to this value for the job to be uberized.

When running uber jobs, MapReduce disables speculative execution and also sets the maximum attempts for tasks to 1.

> **Reducer restrictions**   Currently only map-only jobs and jobs with one reducer are supported for uberization.

Uber jobs are a handy new addition to the MapReduce capabilities, and they only work on YARN. This concludes our look at MapReduce on YARN. Next you'll see examples of other systems running on YARN.

2.3   *YARN applications*

So far you've seen what YARN is, how it works, and how MapReduce 2 works as a YARN application. But this is only the first step of YARN's journey; there are already several projects that work on YARN, and over time, you should expect to see rapid growth in YARN's ecosystem.

At this point, you may be asking yourself why YARN applications are compelling and why the Hadoop community put so much work into YARN's architecture and the port of MapReduce to a YARN application. There are many reasons that we touched on at the start of the chapter, but the most important reason behind this revolutionary change in Hadoop is to open up the platform. Think about how our systems work today—gone are the days when we worked on monolithic systems; instead, we live in a world where we run multiple disparate systems in our datacenters, as shown in figure 2.13.

That's a lot of systems! And chances are that you're already running many of them in production right now. If you're an engineer, you're probably excited about having

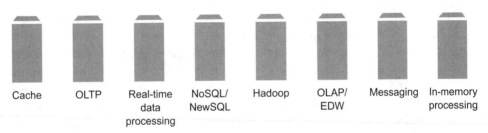

Figure 2.13 Common systems we run today. They are siloed, which complicates data and resource sharing.

all these systems in play, but systems administrators and architects get migraines thinking about the challenges that supporting all these systems brings:

- They have to build the in-house knowledge to administer and keep the systems up and healthy. Systems fail, especially complicated distributed systems, and being open source, many of these systems don't have the tooling to facilitate easy management.
- Data exchange between systems is painful, primarily due to the volume of data and the lack of tooling for the data movement. Large, expensive projects ensue.[14]
- Each system has to solve the same distributed problems, such as fault tolerance, distributed storage, log handling, and resource scheduling.

YARN promises a single cluster that can have its resources managed in a uniform way, support multi-tenant applications and users, and offer elastic computation over shared storage. HBase coupled with Hoya gives us a sneak peek at what the future could look like: strong data locality properties are used for efficient movement of data in and out of HBase; and Hoya, with its YARN integration, provides elastic, on-demand computing, with the ability to run multiple HBase clusters on a single YARN cluster.

In the following sections, you'll be introduced to several systems across a broad spectrum of technologies that are built on YARN. We'll look at one or more examples of these technologies that have been built with YARN compatibility.

2.3.1 NoSQL

NoSQL covers a wide array of technologies, but, in short, they're systems that provide real-time CRUD operations in a way that doesn't hold ACID properties sacred. These systems were created to work around the shortcomings of monolithic OLAP systems, which impeded the ability of system architectures to scale out and provide responsive services.

There are many NoSQL systems out there, but none have been more integrated with Hadoop than HBase. Even prior to YARN, the goal of HBase was to use HDFS for

---

[14] LinkedIn addresses this with a "data plane" architecture highlighted in Jay Kreps' blog post, "The Log: What every software engineer should know about real-time data's unifying abstraction"—take a look at the "unified log" image and the surrounding text for an architectural solution to help reduce these pain points: http://engineering.linkedin.com/distributed-systems/log-what-every-software-engineer-should-know-about-real-time-datas-unifying.

its storage, and HBase benefited from close integration with MapReduce, allowing for batch-processing facilities that often eluded its competitors.

YARN solves two challenges for HBase. HBase and MapReduce 1 coexisting on a cluster brought resource management challenges, as there were no easy ways to guarantee SLAs to both systems. YARN capitalizes on cgroups in Linux, which provide concurrently executing processes with guaranteed access to their required resources. The second opportunity that YARN gave HBase was the ability to run multiple HBase clusters on the same Hadoop cluster. This support is being carried out in a project called Hoya, short for HBase on Yarn.

2.3.2 Interactive SQL

Up until recently, running SQL on Hadoop has been an exercise in patience—kick up your Hive shell, enter your query, and wait, often minutes, until you get a result.[15] Data scientists and analysts would likely not find this to be the most conducive environment for quickly probing and experimenting with data.

There have been several initiatives to work around this issue. Cloudera's solution was to create the Impala project, which bypasses MapReduce altogether and operates by running its own daemon on each slave node in your cluster (colocated with the HDFS slave daemon, the DataNode, for data locality). To help with multi-tenancy on YARN clusters, Cloudera has developed Llama (http://cloudera.github.io/llama/), which aims to work with YARN in such a way that YARN understands the resources that the Impala daemons are utilizing on a cluster.

Hortonworks has taken a different approach—they've focused on making improvements to Hive and have made significant steps toward making Hive more interactive. They've combined their improvements under a project called Stinger (http://hortonworks.com/labs/stinger/), and the most significant change involves bypassing MapReduce and using Tez, a YARN DAG processing framework, to execute their work.

Apache Drill is another SQL-on-Hadoop solution that promises the ability to work over many persistent stores, such as Cassandra and MongoDB. They have an open ticket to add YARN support to the project (https://issues.apache.org/jira/browse/DRILL-142).

Facebook Presto is also in the SQL-on-Hadoop camp, but so far there's no word on whether there will be YARN support.

2.3.3 Graph processing

Modern graph-processing systems allow distributed graph algorithms to execute against large graphs that contain billions of nodes and trillions of edges. Graph operations using traditional MapReduce typically result in one job per iteration,[16] which is

---

[15] The reason Hive queries used to take a long time is that they would be translated to one or more MapReduce jobs, so job startup times (coupled with writing intermediary outputs to and from disk) resulted in long query times.

[16] Giraph in its MapReduce 1 implementation works around this by using long-running map tasks that exchange state with ZooKeeper and pass messages to each other.

slow and cumbersome, as it requires the entire graph data structure to be serialized to and from disk on each iteration.

Apache Giraph, a popular graph-processing project, has worked on Hadoop since version 1 and earlier, and the committers have also updated Giraph so that it runs as a native YARN application.

Apache Hama also has some graph-processing capabilities on YARN.

2.3.4 Real-time data processing

Real-time data processing systems are computational systems that work on unbounded streams of data. The features of these systems are similar to those of MapReduce, as they allow operations such as filtering, projection, joins, and aggregations. A typical use of these systems is to process real-time events occurring in a system, perform some aggregations, and then push the results out to a NoSQL store for retrieval by another system.

Arguably, the real-time data processing system with most traction at the time of writing is Apache Storm, originally built by Nathan Marz, which is a key part of his Lambda Architecture.[17] To bring Storm to YARN, Yahoo has created a project called storm-yarn. This project offers several advantages—not only will this allow multiple Storm clusters to run on YARN, but it promises elasticity for Storm clusters: the ability to quickly provision additional resources for Storm. More details on the project can be seen at https://github.com/yahoo/storm-yarn.

Spark Streaming is another notable real-time data processing project developed as an extension to the Spark API, and it supports consuming data sources such as HDFS, Kafka, Flume, and more. Spark is also supported on YARN. Spark Streaming may become a strong competitor for Storm, notably because once you master Spark, you also know how to do Spark Streaming, and vice versa. This means you have a single programming paradigm for both offline and real-time data analysis.

Other real-time data processing systems with YARN integration are Apache S4, Apache Samza (which came out of LinkedIn), and DataTorrent.

2.3.5 Bulk synchronous parallel

Bulk synchronous parallel (BSP) is a distributed processing method whereby multiple parallel workers independently work on a subset of an overall problem, after which they exchange data among themselves and then use a global synchronization mechanism to wait for all workers to complete before repeating the process. Google Pregel published how their graph processing framework is inspired by BSP, and Apache Giraph uses a similar BSP model for graph iteration.

Apache Hama is a general-purpose BSP implementation that can work on YARN. It also has built-in graph-processing capabilities.

---

[17] The Lambda Architecture plays to the strengths of batch and real-time. Read more in Nathan Marz's book, *Big Data* (Manning, 2014).

2.3.6   *MPI*

MPI (Message Passing Interface) is a mechanism that allows messages to be exchanged on clusters of hosts. Open MPI is an open source MPI implementation. There's currently an open ticket to complete work on integrating Open MPI support into Hadoop (https://issues.apache.org/jira/browse/MAPREDUCE-2911). The work that has been completed so far for this integration is in mpich2-yarn at https://github.com/clarkyzl/mpich2-yarn.

2.3.7   *In-memory*

In-memory computing uses the ever-increasing memory footprint in our systems to quickly perform computing activities such as iterative processing and interactive data mining.

Apache Spark is a popular example that came out of Berkeley. It's a key part of an overall set of solutions that also includes Shark for SQL operations and GraphX for graph processing. Cloudera's CDH5 distribution includes Spark running on YARN.

For additional details on how to run Spark on YARN, see Spark's "Launching Spark on YARN" page at http://spark.apache.org/docs/0.9.0/running-on-yarn.html.

2.3.8   *DAG execution*

Directed Acyclic Graph (DAG) execution engines allow you to model data-processing logic as a DAG and then execute it in parallel over a large dataset.

Apache Tez is an example of a DAG execution engine; it was born out of the need to provide a more generalized MapReduce system that would preserve the parallelism and throughput of MapReduce, and at the same time support additional processing models and optimizations beyond that which MapReduce provides. Examples of Tez's abilities include not imposing a specific data model, so that both the key/value model of MapReduce, as well as the tuple-based models of Hive and Pig, can be supported.

Tez provides a number of advantages over MapReduce, which include eliminating replicated write barriers that exist in MapReduce between multiple jobs—a major performance bottleneck for systems like Hive and Pig. Tez can also support reduce operations without the sorting overhead that MapReduce requires, resulting in more efficient pipelines where sorting isn't necessary for the application. Tez also supports sophisticated operations such as Map-Map-Reduce, or any arbitrary graph of operations, freeing up developers to more naturally express their data pipelines. Tez can also be used to make dynamic data flow choices when executing—for example, based on the size of intermediary data in your flow, you may decide to store it in memory or in HDFS or local disk.

The upshot of all of this is that Tez can shake off the batch-only shackles of MapReduce and support interactive use cases. As an example, the original scope of Tez is a large step in Hortonworks' goal of making Hive interactive—moving from MapReduce to Tez is a key part of that work.

2.4 *Chapter summary*

Hadoop version 2 turns the old way work has been done in Hadoop upside down. No longer are you limited to running MapReduce on your clusters. This chapter covered the essentials that you need to get going with YARN. You looked at why YARN is important in Hadoop, saw a high-level overview of the architecture, and learned about some of the salient YARN configuration properties that you'll need to use.

The advent of YARN has also introduced significant changes in how MapReduce works. MapReduce has been ported into a YARN application, and in section 2.2 you saw how MapReduce executes on Hadoop 2, learned what configuration properties have changed, and also picked up some new features, such as uber jobs.

The last section of this chapter covered some exciting examples of up-and-coming YARN applications to give you a sense of what capabilities you should expect to be able to unleash on your YARN cluster. For additional YARN coverage, feel free to skip ahead to chapter 10 and look at how to develop your very own YARN application!

Now that you understand the lay of the land with YARN, it's time to move on to look at data storage in Hadoop. The focus of the next chapter is on working with common file formats such as XML and JSON, as well as picking file formats better suited for life in Hadoop, such as Parquet and Avro.

Part 2

Data logistics

If you've been thinking about how to work with Hadoop in production settings, you'll benefit from this part of the book, which covers the first set of hurdles you'll need to jump. These chapters detail the often-overlooked yet crucial topics that deal with data management in Hadoop.

Chapter 3 looks at ways to work with data stored in different formats, such as XML and JSON, paving the way for a broader examination of data formats such as Avro and Parquet that work best with big data and Hadoop.

Chapter 4 examines some strategies for laying out your data in HDFS, and partitioning and compacting your data. This chapter also covers ways of working with small files, as well as how compression can save you from many storage and computational headaches.

Chapter 5 looks at ways to manage moving large quantities of data into and out of Hadoop. Examples include working with relational data in RDBMSs, structured files, and HBase.

Data serialization—
working with text
and beyond

This chapter covers

- Working with text, XML, and JSON
- Understanding SequenceFile, Avro, Protocol Buffers, and Parquet
- Working with custom data formats

MapReduce offers straightforward, well-documented support for working with simple data formats such as log files. But MapReduce has evolved beyond log files to more sophisticated data-serialization formats—such as text, XML, and JSON—to the point where its documentation and built-in support runs dry. The goal of this chapter is to document how you can work with common data-serialization formats, as well as to examine more structured serialization formats and compare their fitness for use with MapReduce.

Imagine that you want to work with the ubiquitous XML and JSON data-serialization formats. These formats work in a straightforward manner in most programming languages, with several tools being available to help you with marshaling, unmarshaling, and validating where applicable. Working with XML and JSON in MapReduce, however, poses two equally important challenges. First, MapReduce requires classes that can support reading and writing a particular data-serialization format; if you're working with a custom file format, there's a good chance it doesn't have such classes to support the serialization format you're working with. Second, MapReduce's power lies in its ability to parallelize reading your input data. If your input files are large (think hundreds of megabytes or more), it's crucial that the classes reading your serialization format be able to split your large files so multiple map tasks can read them in parallel.

We'll start this chapter by tackling the problem of how to work with serialization formats such as XML and JSON. Then we'll compare and contrast data-serialization formats that are better suited to working with big data, such as Avro and Parquet. The final hurdle is when you need to work with a file format that's proprietary, or a less common file format for which no read/write bindings exist in MapReduce. I'll show you how to write your own classes to read/write your file format.

> **XML and JSON formats** This chapter assumes you're familiar with the XML and JSON data formats. Wikipedia provides some good background articles on XML and JSON, if needed. You should also have some experience writing MapReduce programs and should understand the basic concepts of HDFS and MapReduce input and output. Chuck Lam's book, *Hadoop in Action* (Manning, 2010), is a good resource on this topic.

Data serialization support in MapReduce is a property of the input and output classes that read and write MapReduce data. Let's start with an overview of how MapReduce supports data input and output.

3.1   *Understanding inputs and outputs in MapReduce*

Your data might be XML files sitting behind a number of FTP servers, text log files sitting on a central web server, or Lucene indexes in HDFS.[1] How does MapReduce support reading and writing to these different serialization structures across the various storage mechanisms?

Figure 3.1 shows the high-level data flow through MapReduce and identifies the actors responsible for various parts of the flow. On the input side, you can see that some work (*Create split*) is performed outside of the map phase, and other work is performed as part of the map phase (*Read split*). All of the output work is performed in the reduce phase (*Write output*).

---

[1] Apache Lucene is an information retrieval project that stores data in an inverted index data structure optimized for full-text search. More information is available at http://lucene.apache.org/.

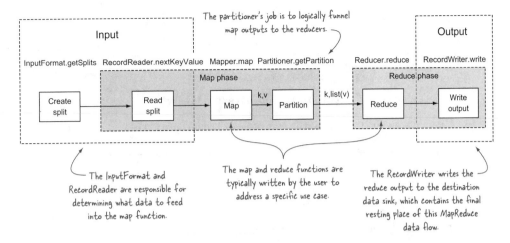

Figure 3.1 **High-level input and output actors in MapReduce**

Figure 3.2 shows the same flow with a map-only job. In a map-only job, the Map-Reduce framework still uses the OutputFormat and RecordWriter classes to write the outputs directly to the data sink.

Let's walk through the data flow and discuss the responsibilities of the various actors. As we do this, we'll also look at the relevant code from the built-in TextInputFormat and TextOutputFormat classes to better understand the concepts. The TextInputFormat and TextOutputFormat classes read and write line-oriented text files.

3.1.1 Data input

The two classes that support data input in MapReduce are InputFormat and RecordReader. The InputFormat class is consulted to determine how the input data should be partitioned for the map tasks, and the RecordReader performs the reading of data from the inputs.

INPUTFORMAT

Every job in MapReduce must define its inputs according to contracts specified in the InputFormat abstract class. InputFormat implementers must fulfill three contracts: they describe type information for map input keys and values, they specify how the input

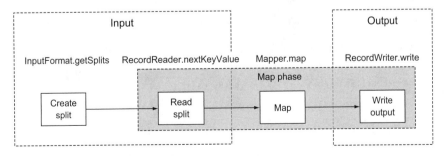

Figure 3.2 **Input and output actors in MapReduce with no reducers**

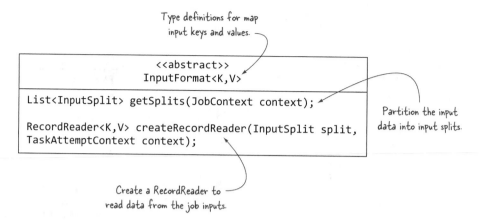

Figure 3.3 The annotated InputFormat class and its three contracts

data should be partitioned, and they indicate the RecordReader instance that should read the data from source. Figure 3.3 shows the InputFormat class and how these three contracts are defined.

Arguably, the most crucial contract is that of determining how to divide the input data. In MapReduce nomenclature, these divisions are referred to as *input splits*. The input splits directly impact the map parallelism, because each split is processed by a single map task. Working with an InputFormat that's unable to create multiple input splits over a single data source (such as a file) will result in a slow map phase, because the file will be processed sequentially.

The TextInputFormat class (view source at http://mng.bz/h728) provides an implementation of the InputFormat class's createRecordReader method, but it delegates the calculation of input splits to its parent class, FileInputFormat. The following code shows the relevant parts of the TextInputFormat class:

```
public class TextInputFormat
            extends FileInputFormat<LongWritable, Text> {

  @Override
  public RecordReader<LongWritable, Text>
    createRecordReader(InputSplit split,
                    TaskAttemptContext context) {
    String delimiter = context.getConfiguration().get(
       "textinputformat.record.delimiter");
    byte[] recordDelimiterBytes = null;

    if (null != delimiter) {
      recordDelimiterBytes = delimiter.getBytes();
    }

    return new LineRecordReader(recordDelimiterBytes);

  }
...
```

The parent class, FileInputFormat, provides all of the input split functionality.

The default record delimiter is newline, but it can be overridden with textinputformat.record.delimiter.

Construct the RecordReader to read the data from the data source.

The code in FileInputFormat (source at http://mng.bz/CZB8) that determines the input splits is a little more complicated. A simplified form of the code is shown in the following example to portray the main elements of the getSplits method:

```
public List<InputSplit> getSplits(JobContext job
                           ) throws IOException {
    List<InputSplit> splits = new ArrayList<InputSplit>();
    List<FileStatus>files = listStatus(job);
    for (FileStatus file: files) {
        Path path = file.getPath();
        BlockLocation[] blkLocations =
        FileSystem.getFileBlockLocations(file, 0, length);
        long splitSize = file.getBlockSize();

        while (splitsRemaining()) {
            splits.add(new FileSplit(path, ...));
        }
    }
    return splits;
}
```

The listStatus method determines all the input files for the job.

Retrieve all of the file blocks.

The size of the splits is the same as the block size for the file. Each file can have a different block size.

Create a split for each file block and add it to the result.

The following code shows how you can specify the InputFormat to use for a MapReduce job:

```
job.setInputFormatClass(TextInputFormat.class);
```

RECORDREADER

You'll create and use the RecordReader class in the map tasks to read data from an input split and to provide each record in the form of a key/value pair for use by mappers. A task is commonly created for each input split, and each task has a single RecordReader that's responsible for reading the data for that input split. Figure 3.4 shows the abstract methods you must implement.

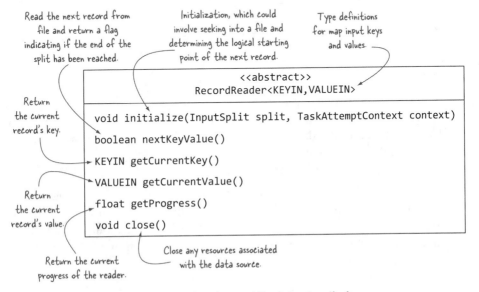

Figure 3.4   The annotated RecordReader class and its abstract methods

As shown previously, the TextInputFormat class creates a LineRecordReader to read records from the input splits. The LineRecordReader directly extends the RecordReader class and uses the LineReader class to read lines from the input split. The LineRecordReader uses the byte offset in the file for the map key, and the contents of the line for the map value. The following example shows a simplified version of the LineRecordReader (source at http://mng.bz/mYO7):

```
public class LineRecordReader
                    extends RecordReader<LongWritable, Text> {
    private LineReader in;
    private LongWritable key = new LongWritable();
    private Text value = new Text();

    public void initialize(InputSplit genericSplit,
                        TaskAttemptContext context) throws IOException {
        FileSplit split = (FileSplit) genericSplit;

        // open the file and seek to the start of the split
        FileSystem fs = file.getFileSystem(job);
        FSDataInputStream fileIn = fs.open(split.getPath());
        fileIn.seek(start);
        in = new LineReader(fileIn, job);

        if (notAtStartOfFile) {
            start += in.readLine(...);
        }
    }

    public boolean nextKeyValue() throws IOException {
        key.set(pos);
        return in.readLine(value, ...) > 0;
    }
}
```

Seek to the start of the input split.

Create a new LineReader that can read lines from a stream.

Open an InputStream to the input split file.

If you aren't at the start of the file, figure out where to start reading lines by reading characters until you hit a newline. At that point you're ready to start supplying lines to the map.

After the initialize method is called, it's called repeatedly by the MapReduce framework until it returns false, which signifies the end of the input split.

Read the next line into the value. If you've gone beyond the end of the input split, return false.

Set the byte offset in the file as the key.

Because the LineReader class is easy, we'll skip that code. The next step is to look at how MapReduce supports data outputs.

3.1.2   Data output

MapReduce uses similar processes for supporting both output and input data. Two classes must exist: an OutputFormat and a RecordWriter. The OutputFormat performs some basic validation of the data sink properties, and the RecordWriter writes each reducer output to the data sink.

OUTPUTFORMAT

Much like the InputFormat class, the OutputFormat class, as shown in figure 3.5, defines the contracts that implementers must fulfill: checking the information related to the job output, providing a RecordWriter, and specifying an output committer, which allows writes to be staged and then made "permanent" upon task or job success. (Output committing is covered in section 3.5.2.)

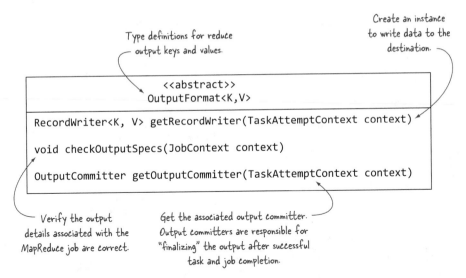

Figure 3.5 The annotated `OutputFormat` class

Just like the `TextInputFormat`, the `TextOutputFormat` also extends a base class, `FileOutput-Format`, which takes care of some complicated logistics such as output committing, which we'll cover later in this chapter. For now, let's take a look at the work that `TextOutputFormat` performs (source at http://mng.bz/lnR0):

```
public class TextOutputFormat<K, V> extends FileOutputFormat<K, V> {
    public RecordWriter<K, V>
        getRecordWriter(TaskAttemptContext job
                        ) throws IOException, InterruptedException {
        boolean isCompressed = getCompressOutput(job);
        String keyValueSeparator= conf.get(
        "mapred.textoutputformat.separator", "\t");

        Path file = getDefaultWorkFile(job, extension);

        FileSystem fs = file.getFileSystem(conf);
        FSDataOutputStream fileOut = fs.create(file, false);

        return new LineRecordWriter<K, V>(
            fileOut, keyValueSeparator);
    }
}
```

The default key/ value separator is the tab character, but this can be changed with the `mapred.textoutput format.separator` configuration setting.

Creates a unique filename for the reducer in a temporary directory.

Creates the output file.

Returns a RecordWriter used to write to the file.

The following code shows how you can specify the `OutputFormat` that should be used for a MapReduce job:

```
job.setOutputFormatClass(TextOutputFormat.class);
```

RECORDWRITER

You'll use the `RecordWriter` to write the reducer outputs to the destination data sink. It's a simple class, as figure 3.6 illustrates.

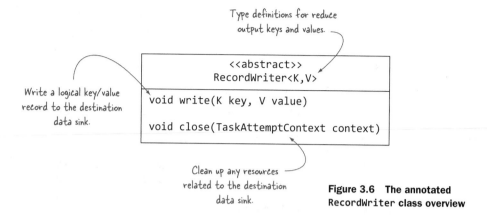

Figure 3.6   **The annotated**
RecordWriter class overview

The TextOutputFormat returns a LineRecordWriter object, which is an inner class of Text-OutputFormat, to perform the writing to the file. A simplified version of that class (source at http://mng.bz/lnR0) is shown in the following example:

```
protected static class LineRecordWriter<K, V>
  extends RecordWriter<K, V> {

  protected DataOutputStream out;

  public synchronized void write(K key, V value)
    throws IOException {

    writeObject(key);
    out.write(keyValueSeparator);
    writeObject(value);
    out.write(newline);
  }

  private void writeObject(Object o) throws IOException {
    out.write(o);
  }
}
```

Whereas on the map side it's the InputFormat that determines how many map tasks are executed, on the reducer side the number of tasks is solely based on the value for mapred.reduce.tasks set by the client (or if it isn't set, the value is picked up from mapred-site.xml, or from mapred-default.xml if it doesn't exist in the site file).

Now that you know what's involved in working with input and output data in Map-Reduce, it's time to apply that knowledge to solving some common data-serialization problems. Your first step in this journey is to learn how to work with common file formats such as XML.

3.2   *Processing common serialization formats*

XML and JSON are industry-standard data interchange formats. Their ubiquity in the technology industry is evidenced by their heavy adoption in data storage and exchange. In this section we'll look at how you can read and write these data formats in MapReduce.

3.2.1　XML

XML has existed since 1998 as a mechanism to represent data that's readable by machine and human alike. It became a universal language for data exchange between systems and is employed by many standards today, such as SOAP and RSS, and it's used as an open data format for products such as Microsoft Office.

TECHNIQUE 8　MapReduce and XML

MapReduce comes bundled with an InputFormat that works with text, but it doesn't come with one that supports XML. Working on a single XML file in parallel in MapReduce is tricky because XML doesn't contain a synchronization marker in its data format.[2]

■ **Problem**

You want to work with large XML files in MapReduce and be able to split and process them in parallel.

■ **Solution**

Mahout's XMLInputFormat can be used to work with XML files in HDFS with MapReduce. It reads records that are delimited by specific XML begin and end tags. This technique also explains how XML can be emitted as output in MapReduce output.

■ **Discussion**

MapReduce doesn't contain built-in support for XML, so we'll turn to another Apache project—Mahout, a machine learning system—to provide an XML InputFormat. To showcase the XML InputFormat, you can write a MapReduce job that uses Mahout's XML input format to read property names and values from Hadoop's configuration files. The first step is to set up the job configuration:

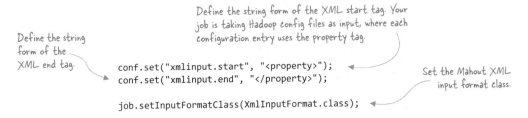

Define the string form of the XML start tag. Your job is taking Hadoop config files as input, where each configuration entry uses the property tag.

Define the string form of the XML end tag.

```
conf.set("xmlinput.start", "<property>");
conf.set("xmlinput.end", "</property>");

job.setInputFormatClass(XmlInputFormat.class);
```

Set the Mahout XML input format class.

Mahout's XML input format is rudimentary; you need to tell it the exact start and end XML tags that will be searched for in the file, and files are split (and records extracted) using the following approach:

---

[2] A synchronization marker is typically some binary data used to demarcate record boundaries. It allows a reader to perform a random seek into a file and determine where the next record starts by reading until a synchronization marker is found.

1 Files are split into discrete sections along HDFS block boundaries for data locality.

2 Each map task operates on a specific input split. The map task seeks to the start of the input split, and then continues to process the file until it hits the first xmlinput.start.

3 The content between xmlinput.start and xmlinput.end is repeatedly emitted until the end of the input split is reached.

Next you need to write a mapper to consume Mahout's XML input format. The XML element in Text form has been supplied, so you'll need to use an XML parser to extract content from the XML.[3]

Listing 3.1   Extracting content with Java's STAX parser

```
public static class Map extends Mapper<LongWritable, Text,
    Text, Text> {

  @Override
  protected void map(LongWritable key, Text value,
                   Mapper.Context context)
    throws
    IOException, InterruptedException {
    String document = value.toString();
    System.out.println("'" + document + "'");
    try {
      XMLStreamReader reader =
          XMLInputFactory.newInstance().createXMLStreamReader(new
            ByteArrayInputStream(document.getBytes()));
      String propertyName = ";
      String propertyValue = ";
      String currentElement = ";
      while (reader.hasNext()) {
        int code = reader.next();
        switch (code) {
          case START_ELEMENT:
            currentElement = reader.getLocalName();
            break;
          case CHARACTERS:
            if (currentElement.equalsIgnoreCase("name")) {
              propertyName += reader.getText();
            } else if (currentElement.equalsIgnoreCase("value")) {
              propertyValue += reader.getText();
            }
            break;
        }
      }
      reader.close();
      context.write(propertyName.trim(), propertyValue.trim());
    } catch (Exception e) {
      log.error("Error processing '" + document + "'", e);
    }
  }
}
```

---

[3] GitHub source: https://github.com/alexholmes/hiped2/blob/master/src/main/java/hip/ch3/xml/
XMLMapReduceReader.java.

The map is given a Text instance, which contains a String representation of the data between the start and end tags. In this code, you use Java's built-in Streaming API for XML (StAX) parser to extract the key and value for each property and output them.

If you run the MapReduce job against Cloudera's core-site.xml and use the HDFS cat command to show the output, you'll see the following:

```
$ hadoop fs -put $HADOOP_HOME/conf/core-site.xml core-site.xml

$ hip hip.ch3.xml.XMLMapReduceReader \
  --input core-site.xml \
  --output output

$ hadoop fs -cat output/part*
fs.default.name hdfs://localhost:8020
hadoop.tmp.dir   /usr/local/hadoop/tmp
...
```

This output shows that you've successfully worked with XML as an input serialization format with MapReduce. Not only that, you can support huge XML files because the input format supports splitting XML.

Writing XML

Having successfully read XML, the next question is how to write XML. In your reducer, you have callbacks that occur before and after your main reduce method is called, which you can use to emit a start and end tag, as shown in the following example.[4]

Listing 3.2 A reducer to emit start and end tags

```
public static class Reduce
    extends Reducer<Text, Text, Text, Text> {

    @Override
    protected void setup(
        Context context)                                      Use the setup method
        throws IOException, InterruptedException {             to write the root
      context.write(new Text("<configuration>"), null);  ◀    element start tag.
    }

    @Override
    protected void cleanup(
        Context context)                                      Use the cleanup method
        throws IOException, InterruptedException {             to write the root
      context.write(new Text("</configuration>"), null);  ◀   element end tag.
    }

    private Text outputKey = new Text();
    public void reduce(Text key, Iterable<Text> values,       Construct a child XML element
                    Context context)                          for each key/value combination
        throws IOException, InterruptedException {             provided in the reducer.
      for (Text value : values) {
        outputKey.set(constructPropertyXml(key, value));  ◀
```

---

[4] GitHub source: https://github.com/alexholmes/hiped2/blob/master/src/main/java/hip/ch3/xml/ XmlMapReduceWriter.java.

```
        context.write(outputKey, null);     ◄─────── Emit the
    }                                                  XML element.
}

    public static String constructPropertyXml(Text name, Text value) {
      return String.format(
        "<property><name>%s</name><value>%s</value></property>",
        name, value);
    }
}
```

This could also be embedded in an OutputFormat, but I'll leave that as a project for you to experiment with. Writing an OutputFormat class is covered in section 3.5.1.

Pig

If you want to work with XML in Pig, the Piggy Bank library[5] (a user-contributed library of useful Pig code) contains an XMLLoader. It works much like this technique and captures all of the content between a start and end tag, supplying it as a single byte array field in a Pig tuple.

Hive

Currently, no means exist for working with XML in Hive. You'd have to write a custom SerDe, which we'll cover in chapter 9. [6]

■ Summary

Mahout's XmlInputFormat certainly helps you work with XML. But it's sensitive to an exact string match of both the start and end element names. If the element tag can contain attributes with variable values, or if the generation of the element can't be controlled and could result in XML namespace qualifiers being used, then this approach may not work for you. Also problematic will be situations where the element name you specify is used as a descendant child element.

If you have control over the XML laid out in the input, this exercise can be simplified by having a single XML element per line. This will let you use the built-in Map-Reduce text-based input formats (such as TextInputFormat), which treat each line as a record and split to preserve that demarcation.

Another option worth considering is that of a preprocessing step, where you could convert the original XML into a separate line per XML element, or convert it into an altogether different data format, such as a SequenceFile or Avro, both of which solve the splitting problem for you.

Now that you have a handle on how to work with XML, let's tackle another popular serialization format, JSON.

3.2.2   *JSON*

JSON shares the machine- and human-readable traits of XML and has existed since the early 2000s. It's less verbose than XML, and it doesn't have the rich typing and validation features available in XML.

---

[5] Piggy Bank—user-defined pig functions: https://cwiki.apache.org/confluence/display/PIG/PiggyBank.

[6] SerDe is a shortened form of Serializer/Deserializer; it's the mechanism that allows Hive to read and write data in HDFS.

TECHNIQUE 9   **MapReduce and JSON**

Imagine you have some code that's downloading JSON data from a streaming REST service, and every hour it writes a file into HDFS. The amount of data being downloaded is large, so each file produced is multiple gigabytes in size.

You've been asked to write a MapReduce job that can take as input these large JSON files. What you have here is a problem in two parts: first, MapReduce doesn't come with an `InputFormat` that works with JSON; second, how does one even go about splitting JSON?

Figure 3.7 shows the problem with splitting JSON. Imagine that MapReduce created a split as shown in the figure. The map task that operates on this input split will perform a seek to the start of the input split, and then needs to determine the start of the next record. With file formats such as JSON and XML, it's challenging to know when the next record starts due to the lack of a synchronization marker, or any other indicator that identifies the start of a record.

JSON is harder to partition into distinct segments than a format such as XML because JSON doesn't have a token (like an end tag in XML) to denote the start or end of a record.

■ **Problem**

You want to work with JSON inputs in MapReduce, and also to ensure that input JSON files can be partitioned for concurrent reads.

■ **Solution**

The Elephant Bird `LzoJsonInputFormat` input format is used as a basis to create an input format class to work with JSON elements. This technique also discusses another approach using my open source project that can work with multiline JSON.

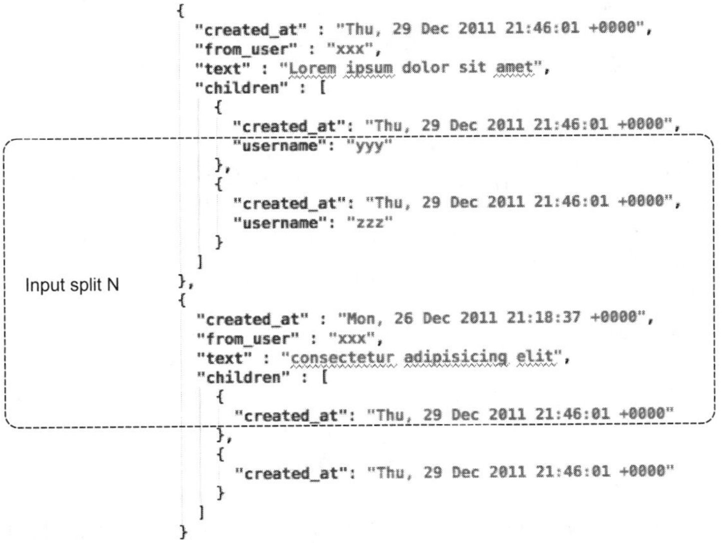

```
{
    "created_at" : "Thu, 29 Dec 2011 21:46:01 +0000",
    "from_user" : "xxx",
    "text" : "Lorem ipsum dolor sit amet",
    "children" : [
        {
            "created_at": "Thu, 29 Dec 2011 21:46:01 +0000",
            "username": "yyy"
        },
        {
            "created_at": "Thu, 29 Dec 2011 21:46:01 +0000",
            "username": "zzz"
        }
    ]
},
{
    "created_at" : "Mon, 26 Dec 2011 21:18:37 +0000",
    "from_user" : "xxx",
    "text" : "consectetur adipisicing elit",
    "children" : [
        {
            "created_at": "Thu, 29 Dec 2011 21:46:01 +0000"
        },
        {
            "created_at": "Thu, 29 Dec 2011 21:46:01 +0000"
        }
    ]
}
```

Input split N

Figure 3.7 Example of issue with JSON and multiple input splits

■ **Discussion**

Elephant Bird (https://github.com/kevinweil/elephant-bird), an open source project that contains useful utilities for working with LZOP compression, has an LzoJsonInputFormat that can read JSON, though it requires that the input file be LZOP-compressed. You can use the Elephant Bird code as a template for your own JSON InputFormat that doesn't have the LZOP compression requirement.

This solution assumes that each JSON record is on a separate line. Your JsonRecord-Format is simple and does nothing other than construct and return a JsonRecordFormat, so we'll skip over that code. The JsonRecordFormat emits LongWritable, MapWritable key/value pairs to the mapper, where the MapWritable is a map of JSON element names and their values.

Let's take a look at how this RecordReader works. It uses the LineRecordReader, which is a built-in MapReduce reader that emits a record for each line. To convert the line to a MapWritable, the reader uses the following method:[7]

```
public static boolean decodeLineToJson(JSONParser parser, Text line,
                                       MapWritable value) {
  try {
    JSONObject jsonObj = (JSONObject)parser.parse(line.toString());
    for (Object key: jsonObj.keySet()) {
      Text mapKey = new Text(key.toString());
      Text mapValue = new Text();
      if (jsonObj.get(key) != null) {
        mapValue.set(jsonObj.get(key).toString());
      }

      value.put(mapKey, mapValue);
    }
    return true;
  } catch (ParseException e) {
    LOG.warn("Could not json-decode string: " + line, e);
    return false;
  } catch (NumberFormatException e) {
    LOG.warn("Could not parse field into number: " + line, e);
    return false;
  }
}
```

The reader uses the json-simple parser (http://code.google.com/p/json-simple/) to parse the line into a JSON object, and then iterates over the keys in the JSON object and puts them, along with their associated values, into a MapWritable. The mapper is given the JSON data in LongWritable, MapWritable pairs and can process the data accordingly.

The following shows an example JSON object:

```
{
  "results" :
    [
      {
        "created_at" : "Thu, 29 Dec 2011 21:46:01 +0000",
```

---

[7] GitHub source: https://github.com/alexholmes/hiped2/blob/master/src/main/java/hip/ch3/json/ JsonInputFormat.java.

```
      "from_user" : "grep_alex",
      "text" : "RT @kevinweil: After a lot of hard work by ..."
    },
    {
      "created_at" : "Mon, 26 Dec 2011 21:18:37 +0000",
      "from_user" : "grep_alex",
      "text" : "@miguno pull request has been merged, thanks again!"
    }
  ]
}
```

This technique assumes one JSON object per line. The following code shows the JSON file you'll work with in this example:

```
{"created_at" : "Thu, 29 Dec 2011 21:46:01 +0000","from_user" : ...
{"created_at" : "Mon, 26 Dec 2011 21:18:37 +0000","from_user" : ...
```

Now copy the JSON file into HDFS and run your MapReduce code. The MapReduce code writes each JSON key/value pair to the output:

```
$ hadoop fs -put test-data/json/tweets.json tweets.json

$ hip hip.ch3.json.JsonMapReduce \
    --input tweets.json \
    --output output
```

```
$ hadoop fs -cat output/part*
text        RT @kevinweil: After a lot of hard work by ...
from_user   grep_alex
created_at  Thu, 29 Dec 2011 21:46:01 +0000
text        @miguno pull request has been merged, thanks again!
from_user   grep_alex
created_at  Mon, 26 Dec 2011 21:18:37 +0000
```

Writing JSON

An approach similar to what we looked at in section 3.2.1 for writing XML could also be used to write JSON.

Pig

Elephant Bird contains a `JsonLoader` and an `LzoJsonLoader`, which you can use to work with JSON in Pig. These loaders work with line-based JSON. Each Pig tuple contains a chararray field for each JSON element in the line.

Hive

Hive contains a `DelimitedJSONSerDe` class which can serialize JSON, but unfortunately can't deserialize it, so you can't load data into Hive using this SerDe.

■ Summary

This solution assumes that the JSON input is structured with one line per JSON object. How would you work with JSON objects that were across multiple lines? An experimental project on GitHub[8] works with multiple input splits over a single JSON file. This approach searches for a specific JSON member and retrieves the containing object.

---

[8] A multiline JSON `InputFormat`: https://github.com/alexholmes/json-mapreduce.

You can also review a Google Code project called hive-json-serde (http://code.google.com/p/hive-json-serde/), which can support both serialization and deserialization.

As you can see, using XML and JSON in MapReduce is kludgy and has rigid requirements about how to lay out your data. Support for these two formats in MapReduce is also complex and error-prone, because neither lends itself naturally to splitting. Clearly, you need to look at alternative file formats that have built-in support for splittability.

The next step is to look at more sophisticated file formats that are better suited to working with MapReduce, such as Avro and SequenceFile.

3.3 *Big data serialization formats*

Unstructured text works well when you're working with scalar or tabular data. Semi-structured text formats such as XML and JSON can model more sophisticated data structures that include composite fields or hierarchical data. But when you're working with big data volumes, you'll need serialization formats with compact serialized forms that natively support partitioning and have schema evolution features.

In this section we'll compare the serialization formats that work best with big data in MapReduce and follow up with how you can use them with MapReduce.

3.3.1 *Comparing SequenceFile, Protocol Buffers, Thrift, and Avro*

In my experience, the following characteristics are important when selecting a data serialization format:

- *Code generation*—Some serialization formats are accompanied by libraries with code-generation abilities that allow you to generate rich objects, making it easier for you to interact with your data. The generated code also provides the added benefit of type-safety to make sure that your consumers and producers are working with the right data types.

- *Schema evolution*—Data models evolve over time, and it's important that your data formats support your need to modify your data models. Schema evolution allows you to add, modify, and in some cases delete attributes, while at the same time providing backward and forward compatibility for readers and writers.

- *Language support*—It's likely that you'll need to access your data in more than one programming language, and it's important that the mainstream languages have support for a data format.

- *Transparent compression*—Data compression is important given the volumes of data you'll work with, and a desirable data format has the ability to internally compress and decompress data on writes and reads. It's a much bigger headache for you as a programmer if the data format doesn't support compression, because it means that you'll have to manage compression and decompression as part of your data pipeline (as is the case when you're working with text-based file formats).

- *Splittability*—Newer data formats understand the importance of supporting multiple parallel readers that are reading and processing different chunks of a large file. It's crucial that file formats contain synchronization markers (and thereby support the ability for a reader to perform a random seek and scan to the start of the next record).

- *Support in MapReduce and the Hadoop ecosystem*—A data format that you select must have support in MapReduce and other critical Hadoop ecosystem projects, such as Hive. Without this support, you'll be responsible for writing the code to make a file format work with these systems.

Table 3.1 compares the more popular data serialization frameworks to see how they stack up against each other. Additional background on these technologies is provided in the following discussion.

Table 3.1 Feature comparison of data serialization frameworks

Library	Code generation	Schema evolution	Language support	Transparent compression	Splittable	Native support in MapReduce	Pig and Hive support
Sequence-File	No	No	Java, Python	Yes	Yes	Yes	Yes
Protocol Buffers	Yes (optional)	Yes	C++, Java, Python, Perl, Ruby	No	No	No	No
Thrift	Yes (mandatory)	Yes	C, C++, Java, Python, Ruby, Perl	No[a]	No	No	No
Avro	Yes (optional)	Yes	C, C++, Java, Python, Ruby, C#	Yes	Yes	Yes	Yes
Parquet	No	Yes	Java, Python (C++ planned in 2.0)	Yes	Yes	Yes	Yes

[a] Thrift does support compression, but not in the Java library.

Let's look at each of these formats in more detail.

SequenceFile

The SequenceFile format was created to work with MapReduce, Pig, and Hive, and therefore integrates well with all of those tools. Its shortcomings are mainly its lack of code generation and versioning support, as well as limited language support.

Protocol Buffers

The Protocol Buffers format has been used heavily by Google for interoperability. Its strengths are its versioning support and compact binary format. Downsides include its lack of support in MapReduce (or in any third-party software) for reading files generated by Protocol Buffers serialization. Not all is lost, however; we'll look at how Elephant Bird uses Protocol Buffers serialization within a higher-level container file in section 3.3.3.

Thrift

Thrift was developed at Facebook as a data-serialization and RPC framework. It doesn't have support in MapReduce for its native data-serialization format, but it can support different wire-level data representations, including JSON and various binary encodings. Thrift also includes an RPC layer with various types of servers, including a nonblocking implementation. We'll ignore the RPC capabilities for this chapter and focus on the data serialization.

Avro

The Avro format is Doug Cutting's creation to help address the shortcomings of SequenceFile.

Parquet

Parquet is a columnar file format with rich Hadoop system support, and it works well with data models such as Avro, Protocol Buffers, and Thrift. Parquet is covered in depth in section 3.4.

Based on certain evaluation criteria, Avro seems to be the best fit as a data serialization framework in Hadoop. SequenceFile is a close second due to its inherent compatibility with Hadoop (it was designed for use with Hadoop).

You can review a useful jvm-serializers project at https://github.com/eishay/jvm-serializers/wiki/, which runs various benchmarks to compare file formats based on items such as serialization and deserialization times. It contains benchmarks for Avro, Protocol Buffers, and Thrift, along with a number of other frameworks.

After looking at how the various data-serialization frameworks compare, we'll dedicate the next few sections to working with them. We'll start off with a look at SequenceFile.

3.3.2   SequenceFile

Because SequenceFile was created for use with MapReduce, this format arguably offers the highest level of integration support in conjunction with MapReduce, Pig, and Hive. SequenceFile is a splittable binary file format that stores data in the form of key/value pairs. All SequenceFiles share the same header format, as shown in figure 3.8.

SequenceFiles come in three types, which vary based on how you apply compression. In addition, each type has its own corresponding `Writer` classes.

Uncompressed

Uncompressed SequenceFiles are written using the `SequenceFile.Writer` class. No advantage exists for this over the compressed formats, because compression generally reduces your storage footprint and is more efficient for reads and writes. The file format is shown in figure 3.9.

Header
Version
Key class name
Value class name
Is compressed?
Is block compressed?
Compression codec
Metadata
Sync

Figure 3.8   SequenceFile header format

Record-compressed

Record-compressed SequenceFiles are written using the `SequenceFile.RecordCompress-Writer` class. When a record is added to the SequenceFile, it's immediately compressed and written to the file. The disadvantage of this approach is that your compression ratio will suffer compared to block compression. This file format, which is essentially the same as that of uncompressed SequenceFiles, is shown in figure 3.9.

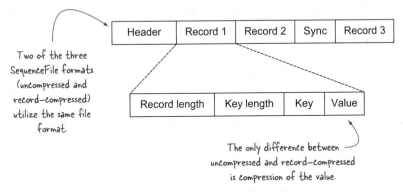

Two of the three SequenceFile formats (uncompressed and record–compressed) utilize the same file format.

The only difference between uncompressed and record–compressed is compression of the value.

Figure 3.9   File format for record-compressed and uncompressed SequenceFiles

Block-compressed

Block-compressed SequenceFiles are written using the `SequenceFile.BlockCompress-Writer` class. By default, the block size is the same as the HDFS block size, although this can be overridden. The advantage to this compression is that it's more aggressive; the whole block is compressed, rather than compressing at the record level. Data isn't written until it reaches the block size, at which point the whole block is compressed, resulting in good overall compression. The file format is shown in figure 3.10.

You only need one `Reader` class (`SequenceFile.Reader`) to read all three types of SequenceFiles. Even the `Writer` is abstracted, because you can call `SequenceFile.create-Writer` to choose the preferred format, and it returns a base class that can be used for writing regardless of compression.

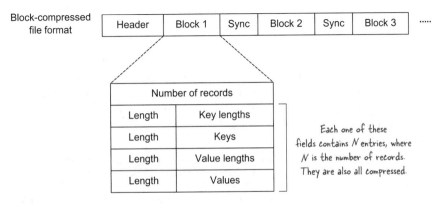

Each one of these fields contains N entries, where N is the number of records. They are also all compressed.

Figure 3.10   Block-compressed SequenceFile format

SequenceFiles have a pluggable serialization framework. Written keys and values must have a related org.apache.hadoop.io.serializer.Serializer and Deserializer for marshaling and unmarshaling. Hadoop comes with four serializers: Avro, Java, Tether (for binary data contained within a TetherData class), and Writable (the default serializer).[9]

> **Custom SequenceFile serialization**   If you want your SequenceFile to contain objects that aren't Writable or Serializable, you'll need to implement your own Serializer and register it. You register it by updating core-site.xml and appending the class name of the custom serialization implementation to the io.serializations property.

SequenceFiles are splittable because a synchronization marker is written approximately every 6 KiB (1 kibibyte = 1024 bytes) in the file for record-based files, and before every block for block-based files.

Now let's look at how to use SequenceFiles in MapReduce.

TECHNIQUE 10   **Working with SequenceFiles**

Working with text in MapReduce can start to get tricky when you have to support complex types of data, which may include nonscalar data types such as lists or dictionaries. In addition, large compressed text files require some additional wrangling if MapReduce's data locality properties are important to you. These challenges can be overcome by using a file format such as SequenceFile.

■ **Problem**

You want to work with a structured file format in MapReduce that you can use to model complex data structures and that also supports compression and splittable inputs.

■ **Solution**

This technique looks at how the SequenceFile file format can be used from both standalone applications and MapReduce.

■ **Discussion**

The SequenceFile format offers a high level of integration with computational tools such as MapReduce and can also model complex data structures. We'll examine how to read and write SequenceFiles, and also how to use them with MapReduce, Pig, and Hive.

We'll work with the stock data for this technique. The most common serialization method used with SequenceFiles is Writable, so you'll need to create a Writable to represent the stock data. The key elements of writing a complex Writable are extending the Writable class and defining serialization and deserialization methods, as shown in the following listing.[10]

---

[9] Writable is an interface in Hadoop used to support general-purpose data serialization, and it's used for sending data across the wire between Hadoop components. Yahoo has a good introduction to Writables at http://developer.yahoo.com/hadoop/tutorial/module5.html#writable.

[10] GitHub source: https://github.com/alexholmes/hiped2/blob/master/src/main/java/hip/ch3/StockPriceWritable.java.

Listing 3.3 A Writable implementation to represent a stock price

```java
public class StockPriceWritable
    implements WritableComparable<StockPriceWritable>, Cloneable  {
  String symbol;
  String date;
  double open;
  double high;
  double low;
  double close;
  int volume;
  double adjClose;

  @Override
  public void write(DataOutput out) throws IOException {
    WritableUtils.writeString(out, symbol);
    WritableUtils.writeString(out, date);
    out.writeDouble(open);
    out.writeDouble(high);
    out.writeDouble(low);
    out.writeDouble(close);
    out.writeInt(volume);
    out.writeDouble(adjClose);
  }

  @Override
  public void readFields(DataInput in) throws IOException {
    symbol = WritableUtils.readString(in);
    date = WritableUtils.readString(in);
    open = in.readDouble();
    high = in.readDouble();
    low = in.readDouble();
    close = in.readDouble();
    volume = in.readInt();
    adjClose = in.readDouble();
  }

  public static StockPriceWritable fromLine(String line)
      throws IOException {
    CSVParser parser = new CSVParser();
    String[] parts = parser.parseLine(line);

    StockPriceWritable stock = new StockPriceWritable(
        parts[0], parts[1], Double.valueOf(parts[2]),
        Double.valueOf(parts[3]),
        Double.valueOf(parts[4]),
        Double.valueOf(parts[5]),
        Integer.valueOf(parts[6]),
        Double.valueOf(parts[7])
    );
    return stock;
  }
}
```

Write out the fields of this Writable in byte form to the output stream.

Read the stock fields in binary form into the Writable fields. Note that this method reads fields in the same order as they were written in the write method.

This helper method engineers a StockPriceWritable from a CSV line. It uses the open source OpenCSV project to parse the CSV.

Now that you have your Writable, you'll need to write some code that will create a SequenceFile. You'll read the stocks file from the local disk, create the StockWritable, and write it to your SequenceFile, using the stock symbol as your key:[11]

Create a new SequenceFile writer, specifying that you want block-level compression. Also set the types for the keys and values you'll be writing (in this case Text and IntWritable). Any Hadoop compression codec can be used with SequenceFiles; see chapter 4 for more details on compression.

Append a record to the SequenceFile.

Read all the lines in the input file and then split them into key/value pairs.

Create the StockPriceWritable instance, using the fromLine helper method in the StockPriceWritable class.

```
SequenceFile.Writer writer =
    SequenceFile.createWriter(conf,
        SequenceFile.Writer.file(outputPath),
        SequenceFile.Writer.keyClass(Text.class),
        SequenceFile.Writer.valueClass(StockPriceWritable.class),
        SequenceFile.Writer.compression(
            SequenceFile.CompressionType.BLOCK,
            new DefaultCodec())
    );
try {
    Text key = new Text();

    for (String line : FileUtils.readLines(inputFile)) {
        StockPriceWritable stock = StockPriceWritable.fromLine(line);

        System.out.println("Stock = " + stock);

        key.set(stock.getSymbol());

        writer.append(key, stock);
    }
} finally {
    writer.close();
}
```

Great! Now how do you go about reading the files created with your writer?[12]

Create a reader that can read records from the SequenceFile. Note that you don't need to specify that you used block-level compression in the file or what key/value types are contained in the file.

The next method on the reader returns true until it hits the end of the file. It also sets the key and value settings.

```
SequenceFile.Reader reader =
    new SequenceFile.Reader(conf,
        SequenceFile.Reader.file(inputFile));

try {
    System.out.println("Is block compressed = " +
            reader.isBlockCompressed());

    Text key = new Text();
    StockPriceWritable value = new StockPriceWritable();

    while (reader.next(key, value)) {
        System.out.println(key + "," + value);
    }
} finally {
    reader.close();
}
```

---

[11] GitHub   source: https://github.com/alexholmes/hiped2/blob/master/src/main/java/hip/ch3/seqfile/writable/SequenceFileStockWriter.java.

[12] GitHub   source: https://github.com/alexholmes/hiped2/blob/master/src/main/java/hip/ch3/seqfile/writable/SequenceFileStockReader.java.

Now you need to prove that it works by writing and reading a file:

```
$ cat test-data/stocks.txt
AAPL,2009-01-02,85.88,91.04,85.16,90.75,26643400,90.75
AAPL,2008-01-02,199.27,200.26,192.55,194.84,38542100,194.84
AAPL,2007-01-03,86.29,86.58,81.90,83.80,44225700,83.80
...
$ hip hip.ch3.seqfile.writable.SequenceFileStockWriter \
    --input  test-data/stocks.txt \
    --output stocks.seqfile

$ hip hip.ch3.seqfile.writable.SequenceFileStockReader \
    --input stocks.seqfile
AAPL,StockPriceWritable[symbol=AAPL,date=2009-01-02,open=85.88,...]
AAPL,StockPriceWritable[symbol=AAPL,date=2008-01-02,open=199.27,...]
AAPL,StockPriceWritable[symbol=AAPL,date=2007-01-03,open=86.29,...]
...
```

How would you process this SequenceFile in MapReduce? Luckily, both SequenceFile-
InputFormat and SequenceFileOutputFormat integrate nicely with MapReduce. Remember earlier in this chapter when we talked about how the default SequenceFile serialization supports Writable classes for serialization? Because Writable is the native data format in MapReduce, using SequenceFiles with MapReduce is totally transparent. See if you agree. The following code shows a MapReduce job with an identity mapper and reducer:[13, 14]

The SequenceFileInputFormat determines the type of Writable keys and values and emits these types as key/value pairs to the mapper.

Specifies an output format for SequenceFiles.

Specifies block-level compression (you can also set this to RECORD or NONE).

Sets the compression codec that should be used; in this case you're using the default codec, which is the DEFLATE compression algorithm used by zip and gzip file formats.

```
Configuration conf = new Configuration();
Job job = new Job(conf);
job.setJarByClass(SequenceFileStockMapReduce.class);
job.setOutputKeyClass(Text.class);
job.setOutputValueClass(IntWritable.class);
job.setInputFormatClass(SequenceFileInputFormat.class);
job.setOutputFormatClass(SequenceFileOutputFormat.class);
SequenceFileOutputFormat.setCompressOutput(job, true);
SequenceFileOutputFormat.setOutputCompressionType(job,
        SequenceFile.CompressionType.BLOCK);
SequenceFileOutputFormat.setOutputCompressorClass(job,
        DefaultCodec.class);

FileInputFormat.setInputPaths(job, new Path(input));
Path outPath = new Path(output);
FileOutputFormat.setOutputPath(job, outPath);
outPath.getFileSystem(conf).delete(outPath, true);

job.waitForCompletion(true);
```

---

[13] GitHub source: https://github.com/alexholmes/hiped2/blob/master/src/main/java/hip/ch3/seqfile/writable/SequenceFileStockMapReduce.java.

[14] An identity function is a mathematical term to denote a function that returns the same value that was used as its argument. In MapReduce this means the same thing—the map identity function emits all the key/value pairs that it is supplied, as does the reducer, without any transformation or filtering. A job that doesn't explicitly set a map or reduce class results in Hadoop using a built-in identity function.

Now you can run the identity MapReduce job against the stocks SequenceFile that you created earlier in this technique:

```
$ hip hip.ch3.seqfile.writable.SequenceFileStockMapReduce \
    --input stocks.seqfile \
    --output output
```

Because all it's doing is echoing the input to the output, you should see identical content in both files. You can make sure that's the case by reading in the job output file.

First of all, how do you verify that the output is a SequenceFile? Easy, just cat it—the first three bytes of a SequenceFile are *SEQ*, followed by a fourth byte containing the SequenceFile version, which is then followed by the key and value classes:

```
$ hadoop fs -cat output/part*
SEQorg.apache.hadoop.io.Text&hip.ch3.StockPriceWritable...
$ reset
```

Linux command to reset your terminal; useful after sending binary data to your screen

Looks good. Now try using the SequenceFile reader code you wrote earlier to dump it to standard output:

```
$ hip hip.ch3.seqfile.writable.SequenceFileStockReader \
    --input output/part-r-00000
AAPL,StockPriceWritable[symbol=AAPL,date=2008-01-02,open=199.27,...]
AAPL,StockPriceWritable[symbol=AAPL,date=2007-01-03,open=86.29,...]
AAPL,StockPriceWritable[symbol=AAPL,date=2009-01-02,open=85.88,...]
...
```

That was easy. Because SequenceFiles are key/value-based, and the default serialization data format for SequenceFiles is Writable, the use of SequenceFiles is completely transparent to your map and reduce classes. We demonstrated this by using MapReduce's built-in identity map and reduce classes with the SequenceFile as input. The only work you had to do was to tell MapReduce to use the SequenceFile-specific input and output format classes, which are built into MapReduce.

Reading SequenceFiles in Pig

By writing your own Writable you created more work for yourself with non-MapReduce tools such as Pig. Pig works well with Hadoop's built-in scalar Writables such as Text and IntWritable, but it doesn't have support for custom Writables. You'll need to write your own LoadFunc to support the StockPriceWritable. This will work well with MapReduce, but Pig's SequenceFileLoader won't work with your custom Writable, which means that you'll need to write your own Pig loader to process your files. The appendix contains details on installing Pig.

The LoadFunc for Pig is straightforward, as can be seen in the following listing.[15]

---

[15] GitHub source: https://github.com/alexholmes/hiped2/blob/master/src/main/java/hip/ch3/seqfile/ writable/SequenceFileStockLoader.java.

Listing 3.4 A Pig loader function that converts a `StockPriceWritable` into a Pig tuple

```
public class SequenceFileStockLoader extends FileInputLoadFunc {

  private SequenceFileRecordReader<Text, StockPriceWritable> reader;

  @Override
  public Tuple getNext() throws IOException {
    boolean next;
    try {
      next = reader.nextKeyValue();
    } catch (InterruptedException e) {
      throw new IOException(e);
    }

    if (!next) return null;

    Object value = reader.getCurrentValue();

    if (value == null) {
      return null;
    }
    if (!(value instanceof StockPriceWritable)) {
      return null;
    }
    StockPriceWritable w = (StockPriceWritable) value;

    return TupleFactory.getInstance().newTuple(Arrays.asList(
        w.getSymbol(), w.getDate(), w.getOpen(),
        w.getHigh(), w.getLow(), w.getClose(),
        w.getVolume(), w.getAdjClose()
    ));
  }

  @SuppressWarnings("unchecked")
  @Override
  public InputFormat getInputFormat() throws IOException {
    return new SequenceFileInputFormat<Text, StockPriceWritable>();
  }

  @SuppressWarnings("unchecked")
  @Override
  public void prepareToRead(RecordReader reader, PigSplit split)
      throws IOException {
    this.reader = (SequenceFileRecordReader) reader;
  }

  @Override
  public void setLocation(String location, Job job)
      throws IOException {
    FileInputFormat.setInputPaths(job, location);
  }
}
```

Now you can try to load and dump the stock SequenceFile in Pig:

```
$ pig
grunt> REGISTER $HIP_HOME/*.jar;
grunt> REGISTER $HIP_HOME/lib/*.jar;
grunt> DEFINE SequenceFileStockLoader
              hip.ch3.seqfile.writable.SequenceFileStockLoader();
grunt> stocks = LOAD 'stocks.seqfile' USING SequenceFileStockLoader;
grunt> dump stocks;
(AAPL,2009-01-02,85.88,91.04,85.16,90.75,26643400,90.75)
(AAPL,2008-01-02,199.27,200.26,192.55,194.84,38542100,194.84)
(AAPL,2007-01-03,86.29,86.58,81.9,83.8,44225700,83.8)
(AAPL,2006-01-03,72.38,74.75,72.25,74.75,28829800,74.75)
(AAPL,2005-01-03,64.78,65.11,62.6,63.29,24714000,31.65)
...
```

Hive

Hive contains built-in support for SequenceFiles, but it has two restrictions. First, it ignores the key portion of each record. Second, out of the box it only works with SequenceFile values that are `Writable`, and it supports them by performing a `toString()` to convert the value into a `Text` form.

In our example, you have a custom `Writable`, so you had to write a Hive SerDe, which deserialized your `Writable` into a form Hive could understand. The resulting data definition language (DDL) statement is as follows:[16]

```
$ export HADOOP_CLASSPATH=$HIP_HOME/hip-<version>.jar

$ hive

hive> CREATE TABLE stocks (
   symbol     string,
   dates       string,
   open       double,
   high       double,
   low        double,
   close      double,
   volume     int,
   adjClose   double
)
ROW FORMAT SERDE 'hip.ch3.StockWritableSerDe'
STORED AS SEQUENCEFILE;

hive> LOAD DATA INPATH 'stocks.seqfile' INTO TABLE stocks;

hive> select * from stocks;

AAPL 2009-01-02 85.88  91.04  85.16  90.75  26643400 90.75
AAPL 2008-01-02 199.27 200.26 192.55 194.84 38542100 194.84
AAPL 2007-01-03 86.29  86.58  81.9   83.8    44225700 83.8
AAPL 2006-01-03 72.38  74.75  72.25  74.75  28829800 74.75
AAPL 2005-01-03 64.78  65.11  62.6   63.29  24714000 31.65
...
```

---

[16] The code for `StockWritableSerDe` is on GitHub at https://github.com/alexholmes/hiped2/blob/master/src/main/java/hip/ch3/StockWritableSerDe.java.

We'll cover custom Hive SerDe examples in more detail in chapter 9.

■ **Summary**

SequenceFiles are useful in that they solve two problems that make using MapReduce challenging: they're natively splittable, and they also have built-in support for compression, which makes it transparent to the user. They're also useful as containers for other file formats that don't integrate as well into MapReduce. The thorn in the side of SequenceFiles is that they lack multilanguage support, which limits the range of tools that can interoperate with your data. But if your data mostly stays in HDFS and is processed with MapReduce (or Hive/Pig), SequenceFiles may be just what you're looking for.

Another challenge for SequenceFiles is their lack of schema evolution when working with Writables—making a change to your Writable won't be backward or forward compatible unless you build that into your implementation. This can be solved by using Protocol Buffers as your key/value type.

This technique looked at how to use SequenceFiles with Writables, which SequenceFile knows how to encode and decode within its file format. How about making SequenceFiles work with data other than Writables?

TECHNIQUE 11   **Using SequenceFiles to encode Protocol Buffers**

Writables are first-class citizens in SequenceFiles, and the APIs have specific methods to read and write Writable instances, which you saw in the previous technique. This doesn't mean that SequenceFiles are limited to working with Writables—in fact, they can work with any data type as long as there's a serialization implementation for your data type that plugs into Hadoop's serialization framework.

Protocol Buffers is a sophisticated data format that Google open-sourced; it provides schema evolution and efficient data-encoding capabilities. (More details on Protocol Buffers are presented in section 3.3.3). In this technique, you'll implement a Protocol Buffers serialization and see how it allows you to work with native Protocol Buffers objects in MapReduce.

■ **Problem**

You want to work with Protocol Buffers data in MapReduce.

■ **Solution**

Write a Protocol Buffers serializer, which enables you to encode Protocol Buffers serialized data within SequenceFiles.

■ **Discussion**

Hadoop uses its own serialization framework to serialize and deserialize data for performance reasons. An example use of this framework is when map outputs are written to disk as part of the shuffle phase. All map outputs must have a corresponding Hadoop serialization class that knows how to read and write data to a stream. Writables, which are the most commonly used data types in MapReduce, have a Writable-Serialization class that uses the readFields and writeFields methods on the Writable interface to perform the serialization.

SequenceFiles use the same serialization framework to serialize and deserialize data within their key/value records, which is why SequenceFiles support Writables out of the box. Therefore, encoding a data type into a SequenceFile is just a matter of writing your own Hadoop serialization instance.

Your first step in getting Protocol Buffers to work with SequenceFiles is to write your own serialization class. Each serialization class must support serialization and deserialization, so let's start with the serializer, whose job is to write records to an output stream.

The following code uses the MessageLite class as the type; it's a superclass of all generated Protocol Buffers classes. The MessageLite interface provides methods to write Protocol Buffers to an output stream and read them from an input stream, as you'll see in the following code:[17]

```java
static class ProtobufSerializer extends Configured implements
    Serializer<MessageLite> {

  private OutputStream out;

  @Override
  public void open(OutputStream out) {
    this.out = out;
  }

  @Override
  public void serialize(MessageLite w) throws IOException {
    w.writeDelimitedTo(out);        ←——
  }

  @Override
  public void close() throws IOException {
    IOUtils.closeStream(out);
  }
}
```

Use a Protocol Buffers method to serialize the object to the output stream.

Next up is the deserializer, whose job is to populate a Protocol Buffers object from an input stream. Things are a little trickier here compared to the serializer, as Protocol Buffers objects can only be engineered via their builder classes: [18]

```java
static class ProtobufDeserializer extends Configured
    implements Deserializer<MessageLite> {

  private Class<? extends MessageLite> protobufClass;
  private InputStream in;

  public ProtobufDeserializer(Configuration conf,
                              Class<? extends MessageLite> c) {
```

The constructor is supplied the class of object being deserialized, which is a MessageLite protobuf class.

[17] GitHub source: https://github.com/alexholmes/hiped2/blob/master/src/main/java/hip/ch3/seqfile/protobuf/ProtobufSerialization.java.

[18] GitHub source: https://github.com/alexholmes/hiped2/blob/master/src/main/java/hip/ch3/seqfile/protobuf/ProtobufSerialization.java.

```
    setConf(conf);
    this.protobufClass = c;
}

@Override
public void open(InputStream in) {
    this.in = in;
}

@Override
public MessageLite deserialize(MessageLite w) throws IOException {

    MessageLite.Builder builder;

    if (w == null) {
        builder = newBuilder();

    } else {
        builder = w.newBuilderForType();

    }

    if (builder.mergeDelimitedFrom(in)) {
        return builder.build();
    }
    return null;
}

public MessageLite.Builder newBuilder() {
    return (MessageLite.Builder)
        MethodUtils.invokeExactStaticMethod(
            protobufClass, "newBuilder");
}

@Override
public void close() throws IOException {
    IOUtils.closeStream(in);
}
}
```

Generate a new Protocol Buffers builder instance if an existing MessageLite wasn't supplied.

Generate a new builder using an existing MessageLite instance.

Populate the builder from the input stream. The method returns a Boolean indicating whether the end of the stream has been reached.

A helper method to engineer a builder object. All Protocol Buffers classes have a static newBuilder method to create builders.

Now you need to configure Hadoop's serialization framework to use your new serializer. This is accomplished by appending your new serializer to the io.serializations property. It's usually good to write a helper method to make this easy for clients. The following example shows the standard serializers bundled with Hadoop 2 being appended with the serialization class you just created. The source for ProtobufSerialization isn't shown here, but all it does is return instances of ProtobufSerializer and ProtobufDeserializer:[19]

```
public static void register(Configuration conf) {
    String[] serializations = conf.getStrings("io.serializations");

    if (ArrayUtils.isEmpty(serializations)) {
```

---

[19] GitHub source: https://github.com/alexholmes/hiped2/blob/master/src/main/java/hip/ch3/seqfile/ protobuf/ProtobufSerialization.java.

```
    serializations = new String[] {
        WritableSerialization.class.getName(),
        AvroSpecificSerialization.class.getName(),
        AvroReflectSerialization.class.getName()
    };
}

    serializations = (String[]) ArrayUtils.add(
      serializations,
      ProtobufSerialization.class.getName()
    );

    conf.setStrings("io.serializations", serializations);
}
```

Next you need to generate a new Protocol Buffers–encoded SequenceFile. The key item here is that you're calling the `register` method (shown in the preceding code) prior to using the SequenceFile writer:[20]

```
Configuration conf = super.getConf();

ProtobufSerialization.register(conf);

SequenceFile.Writer writer =
    SequenceFile.createWriter(conf,
        SequenceFile.Writer.file(outputPath),
        SequenceFile.Writer.keyClass(Text.class),
        SequenceFile.Writer.valueClass(Stock.class),
        SequenceFile.Writer.compression(
            SequenceFile.CompressionType.BLOCK,
            new DefaultCodec())
    );

Text key = new Text();

for (Stock stock : StockUtils.fromCsvFile(inputFile)) {
  key.set(stock.getSymbol());
  writer.append(key, stock);
}
```

On to the MapReduce code. What's great about your new serializer is that the map and reduce classes can work with the Protocol Buffers objects directly. Again, the key thing here is that you're configuring the job to make available the Protocol Buffers serializer. In the following example you use an identity function to demonstrate how Protocol Buffers objects can be used as first-class citizens in MapReduce when encoded in SequenceFiles:[21]

```
        // job driver
        Job job = new Job(conf);
```

---

[20] GitHub source: https://github.com/alexholmes/hiped2/blob/master/src/main/java/hip/ch3/seqfile/protobuf/SequenceFileProtobufWriter.java.

[21] GitHub source: https://github.com/alexholmes/hiped2/blob/master/src/main/java/hip/ch3/seqfile/protobuf/SequenceFileProtobufMapReduce.java.

Specify the Protocol Buffers class as the output value.

Register the Protocol Buffers serialization class.

```
job.setOutputKeyClass(Text.class);
job.setOutputValueClass(Stock.class);
job.setInputFormatClass(SequenceFileInputFormat.class);
job.setOutputFormatClass(SequenceFileOutputFormat.class);
ProtobufSerialization.register(job.getConfiguration());
...

public static class PbMapper extends Mapper<Text, Stock, Text, Stock> {
    @Override
    protected void map(Text key, Stock value, Context context)
                        throws IOException, InterruptedException {
        context.write(key, value);
    }
}

public static class PbReducer
                extends Reducer<Text, Stock, Text, Stock> {

    @Override
    protected void reduce(Text symbol, Iterable<Stock> values,
            Context context) throws IOException, InterruptedException {
        for (Stock stock : values) {
            context.write(symbol, stock);
        }
    }
}
```

The map (and reduce) methods are supplied Protocol Buffers instances.

Similarly, the map and reduce outputs can emit Protocol Buffers instances.

Now you can write a SequenceFile with Protocol Buffers values, run the identity MapReduce job over that data, and then dump the contents of the job output:

```
$ hip hip.ch3.seqfile.protobuf.SequenceFileProtobufWriter \
    --input test-data/stocks.txt \
    --output stocks.pb

$ hip hip.ch3.seqfile.protobuf.SequenceFileProtobufMapReduce \
    --input stocks.pb \
    --output output

$ hip hip.ch3.seqfile.protobuf.SequenceFileProtobufReader \
    --input output/part-r-00000
AAPL,symbol: "AAPL"
date: "2008-01-02"
open: 199.27
...
```

Next up, we'll examine additional ways that you can integrate Protocol Buffers into MapReduce.

3.3.3   *Protocol Buffers*

Google developers invented Protocol Buffers to help them exchange data between services written in multiple languages in a compact and efficient manner. Protocol Buffers is now Google's de facto format for data—there are over 48,000 different message types defined in Google across more than 12,000 .proto files.[22]

---

[22] Protocol Buffers usage statistics taken from Google's Protocol Buffers Developer Guide: http://code.google.com/apis/protocolbuffers/docs/overview.html.

There's been a ticket open since 2008 with the goal of adding native support for Protocol Buffers in MapReduce.[23] As a result, you'll need to turn to alternative methods of working with Protocol Buffers in Hadoop. The previous technique covered one approach that can be used, which is to encode Protocol Buffers within SequenceFiles. Other options exist, such as using either Elephant Bird[24] or Avro, which support Protocol Buffers by wrapping them within their own file formats. Ultimately, these are all stop-gap measures until we get full support for Protocol Buffers in Hadoop.

There are a number of ways that you can work with Protocol Buffers in Hadoop:

- You can serialize Protocol Buffers objects in binary form within SequenceFiles, as was shown in the previous technique.
- Elephant Bird (https://github.com/kevinweil/elephant-bird), an open source project out of Twitter, supports Protocol Buffers within their own binary file format.
- Parquet, a columnar file format that is covered in section 3.4, has support for the Protocol Buffers object model and allows you to effectively write and read Protocol Buffers into a columnar form.

Of these options, Parquet is the recommended way of working with Protocol Buffers—not only does it allow you to work natively with Protocol Buffers, but it also opens up the number of tools that can work with your data (due to Parquet's extensive Hadoop tooling support). This chapter's coverage of Parquet includes a look at how Avro can be used with Parquet, and Parquet can be used in a similar way to support Protocol Buffers.

Thrift is another data format, which, like Protocol Buffers, doesn't have out-of-the-box support with MapReduce. Again, you must rely on other tools to work with Thrift data in Hadoop, as you'll discover in the next section.

3.3.4 *Thrift*

Facebook created Thrift to help with efficient data representation and transport. Facebook uses Thrift for a number of applications, including search, logging, and its ads platform.

The same three options for working with Protocol Buffers also apply to Thrift, and once again, the recommendation is to use Parquet as the file format. Head on over to the section on Parquet (section 3.4) to learn more about how Parquet integrates with these different data models.

Let's look at what's likely the most capable data serialization format of all our options, Avro.

---

[23] See https://issues.apache.org/jira/browse/MAPREDUCE-377.
[24] Using Elephant Bird means you have to use LZOP; ostensibly, it would be possible to derive a version of their classes and remove the LZOP dependency, but it's probably worth looking elsewhere if you're not already using LZOP.

3.3.5 Avro

Doug Cutting created Avro, a data serialization and RPC library, to help improve data interchange, interoperability, and versioning in MapReduce. Avro utilizes a compact binary data format—which you have the option to compress—that results in fast serialization times. Although it has the concept of a schema, similar to Protocol Buffers, Avro improves on Protocol Buffers because its code generation is optional, and it embeds the schema in the container file format, allowing for dynamic discovery and data interactions. Avro has a mechanism to work with schema data that uses generic data types (an example of which can be seen in chapter 4).

The Avro file format is shown in figure 3.11. The schema is serialized as part of the header, which makes deserialization simple and loosens restrictions around users having to maintain and access the schema outside of the Avro data files being interacted with. Each data block contains a number of Avro records, and by default is 16 KB in size.

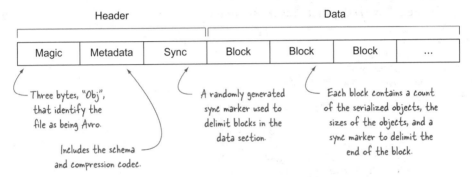

Figure 3.11 Avro container file format

The holy grail of data serialization supports code generation, versioning, and compression, and has a high level of integration with MapReduce. Equally important is schema evolution, and that's the reason why Hadoop SequenceFiles aren't appealing—they don't support the notion of a schema or any form of data evolution.

In this section you'll get an overview of Avro's schema and code-generation capabilities, how to read and write Avro container files, and the various ways Avro can be integrated with MapReduce. At the end we'll also look at Avro support in Hive and Pig.

Let's get rolling with a look at Avro's schema and code generation.

<hr>

TECHNIQUE 12   **Avro's schema and code generation**

Avro has the notion of generic data and specific data:

- *Generic data* allows you to work with data at a low level without having to understand schema specifics.
- *Specific data* allows you to work with Avro using code-generated Avro primitives, which supports a simple and type-safe method of working with your Avro data.

This technique looks at how to work with specific data in Avro.

■ **Problem**

You want to define an Avro schema and generate code so you can work with your Avro records in Java.

■ **Solution**

Author your schema in JSON form, and then use Avro tools to generate rich APIs to interact with your data.

■ **Discussion**

You can use Avro in one of two ways: either with code-generated classes or with its generic classes. In this technique we'll work with the code-generated classes, but you can see an example of how Avro's generic records are used in technique 29 in chapter 4.

> **Getting Avro**   The appendix contains instructions on how to get your hands on Avro.

In the code-generated approach, everything starts with a schema. The first step is to create an Avro schema to represent an entry in the stock data:[25]

```
{
  "name": "Stock",
  "type": "record",
  "namespace": "hip.ch3.avro.gen",
  "fields": [
      {"name": "symbol",   "type": "string"},
      {"name": "date",     "type": "string"},
      {"name": "open",     "type": "double"},
      {"name": "high",     "type": "double"},
      {"name": "low",      "type": "double"},
      {"name": "close",    "type": "double"},
      {"name": "volume",   "type": "int"},
      {"name": "adjClose", "type": "double"}
  ]
}
```

Avro supports code generation for schema data as well as RPC messages (which aren't covered in this book). To generate Java code for a schema, use the Avro tools JAR as follows:

Create a directory for the sources.

Expand the source JAR into the directory.

Tell the Avro tool that you want to generate classes for an Avro schema.

```
$ cd $HIP_HOME && mkdir src && cd src
$ jar -xvf ../hip-2.0.0-sources.jar
$ cd ..
$ java -jar $HIP_HOME/lib/avro-tools-1.7.4.jar \
    compile schema \
    $HIP_HOME/src/hip/ch3/avro/stock.avsc \
    $HIP_HOME/src/hip/ch3/avro/stockavg.avsc \
    $HIP_HOME/src/
```

The input schema file.

The tool supports multiple input schema files.

The output directory where generated code is written.

---

[25] GitHub source: https://github.com/alexholmes/hiped2/blob/master/src/main/java/hip/ch3/avro/stock .avsc.

Generated code will be put into the hip.ch3.avro.gen package. Now that you have generated code, how do you use it to read and write Avro container files?[26]

Listing 3.5 Writing Avro files from outside of MapReduce

Create a writer that can write Avro's data file format.

Indicate the schema that will be used.

Specify that Snappy should be used to compress the data.

```
DataFileWriter<Stock> writer =
    new DataFileWriter<Stock>(
        new SpecificDatumWriter<Stock>());

writer.setCodec(CodecFactory.snappyCodec());
writer.create(Stock.SCHEMA$, outputStream);

for(Stock stock: StockUtils.fromCsvFile(inputFile)) {
    writer.append(stock);
}

IOUtils.closeStream(writer);
IOUtils.closeStream(outputStream);
```

Write each stock to the Avro file.

As you see, you can specify the compression codec that should be used to compress the data. In this example you're using Snappy, which, as shown in chapter 4, is the fastest codec for reads and writes.

The following code example shows how you can marshal a Stock object from a line in the input file. As you can see, the generated Stock class is a POJO with a bunch of setters (and matching getters):

```
public static Stock fromCsv(String line) throws IOException {

    String parts[] = parser.parseLine(line);
    Stock stock = new Stock();

    stock.setSymbol(parts[0]);
    stock.setDate(parts[1]);
    stock.setOpen(Double.valueOf(parts[2]));
    stock.setHigh(Double.valueOf(parts[3]));
    stock.setLow(Double.valueOf(parts[4]));
    stock.setClose(Double.valueOf(parts[5]));
    stock.setVolume(Integer.valueOf(parts[6]));
    stock.setAdjClose(Double.valueOf(parts[7]));

    return stock;
}
```

Now, how about reading the file you just wrote?[27]

Use Avro's file container deserialization class to read from an input stream.

```
DataFileStream<Stock> reader =
    new DataFileStream<Stock>(
```

---

[26] GitHub source: https://github.com/alexholmes/hiped2/blob/master/src/main/java/hip/ch3/avro/
AvroStockFileWrite.java.

[27] GitHub source: https://github.com/alexholmes/hiped2/blob/master/src/main/java/hip/ch3/avro/
AvroStockFileRead.java.

```
        is,
        new SpecificDatumReader<Stock>(Stock.class));

for (Stock a : reader) {
  System.out.println(ToStringBuilder.reflectionToString(a,
      ToStringStyle.SIMPLE_STYLE
  ));
}

IOUtils.closeStream(is);
IOUtils.closeStream(reader);
```

Loop through the Stock objects and use the Apache Commons ToStringBuilder to help dump all the members to the console.

Go ahead and execute this writer and reader pair:

Reads the stock.txt file from the local filesystem and writes the Avro output file stocks.avro to HDFS

```
$ hip hip.ch3.avro.AvroStockFileWrite \
    --input test-data/stocks.txt \
    --output stocks.avro


$ hip hip.ch3.avro.AvroStockFileRead \
    --input stocks.avro
AAPL,2009-01-02,85.88,91.04,85.16,90.75,26643400,90.75
AAPL,2008-01-02,199.27,200.26,192.55,194.84,38542100,194.84
AAPL,2007-01-03,86.29,86.58,81.9,83.8,44225700,83.8
AAPL,2006-01-03,72.38,74.75,72.25,74.75,28829800,74.75
AAPL,2005-01-03,64.78,65.11,62.6,63.29,24714000,31.65
...
```

Reads the Avro file stocks.avro from HDFS and dumps the records to the terminal

Avro comes bundled with some tools to make it easy to examine the contents of Avro files. To view the contents of an Avro file as JSON, simply run this command:

```
$ java -jar $HIP_HOME/lib/avro-tools-1.7.4.jar tojson stocks.avro
{"symbol":"AAPL","date":"2009-01-02","open":85.88,"high":91.04,...
{"symbol":"AAPL","date":"2008-01-02","open":199.27,"high":200.26,...
{"symbol":"AAPL","date":"2007-01-03","open":86.29,"high":86.58,...
...
```

This assumes that the file exists on the local filesystem. Similarly, you can get a JSON representation of your Avro file with the following command:

```
$ java -jar $HIP_HOME/lib/avro-tools-1.7.4.jar getschema stocks.avro
{
  "type" : "record",
  "name" : "Stock",
  "namespace" : "hip.ch3.avro.gen",
  "fields" : [ {
    "name" : "symbol",
    "type" : "string"
  }, {
    "name" : "date",
    "type" : "string"
  }, {
    "name" : "open",
```

```
    "type" : "double"
  }, {
    "name" : "high",
    "type" : "double"
  }, {
    "name" : "low",
    "type" : "double"
  }, {
    "name" : "close",
    "type" : "double"
  }, {
    "name" : "volume",
    "type" : "int"
  }, {
    "name" : "adjClose",
    "type" : "double"
  } ]
}
```

You can run the Avro tools without any options to view all the tools you can use:

```
$ java -jar $HIP_HOME/lib/avro-tools-1.7.4.jar
       compile  Generates Java code for the given schema.
        concat  Concatenates avro files without re-compressing.
    fragtojson  Renders a binary-encoded Avro datum as JSON.
      fromjson  Reads JSON records and writes an Avro data file.
      fromtext  Imports a text file into an avro data file.
       getmeta  Prints out the metadata of an Avro data file.
     getschema  Prints out schema of an Avro data file.
           idl  Generates a JSON schema from an Avro IDL file
        induce  Induce schema/protocol from Java class/interface
                via reflection.
    jsontofrag  Renders a JSON-encoded Avro datum as binary.
       recodec  Alters the codec of a data file.
   rpcprotocol  Output the protocol of a RPC service
    rpcreceive  Opens an RPC Server and listens for one message.
       rpcsend  Sends a single RPC message.
        tether  Run a tethered mapreduce job.
        tojson  Dumps an Avro data file as JSON, one record per line.
        totext  Converts an Avro data file to a text file.
   trevni_meta  Dumps a Trevni file's metadata as JSON.
 trevni_random  Create a Trevni file filled with random instances
                of a schema.
 trevni_tojson  Dumps a Trevni file as JSON.
```

One shortcoming of the tojson tool is that it doesn't support reading data in HDFS. I've therefore bundled a utility with the book's code called AvroDump that can dump a text representation of Avro data in HDFS, which we'll use shortly to examine the output of Avro MapReduce jobs:

```
$ hip hip.util.AvroDump --file stocks.avro
```

This utility supports multiple files (they need to be CSV-delimited) and globbing, so you can use wildcards. The following example shows how you would dump out the contents of a MapReduce job that produced Avro output into a directory called mr-output-dir:

```
$ hip hip.util.AvroDump --file mr-output-dir/part*
```

Let's see how Avro integrates with MapReduce.

TECHNIQUE 13   **Selecting the appropriate way to use Avro in MapReduce**

Avro supports more than one way to work with your Avro data in MapReduce. This technique enumerates the different ways you can work with your data and provides guidance on which situations call for which approach.

■ **Problem**

You want to use Avro in your MapReduce job, but it's unclear which of the available integration options you should choose.

■ **Solution**

Learn more about each integration option, and pick the one best suited for your use case.

■ **Discussion**

There are three ways that you can use Avro in MapReduce, and the specific details on how to use each are discussed in techniques that follow this one. These are the three approaches:

- *Mixed-mode*—Appropriate when you want to mix Avro data with non-Avro data in your job
- *Record-based*—Useful when data is supplied in a non-key/value way
- *Key/value-based*—For when your data must fit a specific model

Let's cover each method in more detail.

Mixed-mode

This use case is for instances where any one of these conditions holds true:

- Your mapper input data isn't in Avro form.
- You don't want to emit intermediate data between your mappers and reducers using Avro.
- Your job output data isn't in Avro form.

In any of these cases, the Avro mapper and reducer classes won't help you, as they are designed with the assumption that Avro data is flowing end-to-end in your MapReduce job. In this case, you'll want to use the regular MapReduce mapper and reducer classes and construct your job in a way that allows you to still work with Avro data.

Record-based

Avro data is record-based, which results in a impedance mismatch when compared with MapReduce, which is key/value-based. To support Avro's record-based roots, Avro comes bundled with a mapper class that isn't key/value-based, and instead only supplies derived classes with a single record.

Key/value-based

If your Avro data internally follows a key/value structure, you can use some Avro-supplied mapper classes that will transform your Avro records and supply them in a key/value form to your mapper. With this method, you're restricted to schemas that literally have "key" and "value" elements.

■ **Summary**

Selecting the right level of integration with Avro is a function of your inputs and outputs, and how you want to work with data inside of Avro. This technique examined three ways of integrating with Avro so that you can pick the right method for your use case. In the following techniques, we'll look at how to use each of these integration methods in your MapReduce jobs.

| TECHNIQUE 14 | **Mixing Avro and non-Avro data in MapReduce** |

This level of Avro integration in MapReduce is suitable in cases where you have non-Avro input and generate Avro outputs, or vice versa, in which case the Avro mapper and reducer classes aren't suitable. In this technique, we'll look at how to work in a mixed-mode fashion with Avro.

■ **Problem**

You want to use Avro in a mixed mode in your MapReduce job, which isn't supported by the Avro-bundled mapper and reducer classes.

■ **Solution**

Use low-level methods to set up your job and drive Avro data through your Map-Reduce job using the regular Hadoop mapper and reducer classes.

■ **Discussion**

Avro comes with some mapper and reducer classes that you can subclass to work with Avro. They're useful in situations where you want your mappers and reducers to exchange Avro objects. But if you don't have a requirement to pass Avro objects between your map and reduce tasks, you're better off using the Avro input and output format classes directly, as you'll see in the following code, which produces an average of all of the opening stock values.

We'll start with a look at the job configuration. Your job is to consume stock data and produce stock averages, both in Avro formats.[28] To do this, you need to set the job

---

[28] Even though this technique is about mixing Avro and non-Avro data together in your jobs, I show Avro being used throughout the job so that you can pick which aspect you wish to integrate into your job. For example, if you have text inputs and Avro outputs, you'd use a regular `TextInputFormat`, and set the Avro output format.

configuration with the schema information for both schemas. You also need to specify Avro's input and output format classes:[29]

Set the Avro schema for the job output files.

Set the Avro schema for the input files that are to be processed.

```
job.set(AvroJob.INPUT_SCHEMA, Stock.SCHEMA$.toString());
job.set(AvroJob.OUTPUT_SCHEMA, StockAvg.SCHEMA$.toString());
job.set(AvroJob.OUTPUT_CODEC, SnappyCodec.class.getName());

job.setInputFormat(AvroInputFormat.class);
job.setOutputFormat(AvroOutputFormat.class);
```

Set the compression codec for this job.

Indicate that the input data is Avro.

The output data is also Avro.

Next up is the Map class. The entire Avro record is supplied as the input key to your map function, because Avro supports records, not key/value pairs (although, as you'll see later, Avro does have a way to provide data to your map function using key/value pairs if your Avro schema has fields called key and value). From an implementation perspective, your map function extracts the necessary fields from the stock record and emits them to the reducer, with the stock symbol and the opening stock price as the key/value pairs:[30]

```
public static class Map extends MapReduceBase
    implements
    Mapper<AvroWrapper<Stock>, NullWritable, Text, DoubleWritable> {

  @Override
  public void map(
    AvroWrapper<Stock> key, NullWritable value,
    OutputCollector<Text, DoubleWritable> output,
    Reporter reporter) throws IOException {

    output.collect(
      new Text(key.datum().symbol.toString()),
      new DoubleWritable(key.datum().open));
  }
}
```

The Avro InputFormat supplies the Avro objects wrapped in an AvroWrapper object. No value is supplied to the mapper.

Convert the Avro data into regular Writable representations for intermediary data.

> **Why is the "old" MapReduce API being used?**   You may have noticed that the example in this technique uses the older org.apache.hadoop.mapred API. This is because the AvroInputFormat and AvroOutputFormat classes used in this technique only support the old API.

---

[29] GitHub source: https://github.com/alexholmes/hiped2/blob/master/src/main/java/hip/ch3/avro/ AvroMixedMapReduce.java.

[30] GitHub source: https://github.com/alexholmes/hiped2/blob/master/src/main/java/hip/ch3/avro/ AvroMixedMapReduce.java.

Finally, the reduce function sums together all of the stock prices for each stock and outputs an average price:[31]

```java
public static class Reduce extends MapReduceBase
    implements Reducer<Text, DoubleWritable, AvroWrapper<StockAvg>,
    NullWritable> {

  @Override
  public void reduce(
    Text key,
    Iterator<DoubleWritable> values,
    OutputCollector<AvroWrapper<StockAvg>, NullWritable> output,     ⟵  The Avro
    Reporter reporter) throws IOException {                              OutputFormat expects
                                                                        AvroWrapper output.
    Mean mean = new Mean();
    while (values.hasNext()) {
      mean.increment(values.next().get());
    }
    StockAvg avg = new StockAvg();
    avg.setSymbol(key.toString());                                  Output the
    avg.setAvg(mean.getResult());                                   AvroWrapper containing
    output.collect(new AvroWrapper<StockAvg>(avg),    ⟵             your StockAvg instance.
      NullWritable.get());
  }
}
```

You can run the MapReduce code as follows:

```
$ hip hip.ch3.avro.AvroMixedMapReduce \
    --input stocks.avro \
    --output output
```

Your MapReduce job is outputting a different Avro object (StockAvg) from the job input. You can verify that the job produced the output you expected by writing some code (not listed) to dump your Avro objects:

```
$ hip hip.util.AvroDump --file output/part*
{"symbol": "AAPL", "avg": 68.631}
{"symbol": "CSCO", "avg": 31.147999999999996}
{"symbol": "GOOG", "avg": 417.47799999999995}
{"symbol": "MSFT", "avg": 44.63100000000001}
{"symbol": "YHOO", "avg": 69.333}
```

■ **Summary**

This technique is useful in cases where you don't want intermediary map outputs in Avro form, or if you have non-Avro inputs or outputs. Next we'll look at the Avro-native way of working with data in MapReduce.

---

[31] GitHub source: https://github.com/alexholmes/hiped2/blob/master/src/main/java/hip/ch3/avro/ AvroMixedMapReduce.java.

TECHNIQUE 15   **Using Avro records in MapReduce**

Avro isn't a native key/value serialization format, unlike SequenceFile, so it can require a little shoehorning to get it to work with MapReduce. In this technique you'll examine the Avro-specific mapper and reducer classes that expose a record-based interface you can use to input and output data.

■ **Problem**

You want to use Avro end-to-end in your MapReduce job, and you also wish to interact with your input and output data in record-oriented form.

■ **Solution**

Extend the AvroMapper and AvroReducer classes to implement your MapReduce job.

■ **Discussion**

Avro comes with two classes that abstract away the key/value nature of MapReduce and instead expose a record-based API. In this technique you'll implement the same MapReduce job as in the prior technique (calculating the average open prices for each stock symbol), and use Avro throughout the job.

First, let's look at the Mapper class, which will extend AvroMapper: [32]

```
public static class Mapper
    extends AvroMapper<Stock, Pair<Utf8, Stock>> {         ◄── Define the input Avro
                                                               type and the intermediate
                                                               output key/value types.
    @Override
    public void map(Stock stock,
                    AvroCollector<Pair<Utf8, Stock>> collector,
                    Reporter reporter) throws IOException {       Generate the output
                                                                  record, which is a pair
        Pair <Utf8, Stock> out =                                  containing the stock
            new Pair<Utf8, Stock>(new Utf8(stock.getSymbol().toString(),   symbol and the stock
                                  stock);                                  Avro object.

        collector.collect(out);      ◄── Output the AvroWrapper
    }                                    containing your StockAvg
}                                                    instance.
```

The first thing to notice is that there are two types defined in the class definition, not four as is the norm in MapReduce. The AvroMapper abstracts away the key/value traits of the mapper inputs and outputs, replacing each with a single type.

If you had a map-only job, the types that you'd define would be the input and output types. But if you're running a full-blown MapReduce job, you'll need to use the Pair class so that you can define the map output key/value pairs. The Pair class requires that an Avro schema exists for the key and value parts, which is why the Utf8 class is used instead of a straight Java string.

---

[32] GitHub source: https://github.com/alexholmes/hiped2/blob/master/src/main/java/hip/ch3/avro/
AvroRecordMapReduce.java.

Let's now take a peek at the AvroReducer implementation. This time there are three types you need to define—the map output key and value types, and the reducer output type:[33]

```
public static class Reducer extends AvroReducer<Utf8, Stock, StockAvg> {
  @Override
  public void reduce(Utf8 symbol, Iterable<Stock> stocks,
                     AvroCollector<StockAvg> collector,
                     Reporter reporter) throws IOException {

    double total = 0.0;                       Iterate over the Avro
    double count = 0;                            Stock objects.
    for (Stock stock: stocks) {      ◄
      total += stock.getOpen();
      count++;
    }
    StockAvg avg = new StockAvg();
    avg.setSymbol(symbol.toString());
    avg.setAvg(total / count);
                                             Output the
    collector.collect(avg);      ◄        StockAvg object.
  }
}
```

Now you can plumb it all together in the driver. Here you'll define the input and output types and the desired output compression, if any:[34]

```
AvroJob.setInputSchema(job, Stock.SCHEMA$);
AvroJob.setMapOutputSchema(job,
  Pair.getPairSchema(Schema.create(Schema.Type.STRING), Stock.SCHEMA$));
AvroJob.setOutputSchema(job, StockAvg.SCHEMA$);

AvroJob.setMapperClass(job, Mapper.class);
AvroJob.setReducerClass(job, Reducer.class);

FileOutputFormat.setCompressOutput(job, true);
AvroJob.setOutputCodec(job, SNAPPY_CODEC);
```

Done! Give it a whirl, and check the outputs after the job completes:

```
$ hip hip.ch3.avro.AvroRecordMapReduce \
    --input stocks.avro \
    --output output

...

$ hip hip.util.AvroDump --file output/part*
{"symbol": "AAPL", "avg": 68.631}
{"symbol": "CSCO", "avg": 31.147999999999996}
```

---

[33] GitHub source: https://github.com/alexholmes/hiped2/blob/master/src/main/java/hip/ch3/avro/AvroRecordMapReduce.java.

[34] GitHub source: https://github.com/alexholmes/hiped2/blob/master/src/main/java/hip/ch3/avro/AvroRecordMapReduce.java.

```
{"symbol": "GOOG", "avg": 417.47799999999995}
{"symbol": "MSFT", "avg": 44.63100000000001}
{"symbol": "YHOO", "avg": 69.333}
```

■ Summary

This technique is handy in situations where you want to keep your data in Avro form throughout the MapReduce job, and you don't have a requirement that your input or output data be key/value-based.

But what if you do need your data be key/value-based, and you still want to use Avro goodies such as compact serialization size and built-in compression?

TECHNIQUE 16 **Using Avro key/value pairs in MapReduce**

MapReduce's native data model is key/value pairs, and as I've mentioned earlier, Avro's is record-based. Avro doesn't have native support for key/value data, but some helper classes exist in Avro to help model key/value data and to use this natively in MapReduce.

■ Problem

You want to use Avro as a data format and container, but you want to model your data using key/value pairs in Avro and use them as native key/value pairs in MapReduce.

■ Solution

Use the AvroKeyValue, AvroKey, and AvroValue classes to work with Avro key/value data.

■ Discussion

Avro has an AvroKeyValue class that encapsulates a generic Avro record containing two records named key and value. AvroKeyValue serves as a helper class so that you can easily read and write key/value data. The types of these records are defined by you.

In this technique you'll repeat the average stock MapReduce job, but this time using Avro's key/value framework. You'll first need to generate the input data for your job. In this case, we'll put the stock symbol in the key and the Stock object in the value:[35]

```
public static void writeToAvro(File inputFile,            Use the helper class to
                            OutputStream outputStream)    generate the schema.
    throws IOException {

  Schema schema = AvroKeyValue.getSchema(
     Schema.create(Schema.Type.STRING), Stock.SCHEMA$);
                                                     Create a generic writer.
  DataFileWriter<GenericRecord> writer =
     new DataFileWriter<GenericRecord>(
         new GenericDatumWriter<GenericRecord>());
                                                     Set the
  writer.setCodec(CodecFactory.snappyCodec());       compression codec.
  writer.create(schema, outputStream);
                                                  Configure the writer
  for (Stock stock : StockUtils.fromCsvFile(inputFile)) {   with the output
                                                           stream and schema.
```

---

[35] GitHub source: https://github.com/alexholmes/hiped2/blob/master/src/main/java/hip/ch3/avro/AvroKeyValueFileWrite.java.

```
    AvroKeyValue<CharSequence, Stock> record
        = new AvroKeyValue<CharSequence, Stock>(
            new GenericData.Record(schema));
    record.setKey(stock.getSymbol());
    record.setValue(stock);

    writer.append(record.get());
  }

  IOUtils.closeStream(writer);
  IOUtils.closeStream(outputStream);
}
```

Create a wrapper object and set the key and value.

Write the encapsulated generic object to the output stream.

Go ahead and generate a file in HDFS containing the stock data in key/value format:

```
$ hip hip.ch3.avro.AvroKeyValueFileWrite \
    --input test-data/stocks.txt \
    --output stocks.kv.avro
```

If you're curious to know the Avro schema definition of the file you just generated, use the tip highlighted in technique 12 to extract the schema from the file. In addition, you can use the AvroDump utility to show the contents of the file:

```
# the "getschema" tool only works with data in the local filesystem,
# so first copy the stocks file from HDFS to local disk
$ hadoop fs -get stocks.kv.avro .
$ java -jar $HIP_HOME/lib/avro-tools-1.7.4.jar getschema stocks.kv.avro
{
  "type" : "record",
  "name" : "KeyValuePair",
  "namespace" : "org.apache.avro.mapreduce",
  "doc" : "A key/value pair",
  "fields" : [ {
    "name" : "key",
    "type" : "string",
    "doc" : "The key"
  }, {
    "name" : "value",
    "type" : {
      "type" : "record",
      "name" : "Stock",
      "namespace" : "hip.ch3.avro.gen",
      "fields" : [ {
        "name" : "symbol",
        "type" : "string"
      }, {
        "name" : "date",
        "type" : "string"
      }, {
        "name" : "open",
        "type" : "double"
      }, {
        "name" : "high",
        "type" : "double"
      }, {
```

```
      "name" : "low",
      "type" : "double"
    }, {
      "name" : "close",
      "type" : "double"
    }, {
      "name" : "volume",
      "type" : "int"
    }, {
      "name" : "adjClose",
      "type" : "double"
    } ]
  },
  "doc" : "The value"
} ]
}
```

```
$ hip hip.util.AvroDump --file stocks.kv.avro
```

```
{"key": "AAPL", "value": {"symbol": "AAPL", "date": "2009-01-02", ...
{"key": "AAPL", "value": {"symbol": "AAPL", "date": "2008-01-02", ...
{"key": "AAPL", "value": {"symbol": "AAPL", "date": "2007-01-03", ...
```

Now for some MapReduce code—you'll define your mapper, reducer, and driver in one shot:[36]

```
public int run(final String[] args) throws Exception {

    ....

    job.setInputFormatClass(AvroKeyValueInputFormat.class);
    AvroJob.setInputKeySchema(job, Schema.create(Schema.Type.STRING));
    AvroJob.setInputValueSchema(job, Stock.SCHEMA$);

    job.setMapOutputKeyClass(Text.class);
    job.setMapOutputValueClass(DoubleWritable.class);

    job.setOutputKeyClass(Text.class);
    job.setOutputValueClass(AvroValue.class);
    job.setOutputFormatClass(AvroKeyValueOutputFormat.class);
    AvroJob.setOutputValueSchema(job, StockAvg.SCHEMA$);

    ...
}

public static class Map extends
    Mapper<AvroKey<CharSequence>, AvroValue<Stock>,
        Text, DoubleWritable> {

    @Override
    public void map(AvroKey<CharSequence> key,
                AvroValue<Stock> value,
                Context context) {
```

---

[36] GitHub source: https://github.com/alexholmes/hiped2/blob/master/src/main/java/hip/ch3/avro/ AvroKeyValueMapReduce.java.

```
      context.write(new Text(key.toString()),
         new DoubleWritable(value.datum().getOpen())));
   }
}

public static class Reduce extends
   Reducer<Text, DoubleWritable, Text, AvroValue<StockAvg>> {

   @Override
   protected void reduce(Text key,
                         Iterable<DoubleWritable> values,
                         Context context) {
      double total = 0.0;
      double count = 0;
      for (DoubleWritable val: values) {
         total += val.get();
         count++;
      }
      StockAvg avg = new StockAvg();
      avg.setSymbol(key.toString());
      avg.setAvg(total / count);
      context.write(key, new AvroValue<StockAvg>(avg));
   }
}
```

As you can see, the AvroKey and AvroValue wrappers are used to supply input data in the mapper, as well as output data in the reducer. The neat thing here is that Avro is smart enough to support Hadoop Writable objects and automatically convert them into their Avro counterparts, which is why you don't need to tell Avro the schema type of the output key.

You can run the MapReduce job with the following command:

```
$ hip hip.ch3.avro.AvroKeyValueMapReduce \
    --input stocks.kv.avro \
    --output output
```

And again, you can view the output with the AvroDump tool:

```
$ hip hip.util.AvroDump --file output/part*
{"key": "AAPL", "value": {"symbol": "AAPL", "avg": 68.631}}
{"key": "CSCO", "value": {"symbol": "CSCO", "avg": 31.148}}
{"key": "GOOG", "value": {"symbol": "GOOG", "avg": 417.478}}
{"key": "MSFT", "value": {"symbol": "MSFT", "avg": 44.631}}
{"key": "YHOO", "value": {"symbol": "YHOO", "avg": 69.333}}
```

■ **Summary**

This concludes our coverage of the three Avro approaches for working with your data in MapReduce. Each of the methods is suited to a particular task, and you can select whichever one works best for your needs.

Let's wrap up our Avro and MapReduce coverage by looking at how you can customize ordering characteristics of Avro data in MapReduce.

TECHNIQUE 17 **Controlling how sorting worksin MapReduce**

If you decide to use Avro data as intermediary map outputs, you may be wondering what control you have over how partitioning, sorting, and grouping work.

■ **Problem**

You want control over how MapReduce sorts your reducer inputs.

■ **Solution**

Modify the Avro schema to alter ordering behavior.

■ **Discussion**

If an Avro object is used as the key output in a mapper, the following happens by default:

- All the fields in the Avro object are used for partitioning, sorting, and grouping.
- The fields are ordered using their ordinal position in the schema. This means that if you have a schema with two elements, the first element in the schema is used for sorting first, followed by the second element.
- Within an element, sorting occurs using comparisons that are specific to the type. So if strings are being compared, the sorting will be lexicographical, and if numbers are being compared, numerical comparison is used.

Some of this behavior can be changed. The following is a modified version of the Stock schema:

```
{
  "name": "Stock",
  "type": "record",
  "namespace": "hip.ch3.avro.gen",
  "fields": [
      {"name": "symbol",   "type": "string"},
      {"name": "date",     "type": "string"},
      {"name": "open",     "type": "double", "order": "descending"},
      {"name": "high",     "type": "double", "order": "ignore"}
  ]
}
```

You can modify the sorting behavior for a field by decorating it with an order attribute and specifying that descending order should be used. Alternatively, you can exclude a field from partitioning, sorting, and grouping by setting the order to ignore.

Note that these are schema-wide settings, and there's no easy way to specify custom partition/sort/group settings on a per-job basis. You can go ahead and write your own partition, sort, and group functions (just like you would for a Writable), but it would be useful if Avro had helper functions to simplify this process.

TECHNIQUE 18 **Avro and Hive**

It wasn't until recently that the Hive project had built-in support for Avro. This technique looks at how you can work with Avro data in Hive.

■ **Problem**

You want to work with Avro data in Hive.

■ **Solution**

Use Hive's Avro Serializer/Deserializer.

■ **Discussion**

Hive version 0.9.1 and newer come bundled with an Avro SerDe, short for Serializer/
Deserializer, which allows Hive to read data in from a table and write it back out to a
table. The appendix has instructions on how to install Hive.

You need to copy the Avro schemas bundled with this book into HDFS, and also
create a directory containing some example Avro stock records:

```
$ hadoop fs -put $HIP_HOME/schema schema

$ hadoop fs -mkdir stock_hive

$ hip hip.ch3.avro.AvroStockFileWrite \
    --input test-data/stocks.txt \
    --output stock_hive/stocks.avro
```

Next, fire up the Hive console and create an external Hive table for the directory you
just created. You also need to specify the location of the Avro schema in HDFS.
Replace YOUR-HDFS-USERNAME with your HDFS username:

```
hive> CREATE EXTERNAL TABLE stocks
➥COMMENT "An Avro stocks table"
➥ROW FORMAT SERDE 'org.apache.hadoop.hive.serde2.avro.AvroSerDe'
➥STORED AS
➥INPUTFORMAT
➥   'org.apache.hadoop.hive.ql.io.avro.AvroContainerInputFormat'
➥OUTPUTFORMAT
➥   'org.apache.hadoop.hive.ql.io.avro.AvroContainerOutputFormat'
➥LOCATION '/user/YOUR-HDFS-USERNAME/stock_hive/'
➥TBLPROPERTIES (
➥  'avro.schema.url'='hdfs:///user/YOUR-HDFS-USERNAME/schema/stock.avsc'
  );
```

AvroSerDe actually supports three ways to define a schema for an Avro table—for this
technique, I picked the method that you'll most likely want to use in production, but
for more details on the other ways to specify a schema, refer to the AvroSerDe site:
https://cwiki.apache.org/confluence/display/Hive/AvroSerDe.

Just like with any Hive table, you can query Hive to describe the schema for a table:

```
hive> describe stocks;

symbol            string
date              string
open              double
high              double
```

```
low                 double
close               double
volume              int
adjclose            double
```

Run a query to verify that everything's working. The following Hive Query Language (HiveQL) will count the number of stock records for each stock symbol:

```
hive> SELECT symbol, count(*) FROM stocks GROUP BY symbol;
```

```
AAPL    10
CSCO    10
GOOG    5
MSFT    10
YHOO    10
```

What if you wanted to write data to an Avro-backed Hive table? The following example shows how you would copy a subset of the records in the stocks table and insert them into a new table. This example also highlights how you'd use the Snappy compression codec for any writes into the new table:

```
hive> SET hive.exec.compress.output=true;
hive> SET avro.output.codec=snappy;


hive> CREATE TABLE google_stocks
➡      COMMENT "An Avro stocks table containing just Google stocks"
➡      ROW FORMAT SERDE 'org.apache.hadoop.hive.serde2.avro.AvroSerDe'
➡      STORED AS
➡      INPUTFORMAT
➡        'org.apache.hadoop.hive.ql.io.avro.AvroContainerInputFormat'
➡      OUTPUTFORMAT
➡        'org.apache.hadoop.hive.ql.io.avro.AvroContainerOutputFormat'
➡      TBLPROPERTIES (
➡          'avro.schema.url'='hdfs:///user/YOUR-USERNAME/schema/stock.avsc'
    );
OK

hive> INSERT OVERWRITE TABLE google_stocks
➡      SELECT * FROM stocks WHERE symbol = 'GOOG';
OK

hive> select * from google_stocks limit 5;
OK
GOOG 2009-01-02 308.6 321.82 305.5 321.32 3610500 321.32
GOOG 2008-01-02 692.87 697.37 677.73 685.19 4306900 685.19
GOOG 2007-01-03 466.0 476.66 461.11 467.59 7706500 467.59
GOOG 2006-01-03 422.52 435.67 418.22 435.23 13121200 435.23
GOOG 2005-01-03 197.4 203.64 195.46 202.71 15844200 202.71
```

For more details on Hive, please refer to chapter 9. Next we'll look at how you'd perform the same sequence of actions in Pig.

TECHNIQUE 19 **Avro and Pig**

Much like Hive, Pig also has built-in support for Avro, which is covered in this technique.

■ **Problem**

You want to read and write Avro data using Pig.

■ **Solution**

Use the AvroStorage class in Pig's Piggy Bank library.

■ **Discussion**

Piggy Bank is a library that contains a useful collection of Pig utilities, one of which is the AvroStorage class you can use to read and write Avro data in HDFS. In this technique you'll mirror the steps you took in the previous Hive technique—you'll read in some stock data, perform some simple aggregations, and store some filtered data back into HDFS.

Before you get started, load some Avro stock data into a directory in HDFS:

```
$ hadoop fs -put $HIP_HOME/schema schema

$ hadoop fs -mkdir stock_pig

$ hip hip.ch3.avro.AvroStockFileWrite \
    --input test-data/stocks.txt \
    --output stock_pig/stocks.avro
```

In Pig-land, your first step is to register the JARs required for AvroStorage to work. You may have to hunt down the specific location of the JARs bundled with the Hadoop distribution that you're using. The locations in the following code assume that Apache Hadoop and Pig were installed under /usr/local:

```
$ pig
REGISTER /usr/local/pig/contrib/piggybank/java/piggybank.jar;
REGISTER /usr/local/hadoop/share/hadoop/common/lib/avro-*.jar;
REGISTER /usr/local/hadoop/share/hadoop/common/lib/jackson-*.jar;
REGISTER /usr/local/hadoop/share/hadoop/common/lib/snappy-*.jar;
REGISTER /usr/local/hadoop/share/hadoop/httpfs/tomcat/webapps/
➥        webhdfs/WEB-INF/lib/json-*.jar;
```

Next, load the stocks into a Pig relation and then display the schema details using the LOAD and DESCRIBE operators:

```
grunt> stocks = LOAD 'stock_pig/' USING
➥org.apache.pig.piggybank.storage.avro.AvroStorage();

grunt> DESCRIBE stocks;
records: {symbol: chararray,date: chararray,open: double,
        high: double,low: double,close: double,volume: int,
        adjClose: double}
```

Notice that you didn't have to supply details about the Avro schema. That's because the Avro container format you used had the schema embedded in the header. If your files don't have the schema embedded, AvroStorage can still support your data, but you'll need to upload the Avro schema to HDFS (like you did in Hive) and use the "schema_file" option—check out the Pig documentation for more details.[37]

To validate that Avro and Pig are working together, you can perform a simple aggregation and count the number of stock records for each stock symbol:

```
grunt> by_symbol = GROUP stocks BY symbol;
grunt> symbol_count = foreach by_symbol generate group, COUNT($1);
grunt> dump symbol_count;

(AAPL,10)
(CSCO,10)
(GOOG,5)
(MSFT,10)
(YHOO,10)
```

The following example shows how you can write out Avro data in Pig. The example filters the Google stocks from the input data and writes them into a new output directory in HDFS. This also shows how you can compress job outputs using Snappy:

```
grunt> SET mapred.compress.map.output true;
grunt> SET mapred.output.compress true;
grunt> SET mapred.output.compression.codec
             org.apache.hadoop.io.compress.SnappyCodec
grunt> SET avro.output.codec snappy;

grunt> google_stocks = FILTER stocks BY symbol == 'GOOG';

grunt> STORE google_stocks INTO 'stock_pig_output/'
   USING org.apache.pig.piggybank.storage.avro.AvroStorage(
       'no_schema_check',
       'data', 'stock_pig/');
```

When writing Avro data to HDFS, you'll need to specify the Avro schema of the data you're persisting. The preceding example uses the data option to tell AvroStorage to use the Avro schema embedded in files under your input directory.

As with loading files, there are various other methods for telling AvroStorage your schema details, and these are documented on Pig's wiki.[38]

■ Summary

The last few techniques have demonstrated how easy and straightforward it is to use Avro with MapReduce, Hive, and Pig. Using Avro to store your data gives you a number of useful free features, such as versioning support, compression, splittability, and code generation. Avro's strong integration with MapReduce, Hive, Pig, and numerous other tools, such as Impala and Flume, means that it's worth consideration as your data format of choice.

---

[37] More Avro and Pig integration details are available on the AvroStorage page: https://cwiki.apache.org/confluence/display/PIG/AvroStorage.

[38] Additional resources on AvroStorage are at https://cwiki.apache.org/confluence/display/PIG/AvroStorage.

Until now we've focused on row-based file formats, which aren't always the best way to lay out data. In the next section you'll learn about the advantages of columnar storage and see examples of Parquet, a columnar storage, in action.

3.4 *Columnar storage*

When data is written to an I/O device (say a flat file, or a table in a relational database), the most common way to lay out that data is row-based, meaning that all the fields for the first row are written first, followed by all the fields for the second row, and so on. This is how most relational databases write out tables by default, and the same goes for most data serialization formats such as XML, JSON, and Avro container files.

Columnar storage works differently—it lays out data by column first, and then by row. All the values of the first field across all the records are written first, followed by the second field, and so on. Figure 3.12 highlights the differences between the two storage schemes in how the data is laid out.

There are two main benefits to storing data in columnar form:

- Systems that read columnar data can efficiently extract a subset of the columns, reducing I/O. Row-based systems typically need to read the entire row even if just one or two columns are needed.
- Optimizations can be made when writing columnar data, such as run-length encoding and bit packing, to efficiently compress the size of the data being written. General compression schemes also work well for compressing columnar data because compression works best on data that has a lot of repeating data, which is the case when columnar data is physically colocated.

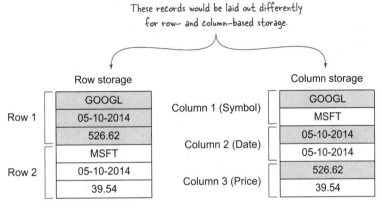

Figure 3.12   How row and column storage systems lay out their data

As a result, columnar file formats work best when working with large datasets where you wish to filter or project data, which is exactly the type of work that's commonly performed in OLAP-type use cases, as well as MapReduce.

The majority of data formats used in Hadoop, such as JSON and Avro, are row-ordered, which means that you can't apply the previously mentioned optimizations when reading and writing these files. Imagine that the data in figure 3.12 was in a Hive table and you were to execute the following query:

```
SELECT AVG(price) FROM stocks;
```

If the data was laid out in a row-based format, each row would have to be read, even though the only column being operated on is price. In a column-oriented store, only the price column would be read, which could result in drastically reduced processing times when you're working with large datasets.

There are a number of columnar storage options that can be used in Hadoop:

- *RCFile* was the first columnar format available in Hadoop; it came out of a collaboration between Facebook and academia in 2009.[39] RCFile is a basic columnar store that supports separate column storage and column compression. It can support projection during reads, but misses out on the more advanced techniques such as run-length encoding. As a result, Facebook has been moving away from RCFile to ORC file.[40]

- *ORC file* was created by Facebook and Hortonworks to address RCFile's shortcomings, and its serialization optimizations have yielded smaller data sizes compared to RCFile.[41] It also uses indexes to enable predicate pushdowns to optimize queries so that a column that doesn't match a filter predicate can be skipped. ORC file is also fully integrated with Hive's type system and can support nested structures.

- *Parquet* is a collaboration between Twitter and Cloudera and employs many of the tricks that ORC file uses to generate compressed files.[42] Parquet is a language-independent format with a formal specification.

RCFile and ORC file were designed to support Hive as their primary usage, whereas Parquet is independent of any other Hadoop tool and tries to maximize compatibility with the Hadoop ecosystem. Table 3.2 shows how these columnar formats integrate with various tools and languages.

---

[39] Yongqiang He, et al., "RCFile: A Fast and Space-efficient Data Placement Structure in MapReduce-based Warehouse Systems," ICDE Conference 2011: www.cse.ohio-state.edu/hpcs/WWW/HTML/publications/papers/TR-11-4.pdf.

[40] Facebook Engineering Blog, "Scaling the Facebook data warehouse to 300 PB," https://code.facebook.com/posts/229861827208629/scaling-the-facebook-data-warehouse-to-300-pb/.

[41] Owen O'Malley, "ORC File Introduction," www.slideshare.net/oom65/orc-fileintro.

[42] Features such as column stats and indexes are planned for the Parquet 2 release.

Table 3.2   Columnar storage formats supported in Hadoop

Format	Hadoop support	Supported object models	Supported programming languages	Advanced compression support
RCFile	MapReduce, Pig, Hive (0.4+), Impala	Thrift, Protocol Buffers[a]	Java	No
ORC file	MapReduce, Pig, Hive (0.11+)	None	Java	Yes
Parquet	MapReduce, Pig, Hive, Impala	Avro, Protocol Buffers, Thrift	Java, C++, Python	Yes

[a]   Elephant Bird provides the ability to use Thrift and Protocol Buffers with RCFile.

For this section, I'll focus on Parquet due to its compatibility with object models such as Avro.

3.4.1   Understanding object models and storage formats

Before we get started with the techniques, we'll cover a few Parquet concepts that are important in understanding the interplay between Parquet and Avro (and Thrift and Protocol Buffers):

- *Object models* are in-memory representations of data. Parquet exposes a simple object model that's supplied more as an example than anything else. Avro, Thrift, and Protocol Buffers are full-featured object models. An example is the Avro Stock class, which was generated by Avro to richly model the schema using Java POJOs.
- *Storage formats* are serialized representations of a data model. Parquet is a storage format that serializes data in columnar form. Avro, Thrift, and Protocol Buffers also have their own storage formats that serialize data in row-oriented formats.[43] Storage formats can be thought of as the at-rest representation of data.
- *Parquet object model converters* are responsible for converting an object model to Parquet's data types, and vice versa. Parquet is bundled with a number of converters to maximize the interoperability and adoption of Parquet.

Figure 3.13 shows how these concepts work in the context of Parquet.

What's unique about Parquet is that it has converters that allow it to support common object models such as Avro. Behind the scenes, the data is stored in Parquet binary form, but when you're working with your data, you're using your preferred object model, such as Avro objects. This gives you the best of both worlds: you can continue to use a rich object model such as Avro to interact with your data, and that data will be efficiently laid out on disk using Parquet.

---

[43] Avro does have a columnar storage format called Trevni: http://avro.apache.org/docs/1.7.6/trevni/spec.html.

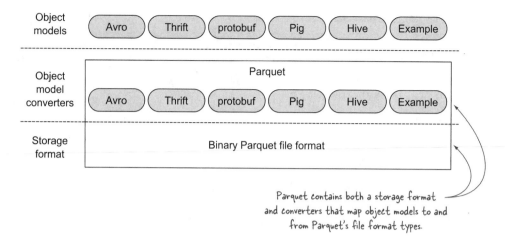

Figure 3.13   Parquet storage format and object model converters

> **Storage format interoperability**   Storage formats generally aren't interoperable. When you're combining Avro and Parquet, you're combining Avro's object model and Parquet's storage format. Therefore, if you have existing Avro data sitting in HDFS that was serialized using Avro's storage format, you can't read that data using Parquet's storage format, as they are two very different ways of encoding data. The reverse is also true—Parquet can't be read using the normal Avro methods (such as the AvroInputFormat in MapReduce); you must use Parquet implementations of input formats and Hive SerDes to work with Parquet data.

To summarize, choose Parquet if you want your data to be serialized in a columnar form. Once you've selected Parquet, you'll need to decide which object model you'll be working with. I recommend you pick the object model that has the most traction in your organization. Otherwise I recommend going with Avro (section 3.3.5 explains why Avro can be a good choice).

> **The Parquet file format**   The Parquet file format is beyond the scope of this book; for more details, take a look at the Parquet project page at https:// github.com/Parquet/parquet-format.

3.4.2   *Parquet and the Hadoop ecosystem*

The goal of Parquet is to maximize support throughout the Hadoop ecosystem. It currently supports MapReduce, Hive, Pig, Impala, and Spark, and hopefully we'll see it being supported by other systems such as Sqoop.

Because Parquet is a standard file format, a Parquet file that's written by any one of these technologies can also be read by the others. Maximizing support across the Hadoop ecosystem is critical to the success of a file format, and Parquet is poised to become the ubiquitous file format in big data.

It's also reassuring that Parquet isn't focused on a particular subset of technologies—in the words of the Parquet home page, "We are not interested in playing favorites" when it comes to ecosystem support (http://parquet.io). This implies that a primary goal of the project is to maximize its support for the tools that you're likely to use, which is important as new tools continue to pop up on our radars.

3.4.3   Parquet block and page sizes

Figure 3.14 shows a high-level representation of the Parquet file format and highlights the key concepts.

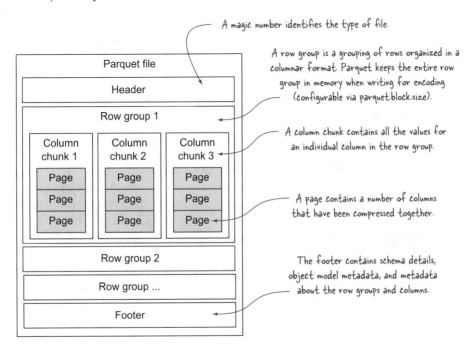

Figure 3.14   Parquet's file format

A more detailed overview of the file format can be seen at the project's home page: https://github.com/Parquet/parquet-format.

TECHNIQUE 20   **Reading Parquet files via the command line**

Parquet is a binary storage format, so using the standard hadoop fs -cat command will yield garbage on the command line. In this technique we'll explore how you can use the command line to not only view the contents of a Parquet file, but also to examine the schema and additional metadata contained in Parquet files.

■ **Problem**

You want to use the command line to examine the contents of a Parquet file.

■ **Solution**

Use the utilities bundled with the Parquet tools.

■ **Discussion**

Parquet is bundled with a tools JAR containing some useful utilities that can dump information in Parquet files to standard output.

Before you get started, you'll need to create a Parquet file so that you can test out the tools. The following example creates a Parquet file by writing Avro records:

```
$ hip hip.ch3.parquet.ParquetAvroStockWriter \
    --input test-data/stocks.txt \
    --output stocks.parquet
```

The first Parquet tool you'll use is cat, which performs a simple dump of the data in the Parquet file to standard output:

```
$ hip --nolib parquet.tools.Main cat stocks.parquet
symbol = AAPL
date = 2009-01-02
open = 85.88
...
```

You can use the Parquet head command instead of cat in the preceding example to emit only the first five records. There's also a dump command that allows you to specify a subset of the columns that should be dumped, although the output isn't as human-readable.

Parquet has its own internal data types and schema that are mapped to external object models by converters. The internal Parquet schema can be viewed using the schema option:

```
$ hip --nolib parquet.tools.Main schema stocks.parquet
message hip.ch3.avro.gen.Stock {
  required binary symbol (UTF8);
  required binary date (UTF8);
  required double open;
  required double high;
  required double low;
  required double close;
  required int32 volume;
  required double adjClose;
}
```

Parquet also allows object models to use the metadata to store information needed for deserialization. Avro, for example, uses the metadata to store the Avro schema, as can be seen in the output of the command that follows:

```
$ hip --nolib parquet.tools.Main meta stocks.parquet
creator: parquet-mr (build 3f25ad97f20...)
extra:   avro.schema = {"type":"record","name":"Stock","namespace" ...

file schema: hip.ch3.avro.gen.Stock
-----------------------------------------------------------------
symbol:      REQUIRED BINARY O:UTF8 R:0 D:0
```

```
date:        REQUIRED BINARY O:UTF8 R:0 D:0
open:        REQUIRED DOUBLE R:0 D:0
high:        REQUIRED DOUBLE R:0 D:0
low:         REQUIRED DOUBLE R:0 D:0
close:       REQUIRED DOUBLE R:0 D:0
volume:      REQUIRED INT32 R:0 D:0
adjClose:    REQUIRED DOUBLE R:0 D:0

row group 1: RC:45 TS:2376
--------------------------------------------------------------
symbol:      BINARY SNAPPY DO:0 FPO:4 SZ:85/84/0.99 VC:45 ENC:PD ...
date:        BINARY SNAPPY DO:0 FPO:89 SZ:127/198/1.56 VC:45 ENC ...
open:        DOUBLE SNAPPY DO:0 FPO:216 SZ:301/379/1.26 VC:45 EN ...
high:        DOUBLE SNAPPY DO:0 FPO:517 SZ:297/379/1.28 VC:45 EN ...
low:         DOUBLE SNAPPY DO:0 FPO:814 SZ:292/379/1.30 VC:45 EN ...
close:       DOUBLE SNAPPY DO:0 FPO:1106 SZ:299/379/1.27 VC:45 E ...
volume:      INT32 SNAPPY DO:0 FPO:1405 SZ:203/199/0.98 VC:45 EN ...
adjClose:    DOUBLE SNAPPY DO:0 FPO:1608 SZ:298/379/1.27 VC:45 E ...
```

Next let's look at how you can write and read Parquet files.

TECHNIQUE 21 Reading and writing Avro data in Parquet with Java

One of the first things you'll want to do when working with a new file format is to understand how a standalone Java application can read and write data. This technique shows how you can write Avro data into a Parquet file and read it back out.

■ **Problem**

You want to read and write Parquet data directly from your Java code outside of Hadoop using an Avro object model.

■ **Solution**

Use the `AvroParquetWriter` and `AvroParquetReader` classes.

■ **Discussion**

Parquet, a columnar storage format for Hadoop, has support for Avro, which allows you to work with your data using Avro classes, and to efficiently encode the data using Parquet's file format so that you can take advantage of the columnar layout of your data. It sounds odd to mix data formats like this, so let's investigate why you'd want to do this and how it works.

Parquet is a storage format, and it has a formal programming language–agnostic specification. You could use Parquet directly without any other supporting data format such as Avro, but Parquet is at heart a simple data format and doesn't support complex types such as maps or unions. This is where Avro comes into play, as it supports these richer types as well as features such as code generation and schema evolution. As a result, marrying Parquet and a rich data format such as Avro creates a perfect match of sophisticated schema capabilities coupled with efficient data encoding.

For this technique, we'll continue to use the Avro Stock schema. First, let's look at how you can write a Parquet file using these Stock objects.[44]

---

[44] GitHub source: https://github.com/alexholmes/hiped2/blob/master/src/main/java/hip/ch3/parquet/ ParquetAvroStockWriter.java.

Use Snappy to compress columns; only Snappy, gzip, and LZO are supported.

The Avro schema.

Create a writer to write out Avro records.

The output file.

```
AvroParquetWriter<Stock> writer =
    new AvroParquetWriter<Stock>(
        outputPath,
        Stock.SCHEMA$,
        CompressionCodecName.SNAPPY,
        ParquetWriter.DEFAULT_BLOCK_SIZE,
        ParquetWriter.DEFAULT_PAGE_SIZE,
        true
    );
```

The amount of memory used to buffer writes—the default is 128 MB.

The page size—the default is 1 MB.

Enable dictionary encoding.

```
for (Stock stock : AvroStockUtils.fromCsvFile(inputFile)) {
    writer.write(stock);
}

writer.close();
```

Write out Stock instances.

The following command generates a Parquet file by executing the preceding code:

```
$ hip hip.ch3.parquet.ParquetAvroStockWriter \
    --input test-data/stocks.txt \
    --output stocks.parquet
```

The previous technique showed you how to use the Parquet tools to dump the file to standard output. But what if you wanted to read the file in Java?[45]

```
ParquetReader<Stock> reader = new AvroParquetReader<Stock>(inputFile);

Stock stock;
while((stock = reader.read()) != null) {
    System.out.println(stock);
}

reader.close()
```

The following command shows the output of the preceding code:

```
$ hip hip.ch3.parquet.ParquetAvroStockReader \
    --input stocks.parquet
AAPL,2009-01-02,85.88,91.04,85.16,90.75,26643400,90.75
AAPL,2008-01-02,199.27,200.26,192.55,194.84,38542100,194.84
AAPL,2007-01-03,86.29,86.58,81.9,83.8,44225700,83.8
...
```

TECHNIQUE 22   **Parquet and MapReduce**

This technique examines how you can work with Parquet files in MapReduce. Using Parquet as a data source as well as a data sink in MapReduce will be covered.

---

[45] GitHub source: https://github.com/alexholmes/hiped2/blob/master/src/main/java/hip/ch3/parquet/ParquetAvroStockReader.java.

■ **Problem**

You want to work with Avro data serialized as Parquet in MapReduce.

■ **Solution**

Use the AvroParquetInputFormat and AvroParquetOutputFormat classes.

■ **Discussion**

The Avro subproject in Parquet comes with MapReduce input and output formats to let you read and write your Avro data using Parquet as the storage format. The following example calculates the average stock price for each symbol:[46]

```java
public int run(final String[] args) throws Exception {

  Path inputPath = new Path(args[0]);
  Path outputPath = new Path(args[1]);

  Configuration conf = super.getConf();

  Job job = new Job(conf);
  job.setJarByClass(AvroParquetMapReduce.class);

  job.setInputFormatClass(AvroParquetInputFormat.class);
  AvroParquetInputFormat.setInputPaths(job, inputPath);

  job.setMapperClass(Map.class);
  job.setReducerClass(Reduce.class);

  job.setMapOutputKeyClass(Text.class);
  job.setMapOutputValueClass(DoubleWritable.class);

  job.setOutputFormatClass(AvroParquetOutputFormat.class);
  FileOutputFormat.setOutputPath(job, outputPath);
  AvroParquetOutputFormat.setSchema(job, StockAvg.SCHEMA$);

  return job.waitForCompletion(true) ? 0 : 1;
}

public static class Map
  extends Mapper<Void, Stock, Text, DoubleWritable> {

  @Override
  public void map(Void key, Stock value, Context context) {
    context.write(new Text(value.getSymbol().toString()),
        new DoubleWritable(value.getOpen())));
  }
}

public static class Reduce
  extends Reducer<Text, DoubleWritable, Void, StockAvg> {

  @Override
  protected void reduce(Text key, Iterable<DoubleWritable> values,
                        Context context) {
```

Set the Avro Parquet input format.

Set the Avro Parquet output format.

Specify the Avro schema for the job outputs.

Parquet doesn't supply an input key, just the value as an Avro object.

Similarly, the output format ignores the key and only uses the Avro value.

---

[46] GitHub source: https://github.com/alexholmes/hiped2/blob/master/src/main/java/hip/ch3/parquet/ AvroParquetMapReduce.java.

```
    Mean mean = new Mean();
    for (DoubleWritable val : values) {
      mean.increment(val.get());
    }
    StockAvg avg = new StockAvg();
    avg.setSymbol(key.toString());
    avg.setAvg(mean.getResult());
    context.write(null, avg);
  }
}
```

Working with Avro in Parquet is very simple, and arguably easier than working with Avro-serialized data.[47] You can run the example:

```
$ hip hip.ch3.parquet.AvroParquetMapReduce \
    --input stocks.parquet \
    --output output
```

Parquet comes with some tools to help you work with Parquet files, and one of them allows you to dump the contents to standard output:

```
$ hdfs -ls output
output/_SUCCESS
output/_metadata
output/part-r-00000.parquet

$ hip --nolib parquet.tools.Main cat output/part-r-00000.parquet
symbol = AAPL
avg = 68.631

symbol = CSCO
avg = 31.148000000000003

symbol = GOOG
avg = 417.47799999999995

symbol = MSFT
avg = 44.63100000000001

symbol = YHOO
avg = 69.333
```

You may have noticed that there's an additional file in the output directory called _metadata. When the Parquet OutputComitter runs upon job completion, it reads the footer of all the output files (which contains the file metadata) and generates this summarized metadata file. This file is used by subsequent MapReduce (or Pig/Hive) jobs to reduce job startup times.[48]

---

[47] The input and output formats supplied with Avro to support Avro's storage format wrap the Avro objects, requiring a level of indirection.

[48] Calculating the input splits can take a long time when there are a large number of input files that need to have their footers read, so having the ability to read a single summary file is a useful optimization.

■ **Summary**

In this technique, you saw how to use code-generated Avro object files with Parquet. If you don't want to work with Avro object files, you have a few options that allow you to work with Avro data generically using Avro's `GenericData` class:

- If you wrote the Avro data using `GenericData` objects, then that's the format in which Avro will supply them to your mappers.
- Excluding the JAR containing your Avro-generated code will also result in `GenericData` objects being fed to your mappers.
- You can trick Avro by mutating the input schema so that Avro can't load the specific class, forcing it to supply the `GenericData` instance instead.

The following code shows how you would perform the third option—you're essentially taking the original schema and duplicating it, but in the process you're supplying a different classname, which Avro won't be able to load (see "foobar" in the first line):[49]

```
Schema schema = Schema.createRecord("foobar",
    Stock.SCHEMA$.getDoc(), Stock.SCHEMA$.getNamespace(), false);
List<Schema.Field> fields = Lists.newArrayList();
for (Schema.Field field : Stock.SCHEMA$.getFields()) {
  fields.add(new Schema.Field(field.name(), field.schema(),
    field.doc(), field.defaultValue(), field.order()));
}
schema.setFields(fields);

AvroParquetInputFormat.setAvroReadSchema(job, schema);
```

What if you want to work with the Parquet data natively? Parquet comes with an example object model that allows you to work with any Parquet data, irrespective of the object model that was used to write the data. It uses a `Group` class to represent records, and provides some basic getters and setters to retrieve fields.

The following code once again shows how to calculate the stock averages. The input is the Avro/Parquet data, and the output is a brand new Parquet schema:[50]

```
private final static String writeSchema = "message stockavg {\n" +
    "required binary symbol;\n" +
    "required double avg;\n" +
    "}";

public void run(Path inputPath, Path outputPath) {
  Configuration conf = super.getConf();

  Job job = new Job(conf);
  job.setJarByClass(ExampleParquetMapReduce.class);

  job.setInputFormatClass(ExampleInputFormat.class);
  FileInputFormat.setInputPaths(job, inputPath);
```

---

[49] GitHub source https://github.com/alexholmes/hiped2/blob/master/src/main/java/hip/ch3/parquet/ AvroGenericParquetMapReduce.java.

[50] GitHub source: https://github.com/alexholmes/hiped2/blob/master/src/main/java/hip/ch3/parquet/ ExampleParquetMapReduce.java.

```
        job.setMapperClass(Map.class);
        job.setReducerClass(Reduce.class);

        job.setMapOutputKeyClass(Text.class);
        job.setMapOutputValueClass(DoubleWritable.class);

        job.setOutputFormatClass(ExampleOutputFormat.class);
        FileOutputFormat.setOutputPath(job, outputPath);
        ExampleOutputFormat.setSchema(
            job,
            MessageTypeParser.parseMessageType(writeSchema));
    }

    public static class Map extends Mapper<Void, Group,
                                           Text, DoubleWritable> {

      @Override
      public void map(Void key, Group value, Context context) {
        context.write(new Text(value.getString("symbol", 0)),
            new DoubleWritable(Double.valueOf(
                                    value.getValueToString(2, 0))));
      }
    }

    public static class Reduce extends Reducer<Text, DoubleWritable,
                                               Void, Group> {

      private SimpleGroupFactory factory;

      @Override
      protected void setup(Context context) {
        factory = new SimpleGroupFactory(
          GroupWriteSupport.getSchema(
            ContextUtil.getConfiguration(context)));
      }

      @Override
      protected void reduce(Text key, Iterable<DoubleWritable> values,
                            Context context) {
        Mean mean = new Mean();
        for (DoubleWritable val : values) {
          mean.increment(val.get());
        }
        Group group = factory.newGroup()
            .append("symbol", key.toString())
            .append("avg", mean.getResult());
        context.write(null, group);
      }
    }
}
```

The example object model is pretty basic and is currently missing some functionality—for example, there are no getters for double types, which is why the preceding code accesses the stock value using the getValueToString method. But there's work afoot to provide better object models, including a POJO adapter.[51]

---

[51] See the GitHub ticket number 325 titled "Pojo Support for Parquet" at https://github.com/Parquet/parquet-mr/pull/325.

TECHNIQUE 23   **Parquet and Hive/Impala**

Parquet comes into its own when utilized in Hive and Impala. Columnar storage is a natural fit for these systems by virtue of its ability to use pushdowns to optimize the read path.[52] This technique shows how Parquet can be used in these systems.

■ **Problem**

You want to be able to work with your Parquet data in Hive and Impala.

■ **Solution**

Use Hive's and Impala's built-in support for Parquet.

■ **Discussion**

Hive requires that data exists in a directory, so you first need to create a directory and copy the stocks Parquet file into it:

```
$ hadoop fs -mkdir parquet_avro_stocks
$ hadoop fs -cp stocks.parquet parquet_avro_stocks
```

Next, you'll create an external Hive table and define the schema. If you're unsure about the structure of your schema, use one of the earlier techniques to view the schema information in the Parquet files that you're working with (use the schema command in the Parquet tools):

```
hive> CREATE EXTERNAL TABLE parquet_stocks(
    symbol string,
    date string,
    open double,
    high double,
    low double,
    close double,
    volume int,
    adjClose double
) STORED AS PARQUET
LOCATION '/user/YOUR_USERNAME/parquet_avro_stocks';
```

> **Hive 0.13**   Support for Parquet as a native Hive store was only added in Hive 0.13 (see https://issues.apache.org/jira/browse/HIVE-5783). If you're using an older version of Hive, you'll need to manually load all the Parquet JARs using the ADD JAR command and use the Parquet input and output formats. Cloudera has an example on its blog; see "How-to: Use Parquet with Impala, Hive, Pig, and Map-Reduce," http://blog.cloudera.com/blog/2014/03/how-to-use-parquet-with-impala-hive-pig-mapreduce/.

You can run a simple query to extract the unique stock symbols from the data:

```
hive> select distinct(symbol) from parquet_stocks;
AAPL
CSCO
GOOG
MSFT
YHOO
```

---

[52] Pushdowns are covered in more detail in the next technique.

You can use the same syntax to create the table in Impala.

TECHNIQUE 24   **Pushdown predicates and projection with Parquet**

Projection and predicate pushdowns involve an execution engine pushing the projection and predicates down to the storage format to optimize the operations at the lowest level possible. This yields space and time advantages, as columns that aren't required for the query don't need to be fetched and supplied to the execution engine.

This is especially useful for columnar stores, as pushdowns allow the storage format to skip over entire column groups that aren't required for the query, and columnar formats can perform this operation very efficiently.

In this technique you'll look at the steps required to use these pushdowns in your Hadoop pipelines.

■ **Problem**

You want to use pushdowns in Hadoop to optimize your jobs.

■ **Solution**

Using Hive and Pig in conjunction with Parquet provides out-of-the-box projection pushdowns. With MapReduce there are some manual steps that you need to take in the driver code to enable pushdowns.

■ **Discussion**

Once again our focus with this technique is Avro. The `AvroParquetInputFormat` has two methods that you can use for predicate and projection pushdowns. In the following example, only two fields of the `Stock` object are projected, and a predicate is added so that only Google stocks are selected:[53]

```
public static class GoogleStockFilter
    implements UnboundRecordFilter {          Create a class that
                                              implements the predicate.
  private final UnboundRecordFilter filter;

  public GoogleStockFilter() {
    filter = ColumnRecordFilter.column("symbol",
            ColumnPredicates.equalTo("GOOG"));     Define the predicate as a
  }                                                filter on Google stocks.

  @Override
  public RecordFilter bind(Iterable<ColumnReader> readers) {
    return filter.bind(readers);
  }
}

public void run(Path inputPath, Path outputPath) {
  Configuration conf = super.getConf();

  Job job = new Job(conf);
  job.setJarByClass(AvroProjectionParquetMapReduce.class);
```

---

[53] GitHub source: https://github.com/alexholmes/hiped2/blob/master/src/main/java/hip/ch3/parquet/
AvroProjectionParquetMapReduce.java.

```
        job.setInputFormatClass(AvroParquetInputFormat.class);
        AvroParquetInputFormat.setInputPaths(job, inputPath);
                                                                          Set the predicate
        // predicate pushdown                                            pushdown for the job.
        AvroParquetInputFormat.setUnboundRecordFilter(
          job, GoogleStockFilter.class);
                                                                       Define a new schema for the
        // projection pushdown                                          projection, based on the
        Schema projection = Schema.createRecord(Stock.SCHEMA$.getName(),   original Stock schema.
            Stock.SCHEMA$.getDoc(), Stock.SCHEMA$.getNamespace(), false);
        List<Schema.Field> fields = Lists.newArrayList();
        for (Schema.Field field : Stock.SCHEMA$.getFields()) {          Project just the stock
          if ("symbol".equals(field.name()) ||                        symbol and opening price.
              "open".equals(field.name())) {
            fields.add(new Schema.Field(field.name(), field.schema(),
                field.doc(),  field.defaultValue(), field.order()));
          }
        }                                                                Set the projection
        projection.setFields(fields);                                   for the job.
        AvroParquetInputFormat.setRequestedProjection(job, projection);


        job.setMapperClass(Map.class);
        job.setReducerClass(Reduce.class);

        job.setMapOutputKeyClass(Text.class);
        job.setMapOutputValueClass(DoubleWritable.class);

        job.setOutputFormatClass(AvroParquetOutputFormat.class);
        FileOutputFormat.setOutputPath(job, outputPath);
        AvroParquetOutputFormat.setSchema(job, StockAvg.SCHEMA$);

        return job.waitForCompletion(true) ? 0 : 1;
                                                         The original Stock
                                                        object is still supplied
    }                                                     to the mapper.

public static class Map extends
    Mapper<Void, Stock, Text, DoubleWritable> {                       Check for null in the case
                                                                      that a record is filtered
    @Override                                                         out due to the predicate.
    public void map(Void key, Stock value, Context context) {
      if (value != null) {
        context.write(new Text(value.getSymbol().toString()),
            new DoubleWritable(value.getOpen())));
      }                                                         Only use the stock and
    }                                                            open fields—all other
  }                                                             fields are null due to the
}                                                                    projection.

public static class Reduce extends Reducer<Text, DoubleWritable,
                                     Void, StockAvg> {

    @Override
    protected void reduce(Text key, Iterable<DoubleWritable> values,
                       Context context) {
      Mean mean = new Mean();
      for (DoubleWritable val : values) {
```

```
        mean.increment(val.get());
      }
      StockAvg avg = new StockAvg();
      avg.setSymbol(key.toString());
      avg.setAvg(mean.getResult());
      context.write(null, avg);
    }
  }
```

> **Predicate filter null values** When the predicate that you supply filters out a record, a `null` value is supplied to your mapper. That's why you have to check for `null` before working with the mapper input.

If you run the job and examine the output, you'll only find the average for the Google stock, demonstrating that the predicate worked:

```
$ hip hip.ch3.parquet.AvroProjectionParquetMapReduce \
    --input stocks.parquet \
    --output output

$ hip --nolib parquet.tools.Main cat output/part-r-00000.parquet
symbol = GOOG
avg = 417.47799999999995
```

■ **Summary**

This technique doesn't include any Hive or Pig pushdown details, as both tools automatically perform these pushdowns as part of their execution. Pushdowns are an important part of your job-optimization work, and if you're using a third-party library or tool that doesn't expose pushdowns when working with Parquet, you can help the community by opening a feature request.

3.4.4 *Parquet limitations*

There are a number of points that you should be aware of when working with Parquet:

- Parquet requires a lot of memory when writing files because it buffers writes in memory to optimize the encoding and compressing of the data. Either increase the heap size (2 GB is recommended), or decrease the `parquet.block.size` configurable if you encounter memory issues when writing Parquet files.
- Using a heavily nested data structure with Parquet will likely limit some of the optimizations that Parquet makes for pushdowns. If possible, try to flatten your schema.
- Hive doesn't yet support `decimal` and `timestamp` data types when working with Parquet because Parquet doesn't support them as native types. Work is being tracked in a JIRA ticket titled "Implement all Hive data types in Parquet" (https://issues.apache.org/jira/browse/HIVE-6384).
- Impala doesn't support nested data in Parquet or complex data types such as maps, structs, or arrays. This should be fixed in the Impala 2.x release.

■ Tools such as Impala work best when a Parquet file contains a single row group and when the entire file fits inside an HDFS block. In reality, it's hard to achieve this goal when you're writing Parquet files in systems such as MapReduce, but it's good to keep this in mind as you're producing Parquet files.

We've covered working with common file formats and working with various data serialization tools for tighter compatibility with MapReduce. It's time to look at how you can support file formats that may be proprietary to your organization, or even public file formats for which no input or output formats exist for MapReduce.

3.5   Custom file formats

In any organization you'll typically find a plethora of custom or uncommon file formats that litter its datacenters. There may be back-end servers dumping out audit files in a proprietary format, or old code or systems that write files using formats that aren't in common use any longer. If you want to work with such data in MapReduce, you'll need to write your own input and output format classes to work with your data. This section will walk you through that process.

3.5.1   Input and output formats

At the start of this chapter, we took a high-level look at the functions of input and output format classes in MapReduce. Input and output classes are required to feed data to map functions and to write the outputs of reduce functions.

TECHNIQUE 25   **Writing input and output formats for CSV**

Imagine you have a bunch of data sitting around in CSV files and you're writing multiple MapReduce jobs that read and write data in CSV form. Because CSV is text, you could use the built-in `TextInputFormat` and `TextOutputFormat`, and handle parsing the CSV in your MapReduce code. This can quickly get tiring, however, and result in the same parsing code being copied and pasted across all of your jobs.

If you thought MapReduce had any built-in CSV input and output formats that could take care of this parsing, you'd be out of luck—there are none.

■ **Problem**

You want to work with CSV in MapReduce and have CSV records presented to you in a richer format than you'd get if you were using a `TextInputFormat` that would supply a string representing a line.

■ **Solution**

Write an input and output format that works with CSV.

■ **Discussion**

We'll cover all of the steps required to write your own format classes to work with CSV input and output. CSV is one of the simpler file formats to work with, which will make it easier to focus on MapReduce format specifics without having to think too much about the file format.

Your custom `InputFormat` and `RecordReader` classes will parse CSV files and supply the data to the mapper in a user-friendly format. You'll also support a custom field separator for non-comma delimiters. Because you don't want to reinvent the wheel, you'll use the CSV parser in the open source OpenCSV project (http:// opencsv.sourceforge.net/), which will take care of quoted fields and ignore separator characters in quoted fields.

> **Overview of `InputFormat` and `OutputFormat`**   I provided a detailed overview of `InputFormat` and `OutputFormat` and their related classes at the start of this chapter. It may be worth looking back at that discussion prior to looking at the code in this technique.

The InputFormat

Your first step is to define the `InputFormat`. The function of `InputFormat` is to validate the set of inputs supplied to the job, identify input splits, and create a `RecordReader` class to read input from the sources. The following code reads the separator (if supplied) from the job configuration and constructs a `CSVRecordReader`:[54]

```
public class CSVInputFormat extends
    FileInputFormat<LongWritable, TextArrayWritable> {

  public static String CSV_TOKEN_SEPARATOR_CONFIG =
      "csvinputformat.token.delimiter";

  @Override
  public RecordReader<LongWritable, TextArrayWritable>
  createRecordReader(InputSplit split,                          Reads (optional) custom
                     TaskAttemptContext context) {              separator for the CSV.
    String csvDelimiter = context.getConfiguration().get(
      CSV_TOKEN_SEPARATOR_CONFIG);

    Character separator = null;
    if(csvDelimiter != null && csvDelimiter.length() == 1) {
      separator = csvDelimiter.charAt(0);
    }
                                                    Creates a RecordReader
                                                           and returns it.
    return new CSVRecordReader(separator);
  }

  @Override
  protected boolean isSplitable(JobContext context, Path file) {
    CompressionCodec codec =                              If the file is compressed, it's
        new CompressionCodecFactory(context.getConfiguration())    not splittable; otherwise it is.
           .getCodec(file);                                   The FileInputFormat parent
    return codec == null;                                           class takes care of
  }                                                          determining splits (by using
                                                               the HDFS block size).
```

---

[54] GitHub source: https://github.com/alexholmes/hiped2/blob/master/src/main/java/hip/ch3/csv/ CSVInputFormat.java.

> **InputFormat and compressed files** In the preceding code, you saw that when the was compressed, a flag was returned to indicate that it couldn't be split. The reason for doing this is that compression codecs aren't splittable, apart from LZOP. But splittable LZOP can't work with regular InputFormat classes— it needs special-case LZOP InputFormat classes. These details are covered in chapter 4.

Your InputFormat class is complete. You extended the FileInputFormat class, which contains code that calculates input splits along HDFS block boundaries, keeping you from having to handle calculating the input splits yourself. The FileInputFormat manages all of the input files and splits for you. Now let's move on to the RecordReader, which will require a little more effort.

RecordReader performs two main functions. It must first open the input source based on the input split supplied, and it optionally seeks into a specific offset in that input split. The second function of the RecordReader is to read individual records from the input source.

In this example, a logical record equates to a line in the CSV file, so you'll use the existing LineRecordReader class in MapReduce to handle working with the file. When the RecordReader is initialized with the InputSplit, it will open the input file, seek to the start of the input split, and keep reading characters until it reaches the start of the next record, which in the case of a line means a newline. The following code shows a simplified version of the LineRecordReader.initialize method:

Extract the byte offset for the start of the input split.

Calculate the byte offset for the end of the input split.

Open an InputStream for the input file.

If the input split doesn't start at byte 0, seek to the starting byte.

Create a LineReader, which the LineRecordReader uses to read each line. The InputStream that was created and on which a seek was performed is passed in to the constructor of the LineReader.

Keep reading until a newline is found, which marks the start of the next record.

```java
public void initialize(InputSplit genericSplit,
                       TaskAttemptContext context) throws IOException {

    start = split.getStart();
    end = start + split.getLength();
    final Path file = split.getPath();

    FileSystem fs = file.getFileSystem(job);
    FSDataInputStream fileIn = fs.open(split.getPath());
    boolean skipFirstLine = false;
    if (start != 0) {
      skipFirstLine = true;
      --start;
      fileIn.seek(start);
    }
    in = new LineReader(fileIn, job);
    if (skipFirstLine) {
      start += in.readLine(new Text(), 0,
              (int)Math.min((long)Integer.MAX_VALUE, end - start));
    }
}
```

The LineRecordReader returns key/value pairs for each line in LongWritable/Text form. Because you'll want to provide some functionality in the Record Reader, you need to encapsulate the LineRecordReader within your class. The RecordReader needs to supply a key/value pair representation of the record to the mapper, and in this case the key is the byte offset in the file, and the value is an array containing the tokenized parts of the CSV line:[55]

```
public static class CSVRecordReader
        extends RecordReader<LongWritable, TextArrayWritable> {
    private LineRecordReader reader;
    private TextArrayWritable value;
    private final CSVParser parser;

    public CSVRecordReader(Character csvDelimiter) {
        this.reader = new LineRecordReader();
        if (csvDelimiter == null) {
            parser = new CSVParser();
        } else {
            parser = new CSVParser(csvDelimiter);
        }
    }

    @Override
    public void initialize(InputSplit split,
                           TaskAttemptContext context)
        throws IOException, InterruptedException {
        reader.initialize(split, context);
    }
```

The RecordReader class is responsible for reading records from the input file. It emits keys in the form of the file offset in the file, and the values are an array of tokens in the CSV line.

Create the CSV parser (courtesy of the OpenCSV project).

Use LineRecordReader to perform the heavy lifting. It will open the file specified in the InputSplit and seek to the start of the split.

Next you need to provide methods to read the next record and to get at the key and value for that record:[56]

Use LineRecordReader to read the next record. LineRecordReader.nextKeyValue will return a NULL once the end of the split has been reached.

If the LineRecordReader supplied a new record, process the line.

```
    @Override
    public boolean nextKeyValue()
            throws IOException, InterruptedException {
        if (reader.nextKeyValue()) {
            loadCSV();
            return true;
        } else {
            value = null;
            return false;
        }
    }

    private void loadCSV() {
        String line = reader.getCurrentValue().toString();
        String[] tokens = parser.parseLine(line);
        if (transformer != null) {
            for (int i = 0; i < tokens.length; i++) {
                tokens[i] = transformer.transform(line, i, tokens[i]);
            }
```

Tokenize the line and store the tokens in an array.

Use OpenCSV's parse method to tokenize the line and return an array of fields.

---

[55] GitHub source: https://github.com/alexholmes/hiped2/blob/master/src/main/java/hip/ch3/csv/CSVInputFormat.java.

[56] GitHub source: https://github.com/alexholmes/hiped2/blob/master/src/main/java/hip/ch3/csv/CSVInputFormat.java.

```
      }
      value = new TextArrayWritable(convert(tokens));
    }

    private Text[] convert(String[] s) {
      Text t[] = new Text[s.length];
      for(int i=0; i < t.length; i++) {
        t[i] = new Text(s[i]);
      }
      return t;
    }

    @Override
    public LongWritable getCurrentKey()
        throws IOException, InterruptedException {
      return reader.getCurrentKey();
    }

    @Override
    public TextArrayWritable getCurrentValue()
        throws IOException, InterruptedException {
      return value;
    }
  }
```

Proxy the request for the key to the LineRecordReader, which returns the byte offset of the line in the file.

Return the version of the value, which is the array of tokens.

At this point, you've created an InputFormat and a RecordReader that both can work with CSV files. Now that you've completed the InputFormat, it's time to move on to the OutputFormat.

OutputFormat

OutputFormat classes follow a pattern similar to InputFormat classes; the OutputFormat class handles the logistics around creating the output stream and then delegates the stream writes to the RecordWriter.

The CSVOutputFormat indirectly extends the FileOutputFormat class (via TextOutput-Format), which handles all of the logistics related to creating the output filename, creating an instance of a compression codec (if compression was enabled), and output committing, which we'll discuss shortly.

That leaves the OutputFormat class with the tasks of supporting a custom field delimiter for your CSV output file, and of creating a compressed OutputStream if required. It must also return your CSVRecordWriter, which will write CSV lines to the output stream:[57]

```
public class CSVOutputFormat extends
    TextOutputFormat<TextArrayWritable, NullWritable> {

    public static String CSV_TOKEN_SEPARATOR_CONFIG =
        "csvoutputformat.token.delimiter";

    @Override
    public RecordWriter getRecordWriter(TaskAttemptContext job)
```

The OutputFormat expects keys as TextArrayWritable and NullWritable values.

Define a configuration constant so that users can specify a custom CSV separator character.

---

[57] GitHub source: https://github.com/alexholmes/hiped2/blob/master/src/main/java/hip/ch3/csv/CSVOutputFormat.java.

```
      throws IOException, InterruptedException {
  Configuration conf = job.getConfiguration();
  boolean isCompressed = getCompressOutput(job);
  String
      keyValueSeparator =
      conf.get(CSV_TOKEN_SEPARATOR_CONFIG, ",");
  if (!isCompressed) {
    FSDataOutputStream fileOut = fs.create(file, false);
    return new CSVRecordWriter(fileOut,
        keyValueSeparator);
  } else {
    FSDataOutputStream fileOut = fs.create(file, false);
    return new CSVRecordWriter(
        new DataOutputStream(codec.createOutputStream(fileOut)),
        keyValueSeparator);
  }
}
```

Read a custom separator from configuration, and if none exists, use the default of a comma.

Create an uncompressed output stream for the reducer and construct a CSVRecordReader to write the reducer output.

Create a compressed output stream using the configured compression codec for the job and construct a CSVRecordReader to write the reducer output.

In the following code, your RecordWriter writes each record emitted by the reducer to the output destination. You require that the reducer output key be in array form representing each token in the CSV line, and you specify that the reducer output value must be a NullWritable, which means that you don't care about the value part of the output.

Let's take a look at the CSVRecordWriter class. The constructor, which only sets the field separator and the output stream, is excluded, as shown in the following listing.[58]

Listing 3.6   A RecordWriter that produces MapReduce output in CSV form

```
protected static class CSVRecordWriter
    extends RecordWriter<TextArrayWritable, NullWritable> {
  private static final String utf8 = "UTF-8";
  private static final byte[] newline;

  protected DataOutputStream out;
  private final String csvSeparator;

  @Override
  public void write(TextArrayWritable key, NullWritable value)
      throws IOException, InterruptedException {
    if (key == null) {
      return;
    }
    boolean first = true;
    for (Writable field : key.get()) {
      writeObject(first, field);
      first = false;
    }
    out.write(newline);
  }
```

The write method is called for each record emitted by the reducer. Iterate through all of the fields in the array, and call the writeObject to handle writing the field to the output stream. When this is complete, write the newline string to the stream.

---

[58] GitHub source: https://github.com/alexholmes/hiped2/blob/master/src/main/java/hip/ch3/csv/
CSVOutputFormat.java.

```
/**
 * Write the object to the byte stream, handling Text as a special
 * case.
 *
 * @param o the object to print
 * @throws IOException if the write throws, we pass it on
 */
private void writeObject(boolean first, Writable o)
  throws IOException {

  if(!first) {
    out.write(csvSeparator.getBytes(utf8));          ◄─── Write the CSV separator.
  }

  boolean encloseQuotes = false;
  if (o.toString().contains(csvSeparator)) {
    encloseQuotes = true;
  }
                                                  Write quotes if the field contains
                                                        the separator character.
  if(encloseQuotes) {
    out.write("\".getBytes(utf8));          ◄───
  }
    if (o instanceof Text) {
      Text to = (Text) o;
      out.write(to.getBytes(), 0, to.getLength());   ◄─── Write the field.
    } else {
      out.write(o.toString().getBytes(utf8));
    }
  if(encloseQuotes) {
    out.write("\".getBytes(utf8));
  }
}
```

Now you need to apply the new input and output format classes in a MapReduce job.

MapReduce

Your MapReduce job will take CSV as input, and it'll produce CSV that's separated by colons, not commas. The job will perform identity map and reduce functions, which means that you won't be changing the data as it passes through MapReduce. Your input file will be delimited with the tab character, and your output file will be comma-separated. Your input and output format classes will support the notion of custom delimiters via Hadoop configuration properties.

The MapReduce code is as follows:[59]

Indicate the separator character for the CSV input file.

Indicate the separator character for the CSV output file, which in this case is a colon.

```
conf.set(CSVInputFormat.CSV_TOKEN_SEPARATOR_CONFIG, ",");     ◄───
conf.set(CSVOutputFormat.CSV_TOKEN_SEPARATOR_CONFIG, ":");    ◄───

Job job = new Job(conf);
job.setJarByClass(CSVMapReduce.class);
job.setMapperClass(Map.class);
job.setReducerClass(Reduce.class);
```

---

[59] GitHub source: https://github.com/alexholmes/hiped2/blob/master/src/main/java/hip/ch3/csv/
CSVMapReduce.java.

```
job.setInputFormatClass(CSVInputFormat.class);
job.setOutputFormatClass(CSVOutputFormat.class);

job.setMapOutputKeyClass(LongWritable.class);
job.setMapOutputValueClass(TextArrayWritable.class);

job.setOutputKeyClass(TextArrayWritable.class);
job.setOutputValueClass(NullWritable.class);
```

Set the InputFormat class.

Set the OutputFormat class.

The map and reduce functions don't do much other than echo their inputs to output, but include them so you can see how to work with the CSV in your MapReduce code:[60]

```
public static class Map
    extends Mapper<LongWritable, TextArrayWritable,
    LongWritable, TextArrayWritable> {

  @Override
  protected void map(LongWritable key, TextArrayWritable value,
                     Context context)
      throws
      IOException, InterruptedException {
    context.write(key, value);
  }
}

public static class Reduce
    extends Reducer<LongWritable, TextArrayWritable,
    TextArrayWritable, NullWritable> {

  public void reduce(LongWritable key,
                     Iterable<TextArrayWritable> values,
                     Context context)
      throws IOException, InterruptedException {
    for (TextArrayWritable val : values) {
      context.write(val, NullWritable.get());
    }
  }
}
```

You can see the TextArrayWritable being supplied as input to the mapper.

The TextArrayWritable is also used as output.

If you run this example MapReduce job against a tab-delimited file, you can examine the mapper output and see if the results are as expected:

```
$ hadoop fs -put test-data/stocks.txt stocks.txt
$ hip hip.ch3.csv.CSVMapReduce \
    --input stocks.txt \
    --output output

$ hadoop fs -cat output/part*
AAPL:2009-01-02:85.88:91.04:85.16:90.75:26643400:90.75
AAPL:2008-01-02:199.27:200.26:192.55:194.84:38542100:194.84
AAPL:2007-01-03:86.29:86.58:81.90:83.80:44225700:83.80
...
```

---

[60] GitHub source: https://github.com/alexholmes/hiped2/blob/master/src/main/java/hip/ch3/csv/CSVMapReduce.java.

You now have a functional `InputFormat` and `OutputFormat` that can consume and produce CSV in MapReduce.

Pig

Pig's piggybank library contains a `CSVLoader` that can be used to load CSV files into tuples. It supports double-quoted fields in the CSV records and provides each item as a byte array.

There's a GitHub project called csv-serde (https://github.com/ogrodnek/csv-serde), which has a Hive SerDe that can both serialize and deserialize CSV. Like the previous `InputFormat` example, it also uses the OpenCSV project for reading and writing CSV.

■ Summary

This technique demonstrated how you can write your own MapReduce format classes to work with text-based data. Work is currently underway in MapReduce to add a CSV input format (see https://issues.apache.org/jira/browse/MAPREDUCE-2208).

Arguably, it would have been simpler to use the `TextInputFormat` and split the line in the mapper. But if you need to do this multiple times, you're likely suffering from the copy-paste antipattern, because the same code to tokenize the CSV likely exists in multiple locations. If the code is written with code reuse in mind, you'll be covered.

We've looked at how you can write your own I/O format classes to work with a custom file format in MapReduce. Now we need to look at a crucial aspect of working with output formats—output committing.

3.5.2   *The importance of output committing*

In the CSV `OutputFormat` example in the previous technique, you extended `FileOutput-Format`, which takes care of committing output after the task has succeeded. Why do you need commits in MapReduce, and why should you care?

As a job and its tasks are executing, they will start writing job output at some point. Tasks and jobs can fail, they can be restarted, and they can also be speculatively executed.[61] To allow `OutputFormats` to correctly handle these scenarios, MapReduce has the notion of an `OutputCommitter`, which is a mechanism by which MapReduce invokes a callback when an individual task as well as the overall job have completed.

Most `OutputFormats` in MapReduce use `FileOutputFormat`, which uses `FileOutput-Committer` for its output committing. When the `FileOutputFormat` is initially consulted about the location of the output files, it delegates the decision of where the output should be located to the `FileOutputCommitter`, which in turn specifies that the output should go to a temporary directory under the job output directory (<job-output>/_temporary/<task-attempt-id>). Only after the overall task has completed will the `FileOutputCommitter` be notified, at which point the temporary output is moved to the

---

[61] Speculative executing is when MapReduce executes multiple tasks for the same input data to guard against slow or misbehaving nodes slowing down the overall job. By default, both map-side and reduce-side speculative execution is enabled. The `mapred.map.tasks.speculative.execution` and `mapred.reduce.tasks.speculative.execution` control this behavior.

job output directory. When the overall job has successfully completed, the `FileOutput-Committer` is again notified, and this time it touches a `_SUCCESS` file in the job output directory to help downstream processors know the job succeeded.

This is great if your data sink is HDFS, where you can use `FileOutputFormat` and its committing mechanism. Things start to get trickier when you're working with data sources other than files, such as a database. If, in such cases, idempotent writes (where the same operation can be applied multiple times without changing the result) are necessary, you'll need to factor that into the design of your destination data store or `OutputFormat`.

This topic is examined in more detail in chapter 5, which covers exporting data from Hadoop to databases.

3.6   *Chapter summary*

The goal for this chapter was to show you how to work with common file formats such as XML and JSON in MapReduce. We also looked at more sophisticated file formats such as SequenceFile, Avro, and Parquet, which provide useful features for working with big data, such as versioning, compression, and complex data structures. We also walked through the process of working with custom file formats to ensure they'll work in MapReduce.

At this point, you're equipped to work with any file format in MapReduce. Now it's time to look at some storage patterns so you can effectively work with your data and optimize storage and disk/network I/O.

Organizing and
optimizing data in HDFS

In the previous chapter, we looked at how to work with different file formats in MapReduce and which ones were ideally suited for storing your data. Once you've honed in on the data format that you'll be using, it's time to start thinking about how you'll organize your data in HDFS. It's important that you give yourself enough time early on in the design of your Hadoop system to understand how your data will be accessed so that you can optimize for the more important use cases that you'll be supporting.

There are numerous factors that will impact your data organization decisions, such as whether you'll need to provide SQL access to your data (likely, you will), which fields will be used to look up the data, and what access-time SLAs you'll need to support. At the same time, you need to make sure that you don't apply unnecessary heap pressure on the HDFS NameNode with a large number of small files, and you also need to learn how to work with huge input datasets.

This chapter is dedicated to looking at ways to efficiently store and access big data in HDFS. I'll first cover ways you can lay out data in HDFS and present some methods for partitioning and combining data to relieve NameNode heap pressure. Then I'll discuss some data access patterns to help you work with disparate data as well as huge data sets. And finally, we'll look at compression as a big data pattern to maximize your storage and processing capabilities.

> **Chapter prerequisites** This chapter assumes you have a basic understanding of HDFS concepts and that you have experience working directly with HDFS. If you need to become familiar with the topic, *Hadoop in Action* by Chuck Lam (Manning, 2010) offers the background information you'll need on HDFS.

We'll start things off with a look at how you can organize and manage your data.

4.1   Data organization

Data organization is one of the most challenging aspects of working with Hadoop. You have pressure from different groups in your organization, such as data scientists and your cluster administrators, each coming to you with competing requirements. What's more, these requirements often come after your data applications are in production and you've already amassed large amounts of data.

There are multiple dimensions to data organization in Hadoop. You first need to decide how to organize your data in HDFS, after which you'll be faced with operational issues such as how to partition and compact your data. You'll need to decide whether to enable Kerberos to secure your cluster and how to manage and communicate data changes. These are all complex issues, and the goal of this chapter is to focus on some of the more challenging aspects of data organization, including data partitioning and compaction, starting off with how you can structure your data in HDFS.

4.1.1   Directory and file layout

Having a cluster-wide standard that defines how data is organized is a worthwhile pursuit, as it makes it easier to discover where data is located, and it also helps apply structure and manage common areas that you want to address with data storage in general. Because we're working within the confines of what a filesystem can express, a common approach to arranging data is to create a hierarchy of tiers that aligns with your organizational or functional structure. For example, if you work on the analytics team and you're bringing a new dataset to the cluster, then one way to organize your directory would be as shown in figure 4.1.

Data revolution

Hopefully you've settled on a data format such as Avro, which offers you the ability to evolve your schema over time. That's great, but how do you support a move to the

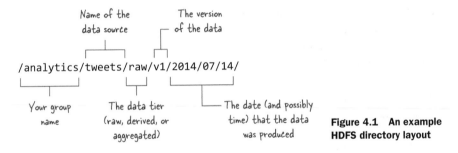

Figure 4.1 An example HDFS directory layout

Next Big Data Format, which will no doubt arrive as soon as everyone has migrated to Avro? Well, you can look to other software fields where semantic versioning concepts permeate interfaces such as URLs and adopt a similar strategy in your directory structure. By sticking a version number in your structure, you can give yourself the flexibility to move to the data format of tomorrow and communicate the differing file formats using the directory path.

Once you've embraced putting a version number in your directory, the only challenge left is communicating future changes to the consumers of your data. If this becomes a challenge, you may want to look at HCatalog as a way to abstract away data formats from your clients.

Partitioning by date and other fields

You may need your directory structure to model your organizational and data evolution needs, but why would you need further partitioning by date? This is a technique that Hive used early on to help speed up queries. If you put all of your data into a single directory, you're essentially doing the Hadoop equivalent of a full table scan every time you need to access the data. Instead, it's smarter to partition your data based on how you expect your data to be accessed.

It can be hard to know ahead of time exactly how data is going to be accessed, but a reasonable first attempt at partitioning is to segment data by the date when it was generated. If your data doesn't have a date, then talk to the data producers about adding one, as the time at which an event or record was created is a critical data point that should always be captured.

4.1.2 Data tiers

In his 2012 Strata talk, Eric Sammer presented the idea of storing different tiers of data.[1] This is a powerful concept, and it also ties in nicely with one of the primary tenets of Nathan Marz's Lambda Architecture—that of never deleting or modifying your raw data.

At first glance, this may not seem to make any sense—surely once you extract the important parts of a data source, you can discard the rest! While it may seem wasteful to keep around raw data, especially if there are parts that aren't being actively used,

---

[1] Eric Sammer, "Large scale ETL with Hadoop," www.slideshare.net/OReillyStrata/large-scale-etl-with-hadoop.

ask yourself this question—could some organizational value be extracted from the data in the future? It's hard to answer this with a resounding "no."

There are also occasionally bugs in our software. Imagine that you're streaming data from the Twitter fire hose, producing some aggregations and discarding the source data. What happens if you discover a bug in your aggregation logic? You have no way to go back and regenerate the aggregated data.

Therefore, it's recommended that you think of your data in terms of the following tiers:

- *Raw data* is the first tier. It's the unaltered data you capture from the source. Data at this tier should never be modified because there's a chance that your logic that produces derivatives or aggregations has bugs, and if you discard the raw data, you'll remove your ability to regenerate your derived data upon discovering your bugs.
- *Derived data* is created from the raw data. Here you can perform deduplication, sanitation, and any other cleansing.
- *Aggregated data* is calculated from the derived data and will likely be fed into systems such as HBase or your NoSQL system of choice for real-time access to your data, both in production and for analytical purposes.

Data tiers should also be expressed in your directory layout so that users can easily differentiate between the tiers.

Once you've decided on a directory layout for partitioning your data, the next step is figuring out how you're going to get your data into these partitions. That's covered next.

4.1.3   *Partitioning*

Partitioning is the process by which you take a dataset and split it into distinct parts. These parts are the partitions, and they represent a meaningful division of your data. An example of a common partition in data is time, as it allows those querying the data to narrow in on a specific window of time. The previous section included time as a key element in deciding how to lay out your data in HDFS.

Great! You have a large dataset in HDFS and you need to partition it. How do you go about doing that? In this section I'll present two methods you can employ to partition your data.

TECHNIQUE 26   **Using MultipleOutputs to partition your data**

Imagine a situation where you have stock prices being streamed into HDFS, and you want to write a MapReduce job to partition your stock data based on the day of the stock quote. To do this, you'll need to write to multiple output files in a single task. Let's look at how you can make that happen.

■ **Problem**

You need to partition your data, but most output formats only create a single output file per task.

■ **Solution**

Use the MultipleOutputs class bundled with MapReduce.

■ **Discussion**

The MultipleOutputs class in Hadoop bypasses the normal channel by which outputs are produced in Hadoop. It provides a separate API to write partitioned outputs, and it writes output directly to the task attempt directory in HDFS. This is powerful, as you can continue to collect output using the standard write method on the Context object supplied to your job, and also use MultipleOutputs to write partitioned output. Of course, you can also choose to only use the MultipleOutputs class and ignore the standard Context-based output.

In this technique, you'll use MultipleOutputs to partition stocks by their quote date. The first step is to set up MultipleOutputs for use in your job. In your driver, you'll indicate the output format and the key and value types:

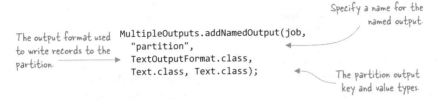

The output format used to write records to the partition.

```
MultipleOutputs.addNamedOutput(job,
    "partition",
    TextOutputFormat.class,
    Text.class, Text.class);
```

Specify a name for the named output.

The partition output key and value types.

> **Why do you need to name the output in the driver?**   You may be wondering why MultipleOutputs requires you to specify a output name (partition in the preceding example). This is because MultipleOutputs supports two modes of operation—static partitions and dynamic partitions.
>
> *Static partitions* work well if you know ahead of time the partition names; this gives you the additional flexibility of specifying a different output format for each partition (you'd just have multiple calls to MultipleOutputs.addNamedOutput with different named outputs). With static partitions, the output name you specify when calling addNamedOutput is the same name that you use when emitting output in your mapper or reducer.
>
> This technique focuses on *dynamic partitions*, which you're likely to find more useful, because in most cases you won't know the partitions ahead of time. In this case, you still need to supply a output name, but for all intents and purposes, it's ignored, as you can dynamically specify the partition name in your mapper or reducer.

As you can see in the following code, your map (or reduce) class, will get a handle to a MultipleOutputs instance and then use its write method to write partitioned outputs. Notice that the third argument is the partition name, which is the stock date:[2]

---

[2] GitHub source: https://github.com/alexholmes/hiped2/blob/master/src/main/java/hip/ch4/ MultipleOutputsJob.java.

```
public static class Map extends Mapper<LongWritable, Text, Text, Text> {

  private MultipleOutputs output;

  @Override
  protected void setup(Context context) {
    output = new MultipleOutputs(context);
  }

  @Override
  protected void map(LongWritable key, Text value, Context context)
      throws IOException, InterruptedException {

    StockPriceWritable stock =
        StockPriceWritable.fromLine(value.toString());

    output.write(value, null, stock.getDate());
  }

  @Override
  protected void cleanup(Context context) throws IOException, InterruptedException {
    output.close();
  }
}
```

Get a handle to the MultipleOutputs instance.

Use a helper class to extract the stock date from the input record.

Write out the partitioned record, indicating that the stock date should be used as the partition.

Flush and close all HDFS file handles.

> **Don't forget the close method!**　It's important that you call the close method on MultipleOutputs in the cleanup method of your task. Otherwise it's possible that you'll have data missing from your output or even a corrupt file.

Let's take a peek at this class in action. As you can see in the following output, running the previous example produces a number of partitioned files for the single mapper. You can also see the original map output file, which is empty because you haven't emitted any records using the Context object:

```
$ hip hip.ch4.MultipleOutputsJob --input stocks.txt --output out1

$ hadoop fs -ls -R out1
out1/2000-01-03-m-00000
out1/2001-01-02-m-00000
out1/2002-01-02-m-00000
out1/2003-01-02-m-00000
out1/2004-01-02-m-00000
out1/2005-01-03-m-00000
out1/2006-01-03-m-00000
out1/2007-01-03-m-00000
out1/2008-01-02-m-00000
out1/2009-01-02-m-00000
out1/_SUCCESS
out1/part-m-00000
```

In this example you used a map-only job, but in production you'll probably want to limit the number of tasks that create partitions. There are two ways you can do this:

- Use the CombineFileInputFormat or a custom input format to limit the number of mappers in your job.
- Use a reducer where you can explicitly specify a reasonable number of reducers.

Summary

There are plenty of things to like about MultipleOutputs: its support for both "old" and "new" MapReduce APIs and its support for multiple output format classes. But using MultipleOutputs does carry with it some constraints that you should be aware of:

- Be cautious when using MultipleOutputs in a mapper—remember that you'll end up with NumberOfMappers * NumberOfPartition output files, which in my experience can bring down clusters with large numbers of both values!
- Each partition incurs the overhead of an HDFS file handle for the duration of the task.
- You can often end up with a large number of small files that accumulate across multiple uses of your partitioner. You'll probably want to make sure that you have a compaction strategy in place to mitigate this problem (see section 4.1.4 for more details).
- Although Avro comes with the AvroMultipleOutputs class, it's quite slow due to some inefficiencies in the code.

In addition to the MultipleOutputs approach, Hadoop also comes with a MultipleOutputFormat class that has features similar to MultipleOutputs. Its primary pitfalls are that it only supports the old MapReduce API and only one output format can be used for all the partitions.

Another partitioning strategy that you can employ is to use the MapReduce partitioner, which can help mitigate the large number of files that may be produced using MultipleOutputs.

TECHNIQUE 27 Using a custom MapReduce partitioner

Another partitioning approach is to use the partitioning facilities built into MapReduce. By default, MapReduce uses a hash partitioner that calculates the hash of each map output key and performs a modulo over the number of reducers to determine which reducer the record should be sent to. You can control how partitioning occurs by writing your own custom partitioner and then route records according to your partitioning scheme.

This technique has an added benefit over the previous technique in that you'll generally end up with fewer output files because each reducer will only create a single output file, as opposed to MultipleOutputs, where each map or reduce task will generate *N* output files—one for each partition.

Problem

You want to partition your input data.

Solution

Write a custom partitioner that partitions records to the appropriate reducer.

Discussion

Let's look at the custom partitioner first. It exposes a helper method to the MapReduce driver that allows you to define a mapping from a date to a partition, and it writes this mapping to the job configuration. Then, when MapReduce loads the partitioner,

MapReduce calls the setConf method; in this partitioner you'll read the mappings into a map, which is subsequently used when partitioning.[3]

```
public static class DatePartitioner extends Partitioner<Text, Text>
                                    implements Configurable {
  public static final String CONF_PARTITIONS = "partition.map";
  public static final String PARTITION_DELIM = ":";
  private Configuration conf;
  private java.util.Map<Text, Integer> datePartitions =
      Maps.newHashMap();


  public static void addPartitionToConfig(
      Configuration conf,  String date, int partition) {

    String addition = String.format("%s%s%d",
                          date, PARTITION_DELIM, partition);
    String existing = conf.get(CONF_PARTITIONS);
    conf.set(CONF_PARTITIONS, existing == null
        ? addition : existing + "," + addition);
  }


  @Override
  public void setConf(Configuration conf) {
    this.conf = conf;
    for (String partition : conf.getStrings(CONF_PARTITIONS)) {
      String[] parts = partition.split(PARTITION_DELIM);
      datePartitions.put(new Text(parts[0]),
          Integer.valueOf(parts[1]));
    }
  }


  @Override
  public int getPartition(Text date, Text stock, int numPartitions) {
    return datePartitions.get(date);
  }

  @Override
  public Configuration getConf() {
    return conf;
  }
}
```

A helper function for the driver to add date-to-reducer partitions.

Load the date-to-reducer details from configuration into a map.

For each map output, pull the reducer (partition) that the record should be sent to.

Your driver code needs to set up the custom partitioner configuration. The partitions in this example are dates, and you want to make sure that each reducer will correspond to a unique date. The stocks example data has 10 unique dates, so you configure your job with 10 reducers. You also call the partition helper function that was defined previously to set up the configuration that maps each unique date to a unique reducer.[4]

---

[3] GitHub source: https://github.com/alexholmes/hiped2/blob/master/src/main/java/hip/ch4/
CustomPartitionerJob.java.

[4] GitHub source: https://github.com/alexholmes/hiped2/blob/master/src/main/java/hip/ch4/
CustomPartitionerJob.java.

```
Configuration conf = super.getConf();
List<String> dates = Lists.newArrayList("2000-01-03",
    "2001-01-02", "2002-01-02", "2003-01-02", "2004-01-02",
    "2005-01-03", "2006-01-03", "2007-01-03", "2008-01-02",
    "2009-01-02");

for (int partition=0; partition < dates.size(); partition++) {
  DatePartitioner.addPartitionToConfig(conf,
      dates.get(partition), partition);
}

Job job = new Job(conf);

job.setPartitionerClass(DatePartitioner.class);

...
```

Define the 10 dates that correspond to the input data.

For each date, indicate the reducer (partition) that the date is associated with.

Specify the custom reducer that will be used for the job.

The mapper does little other than extract the stock date from the input data and emit it as the output key:[5]

```
public static class Map extends Mapper<LongWritable, Text, Text, Text> {

  private Text date = new Text();

  @Override
  protected void map(LongWritable key, Text value, Context context)
      throws IOException, InterruptedException {
    StockPriceWritable stock =
        StockPriceWritable.fromLine(value.toString());

    date.set(stock.getDate());
    context.write(date, value);
  }
}
```

Emit the date as the output key and the stock as the output value.

The command to run the preceding example is as follows:

```
$ hip hip.ch4.CustomPartitionerJob --input stocks.txt --output output
```

This job will generate 10 output files, each containing the stocks for that day.

■ **Summary**

Using the MapReduce framework to naturally partition your data gives you a couple of advantages:

- Data in your partitions will be sorted because the shuffle will ensure that all data streamed to a reducer will be sorted. This allows you to use optimized join strategies on your data.
- You can deduplicate data in the reducer, again as a benefit of the shuffle phase.

---

[5] GitHub source: https://github.com/alexholmes/hiped2/blob/master/src/main/java/hip/ch4/
CustomPartitionerJob.java.

The main problem to look out for with this technique is data skew. You want to make sure that you can spread the load across reducers as much as possible, which may be a challenge if there's a natural skew in your data. For example, if your partitions are days, then it's possible that the majority of your records will be for a single day, and you may have only a few records for either a previous or following day. In this case, you'll ideally want to partition records in a way that allocates the majority of the reducers to a single day, and then maybe one or two for the previous or following days. You can also sample your inputs and dynamically determine the optimal number of reducers based on your sample data.

Once you've produced your partitioned output, the next challenge is how to deal with the potentially large number of small files that have resulted from the partitioning.

4.1.4   Compacting

Sometimes having small files in HDFS can't be avoided—maybe you're using a partitioning technique similar to those described previously, or maybe your data organically lands in HDFS in small file sizes. Either way, you'll be exposing some weaknesses in HDFS and MapReduce, including the following:

- Hadoop's NameNode keeps all the HDFS metadata in memory for fast metadata operations. Yahoo! estimated that each file, on average, occupies 600 bytes of space in memory,[6] which translates to a metadata overhead of one billion files amounting to 60 GB, all of which needs to be stored in the NameNode's memory. That's a lot of memory for a single process, even with today's mid-tier server RAM capacities.

- If your input to a MapReduce job is a large number of files, the number of mappers that will run (assuming your files are text or splittable) would be equivalent to the number of blocks that these files occupy. If you run a MapReduce job whose input is thousands or millions of files, your job will spend more time at the kernel layer dealing with creating and destroying your map task processes than it will on its work.

- Finally, if you're running in a controlled environment where there's a scheduler, you may have a cap on the number of tasks your MapReduce job can use. Because each file (by default) results in at least one map task, this could cause your job to be rejected by the scheduler.

If you're thinking you won't have this problem, think again. What percentage of your files are smaller than the HDFS block size?[7] And how much smaller are they—50%, 70%, 90%? What if your big data project takes off and suddenly you need to be able to scale to handle

---

[6] According to Yahoo! statistics, each block or file inode uses less than 200 bytes of memory, and on average each file occupies 1.5 blocks with a 3x replication factor. See Yahoo!'s page titled "Scalability of the Hadoop Distributed File System," http://developer.yahoo.com/blogs/hadoop/posts/2010/05/scalability_of_the _hadoop_dist/ and a JIRA ticket titled "Name-node memory size estimates and optimization proposal," https://issues.apache.org/jira/browse/HADOOP-1687.

[7] The default block size is 1,238 MB. Check the value of `dfs.block.size` to see what it's set to in your cluster.

datasets that are several orders of magnitude greater in size? Isn't that why you use Hadoop in the first place? To scale, you want to be able to add more nodes and then get back to your morning coffee. You don't want to have to go back and redesign your use of Hadoop and deal with migrating your files. Thinking and preparing for this eventuality is best done early in your design phase.

This section examines some techniques that you can use to combine your data in HDFS. I'll start off by discussing a utility called filecrush, which can compact small files together to create a smaller number of larger files. I'll also show you how Avro can be used as a container format to store files that can't be easily compacted, such as binary files.

TECHNIQUE 28 Using filecrush to compact data

Compacting is the act of combining small files together to produce larger files—this helps alleviate heap pressure on the NameNode. In this technique, you'll learn about an open source utility you can use to compact data and help keep your cluster administrator happy.

> **Compatibility with Hadoop versions** Currently the filecrush utility only works with Hadoop version 1. I'm writing a simple file compacter that's compatible with Hadoop 2 at https://github.com/alexholmes/hdfscompact.

■ **Problem**

You want to combine small files to reduce the metadata that the NameNode needs to keep in memory.

■ **Solution**

Use the filecrush utility.

■ **Discussion**

The filecrush utility[8] combines or compacts multiple small files to form larger files. The utility is quite sophisticated and gives you the ability to

- Determine the size threshold below which files will be compacted (and by association, leave files that are large enough alone)
- Specify the maximum size of the compacted files
- Work with different input and output formats and different input and output compression codecs (useful for moving to a different file format or compression codec)
- Swap smaller files with newer compacted files in place

We'll use filecrush on a straightforward example—we'll crush a single directory of small text files and replace them with gzipped SequenceFiles.

First, artificially create 10 input files in a directory in HDFS:

```
$ hadoop fs -mkdir crusher-dir
$ for i in `seq 1 10`; do
    hadoop fs -put test-data/stocks.txt crusher-dir/stocks$i.txt
done
```

---

[8] The filecrush GitHub project page is located at https://github.com/edwardcapriolo/filecrush.

Now run filecrush. In this example, you'll replace the small files with the new large file, and also convert from a text file to a compressed SequenceFile:

Write the output file into the input directory and move the input files out of the way.

This is a hack required to get the utility to work with Hadoop 2. Replace the value with your HDFS block size.

The compression codec for the output files.

The input file format.

The input and output directories.

The output file format.

A 14-digit timestamp that's used to generate unique output filenames.

```
$ hadoop jar ./filecrush-2.2.2-SNAPSHOT.jar \
    com.m6d.filecrush.crush.Crush \
    -Ddfs.block.size=128000000 \
    --clone \
    --compress gzip \
    --input-format text \
    --output-format sequence \
    crusher-dir crusher-out \
    `date +%Y%m%d%H%M%S`
```

After running filecrush, you'll observe that the files in the input directory have been replaced by a single SequenceFile:

```
$ hadoop fs -ls -R crusher-dir
crusher-dir/crushed_file-20140713162739-0-0
```

You can also run the text Hadoop command to view the text representation of the SequenceFile:

```
$ hadoop fs -text crusher-dir/crushed_file-20140713162739-0-0
```

You'll also notice that the original small files have all been moved to the output directory that you specified in your command:

```
$ hadoop fs -ls -R crusher-out
crusher-out/user/aholmes/crusher-dir/stocks1.txt
crusher-out/user/aholmes/crusher-dir/stocks10.txt
crusher-out/user/aholmes/crusher-dir/stocks2.txt
...
```

If you had run filecrush without the --clone option, the input files would have remained intact, and the crushed file would have been written to the output directory.

Input and output file size thresholds

How does filecrush determine whether files need to be crushed? It looks at each file in the input directory and compares it to the block size (or in Hadoop 2, the size that you specified in -Ddfs.block.size in the command). If the file is less than 75% of the block size, it will be crushed. This threshold can be customized by supplying the --threshold argument—for example, if you wanted to raise the value to 85%, you'd specify --threshold 0.85.

Similarly, filecrush uses the block size to determine the output file sizes. By default, it won't create output files that occupy more than eight blocks, but this can be customized with the `--max-file-blocks` argument.

■ **Summary**

Filecrush is a simple and quick way to combine small files together. It supports any type of input or output files as long as there are associated input format and output format classes. Unfortunately, it doesn't work with Hadoop 2, and there hasn't been much activity in the project over the last few years, so these points may rule out this utility for your environment.

The example presented in this technique works well in situations where the directory being crushed is an external Hive table, or if you're running it against a directory in a standard location where other users in a cluster expect your data to exist.

Currently, the filecrush project doesn't work with Hadoop 2. If you're looking for a solution for Hadoop 2, take a look at another HDFS compactor that I'm currently working on at https://github.com/alexholmes/hdfscompact.

Because filecrush requires input and output formats, one use case where it falls short is if you're working with binary data and you need a way to combine small binary files together.

TECHNIQUE 29 Using Avro to store multiple small binary files

Let's say that you're working on a project akin to Google Images, where you crawl the web and download image files from websites. Your project is internet-scale, so you're downloading millions of files and storing them individually in HDFS. You already know that HDFS doesn't work well with a large number of small files, but you're dealing with binary data, so the previous technique doesn't fit your needs.

This technique shows how you can use Avro as a container file format for binary data in HDFS.

■ **Problem**

You want to store a large number of binary files in HDFS, and to do so without hitting the NameNode memory limits.

■ **Solution**

The easiest way to work with small binary files in HDFS is to package them into a larger containing file. For this technique, you'll read all of the files in a directory stored on local disk and save them in a single Avro file in HDFS. You'll also see how to use the Avro file in MapReduce to process the contents of the original files.

■ **Discussion**

Figure 4.2 shows the first part of this technique, where you create the Avro file in HDFS. In doing so, you create fewer files in HDFS, which means less data to be stored in NameNode memory, which also means you can store more stuff.

Avro is a data serialization and RPC library invented by Doug Cutting, the creator of Hadoop. Avro has strong schema-evolution capabilities that give it an advantage

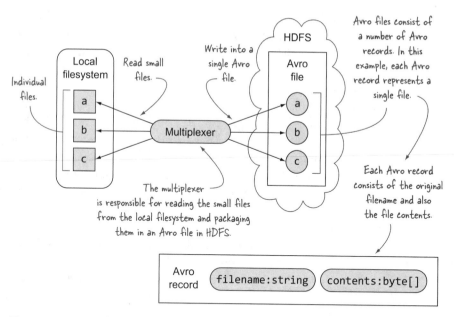

Figure 4.2 Storing small files in Avro allows you to store more.

over competitors such as SequenceFile. Avro and its competitors were covered extensively in chapter 3.

Take a look at the Java code in the following listing, which will create the Avro file.[9]

Listing 4.1   Read a directory containing small files and produce a single Avro file in HDFS

Avro uses JSON to define the data structure schema, which in this example is defined in the SCHEMA_JSON variable. You define two items per record: the filename you're storing, and the raw contents of the file.

```java
public class SmallFilesWrite {

    public static final String FIELD_FILENAME = "filename";
    public static final String FIELD_CONTENTS = "contents";
    private static final String SCHEMA_JSON =
            "{\"type\": \"record\", \"name\": \"SmallFilesTest\", "
            + "\"fields\": ["
            + "{\"name\":\"" + FIELD_FILENAME
            + "\", \"type\":\"string\"},"
            + "{\"name\":\"" + FIELD_CONTENTS
            + "\", \"type\":\"bytes\"}]}";
    public static final Schema SCHEMA = Schema.parse(SCHEMA_JSON);

    public static void writeToAvro(File srcPath,
            OutputStream outputStream)
            throws IOException {
        DataFileWriter<Object> writer =
            new DataFileWriter<Object>(
                new GenericDatumWriter<Object>())
                .setSyncInterval(100);
```

Create an Avro writer.

---

[9] GitHub source: https://github.com/alexholmes/hiped2/blob/master/src/main/java/hip/ch4/SmallFilesWrite.java.

For each file in the input directory, create a new Avro record specifying your schema. Then write the filename and contents to the record using the names you defined in the schema.

Compress Avro content using the Snappy codec.

Associate the schema and output stream with the writer.

GenericRecord is Avro's generic wrapper around a single record.

Set the raw file bytes in the record.

Set the filename field for the record.

Write the record to the writer (and its associated stream, which in this case will write into HDFS).

As you're writing the file contents, you'll also produce an MD5 hash so that later you can visually compare that your writing and reading are correct.

```java
writer.setCodec(CodecFactory.snappyCodec());
writer.create(SCHEMA, outputStream);
for (Object obj :
        FileUtils.listFiles(srcPath, null, false)) {
    File file = (File) obj;
    String filename = file.getAbsolutePath();
    byte content[] = FileUtils.readFileToByteArray(file);
    GenericRecord record = new GenericData.Record(SCHEMA);

    record.put(FIELD_FILENAME, filename);
    record.put(FIELD_CONTENTS, ByteBuffer.wrap(content));
    writer.append(record);
    System.out.println(
            file.getAbsolutePath()
            + ": "
            + DigestUtils.md5Hex(content));
}

IOUtils.cleanup(null, writer);
IOUtils.cleanup(null, outputStream);
}

public static void main(String... args) throws Exception {
    Configuration config = new Configuration();
    FileSystem hdfs = FileSystem.get(config);

    File sourceDir = new File(args[0]);
    Path destFile = new Path(args[1]);

    OutputStream os = hdfs.create(destFile);
    writeToAvro(sourceDir, os);
}
}
```

Compression dependency   To run the code in this chapter, you'll need to have both the Snappy and LZOP compression codecs installed on your host. Please refer to the appendix for details on how to install and configure them.

Let's see what happens when you run this script against Hadoop's config directory (replace $HADOOP_CONF_DIR with the directory containing your Hadoop configuration files):

```
$ hip hip.ch4.SmallFilesWrite $HADOOP_CONF_DIR test.avro
/etc/hadoop/conf/ssl-server.xml.example: cb6f1b218...
/etc/hadoop/conf/log4j.properties: 6920ca49b9790cb...
/etc/hadoop/conf/fair-scheduler.xml: b3e5f2bbb1d6c...
...
```

Looks promising—let's make sure that the output file is in HDFS:

```
$ hadoop fs -ls test.avro
2011-08-20 12:38 /user/aholmes/test.avro
```

To be sure everything's working as expected, you can also write some code that will read the Avro file from HDFS and output the MD5 hash for each file's content:[10]

Create an Avro reader object by supplying the InputStream of the file in HDFS. Note that you don't need to supply schema information because Avro encodes that in the Avro file.

```java
public class SmallFilesRead {

    private static final String FIELD_FILENAME = "filename";
    private static final String FIELD_CONTENTS = "contents";

    public static void readFromAvro(InputStream is) throws IOException {
        DataFileStream<Object> reader =
            new DataFileStream<Object>(
                is, new GenericDatumReader<Object>());
        for (Object o : reader) {
            GenericRecord r = (GenericRecord) o;
            System.out.println(
                r.get(FIELD_FILENAME) +
                    ": " +
                    DigestUtils.md5Hex(
                        ((ByteBuffer) r.get(FIELD_CONTENTS)).array()));
        }
        IOUtils.cleanup(null, is);
        IOUtils.cleanup(null, reader);
    }

    public static void main(String... args) throws Exception {
        Configuration config = new Configuration();
        FileSystem hdfs = FileSystem.get(config);

        Path destFile = new Path(args[0]);

        InputStream is = hdfs.open(destFile);
        readFromAvro(is);
    }
}
```

Loop through every record in the Avro file.

Retrieve the filename and content from the record.

Cast each record to a GenericRecord instance.

This code is simpler than the write. Because Avro writes the schema into every Avro file, you don't need to give Avro any information about the schema as part of deserialization. Give the code a spin:

```
$ hip hip.ch4.SmallFilesRead test.avro
/etc/hadoop/conf/ssl-server.xml.example: cb6f1b21...
/etc/hadoop/conf/fair-scheduler.xml: b3e5f2bbb1d6...
...
```

The hashes are the same as those you generated with the write, so things are looking good.

At this point you have Avro files in HDFS. Even though this chapter is about HDFS, the next thing you'll likely want to do is process the files that you wrote in MapReduce. Let's look at how to do that, writing a map-only MapReduce job that can read the Avro records as input and write out a text file containing the filenames and MD5 hashes of the file contents, as shown in figure 4.3.

---

[10] GitHub source: https://github.com/alexholmes/hiped2/blob/master/src/main/java/hip/ch4/SmallFilesRead.java.

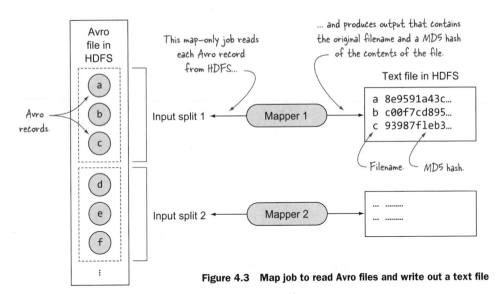

Figure 4.3 Map job to read Avro files and write out a text file

The next listing shows the code for this MapReduce job.[11]

Listing 4.2 A MapReduce job that takes as input Avro files containing the small files

```
public class SmallFilesMapReduce {

  public static void main(String... args) throws Exception {
    JobConf job = new JobConf();
    job.setJarByClass(SmallFilesMapReduce.class);
    Path input = new Path(args[0]);
    Path output = new Path(args[1]);

    output.getFileSystem(job).delete(output, true);

    AvroJob.setInputSchema(job, SmallFilesWrite.SCHEMA);
    job.setInputFormat(AvroInputFormat.class);

    job.setOutputFormat(TextOutputFormat.class);

    job.setMapperClass(Map.class);

    FileInputFormat.setInputPaths(job, input);
    FileOutputFormat.setOutputPath(job, output);

    job.setNumReduceTasks(0);

    JobClient.runJob(job);
  }

  public static class Mapper implements
      Mapper<AvroWrapper<GenericRecord>, NullWritable,
```

Avro has a convenience method to help set the appropriate job configuration settings for Avro input files.

Set the Avro-specific input format for your job.

The Avro file uses the basic building-block GenericRecord objects, so you define this type as your input type for the mapper.

---

[11] GitHub source: https://github.com/alexholmes/hiped2/blob/master/src/main/java/hip/ch4/
SmallFilesMapReduce.java.

```
        Text, Text> {
    @Override
    public void map(AvroWrapper<GenericRecord> key,
                    NullWritable value,
                    OutputCollector<Text, Text> output,
                    Reporter reporter) throws IOException {
      outKey.set(
        key.datum().get(
          SmallFilesWrite.FIELD_FILENAME).toString());
      outValue.set(DigestUtils.md5Hex(
        ((ByteBuffer) key.datum().get(SmallFilesWrite.FIELD_CONTENTS))
          .array())));

      output.collect(outKey, outValue);
    }
  }
}
```

Extract your data from the GenericRecord using the simple get methods.

If you run this MapReduce job over the Avro file you created earlier, the job log files will contain your filenames and hashes:

```
$ hip hip.ch4.SmallFilesMapReduce \
    --input test.avro \
    --output output

$ hadoop fs -cat output/part*

/etc/hadoop/conf/capacity-scheduler.xml: 0601a2..
/etc/hadoop/conf/taskcontroller.cfg: 5c2c191420...
/etc/hadoop/conf/configuration.xsl: e4e5e17b4a8...
...
```

Compare the hashes here with the output of the SmallFilesRead utility executed earlier in this technique, and you'll see they are the same, which verifies that the files are identical.

In this technique, it was assumed that you were working with a file format (such as image files) that couldn't have separate files concatenated together. If your files can be concatenated, you should consider that option. If you go this route, try your best to make sure that the file size is at least as large as the HDFS block size to minimize the data stored in NameNode.

■ **Summary**

You could have used Hadoop's SequenceFile as a mechanism to hold your small files. SequenceFile is a more mature technology, having been around longer than Avro files. But SequenceFiles are Java-specific, and they don't provide the rich interoperability and versioning semantics you get with Avro.

Google's Protocol Buffers, as well as Apache Thrift (which originated from Facebook), can also be used to store small files. But neither has a input format that works with native Thrift or Protocol Buffers files.

Another approach you could use is to write the files into a zip file. The downsides to this approach are first that you'd have to write a custom input format[12] to process the zip file, and second that zip files aren't splittable (as opposed to Avro files and

---

[12] There has been a ticket open since 2008 asking for a zip input format implementation; see https://issues.apache.org/jira/browse/MAPREDUCE-210.

SequenceFiles). This could be mitigated by generating multiple zip files and attempting to make them close to the HDFS block size.

Hadoop also has a `CombineFileInputFormat` that can feed multiple input splits (across multiple files) into a single map task, which greatly decreases the number of map tasks needed to run.

You also could have created a tarball file containing all the files, and then produced a separate text file that contained the locations of the tarball file in HDFS. This text file would be supplied as the input to the MapReduce job, and the mapper would open the tarball directly. But that approach would circumvent the locality in Map-Reduce, because the mappers would be scheduled to execute on the node that contained the text file, and would therefore likely need to read the tarball blocks from remote HDFS nodes, incurring unnecessary network I/O.

Hadoop Archive files (HARs) are Hadoop files specifically created to solve the problem of small files. They are a virtual filesystem that sits on top of HDFS. The disadvantages of HAR files are that they can't be optimized for local disk access in Map-Reduce, and they can't be compressed.

Hadoop version 2 supports HDFS Federation, where HDFS is partitioned into multiple distinct namespaces, with each independently managed by a separate NameNode. This, in effect, means that the overall impact of keeping block information in memory can be spread across multiple NameNodes, thereby supporting a much larger number of small files. Hortonworks has a good blog post that contains more details about HDFS Federation ("An Introduction to HDFS Federation" [August 23, 2011], http://hortonworks.com/an-introduction-to-hdfs-federation/).

Finally, MapR, which provides a Hadoop distribution, has its own distributed filesystem that supports large numbers of small files. Using MapR for your distributed storage is a big change to your system, so it's unlikely you'll move to MapR to mitigate this problem with HDFS.

You may encounter times when you'll want to work with small files in Hadoop, and using them directly would result in bloated NameNode memory use and MapReduce jobs that run slowly. This technique helps you mitigate these issues by packaging small files into larger container files. I picked Avro for this technique because of its support for splittable files and compression and its expressive schema language, which will help with versioning.

What if you have the opposite problem, where your files are big and you want to be more efficient about how you store your data? Our coverage of compression in Hadoop (section 4.2) will come to your rescue in these situations. But before we get to that section, let's continue with our look at data organization and discover some tips on how to move data atomically in HDFS.

4.1.5 *Atomic data movement*

Activities such as partitioning and compacting tend to follow a similar pattern—they produce output files in a staging directory, and then need to atomically move them to their final destination once all the output files have been successfully staged. This may bring up some questions:

- What trigger do you use to determine that you're ready to perform the atomic move?
- How do you move data atomically in HDFS?
- What impact does your data movement have on any readers of the final data?

It may be tempting to perform the atomic move as a postprocessing step within your MapReduce driver, but what will happen if the client process dies before the MapReduce application completes? This is where using the OutputCommitter in Hadoop is useful, because you can perform any atomic file movement as part of your job, as opposed to using the driver. An example of the OutputCommitter is shown in section 3.5.2.

The next question is how you can move data atomically in HDFS. For the longest time, it was thought that the rename method on the DistributedFileSystem class (which is the concrete implementation supporting HDFS) was atomic. But it turns out that there are situations where this isn't an atomic operation. This was remedied in HADOOP-6240, but for backward compatibility reasons, the rename method wasn't updated. As a result, the rename method is still not truly atomic; instead, you need to use a new API. As you can see, the code is cumbersome and it only works with newer versions of Hadoop:

```
DistributedFileSystem fs = (DistributedFileSystem) FileSystem.get(new Configuration());

fs.rename(src, dest, Options.Rename.NONE);
```

One thing that's missing from HDFS is the ability to atomically swap directories. This would be useful in situations such as compacting, where you need to replace the entire contents of a directory that is being used by other processes such as Hive. There's an open JIRA ticket titled "Atomic Directory Swapping Operation" (https://issues.apache.org/jira/browse/HDFS-5902) that will hopefully provide this ability in the future.

It's important that you factor the points discussed here into the design of your system. And if you're using a third-party utility or library, try to determine whether it's atomically moving data.

This concludes our look at data organization techniques. Let's switch to another important data management topic in Hadoop, that of data compression.

4.2 *Efficient storage with compression*

Data compression is a mechanism that reduces data to a more compact form to save on storage space and to make it more efficient to transfer the data. Compression is an important aspect of dealing with files, and it becomes all the more important when dealing with the data sizes that Hadoop supports. Your goal with Hadoop is to be as efficient as possible when working with your data, and picking a suitable compression codec will result in your jobs running faster and allow you to store more data in your cluster.[13]

TECHNIQUE 30 **Picking the right compression codec for your data**

Using compression with HDFS isn't as transparent as it is on filesystems such as ZFS,[14] especially when dealing with compressed files that can be split (more on that later in this chapter). One of the advantages of working with file formats such as Avro and Sequence-File is their built-in compression support, making compression almost completely transparent to users. But you lose that luxury when working with file formats such as text.

■ **Problem**

You want to evaluate and determine the optimal compression codec for use with your data.

■ **Solution**

Snappy, a compression codec from Google, offers the best combination of compressed size and read/write execution times. But LZOP is the best codec when working with large compressed files that must support splittability.

■ **Discussion**

Let's kick things off with a quick look at the compression codecs available for use in Hadoop, shown in table 4.1.

Table 4.1 Compression codecs

Codec	Background
Deflate	Deflate is similar to zlib, which is the same compression algorithm that gzip uses but without the gzip headers.
gzip	The gzip file format consists of a header and a body, which contains a Deflate-compressed payload.
bzip2	bzip2 is a space-efficient compression codec.
LZO	LZO is a block-based compression algorithm that allows the compressed data to be split.
LZOP	LZOP is LZO with additional headers. At one time, LZO/LZOP came bundled with Hadoop, but they have since been removed due to GPL licensing restrictions.
LZ4	LZ4 is a speedy derivative of the same compression algorithm on which LZO is based.
Snappy	Snappy (http://code.google.com/p/hadoop-snappy/) is a recent addition to the codec options in Hadoop. It's Google's open source compression algorithm. Google uses it for compressing data in both MapReduce and BigTable.[a] Snappy's main drawback is that it's not splittable. If you're working with file formats that support splitting, such as Avro or Parquet, or your file sizes are smaller than or equal to your HDFS block size, you can ignore this drawback.

[a] BigTable is Google's proprietary database system; see Fay Chang et al., "Bigtable: A Distributed Storage System for Structured Data," http://research.google.com/archive/bigtable.html.

---

[13] A compression codec is a programming implementation capable of reading and writing a given compression format.

[14] ZFS, short for Z File System, is a filesystem developed by Sun Microsystems that provides innovative features to enhance data integrity.

To properly evaluate the codecs, you first need to specify your evaluation criteria, which should be based on functional and performance traits. For compression, your criteria are likely to include the following:

- *Space/time trade-off*—Generally, the more computationally expensive compression codecs yield better compression ratios, resulting in smaller compressed outputs.
- *Splittability*—Can a compressed file be split for use by multiple mappers? If a compressed file can't be split, only a single mapper will be able to work on it. If that file spans multiple blocks, you'll lose out on data locality because the map will likely have to read blocks from remote DataNodes, incurring the overhead of network I/O.
- *Native compression support*—Is there a native library that performs compression and decompression? This will usually outperform a compression codec written in Java with no underlying native library support.

Table 4.2 compares the compression codecs currently available (we'll cover the space/time comparison in the next section).

Table 4.2   Comparison of compression codecs

Codec	Extension	Licensing	Splittable	Java-only compression support	Native compression support
Deflate	.deflate	zlib	No	Yes	Yes
gzip	.gz	GNU GPL	No	Yes	Yes
bzip2	.gz	BSD	Yes [a]	Yes	Yes[b]
LZO	.lzo_deflate	GNU GPL	No	No	Yes
LZOP	.lzo	GNU GPL	Yes [c]	No	Yes
LZ4	.lz4	New BSD	No	No	Yes
Snappy	.gz	New BSD	No	No	Yes

[a] The Java version of bzip2 is splittable in Hadoop 2 and 1.1.0 onward (see https://issues.apache.org/jira/browse/HADOOP-4012). The native version isn't currently splittable.

[b] Native bzip2 support was added in Hadoop 2.1 (see https://issues.apache.org/jira/browse/HADOOP-8462).

[c] LZOP files aren't natively splittable. You need to preprocess them to create an index file, which is then used by their respective `CompressionCodec` implementations to determine the file splits. We'll cover how you can achieve this in technique 32.

Native vs. Java bzip2   Native support for bzip2 was recently added to Hadoop (starting from versions 2.0 and 1.1.0). Native bzip2 support is the default, but it doesn't support splittability. If you need splittability with bzip2, you'll need to enable the Java bzip2, which can be specified by setting `io.compression` `.codec.bzip2.library` to `java-builtin`.

Now that you understand the codecs, how do they square up when looking at their space/time trade-offs? I used a 100 MB (10^8) Wikipedia XML file (enwik8.zip from http://mattmahoney.net/dc/textdata.html), to compare the codec run times and their compression sizes. The results of these tests can be seen in table 4.3.

Table 4.3 Performance comparison of compression codecs on a 100 MB text file

Codec	Compression time (secs)	Decompression time (secs)	Compressed file size	Compressed percentage
Deflate	9.21	1.02	36,548,921	36.55%
gzip	9.09	0.90	36,548,933	36.55%
bzip2 (Java)	47.33	6.45	29,007,274	29.01%
bzip2 (native)	11.59	4.66	29,008,758	29.01%
LZO	2.10	0.46	53,926,001	53.93%
LZOP	2.09	0.45	53,926,043	53.93%
LZ4	1.72	0.28	57,337,587	57.34%
Snappy	1.75	0.29	58,493,673	58.49%

Running your own tests   When you're performing your own evaluation, I recommend you perform your tests using your own data, and preferably on hosts similar to your production nodes. This way you'll have a good sense of the expected compression and run times for the codecs.

Also make sure your cluster has native codecs enabled. You can check this by running the following command:

```
$ hadoop checknative -a
```

Figure 4.4 shows the compressed sizes in bar graph form.

Figure 4.5 shows the compressed times in bar graph form. These times will vary significantly based on hardware, and they're only supplied here to give a sense of how they relate to each other.

What do the space and time results tell you? If squeezing as much data into your cluster as possible is your top priority and you can live with long compression times, then bzip2 may be the right codec for you. If you want to compress your data but introduce the least amount of CPU overhead when it comes to reading and writing compressed files, you should look at LZ4. Anyone looking for a balance between compression and execution times would have to eliminate the Java version of bzip2 from the picture.

Being able to split your compressed files is important, and here you have to choose between bzip2 and LZOP. The native bzip2 codec doesn't support splitting, and the Java bzip2 times will likely give most people pause. The only advantage of bzip2 over LZOP is that its Hadoop integration is much easier to work with than LZOP's.

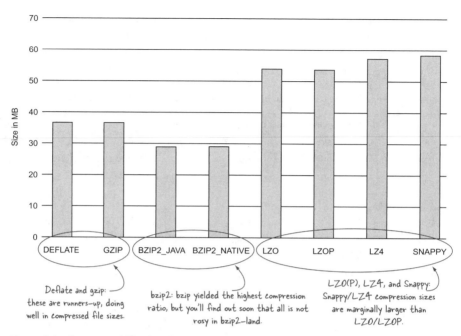

Figure 4.4   Compressed file sizes for a single 100 MB text file (smaller values are better)

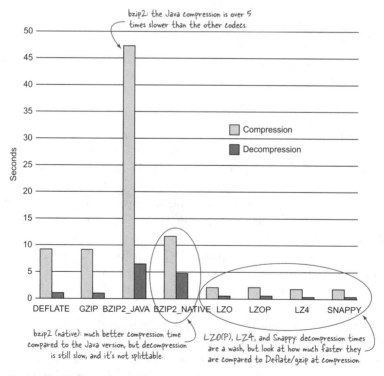

Figure 4.5   Compression and decompression times for a single 100 MB text file (smaller values are better)

Although LZOP is the natural winner here, it requires some effort to work with, as you'll see in technique 32.

■ **Summary**

The best codec for you will depend on your criteria. LZ4 is the most promising codec if you don't care about splitting your files, and LZOP is what you should be looking at if you want splittable files.

Another factor to consider is the long-term storage retention required for the data. If you're keeping data for a long time, you'll probably want to maximize the compression of your files, for which I would recommend a zlib-based codec (such as gzip). Because gzip isn't splittable, though, it would be prudent to use it in combination with a block-based file format such as Avro or Parquet so that your data can still be split. Or you could size your outputs so they occupy a single block in HDFS so that splittability isn't a concern.

Bear in mind that compressed sizes will vary based on whether your file is text or binary and depending on its contents. To get accurate numbers, you should run similar tests against your own data.

Compressing data in HDFS has many benefits, including reduced file sizes and faster MapReduce job runtimes. A number of compression codecs are available for use in Hadoop, and I evaluated them based on features and performance. Now you're ready to start using compression. Let's look at how you can compress files and use them with tools such as MapReduce, Pig, and Hive.

TECHNIQUE 31   **Compression with HDFS, MapReduce, Pig, and Hive**

Because HDFS doesn't provide built-in support for compression, it can be a challenge to work with compression in Hadoop. The onus falls on you to figure out how to work with compressed files. Also, splittable compression isn't for the faint of heart, because it doesn't come out of the box with Hadoop.[15] If you're dealing with medium-size files that compress down to near-HDFS block size, this technique will be the quickest and simplest way to reap the benefits of compression in Hadoop.

■ **Problem**

You want to read and write compressed files in HDFS and also use them with Map-Reduce, Pig, and Hive.

■ **Solution**

Working with compressed files in MapReduce involves updating the MapReduce configuration file mapred-site.xml and registering the compression codec you're using. After you do this, working with compressed input files in MapReduce requires no additional steps, and producing compressed MapReduce output is a matter of setting the `mapred.output.compress` and `mapred.output.compression.codec` MapReduce properties.

---

[15] Technically, you can get out-of-the-box splittable compression with bzip2, but its performance traits, as shown earlier in this section, rule it out as a serious compression codec.

■ **Discussion**

The first step is to figure out how to read and write files using any of the codecs evaluated earlier in this chapter. All of the codecs detailed in this chapter are bundled with Hadoop except for LZO/LZOP and Snappy, so if you want to work with those three, you'll need to download and build them yourself (I'll walk you through how to work with LZO/LZOP later in this section).

To use the compression codecs, you need to know their class names, which are listed in table 4.4.

Table 4.4   Codec classes

Codec	Class	Default extension
Deflate	org.apache.hadoop.io.compress.DeflateCodec	deflate
gzip	org.apache.hadoop.io.compress.GzipCodec	gz
bzip2	org.apache.hadoop.io.compress.BZip2Codec	bz2
LZO	com.hadoop.compression.lzo.LzoCodec	lzo_deflate
LZOP	com.hadoop.compression.lzo.LzopCodec	lzo
LZ4	org.apache.hadoop.io.compress.Lz4Codec	lz4
Snappy	org.apache.hadoop.io.compress.SnappyCodec	snappy

Using compression in HDFS

How would you compress an existing file in HDFS using any one of the codecs mentioned in the previous table? The following code supports doing that:[16]

Construct an instance of the codec with the help of Hadoop's ReflectionUtils.

Read the compression codec from your input arguments.

Each codec has a default extension (listed in table 4.4), and it's a best practice to use that extension when writing a compressed file.

Use the codec to create a compressed output stream.

```
Configuration config = new Configuration();
FileSystem hdfs = FileSystem.get(config);

Class<?> codecClass = Class.forName(args[2]);
CompressionCodec codec = (CompressionCodec)
    ReflectionUtils.newInstance(codecClass, config);

InputStream is = hdfs.open(new Path(args[0]));
OutputStream os = hdfs.create(
    new Path(args[0] + codec.getDefaultExtension()));

OutputStream cos = codec.createOutputStream(os);

IOUtils.copyBytes(is, cos, config, true);

IOUtils.closeStream(os);
IOUtils.closeStream(is);
```

Use any standard Java OutputStream writing mechanism to write to the compressed stream; here you're using a utility provided by Hadoop. The last argument indicates whether the input and output streams should be closed after the copy has completed.

---

[16] GitHub source: https://github.com/alexholmes/hiped2/blob/master/src/main/java/hip/ch4/CompressedFileWrite.java.

Codec caching   One of the overheads to using compression codecs is that they can be expensive to create. When you use the Hadoop `ReflectionUtils` class, some of the reflection overhead associated with creating the instance will be cached in `ReflectionUtils`, which should speed up subsequent creation of the codec. A better option would be to use the `CompressionCodecFactory`, which provides caching of the codecs themselves.

Reading this compressed file is as simple as writing it:[17]

```
InputStream is = hdfs.open(new Path(args[0]));

Class<?> codecClass = Class.forName(args[1]);
CompressionCodec codec = (CompressionCodec)
    ReflectionUtils.newInstance(codecClass, config);

InputStream cis = codec.createInputStream(is);

IOUtils.copyBytes(cis, System.out, config, true);

IOUtils.closeStream(is);
```

Use the codec's createInputStream to return an InputStream for reading.

Super simple. Now that you can create compressed files, let's look at how you can work with them in MapReduce.

Using compression in MapReduce

To work with compressed files in MapReduce, you need to set some configuration options for your job. For the sake of brevity, let's assume identity mappers and reducers[18] in this example:[19]

```
Class<?> codecClass = Class.forName(args[2]);

conf.setBoolean("mapred.output.compress", true);

conf.setBoolean("mapred.compress.map.output", true);

conf.setClass("mapred.output.compression.codec",
    codecClass,
    CompressionCodec.class);
```

Compress the reducer output.

Compress the mapper output.

The compression codec for compressing mapper output.

The only differences between a MapReduce job that works with uncompressed versus compressed I/O are the three annotated lines in the previous example.

Not only can a job's input and output be compressed, but so can the intermediate map output, because it's spilled first to disk, and then eventually over the network to the reducer. The effectiveness of compressing the map output will ultimately depend on the type of data being emitted, but as a general rule, you should see some job speed-up by making this change.

---

[17] GitHub source: https://github.com/alexholmes/hiped2/blob/master/src/main/java/hip/ch4/ CompressedFileRead.java.

[18] An identity task is one that emits all of the input it receives as output, without any transformation or filtering.

[19] GitHub source: https://github.com/alexholmes/hiped2/blob/master/src/main/java/hip/ch4/ CompressedMapReduce.java.

Why didn't you have to specify the compression codec for the input file in the preceding code? By default the FileInputFormat class uses the CompressionCodecFactory to determine if the input file extension matches any of the registered codecs. If it finds a codec that's associated with that file extension, it automatically uses that codec to decompress the input files.

How does MapReduce know which codecs to use? You need to specify the codecs in mapred-site.xml. The following code shows how to register all of the codecs we've evaluated. Remember that other than gzip, Deflate, and bzip2, all compression codecs need to be built and made available on your cluster before you can register them:

```
<property>
  <name>io.compression.codecs</name>
  <value>
    org.apache.hadoop.io.compress.GzipCodec,
    org.apache.hadoop.io.compress.DefaultCodec,
    org.apache.hadoop.io.compress.BZip2Codec,
    com.hadoop.compression.lzo.LzoCodec,
    com.hadoop.compression.lzo.LzopCodec,
    org.apache.hadoop.io.compress.SnappyCodec
  </value>
</property>
<property>
  <name>
    io.compression.codec.lzo.class
  </name>
  <value>
    com.hadoop.compression.lzo.LzoCodec
  </value>
</property>
```

Now that you've mastered compression with MapReduce, it's time to look higher up the Hadoop stack. Because compression can also be used in conjunction with Pig and Hive, let's see how you can mirror your MapReduce compression accomplishment using Pig and Hive. (As I'll show in chapter 9, Hive is a higher-level language that abstracts away some of the complex details of MapReduce.)

Using compression in Pig

If you're working with Pig, there's no extra effort required to use compressed input files. All you need to do is ensure your filename extension maps to the appropriate compression codec (see table 4.4). The following example gzips a local password file, loads it into Pig, and dumps out the usernames:

```
$ gzip -c /etc/passwd > passwd.gz
$ hadoop fs -put passwd.gz passwd.gz

$ pig
grunt> A = load 'passwd.gz' using PigStorage(':');

grunt> B = foreach A generate $0 as id;
grunt> DUMP B;
```

Ending your filename with the .gz extension results in the underlying MapReduce output format recognizing the file as being gzipped and using the appropriate compression codec to decompress the contents.

```
(root)
(bin)
(daemon)
...
```

Writing out a gzipped file is the same—make sure you specify the extension for a compression codec. The following example stores the results of Pig relation B in a file in HDFS, and then copies them to the local filesystem to examine the contents:

```
grunt> STORE B INTO 'passwd-users.gz';

# Ctrl+C to break out of Pig shell

$ hadoop fs -get passwd-users.gz/part-m-00000.gz .

$ gunzip -c part-m-00000.gz
root
bin
daemon
...
```

That was straightforward—let's hope things are equally smooth with Hive.

Using compression in Hive

As with Pig, all you need to do is specify the codec extension when defining the filename:

```
hive> CREATE TABLE apachelog (...);

hive> LOAD DATA INPATH /user/aholmes/apachelog.txt.gz
    OVERWRITE INTO TABLE apachelog;
```

As with the Pig example, the .gz filename extension triggers the appropriate compression codec for decompression.

The previous example loaded a gzipped file into Hive. In this situation, Hive moves the file being loaded into Hive's warehouse directory and continues to use the raw file as its storage for the table.

What if you want to create another table and also specify that it should be compressed? The following example achieves this by setting some Hive configs to enable MapReduce compression (because a MapReduce job will be executed to load the new table in the last statement):

```
hive> SET hive.exec.compress.output=true;
hive> SET hive.exec.compress.intermediate = true;
hive> SET mapred.output.compression.codec =
  org.apache.hadoop.io.compress.GzipCodec;

hive> CREATE TABLE apachelog_backup (...);

hive> INSERT OVERWRITE TABLE apachelog_backup SELECT * FROM apachelog;
```

You can verify that Hive is indeed compressing the storage for the new apachelog_backup table by looking at it in HDFS:

```
$ hadoop fs -ls /user/hive/warehouse/apachelog_backup
/user/hive/warehouse/apachelog_backup/000000_0.gz
```

It should be noted that Hive recommends using SequenceFile as the output format for tables because SequenceFile blocks can be individually compressed.

■ **Summary**

This technique provides a quick and easy way to get compression running in Hadoop. It works well for files that aren't too large because it offers a fairly transparent way of working with compression.

If your compressed file sizes are much larger than the HDFS block size, read on for compression techniques that can split your files.

TECHNIQUE 32   **Splittable LZOP with MapReduce, Hive, and Pig**

Imagine that you're working with large text files that, even when compressed, are many times larger than the HDFS block size. To avoid having one map task process an entire large compressed file, you'll need to pick a compression codec that can support splitting that file.

LZOP fits the bill, but working with it is more complex than the examples detailed in the previous technique because LZOP is not in and of itself splittable. "Wait," you may be thinking, "didn't you state earlier that LZOP is splittable?" LZOP is block-based, but you can't perform a random seek into an LZOP file and determine the next block's starting point. This is the challenge we'll tackle in this technique.

■ **Problem**

You want to use a compression codec that will allow MapReduce to work in parallel on a single compressed file.

■ **Solution**

In MapReduce, splitting large LZOP-compressed input files requires the use of LZOP-specific input format classes, such as `LzoInputFormat`. The same principle applies when working with LZOP-compressed input files in both Pig and Hive.

■ **Discussion**

The LZOP compression codec is one of only two codecs that allow for compressed files to be split, and therefore to be worked on in parallel by multiple reducers. The other codec, bzip2, suffers from compression times that are so slow they arguably render the codec unusable. LZOP also offers a good compromise between compression and speed.

> **What's the difference between LZO and LZOP?**   Both LZO and LZOP codecs are supplied for use with Hadoop. LZO is a stream-based compression store that doesn't have the notion of blocks or headers. LZOP has the notion of blocks (that are checksummed), and therefore is the codec you want to use, especially if you want your compressed output to be splittable. Confusingly, the Hadoop codecs by default treat files ending with the .lzo extension to be LZOP-encoded, and files ending with the .lzo_deflate extension to be LZO-encoded. Also, much of the documentation seems to use LZO and LZOP interchangeably.

Preparing your cluster for LZOP

Unfortunately, Hadoop doesn't bundle LZOP for licensing reasons.[20]

Getting all the prerequisites compiled and installed on your cluster is laborious, but rest assured that there are detailed instructions in the appendix. To compile and run the code in this section, you'll need to follow the instructions in the appendix.

Reading and writing LZOP files in HDFS

We covered how to read and write compressed files in section 4.2. To perform the same activity with LZOP requires you to specify the LZOP codec in your code. This code is shown in the following listing.[21]

Listing 4.3 Methods to read and write LZOP files in HDFS

```java
public static Path compress(Path src,
                            Configuration config)
    throws IOException {
  Path destFile =
    new Path(
        src.toString() +
            new LzopCodec().getDefaultExtension());

  LzopCodec codec = new LzopCodec();
  codec.setConf(config);

  FileSystem hdfs = FileSystem.get(config);
  InputStream is = null;
  OutputStream os = null;
  try {
    is = hdfs.open(src);
    os = codec.createOutputStream(hdfs.create(destFile));

    IOUtils.copyBytes(is, os, config);
  } finally {
    IOUtils.closeStream(os);
    IOUtils.closeStream(is);
  }
  return destFile;
}

public static void decompress(Path src, Path dest,
                              Configuration config)
    throws IOException {
  LzopCodec codec = new LzopCodec();
  codec.setConf(config);

  FileSystem hdfs = FileSystem.get(config);
  InputStream is = null;
  OutputStream os = null;
  try {
```

---

[20] LZOP used to be included with Hadoop, but with the work performed in JIRA ticket https://issues.apache.org/jira/browse/HADOOP-4874, it was removed from Hadoop version 0.20 and newer releases due to LZOP's GPL licensing limiting its redistribution.

[21] GitHub source: https://github.com/alexholmes/hiped2/blob/master/src/main/java/hip/ch4/LzopFileReadWrite.java.

```
    is = codec.createInputStream(hdfs.open(src));
    os = hdfs.create(dest);

    IOUtils.copyBytes(is, os, config);
  } finally {
    IOUtils.closeStream(os);
    IOUtils.closeStream(is);
  }
}
```

Let's write and read an LZOP file, and then make sure that LZOP utilities can work with the generated file (replace $HADOOP_CONF_HOME with the location of your Hadoop config directory):

```
$ hadoop fs -put $HADOOP_CONF_DIR/core-site.xml core-site.xml
$ hip hip.ch4.LzopFileReadWrite core-site.xml
```

The preceding code will generate a core-site.xml.lzo file in HDFS.

Now make sure you can use this LZOP file with the lzop binary. Install an lzop binary on your host.[22] Copy the LZOP file from HDFS to local disk, uncompress it with the native lzop binary, and compare it with the original file:

```
$ hadoop fs -get core-site.xml.lzo /tmp/core-site.xml.lzo
$ lzop -l /tmp/core-site.xml.lzo
method        compressed  uncompr. ratio uncompressed_name
LZO1X-1            454         954 47.6% core-site.xml
# cd /tmp
$ lzop -d core-site.xml.lzo
$ ls -ltr
-rw-r--r-- 1 aholmes aholmes    954 May 5 09:05 core-site.xml
-rw-r--r-- 1 aholmes aholmes    504 May 5 09:05 core-site.xml.lzo
$ diff core-site.xml $HADOOP_CONF_DIR/conf/core-site.xml
$
```

The diff verified that the file compressed with the LZOP codec could be decompressed with the lzop binary.

Now that you have your LZOP file, you need to index it so that it can be split.

Creating indexes for your LZOP files

Earlier I made the paradoxical statement that LZOP files can be split, but that they're not natively splittable. Let me clarify what that means—the lack of block-delimiting synchronization markers means you can't do a random seek into an LZOP file and start reading blocks. But because internally it does use blocks, all you need is a preprocessing step that can generate an index file containing the block offsets.

The LZOP file is read in its entirety, and block offsets are written to the index file as the read is occurring. The index file format, shown in figure 4.6, is a binary file containing a consecutive series of 64-bit numbers that indicate the byte offset for each block in the LZOP file.

---

[22] For RedHat and Centos, you can install the rpm from http://pkgs.repoforge.org/lzop/lzop-1.03-1.el5.rf .x86_64.rpm.

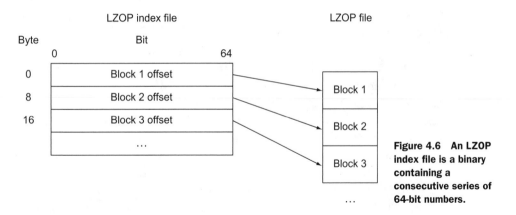

Figure 4.6 An LZOP index file is a binary containing a consecutive series of 64-bit numbers.

You can create index files in one of two ways, as shown in the following two code snippets. If you want to create an index file for a single LZOP file, here is a simple library call that will do this for you:

```
shell$ hadoop com.hadoop.compression.lzo.LzoIndexer core-site.xml.lzo
```

The following option works well if you have a large number of LZOP files and you want a more efficient way to generate the index files. The indexer runs a MapReduce job to create the index files. Both files and directories (which are scanned recursively for LZOP files) are supported:

```
shell$ hadoop  \
       com.hadoop.compression.lzo.DistributedLzoIndexer  \
       core-site.xml.lzo
```

Both approaches depicted in figure 4.6 will generate an index file in the same directory as the LZOP file. The index filename is the original LZOP filename suffixed with .index. Running the previous commands would yield the filename core-site.xml.lzo.index.

Now let's look at how you can use the LzoIndexer in your Java code. The following code (from the main method of LzoIndexer) will result in the index file being created synchronously:

```
LzoIndexer lzoIndexer = new LzoIndexer(new Configuration());
for (String arg: args) {
  try {
    lzoIndexer.index(new Path(arg));
  } catch (IOException e) {
    LOG.error("Error indexing " + arg, e);
  }
}
```

With the DistributedLzoIndexer, the MapReduce job will launch and run with *N* mappers, one for each .lzo file. No reducers are run, so the (identity) mapper, via the custom LzoSplitInputFormat and LzoIndexOutputFormat, writes the index files directly.

If you want to run the MapReduce job from your own Java code, you can use the DistributedLzoIndexer code as an example.

You need the LZOP index files so that you can split LZOP files in your MapReduce, Pig, and Hive jobs. Now that you have the aforementioned LZOP index files, let's look at how you can use them with MapReduce.

MapReduce and LZOP

After you've created index files for your LZOP files, it's time to start using your LZOP files with MapReduce. Unfortunately, this brings us to the next challenge: none of the existing, built-in Hadoop-file-based input formats will work with splittable LZOP because they need specialized logic to handle input splits using the LZOP index file. You need specific input format classes to work with splittable LZOP.

The LZOP library provides an LzoTextInputFormat implementation for line-oriented LZOP-compressed text files with accompanying index files.[23]

The following code shows the steps required to configure the MapReduce job to work with LZOP. You would perform these steps for a MapReduce job that had text LZOP inputs and outputs:[24]

```
job.setInputFormatClass(LzoTextInputFormat.class);
job.setOutputFormatClass(TextOutputFormat.class);

job.getConfiguration().setBoolean("mapred.output.compress", true);
job.getConfiguration().setClass("mapred.output.compression.codec",
    LzopCodec.class, CompressionCodec.class);
```

Compressing intermediary map output will also speed up the overall execution time of your MapReduce jobs:

```
conf.setBoolean("mapred.compress.map.output", true);
conf.setClass("mapred.map.output.compression.codec",
    LzopCodec.class,
    CompressionCodec.class);
```

You can easily configure your cluster to always compress your map output by editing hdfs-site.xml:

```
<property>
    <name>mapred.compress.map.output</name>
    <value>true</value>
  </property>
  <property>
    <name>mapred.map.output.compression.codec</name>
    <value>com.hadoop.compression.lzo.LzopCodec</value>
</property>
```

The number of splits per LZOP file is a function of the number of LZOP blocks that the file occupies, not the number of HDFS blocks that the file occupies.

---

[23] The LZOP input formats also work well with LZOP files that don't have index files.

[24] GitHub source: https://github.com/alexholmes/hiped2/blob/master/src/main/java/hip/ch4/LzopMapReduce.java.

Now that we've covered MapReduce, let's look at how Pig and Hive can work with splittable LZOP.

Pig and Hive

Elephant Bird,[25] a Twitter project containing utilities to work with LZOP, provides a number of useful MapReduce and Pig classes. Elephant Bird has an `LzoPigStorage` class that works with text-based, LZOP-compressed data in Pig.

Hive can work with LZOP-compressed text files by using the `com.hadoop.mapred` `.DeprecatedLzoTextInputFormat` input format class found in the LZO library.

■ Summary

Working with splittable compression in Hadoop is tricky. If you're fortunate enough to be able to store your data in Avro or Parquet, they offer the simplest way to work with files that can be easily compressed and split. If you want to compress other file formats and need them to be split, LZOP is the only real candidate.

As I mentioned earlier, the Elephant Bird project provides some useful LZOP input formats that will work with LZOP-compressed file formats such as XML and plain text. If you need to work with an LZOP-compressed file format that isn't supported by either Todd Lipcon's LZO project or Elephant Bird, you'll have to write your own input format. This is a big hurdle for developers. I hope at some point Hadoop will be able to support compressed files with custom splitting logic so that end users don't have to write their own input formats for compression.

Compression is likely to be a hard-and-fast requirement for any production environment where resources are always scarce. Compression also allows faster execution times for your computational jobs, so it's a compelling aspect of storage. In the previous section I showed you how to evaluate and pick the codec best suited for your data. We also covered how to use compression with HDFS, MapReduce, Pig, and Hive. Finally, we tackled the tricky subject of splittable LZOP compression.

4.3   Chapter summary

Big data in the form of large numbers of small files brings to light a limitation in HDFS, and in this chapter we worked around it by looking at how you can package small files into larger Avro containers.

Compression is a key part of any large cluster, and we evaluated and compared the different compression codecs. I recommended codecs based on various criteria and also showed you how to compress and work with these compressed files in MapReduce, Pig, and Hive. We also looked at how to work with LZOP to achieve compression as well as blazing-fast computation with multiple input splits.

This and the previous chapter were dedicated to looking at techniques for picking the right file format and working effectively with big data in MapReduce and HDFS. It's now time to apply this knowledge and look at how to move data in and out of Hadoop. That's covered in the next chapter.

---

[25] See the appendix for more details on Elephant Bird.

Moving data into and out of Hadoop

This chapter covers

- Understanding key design considerations for data ingress and egress tools
- Low-level methods for moving data into and out of Hadoop
- Techniques for moving log files and relational and NoSQL data, as well as data in Kafka, in and out of HDFS

Data movement is one of those things that you aren't likely to think too much about until you're fully committed to using Hadoop on a project, at which point it becomes this big scary unknown that has to be tackled. How do you get your log data sitting across thousands of hosts into Hadoop? What's the most efficient way to get your data out of your relational and No/NewSQL systems and into Hadoop? How do you get Lucene indexes generated in Hadoop out to your servers? And how can these processes be automated?

Welcome to chapter 5, where the goal is to answer these questions and set you on your path to worry-free data movement. In this chapter you'll first see how data across a broad spectrum of locations and formats can be moved into Hadoop, and then you'll see how data can be moved out of Hadoop.

This chapter starts by highlighting key data-movement properties, so that as you go through the rest of this chapter you can evaluate the fit of the various tools. It goes on to look at low-level and high-level tools that can be used to move your data. We'll start with some simple techniques, such as using the command line and Java for ingress,[1] but we'll quickly move on to more advanced techniques like using NFS and DistCp.

Once the low-level tooling is out of the way, we'll survey higher-level tools that have simplified the process of ferrying data into Hadoop. We'll look at how you can automate the movement of log files with Flume, and how Sqoop can be used to move relational data. So as not to ignore some of the emerging data systems, you'll also be introduced to methods that can be employed to move data from HBase and Kafka into Hadoop.

We'll cover a lot of ground in this chapter, and it's likely that you'll have specific types of data you need to work with. If this is the case, feel free to jump directly to the section that provides the details you need.

Let's start things off with a look at key ingress and egress system considerations.

5.1 Key elements of data movement

Moving large quantities of data in and out of Hadoop offers logistical challenges that include consistency guarantees and resource impacts on data sources and destinations. Before we dive into the techniques, however, we need to discuss the design elements you should be aware of when working with data movement.

Idempotence

An idempotent operation produces the same result no matter how many times it's executed. In a relational database, the inserts typically aren't idempotent, because executing them multiple times doesn't produce the same resulting database state. Alternatively, updates often are idempotent, because they'll produce the same end result.

Any time data is being written, idempotence should be a consideration, and data ingress and egress in Hadoop are no different. How well do distributed log collection frameworks deal with data retransmissions? How do you ensure idempotent behavior in a MapReduce job where multiple tasks are inserting into a database in parallel? We'll examine and answer these questions in this chapter.

Aggregation

The data aggregation process combines multiple data elements. In the context of data ingress, this can be useful because moving large quantities of small files into HDFS potentially translates into NameNode memory woes, as well as slow MapReduce execution times. Having the ability to aggregate files or data together mitigates this problem and is a feature to consider.

---

[1] *Ingress* and *egress* refer to data movement into and out of a system, respectively.

Data format transformation

The data format transformation process converts one data format into another. Often your source data isn't in a format that's ideal for processing in tools such as Map-Reduce. If your source data is in multiline XML or JSON form, for example, you may want to consider a preprocessing step. This would convert the data into a form that can be split, such as one JSON or XML element per line, or convert it into a format such as Avro. Chapter 3 contains more details on these data formats.

Compression

Compression not only helps by reducing the footprint of data at rest, but also has I/O advantages when reading and writing data.

Availability and recoverability

Recoverability allows an ingress or egress tool to retry in the event of a failed operation. Because it's unlikely that any data source, sink, or Hadoop itself can be 100% available, it's important that an ingress or egress action be retried in the event of failure.

Reliable data transfer and data validation

In the context of data transportation, checking for correctness is how you verify that no data corruption occurred as the data was in transit. When you work with heterogeneous systems such as Hadoop data ingress and egress, the fact that data is being transported across different hosts, networks, and protocols only increases the potential for problems during data transfer. A common method for checking the correctness of raw data, such as storage devices, is Cyclic Redundancy Checks (CRCs), which are what HDFS uses internally to maintain block-level integrity.

In addition, it's possible that there are problems in the source data itself due to bugs in the software generating the data. Performing these checks at ingress time allows you to do a one-time check, instead of dealing with all the downstream consumers of the data that would have to be updated to handle errors in the data.

Resource consumption and performance

Resource consumption and performance are measures of system resource utilization and system efficiency, respectively. Ingress and egress tools don't typically impose significant load (resource consumption) on a system, unless you have appreciable data volumes. For performance, the questions to ask include whether the tool performs ingress and egress activities in parallel, and if so, what mechanisms it provides to tune the amount of parallelism. For example, if your data source is a production database and you're using MapReduce to ingest that data, don't use a large number of concurrent map tasks to import data.

Monitoring

Monitoring ensures that functions are performing as expected in automated systems. For data ingress and egress, monitoring breaks down into two elements: ensuring that the processes involved in ingress and egress are alive, and validating that source and destination data are being produced as expected. Monitoring should also include verifying that the data volumes being moved are at expected levels; unexpected drops or highs in your data will alert you to potential system issues or bugs in your software.

Speculative execution

MapReduce has a feature called *speculative execution* that launches duplicate tasks near the end of a job for tasks that are still executing. This helps prevent slow hardware from impacting job execution times. But if you're using a map task to perform inserts into a relational database, for example, you should be aware that you could have two parallel processes inserting the same data.[2]

On to the techniques. Let's start with how you can leverage Hadoop's built-in ingress mechanisms.

5.2 Moving data into Hadoop

The first step in working with data in Hadoop is to make it available to Hadoop. There are two primary methods that can be used to move data into Hadoop: writing external data at the HDFS level (a data push), or reading external data at the MapReduce level (more like a pull). Reading data in MapReduce has advantages in the ease with which the operation can be parallelized and made fault tolerant. Not all data is accessible from MapReduce, however, such as in the case of log files, which is where other systems need to be relied on for transportation, including HDFS for the final data hop.

In this section we'll look at methods for moving source data into Hadoop. I'll use the design considerations in the previous section as the criteria for examining and understanding the different tools.

We'll get things started with a look at some low-level methods you can use to move data into Hadoop.

5.2.1 Roll your own ingest

Hadoop comes bundled with a number of methods to get your data into HDFS. This section will examine various ways that these built-in tools can be used for your data movement needs. The first and potentially easiest tool you can use is the HDFS command line.

> **Picking the right ingest tool for the job**   The low-level tools in this section work well for one-off file movement activities, or when working with legacy data sources and destinations that are file-based. But moving data in this way is quickly becoming obsolete by the availability of tools such as Flume and Kafka (covered later in this chapter), which offer automated data movement pipelines.
>
> Kafka is a much better platform for getting data from A to B (and B can be a Hadoop cluster) than the old-school "let's copy files around!" With Kafka, you only need to pump your data into Kafka, and you have the ability to consume the data in real time (such as via Storm) or in offline/batch jobs (such as via Camus).

---

[2] Map- and reduce-side speculative execution can be disabled via the `mapreduce.map.speculative` and `mapreduce.reduce.speculative` configurables in Hadoop 2.

> File-based ingestion flows are, to me at least, a relic of the past (because every-body knows how scp works :-P), and they primarily exist for legacy reasons—the upstream data sources may have existing tools to create file snapshots (such as dump tools for the database), and there's no infrastructure to migrate or move the data into a real-time messaging system such as Kafka.

TECHNIQUE 33   **Using the CLI to load files**

If you have a manual activity that you need to perform, such as moving the examples bundled with this book into HDFS, then the HDFS command-line interface (CLI) is the tool for you. It'll allow you to perform most of the operations that you're used to performing on a regular Linux filesystem. In this section we'll focus on copying data from a local filesystem into HDFS.

■ **Problem**

You want to copy files into HDFS using the shell.

■ **Solution**

The HDFS command-line interface can be used for one-off moves, or it can be incorporated into scripts for a series of moves.

■ **Discussion**

Copying a file from local disk to HDFS is done with the hadoop command:

```
$ hadoop fs -put local-file.txt hdfs-file.txt
```

The behavior of the Hadoop -put command differs from the Linux cp command—in Linux if the destination already exists, it is overwritten; in Hadoop the copy fails with an error:

```
put: `hdfs-file.txt': File exists
```

The -f option must be added to force the file to be overwritten:

```
$ hadoop fs -put -f local-file.txt hdfs-file.txt
```

Much like with the Linux cp command, multiple files can be copied using the same command. In this case, the final argument must be the directory in HDFS into which the local files are copied:

```
$ hadoop fs -put local-file1.txt local-file2.txt /hdfs/dest/
```

You can also use Linux pipes to pipe the output of a command into an HDFS file—use the same -put command and add a separate hyphen after it, which tells Hadoop to read the input from standard input:

```
$ echo "the cat sat on the mat" | hadoop fs -put - hdfs-file.txt
```

To test for the existence of a file or directory, use the -test command with either the -e or -d option to test for file or directory existence, respectively. The exit code of the command is 0 if the file or directory exists, and 1 if it doesn't:

```
$ hadoop fs -test -e hdfs-file.txt
$ echo $?
1
$ hadoop fs -touchz hdfs-file.txt
$ hadoop fs -test -e hdfs-file.txt
$ echo $?
0
$ hadoop fs -test -d hdfs-file.txt
$ echo $?
1
```

If all you want to do is "touch" a file in HDFS (create a new empty file), the touchz option is what you're looking for:

```
$ hadoop fs -touchz hdfs-file.txt
```

There are many more operations supported by the fs command—to see the full list, run the command without any options:

```
$ hadoop fs
Usage: hadoop fs [generic options]
    [-appendToFile <localsrc> ... <dst>]
    [-cat [-ignoreCrc] <src> ...]
    [-checksum <src> ...]
    [-chgrp [-R] GROUP PATH...]
    [-chmod [-R] <MODE[,MODE]... | OCTALMODE> PATH...]
    [-chown [-R] [OWNER][:[GROUP]] PATH...]
    [-copyFromLocal [-f] [-p] <localsrc> ... <dst>]
    [-copyToLocal [-p] [-ignoreCrc] [-crc] <src> ... <localdst>]
    [-count [-q] <path> ...]
    [-cp [-f] [-p] <src> ... <dst>]
    [-createSnapshot <snapshotDir> [<snapshotName>]]
    [-deleteSnapshot <snapshotDir> <snapshotName>]
    [-df [-h] [<path> ...]]
    [-du [-s] [-h] <path> ...]
    [-expunge]
    [-get [-p] [-ignoreCrc] [-crc] <src> ... <localdst>]
    [-getmerge [-nl] <src> <localdst>]
    [-help [cmd ...]]
    [-ls [-d] [-h] [-R] [<path> ...]]
    [-mkdir [-p] <path> ...]
    [-moveFromLocal <localsrc> ... <dst>]
    [-moveToLocal <src> <localdst>]
    [-mv <src> ... <dst>]
    [-put [-f] [-p] <localsrc> ... <dst>]
    [-renameSnapshot <snapshotDir> <oldName> <newName>]
    [-rm [-f] [-r|-R] [-skipTrash] <src> ...]
    [-rmdir [--ignore-fail-on-non-empty] <dir> ...]
    [-setrep [-R] [-w] <rep> <path> ...]
    [-stat [format] <path> ...]
    [-tail [-f] <file>]
```

```
[-test -[defsz] <path>]
[-text [-ignoreCrc] <src> ...]
[-touchz <path> ...]
[-usage [cmd ...]]
```

The CLI is designed for interactive HDFS activities, and it can also be incorporated into scripts for some tasks you wish to automate. The disadvantage of the CLI is that it's low-level and doesn't have any automation mechanisms built in, so you'll need to look elsewhere if that's your goal. It also requires a fork for each command, which may be fine if you're using it in a bash script, but it likely isn't what you want to use if you're trying to integrate HDFS functionality into a Python or Java application. In that case, the overhead of launching an external process for each command, in addition to the brittle nature of launching and interacting with an external process, is likely something you'll want to avoid.

The next technique is more suited to working with HDFS in programming languages such as Python.

TECHNIQUE 34   **Using REST to load files**

The CLI is handy for quickly running commands and for scripting. However, it incurs the overhead of forking a separate process for each command, which is overhead that you'll probably want to avoid, especially if you're interfacing with HDFS in a programming language. This technique covers working with HDFS in languages other than Java (which is covered in a subsequent section).

■ **Problem**

You want to be able to interact with HDFS from a programming language that doesn't have a native interface to HDFS.

■ **Solution**

Use Hadoop's WebHDFS interface, which offers a full-featured REST API for HDFS operations.

■ **Discussion**

Before you get started, you'll need to make sure WebHDFS is enabled on your cluster (by default it's not). This is governed by the dfs.webhdfs.enabled property. If it's not enabled, you'll need to update hdfs-site.xml and add the following:

```
<property>
    <name>dfs.webhdfs.enabled</name>
    <value>true</value>
</property>
```

In this technique, we'll cover running WebHDFS on an unsecured Hadoop cluster.[3] If you're working on a secure Hadoop cluster, you won't supply the user.name argument;

---

[3] In an unsecured Hadoop cluster (which is the default setup), any user can masquerade as another user in the cluster. This is especially problematic with WebHDFS, which exposes the username directly in the URL, making it trivial to enter some other user's name. Hadoop security in the form of Kerberos will prevent this from happening because it requires that users be authenticated via LDAP or Active Directory prior to interacting with Hadoop.

instead you'll authenticate with Kerberos using `kinit` prior to interacting with Web-HDFS, and then supply `--negotiate -u:youruser` in the curl command line.

> **Warning: Running WebHDFS on an unsecured cluster** If WebHDFS is enabled for a cluster where security is turned off, then it can easily be used to run commands as arbitrary users in your cluster (simply change the username in the URL to be any user in the cluster). It's recommended that you only run WebHDFS with security turned on.

Because you're using HTTP to communicate with the NameNode in this technique, you'll need to know the host and port that the NameNode RPC service is running on. This is configured with the `dfs.namenode.http-address` property. In a pseudo-distributed setup, this is most likely set to `0.0.0.0:50070`. We'll assume a pseudo-distributed setup for the rest of this technique—substitute the appropriate host and port for your setup.

You can start by creating a file in HDFS using the CLI:

```
$ echo "the cat sat on the mat" | hadoop fs -put - /tmp/hdfs-file.txt
```

You can use WebHDFS to get at all sorts of interesting metadata about the file (replace aholmes in the following URL with your username):

```
$ curl -L "http://0.0.0.0:50070/webhdfs/v1/tmp/hdfs-file.txt?
  op=GETFILESTATUS&user.name=aholmes"
{"FileStatus":{
  "accessTime":1389106989995,
  "blockSize":134217728,
  "childrenNum":0,
  "fileId":21620,
  "group":"supergroup",
  "length":23,
  "modificationTime":1389106990223,
  "owner":"aholmes",
  "pathSuffix":"",
  "permission":"644",
  "replication":1,
  "type":"FILE"
}}
```

The syntax for commands is composed of two parts: first the path, followed by the operation being performed. You also need to supply the username that you wish to execute the operation as; otherwise HDFS will assume you're an anonymous user with restricted access. Figure 5.1 highlights these parts of the URL path.

The path being operated on.

The operation being performed on the path.

The user that you wish to execute the command as. Only required if Kerberos isn't configured for your cluster.

Figure 5.1
Dissecting the
WebHDFS URL path

Reading the file from HDFS is just a matter of specifying OPEN as the operation:

```
$ curl -L "http://0.0.0.0:50070/webhdfs/v1/tmp/hdfs-file.txt?
op=OPEN&user.name=aholmes"
the cat sat on the mat
```

Writing a file using WebHDFS is a two-step process. The first step informs the Name-Node of your intent to create a new file. You do that with an HTTP PUT command:

```
$ echo "the cat sat on the mat" > local.txt
$ curl -i -X PUT "http://0.0.0.0:50070/webhdfs/v1/tmp/new-file.txt?
op=CREATE&user.name=aholmes"

HTTP/1.1 307 TEMPORARY_REDIRECT
...
Location: http://localhost.localdomain:50075/webhdfs/v1/tmp/
new-file.txt?op=CREATE&user.name=aholmes&
namenoderpcaddress=localhost:8020&overwrite=false
...
```

At this point, the file hasn't been written yet—you just gave the NameNode the opportunity to determine which DataNode you'll be writing to, which was specified in the "Location" header in the response. You'll need to grab that URL and then issue a second HTTP PUT to perform the actual write:

```
$ curl -i -X PUT -T local.txt \
"http://localhost.localdomain:50075/webhdfs/v1/tmp/new-file.txt?
op=CREATE&user.name=aholmes&namenoderpcaddress=localhost:8020
&overwrite=false"
```

You can verify that the write was successful with a read of the file:

```
$ hadoop fs -cat /tmp/new-file.txt
the cat sat on the mat
```

WebHDFS supports all the HDFS operations that you can perform using the regular command line,[4] and it's more useful because it gives you access to metadata in a structured JSON form, which makes it easier to parse the data.

It's worth mentioning some additional features provided by WebHDFS. First, data locality is present for the first block of the file. The NameNode redirects the client to the DataNode that hosts the first block, giving you strong data locality. For subsequent blocks in the file, the DataNode acts as a proxy and streams data to and from the node that holds the block's data.

WebHDFS is also integrated with Hadoop's secure authentication, meaning that you can enable Kerberos and use the delegation tokens in your HTTP requests. Additionally, the API will maintain wire-level compatibility across Hadoop releases, meaning that

---

[4] See the WebHDFS REST API page (http://hadoop.apache.org/docs/stable/hadoop-project-dist/hadoop-hdfs/WebHDFS.html) for the full set of operations you can perform.

the commands you issue today will work with future versions of Hadoop (and vice versa). This is a useful tool for accessing multiple clusters running different versions of Hadoop.

There are several projects that provide WebHDFS libraries in various languages (listed in table 5.1) to make it easier for you to get up and running with it.[5]

Table 5.1 WebHDFS libraries

Language	Link
C	libwebhdfs (bundled with Hadoop)
Python	https://github.com/drelu/webhdfs-py
Ruby	https://github.com/kzk/webhdfs https://rubygems.org/gems/webhdfs
Perl	http://search.cpan.org/~afaris/Apache-Hadoop-WebHDFS-0.04/lib/Apache/Hadoop/WebHDFS.pm

WebHDFS is useful when the client has access to all the NameNodes and DataNodes. In locked-down environments, this may not be the case, and you may need to look at HttpFS.

TECHNIQUE 35 Accessing HDFS from behind a firewall

Production Hadoop environments are often locked down to protect the data in these clusters. Part of the security procedures could include putting your cluster behind a firewall, which is a nuisance if you're trying to read from or write to HDFS from outside of the firewall. This technique looks at the HttpFS gateway, which can provide HDFS access using HTTP (which is often opened up on firewalls).

■ **Problem**

You want to write to HDFS, but there's a firewall restricting access to the NameNode and/or the DataNodes.

■ **Solution**

Use the HttpFS gateway, which is a standalone server that provides access to HDFS over HTTP. Because it's a separate service and it's HTTP, it can be configured to run on any host that has access to the Hadoop nodes, and you can open a firewall rule to allow traffic to the service.

■ **Discussion**

HttpFS is useful because not only does it allow you use REST to access HDFS, but it has a complete Hadoop filesystem implementation, which means you can use the CLI and native HDFS Java clients to talk to HDFS, as shown in figure 5.2.

---

[5] In fact, a new C client was written in Hadoop 2 called libwebhdfs to leverage WebHDFS. See https://issues.apache.org/jira/browse/HDFS-2656.

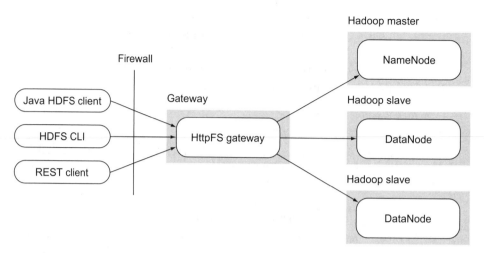

Figure 5.2   The HttpFS gateway architecture

To get HttpFS up and running, you're going to have to designate a proxy user. This is the user that will run the HttpFS process, and this user will also be configured in Hadoop as the proxy user.

Suppose you have a user called foxyproxy that you're going to designate as your proxy user. You'd update your core-site.xml with this:

```
<property>
    <name>hadoop.proxyuser.foxyproxy.hosts</name>
    <value>localhost</value>
  </property>
  <property>
    <name>hadoop.proxyuser.foxyproxy.groups</name>
    <value>*</value>
</property>
```

The hosts that the proxy user is allowed to connect from

The groups that the proxy user is allowed to impersonate

Basically, what you've done here is indicate that Hadoop should only accept proxy requests from host localhost, and that foxyproxy can impersonate any user (you can lock down the set of users that can be impersonated by supplying a comma-separated list of group names). Change the username, host, and group values so that they make sense in your environment.

Once you've made your changes to core-site.xml, you'll have to bounce Hadoop. Next you'll need to start the HttpFS process:

```
$ sbin/httpfs.sh start
```

Now you can issue the same curl commands that you used in the previous technique with WebHDFS. This is one of the nice things about the HttpFS gateway—the syntax is exactly the same. To perform a directory listing on the root directory, you'd do the following:

```
$ curl -i "http://localhost:14000/webhdfs/v1/?user.name=poe&
op=LISTSTATUS"

HTTP/1.1 200 OK
Server: Apache-Coyote/1.1
Set-Cookie: hadoop.auth="u=poe&p=poe&t=simple&e=13...
Content-Type: application/json
Transfer-Encoding: chunked
Date: Fri, 10 Jan 2014 00:09:00 GMT

{"FileStatuses":{"FileStatus":[
  {"pathSuffix":"input",
    "type":"DIRECTORY","length":0,"owner":"aholmes",
    "group":"supergroup","permission":"755","accessTime":0,
    "modificationTime":1388197364463,"blockSize":0,"replication":0},
  {"pathSuffix":"tmp","type":"DIRECTORY","length":0,"owner":"aholmes",
    "group":"supergroup","permission":"755","accessTime":0,
    "modificationTime":1389108717540,"blockSize":0,"replication":0},
  {"pathSuffix":"user","type":"DIRECTORY","length":0,"owner":"aholmes",
    "group":"supergroup","permission":"755","accessTime":0,
    "modificationTime":1388199399483,"blockSize":0,"replication":0}]}}
```

The only difference between this curl command and the ones you used in the previous technique is the port number. HttpFS by default runs on port 14000, but this can be changed by editing `httpfs-env.sh`. Some of the more interesting properties that can be changed in the file are shown in table 5.2.

Table 5.2 HttpFS properties

Property	Default value	Description
HTTPFS_HTTP_PORT	14000	The HTTP port that HttpFS listens on.
HTTPFS_ADMIN_PORT	14001	The admin port for HttpFS.
HTTPFS_LOG	${HTTPFS_HOME}/logs	The logs directory for HttpFS.
HTTPFS_HTTP_HOSTNAME	`hostname -f`	The command used to determine which host HttpFS is running on. This information is passed to the NameNode so it can compare this to the value of hadoop.proxyuser.${user}.hosts that you configured earlier in core-site.xml.

There are additional Kerberos and user- and group-level settings that can be configured in httpfs-site.xml.[6]

---

[6] Consult the "HttpFS configuration properties" web page at http://hadoop.apache.org/docs/stable/hadoop-hdfs-httpfs/httpfs-default.html.

Differences between WebHDFS and HttpFS

The primary difference between WebHDFS and HttpFS is the accessibility of the client to all the data nodes. If your client has access to all the data nodes, then WebHDFS will work for you, as reading and writing files involves the client talking directly to the data nodes for data transfer. On the other hand, if you're behind a firewall, your client probably doesn't have access to all the data nodes, in which case the HttpFS option will work best for you. With HttpFS, the server will talk to the data nodes, and your client just needs to talk to the single HttpFS server.

If you have a choice, pick WebHDFS because there's an inherent advantage in clients talking directly to the data nodes—it allows you to easily scale the number of concurrent clients across multiple hosts without hitting the network bottleneck of all the data being streamed via the HttpFS server. This is especially true if your clients are running on the data nodes themselves, as you'll be using the data locality benefits of WebHDFS by directly streaming any locally hosted HDFS data blocks from the local filesystem instead of over the network.

TECHNIQUE 36   Mounting Hadoop with NFS

Often it's a lot easier to work with Hadoop data if it's accessible as a regular mount to your filesystem. This allows you to use existing scripts, tools, and programming languages and to interact with your data in HDFS. This section looks at how you can easily copy data in and out of HDFS using an NFS mount.

■ **Problem**

You want to treat HDFS as a regular Linux filesystem and use standard Linux tools to interact with HDFS.

■ **Solution**

Use Hadoop's NFS implementation to access data in HDFS.

■ **Discussion**

Prior to Hadoop 2.1, the only way to NFS-mount HDFS was with FUSE. It wasn't recommended for general use due to various performance and reliability issues. It also introduced an additional burden of requiring the driver to be installed on any client machine (in other words, it didn't provide an NFS gateway).

The new NFS implementation in Hadoop addresses all of the shortcomings with the old FUSE-based system. It's a proper NFSv3 implementation, and it allows you to run one or more NFS gateways for increased availability and throughput.

Figure 5.3 shows the various Hadoop NFS components in action.

To get the NFS services up and running, you'll first need to stop the NFS services running on your host. On Linux systems this can be achieved with the following commands:

```
$ service portmap stop
$ service nfs stop
$ service rpcbind stop
```

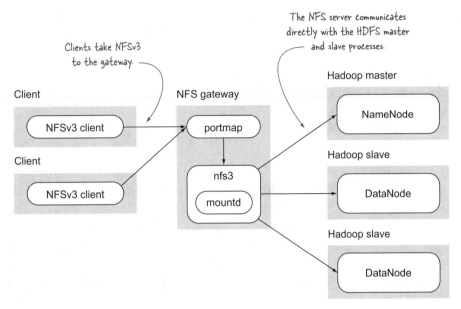

Figure 5.3 Hadoop NFS

Next you need to start the Hadoop NFS services. The first service you'll launch is port-map, which provides a registry service for protocols and their associated transports and ports. It runs on a restricted port, so it needs to be launched as a root user:

```
$ sudo hadoop-daemon.sh start portmap
```

Next you need to start the actual NFS service. It's important that the user running this service be the same user that you use to run HDFS:

```
$ hadoop-daemon.sh start nfs3
```

Verify that the services are running by running rpcinfo and showmount—you should see output similar to the following:

```
$ /usr/sbin/rpcinfo -p localhost
   program vers proto   port
    100005    1   tcp   4242  mountd
    100000    2   udp    111  portmapper
    100005    3   tcp   4242  mountd
    100005    2   udp   4242  mountd
    100003    3   tcp   2049  nfs
    100000    2   tcp    111  portmapper
    100005    3   udp   4242  mountd
    100005    1   udp   4242  mountd
    100005    2   tcp   4242  mountd

$ /usr/sbin/showmount -e localhost
Export list for localhost:
/ *
```

Now you need to mount HDFS on a directory on your host. In the following example I've picked /hdfs as the mount directory. The second mount command verifies that the mount has been created:

```
$ sudo mkdir /hdfs
$ sudo mount -t nfs -o vers=3,proto=tcp,nolock localhost:/  /hdfs

$ mount | grep hdfs
localhost:/ on /hdfs type nfs (rw,nfsvers=3,proto=tcp,nolock,
  addr=127.0.0.1)
```

You're all set! Now you can manipulate HDFS directly using the mounted filesystem.

There are a few things to consider when using the NFS gateway:

- HDFS is an append-only filesystem. You can append to files, but you can't perform random writes. If you have a hard-and-fast requirement that you need to work with Hadoop using a filesystem that supports random writes, you should take a look at MapR's distribution of Hadoop.
- Hadoop version 2.2 doesn't support secure Hadoop (Kerberos), and there's an open ticket to add that support.[7]
- Support for proxy users isn't available until Hadoop 2.4 (or 3). This essentially means that previous versions of Hadoop will execute all commands as superuser, because there's a requirement that the NFS gateway run as the same user as HDFS itself.

Due the these restrictions, it's advised that the NFS gateway be reserved for experimental use, or for use in a single-tenant cluster where user-level security isn't a concern.

TECHNIQUE 37   Using DistCp to copy data within and between clusters

Imagine that you have a large amount of data you want to move into or out of Hadoop. With most of the techniques in this section, you have a bottleneck because you're funneling the data through a single host, which is the host on which you're running the process. To optimize data movement as much as possible, you want to leverage MapReduce to copy data in parallel. This is where DistCp comes into play, and this technique examines several ways that you can use DistCp to efficiently copy data between Hadoop clusters, as well as into and out of an NFS mount.

■ Problem

You want to efficiently copy large amounts of data between Hadoop clusters and have the ability for incremental copies.

■ Solution

Use DistCp, a parallel file-copy tool built into Hadoop.

---

[7] Kerberos support in the NFS gateway is being tracked in https://issues.apache.org/jira/browse/HDFS-5539.

■ **Discussion**

In this section, we'll start by covering the important configuration aspects of DistCp. After that, we'll go on to look at specific scenarios where you'll want to use DistCp, and the best way to configure and run it.

> **DistCp version 2**   This technique covers the newer version of DistCp available in Hadoop 2, called DistCp 2. This code was backported into Hadoop 1.2.0 and is available by using `distcp2` as the command—on Hadoop 2 it replaces the existing DistCp so the normal `distcp` command can be used.

DistCp 2 supports the same set of command-line arguments as the legacy version of DistCp, but brings with it a number of useful advantages:

- Reduced setup and execution time when working with a large number of files, as the driver no longer needs to preprocess all the inputs (this is now deferred to the mappers).
- It now has a full-featured Java interface and removes the need for Java clients to serialize arguments into strings.
- Atomic commits allow all-or-none copying semantics.
- Using option `-update` to skip files that already exist in the destination will result in file attributes being changed if they differ from the source files.
- Empty directories are no longer skipped as part of the copy.

DistCp utilizes a map-only MapReduce job to perform a copy. A very simple example follows, where it's used within a single Hadoop cluster to copy the source directory, /hello, into a destination directory, /world:

```
$ hadoop distcp /hello /world
```

This command will create the /world directory if it doesn't already exist, and then copy the contents of /hello (all its files and directories recursively) into /world. You may be wondering how DistCp deals with files that already exist in the destination—keep on reading for details.

Dealing with destination files that already exist

Files and directories that already exist in the destination are left untouched (even if the files are different). You can change this behavior by adding the arguments shown in table 5.3.

Table 5.3   DistCp arguments that impact where files are copied, and the behavior should destination files preexist

Argument	Description
None (neither `-update` nor `-overwrite`)	Source files are never recopied if the destination already exists.

Table 5.3   DistCp arguments that impact where files are copied, and the behavior should destination files preexist *(continued)*

Argument	Description
-update	Source files are recopied if any of the following are true: ■ Source and destination file sizes are different. ■ Source and destination file CRCs don't match.[a] ■ Source and destination file block sizes don't match.
-overwrite	Source files are always recopied if the destination file already exists.

[a]   File CRC checks can be turned off with the -skipcrccheck argument.

You can see the number of files that are skipped by looking at the SKIP counter that's dumped to standard output when the job completes:

```
org.apache.hadoop.tools.mapred.CopyMapper$Counter
    BYTESSKIPPED=24
    SKIP=2
```

Another factor to understand about the -update and -overwrite arguments is that they subtly change the behavior of what is copied. Without these options, if the source is a directory, that directory is created under the destination directory. With either the -update or -overwrite arguments, only the files and subdirectories are copied, and not the source directory. This is best demonstrated with an example:

```
# create a source directory and file
$ hadoop fs -mkdir /src
$ hadoop fs -touchz /src/file1.txt

# create a destination directory
$ hadoop fs -mkdir /dest

# run a distcp without any options
$ hadoop distcp /src /dest
$ hadoop fs -ls -R /dest
/dest/src
/dest/src/file1.txt

# now run the same command again with
# the -update argument
$ hadoop distcp -update /src /dest
$ hadoop fs -ls -R /dest
/dest/file1.txt
/dest/src
/dest/src/file1.txt
```

Ignoring errors

When you're using DistCp to copy over a large number of files, it's wise to execute the command with the -i flag to ignore errors. This way a single error won't cause your entire copy process to fail, and you can reattempt to copy any failed files by reissuing the same DistCp command with the -update option.

Dynamic copy strategy

The default behavior for DistCp is to preallocate work for each mapper by evenly spreading all the files in such a way that all the mappers are copying approximately the same number of bytes. In theory, this sounds like a great way to fairly allocate work, but in reality, factors such as differing hardware, hardware errors, and poor configuration often results in long-tail job execution, where a handful of straggler mappers take much longer than the others.

With DistCp 2 you can use an alternative strategy, where the mappers pick up work directly as opposed to having it preallocated. This is called the *dynamic copy strategy*, and it's activated with the -strategy dynamic argument. The net effect of adding this argument is improved copy times, as the faster mappers can pick up the slack of the slower mappers.

Atomic commits

Another useful feature in DistCp 2 is the notion of atomic commits. The default behavior of DistCp is for each file to be written to a temporary file and then moved to the final destination. This means that there would be no way to undo any files that were copied prior to an error encountered in the job.

Atomic commits therefore allow you to defer the actual "commit" until the end of the job when all files have been copied so that you don't see any partial writes if an error is encountered. This feature can be enabled using the -atomic argument.

Parallelism and number of mappers

Currently the most granular unit of work for DistCp is at the file level. Therefore, only one mapper will be used to copy each file, regardless of how large the files are. Bumping up the number of mappers for a job won't have any effect on speeding up the copy.

By default, DistCp runs with 20 mappers, and which files each mapper copies are determined by the copy strategy you have selected. The Hadoop developers put some thought into the default setting for the number of mappers—choosing the right value is a function of how much network bandwidth you want to utilize (discussed next), and how many tasks you want to occupy during the copy.

You can change the number of mappers by specifying -m followed by your desired value.

Bandwidth

A final consideration worth mentioning is the network bandwidth used during a copy. Large copies can saturate and overwhelm the network between clusters. One way to keep on the good side of the network operations folks in your organization is to use the -bandwidth argument to specify a cap on the amount of bandwidth each map task consumes during a copy. The value for this argument is in megabytes per second (MBps).

Additional options

So far we've looked at some of the more interesting options in DistCp. To see the full list of options, you can run the distcp command without any options, or head on over to the online Hadoop docs at http://hadoop.apache.org/docs/r1.2.1/distcp2.html.

Copying data from an NFS mount into HDFS

DistCp may be a good fit if you have files sitting on a filer or a NAS that you want to copy into HDFS. This will only work if all the DataNodes have the data mounted, because the DistCp mappers running on the DataNodes require access to both the source and destination. The following example shows how you would perform the copy. Note the `file` scheme used to tell Hadoop that the local filesystem should be used as the source:

```
$ hadoop distcp file://my_filer/source /dest
```

Copying data within the same cluster

In what situations would you use DistCp in place of a regular `hadoop fs -cp` command? The regular `cp` command is a single-threaded approach to copying data—it goes file by file, and streams the data from the server to the client and back out to the server. Compare that to DistCp, which launches a MapReduce job that uses multiple mappers to perform the copy. As a rule of thumb, you should use the regular copy process when dealing with tens of GBs and consider DistCp when working with hundreds of GBs or more.

When the same cluster is both the source and the destination, nothing special is required to qualify the source or destination:

```
$ hadoop distcp /source /dest
```

Copying between two clusters running the same version of Hadoop

Now let's look at copying data between two clusters running the same version of Hadoop. This approach optimizes for the fact that they're both running the same version of Hadoop by using Hadoop-native filesystem reads and writes, which emphasize data locality. Unfortunately the Hadoop RPC is sensitive to the fact that the client and server versions are identical, so this won't work if the versions differ. In that situation you'll need to skip to the next subsection.

Imagine that you have two HDFS setups, one running on nn1 and the other on nn2, and both NameNodes are running on the default RPC port.[8] Copying files from the /source to the /dest directories between the clusters would be achieved with the following command:

```
$ hadoop distcp hdfs://nn1:8020/source hdfs://nn2:8020/dest
```

With two clusters in play, you may be wondering which cluster you should use to run DistCp. If you have a firewall sitting between the clusters and ports can only be opened in one direction, then you'll have to run the job on the cluster that has read or write access to the other cluster.

Next let's look at how to run DistCp between clusters on different Hadoop versions.

---

[8] To figure out the actual host and port for each NameNode, examine the value of `fs.default.name` or `fs.defaultFS` in core-site.xml.

Copying between clusters running different versions of Hadoop

The previous approach won't work when your clusters are running different versions of Hadoop. Hadoop's RPC doesn't have backward or forward compatibility built into it, so a newer version of the Hadoop client can't talk to an older version of a Hadoop cluster, and vice versa.

With recent versions of Hadoop, you have two options for the copy: the older HFTP and the newer WebHDFS. Let's first look at the legacy method, HFTP.

HFTP is a version-independent interface on HDFS that uses HTTP as the transport mechanism. It offers a read-only view into HDFS, so by definition this means that you'll have to always use it as the source in your DistCp. It's enabled via the hftp scheme in the NameNode URI, as seen in the following example:

```
$ hadoop distcp hftp://nn1:50070/source hdfs://nn2:8020/dest
```

Look at hdfs-site.xml (and hdfs-default.xml if you don't see it in hdfs-site.xml) to figure out the host and port to use for HFTP (specifically dfs.http.port, or dfs.namenode .http-address if it's not set). If securing the data in transit is important to you, look at using the HFTPS scheme, which uses HTTPS for transport (configure or examine dfs.hftp.https.port, which if not set will default to dfs.https.port for the port).

With HFTP(S), you'll have to run the DistCp command on the destination cluster so that HDFS writes using the same Hadoop client version as the destination. But what if this is too constrained for your environment—what if you have a firewall that doesn't allow you to run DistCp on the destination? That's where WebHDFS comes into play.

WebHDFS has the advantage over HFTP of providing both a read and write interface. You can use it for either the source or destination in your DistCp, as shown here:

```
$ hadoop distcp hdfs://nn1:50070/source webhdfs://nn2:50070/dest
```

WebHDFS has an additional benefit in the form of data locality—it uses HTTP redirection when reading and writing data so that reads and writes are performed with the actual DataNode that stores the data. It's highly recommended that you use WebHDFS rather than HFTP for both its writing abilities and the performance improvements.

Examine the value of dfs.namenode.http-address to determine the host and port that you should use with WebHDFS.

Other destinations

DistCp works with any implementation of the Hadoop filesystem interface; table 5.4 shows the most popular implementations that are bundled with Hadoop.

Table 5.4   URI schemes and their related Hadoop filesystem implementations

Scheme	Details
hdfs	Provides native access to Hadoop's own HDFS. The only downside is that backward and forward compatibility aren't supported.
file	Used to read and write from the local filesystem.
hftp and hsftp	A legacy, read-only view on top of HDFS that emphasized API compatibility to support any version of Hadoop. It was the old-school way of copying data between clusters running different versions of Hadoop. hsftp provides an implementation that uses HTTPS for transport for added security.
webhdfs	Can be used with both WebHDFS (see technique 34) if your client has access to the Hadoop cluster, and the HttpFS gateway (see technique 35) for accessing HDFS from behind a firewall. This is the replacement for the read-only hftp implementation. It supports a read and write interface to HDFS. In addition, this filesystem can be used to read and write between different versions of Hadoop.
ftp	Uses FTP as the storage implementation.
s3 and s3n	Provides access to Amazon's S3 filesystem. s3n provides native access to S3, whereas the s3 scheme stores data in a block-based manner to work around S3's maximum file-size constraints.

■ **Summary**

DistCp is a powerful tool for moving data into and between Hadoop filesystems. Features such as incremental copies enable it to be used in a near-continuous fashion to synchronize directories on two systems. And its ability to copy data between Hadoop versions means that it's a very popular way of synchronizing data across multiple Hadoop clusters.

> **Executing DistCp** When you're running a DistCp command, it's recommended that you execute it within a screen session,[9] or at least use nohup to redirect the output to a local file.

One limitation of DistCp is that it supports multiple source directories but only a single destination directory. This means you can't use a single DistCp job to perform a one-directional synchronization between clusters (unless you only need to sync a single directory). In this situation, you could run multiple DistCp jobs, or you could run a single job and sync to a staging directory, and then follow up the copy with a fs -mv to move the staged files into the ultimate destinations.

TECHNIQUE 38   **Using Java to load files**

Let's say you've generated a number of Lucene indexes in HDFS and you want to pull them out to an external host. Maybe, as part of pulling the data out, you want to manipulate the files in some way using Java. This technique shows how the Java HDFS API can be used to read and write data in HDFS.

---

[9] Screen is a Linux utility that manages virtual shells and allows them to persist even when the parent shell has terminated. Matt Cutts has an excellent overview on his site called "A quick tutorial on screen," www.mattcutts.com/blog/a-quick-tutorial-on-screen/.

■ **Problem**

You want to incorporate writing to HDFS into your Java application.

■ **Solution**

Use the Hadoop Java API to access data in HDFS.

■ **Discussion**

The HDFS Java API is nicely integrated with Java's I/O model, which means you can work with regular InputStreams and OutputStreams for I/O. To perform filesystem-level operations such as creating, opening, and removing files, Hadoop has an abstract class called FileSystem, which is extended and implemented for specific filesystems that can be leveraged in Hadoop.

Earlier, in technique 33, you saw an example of how you can use the CLI to stream data from standard input to a file in HDFS:

```
$ echo "hello world" | hadoop fs -put - hdfs-file.txt
```

Let's explore how to do that in Java. There are two main parts to writing the code that does this: getting a handle to the FileSystem and creating the file, and then copying the data from standard input to the OutputStream:

You need a handle to a Configuration object before you can get a handle to a Hadoop filesystem. Creating a Configuration object using the constructor as shown here results in the classpath being searched to load the core-site.xml and hdfs-site.xml files.

Create a Path instance that represents the file you'll be writing to. The Path class is the HDFS representation of a file or directory in a Hadoop filesystem.

Get a handle to a concrete FileSystem. Note that you don't specify which filesystem implementation is used. Instead, this is determined at runtime by loading the configuration properties.

Create a new file, which returns an OutputStream that you can write to.

```
Path output = new Path("output.txt");

Configuration conf = new Configuration();

FileSystem fs = FileSystem.get(conf);

FSDataOutputStream out = fs.create(output, false);

try {
  IOUtils.copyBytes(System.in, out, getConf(), false);
} finally {
  out.close();
}
```

Use the Apache commons I/O library to copy data from standard input to the destination stream.

You can see how this code works in practice by running the following command:

```
$ echo "the cat" | hip hip.ch5.CopyStreamToHdfs --output test.txt

$ hadoop fs -cat test.txt
the cat
```

Let's circle back into the code to understand how it worked. The following code snippet was used to get a handle to the FileSystem. But how did Hadoop know which concrete filesystem to return?

```
FileSystem fs = FileSystem.get(conf);
```

The key is in the conf object that's passed into the get method. What's happening is that the FileSystem class examines the value of the fs.defaultFS property,[10] which contains a URI identifying the filesystem that should be used. By default, this is configured to be the local filesystem (file:///), which is why if you try running Hadoop out of the box without any configuration, you'll be using your local filesystem and not HDFS.

In a pseudo-distributed setup like the one in the appendix, one of the first things you would do is configure core-site.xml with an HDFS filesystem:

```
<property>
    <name>fs.default.name</name>
    <value>hdfs://localhost:8020</value>
</property>
```

Hadoop takes the scheme from the URL (hdfs in the preceding example) and performs a lookup to discover the concrete filesystem. There are two ways that a filesystem can be discovered:

- Built-in filesystems are automatically discovered, and their getScheme methods are called to determine their schemes. In the example of HDFS, the implementation class is org.apache.hadoop.hdfs.DistributedFileSystem and the getScheme method returns hdfs.
- Filesystems that aren't built into Hadoop can be identified by updating coresite .xml with fs.$scheme.impl, where $scheme would be replaced with the scheme identified in the URI.

The FileSystem class has a number of methods for manipulating a filesystem—some of the more commonly used methods are listed here:

```
static FileSystem get(Configuration conf)
static LocalFileSystem getLocal(Configuration conf)
static FSDataOutputStream create(FileSystem fs, Path file)
FSDataInputStream open(Path f, int bufferSize)
boolean delete(Path f, boolean recursive)
boolean mkdirs(Path f)
void copyFromLocalFile(Path src, Path dst)
void copyToLocalFile(Path src, Path dst)
FileStatus getFileStatus(Path f)
void close()
```

5.2.2 Continuous movement of log and binary files into HDFS

Log data has long been prevalent across all applications, but with Hadoop came the ability to process the large volumes of log data produced by production systems. Various systems produce log data, from network devices and operating systems to web servers and applications. These log files all offer the potential for valuable insights into how systems and applications operate, as well as how they're used. What unifies log files is that they tend to be in text form and line-oriented, making them easy to process.

---

[10] fs.default.name is the deprecated property used in Hadoop 1.

In the previous section we covered low-level methods that you can use to copy data into Hadoop. Rather than build your own data-movement tools using these methods, this section introduces some higher-level tools that simplify moving your log and binary data into Hadoop. Tools like Flume, Sqoop, and Oozie provide mechanisms to periodically (or continuously) move data from various data sources such as files, relational databases, and messaging systems into Hadoop, and they've already solved many of the hard problems of dealing with multiple data sources spread across different hosts.

Let's get started by looking at how Flume can be used to ingest log files into HDFS.

> **Preferred data-movement methods**   The techniques in this section work well if you're working in a constrained legacy environment where you have files that you need to automatically move into HDFS.
>
> An alternative architecture would be to use Kafka as a mechanism to transport your data, which would allow you to decouple the producers from the consumers and at the same time enable multiple consumers to operate on the data in different ways. In this situation, you'd use Kafka to both land data on Hadoop and provide a feed into a real-time data-streaming system such as Storm or Spark Streaming, which you could then use to perform near-real-time computations. One scenario that this enables is a Lambda Architecture, which allows you to calculate aggregated data in real time in small increments, and to use the batch tier to perform functions such as error correction and adding new data points, thus playing to the strengths of both real-time and batch systems.

TECHNIQUE 39   Pushing system log messages into HDFS with Flume

A bunch of log files are being produced by multiple applications and systems across multiple servers. There's no doubt there's valuable information to be mined from these logs, but your first challenge is a logistical one of moving these logs into your Hadoop cluster so that you can perform some analysis.

> **Versioning caveat emptor**   This section on Flume covers release 1.4. As with all software, there are no guarantees that the techniques, code, and configuration covered here will work out of the box with different versions of Flume. Further, Flume 1.4 requires some updates to get it to work with Hadoop 2— see the Flume section in the appendix for more details.

■ **Problem**

You want to push all of your production server's system log files into HDFS.

■ **Solution**

For this technique you'll use Flume, a data collection system, to push a Linux log file into HDFS.

■ **Discussion**

Flume, at its heart, is a log file collection and distribution system, and collecting system logs and transporting them to HDFS is its bread and butter. Your first step in this technique will involve capturing all data appended to /var/log/messages and transporting it to HDFS. You'll run a single Flume agent (more details on what that means later), which will do all this work for you.

A Flume agent needs a configuration file to tell it what to do, so let's go ahead and define one for this use case:

```
# define source, channel and sink
agent1.sources = tail_source1
agent1.channels = ch1
agent1.sinks = hdfs_sink1

# define tail source
agent1.sources.tail_source1.type = exec
agent1.sources.tail_source1.channels = ch1
agent1.sources.tail_source1.shell = /bin/bash -c
agent1.sources.tail_source1.command = tail -F /var/log/messages
agent1.sources.tail_source1.interceptors = ts
agent1.sources.tail_source1.interceptors.ts.type = timestamp

# define in-memory channel
agent1.channels.ch1.type = memory
agent1.channels.ch1.capacity = 100000
agent1.channels.ch1.transactionCapacity = 1000

# define HDFS sink properties
agent1.sinks.hdfs_sink1.type = hdfs
agent1.sinks.hdfs_sink1.hdfs.path = /flume/%y%m%d/%H%M%S
agent1.sinks.hdfs_sink1.hdfs.fileType = DataStream
agent1.sinks.hdfs_sink1.channel = ch1
```

We'll examine the contents of this file shortly, but before we do that, let's see Flume in action.

> **System prerequisites** For the following example to work, you'll need to make sure that you're working on a host that has access to a Hadoop cluster (see the appendix if you need to get up one up and running), and that your HADOOP_HOME is configured appropriately. You'll also need to have Flume downloaded and installed and have FLUME_HOME set to point to the installation directory.

Copy the preceding file into your Flume conf directory using the filename tail-hdfs-part1.conf. Once you do that, you're ready to start an instance of a Flume agent:

```
$ ${FLUME_HOME}/bin/flume-ng agent \
  --conf ${FLUME_HOME}/conf/ \
  -f ${FLUME_HOME}/conf/tail-hdfs-part1.conf \
  -Dflume.root.logger=DEBUG,console \
  -n agent1
```

This should generate a lot of output, but ultimately you should see output similar to the following, indicating that everything came up OK:

```
Component type: CHANNEL, name: ch1 started
Exec source starting with command:tail -F /var/log/messages
Component type: SINK, name: hdfs_sink1 started
```

At this point, you should start to see some data appearing in HDFS:

```
$ hadoop fs -lsr /flume
/flume/140120/195155/FlumeData.1390265516304.tmp
```

The .tmp suffix means that Flume has the file open and will continue to write to it. Once it's done, it'll rename the file and remove the suffix:

```
/flume/140120/195155/FlumeData.1390265516304
```

You can cat this file to examine its contents—the contents should line up with `tail /var/log/messages`.

If you got this far, you've completed your first data move with Flume!

Dissecting a Flume agent

Let's take a few steps back and examine what you did. There were two main parts to your work: defining the Flume configuration file, and running the Flume agent. The Flume configuration file contains details on your *sources*, *channels*, and *sinks*. These are all Flume concepts that impact different parts of Flume's data flow. Figure 5.4 shows these concepts in action in a Flume agent.

Let's step through these Flume concepts and look at their purpose and how they work.

Sources

Flume *sources* are responsible for reading data from external clients or from other Flume sinks. A unit of data in Flume is defined as an *event*, which is essentially a payload and

Host

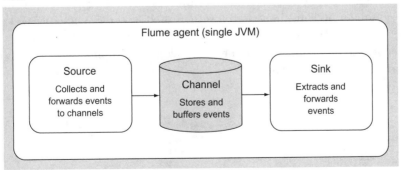

Figure 5.4   Flume components illustrated within the context of an agent

optional set of metadata. A Flume source sends these events to one or more Flume channels, which deal with storage and buffering.

Flume has an extensive set of built-in sources, including HTTP, JMS, and RPC, and you encountered one of them just a few moments ago.[11] Let's take a look at the source-specific configuration properties that you set:

```
agent1.sources = tail_source1

# define tail source
agent1.sources.tail_source1.type = exec
agent1.sources.tail_source1.channels = ch1
agent1.sources.tail_source1.shell = /bin/bash -c
agent1.sources.tail_source1.command = tail -F /var/log/messages
agent1.sources.tail_source1.interceptors = ts
agent1.sources.tail_source1.interceptors.ts.type = timestamp
```

The exec source allows you to execute a Unix command, and each line emitted in standard output is captured as an event (standard error is ignored by default). In the preceding example, the `tail -F` command is used to capture system messages as they are produced.[12] If you have more control over your files (if, for example, you can move them into a directory after all writes have completed), consider using Flume's spooling directory source (called `spooldir`), as it offers reliability semantics that you don't get with the exec source.

> **Only use `tail` for testing** Using `tail` for anything other than testing is discouraged.

Another feature highlighted in this configuration is interceptors, which allow you to add metadata to events. Recall that the data in HDFS was organized according to a timestamp—the first part was the date, and the second part was the time:

```
/flume/140120/195155/FlumeData.1390265516304
```

You were able to do this because you modified each event with a timestamp interceptor, which inserted into the event header the time in milliseconds when the source processed the event. This timestamp was then used by the Flume HDFS sink to determine where an event was written.

To conclude our brief dive into Flume sources, let's summarize some of the interesting abilities that they provide:

---

[11] The full set of Flume sources can be seen at http://flume.apache.org/FlumeUserGuide.html#flume-sources.
[12] Use of the capital F in `tail` means that `tail` will continue to retry opening the file, which is useful in situations where the file is rotated.

- *Transactional semantics*, which allow data to be reliably moved with at-least-once semantics. Not all data sources support this.[13]
- *Interceptors*, which provide the ability to modify or drop events. They are useful for annotating events with host, time, and unique identifiers, which are useful for deduplication.
- *Selectors*, which allow events to be fanned out or multiplexed in various ways. You can fan out events by replicating them to multiple channels, or you can route them to different channels based on event headers.

Channels

Flume *channels* provide data storage facilities inside an agent. Sources add events to a channel, and sinks remove events from a channel. Channels provide durability properties inside Flume, and you pick a channel based on which level of durability and throughput you need for your application.

There are three channels bundled with Flume:

- *Memory channels* store events in an in-memory queue. This is very useful for high-throughput data flows, but they have no durability guarantees, meaning that if an agent goes down, you'll lose data.
- *File channels* persist events to disk. The implementation uses an efficient write-ahead log and has strong durability properties.
- *JDBC channels* store events in a database. This provides the strongest durability and recoverability properties, but at a cost to performance.

In the previous example, you used an in-memory channel and capped the number of events that it would store at 100,000. Once the maximum number of events is reached in a memory channel, it will start refusing additional requests from sources to add more events. Depending on the type of source, this means that the source will either retry or drop the event (the exec source will drop the event):

```
agent1.channels = ch1

# define in-memory channel
agent1.channels.ch1.type = memory
agent1.channels.ch1.capacity = 100000
agent1.channels.ch1.transactionCapacity = 1000
```

Additional details on Flume channels can be seen at http://flume.apache.org/FlumeUserGuide.html#flume-channels.

Sinks

A Flume *sink* drains events out of one or more Flume channels and will either forward these events to another Flume source (in a multihop flow), or handle the events in a sink-specific manner. There are a number of sinks built into Flume, including HDFS, HBase, Solr, and Elasticsearch.

---

[13] The exec source used in this technique is an example of a source that doesn't provide any data-reliability guarantees.

In the previous example, you configured the flow to use an HDFS sink:

```
agent1.sinks = hdfs_sink1

# define HDFS sink properties
agent1.sinks.hdfs_sink1.type = hdfs
agent1.sinks.hdfs_sink1.hdfs.path = /flume/%y%m%d/%H%M%S
agent1.sinks.hdfs_sink1.hdfs.fileType = DataStream
agent1.sinks.hdfs_sink1.channel = ch1
```

You configured the sink to write files based on a timestamp (note the %y and other timestamp aliases). You could do this because you decorated the events with a timestamp interceptor in the exec source. In fact, you can use any header value to determine the output location for events (for example, you can add a host interceptor and then write files according to which host produced the event).

The HDFS sink can be configured in various ways to determine how files are rolled. When a sink reads the first event, it will open a new file (if one isn't already open) and write to it. By default, the sink will continue to keep the file open and write events into it for 30 seconds, after which it will close it out. The rolling behavior can be changed with the properties in table 5.5.

Table 5.5   Rollover properties for Flume's HDFS sink

Property	Default value	Description
hdfs.rollInterval	30	Number of seconds to wait before rolling current file (0 = never roll based on time interval)
hdfs.rollSize	1024	File size to trigger roll, in bytes (0 = never roll based on file size)
hdfs.rollCount	10	Number of events written to file before it rolls (0 = never roll based on number of events)
hdfs.idleTimeout	0	Timeout after which inactive files get closed (0 = disable automatic closing of idle files)
hdfs.batchSize	100	Number of events written to file before it's flushed to HDFS

> **Default settings for the HDFS sink**   The default HDFS sink settings shouldn't be used in production, as they'll result in a large number of potentially small files. It's recommended that you either bump up the values or use a downstream compaction job to coalesce these small files.

The HDFS sink allows you to specify how events are serialized when writing files. By default, they're serialized in text format, without any headers added by interceptors. If, for example, you want to write data in Avro, which also includes event headers, you can use the serializer configuration to do this. In doing so, you can also specify a Hadoop compression codec that Avro uses internally to compress data:

```
agent1.sinks.hdfs_sink1.serializer = avro_event
agent1.sinks.hdfs_sink1.serializer.compressionCodec = snappy
```

■ Summary

Reliability in Flume is determined by the type of channel you use, whether your data sources have the ability to retransmit events, and whether you multiplex events to multiple sources to mitigate against unrecoverable node failure. In this technique, the memory channel and exec source were used, but neither provides reliability in the face of failure. One way to add that reliability would be to replace the exec source with a spooling directory source and replace the memory channel with a disk channel.

You've used Flume on a single machine running a single agent with a single source, channel, and sink. But Flume can support a fully distributed setup where you have agents running on multiple hosts with multiple agent hops between the source and final destinations. Figure 5.5 shows one example of how Flume can function in a distributed environment.

The goal of this technique is to move data into HDFS. Flume, however, can support various data sinks, including HBase, a file roll, Elasticsearch, and Solr. Using Flume to write to Elasticsearch or Solr enables a powerful near-real-time indexing strategy.

Flume, then, is a very powerful data movement project, which can easily support moving your data into HDFS as well as many other locations. It moves data continuously and

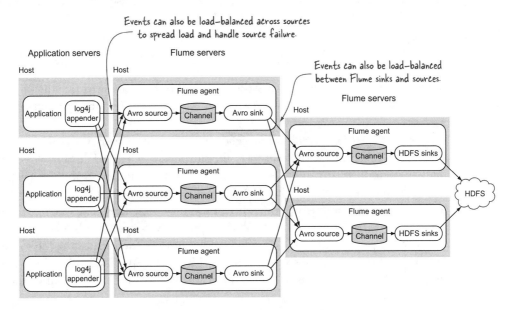

Figure 5.5   A Flume setup that uses load balancing and fan-in to move log4j logs into HDFS

supports various levels of resiliency to work around failures in your systems. And it's a simple system to configure and run.

One area that Flume isn't really optimized for is working with binary data. It can support moving binary data, but it loads the entire binary event into memory, so moving files that are gigabytes in size or larger won't work. The next technique looks at how such data can be moved into HDFS.

TECHNIQUE 40   **An automated mechanism to copy files into HDFS**

You've learned how to use log-collecting tools like Flume to automate moving data into HDFS. But these tools don't support working with semistructured or binary data out of the box. In this technique, we'll look how to automate moving such files into HDFS.

Production networks typically have network silos where your Hadoop clusters are segmented away from other production applications. In such cases, it's possible that your Hadoop cluster won't be able to pull data from other data sources, leaving you with no option but to push data into Hadoop.

You need a mechanism to automate the process of copying files of any format into HDFS, similar to the Linux tool rsync. The mechanism should be able to compress files written in HDFS and offer a way to dynamically determine the HDFS destination for data-partitioning purposes.

Existing file transportation mechanisms such as Flume, Scribe, and Chukwa are geared toward supporting log files. What if you have different formats for your files, such as semistructured or binary? If the files were siloed in a way that the Hadoop slave nodes couldn't directly access, then you couldn't use Oozie to help with file ingress either.

■ **Problem**

You need to automate the process by which files on remote servers are copied into HDFS.

■ **Solution**

The open source HDFS File Slurper project can copy files of any format into and out of HDFS. This technique covers how it can be configured and used to copy data into HDFS.

■ **Discussion**

You can use the HDFS File Slurper project (which I wrote) to assist with your automation (https://github.com/alexholmes/hdfs-file-slurper). The HDFS File Slurper is a simple utility that supports copying files from a local directory into HDFS and vice versa.

Figure 5.6 provides a high-level overview of the Slurper (my nickname for the project), with an example of how you can use it to copy files. The Slurper reads any files that exist in a source directory and optionally consults with a script to determine the file placement in the destination directory. It then writes the file to the destination, after which there's an optional verification step. Finally, the Slurper moves the source file to a completed folder upon successful completion of all of the previous steps.

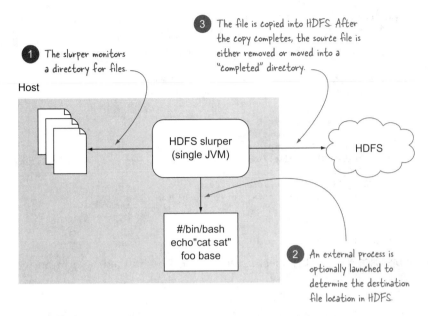

Figure 5.6 HDFS File Slurper data flow for copying files

With this technique, there are a few challenges you need to make sure to address:

- How do you effectively partition your writes to HDFS so that you don't lump everything into a single directory?
- How do you determine that your data in HDFS is ready for processing (to avoid reading files that are mid-copy)?
- How do you automate regular execution of your utility?

Your first step is to download the latest HDFS File Slurper tarball from https://github.com/alexholmes/hdfs-file-slurper/releases and install it on a host that has access to both a Hadoop cluster and a local install of Hadoop:

```
$ sudo tar -xzf target/hdfs-slurper-<version>-package.tar.gz \
  -C /usr/local/

$ sudo ln -s /usr/local/hdfs-slurper-<version> \
    /usr/local/hdfs-slurper
```

Configuration

Before you can run the code, you'll need to edit /usr/local/hdfs-slurper/conf/slurper-env.sh and set the location of the hadoop script. The following code is an example of what slurper-eng.sh file looks like if you followed the Hadoop installation instructions in the appendix:

```
$ cat /usr/local/hdfs-slurper/conf/slurper-env.sh
export HADOOP_BIN=/usr/local/hadoop/bin/hadoop
```

The Slurper comes bundled with a /usr/local/hdfs-slurper/conf/slurper.conf file, which contains details on the source and destination directories, along with other options. The file contains the following default settings, which you can change:

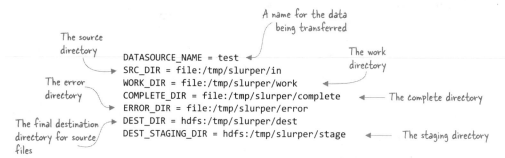

Let's take a closer look at these settings:

- DATASOURCE_NAME—This specifies the name for the data being transferred. It's used for the log filename when launched via the Linux init daemon management system, which we'll cover shortly.

- SRC_DIR—This specifies the source directory. Any files moved into here are automatically copied to the destination directory (with an intermediary hop to the staging directory).

- WORK_DIR—This is the work directory. Files from the source directory are moved here before the copy to the destination starts.

- COMPLETE_DIR—This specifies the complete directory. After the copy has completed, the file is moved from the work directory into this directory. Alternatively, the --remove-after-copy option can be used to delete the source file, in which case the --complete-dir option shouldn't be supplied.

- ERROR_DIR—This is the error directory. Any errors encountered during the copy result in the source file being moved into this directory.

- DEST_DIR—This sets the final destination directory for source files.

- DEST_STAGING_DIR—This specifies the staging directory. A file is first copied into this directory, and once the copy succeeds, the Slurper moves the copy into the destination to avoid the possibility of the destination directory containing partially written files (in the event of failure).

You'll notice that all of the directory names are HDFS URIs. HDFS distinguishes between different filesystems in this way. The file:/ URI denotes a path on the local filesystem, and the hdfs:/ URI denotes a path in HDFS. In fact, the Slurper supports any Hadoop filesystem, as long as you configure Hadoop to use it.

Running

Let's create a local directory called /tmp/slurper/in, write an empty file into it, and run the Slurper:

```
$ mkdir -p /tmp/slurper/in
$ touch /tmp/slurper/in/test-file.txt

$ cd /usr/local/hdfs-slurper/
$ bin/slurper.sh  --config-file conf/slurper.conf

Copying source file 'file:/tmp/slurper/work/test-file.txt'
to staging destination 'hdfs:/tmp/slurper/stage/1354823335'

Moving staging file 'hdfs:/tmp/slurper/stage/1354823335'
to destination 'hdfs:/tmp/slurper/dest/test-file.txt'

File copy successful, moving source
file:/tmp/slurper/work/test-file.txt to completed file
file:/tmp/slurper/complete/test-file.txt

$ hadoop fs -ls /tmp/slurper/dest
/tmp/slurper/dest/test-file.txt
```

A key feature in the Slurper's design is that it doesn't work with partially written files. Files must be atomically moved into the source directory (file moves in both the Linux and HDFS filesystems are atomic).[14] Alternatively, you can write to a filename that starts with a period (.), which is ignored by the Slurper, and after the file write completes, you can rename the file to a name without the period prefix.

Be aware that copying multiple files with the same filename will result in the destination being overwritten—the onus is on the user to make sure that files are unique to prevent this from happening.

Dynamic destination paths

The previous approach works well if you're moving a small number of files into HDFS on a daily basis. But if you're dealing with a large volume of files, you'll want to think about partitioning them into separate directories. This has the benefit of giving you more fine-grained control over the input data for your MapReduce jobs, as well as helping with the overall organization of your data in the filesystem (you wouldn't want all the files on your computer to reside in a single flat directory).

How can you have more dynamic control over the destination directory and the filename that the Slurper uses? The Slurper configuration file has a SCRIPT option (which is mutually exclusive of the DEST_DIR option), where you can specify a script that provides dynamic mapping of the source files to destination files.

Let's assume that the files you're working with contain a date in the filename, and you've decided that you want to organize your data in HDFS by date. You can write a script to perform this mapping activity. The following example is a Python script that does this:

---

[14] Moving files is atomic only if both the source and destination are on the same partition. In other words, moving a file from an NFS mount to a local disk results in a copy, which isn't atomic.

```
#!/usr/bin/python

import sys, os, re

# read the local file from standard input
input_file=sys.stdin.readline()

# extract the filename from the file
filename = os.path.basename(input_file)

# extract the date from the filename
match=re.search(r'([0-9]{4})([0-9]{2})([0-9]{2})', filename)

year=match.group(1)
mon=match.group(2)
day=match.group(3)

# construct our destination HDFS file
hdfs_dest="hdfs:/data/%s/%s/%s/%s" % (year, mon, day, filename)

# write it to standard output
print hdfs_dest,
```

Now you can update /usr/local/hdfs-slurper/conf/slurper.conf, set SCRIPT, and comment out DEST_DIR, which results in the following entry in the file:

```
# DEST_DIR = hdfs:/tmp/slurper/dest

SCRIPT = /usr/local/hdfs-slurper/bin/sample-python.py
```

If you run the Slurper again, you'll notice that the destination path is now partitioned by date by the Python script:

```
$ touch /tmp/slurper/in/apache-20110202.log

$ bin/slurper.sh  --config-file conf/slurper.conf

Launching script '/usr/local/hdfs-slurper/bin/sample-python.py' and
piping the following to stdin 'file:/tmp/slurper/work/apache-20110202.log'
...
Moving staging file 'hdfs:/tmp/slurper/stage/675861557' to destination
'hdfs:/data/2011/02/02/apache-20110202.log'
```

Compression and verification

What if you want to compress the output file in HDFS and also verify that the copy is correct? You'll need to use the COMPRESSION_CODEC option, whose value is a class that implements the CompressionCodec interface. If your compression codec is LZO or LZOP, you can also add a CREATE_LZO_INDEX option so that LZOP indexes are created. If you don't know what this means, take a look at the LZO coverage in chapter 4.

Also available is a verification feature, which rereads the destination file after the copy has completed and ensures that the checksum of the destination file matches the source file. This results in longer processing times, but it adds an additional level of assurance that the copy was successful.

The following configuration fragment shows the LZOP codec, LZO indexing, and file verification enabled:

```
COMPRESSION_CODEC = com.hadoop.compression.lzo.LzopCodec
CREATE_LZO_INDEX = true
VERIFY = true
```

Let's run the Slurper again:

```
$ touch /tmp/slurper/in/apache-20110202.log

$ bin/slurper.sh  --config-file conf/slurper.conf

Verifying files
CRC's match (0)
Moving staging file 'hdfs:/tmp/slurper/stage/535232571'
to destination 'hdfs:/data/2011/02/02/apache-20110202.log.snappy'
```

Continuous operation

Now that you have the basic mechanics in place, your final step is to run the tool as a daemon so that it continuously looks for files to transfer. To do this, you can use a script called bin/slurper-inittab.sh, which is designed to work with the inittab respawn.[15]

This script won't create a PID file or perform a nohup—neither makes sense in the context of respawn, because inittab is managing the process. It uses the DATASOURCE_NAME configuration value to create the log filename. This means that multiple Slurper instances can all be launched with different config files logging to separate log files.

■ Summary

The Slurper is a handy tool for data ingress from a local filesystem to HDFS. It also supports data egress by copying from HDFS to the local filesystem. It can be useful in situations where MapReduce doesn't have access to the filesystem and the files being transferred are in a form that doesn't work with tools such as Flume.

Now let's look at automated pulls for situations where MapReduce or HDFS has access to your data sources.

TECHNIQUE 41　Scheduling regular ingress activities with Oozie

If your data is sitting on a filesystem, web server, or any other system accessible from your Hadoop cluster, you'll need a way to periodically pull that data into Hadoop. Tools exist to help with pushing log files and pulling from databases (which we'll cover in this chapter), but if you need to interface with some other system, it's likely you'll need to handle the data ingress process yourself.

Oozie versions　This technique covers using Oozie version 4.0.0.

---

[15] Inittab is a Linux process-management tool that you can configure to supervise and restart a process if it goes down. See INITTAB(5) in the Linux System Administrator's Manual: http://unixhelp.ed.ac.uk/CGI/man-cgi?inittab+5 .

There are two parts to this data ingress process: how you import data from another system into Hadoop, and how you regularly schedule the data transfer.

■ **Problem**

You want to automate a daily task to download content from an HTTP server into HDFS.

■ **Solution**

Oozie can be used to move data into HDFS, and it can also be used to execute post-ingress activities such as launching a MapReduce job to process the ingested data. Now an Apache project, Oozie started life inside Yahoo!. It's a Hadoop workflow engine that manages data processing activities. Oozie also has a coordinator engine that can start workflows based on data and time triggers.

■ **Discussion**

In this technique, you'll perform a download from a number of URLs every 24 hours, using Oozie to manage the workflow and scheduling. The flow for this technique is shown in figure 5.7. You'll use Oozie's triggering capabilities to kick off a MapReduce job every 24 hours. The appendix contains Oozie installation instructions.

The first step is to look at the coordinator XML configuration file. This file is used by Oozie's coordination engine to determine when it should kick off a workflow. Oozie uses a template engine and expression language to perform parameterization, as you'll see in the following code. Create a file called coordinator.xml with the following content:[16]

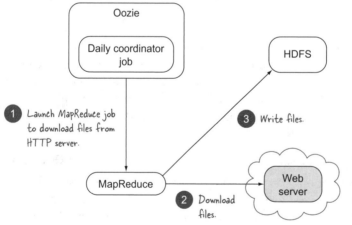

Figure 5.7   Data flow for this Oozie technique

---

[16] GitHub source: https://github.com/alexholmes/hiped2/blob/master/src/main/oozie/http-download/coordinator.xml.

Listing 5.1 Using a template engine to perform parameterization with Oozie

The materialized starting date for the job.

The end date for job.

Specifies how many workflows can execute concurrently.

Input filename for the MapReduce job.

Specifies how often the coordinator is scheduled to run, expressed in minutes. The coord qualifier provides access to some Oozie-defined functions, such as days, which provides the number of minutes in a day.

Output directory for the MapReduce job.

```
<coordinator-app name="http-download"
    frequency="${coord:days(1)}"
    start="${start}"
    end="${end}"
    timezone="UTC"
    xmlns="uri:oozie:coordinator:0.2">

    <controls>
        <concurrency>1</concurrency>
    </controls>

    <action>
        <workflow>
            <app-path>${workingDirectory}</app-path>
            <configuration>
                <property>
                    <name>inputData</name>
                    <value>
${nameNode}/user/${coord:user()}/http-download/input-urls.txt
                    </value>
                </property>
                <property>
                    <name>outputData</name>
                    <value>
${nameNode}/user/${coord:user()}/http-download/output/
${coord:formatTime(coord:nominalTime(), "yyyy/MM/dd")}
                    </value>
                </property>
            </configuration>
        </workflow>
    </action>
</coordinator-app>
```

What can be confusing about Oozie's coordinator is that the start and end times don't relate to the actual times when the jobs will be executed. Rather, they refer to the dates that will be created ("materialized") for each workflow execution. This is useful in situations where you have data being generated at periodic intervals and you want to be able to go back in time to a certain point and perform some work on that data. In this example, you don't want to go back in time, but instead want to schedule a job every 24 hours going forward. But you won't want to wait until the next day, so you can set the start date to be yesterday, and the end date to be some far-off date in the future.

Next you need to define the actual workflow, which will be executed for every interval in the past, and, going forward, when the wall clock reaches an interval. To do this, create a file called workflow.xml with the content shown in the next listing.[17]

---

[17] GitHub source: https://github.com/alexholmes/hiped2/blob/master/src/main/oozie/http-download/ workflow.xml.

Listing 5.2   Defining the past workflow using Oozie's coordinator

```
<workflow-app xmlns="uri:oozie:workflow:0.1" name="download-http">
  <start to="download-http"/>
  <action name="download-http">
    <map-reduce>
      <name-node>${nameNode}</name-node>
      <prepare>
        <delete path="${outputData}"/>
      </prepare>
      <configuration>
        <property>
          <name>mapred.mapper.class</name>
          <value>hip.ch5.http.HttpDownloadMap</value>
        </property>
        <property>
          <name>mapred.input.dir</name>
          <value>${inputData}</value>
        </property>
        <property>
          <name>mapred.output.dir</name>
          <value>${outputData}</value>
        </property>
      </configuration>
    </map-reduce>
    <ok to="end"/>
    <error to="fail"/>
  </action>
  <kill name="fail">
    <message>Map/Reduce failed, error
      message[${wf:errorMessage(wf:lastErrorNode())}]
    </message>
  </kill>
  <end name="end"/>
</workflow-app>
```

Delete output directory before running MapReduce job

Map class

Input directory for job

Output directory for job

Action needed if job fails; logs error message

Working with the new MapReduce APIs in Oozie   By default, Oozie expects that your map and reduce classes use the "old" MapReduce APIs. If you want to use the "new" APIs, you need to specify additional properties:

```
<property>
  <name>mapred.mapper.new-api</name>
  <value>true</value>
</property>

<property>
  <name>mapred.reducer.new-api</name>
  <value>true</value>
</property>
<property>
  <name>mapreduce.map.class</name>
  <value>YOUR-NEW-API-MAP-CLASSNAME</value>
</property>
<property>
  <name>mapreduce.reduce.class</name>
  <value>YOUR-NEW-API-REDUCE-CLASSNAME</value>
</property>
```

The last step is to define your properties file, which specifies how to get to HDFS, MapReduce, and the location of the two XML files previously identified in HDFS. Create a file called job.properties, as shown in the following code:

```
nameNode=hdfs://localhost:8020
jobTracker=0.0.0.0:8032
queueName=default

start=2014-01-23T00:00Z
end=2026-11-29T00:00Z

workingDirectory=${nameNode}/user/${user.name}/http-download

oozie.coord.application.path=${nameNode}/user/${user.name}
    /http-download
```

HDFS location of two XML files

> **JobTracker property for different Hadoop versions** If you're targeting Hadoop 1, you should use the JobTracker RPC port in the `jobTracker` property (the default is 8021). Otherwise use the YARN ResourceManager RPC port (the default is 8032).

In the previous snippet, the location in HDFS indicates where the coordinator.xml and workflow.xml files that you wrote earlier in this chapter are. Now you need to copy the XML files, your input file, and the JAR file containing your MapReduce code into HDFS:

```
$ hadoop fs -put oozie/http-download http-download
$ hadoop fs -put test-data/ch5/http-download/input/* http-download/
$ hadoop fs -mkdir http-download/lib
$ hadoop fs -put hip-2.0.0.jar http-download/lib/
```

Finally, run your job in Oozie:

```
$ oozie job -config src/main/oozie/http-download/job.properties \
  -run
job: 0000006-140124164013396-oozie-ahol-C
```

You can use the job ID to get some information about the job:

```
$ oozie job -info 0000006-140124164013396-oozie-ahol-C
Job ID : 0000006-140124164013396-oozie-ahol-C
------------------------------------------------
Job Name    : http-download
App Path    : hdfs://localhost:8020/user/aholmes/http-download
Status      : RUNNING
Start Time  : 2014-01-23 00:00 GMT
End Time    : 2026-11-29 00:00 GMT
Pause Time  : -
Concurrency : 1
------------------------------------------------
ID              Status    Created             Nominal Time
0000006-1401241... SUCCEEDED 2014-02-16 20:50 GMT 2014-01-23 00:00 GMT
------------------------------------------------
```

This output tells you that the job resulted in one run, and you can see the nominal time for the run. The overall state is RUNNING, which means that the job is waiting for the next interval to occur. When the overall job has completed (after the end date has been reached), the status will transition to SUCCEEDED.

You can confirm that there is an output directory in HDFS corresponding to the materialized date:

```
$ hadoop fs -lsr http-download/output

http-download/output/2014/01/23
```

As long as the job is running, it'll continue to execute until the end date, which in this example has been set as the year 2026. If you wish to stop the job, use the -suspend option:

```
$ oozie job -suspend 0000006-140124164013396-oozie-ahol-C
```

Oozie also has the ability to resume suspended jobs, as well as to kill a workflow, using the -resume and -kill options, respectively.

■ **Summary**

I showed you one example of the use of the Oozie coordinator, which offers cron-like capabilities to launch periodic Oozie workflows. The Oozie coordinator can also be used to trigger a workflow based on data availability (if no data is available, the workflow isn't triggered). For example, if you had an external process, or even MapReduce generating data on a regular basis, you could use Oozie's data-driven coordinator to trigger a workflow, which could aggregate or process that data.

In this section, we covered three automated mechanisms that can be used for data ingress purposes. The first technique covered Flume, a powerful tool for shipping your log data into Hadoop, and the second technique looked at the HDFS File Slurper, which automates the process of pushing data into HDFS. The final technique looked at how Oozie could be used to periodically launch a MapReduce job to pull data into HDFS or MapReduce.

At this point in our exploration of data ingress, we've looked at pushing log files, pushing files from regular filesystems, and pulling files from web servers. Another data source that will be of interest to most organizations is relational data sitting in OLTP databases. Next up is a look at how you can access that data.

5.2.3   *Databases*

Most organizations' crucial data exists across a number of OLTP databases. The data stored in these databases contains information about users, products, and a host of other useful items. If you wanted to analyze this data, the traditional way to do so would be to periodically copy that data into an OLAP data warehouse.

Hadoop has emerged to play two roles in this space: as a replacement to data warehouses, and as a bridge between structured and unstructured data and data warehouses. Figure 5.8 shows the first role, where Hadoop is used as a large-scale

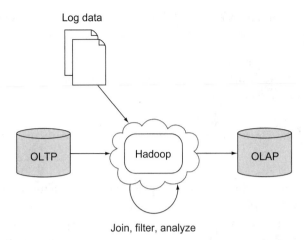

Figure 5.8   **Using Hadoop for data ingress, joining, and egress to OLAP**

joining and aggregation mechanism prior to exporting the data to an OLAP system (a commonly used platform for business intelligence applications).

Facebook is an example of an organization that has successfully utilized Hadoop and Hive as an OLAP platform for working with petabytes of data. Figure 5.9 shows an architecture similar to that of Facebook's. This architecture also includes a feedback loop into the OLTP system, which can be used to push discoveries made in Hadoop, such as recommendations for users.

In either usage model, you need a way to bring relational data into Hadoop, and you also need to export it into relational databases. In this section, you'll use Sqoop to streamline moving your relational data into Hadoop.

TECHNIQUE 42   Using Sqoop to import data from MySQL

Sqoop is a project that you can use to move relational data into and out of Hadoop. It's a great high-level tool as it encapsulates the logic related to the movement of the relational data into Hadoop—all you need to do is supply Sqoop the SQL queries that

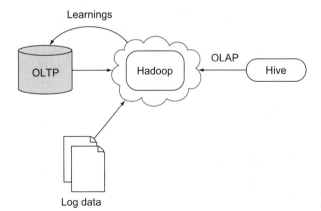

Figure 5.9   **Using Hadoop for OLAP and feedback to OLTP systems**

will be used to determine which data is exported. This technique provides the details on how you can use Sqoop to move some stock data in MySQL to HDFS.

> **Versioning**   This section uses version 1.4.4 of Sqoop. The code and scripts used in this technique may not work with other versions of Sqoop, especially Sqoop 2, which is implemented as a web application.

■ Problem

You want to load relational data into your cluster and ensure your writes are efficient and also idempotent.

■ Solution

In this technique, we'll look at how you can use Sqoop as a simple mechanism to bring relational data into Hadoop clusters. We'll walk through the process of importing data from MySQL into Sqoop. We'll also cover bulk imports using the fast connector (connectors are database-specific components that provide database read and write access).

■ Discussion

Sqoop is a relational database import and export system. It was created by Cloudera and is currently an Apache project in incubation status.

When you perform an import, Sqoop can write to HDFS, Hive, and HBase, and for exports it can do the reverse. Importing is divided into two activities: connecting to the data source to gather some statistics, and then firing off a MapReduce job that performs the actual import. Figure 5.10 shows these steps.

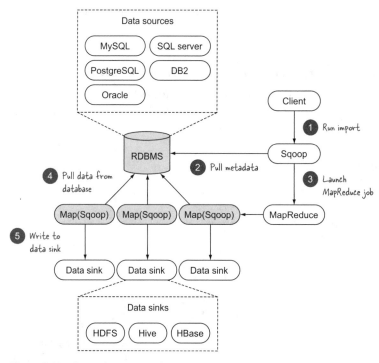

Figure 5.10   Sqoop import overview: connecting to the data source and using MapReduce

Sqoop has the notion of *connectors*, which contain the specialized logic needed to read and write to external systems. Sqoop comes with two classes of connectors: *common connectors* for regular reads and writes, and *fast connectors* that use database-proprietary batch mechanisms for efficient imports. Figure 5.11 shows these two classes of connectors and the databases that they support.

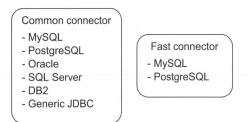

Figure 5.11   Sqoop connectors used to read and write to external systems

Before you can continue, you'll need access to a MySQL database and the MySQL JDBC JAR will need to be available.[18] The following script will create the necessary MySQL user and schema and load the data for this technique. The script creates a `hip_sqoop_user` MySQL user, and creates a sqoop_test database with three tables: stocks, stocks_export, and stocks_staging. It then loads the stocks sample data into the stocks table. All of these steps are performed by running the following command:

```
$ bin/prep-sqoop-mysql
```

Here's a quick peek at what the script does:

```
$ mysql -u hip_sqoop_user -p
<enter "password" for the password>
mysql> use sqoop_test;
mysql> show tables;
+----------------------+
| Tables_in_sqoop_test |
+----------------------+
| stocks               |
| stocks_export        |
| stocks_staging       |
+----------------------+
3 rows in set (0.00 sec)

mysql> select * from stocks;
+----+--------+------------+------------+------------+-----------+---
| id | symbol | quote_date | open_price | high_price | low_price |...
+----+--------+------------+------------+------------+-----------+---
|  1 | AAPL   | 2009-01-02 |      85.88 |      91.04 |     85.16 |...
|  2 | AAPL   | 2008-01-02 |     199.27 |     200.26 |    192.55 |...
|  3 | AAPL   | 2007-01-03 |      86.29 |      86.58 |      81.9 |...
  ...
```

Follow the instructions in the appendix to install Sqoop. Those instructions also contain important steps for installing Sqoop dependencies, such as MySQL JDBC drivers.

_____

[18] MySQL installation instructions can be found in the appendix, if you don't already have it installed. That section also includes a link to get the JDBC JAR.

Your first Sqoop command will be a basic import, where you'll specify connection information for your MySQL database and the table you want to export:

```
$ sqoop import \
    --username hip_sqoop_user \
    --password password \
    --connect jdbc:mysql://localhost/sqoop_test \
    --table stocks
```

> **MySQL table names** MySQL table names in Linux are case-sensitive. Make sure that the table name you supply in the Sqoop commands uses the correct case.

By default, Sqoop uses the table name as the destination in HDFS for the MapReduce job that it launches to perform the import. If you run the same command again, the MapReduce job will fail because the directory already exists.

Let's take a look at the stocks directory in HDFS:

```
$ hadoop fs -ls stocks
624 2011-11-24 11:07 /user/aholmes/stocks/part-m-00000
644 2011-11-24 11:07 /user/aholmes/stocks/part-m-00001
642 2011-11-24 11:07 /user/aholmes/stocks/part-m-00002
686 2011-11-24 11:07 /user/aholmes/stocks/part-m-00003

$ hadoop fs -cat stocks/part-m-00000
1,AAPL,2009-01-02,85.88,91.04,85.16,90.75,26643400,90.75
2,AAPL,2008-01-02,199.27,200.26,192.55,194.84,38542100,194.84
3,AAPL,2007-01-03,86.29,86.58,81.9,83.8,44225700,83.8
...
```

Import data formats

Sqoop has imported the data as comma-separated text files. It supports a number of other file formats, which can be activated with the arguments listed in table 5.6.

Table 5.6 Sqoop arguments that control the file formats of import commands

Argument	Description
--as-avrodatafile	Data is imported as Avro files.
--as-sequencefile	Data is imported as SequenceFiles.
--as-textfile	The default file format; data is imported as CSV text files.

If you're importing large amounts of data, you may want to use a file format such as Avro, which is a compact data format, and use it in conjunction with compression. The following example uses the Snappy compression codec in conjunction with Avro files. It also writes the output to a different directory from the table name by using the --target-dir option and specifies that a subset of rows should be imported by using the --where option. Specific columns to be extracted can be specified with --columns:

```
$ sqoop import \
    --username hip_sqoop_user \
    --password password \
    --as-avrodatafile \
    --compress \
    --compression-codec org.apache.hadoop.io.compress.SnappyCodec \
    --connect jdbc:mysql://localhost/sqoop_test \
    --table stocks \
    --where "symbol = 'AAPL'" \
    --columns "symbol,quote_date,close_price" \
    --target-dir mystocks
```

Note that the compression that's supplied on the command line must be defined in the config file, core-site.xml, under the `io.compression.codecs` property. The Snappy compression codec requires you to have the Hadoop native libraries installed. See chapter 4 for more details on compression setup and configuration.

You can introspect the structure of the Avro file to see how Sqoop has laid out the records by using the AvroDump tool introduced in technique 12. Sqoop uses Avro's `GenericRecord` for record-level storage (more details on that in chapter 3). If you run AvroDump against the Sqoop-generated files in HDFS, you'll see the following:

```
$ hip hip.util.AvroDump --file mystocks/part-m-00000.avro
{"symbol": "AAPL", "quote_date": "2009-01-02", "close_price": 90.75}
{"symbol": "AAPL", "quote_date": "2008-01-02", "close_price": 194.84}
{"symbol": "AAPL", "quote_date": "2007-01-03", "close_price": 83.8}
```

> **Using Sqoop in conjunction with SequenceFiles**   One of the things that makes SequenceFiles hard to work with is that there isn't a generic way to access data in a SequenceFile. You must have access to the `Writable` class that was used to write the data. In Sqoop's case, it code-generates this file, which introduces a major problem: if you move to a newer version of Sqoop, and that version modifies the code generator, there's a chance your older code-generated class won't work with SequenceFiles generated with the newer version of Sqoop. You'll either need to migrate all of your old SequenceFiles to the new version, or have code that can work with different versions of these Sequence-Files. Due to this restriction, I don't recommend using SequenceFiles with Sqoop. If you're looking for more information on how SequenceFiles work, run the Sqoop import tool and look at the stocks.java file that's generated within your working directory.

You can take things a step further and specify the entire query with the `--query` option as follows:

Bash by default performs globbing, meaning that it'll expand wildcards like *. Use GLOBIGNORE to turn this off so that the next line generates the SQL correctly.

```
$ GLOBIGNORE=*
$ read -d '' query << "EOF"
select * from stocks
where symbol in ("AAPL", "GOOG")
```

Store your query in the query variable. The $CONDITIONS is a Sqoop macro that must be present in the WHERE clause of the query. Sqoop replaces $CONDITIONS with relevant LIMIT and OFFSET options when issuing MySQL queries.

```
    and quote_date between "2007-01-01" AND "2007-12-31"
    AND $CONDITIONS
EOF
```

```
$ sqoop import \
    --username hip_sqoop_user \
    --password password \
    --query "$query" \
    --split-by id \
    --connect jdbc:mysql://localhost/sqoop_test \
    --target-dir cstocks
```

This argument must be supplied so that Sqoop can determine which table column to use for splitting.

Securing passwords

Up until now you've been using passwords in the clear on the command line. This is a security hole, because other users on the host can easily list the running processes and see your password. Luckily Sqoop has a few mechanisms that you can use to avoid leaking your password.

The first approach is to use the -P option, which will result in Sqoop prompting you for the password. This is the most secure approach, as it doesn't require you to store your password, but it means you can't automate your Sqoop commands.

The second approach is to use the --password-file option, where you specify a file that contains your password. Note that this file must exist in the configured filesystem (mostly likely HDFS), not on a disk local to the Sqoop client. You'll probably want to lock the file down so that only you have read access to this file. This still isn't the most secure option, as root users on the filesystem would still be able to pry into the file, and unless you're running secure Hadoop, it's fairly easy even for non-root users to gain access.

The last option is to use an options file. Create a file called ~/.sqoop-import-opts:

```
import
--username
hip_sqoop_user
--password
password
```

Don't forget to lock down the file to avoid prying eyes:

```
$ chmod 600 ~/.sqoop-import
```

Then you can supply this filename to your Sqoop job via the --options-file option, and Sqoop will read the options specified in the file, which means you don't need to supply them on the command line:

```
$ sqoop \
    --options-file ~/.sqoop-import-opts \
    --connect jdbc:mysql://localhost/sqoop_test \
    --table stocks
```

Data splitting

How is Sqoop able to parallelize imports across multiple mappers?[19] In figure 5.10 I showed how Sqoop's first step is to pull metadata from the database. It inspects the table being imported to determine the primary key, and runs a query to determine the lower and upper bounds of the data in the table (see figure 5.12). A somewhat even distribution of data within the minimum and maximum keys is assumed by Sqoop as it divides the delta (the range between the minimum and maximum keys) by the number of mappers. Each mapper is then fed a unique query containing a range of the primary key.

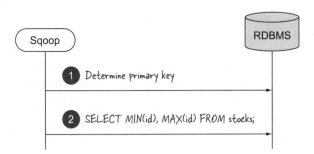

Figure 5.12 Sqoop preprocessing steps to determine query splits

You can configure Sqoop to use a nonprimary key with the `--split-by` argument. This can be useful in situations where the primary key doesn't have an even distribution of values between the minimum and maximum values. For large tables, however, you need to be careful that the column specified in `--split-by` is indexed to ensure optimal import times.

You can use the `--boundary-query` argument to construct an alternative query to determine the minimum and maximum values.

Incremental imports

You can also perform incremental imports. Sqoop supports two types: `append` works for numerical data that's incrementing over time, such as auto-increment keys; `lastmodified` works on timestamped data. In both cases you need to specify the column using `--check-column`, the mode via the `--incremental` argument (the value must be either `append` or `lastmodified`), and the actual value to use to determine the incremental changes via `--last-value`.

For example, if you want to import stock data that's newer than January 1, 2005, you'd do the following:

```
$ sqoop  import \
    --username hip_sqoop_user \
    --password password \
    --check-column "quote_date" \
    --incremental "lastmodified" \
```

---

[19] By default Sqoop runs with four mappers. The number of mappers can be controlled with the `--num-mappers` argument.

```
    --last-value "2005-01-01" \
    --connect jdbc:mysql://localhost/sqoop_test \
    --table stocks
...
tool.ImportTool:  --incremental lastmodified
tool.ImportTool:  --check-column quote_date
tool.ImportTool:  --last-value 2014-02-17 07:58:39.0
tool.ImportTool: (Consider saving this with 'sqoop job --create')
...
```

Assuming that there's another system that's continuing to write into the stocks table, you'd use the --last-value output of this job as the input to the subsequent Sqoop job so that only rows newer than that date will be imported.

Sqoop jobs and the metastore

You can see in the command output the last value that was encountered for the increment column. How can you best automate a process that can reuse that value? Sqoop has the notion of a *job*, which can save this information and reuse it in subsequent executions:

```
$ sqoop job --create stock_increment -- import \      ◄───   Create a new saved job with id
    --append \                                               "stock_increment." Arguments
    --check-column "quote_date" \                            that appear after the double-
    --incremental "lastmodified" \                           hyphen are treated as regular
    --last-value "2005-01-01" \                              Sqoop arguments.
    --connect jdbc:mysql://localhost/sqoop_test \
    --username hip_sqoop_user \
    --table stocks
```

Executing the preceding command creates a named job in the Sqoop *metastore*, which keeps track of all jobs. By default, the metastore is contained in your home directory under .sqoop and is only used for your own jobs. If you want to share jobs between users and teams, you'll need to install a JDBC-compliant database for Sqoop's metastore and use the --meta-connect argument to specify its location when issuing job commands.

The job create command executed in the previous example didn't do anything other than add the job to the metastore. To run the job, you need to explicitly execute it as shown here:

```
$ sqoop job --list          ◄──────     Lists all jobs in
Available jobs:                         the metastore
  stock_increment

$ sqoop job --exec stock_increment      ◄────────  Executes your job

$ sqoop job --show stock_increment      ◄────
incremental.last.value = 2014-02-17 15:18:54.0         Shows metadata
         ...                                        information about
                                                          your job
```

The metadata displayed by the --show argument includes the last value of your incremental column. This is actually the time when the command was executed, and not the last value in the table. If you're using this feature, make sure that the database server and any clients interacting with the server (including the Sqoop client) have their clocks synced with the Network Time Protocol (NTP).

Sqoop will prompt for a password when running the job. To make this work in an automated script, you'll need to use Expect, a Linux automation tool, to supply the password from a local file when it detects Sqoop prompting for a password. An Expect script that works with Sqoop can be found on GitHub at https://github.com/alexholmes/ hadoop-book/blob/master/bin/sqoop-job.exp.

Sqoop jobs can also be deleted as shown here:

```
$ sqoop job --delete stock_increment
```

Fast MySQL imports
What if you want to bypass JDBC altogether and use the fast MySQL Sqoop connector for a high-throughput load into HDFS? This approach uses the `mysqldump` utility shipped with MySQL to perform the load. You must make sure that `mysqldump` is in the path of the user running the MapReduce job. To enable use of the fast connector you must specify the `--direct` argument:

```
$ sqoop --options-file ~/.sqoop-import-opts \
    --direct \
    --connect jdbc:mysql://localhost/sqoop_test \
    --table stocks
```

What are the disadvantages of fast connectors? Fast connectors only work with text output files—specifying Avro or SequenceFile as the output format of the import won't work.

Importing to Hive
The final step in this technique is to use Sqoop to import your data into a Hive table. The only difference between an HDFS import and a Hive import is that the Hive import has a postprocessing step where the Hive table is created and loaded, as shown in figure 5.13.

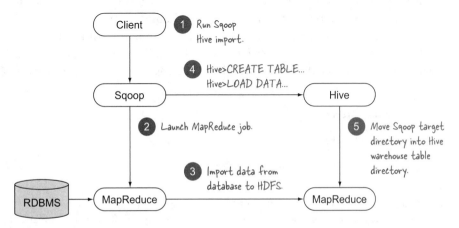

Figure 5.13   The Sqoop Hive import sequence of events

When data is loaded into Hive from an HDFS file or directory, as in the case of Sqoop Hive imports (step 4 in the figure), Hive moves the directory into its warehouse rather than copying the data (step 5) for the sake of efficiency. The HDFS directory that the Sqoop MapReduce job writes to won't exist after the import.

Hive imports are triggered via the `--hive-import` argument. Just like with the fast connector, this option isn't compatible with the `--as-avrodatafile`[20] and `--as-sequencefile` options:

```
$ sqoop --options-file ~/.sqoop-import-opts \
    --hive-import \
    --connect jdbc:mysql://localhost/sqoop_test \
    --table stocks

$ hive
hive> select * from stocks;
OK
1 AAPL  2009-01-02  85.88  91.04   85.16   90.75  26643400  90.75
2 AAPL  2008-01-02 199.27 200.26  192.55  194.84  38542100 194.84
3 AAPL  2007-01-03  86.29  86.58   81.9    83.8    44225700  83.8
4 AAPL  2006-01-03  72.38  74.75   72.25   74.75   28829800  74.75
...
```

> **Importing strings containing Hive delimiters**   You'll likely have downstream processing issues if you're importing columns that can contain any of Hive's delimiters (the \n, \r, and \01 characters). You have two options in such cases: either specify `--hive-drop-import-delims`, which will remove conflicting characters as part of the import, or specify `--hive-delims-replacement`, which will replace them with a different character.

If the Hive table already exists, the data will be appended to the existing table. If this isn't the desired behavior, you can use the `--hive-overwrite` argument to indicate that the existing table should be replaced with the imported data.

You can also tell Sqoop to compress data being written to Hive tables. Sqoop currently only supports text outputs for Hive, so the LZOP compression codec is the best option here as it can be split in Hadoop (see chapter 4 for details).[21] The following example shows how to use `--hive-overwrite` in conjunction with LZOP compression. For this to work, you'll need to have LZOP built and installed on your cluster, because it isn't bundled with Hadoop (or CDH) by default. Refer to chapter 4 for more details:

```
$ hive
hive> drop table stocks;

$ hadoop fs -rmr stocks

$ sqoop --options-file ~/.sqoop-import-opts \
```

---

[20] See https://issues.apache.org/jira/browse/SQOOP-324 for a potential future fix.
[21] bzip2 is also a splittable compression codec that can be used in Hadoop, but its write performance is so poor that in practice it's rarely used.

```
--hive-import \
--hive-overwrite \
--compress \
--compression-codec com.hadoop.compression.lzo.LzopCodec \
--connect jdbc:mysql://localhost/sqoop_test \
--table stocks
```

Finally, you can use the `--hive-partition-key` and `--hive-partition-value` arguments to create different Hive partitions based on the value of a column being imported. For example, if you want to partition your input by stock name, you do the following:

```
$ hive
hive> drop table stocks;

$ hadoop fs -rmr stocks

$ read -d '' query << "EOF"
SELECT id, quote_date, open_price
FROM stocks
WHERE symbol = "AAPL" AND $CONDITIONS
EOF

$ sqoop --options-file ~/.sqoop_import_options.txt \
    --query "$query" \
    --split-by id \
    --hive-import \
    --hive-table stocks \
    --hive-overwrite \
    --hive-partition-key symbol \
    --hive-partition-value "AAPL" \
    --connect jdbc:mysql://localhost/sqoop_test \
    --target-dir stocks

$ hadoop fs -lsr /user/hive/warehouse
/user/hive/warehouse/stocks/symbol=AAPL/part-m-00000
/user/hive/warehouse/stocks/symbol=AAPL/part-m-00001
...
```

Now, the previous example isn't optimal by any means. Ideally, a single import would be able to create multiple Hive partitions. Because you're limited to specifying a single key and value, you'd need to run the import once per unique partition value, which is laborious. You'd be better off importing into a nonpartitioned Hive table, and then retroactively creating partitions on the table after it had been loaded.

Also, the SQL query that you supply to Sqoop must also take care of filtering out the results, so that only those that match the partition are included. In other words, it would have been useful if Sqoop had updated the `WHERE` clause with `symbol = "AAPL"` rather than you having to do this yourself.

Continuous Sqoop execution

If you need to regularly schedule imports into HDFS, Oozie has Sqoop integration that will allow you to periodically perform imports and exports. A sample Oozie work-flow.xml example follows:

```
<workflow-app xmlns="uri:oozie:workflow:0.2" name="sqoop-wf">
  <start to="sqoop-node"/>

  <action name="sqoop-node">
    <sqoop xmlns="uri:oozie:sqoop-action:0.2">
      <job-tracker>${jobTracker}</job-tracker>
      <name-node>${nameNode}</name-node>
      <prepare>
        <delete path="${nameNode}/output-data/sqoop"/>
        <mkdir path="${nameNode}/output-data/sqoop"/>
      </prepare>
      <command>import
       --username hip_sqoop_user
       --password password
       --connect jdbc:mysql://localhost/sqoop_test
       --table stocks --target-dir  ${nameNode}/output-data/sqoop
       -m 1
      </command>
    </sqoop>
    <ok to="end"/>
    <error to="fail"/>
  </action>

  <kill name="fail">
    <message>Sqoop failed, error message
      [${wf:errorMessage(wf:lastErrorNode())}]</message>
  </kill>
  <end name="end"/>
</workflow-app>
```

Single and double quotes aren't supported within the <command> element, so if you need to specify arguments that contain spaces, you'll need to use the <arg> element instead:

```
<arg>import</arg>
<arg>--username</arg>
<arg>hip_sqoop_user</arg>
<arg>--password</arg>
...
```

One other consideration when using Sqoop from Oozie is that you'll need to make the JDBC driver JAR available to Oozie. You can either copy the JAR into the workflow's lib/ directory or update your Hadoop installation's lib directory with the JAR.

■ **Summary**

Obviously, for Sqoop to work, your Hadoop cluster nodes need to have access to the MySQL database. Common sources of error are either misconfiguration or lack of connectivity from the Hadoop nodes. It's probably wise to log on to one of the Hadoop nodes and attempt to connect to the MySQL server using the MySQL client, or attempt access with the mysqldump utility (if you're using a fast connector).

Another important point when using a fast connector is that it's assumed that mysqldump is installed on each Hadoop node and is in the path of the user running the map tasks.

This wraps up our review of using Sqoop to import data from relational databases into Hadoop. We'll now transition from relational stores to a NoSQL store, HBase, which excels at data interoperability with Hadoop because it uses HDFS to store its data.

5.2.4 HBase

Our final foray into moving data into Hadoop involves taking a look at HBase. HBase is a real-time, distributed, data storage system that's often either colocated on the same hardware that serves as your Hadoop cluster or is in close proximity to a Hadoop cluster. Being able to work with HBase data directly in MapReduce, or to push it into HDFS, is one of the huge advantages when picking HBase as a solution.

In the first technique, I'll show you how to use a tool that HBase is bundled with to save an HBase table into HDFS.

<hr/>

TECHNIQUE 43   **HBase ingress into HDFS**

<hr/>

What if you had customer data sitting in HBase that you wanted to use in MapReduce in conjunction with data in HDFS? You could write a MapReduce job that takes as input the HDFS dataset and pulls data directly from HBase in your map or reduce code. But in some cases it may be more useful to take a dump of the data in HBase directly into HDFS, especially if you plan to utilize that data in multiple MapReduce jobs and the HBase data is immutable or changes infrequently.

■ **Problem**

You want to get HBase data into HDFS.

■ **Solution**

HBase includes an `Export` class that can be used to import HBase data into HDFS in SequenceFile format. This technique also walks through code that can be used to read the imported HBase data.

■ **Discussion**

Before we get started with this technique, you need to get HBase up and running.[22]

To be able to export data from HBase you first need to load some data into HBase. The loader creates an HBase table called stocks_example with a single column family, `details`. You'll store the HBase data as Avro binary-serialized data. I won't show the code here, but it's available on GitHub.[23]

Run the loader and use it to load the sample stock data into HBase:

```
$ hip hip.ch5.hbase.HBaseWriter \
    --input test-data/stocks.txt
```

You can use the HBase shell to look at the results of the load. The `list` command, without any arguments, will show you all of the tables in HBase, and the `scan` command, with a single argument, will dump all of the contents of a table:

<hr/>

[22] The appendix contains installation instructions and additional resources for working with HBase.

[23] GitHub source: https://github.com/alexholmes/hiped2/blob/master/src/main/java/hip/ch5/hbase/HBaseWriter.java.

```
$ hbase shell

hbase(main):012:0> list
TABLE
stocks_example
1 row(s) in 0.0100 seconds

hbase(main):007:0> scan 'stocks_example'
ROW                COLUMN+CELL
AAPL2000-01-03     column=details:stockAvro, timestamp=1322315975123,...
AAPL2001-01-02     column=details:stockAvro, timestamp=1322315975123,...
...
```

With your data in place, you're ready to export it to HDFS. HBase comes with an
`org.apache.hadoop.hbase.mapreduce.Export` class that will dump an HBase table. An
example of using the `Export` class is shown in the following snippet. With this command, you can export the whole HBase table:

```
$ hip org.apache.hadoop.hbase.mapreduce.Export \
    stocks_example \
    output
```

HBase table to export

HDFS directory where exported table is written

The `Export` class also supports exporting only a single column family, and it can also
compress the output:

Specify the output should be compressed.

```
$ hip org.apache.hadoop.hbase.mapreduce.Export \
    -D hbase.mapreduce.scan.column.family=details \
    -D mapred.output.compress=true \
    -D mapred.output.compression.codec=\
org.apache.hadoop.io.compress.SnappyCodec \
    stocks_example output
```

Specify column family to be exported.

Set the compression codec, in this case Snappy. Snappy's a good fit here because the SequenceFile internally applies the compression, and the compressed content doesn't need to be split.

The `Export` class writes the HBase output in the SequenceFile format, where the HBase
row key is stored in the SequenceFile record key using `org.apache.hadoop.hbase.io`
`.ImmutableBytesWritable`, and the HBase value is stored in the SequenceFile record
value using `org.apache.hadoop.hbase.client.Result`.

What if you want to process that exported data in HDFS? The following listing
shows an example of how you'd read the HBase SequenceFile and extract the Avro
stock records.[24]

---

[24] GitHub source: https://github.com/alexholmes/hiped2/blob/master/src/main/java/hip/ch5/hbase/
ExportedReader.java.

Listing 5.3   Reading the HBase SequenceFile to extract Avro stock records

```
...
import static com.manning.hip.ch5.HBaseWriteAvroStock.*;

public class HBaseExportedStockReader {
  public static void main(String... args) throws IOException {
    read(new Path(args[0]));
  }

  public static void read(Path inputPath) throws IOException {
    Configuration conf = new Configuration();
    FileSystem fs = FileSystem.get(conf);

    SequenceFile.Reader reader =                        ◄———————— Prepare the SequenceFile reader.
        new SequenceFile.Reader(fs, inputPath, conf);

    HBaseScanAvroStock.AvroStockReader stockReader =   ◄——— Prepare the Avro reader.
        new HBaseScanAvroStock.AvroStockReader();

    try {
      ImmutableBytesWritable key = new ImmutableBytesWritable();
      Result value = new Result();

      while (reader.next(key, value)) {                        Decode the byte array contents of
        Stock stock = stockReader.decode(value.getValue( ◄——  the HBase column family/qualifier
          STOCK_DETAILS_COLUMN_FAMILY_AS_BYTES,                value into your Avro Stock bean. The
          STOCK_COLUMN_QUALIFIER_AS_BYTES));                   constants used here are defined in the
                                                               HBaseWriteAvroStock class.
        System.out.println(new String(key.get()) + ": " +  ◄—
        ToStringBuilder
            .reflectionToString(stock, ToStringStyle.SIMPLE_STYLE));
      }
    } finally {                                         Write out row key and Stock
      reader.close();                                    object to standard out.
    }
  }
}
```

Iterate through all SequenceFile records.

You can run the code against the HDFS directory that you used for the export and view
the results:

```
$ hip hip.ch5.hbase.ExportedReader \
    --input output/part-m-00000
AAPL2000-01-03: AAPL,2000-01-03,104.87,...
AAPL2001-01-02: AAPL,2001-01-02,14.88,...
AAPL2002-01-02: AAPL,2002-01-02,22.05,...
...
```

The HBaseExportedStockReader class is able to read and dump out the contents of the
SequenceFile used by HBase's Export class.

Exporting data from HBase into HDFS is made easier with the built-in HBase Export
class. But what if you don't want to write HBase data into HDFS, but instead want to

process it directly in a MapReduce job? Let's look at how you can use HBase as a data source for a MapReduce job.

TECHNIQUE 44   **MapReduce with HBase as a data source**

The built-in HBase exporter writes out HBase data using SequenceFile, which isn't supported by programming languages other than Java and doesn't support schema evolution. It also only supports a Hadoop filesystem as the data sink. If you want to have more control over HBase data extracts, you may have to look beyond the built-in HBase facilities.

■ **Problem**

You want to operate on HBase directly within your MapReduce jobs without the intermediary step of copying the data into HDFS.

■ **Solution**

HBase has a `TableInputFormat` class that can be used in your MapReduce job to pull data directly from HBase.

■ **Discussion**

HBase provides an `InputFormat` class called `TableInputFormat`, which can use HBase as a data source in MapReduce. The following listing shows a MapReduce job that uses this input format (via the `TableMapReduceUtil.initTableMapperJob` call) to read data from HBase.[25]

Listing 5.4   Importing HBase data into HDFS using MapReduce

```
public class HBaseSourceMapReduce extends
    TableMapper<Text, DoubleWritable> {

    private HBaseScanAvroStock.AvroStockReader stockReader;
    private Text outputKey = new Text();
    private DoubleWritable outputValue = new DoubleWritable();

    @Override
    protected void setup(
        Context context)
        throws IOException, InterruptedException {
      stockReader = new HBaseScanAvroStock.AvroStockReader();
    }

    @Override
    public void map(ImmutableBytesWritable row, Result columns,
                    Context context)
        throws IOException, InterruptedException {
      for (KeyValue kv : columns.list()) {
        byte[] value = kv.getValue();

        Stock stock = stockReader.decode(value);

        outputKey.set(stock.symbol.toString());
```

Iterate through all values for row key and scan criteria (defined in the main method).

Extract the value.

Extract the Avro object from the column value.

---

[25] GitHub source: https://github.com/alexholmes/hiped2/blob/master/src/main/java/hip/ch5/hbase/ImportMapReduce.java.

Output the stock symbol and closing price.

Create an HBase Scan object, which HBase will use to filter the table contents based on the supplied criteria. In this case, you're specifying the column family and qualifier that you want to scan.

```
            outputValue.set(stock.close);
            context.write(outputKey, outputValue);
        }
    }

    public static void main(String[] args) throws Exception {
        Configuration conf = new Configuration();

        Scan scan = new Scan();
        scan.addColumn(STOCK_DETAILS_COLUMN_FAMILY_AS_BYTES,
            STOCK_COLUMN_QUALIFIER_AS_BYTES);
        Job job = new Job(conf);

        job.setJarByClass(HBaseSourceMapReduce.class);

        TableMapReduceUtil.initTableMapperJob(
            STOCKS_TABLE_NAME,
            scan,
            HBaseSourceMapReduce.class,
            ImmutableBytesWritable.class,
            Put.class,
            job);

        job.setNumReduceTasks(0);
        ...
```

Use HBase's helper method to set up the map configuration parameters for the job.

The Scan object that you defined earlier.

The HBase table name that's the data source for the job.

The class name of the mapper.

The class of the map output key.

You can run this MapReduce job as follows:

```
$ hip hip.ch5.hbase.ImportMapReduce --output output
```

A quick peek in HDFS should tell you whether or not your MapReduce job worked as expected:

```
$ hadoop fs -cat output/part*
AAPL    111.94
AAPL    14.88
AAPL    23.3
```

This output confirms that the MapReduce job works as expected.

■ **Summary**

The TableInputFormat class examines HBase and creates an input split for each HBase table region. If there are 10 HBase regions, 10 map tasks will execute. The input format also includes the server that hosts the region in the input split, which means that the map tasks will be scheduled to execute on the same nodes as the HRegionServer hosting the data. This gives you locality at the HBase level, but also at the HDFS level. Data being read from the region will likely be coming from local disk, because after some time, all of a region's data will be local to it. This all assumes that the HRegion-Servers are running on the same hosts as the DataNodes.

Our focus over the last couple of sections has been on persistent stores, covering relational databases and HBase, a NoSQL store. We're now going to change directions and look at how a publish-subscribe system can be leveraged to move data into Hadoop.

5.2.5 *Importing data from Kafka*

Kafka, a distributed publish-subscribe system, is quickly becoming a key part of our data pipelines thanks to its strong distributed and performance properties. It can be used for many functions, such as messaging, metrics collection, stream processing, and log aggregation. Another effective use of Kafka is as a vehicle to move data into Hadoop. This is useful in situations where you have data being produced in real time that you want to land in Hadoop.

A key reason to use Kafka is that it decouples data producers and consumers. It notably allows you to have multiple independent producers (possibly written by different development teams), and, likewise, multiple independent consumers (again possibly written by different teams). Also, consumption can be real-time/synchronous or batch/offline/asynchronous. The latter property is a big differentiator when you're looking at other pub-sub tools like RabbitMQ.

Kafka has a handful of concepts that you'll need to understand:

- *Topics*—A topic is a feed of related messages.
- *Partitions*—Each topic is made up of one or more partitions, which are ordered sequences of messages backed by log files.[26]
- *Producers and consumers*—Producers and consumers write messages to and read them from partitions.
- *Brokers*—Brokers are the Kafka processes that manage topics and partitions and serve producer and consumer requests.

Kafka does not guarantee "total" ordering for a topic—instead, it only guarantees that the individual partitions that make up a topic are ordered. It's up to the consumer application to enforce, if needed, a "global" per-topic ordering.

Figure 5.14 shows a conceptual model of how Kafka works and figure 5.15 shows an example of how partitions could be distributed in an actual Kafka deployment.

To support fault tolerance, topics can be replicated, which means that each partition can have a configurable number of replicas on different hosts. This provides increased fault tolerance and means that a single server dying isn't catastrophic for your data or for the availability of your producers and consumers.

> **Versioning** Technique 45 employs Kafka version 0.8 and the 0.8 branch of Camus.

This wraps up our quick dive into how Kafka works. For more details, please refer to Kafka's online documentation.

---

[26] I'm not talking about logging files here; Kafka employs log files to store data flowing through Kafka.

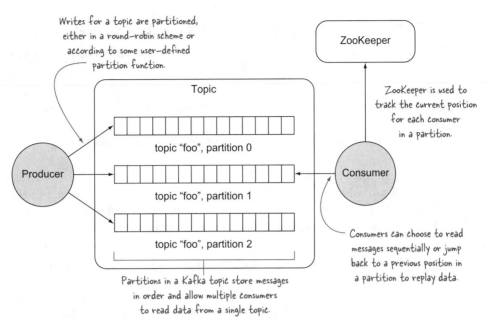

Figure 5.14 Conceptual Kafka model showing producers, topics, partitions, and consumers

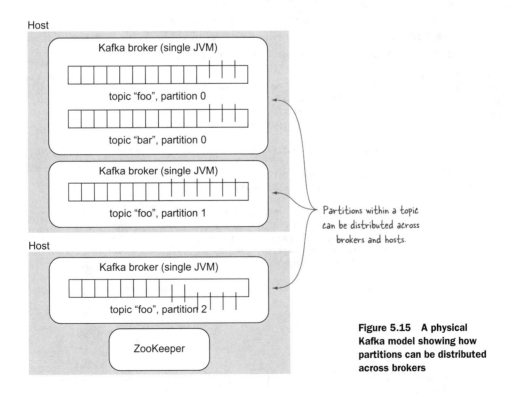

Figure 5.15 A physical Kafka model showing how partitions can be distributed across brokers

TECHNIQUE 45   **Using Camus to copy Avro data from Kafka into HDFS**

This technique is useful in situations where you already have data flowing in Kafka for other purposes and you want to land that data in HDFS.

■ **Problem**

You want to use Kafka as a data-delivery mechanism to get your data into HDFS.

■ **Solution**

Use Camus, a LinkedIn-developed solution for copying data in Kafka into HDFS.

■ **Discussion**

Camus is an open-source project developed by LinkedIn. Kafka is heavily deployed at LinkedIn, and where Camus is used as a tool to copy data from Kafka into HDFS.

Out of the box, Camus supports two data formats in Kafka: JSON and Avro. In this technique we're going to get Camus working with Avro data. Camus's built-in support of Avro requires that Kafka publishers write the Avro data in a proprietary way, so for this technique we're going to assume that you want to work with vanilla Avro-serialized data in Kafka.

There are three parts to getting this technique to work: you'll first write some Avro data into Kafka, then you'll write a simple class to help Camus deserialize your Avro data, and finally you'll run a Camus job to perform the data import.

Writing data into Kafka

To get going, you'll write some Avro records into Kafka. In the following code, you set up a Kafka producer by configuring some required Kafka properties, load some Avro records from file, and write them out to Kafka:[27]

Set the serializer class for messages. In this example you use the default encoder, which accepts and writes bytes.

Specify the CSV-delimited list of Kafka brokers.

Create a new Kafka producer to write messages.

Convert the Avro object to a byte array and wrap it in a Kafka message.

Write the message to Kafka.

```
Properties props = new Properties();
props.put("metadata.broker.list", "localhost:9092");
props.put("serializer.class",
    kafka.serializer.DefaultEncoder.class.getName());

ProducerConfig config = new ProducerConfig(props);

Producer<Integer, byte[]> producer =
    new Producer<Integer, byte[]>(config);

for (String line : FileUtils.readLines(inputFile)) {
    Stock stock = AvroStockFileWrite.createStock(line);
    KeyedMessage<Integer, byte[]> msg =
        new KeyedMessage<Integer, byte[]>(kTopic, toBytes(stock));
    producer.send(msg);
}
producer.close();
```

---

[27] The complete set of Kafka properties you can set can be viewed in the Kafka documentation: https://kafka.apache.org/documentation.html.

You can load the sample stock data into a Kafka topic called test with the following command:

```
$ hip hip.ch5.kafka.KafkaAvroWriter \
    --stocksfile test-data/stocks.txt \
    --broker-list localhost:9092 \
    --topic test
```

The Kafka console consumer can be used to verify that the data has been written to Kafka. This will dump the binary Avro data to your console:

```
$ kafka-console-consumer.sh \
    --zookeeper localhost:2181 \
    --topic test \
    --from-beginning
```

Once that's done, you're ready for the next part—writing some Camus code so that you can read these Avro records in Camus.

Writing a Camus decoder and schema registry

There are three Camus concepts that you need to understand:

- *Decoders*—The decoder's job is to convert raw data pulled from Kafka into a Camus format.
- *Encoders*—Encoders serialize decoded data into the format that will be stored in HDFS.
- *Schema registry*—The schema registry provides schema information about Avro data being encoded.

As mentioned earlier, Camus supports Avro data, but it does so in a way that requires Kafka producers to write data using the Camus KafkaAvroMessageEncoder class, which prefixes the Avro-serialized binary data with some proprietary data, presumably so that the decoder in Camus can verify that it was written by that class.

In this example you're serializing using the straight Avro serialization, so you need to write your own decoder. Luckily this is simple to do:

```
import com.linkedin.camus.coders.CamusWrapper;
import com.linkedin.camus.coders.MessageDecoder;
import hip.ch5.avro.gen.Stock;
import org.apache.avro.generic.GenericData;
import org.apache.avro.generic.GenericDatumReader;
import org.apache.avro.io.DatumReader;
import org.apache.avro.io.DecoderFactory;

import java.io.IOException;

/**
 */
public class StockMessageDecoder
  extends MessageDecoder<byte[], GenericData.Record> {
```

Decoders must implement this interface and specify the input and output types.

```
DecoderFactory factory = DecoderFactory.get();        ◄─── The Avro decoder
                                                             factory.
@Override
public CamusWrapper<GenericData.Record> decode(byte[] bytes) {        ─── Create an
                                                                          Avro reader.
    DatumReader<GenericData.Record> reader =                   ◄───
      new GenericDatumReader<GenericData.Record>(Stock.SCHEMA$);

    GenericData.Record record =                          ◄──── Deserialize the binary data
      reader.read(null, factory.binaryDecoder(bytes, null));        into an Avro record.

    return new CamusWrapper<GenericData.Record>(record);    ◄─── Wrap the record in a
  }                                                              Camus wrapper class.
}
```

> **Versioning**   You may have noticed that we wrote a specific Avro record into
> Kafka, but in Camus we're reading the record as a generic Avro record, not a
> specific Avro record. This is due to the fact that the CamusWrapper class only
> supports generic Avro records. Otherwise, specific Avro records would have
> been simpler to work with, as you can work with generated code and have all
> the type-safety goodness that comes along with that.

The CamusWrapper object is an envelope for the data being extracted from Kafka. The
reason this class exists is that it allows you to stick metadata into the envelope, such as
a timestamp, a server name, and the service details. It's highly recommended that any
data you work with have some meaningful timestamp associated with each record (typically this would be the time at which the record was created or generated). You can
then use a CamusWrapper constructor that accepts the timestamp as an argument:

```
public CamusWrapper(R record, long timestamp) { ... }
```

If the timestamp isn't set, then Camus will create a new timestamp at the time the
wrapper is created. This timestamp and other metadata is used in Camus when determining the HDFS location of output records. You'll see an example of this shortly.

Next you need to write a schema registry so that the Camus Avro encoder knows the
schema details for the Avro records being written to HDFS. When registering the schema,
you also specify the name of the Kafka topic from which the Avro record was pulled:

```
import com.linkedin.camus.schemaregistry.AvroMemorySchemaRegistry;
import hip.ch5.avro.gen.Stock;

public class StockSchemaRegistry extends AvroMemorySchemaRegistry {
  public StockSchemaRegistry() {
    super();
    // register the schema for the topic
    super.register("test", Stock.SCHEMA$);
  }
}
```

That's it for the coding side of things! Let's move on and see Camus in action.

Running Camus

Camus runs as a MapReduce job on the Hadoop cluster where you want to import the Kafka data. You need to feed a bunch of properties to Camus, and you can do so using the command line, or alternatively using a properties file. We'll use the properties file for this technique:

```
# comma-separated brokers in "host:port" format
kafka.brokers=localhost:9092

# Name of the client as seen by kafka
kafka.client.name=hip

# Top-level data output directory in HDFS
etl.destination.path=/tmp/camus/dest

# HDFS location where you want to keep execution files,
# i.e. offsets, error logs, and count files
etl.execution.base.path=/tmp/camus/work

# Where completed Camus job output directories are kept,
# usually a sub-dir in the base.path
etl.execution.history.path=/tmp/camus/history

# The decoder class
camus.message.decoder.class=hip.ch5.kafka.camus.StockMessageDecoder

# The HDFS serializer
etl.record.writer.provider.class=\
com.linkedin.camus.etl.kafka.common.AvroRecordWriterProvider

# The schema registry
kafka.message.coder.schema.registry.class=
hip.ch5.kafka.camus.StockSchemaRegistry

# Max hadoop tasks to use, each task can pull multiple topic partitions
mapred.map.tasks=2
```

As you can see from the properties, you don't need to explicitly tell Camus which topics you want to import. Camus automatically communicates with Kafka to discover the topics (and partitions), and the current start and end offsets.

If you want control over exactly which topics are imported, you can whitelist (to limit the topics) or blacklist (to exclude topics) using `kafka.whitelist.topics` and `kafka.blacklist.topics`, respectively. Multiple topics can be specified using a comma as the delimiter. Regular expressions are also supported, as shown in the following example, which matches on topic "topic1" or any topics that start with "abc" followed by one or more digits. Blacklists can be specified using the exact same syntax for the value:

```
kafka.whitelist.topics=topic1,abc[0-9]+
```

Once your properties are all set, you're ready to run the Camus job:

```
$ CAMUS_HOME=<your Camus directory>
$ HIP_HOME=<your Hadoop in Practice directory>

$ LIBJARS="$CAMUS_HOME/camus-example/target/
```

```
camus-example-0.1.0-SNAPSHOT-shaded.jar"
$ LIBJARS=$LIBJARS=",$HIP_HOME/target/hip-2.0.0.jar"
$ export HADOOP_CLASSPATH=`echo ${LIBJARS} | sed s/,/:/g`

hadoop com.linkedin.camus.etl.kafka.CamusJob \
  -libjars ${LIBJARS} \
  -P $HIP_HOME/conf/camus-avro.conf
```

This will result in the Avro data landing in HDFS. Let's take a look at what's in HDFS:

```
$ hadoop fs -lsr /tmp/camus

/tmp/camus/dest/test/hourly/2014/03/03/01/test.0.0.45.100.avro

/tmp/camus/history/2014-03-03-09-36-02/errors-m-00000
/tmp/camus/history/2014-03-03-09-36-02/offsets-m-00000
/tmp/camus/history/2014-03-03-09-36-02/offsets-previous
/tmp/camus/history/2014-03-03-09-36-02/requests.previous
```

The first file is the file that you're interested in, as it contains the data that's been imported. The other files are there for Camus's housekeeping.

The data files in HDFS can be viewed using the AvroDump utility:

```
$ hip hip.util.AvroDump \
 --file /tmp/camus/dest/test/hourly/2014/03/03/01/test.0.0.45.100.avro
```

So what actually happened when the Camus job was running? The Camus import process is executed as a MapReduce job, as seen in figure 5.16.

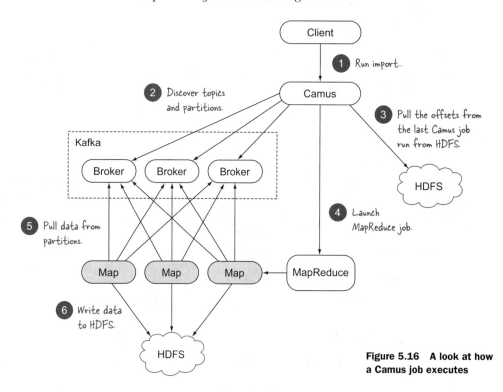

Figure 5.16   A look at how a Camus job executes

As Camus tasks in MapReduce succeed, the Camus OutputCommitter (a MapReduce construct that allows for custom work to be performed upon task completion) atomically moves the tasks' data files to the destination directory. The OutputCommitter additionally creates the offset files for all the partitions that the tasks were working on. It's possible that other tasks in the same job may fail, but this doesn't impact the state of tasks that succeed—the data and offset outputs of successful tasks will still exist, so that subsequent Camus executions will resume processing from the last-known successful state.

Next, let's take a look at where Camus writes the imported data and how you can control the behavior.

Data partitioning

Earlier you saw the location where Camus imported the Avro data sitting in Kafka. Let's take a closer look at the HDFS path structure, shown in figure 5.17, and see what you can do to determine the location.

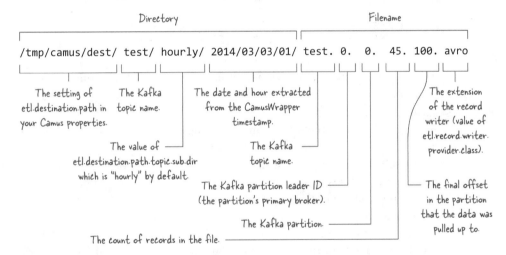

Figure 5.17 Dissecting the Camus output path for exported data in HDFS

The date/time part of the path is determined by the timestamp extracted from the CamusWrapper. You'll recall from our earlier discussion that you can extract timestamps from your records in Kafka in your MessageDecoder and supply them to the CamusWrapper, which will allow your data to be partitioned by dates that are meaningful to you, as opposed to the default, which is simply the time at which the Kafka record is read in MapReduce.

Camus supports a pluggable partitioner, which allows you to control the part of the path shown in figure 5.18.

```
/tmp/camus/dest/ test/hourly/2014/03/03/01/ test.0.0.45.100.avro
```

This part of the output path can be controlled with a custom partitioner.   **Figure 5.18 The Camus partitioner path**

The Camus `Partitioner` interface provides two methods that you must implement:

```
public interface Partitioner {
    /**
     * Encode partition values into a string, to be embedded
     * into the working filename.
     * Encoded values cannot use '/' or ':'.
     */
    String encodePartition(JobContext context, IEtlKey etlKey);

    /**
     * Return a string representing the partitioned directory
     * structure where the .avro files will be moved.
     *
     * For example, if you were using Hive style partitioning,
     * a timestamp based partitioning scheme would return
     *    topic-name/year=2012/month=02/day=04/hour=12
     *
     */
    String generatePartitionedPath(JobContext context, String topic,
        int brokerId, int partitionId, String encodedPartition);
}
```

As an example, a custom partitioner could create a path that could be leveraged for Hive partitions.

■ Summary

Camus provides a complete solution to landing data from Kafka in HDFS, and it takes care of maintaining state and error handling when things go wrong. It can be easily automated by integrating it with Azkaban or Oozie, and it performs some simple data-management facilities by organizing HDFS data based on the time that messages are ingested. It's worth mentioning that when it comes to ETL, it's bare-boned in its features compared to Flume.

Kafka comes bundled with a mechanism that pulls data into HDFS. It has a `KafkaETLInputFormat` input format class that can be used to pull data from Kafka in a MapReduce job. It requires you to write the MapReduce job to perform the import, but the advantage is that you can use the data directly in your MapReduce flow, as opposed to using HDFS as intermediary storage for your data.

The Flume project is also in the process of adding a Kafka source and sink, although at the time of writing that work is still in progress.[28] Once this is ready for production, you'll be able to leverage all the other goodies that Flume offers, such as Morphlines and Solr indexing as part of moving Kafka data into Hadoop.

That concludes our examination of how to move data into Hadoop. We covered a broad range of data types, tools, and technologies. Next we're going to flip things around and look at how to get data that resides in Hadoop out to other systems, such as filesystems and other stores.

---

[28] For more details on Flume and Kafka see https://issues.apache.org/jira/browse/FLUME-2242.

5.3   Moving data out of Hadoop

Once you've used Hadoop to perform some critical function, be it data mining or data aggregations, the next step is typically to externalize that data into other systems in your environment. For example, it's common to rely on Hadoop to perform offline aggregations on data that's pulled from your real-time systems, and then to feed the derived data back into your real-time systems. A more concrete example would be building recommendations based on user-behavior patterns.

This section examines some of the more common scenarios where you want to get data out of Hadoop, and the tools that will help you with that work. We'll start with a look at the lower-level tools that exist, most of which are built into Hadoop, and then go on to look at how to push data to relational databases and HBase.

To start off, we'll look at how to copy files out of Hadoop using the command line.

5.3.1   Roll your own egress

This section covers some built-in mechanisms in Hadoop for copying data out of HDFS. These techniques can either be manually executed, or you'll need to automate them using a scheduling system such as Azkaban, Oozie, or even cron.

TECHNIQUE 46   Using the CLI to extract files

Imagine that you've run some jobs in Hadoop to aggregate some data, and now you want to get it out. One method you can use is the HDFS command-line interface (CLI) to pull out directories and files into your local filesystem. This technique covers some basic CLI commands that can help you out.

■ **Problem**

You want to copy files from HDFS to a local filesystem using the shell.

■ **Solution**

The HDFS CLI can be used for one-off moves, or the same commands can be incorporated into scripts for more regularly utilized moves.

■ **Discussion**

Copying a file from HDFS to local disk is achieved via the hadoop command:

```
$ hadoop fs -get hdfs-file.txt local-file.txt
```

The behavior of the Hadoop put command differs from the Linux cp command—in Linux if the destination already exists, it's overwritten; in Hadoop the copy fails with an error:

```
put: `hdfs-file.txt': File exists
```

The -f option must be added to force the file to be overwritten:

```
$ hadoop fs -get -f hdfs-file.txt local-file.txt
```

Much like with the Linux `cp` command, multiple files can be copied using the same command. In this case, the final argument must be the directory in the local filesystem into which the HDFS files are copied:

```
$ hadoop fs -get hdfs-file1.txt hdfs-file2.txt /local/dest/
```

Often, one is copying a large number of files from HDFS to local disk—an example is a MapReduce job output directory that contains a file for each task. If you're using a file format that can be concatenated, you can use the -getmerge command to combine multiple files. By default, a newline is added at the end of each file during concatenation:

```
$ hdfs fs -getmerge hdfs-dir/part* /local/output.txt
```

There are many more operations supported by the `fs` command—to see the full list, run the command without any options.

The challenge with using the CLI is that it's very low-level, and it won't be able to assist you with your automation needs. Sure, you could use the CLI within shell scripts, but once you graduate to more sophisticated programming languages, forking a process for every HDFS command isn't ideal. In this situation you may want to look at using the REST, Java, or C HDFS APIs. The next technique looks at the REST API.

TECHNIQUE 47   Using REST to extract files

Using the CLI is handy for quickly running commands and for scripting, but it incurs the overhead of forking a separate process for each command, which is overhead that you'll probably want to avoid, especially if you're interfacing with HDFS in a programming language. This technique covers working with HDFS in languages other than Java.

■ **Problem**

You want to be able to interact with HDFS from a programming language that doesn't have a native interface to HDFS.

■ **Solution**

Use Hadoop's WebHDFS interface, which offers a full-featured REST API for HDFS operations.

■ **Discussion**

Before you get started, you'll need to enable WebHDFS on your cluster—see technique 34 for details on how to do that.

Let's start by creating a file in HDFS using the CLI:

```
$ echo "the cat sat on the mat" | hadoop fs -put - /tmp/hdfs-file.txt
```

Reading the file from HDFS is a matter of specifying OPEN as the operation:

```
$ curl -L "http://0.0.0.0:50070/webhdfs/v1/tmp/hdfs-file.txt?the cat sat on the mat
➥                      op=OPEN&user.name=aholmes"
```

Consult technique 34 for additional information on using WebHDFS, including how it can be leveraged in different programming languages.

TECHNIQUE 48   Reading from HDFS when behind a firewall

Production Hadoop environments are often locked down to protect the data residing in these clusters. Part of the security procedures could include putting your cluster behind a firewall, and this can be a nuisance if the destination for your Hadoop cluster is outside of the firewall. This technique looks at using the HttpFS gateway to provide HDFS access over port 80, which is often opened up on firewalls.

■ **Problem**

You want to pull data out of HDFS, but you're sitting behind a firewall that's restricting access to HDFS.

■ **Solution**

Use the HttpFS gateway, which is a standalone server that provides access to HDFS over HTTP. Because it's a separate service and it's HTTP, it can be configured to run on any host that has access to the Hadoop nodes, and you can open a firewall rule to allow traffic to the service.

■ **Discussion**

HttpFS is useful because not only can you use REST to access HDFS, but it has a complete Hadoop filesystem implementation, which means you can use the CLI and native HDFS Java clients to talk to HDFS. Consult technique 35 for instructions on how to get HttpFS up and running.

Once it's running, you can issue the same curl commands that you used in the previous technique with WebHDFS (the only difference is URL host and port, which need to point to where your HttpFS is deployed). This is one of the nice things about the HttpFS gateway—the syntax is exactly the same.

To dump the contents of the file /tmp/hdfs-file.txt, you'd do the following:

```
$ curl -L "http://0.0.0.0:140000/webhdfs/v1/tmp/hdfs-file.txt?the cat sat on the mat
➥                      op=OPEN&user.name=aholmes"
```

Swing on over to technique 35 for additional details on how HttpFS works.

TECHNIQUE 49   Mounting Hadoop with NFS

Often it's a lot easier to work with Hadoop data if it's accessible as a regular mount to your filesystem. This allows you to use existing scripts, tools, and programming languages and easily interact with your data in HDFS. This section looks at how you can easily copy data out of HDFS using an NFS mount.

■ **Problem**

You want to treat HDFS as a regular Linux filesystem and use standard Linux tools to interact with HDFS.

■ **Solution**

Use Hadoop's NFS implementation to access data in HDFS.

■ **Discussion**

Technique 36 has setup instructions for NFS access to HDFS. Once that's set up, you can perform normal filesystem operations such as copying files from HDFS to a local filesystem. The following example shows this, assuming that HDFS is mounted under /hdfs:

```
$ cp /hdfs/tmp/foo.txt ~/
```

For more details on how NFS works in Hadoop, head on over to technique 36.

TECHNIQUE 50   **Using DistCp to copy data out of Hadoop**

Imagine that you have a large amount of data you want to move out of Hadoop. With most of the techniques in this section, you have a bottleneck because you're funneling the data through a single host, which is the host on which you're running the process. To optimize data movement as much as possible, you want to leverage MapReduce to copy data in parallel. This is where DistCp comes into play, and this technique examines one way you can pull out data to an NFS mount.

■ **Problem**

You want to efficiently pull data out of Hadoop and parallelize the copy.

■ **Solution**

Use DistCp.

■ **Discussion**

Technique 37 covers DistCp in detail and includes details on how to copy data between different Hadoop clusters. But DistCp can't be used to copy data from Hadoop to a local filesystem (or vice versa), because DistCp runs as a MapReduce job, and your cluster won't have access to your local filesystem. Depending on your situation you have a couple of options:

- Use the HDFS File Slurper to copy the local files.
- Copy your files to an NFS that's also available to all the DataNodes in your cluster.

If you go with the second option, you can use DistCp and write to a locally mounted NFS mount on each DataNode, an example of which follows:

```
$ hadoop distcp \
  hdfs://src \
  file://mount1/dest
```

Note that your NFS system may not handle a large number of parallel reads or writes, so you'll likely want to run this with a smaller number of mappers than the default of 20—the following example runs with 5 mappers:

```
$ hadoop distcp \
  -m 5 \
  hdfs://src \
  file://mount1/dest
```

| TECHNIQUE 51 | **Using Java to extract files** |

Let's say you've generated a number of Lucene indexes in HDFS, and you want to pull them out to an external host. Maybe you want to manipulate the files in some way using Java. This technique shows how the Java HDFS API can be used to read data in HDFS.

■ **Problem**

You want to copy files in HDFS to the local filesystem.

■ **Solution**

Use Hadoop's filesystem API to copy data out of HDFS.

■ **Discussion**

The HDFS Java API is nicely integrated with Java's I/O model, which means you can work with regular input streams and output streams for I/O.

To start off, you need to create a file in HDFS using the command line:

```
$ echo "hello world" | hadoop fs -put - hdfs-file.txt
```

Now copy that file to the local filesystem using the command line:

```
$ hadoop fs -get hdfs-file.txt local-file.txt
```

Let's explore how you can replicate this copy in Java. There are two main parts to writing the code to do this—the first part is getting a handle to the FileSystem and creating the file, and the second part is copying the data from standard input to the OutputStream:

Open a file in HDFS and get a handle to it.

Get a handle to a Hadoop filesystem. You don't specify which filesystem implementation is used; this is determined at runtime by loading the configuration properties.

```
FileSystem fs = FileSystem.get(conf);
InputStream is = fs.open(inputFile);
OutputStream os = FileUtils.openOutputStream(outputFile);

IOUtils.copyBytes(is, os, getConf(), true);
```

Create a local file and open a stream.

Use a helper class in Hadoop to copy the bytes between the streams. It'll automatically close the streams once the copy has completed, as specified by the last argument.

You can see how this code works in practice by running the following command:

```
$ echo "the cat" | hadoop fs -put - hdfs-file.txt

$ hip hip.ch5.CopyHdfsFileToLocal \
    --input hdfs-file.txt \
    --output local-file.txt

$ cat local-file.txt
the cat
```

So far we've covered the low-level tools that are bundled with Hadoop to help you pull out data. Next we'll look at a method for near-continuous movement of data from HDFS to a local filesystem.

5.3.2 Automated file egress

Up until now you've seen different options for copying data out of HDFS. Most of these mechanisms don't have automation or scheduling capabilities; they're ulti-mately low-level methods for accessing data. If you're looking to automate your data copy, you can wrap one of these low-level techniques inside of a scheduling engine such as cron or Quartz. However, if you're looking for out-of-the-box automation, then this section is for you.

Earlier in this chapter we looked at two mechanisms that can move semistructured and binary data into HDFS: the open source HDFS File Slurper project, and Oozie, which triggers a data ingress workflow. The challenge in using a local filesystem for egress (and ingress for that matter) is that map and reduce tasks running on clusters won't have access to the filesystem on a specific server. You have three broad options for moving data from HDFS to a filesystem:

- You can host a proxy tier on a server, such as a web server, which you would then write to using MapReduce.
- You can write to the local filesystem in MapReduce and then, as a postprocess-ing step, trigger a script on the remote server to move that data.
- You can run a process on the remote server to pull data from HDFS directly.

The third option is the preferred approach because it's the simplest and most effi-cient, and as such it's the focus of this section. We'll look at how you can use the HDFS File Slurper to automatically move files from HDFS out to a local filesystem.

TECHNIQUE 52   **An automated mechanism to export files from HDFS**

Let's say you have files being written in HDFS by MapReduce, and you want to auto-mate their extraction to a local filesystem. This kind of feature isn't supported by any Hadoop tools, so you have to look elsewhere.

■ **Problem**

You want to automate moving files from HDFS to a local filesystem.

■ **Solution**

The HDFS File Slurper can be used to copy files from HDFS to a local filesystem.

■ **Discussion**

The goal here is to use the HDFS File Slurper project (https://github.com/alexholmes/hdfs-file-slurper) to assist with the automation. We covered the HDFS File Slurper in detail in technique 40—please read that section before continuing with this technique.

In addition to the way you used it in technique 40, the HDFS Slurper also supports moving data from HDFS out to a local directory. All you need to do is flip around the source and destination directories, as you can see from the following subsection of the Slurper's configuration file:

```
SRC_DIR = hdfs:/tmp/slurper/in
WORK_DIR = hdfs:/tmp/slurper/work
COMPLETE_DIR = hdfs:/tmp/slurper/complete
ERROR_DIR = hdfs:/tmp/slurper/error
DEST_STAGING_DIR = file:/tmp/slurper/stage
DEST_DIR = file:/tmp/slurper/dest
```

You'll notice that not only is the source directory in HDFS, but also the work, complete, and error directories are there. This is because you need to be able to atomically move files between directories without incurring the expensive overhead of copying the files across filesystems.

■ **Summary**

At this point you may wonder how you can trigger the Slurper to copy a directory that was just written with a MapReduce job. When a MapReduce job completes successfully, it creates a file called _SUCCESS in the job output directory. This would seem like the perfect trigger to kick off an egress process to copy that content to a local filesystem. As it turns out, Oozie has a mechanism that can trigger a workflow when it detects these Hadoop "success" files, but again the challenge here is that any work performed by Oozie is performed in MapReduce, so it can't be used to perform the transfer directly.

You could write your own script that polls HDFS for completed directories and then triggers a file copy process. That file copy process could be the Slurper or a simple `hadoop fs -get` command if the source files need to be kept intact.

In the next topic we'll look at writing data from Hadoop out to relational databases.

5.3.3 *Databases*

Databases are usually the target of Hadoop data egress in one of two circumstances: either when you move data back into production databases to be used by production systems, or when you move data into OLAP databases to perform business intelligence and analytics functions.

In this section we'll use Apache Sqoop to export data from Hadoop to a MySQL database. Sqoop is a tool that simplifies database imports and exports. Sqoop is covered in detail in technique 42.

We'll walk through the process of exporting data from HDFS to Sqoop. We'll also cover methods for using the regular connector, as well as how to perform bulk imports using the fast connector.

TECHNIQUE 53   **Using Sqoop to export data to MySQL**

Hadoop excels at performing operations at scales that defeat most relational databases, so it's common to extract OLTP data into HDFS, perform some analysis, and then export it back out to a database.

■ **Problem**

You want to write data to relational databases, and at the same time ensure that writes are idempotent.

■ **Solution**

This technique covers how Sqoop can be used to export text files to a relational database and also looks at how Sqoop can be configured to work with files with custom field and record delimiters. We'll also cover idempotent exports to make sure that failed exports don't leave your database in an inconsistent state.

■ **Discussion**

This technique assumes you've already followed the instructions in technique 42 to install MySQL and create the schema.

Sqoop exports require that the database table you're exporting into already exists. Sqoop can support both inserts and updates of rows in the table.

Exporting data to a database shares many of the arguments that we examined in the import section. The differences are that exports require the `--export-dir` argument to determine the HDFS directory to export. You'll also create another options file for exports to keep from insecurely supplying the password on the command line:

```
$ cat > ~/.sqoop_export_options.txt << EOF
export
--username
hip_sqoop_user
--password
password
--connect
jdbc:mysql://localhost/sqoop_test
EOF
$ chmod 700 ~/.sqoop_export_options.txt
```

Your first step will be to export data from MySQL to HDFS to ensure you have a good starting point, as shown in the following commands:

```
$ hadoop fs -rmr stocks
$ sqoop --options-file ~/.sqoop_import_options.txt \
  --connect jdbc:mysql://localhost/sqoop_test --table stocks
```

The result of the Sqoop import is a number of CSV files in HDFS, as you can see in the following code:

```
$ hadoop fs -cat stocks/part-m-00000 | head
1,AAPL,2009-01-02,85.88,91.04,85.16,90.75,26643400,90.75
2,AAPL,2008-01-02,199.27,200.26,192.55,194.84,38542100,194.84
...
```

For the Sqoop export from HDFS to MySQL, you'll specify that the target table should be stocks_export and that it should export data from the HDFS stocks directory:

```
$ sqoop --options-file ~/.sqoop_export_options.txt \
  --export-dir stocks \
  --table stocks_export
```

By default, Sqoop exports will perform an INSERT into the target database table. It can support updates with the --update-mode argument. A value of updateonly means that if there's no matching key, the updates will fail. A value of allowinsert results in an insert if a matching key doesn't exist. The table column name that's used to perform the update is supplied in the --update-key argument.

The following example indicates that only an update should be attempted, using the primary key for the update:

```
$ sqoop --options-file ~/.sqoop_export_options.txt \
    --update-mode updateonly \
    --update-key id \
    --export-dir stocks \
    --table stocks_export
```

Input data formatting

You can use several options to override the default Sqoop settings for parsing the input data. Table 5.7 lists these options.

Table 5.7 Formatting options for input data

Argument	Default	Description
--input-enclosed-by	(None)	The field enclosing character. Every field must be enclosed with this character. (If the field enclosing character can occur inside a field, the --input-optionally-enclosed-by option should be used to enclose that field.)
--input-escaped-by	(None)	Escape character, where the next character is extracted literally and isn't parsed.
--input-fields-⇥ terminated-by	,	The field separator.
--input-lines-⇥ terminated-by	\n	The line terminator.
--input-optionally-⇥ enclosed-by	(None)	The field enclosing character. This argument is the same as --input-enclosed-by, except that it's applied only to fields that contain the field separator character. For example, in CSV it's common for fields to be enclosed by double quotes only when they contain commas.

Idempotent exports

The Sqoop map tasks that perform the exports use multiple transactions for their database writes. If a Sqoop export MapReduce job fails, your table could contain partial writes. For idempotent database writes, Sqoop can be instructed to perform the MapReduce writes to the staging table. After successful job completion, the staging table is moved to the target table in a single transaction, which is idempotent. You can see the sequence of events in figure 5.19.

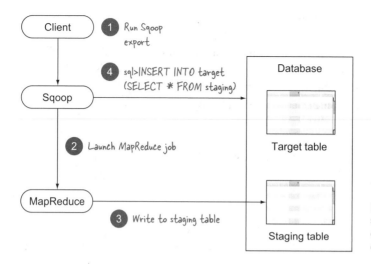

Figure 5.19 Sqoop staging sequence of events, which helps ensure idempotent writes

In the following example, the staging table is stocks_staging, and you're also telling Sqoop to clear it out before the MapReduce job starts with the --clear-staging-table argument:

```
$ sqoop --options-file ~/.sqoop_export_options.txt \
        --export-dir stocks \
        --table stocks_export \
        --staging-table stocks_staging \
        --clear-staging-table
```

Direct exports

You used the fast connector in the import technique, which was an optimization that used the mysqldump utility. Sqoop exports also support using the fast connector, which uses the mysqlimport tool. As with mysqldump, all of the nodes in your cluster need to have mysqlimport installed and available in the path of the user that's used to run MapReduce tasks. And as with the import, the --direct argument enables utilization of the fast connectors:

```
$ sqoop --options-file ~/.sqoop_export_options.txt \
        --direct \
        --export-dir stocks \
        --table stocks_export
```

Idempotent exports with mysqlimport

Sqoop doesn't support using fast connectors in conjunction with a staging table, which is how you achieve idempotent writes with regular connectors. But it's still possible to achieve idempotent writes with fast connectors with a little extra work at your end. You need to use the fast connector to write to a staging table, and then trigger the INSERT statement, which atomically copies the data into the target table. The steps would look like the following:

```
$ sqoop --options-file ~/.sqoop_export_options.txt \
        --direct \
        --export-dir stocks \
        --table stocks_staging

$ mysql --host=localhost \
        --user=hip_sqoop_user \
        --password=password \
        -e "INSERT INTO stocks_export (SELECT * FROM stocks_staging)"\
        sqoop_test
```

This breaks the earlier rule about exposing credentials on the command line, but it's easy to write a wrapper script that can read these settings from a configuration file.

■ **Summary**

Sqoop provides a simplified usage model compared to using the DBInputFormat format classes that are provided in MapReduce. But using the DBInputFormat classes will give you the added flexibility to transform or preprocess your data in the same MapReduce job that performs the database export. The advantage of Sqoop is that it doesn't require you to write any code, and it has some useful notions, such as staging, to help you achieve your idempotent goals.

The final step in this section, and in the chapter, is to look at exporting data to HBase.

5.3.4 *NoSQL*

MapReduce is a powerful and efficient way to bulk-load data into external systems. So far we've covered how Sqoop can be used to load relational data, and now we'll look at NoSQL systems, and specifically HBase.

Apache HBase is a distributed key/value, column-oriented data store. Earlier in this chapter we looked at how to import data from HBase into HDFS, as well as how to use HBase as a data source for a MapReduce job.

The most efficient way to load data into HBase is via its built-in bulk-loading mechanism, which is described in detail on the HBase wiki page titled "Bulk Loading" at https://hbase.apache.org/book/arch.bulk.load.html. But this approach bypasses the write-ahead log (WAL), which means that the data being loaded isn't replicated to slave HBase nodes.

HBase also comes with an org.apache.hadoop.hbase.mapreduce.Export class, which will load HBase tables from HDFS, similar to how the equivalent import worked earlier in this chapter. But you must have your data in SequenceFile form, which has disadvantages, including no support for versioning.

You can also use the TableOutputFormat class in your own MapReduce job to export data to HBase, but this approach is slower than the bulk-loading tool.

We've now concluded our examination of Hadoop egress tools. We covered how you can use the HDFS File Slurper to move data out to a filesystem and how to use Sqoop for idempotent writes to relational databases, and we wrapped up with a look at ways to move Hadoop data into HBase.

5.4   *Chapter summary*

Moving data in and out of Hadoop is a critical part of the Hadoop architecture. In this chapter we covered a broad spectrum of techniques that you can use to perform data ingress and egress activities and that work with a variety of data sources. Of note, we covered Flume, a data collection and distribution solution, Sqoop, a tool for moving relational data in and out of Hadoop, and Camus, a tool for ingesting Kafka data into HDFS.

Now that your data is tucked away in HDFS, it's time to look at some interesting processing patterns that you can apply to that data.

Part 3

Big data patterns

Now that you've gotten to know Hadoop and know how to best organize, move, and store your data in Hadoop, you're ready to explore part 3 of this book, which examines the techniques you need to know to streamline your big data computations.

In chapter 6 we'll examine techniques for optimizing MapReduce operations, such as joining and sorting on large datasets. These techniques make jobs run faster and allow for more efficient use of computational resources.

Chapter 7 examines how graphs can be represented and utilized in MapReduce to solve algorithms such as friends-of-friends and PageRank. It also covers how data structures such as Bloom filters and HyperLogLog can be used when regular data structures can't scale to the data sizes that you're working with.

Chapter 8 looks at how to measure, collect, and profile your MapReduce jobs and identify areas in your code and hardware that could be causing jobs to run longer than they should. It also tames MapReduce code by presenting different approaches to unit testing. Finally, it looks at how you can debug any MapReduce job, and offers some anti-patterns you'd best avoid.

Applying MapReduce patterns to big data

With your data safely in HDFS, it's time to learn how to work with that data in MapReduce. Previous chapters showed you some MapReduce snippets in action when working with data serialization. In this chapter we'll look at how to work effectively with big data in MapReduce to solve common problems.

> **MapReduce basics** If you want to understand the mechanics of MapReduce and how to write basic MapReduce programs, it's worth your time to read *Hadoop in Action* by Chuck Lam (Manning, 2010).

MapReduce contains many powerful features, and in this chapter we'll focus on joining, sorting, and sampling. These three patterns are important because they're natural operations you'll want to perform on your big data, and the goal of your clusters should be to squeeze as much performance as possible out of your MapReduce jobs.

The ability to *join* disparate and sparse data is a powerful MapReduce feature, but an awkward one in practice, so we'll also look at advanced techniques for optimizing join operations with large datasets. Examples of joins include combining log files with reference data from a database and inbound link calculations on web graphs.

Sorting in MapReduce is also a black art, and we'll dive into the depths of Map-Reduce to understand how it works by examining two techniques that everyone will encounter at some point: secondary sorting and total order sorting. We'll wrap things up with a look at *sampling* in MapReduce, which provides the opportunity to quickly iterate over a large dataset by working with a small subset of that data.

6.1   Joining

Joins are relational constructs used to combine relations together (you're probably familiar with them in the context of databases). In MapReduce, joins are applicable in situations where you have two or more datasets you want to combine. An example would be when you want to combine your users (which you extracted from your OLTP database) with your log files (which contain user activity details). Various scenarios exist where it would be useful to combine these datasets together, such as these:

- You want to aggregate data based on user demographics (such as differences in user habits, comparing teenagers and users in their 30s).

- You want to send an email to users who haven't used the website for a pre-scribed number of days.

- You want to create a feedback loop that examines a user's browsing habits, allowing your system to recommend previously unexplored site features to the user.

All of these scenarios require you to join datasets together, and the two most common types of joins are inner joins and outer joins. *Inner joins* compare all tuples in relations *L* and *R*, and produce a result if a join predicate is satisfied. In contrast, *outer joins* don't require both tuples to match based on a join predicate, and instead can retain a record from *L* or *R* even if no match exists. Figure 6.1 illustrates the different types of joins.

In this section we'll look at three joining strategies in MapReduce that support the two most common types of joins (inner and outer). These three strategies perform

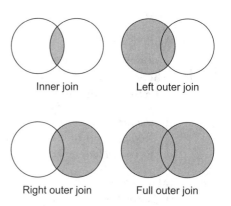

Figure 6.1   Different types of joins combining relations, shown as Venn diagrams. The shaded areas show data that is retained in the join.

the join either in the map phase or in the reduce phase by taking advantage of the MapReduce sort-merge architecture:

- *Repartition join*—A reduce-side join for situations where you're joining two or more large datasets together
- *Replication join*—A map-side join that works in situations where one of the datasets is small enough to cache
- *Semi-join*—Another map-side join where one dataset is initially too large to fit into memory, but after some filtering can be reduced down to a size that can fit in memory

After we cover these joining strategies, we'll look at a decision tree so you can determine the best join strategy for your situation.

Join data

The techniques will all utilize two datasets to perform the join—users and logs. The user data contains user names, ages, and states. The complete dataset follows:

```
anne     22    NY
joe      39    CO
alison   35    NY
mike     69    VA
marie    27    OR
jim      21    OR
bob      71    CA
mary     53    NY
dave     36    VA
dude     50    CA
```

The logs dataset shows some user-based activity that could be extracted from application or webserver logs. The data includes the username, an action, and the source IP address. Here's the complete dataset:

```
jim      logout       93.24.237.12
mike     new_tweet    87.124.79.252
bob      new_tweet    58.133.120.100
mike     logout       55.237.104.36
jim      new_tweet    93.24.237.12
marie    view_user    122.158.130.90
jim      login        198.184.237.49
marie    login        58.133.120.100
```

Let's get started by looking at which join method you should pick given your data.

TECHNIQUE 54 **Picking the best join strategy for your data**

Each of the join strategies covered in this section has different strengths and weaknesses, and it can be challenging to determine which one is best suited for the data you're working with. This technique takes a look at different traits in the data and uses that information to pick the optimal approach to join your data.

- **Problem**

You want to select the optimal method to join your data.

- **Solution**

Use a data-driven decision tree to pick the best join strategy.

- **Discussion**

Figure 6.2 shows a decision tree you can use.[1]

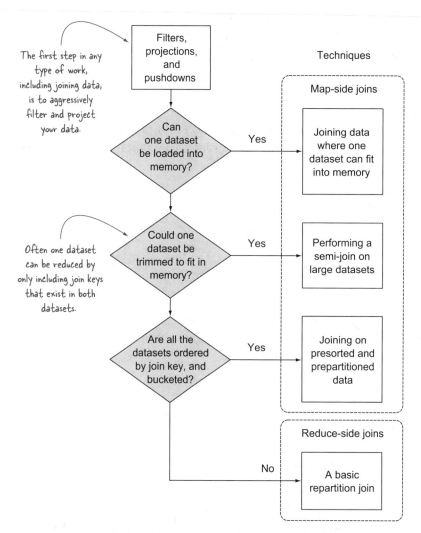

Figure 6.2   Decision tree for selecting a join strategy

---

[1] This decision tree is modeled after the one presented by Spyros Blanas et al., in "A Comparison of Join Algorithms for Log Processing in MapReduce," http://pages.cs.wisc.edu/~jignesh/publ/hadoopjoin.pdf.

The decision tree can be summarized in the following three points:

- If one of your datasets is small enough to fit into a mapper's memory, the map-only replicated join is efficient.
- If both datasets are large and one dataset can be substantially reduced by prefiltering elements that don't match the other, the semi-join works well.
- If you can't preprocess your data and your data sizes are too large to cache—which means you have to perform the join in the reducer—repartition joins need to be used.

Regardless of which strategy you pick, one of the most fundamental activities you should be performing in your joins is using filters and projections.

TECHNIQUE 55 Filters, projections, and pushdowns

In this technique, we'll examine how you can effectively use filters and projections in your mappers to cut down on the amount of data that you're working with, and spilling, in MapReduce. This technique also examines a more advanced optimization called pushdowns, which can further improve your data pipeline.

■ **Problem**

You're working with large data volumes and you want to efficiently manage your input data to optimize your jobs.

■ **Solution**

Filter and project your data to only include the data points you'll be using in your work.

■ **Discussion**

Filtering and projecting data is the biggest optimization you can make when joining data, and when working with data in general. This is a technique that applies to any OLAP activity, and it's equally effective in Hadoop.

Why are filtering and projection so important? They cut down on the amount of data that a processing pipeline needs to handle. Having less data to work with is important, especially when you're pushing that data across network and disk boundaries. The shuffle step in MapReduce is expensive because data is being written to local disk and across the network, so having fewer bytes to push around means that your jobs and the MapReduce framework have less work to do, and this translates to faster jobs and less pressure on the CPU, disk, and your networking gear.

Figure 6.3 shows a simple example of how filtering and projection works.

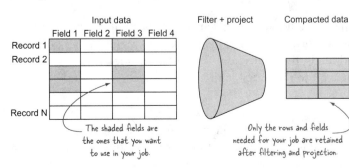

Figure 6.3 Using filters and projections to reduce data sizes

Filters and projections should be performed as close to the data source as possible; in MapReduce this work is best performed in the mappers. The following code shows an example of a filter that excludes users under 30 and only projects their names and states:

```
@Override
protected void map(LongWritable offset, Text value, Context context) {

    User user = User.fromText(value);
    if (user.getAge() >= 30) {                        ◄............  Filter out users that
      context.write(new Text(user.getName()),                       are younger than 30.
          new Text(user.getState())));      ◄
    }
}                                                   Project just the
                                                    name and state.
```

The challenge with using filters in joins is that it's possible that not all of the datasets you're joining will contain the fields you want to filter on. If this is the case, take a look at technique 61, which discusses using a Bloom filter to help solve this challenge.

Pushdowns

Projection and predicate pushdowns take filtering further by pushing the projections and predicates down to the storage format. This is even more efficient, especially when working with storage formats that can skip over records or entire blocks based on the pushdowns.

Table 6.1 lists the various storage formats and whether they support pushdowns.

Table 6.1   Storage formats and their pushdown support

Format	Projection pushdown supported?	Predicate pushdown supported?
Text (CSV, JSON, etc.)	No	No
Protocol Buffers	No	No
Thrift	No	No
Avro[a]	No	No
Parquet	Yes	Yes

[a] Avro has both row-major and column-major storage formats.

> **Further reading on pushdowns**   Chapter 3 contains additional details on how Parquet pushdowns can be used in your jobs.

It's pretty clear that a big advantage of Parquet is its ability to support both types of pushdowns. If you're working with huge datasets and regularly work on only a subset of the records and fields, then you should consider Parquet as your storage format.

It's time to move on to the actual joining techniques.

6.1.1   Map-side joins

Our coverage of joining techniques will start with a look at performing joins in the mapper. The reason we'll cover these techniques first is that they're the optimal join strategies if your data can support map-side joins. Reduce-size joins are expensive by comparison due to the overhead of shuffling data between the mappers and reducers. As a general policy, map-side joins are preferred.

In this section we'll look at three different flavors of map-side joins. Technique 56 works well in situations where one of the datasets is already small enough to cache in memory. Technique 57 is more involved, and it also requires that one dataset can fit in memory after filtering out records where the join key exists in both datasets. Technique 58 works in situations where your data is sorted and distributed across your files in a certain way.

TECHNIQUE 56   Joining data where one dataset can fit into memory

A replicated join is a map-side join, and it gets its name from its function—the smallest of the datasets is replicated to all the map hosts. The replicated join depends on the fact that one of the datasets being joined is small enough to be cached in memory.

■ **Problem**

You want to perform a join on data where one dataset can fit into your mapper's memory.

■ **Solution**

Use the distributed cache to cache the smaller dataset and perform the join as the larger dataset is streamed to the mappers.

■ **Discussion**

You'll use the distributed cache to copy the small dataset to the nodes running the map tasks[2] and use the initialization method of each map task to load it into a hashtable. Use the key from each record fed to the map function from the large dataset to look up the small dataset hashtable, and perform a join between the large dataset record and all of the records from the small dataset that match the join value. Figure 6.4 shows how the replicated join works in MapReduce.

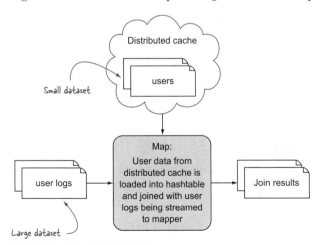

Figure 6.4   Map-only replicated join

---

[2]   Hadoop's distributed cache copies files located on the MapReduce client host or files in HDFS to the slave nodes before any map or reduce tasks are executed on the nodes. Tasks can read these files from their local disk to use as part of their work.

The following code performs this join:[3]

```java
public void run(Path usersPath, Path userLogsPath, Path outputPath) {

  Configuration conf = super.getConf();

  Job job = new Job(conf);

  job.setJarByClass(ReplicatedJoin.class);
  job.setMapperClass(JoinMap.class);

  job.addCacheFile(usersPath.toUri());
  job.getConfiguration().set(
    JoinMap.DISTCACHE_FILENAME, usersPath.getName());

  job.setNumReduceTasks(0);

  FileInputFormat.setInputPaths(job, userLogsPath);
  FileOutputFormat.setOutputPath(job, outputPath);

  job.waitForCompletion(true);
}

public static class JoinMap
             extends Mapper<LongWritable, Text, Text, Text> {
  public static final String DISTCACHE_FILENAME = "distcachefile";
  private Map<String, User> users = new HashMap<String, User>();

  @Override
  protected void setup(Context context)
      throws IOException, InterruptedException {

    URI[] files = context.getCacheFiles();

    final String distributedCacheFilename =
        context.getConfiguration().get(DISTCACHE_FILENAME_CONFIG);

    for (URI uri: files) {
      File path = new File(uri.getPath());

      if (path.getName().equals(distributedCacheFilename)) {
        loadCache(path);
        break;
      }
    }
  }

  private void loadCache(File file) throws IOException {
    for(String line: FileUtils.readLines(file)) {
      User user = User.fromString(line);
      users.put(user.getName(), user);
    }
  }
}
```

Add the users file to the distributed cache. (annotation pointing to `job.addCacheFile(usersPath.toUri());`)

Save the users filename to the job config. (annotation pointing to `job.getConfiguration().set(...)`)

The larger user log file is the job input. (annotation pointing to `FileInputFormat.setInputPaths(job, userLogsPath);`)

Extract the user filename from the job config. (annotation pointing to `final String distributedCacheFilename = ...`)

Loop through all the files in the distributed cache searching for your file. (annotation pointing to `for (URI uri: files) {`)

When your file is found, load the users into memory. (annotation pointing to `loadCache(path);`)

---

[3] GitHub   source: https://github.com/alexholmes/hiped2/blob/master/src/main/java/hip/ch6/joins/replicated/simple/ReplicatedJoin.java.

```
@Override
protected void map(LongWritable offset, Text value, Context context)
    throws IOException, InterruptedException {

  UserLog userLog = UserLog.fromText(value);
  User user = users.get(userLog.getName());
  if (user != null) {
    context.write(
        new Text(user.toString()),
        new Text(userLog.toString()));
  }
 }
}
```

If the user exists in both datasets, emit the combined records.

To perform this join, you first need to copy the two files you're going to join to your home directory in HDFS:

```
$ hadoop fs -put test-data/ch6/users.txt .
$ hadoop fs -put test-data/ch6/user-logs.txt .
```

Next, run the job and examine its output once it has completed:

```
$ hip hip.ch6.joins.replicated.simple.ReplicatedJoin \
    --users users.txt \
    --user-logs user-logs.txt \
    --output output

$ hadoop fs -cat output/part*
jim     21  OR  jim    logout    93.24.237.12
mike    69  VA  mike   new_tweet 87.124.79.252
bob     71  CA  bob    new_tweet 58.133.120.100
mike    69  VA  mike   logout    55.237.104.36
jim     21  OR  jim    new_tweet 93.24.237.12
marie   27  OR  marie  view_user 122.158.130.90
jim     21  OR  jim    login     198.184.237.49
marie   27  OR  marie  login     58.133.120.100
```

Hive

Hive joins can be converted to map-side joins by configuring the job prior to execution. It's important that the largest table be the last table in the query, as that's the table that Hive will stream in the mapper (the other tables will be cached):

```
set hive.auto.convert.join=true;

SELECT /*+ MAPJOIN(l) */ u.*, l.*
FROM users u
JOIN user_logs l ON u.name = l.name;
```

> **De-emphasizing map-join hint** Hive 0.11 implemented some changes that ostensibly removed the need to supply map-join hints as part of the SELECT statement, but it's unclear in which situations the hint is no longer needed (see https://issues.apache.org/jira/browse/HIVE-3784).

Map-side joins are not supported for full or right outer joins; they'll execute as repartition joins (reduce-side joins).

■ **Summary**

Both inner and outer joins can be supported with replicated joins. This technique implemented an inner join, because only records that had the same key in both datasets were emitted. To convert this into an outer join, you could emit values being streamed to the mapper that don't have a corresponding entry in the hashtable, and you could similarly keep track of hashtable entries that were matched with streamed map records and use the cleanup method at the end of the map task to emit records from the hashtable that didn't match any of the map inputs.

Is there a way to further optimize map-side joins in cases where the dataset is small enough to cache in memory? It's time to look at semi-joins.

TECHNIQUE 57   **Performing a semi-join on large datasets**

Imagine a situation where you're working with two large datasets that you want to join, such as user logs and user data from an OLTP database. Neither of these datasets is small enough to cache in a map task's memory, so it would seem you'll have to resign yourself to performing a reduce-side join. But not necessarily—ask yourself this question: would one of the datasets fit into memory if you were to remove all records that didn't match a record from the other dataset?

In our example there's a good chance that the users that appear in your logs are a small percentage of the overall set of users in your OLTP database, so by removing all the OLTP users that don't appear in your logs, you could get the dataset down to a size that fits into memory. If this is the case, a semi-join is the solution. Figure 6.5 shows the three MapReduce jobs you need to execute to perform a semi-join.

Let's look at what's involved in writing a semi-join.

■ **Problem**

You want to join large datasets together and at the same time avoid the overhead of the shuffle and sort phases.

■ **Solution**

In this technique you'll use three MapReduce jobs to join two datasets together to avoid the overhead of a reducer-side join. This technique is useful in situations where you're working with large datasets, but where a job can be reduced down to a size that can fit into the memory of a task by filtering out records that don't match the other dataset.

■ **Discussion**

In this technique you'll break down the three jobs illustrated in figure 6.5.

Job 1

The function of the first MapReduce job is to produce a set of unique user names that exist in the log files. You do this by having the map function perform a projection of the user name, and in turn use the reducers to emit the user name. To cut down on the amount of data transferred between the map and reduce phases, you'll have the

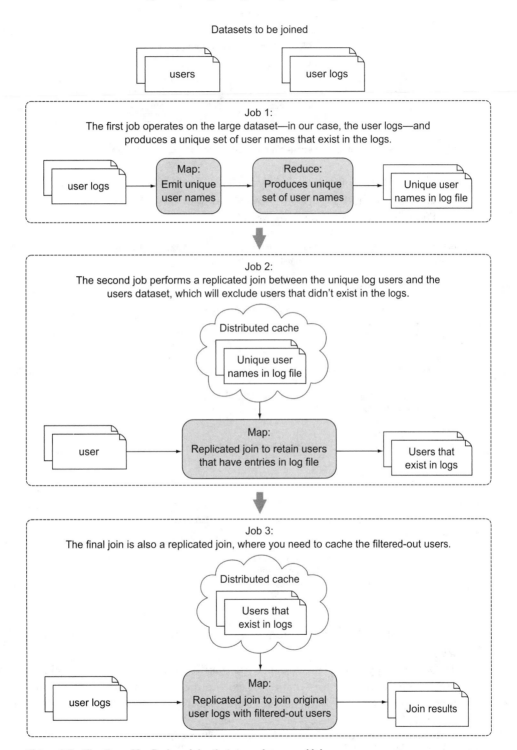

Figure 6.5 The three MapReduce jobs that comprise a semi-join

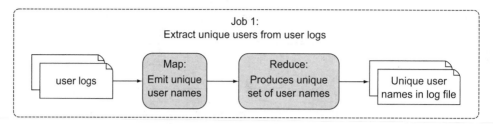

Figure 6.6   The first job in the semi-join produces a unique set of user names that exist in the log files.

map task cache all of the user names in a HashSet and emit the values of the HashSet in the cleanup method. Figure 6.6 shows the flow of this job.

The following code shows the MapReduce job:[4]

```java
public static class Map extends Mapper<Text, Text, Text, NullWritable> {
    private Set<String> keys = new HashSet<String>();        // Create the HashSet to
                                                              // cache the user names.
    @Override
    protected void map(Text key, Text value, Context context)
        throws IOException, InterruptedException {
      keys.add(key.toString());         // Add the user name
    }                                    // to the cache.

    @Override
    protected void cleanup(
        Context context)
        throws IOException, InterruptedException {
      Text outputKey = new Text();
      for(String key: keys) {
        outputKey.set(key);
        context.write(outputKey, NullWritable.get());     // Emit the cached user
      }                                                   // names from the mapper.
    }
}

public static class Reduce
    extends Reducer<Text, NullWritable, Text, NullWritable> {
    @Override
    protected void reduce(Text key, Iterable<NullWritable> values,
                          Context context)
        throws IOException, InterruptedException {          // Emit each user name
      context.write(key, NullWritable.get());               // once from the reducer.
    }
}
```

The result of the first job is a unique set of users that appear in the log files.

Job 2

The second step is an elaborate filtering MapReduce job, where the goal is to remove users from the user dataset that don't exist in the log data. This is a map-only job that uses a replicated join to cache the user names that appear in the log files and join

---

[4] GitHub source: https://github.com/alexholmes/hiped2/blob/master/src/main/java/hip/ch6/joins/semijoin/UniqueHashedKeyJob.java.

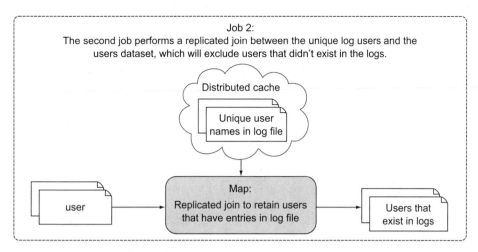

Figure 6.7   The second job in the semi-join removes users from the user dataset missing from the log data.

them with the user dataset. The unique user output from job 1 will be substantially smaller than the entire user dataset, which makes it the natural selection for caching. Figure 6.7 shows the flow of this job.

This is a replicated join, just like the one you saw in the previous technique. For that reason I won't include the code here, but you can easily access it on GitHub.[5]

Job 3

In this final step you'll combine the filtered users produced from job 2 with the original user logs. The filtered users should now be few enough to stick into memory, allowing you to put them in the distributed cache. Figure 6.8 shows the flow of this job.

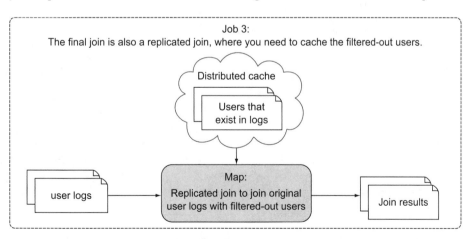

Figure 6.8   The third job in the semi-join combines the users produced from job 2 with the original user logs.

---

[5] GitHub source: https://github.com/alexholmes/hiped2/blob/master/src/main/java/hip/ch6/joins/semijoin/ReplicatedFilterJob.java.

Again you're using the replicated join to perform this join, so I won't show the code for that here—please refer to the previous technique for more details on replicated joins, or go straight to GitHub for the source of this job.[6]

Run the code and look at the output produced by each of the previous steps:

```
$ hip hip.ch6.joins.semijoin.Main \
  --users users.txt \                      The output directory shows three
  --user-logs user-logs.txt \              subdirectories corresponding to
  --output output                          the three jobs you ran.

$ hadoop fs -ls output       ◄
/user/aholmes/output/filtered
/user/aholmes/output/result
/user/aholmes/output/unique
                                           The output of the first
$ hadoop fs -cat output/unique/part*   ◄   job is the unique user
bob                                        names in the log file.
jim
marie
mike
                                           The second job's output shows
$ hadoop fs -cat output/filtered/part*  ◄  the users file filtered by users
mike   69  VA                              that were in the log file.
marie  27  OR
jim    21  OR
bob    71  CA


$ hadoop fs -cat output/result/part*  ◄
jim    logout     93.24.237.12      21  OR    The final output has the results
mike   new_tweet  87.124.79.252  69  VA        of the join between the user
bob    new_tweet  58.133.120.100  71  CA        logs and the filtered users.
mike   logout     55.237.104.36   69  VA
jim    new_tweet  93.24.237.12    21  OR
marie  view_user  122.158.130.90  27  OR
jim    login      198.184.237.49  21  OR
marie  login      58.133.120.100  27  OR
```

The output shows the logical progression of the jobs in the semi-join and the final join output.

■ **Summary**

In this technique we looked at how to use a semi-join to combine two datasets together. The semi-join construct involves more steps than the other joins, but it's a powerful way to use a map-side join even when working with large datasets (with the caveat that one of the datasets must be reduced to a size that fits in memory).

With these three join strategies in hand, you may be wondering which one you should use in what circumstances.

---

[6] GitHub source: https://github.com/alexholmes/hiped2/blob/master/src/main/java/hip/ch6/joins/semijoin/FinalJoinJob.java.

TECHNIQUE 58   Joining on presorted and prepartitioned data

Map-side joins are the most efficient techniques, and the previous two map-side strategies both required that one of the datasets could be loaded into memory. What if you're working with large datasets that can't be reduced down to a smaller size as required by the previous technique? In this case, a composite map-side join may be viable, but only if all of the following requirements are met:

- None of the datasets can be loaded in memory in its entirety.
- The datasets are all sorted by the join key.
- Each dataset has the same number of files.
- File *N* in each dataset contains the same join key *K*.
- Each file is less than the size of an HDFS block, so that partitions aren't split. Or alternatively, the input split for the data doesn't split files.

Figure 6.9 shows an example of sorted and partitioned files that lend themselves to composite joins. This technique will look at how you can use the composite join in your jobs.

■ **Problem**

You want to perform a map-side join on sorted, partitioned data.

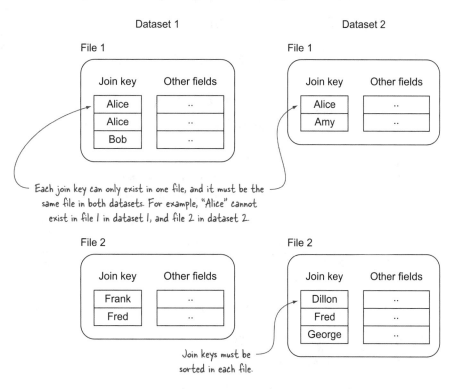

Figure 6.9   An example of sorted files used as input for the composite join

■ **Solution**

Use the `CompositeInputFormat` bundled with MapReduce.

■ **Discussion**

The `CompositeInputFormat` is quite powerful and supports both inner and outer joins. The following example shows how an inner join would be performed on your data:[7]

```
public void run(Path usersPath, Path userLogsPath, Path outputPath) {

    Configuration conf = super.getConf();

    Job job = new Job(conf);

    job.setJarByClass(CompositeJoin.class);
    job.setMapperClass(JoinMap.class);

    job.setInputFormatClass(CompositeInputFormat.class);
    job.getConfiguration().set(CompositeInputFormat.JOIN_EXPR,
        CompositeInputFormat.compose("inner",
            KeyValueTextInputFormat.class, usersPath, userLogsPath)
    );

    job.setNumReduceTasks(0);

    FileOutputFormat.setOutputPath(job, outputPath);

    job.waitForCompletion(true);
}

public static class JoinMap extends Mapper<Text, TupleWritable,
                                            Text, Text> {
    @Override
    protected void map(Text key, TupleWritable value, Context context) {
        context.write(key,
            new Text(StringUtils.join(value.get(0), value.get(1))));
    }
}
```

Configure the CompositeInputFormat.

Specify the input format.

Specify that an inner join should be performed (outer joins are also supported).

Specify the input format and input locations for the datasets being joined. The key emitted by the input format is used as the join key, so use of the KeyValueInputFormat results in the join key being the first token of each input line.

Extract and emit the join value from both datasets.

The composite join requires the input files to be sorted by key (which is the user name in our example), so before you run the example you'll need to sort the two files and upload them to HDFS:

```
$ sort -k1,1 test-data/ch6/users.txt > users-sorted.txt
$ sort -k1,1 test-data/ch6/user-logs.txt > user-logs-sorted.txt
$ hadoop fs -put users-sorted.txt .
$ hadoop fs -put user-logs-sorted.txt .
```

Next, run the job and examine its output once it has completed:

```
$ hip hip.ch6.joins.composite.CompositeJoin \
    --users users-sorted.txt \
    --user-logs user-logs-sorted.txt \
```

---

[7] GitHub source: https://github.com/alexholmes/hiped2/blob/master/src/main/java/hip/ch6/joins/composite/CompositeJoin.java.

```
    --output output

$ hadoop fs -cat output/part*
bob    71  CA  new_tweet  58.133.120.100
jim    21  OR  login      198.184.237.49
jim    21  OR  logout     93.24.237.12
jim    21  OR  new_tweet  93.24.237.12
marie  27  OR  login      58.133.120.100
marie  27  OR  view_user  122.158.130.90
mike   69  VA  logout     55.237.104.36
mike   69  VA  new_tweet  87.124.79.252
```

Hive

Hive supports a map-side join called a *sort-merge join*, which operates in much the same way as this technique. It also requires all the keys to be sorted in both tables, and the tables must be bucketized into the same number of buckets. You need to specify a number of configurables and also use the MAPJOIN hint to enable this behavior:

```
set hive.input.format=
org.apache.hadoop.hive.ql.io.BucketizedHiveInputFormat;
set hive.optimize.bucketmapjoin = true;
set hive.optimize.bucketmapjoin.sortedmerge = true;

SELECT /*+ MAPJOIN(l) */ u.*, l.*
FROM users u
JOIN user_logs l ON u.name = l.name;
```

■ Summary

The composite join actually supports *N*-way joins, so more than two datasets can be joined. But all datasets must conform to the same set of restrictions that were discussed at the start of this technique.

Because each mapper works with two or more data inputs, data locality can only exist with one of the datasets, so the remaining ones must be streamed from other data nodes.

This join is certainly restrictive in terms of how your data must exist prior to running the join, but if your data is already laid out that way, then this is a good way to join data and avoid the overhead of the shuffle in reducer-based joins.

6.1.2 Reduce-side joins

If none of the map-side techniques work for your data, you'll need to use the shuffle in MapReduce to sort and join your data together. The following techniques present a number of tips and tricks for your reduce-side joins.

TECHNIQUE 59   A basic repartition join

The first technique is a basic reduce-side join, which allows you to perform inner and outer joins.

■ Problem

You want to join together large datasets.

■ **Solution**

Use a reduce-side repartition join.

■ **Discussion**

A repartition join is a reduce-side join that takes advantage of MapReduce's sort-merge to group together records. It's implemented as a single MapReduce job, and it can support an *N*-way join, where *N* is the number of datasets being joined.

The map phase is responsible for reading the data from the various datasets, determining the join value for each record, and emitting that join value as the output key. The output value contains data that you'll want to include when you combine datasets together in the reducer to produce the job output.

A single reducer invocation receives all of the values for a join key emitted by the map function, and it partitions the data into *N* partitions, where *N* is the number of datasets being joined. After the reducer has read all of the input records for the join value and partitioned them in memory, it performs a Cartesian product across all partitions and emits the results of each join. Figure 6.10 shows the repartition join at a high level.

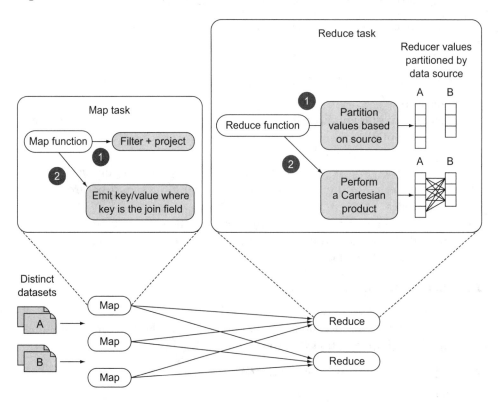

Figure 6.10   A basic MapReduce implementation of a repartition join

There are a number of things that your MapReduce code will need to be able to support for this technique:

- It needs to support multiple map classes, each handling a different input dataset. This is accomplished by using the `MultipleInputs` class.
- It needs a way to mark records being emitted by the mappers so that they can be correlated with the dataset of their origin. Here you'll use the htuple project to easily work with composite data in MapReduce.[8]

The code for the repartition join follows:[9]

```
enum ValueFields {              ◀———  Create an enum to easily
  DATASET,                            reference fields in the
  DATA                                map output tuple.
}

public static final int USERS = 0;      ◀———  Create constants to
public static final int USER_LOGS = 1;        represent each dataset.

public void run(Path usersPath, Path userLogsPath, Path outputPath) {

  Configuration conf = super.getConf();
                                                        Specify the mapper
  Job job = new Job(conf);                              for each dataset.
  job.setJarByClass(SimpleRepartitionMapReduce.class);   ◀———

  MultipleInputs.addInputPath(job, usersPath,
    TextInputFormat.class, UserMap.class);
  MultipleInputs.addInputPath(job, userLogsPath,
    TextInputFormat.class, UserLogMap.class);

  job.setReducerClass(Reduce.class);

  job.setMapOutputKeyClass(Text.class);
  job.setMapOutputValueClass(Tuple.class);

  FileOutputFormat.setOutputPath(job, outputPath);

  job.waitForCompletion(true);
}

public static class UserMap extends Mapper
  <LongWritable, Text, Text, Tuple> {

  @Override
  public void map(LongWritable key, Text value, Context context) {
    User user = User.fromText(value);
```

---

[8] htuple (http://htuple.org) is an open source project that was designed to make it easier to work with tuples in MapReduce. It was created to simplify secondary sorting, which is onerous in MapReduce.

[9] GitHub source: https://github.com/alexholmes/hiped2/blob/master/src/main/java/hip/ch6/joins/repartition/SimpleRepartitionJoin.java.

```java
      Tuple outputValue = new Tuple();
      outputValue.setInt(ValueFields.DATASET, USERS);
      outputValue.setString(ValueFields.DATA, value.toString());

      context.write(new Text(user.getName()), outputValue);
  }
}

public static class UserLogMap extends Mapper
  <LongWritable, Text, Text, Tuple> {

  @Override
  public void map(LongWritable key, Text value, Context context) {
    UserLog userLog = UserLog.fromText(value);

    Tuple outputValue = new Tuple();
    outputValue.setInt(ValueFields.DATASET, USER_LOGS);
    outputValue.setString(ValueFields.DATA, value.toString());

    context.write(new Text(userLog.getName()), outputValue);
  }
}

public static class Reduce extends Reducer<Text, Tuple, Text, Text> {

  List<String> users;
  List<String> userLogs;

  @Override
  protected void reduce(Text key, Iterable<Tuple> values,
                        Context context) {
    users = Lists.newArrayList();
    userLogs = Lists.newArrayList();

    for (Tuple tuple: values) {
      switch (tuple.getInt(ValueFields.DATASET)) {
        case USERS: {
          users.add(tuple.getString(ValueFields.DATA));
          break;
        }
        case USER_LOGS: {
          userLogs.add(tuple.getString(ValueFields.DATA));
          break;
        }
      }
    }

    for (String user: users) {
      for (String userLog: userLogs) {
        context.write(new Text(user), new Text(userLog));
      }
    }

  }
}
```

Identify "users" as the originating dataset in the output tuple.

Identify "user logs" as the originating dataset in the output tuple.

Partition the inputs into the appropriate list.

Perform a Cartesian product for the inner join.

You can use the following commands to run the job and view the job outputs:

```
$ hip hip.ch6.joins.repartition.SimpleRepartitionJoin \
    --users users.txt \
    --user-logs user-logs.txt \
    --output output

$ hadoop fs -cat output/part*
jim     21  OR  jim     login       198.184.237.49
jim     21  OR  jim     new_tweet   93.24.237.12
jim     21  OR  jim     logout      93.24.237.12
mike    69  VA  mike    logout      55.237.104.36
mike    69  VA  mike    new_tweet   87.124.79.252
bob     71  CA  bob     new_tweet   58.133.120.100
marie   27  OR  marie   login       58.133.120.100
marie   27  OR  marie   view_user   122.158.130.90
```

■ Summary

Hadoop comes bundled with a `hadoop-datajoin` module, which is a framework for repartition joins. It includes the main plumbing for handling multiple input datasets and performing the join.

The example shown in this technique as well as the `hadoop-datajoin` code are the most basic form of repartition joins. Both require that all the data for a join key be loaded into memory before the Cartesian product can be performed. This may work well for your data, but if you have join keys with cardinalities that are larger than your available memory, then you're out of luck. The next technique looks at a way you can possibly work around this problem.

TECHNIQUE 60   Optimizing the repartition join

The previous implementation of the repartition join is not space-efficient; it requires all of the output values for a given join value to be loaded into memory before it can perform the multiway join. It's more efficient to load the smaller of the datasets into memory and then iterate over the larger datasets, performing the join along the way.

■ Problem

You want to perform a repartition join in MapReduce, but you want to do so without the overhead of caching all the records in the reducer.

■ Solution

This technique uses an optimized repartition join framework that caches just one of the datasets being joined to reduce the amount of data cached in the reducers.

■ Discussion

This optimized join only caches records from the smaller of the two datasets to cut down on the memory overhead of caching all the records. Figure 6.11 shows the improved repartition join in action.

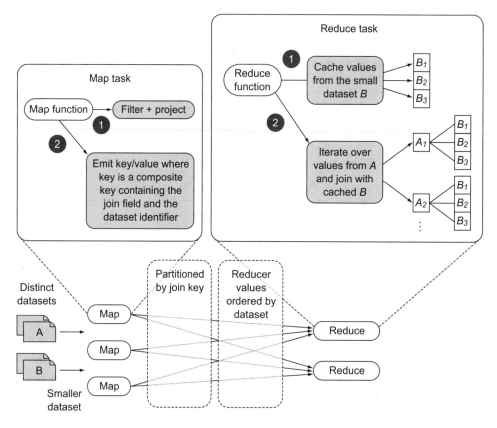

Figure 6.11 An optimized MapReduce implementation of a repartition join

There are a few differences between this technique and the simpler repartition join shown in the previous technique. In this technique you're using a secondary sort to ensure that all the records from the small dataset arrive at the reducer before all the records from the larger dataset. To accomplish this, you'll emit tuple output keys from the mapper containing the user name being joined on and a field identifying the originating dataset.

The following code shows a new enum containing the fields that the tuple will contain for the map output keys. It also shows how the user mapper populates the tuple fields:[10]

```
enum KeyFields {
  USER,
  DATASET
}
```

---

[10] GitHub source: https://github.com/alexholmes/hiped2/blob/master/src/main/java/hip/ch6/joins/repartition/StreamingRepartitionJoin.java.

```
Tuple outputKey = new Tuple();
outputKey.setString(KeyFields.USER, user.getName());
outputKey.setInt(KeyFields.DATASET, USERS);
```

The MapReduce driver code will need to be updated to indicate which fields in the tuple should be used for sorting, partitioning, and grouping:[11]

- The partitioner should only partition based on the user name, so that all the records for a user arrive at the same reducer.
- Sorting should use both the user name and dataset indicator, so that the smaller dataset is ordered first (by virtue of the fact that the USERS constant is a smaller number than the USER_LOGS constant, resulting in the user records being sorted before the user logs).
- The grouping should group on users so that both datasets are streamed to the same reducer invocation:

```
ShuffleUtils.configBuilder()
    .setPartitionerIndices(KeyFields.USER)
    .setSortIndices(KeyFields.USER, KeyFields.DATASET)
    .setGroupIndices(KeyFields.USER)
    .configure(job.getConfiguration());
```

Finally, you'll modify the reducer to cache the incoming user records, and then join them with the user logs:[12]

```
@Override
protected void reduce(Tuple key, Iterable<Tuple> values,
                      Context context){
  users = Lists.newArrayList();

  for (Tuple tuple : values) {
    switch (tuple.getInt(ValueFields.DATASET)) {
      case USERS: {
        users.add(tuple.getString(ValueFields.DATA));
        break;
      }
      case USER_LOGS: {
        String userLog = tuple.getString(ValueFields.DATA);
        for (String user : users) {
          context.write(new Text(user), new Text(userLog));
        }
        break;
      }
    }
  }
}
```

---

[11] Secondary sort is covered in more detail in section 6.2.1.

[12] GitHub source: https://github.com/alexholmes/hiped2/blob/master/src/main/java/hip/ch6/joins/repartition/StreamingRepartitionJoin.java.

You can use the following commands to run the job and view the job's output:

```
$ hip hip.ch6.joins.repartition.StreamingRepartitionJoin \
    --users users.txt \
    --user-logs user-logs.txt \
    --output output

$ hadoop fs -cat output/part*
bob     71  CA  bob    new_tweet 58.133.120.100
jim     21  OR  jim    logout    93.24.237.12
jim     21  OR  jim    new_tweet 93.24.237.12
jim     21  OR  jim    login     198.184.237.49
marie   27  OR  marie  view_user 122.158.130.90
marie   27  OR  marie  login     58.133.120.1
mike    69  VA  mike   new_tweet 87.124.79.252
mike    69  VA  mike   logout    55.237.104.36
```

Hive

Hive can support a similar optimization when performing repartition joins. Hive can cache all the datasets for a join key and then stream the large dataset so that it doesn't need to be stored in memory.

Hive assumes that the largest dataset is specified last in your query. Imagine you had two tables called users and user_logs, and user_logs was much larger. To join these tables, you'd make sure that the user_logs table was referenced as the last table in the query:

```
SELECT u.*, l.*
FROM users u
JOIN user_logs l ON u.name = l.name;
```

If you don't want to rearrange your query, you can alternatively use the STREAMTABLE hint to tell Hive which table is larger:

```
SELECT /*+ STREAMTABLE(l) */ u.*, l.*
FROM user_logs l
JOIN users u ON u.name = l.name;
```

■ Summary

This join implementation improves on the earlier technique by buffering only the values of the smaller dataset. But it still suffers from the problem of all the data being transmitted between the map and reduce phases, which is an expensive network cost to incur.

Further, the previous technique can support *N*-way joins, but this implementation only supports two-way joins.

A simple mechanism to reduce further the memory footprint of the reduce-side join is to be aggressive about projections and filters in the map function, as discussed in technique 55.

TECHNIQUE 61 **Using Bloom filters to cut down on shuffled data**

Imagine that you wanted to perform a join over a subset of your data according to some predicate, such as "only users that live in California." With the repartition job techniques covered so far, you'd have to perform that filter in the reducer, because only one dataset (the users) has details about the state—the user logs don't have that information.

In this technique we'll look at how a Bloom filter can be used on the map side, which can have a big impact on your job execution time.

■ **Problem**

You want to filter data in a repartition join, but to push that filter to the mappers.

■ **Solution**

Use a preprocessing job to create a Bloom filter, and then load the Bloom filter in the repartition job to filter out records in the mappers.

■ **Discussion**

A Bloom filter is a useful probabilistic data structure that provides membership qualities much like a set—the difference is that membership lookups only provide a definitive "no" answer, as it's possible to get false positives. Nevertheless, they require a lot less memory compared to a HashSet in Java, so they're well-suited to work with very large datasets.

> **More about Bloom filters** Chapter 7 provides details on how Bloom filters work and how to use MapReduce to create a Bloom filter in parallel.

Your goal in this technique is to perform a join only on users that live in California. There are two steps to this solution—you'll first run a job to generate the Bloom filter, which will operate on the user data and be populated with users that live in California. This Bloom filter will then be used in the repartition join to discard users that don't exist in the Bloom filter. The reason you need this Bloom filter is that the mapper for the user logs doesn't have details on the users' states.

Figure 6.12 shows the steps in this technique.

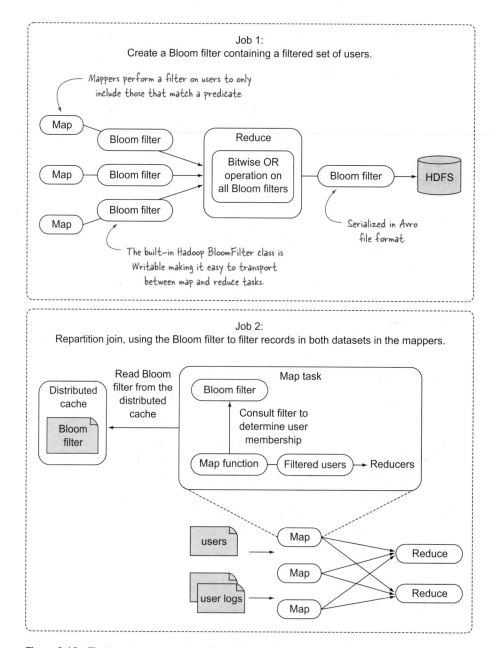

Figure 6.12   The two-step process to using a Bloom filter in a repartition join

Step 1: Creating the Bloom filter

The first job creates the Bloom filter containing names of users that are in California.
The mappers generate intermediary Bloom filters, and the reducer combines them

together into a single Bloom filter. The job output is an Avro file containing the serialized Bloom filter:[13]

```
public static class Map extends Mapper<LongWritable, Text,
                                        NullWritable, BloomFilter> {
  private BloomFilter filter =
            new BloomFilter(1000, 5, Hash.MURMUR_HASH);

  @Override
  protected void map(LongWritable key, Text value, Context context) {
    User user = User.fromText(value);
    if ("CA".equals(user.getState())) {            Only add users that live
      filter.add(new Key(user.getName().getBytes()));    in California to the
    }                                                        Bloom filter.
  }

  @Override
  protected void cleanup(Context context) {        Once the mapper is
    context.write(NullWritable.get(), filter);     complete, emit the
  }                                                    Bloom filter.
}

public static class Reduce
    extends Reducer<NullWritable, BloomFilter,
                    AvroKey<GenericRecord>, NullWritable> {

  private BloomFilter filter =
            new BloomFilter(1000, 5, Hash.MURMUR_HASH);

  @Override
  protected void reduce(NullWritable key,
            Iterable<BloomFilter> values, Context context) {
    for(BloomFilter bf: values) {
      filter.or(bf);                           Combine all the Bloom
    }                                          filters together in
  }                                                the reducer.

  @Override
  protected void cleanup(Context context) {
    context.write(                            Emit the consolidated
      new AvroKey<GenericRecord>(                 Bloom filter.
            AvroBytesRecord.toGenericRecord(filter)),
            NullWritable.get());
  }
}
```

Step 2: The repartition join

The repartition join is identical to the repartition join presented in technique 59—the only difference is that the mappers now load the Bloom filter generated in the first step, and when processing the map records, they perform a membership query against the Bloom filter to determine whether the record should be sent to the reducer.

---

[13] GitHub source: https://github.com/alexholmes/hiped2/blob/master/src/main/java/hip/ch6/joins/bloom/BloomFilterCreator.java.

The reducer is unchanged from the original repartition join, so the following code shows two things: the abstract mapper that generalizes the loading of the Bloom filter and the filtering and emission, and the two subclasses that support the two datasets being joined:[14]

```java
public static abstract class AbstractFilterMap
    extends Mapper<LongWritable, Text, Text, Tuple> {
  public static final String DISTCACHE_FILENAME = "bloomjoin...";
  private BloomFilter filter;

  abstract String getUsername(Text value);
  abstract int getDataset();

  @Override
  protected void setup(Context context)
      throws IOException, InterruptedException {
    final String bloomfile =
        context.getConfiguration().get(DISTCACHE_FILENAME);
    filter = BloomFilterCreator.fromFile(new File(bloomfile));
  }

  @Override
  protected void map(LongWritable offset, Text value, Context context)
      throws IOException, InterruptedException {
    String user = getUsername(value);
    if (filter.membershipTest(new Key(user.getBytes()))) {
      Tuple outputValue = new Tuple();
      outputValue.setInt(ValueFields.DATASET, getDataset());
      outputValue.setString(ValueFields.DATA, value.toString());

      context.write(new Text(user), outputValue);
    }
  }
}

public static class UserMap extends AbstractFilterMap {
  @Override
  String getUsername(Text value) {
    return User.fromText(value).getName();
  }

  @Override
  int getDataset() {
    return USERS;
  }
}

public static class UserLogMap extends AbstractFilterMap {
  @Override
  String getUsername(Text value) {
    return UserLog.fromText(value).getName();
  }
```

Load the Bloom filter from the distributed cache.

Extract the user name from a concrete subclass.

The dataset value of the tuple is fetched from the concrete subclass.

Only emit a value if the user name exists in the Bloom filter.

The user mapper extracts the user name and also identifies the data source for the records.

The user logs mapper similarly extracts the user name and tags the data source.

---

[14] GitHub source: https://github.com/alexholmes/hiped2/blob/master/src/main/java/hip/ch6/joins/bloom/BloomJoin.java.

```
@Override
int getDataset() {
  return USER_LOGS;
}
}
```

The following commands run the two jobs and dump the output of the join:

```
$ hip hip.ch6.joins.bloom.BloomFilterCreator \
    --users users.txt \
    --output bloom-output
```
First run the job to create the Bloom filter, retaining only users that live in California.

```
$ hip hip.ch6.joins.bloom.BloomJoin \
    --users users.txt \
    --user-logs user-logs.txt \
    --bloom-file bloom-output/part-r-00000.avro \
    --output output
```
Perform the repartition join, using the Bloom filter in the mappers to filter data sent to the reducers.

```
$ hadoop fs -cat output/part*
bob  71  CA  bob  new_tweet  58.133.120.100
```
The user data only had two users in California, and only Bob had a log entry, so only one record is in the final inner-join output.

■ **Summary**

This technique presented an effective method of performing a map-side filter on both datasets to minimize the network I/O between mappers and reducers. It also reduces the amount of data that needs to be spilled to and from disk in both the mappers and reducers as part of the shuffle. Filters are often the simplest and most optimal method of speeding up and optimizing your jobs, and they work just as well for repartition joins as they do for other MapReduce jobs.

Why not use a hashtable rather than a Bloom filter to represent the users? To construct a Bloom filter with a false positive rate of 1%, you need just 9.8 bits for each element in the data structure. Compare this with the best-case use of a HashSet containing integers, which requires 8 bytes. Or if you were to have a HashSet that only reflected the presence of an element that ignores collision, you'd end up with a Bloom filter with a single hash, yielding higher false positives.

Version 0.10 of Pig will include support for Bloom filters in a mechanism similar to that presented here. Details can be viewed in the JIRA ticket at https:// issues.apache.org/jira/browse/PIG-2328.

In this section you learned that Bloom filters offer good space-constrained set membership capabilities. We looked at how you could create Bloom filters in Map-Reduce, and you also applied that code to a subsequent technique, which helped you optimize a MapReduce semi-join.

6.1.3   *Data skew in reduce-side joins*

This section covers a common issue that's encountered when joining together large datasets—that of data skew. There are two types of data skew that could be present in your data:

- High join-key cardinality, where you have some join keys that have a large number of records in one or both of the datasets. I call this *join-product skew.*
- Poor hash partitioning, where a minority of reducers receive a large percentage of the overall number of records. I refer to this as *hash-partitioning skew.*

In severe cases, join-product skews can result in heap exhaustion issues due to the amount of data that needs to be cached. Hash-partitioning skew manifests itself as a join that takes a long time to complete, where a small percentage of the reducers take significantly longer to complete compared to the majority of the reducers.

The techniques in this section examine these two situations and present recommendations for combating them.

TECHNIQUE 62   **Joining large datasets with high join-key cardinality**

This technique tackles the problem of join-product skew, and the next technique examines hash-partitioning skew.

■ **Problem**

Some of your join keys are high-cardinality, which results in some of your reducers running out of memory when trying to cache these keys.

■ **Solution**

Filter out these keys and join them separately or spill them out in the reducer and schedule a follow-up job to join them.

■ **Discussion**

If you know ahead of time which keys are high-cardinality, you can separate them out into a separate join job, as shown in figure 6.13.

If you don't know the high-cardinality keys, you may have to build some intelligence into your reducers to detect these keys and write them out to a side-effect file, which is joined by a subsequent job, as illustrated in figure 6.14.

> **Hive 0.13**   The skewed key implementation was flawed in Hive versions before 0.13 (https://issues.apache.org/jira/browse/HIVE-6041).

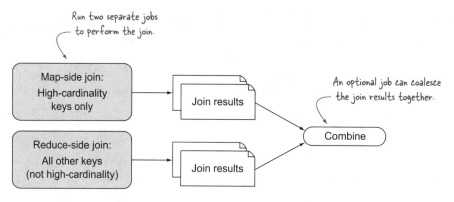

Figure 6.13   Dealing with skew when you know the high-cardinality key ahead of time

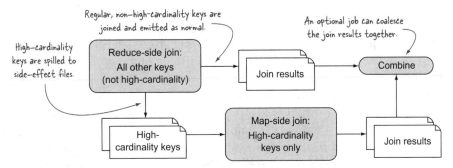

Figure 6.14   Dealing with skew when you don't know high-cardinality keys ahead of time

Hive

Hive supports a skew-mitigation strategy similar to the second approach presented in this technique. It can be enabled by specifying the following configurables prior to running the job:

```
SET hive.optimize.skewjoin = true;
SET hive.skewjoin.key = 100000;
```

If Hive sees more than the specified number of rows with the same key in the join operator, the key is considered skewed.

Enable skew join-optimization.

You can optionally set some additional configurables to control the map-side join that operates on the high-cardinality keys:

```
SET hive.skewjoin.mapjoin.map.tasks = 10000;
SET hive.skewjoin.mapjoin.min.split = 33554432;
```

Determine the minimum split size for the follow-up map join.

Determine the number of map tasks used in the follow-up map join job for a skew join.

Finally, if you're using a GROUP BY in your SQL, you may also want to consider enabling the following configuration to handle skews in the grouped data:

```
SET hive.groupby.skewindata = true;
```

■ Summary

The options presented in this technique assume that for a given join key, only one dataset has high-cardinality occurrences; hence the use of a map-side join that caches the smaller of the datasets. If both datasets are high-cardinality, then you're facing an expensive Cartesian product operation that will be slow to execute, as it doesn't lend itself to the MapReduce way of doing work (meaning it's not inherently splittable and parallelizable). In this case, you are essentially out of options in terms of optimizing the actual join. You should reexamine whether any back-to-basics techniques, such as filtering or projecting your data, can help alleviate the time required to execute the join.

The next technique looks at a different type of skew that can be introduced into your application as a result of using the default hash partitioner.

TECHNIQUE 63   ### Handling skews generated by the hash partitioner

The default partitioner in MapReduce is a hash partitioner, which takes a hash of each map output key and performs a modulo against the number of reducers to determine the reducer the key is sent to. The hash partitioner works well as a general partitioner, but it's possible that some datasets will cause the hash partitioner to overload some reducers due to a disproportionate number of keys being hashed to the same reducer.

This is manifested by a small number of straggling reducers taking much longer to complete compared to the majority of reducers. In addition, when you examine the straggler reducer counters, you'll notice that the number of groups sent to the stragglers is much higher than the others that have completed.

> **Differentiating between skew caused by high-cardinality keys versus a hash partitioner** You can use the MapReduce reducer counters to identify the type of data skew in your job. Skews introduced by a poorly performing hash partitioner will have a much higher number of groups (unique keys) sent to these reducers, whereas the symptoms of high-cardinality keys causing skew is evidenced by the roughly equal number of groups across all reducers but a much higher number of records for skewed reducers.

- **Problem**

Your reduce-side joins are taking a long time to complete, with several straggler reducers taking significantly longer to complete than the majority.

- **Solution**

Use a range partitioner or write a custom partitioner that siphons skewed keys to a reserved set of reducers.

- **Discussion**

The goal of this solution is to dispense with the default hash partitioner and replace it with something that works better with your skewed data. There are two options you can explore here:

- You can use the sampler and `TotalOrderPartitioner` that comes bundled with Hadoop, which replaces the hash partitioner with a range partitioner.
- You can write a custom partitioner that routes keys with data skew to a set of reducers reserved for skewed keys.

Let's explore both options and look at how you'd use them.

Range partitioning

A range partitioner will distribute map outputs based on a predefined range of values, where each range maps to a reducer that will receive all outputs within that range. This is exactly how the `TotalOrderPartitioner` works. In fact, the `TotalOrderPartitioner` is used by TeraSort to evenly distribute words across all the reducers to minimize straggling reducers.[15]

---

[15] TeraSort is a Hadoop benchmarking tool that sorts a terabyte of data.

For range partitioners such as the `TotalOrderPartitioner` to do their work, they need to know the output key ranges for a given job. The `TotalOrderPartitioner` is accompanied by a sampler that samples the input data and writes these ranges to HDFS, which is then used by the `TotalOrderPartitioner` when partitioning. More details on how to use the `TotalOrderPartitioner` and the sampler are covered in section 6.2.

Custom partitioner

If you already have a handle on which keys exhibit data skew, and that set of keys is static, you can write a custom partitioner to push these high-cardinality join keys to a reserved set of reducers. Imagine that you're running a job with ten reducers—you could decide to use two of them for keys that are skewed, and then hash partition all other keys across the remainder of the reducers.

■ Summary

Of the two approaches presented here, range partitioning is quite possibly the best solution, as it's likely that you won't know which keys are skewed, and it's also possible that the keys that exhibit skew will change over time.

It's possible to have reduce-side joins in MapReduce because they sort and correlate the map output keys together. In the next section, we'll look at common sorting techniques in MapReduce.

6.2   Sorting

The magic of MapReduce occurs between the mappers and reducers, where the framework groups together all the map output records that were emitted with the same key. This MapReduce feature allows you to aggregate and join your data and implement powerful data pipelines. To execute this feature, MapReduce internally partitions, sorts, and merges data (which is part of the shuffle phase), and the result is that each reducer is streamed an ordered set of keys and accompanying values.

In this section we'll explore two particular areas where you'll want to tweak the behavior of MapReduce sorting.

First we'll look at the secondary sort, which allows you to sort values for a reducer key. Secondary sorts are useful when you want some data to arrive at your reducer ahead of other data, as in the case of the optimized repartition join in technique 60. Secondary sorts are also useful if you want your job output to be sorted by a secondary key. An example of this is if you want to perform a primary sort of stock data by stock symbol, and then perform a secondary sort on the time of each stock quote during a day.

The second scenario we'll cover in this section is sorting data across all the reducer outputs. This is useful in situations where you want to extract the top or bottom N elements from a dataset.

These are important areas that allow you to perform some of the joins that we looked at earlier in this chapter. But the applicability of sorting isn't limited to joins; sorting also allows you to provide a secondary sort over your data. Secondary sorts are used in many of the techniques in this book, ranging from optimizing the repartition join to graph algorithms such as friends-of-friends.

6.2.1 *Secondary sort*

As you saw in the discussion of joining in section 6.1, you need secondary sorts to allow some records to arrive at a reducer ahead of other records. Secondary sorts require an understanding of both data arrangement and data flows in MapReduce. Figure 6.15 shows the three elements that affect data arrangement and flow (partitioning, sorting, and grouping) and how they're integrated into MapReduce.

The partitioner is invoked as part of the map output collection process, and it's used to determine which reducer should receive the map output. The sorting RawComparator

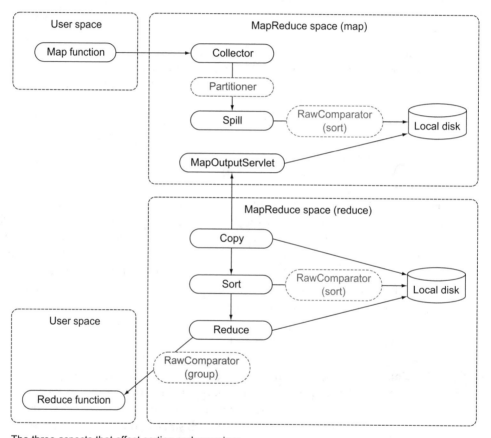

The three aspects that affect sorting and grouping:

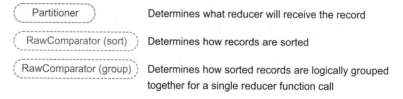

Partitioner — Determines what reducer will receive the record

RawComparator (sort) — Determines how records are sorted

RawComparator (group) — Determines how sorted records are logically grouped together for a single reducer function call

Figure 6.15 An overview of where sorting, partitioning, and grouping occur in MapReduce

is used to sort the map outputs within their respective partitions, and it's used in both the map and reduce sides. Finally, the grouping `RawComparator` is responsible for determining the group boundaries across the sorted records.

The default behavior in MapReduce is for all three functions to operate on the entire output key emitted by map functions.

TECHNIQUE 64 Implementing a secondary sort

Secondary sorts are useful when you want some of the values for a unique map key to arrive at a reducer ahead of other values. You can see the value of secondary sorting in other techniques in this book, such as the optimized repartition join (technique 60), and the friends-of-friends algorithm discussed in chapter 7 (technique 68).

■ **Problem**

You want to order values sent to a single reducer invocation for each key.

■ **Solution**

This technique covers writing your partitioner, sort comparator, and grouping comparator classes, which are required for secondary sorting to work.

■ **Discussion**

In this technique we'll look at how to use secondary sorts to order people's names. You'll use the primary sort to order people's last names, and the secondary sort to order their first names.

To support secondary sort, you need to create a composite output key, which will be emitted by your map functions. The composite key will contain two parts:

- The *natural key*, which is the key to use for joining purposes
- The *secondary key*, which is the key to use to order all of the values sent to the reducer for the natural key

Figure 6.16 shows the composite key for the names. It also shows a composite value that provides reducer-side access to the secondary key.

Let's go through the partitioning, sorting, and grouping phases and implement them to sort the names. But before that, you need to write your composite key class.

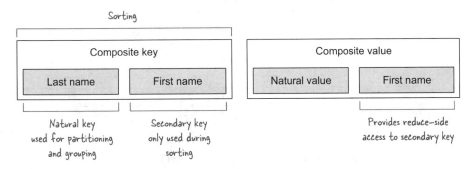

Figure 6.16   The user composite key and value

Composite key

The composite key contains both the first and last name. It extends `WritableComparable`, which is recommended for `Writable` classes that are emitted as keys from map functions:[16]

```java
public class Person implements WritableComparable<Person> {

  private String firstName;
  private String lastName;

  @Override
  public void readFields(DataInput in) throws IOException {
    this.firstName = in.readUTF();
    this.lastName = in.readUTF();
  }

  @Override
  public void write(DataOutput out) throws IOException {
    out.writeUTF(firstName);
    out.writeUTF(lastName);
  }
...
```

Figure 6.17 shows the configuration names and methods that you'll call in your code to set the partitioning, sorting, and grouping classes. The figure also shows what part of the composite key each class uses.

Let's look at the implementation code for each of these classes.

Partitioner

The partitioner is used to determine which reducer should receive a map output record. The default MapReduce partitioner (`HashPartitioner`) calls the hashCode

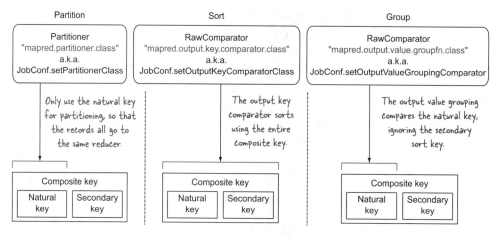

Figure 6.17 Partitioning, sorting, and grouping settings and key utilization

---

[16] GitHub source: https://github.com/alexholmes/hiped2/blob/master/src/main/java/hip/ch6/sort/secondary/Person.java.

method of the output key and performs a modulo with the number of reducers to determine which reducer should receive the output. The default partitioner uses the entire key, which won't work for your composite key, because it will likely send keys with the same natural key value to different reducers. Instead, you need to write your own `Partitioner` that partitions on the natural key.

The following code shows the `Partitioner` interface you must implement. The get-Partition method is passed the key, value, and number of partitions (also known as *reducers*):

```
public interface Partitioner<K2, V2> extends JobConfigurable {
  int getPartition(K2 key, V2 value, int numPartitions);
}
```

Your partitioner will calculate a hash based on the last name in the `Person` class and perform a modulo of that with the number of partitions (which is the number of reducers):[17]

```
public class PersonNamePartitioner extends
    Partitioner<Person, Text> {

  @Override
  public int getPartition(Person key, Text value, int numPartitions) {
    return Math.abs(key.getLastName().hashCode() * 127) %
        numPartitions;
  }
}
```

Sorting

Both the map and reduce sides participate in sorting. The map-side sorting is an optimization to help make the reducer sorting more efficient. You want MapReduce to use your entire key for sorting purposes, which will order keys according to both the last name and the first name.

In the following example, you can see the implementation of the `WritableComparator`, which compares users based on their last name and their first name:[18]

```
public class PersonComparator extends WritableComparator {
  protected PersonComparator() {
    super(Person.class, true);
  }

  @Override
  public int compare(WritableComparable w1, WritableComparable w2) {

    Person p1 = (Person) w1;
    Person p2 = (Person) w2;
```

---

[17] GitHub source: https://github.com/alexholmes/hiped2/blob/master/src/main/java/hip/ch6/sort/secondary/PersonNamePartitioner.java.

[18] GitHub source: https://github.com/alexholmes/hiped2/blob/master/src/main/java/hip/ch6/sort/secondary/PersonComparator.java.

```
    int cmp = p1.getLastName().compareTo(p2.getLastName());
    if (cmp != 0) {
      return cmp;
    }

    return p1.getFirstName().compareTo(p2.getFirstName());
  }
}
```

Grouping

Grouping occurs when the reduce phase is streaming map output records from local disk. Grouping is the process by which you can specify how records are combined to form one logical sequence of records for a reducer invocation.

When you're at the grouping stage, all of the records are already in secondary-sort order, and the grouping comparator needs to bundle together records with the same last name:[19]

```
public class PersonNameComparator extends WritableComparator {

  protected PersonNameComparator() {
    super(Person.class, true);
  }

  @Override
  public int compare(WritableComparable o1, WritableComparable o2) {

    Person p1 = (Person) o1;
    Person p2 = (Person) o2;

    return p1.getLastName().compareTo(p2.getLastName());

  }
}
```

MapReduce

The final steps involve telling MapReduce to use the partitioner, sort comparator, and group comparator classes:[20]

```
job.setPartitionerClass(PersonNamePartitioner.class);
job.setSortComparatorClass(PersonComparator.class);
job.setGroupingComparatorClass(PersonNameComparator.class);
```

To complete this technique, you need to write the map and reduce code. The mapper creates the composite key and emits that in conjunction with the first name as the output value. The reducer produces output identical to the input:[21]

---

[19] GitHub source: https://github.com/alexholmes/hiped2/blob/master/src/main/java/hip/ch6/sort/secondary/PersonNameComparator.java.

[20] GitHub source: https://github.com/alexholmes/hiped2/blob/master/src/main/java/hip/ch6/sort/secondary/SortMapReduce.java.

[21] GitHub source: https://github.com/alexholmes/hiped2/blob/master/src/main/java/hip/ch6/sort/secondary/SortMapReduce.java.

```java
public static class Map extends Mapper<Text, Text, Person, Text> {

  private Person outputKey = new Person();

  @Override
  protected void map(Text lastName, Text firstName, Context context)
      throws IOException, InterruptedException {
    outputKey.set(lastName.toString(), firstName.toString());
    context.write(outputKey, firstName);
  }
}

public static class Reduce extends Reducer<Person, Text, Text, Text> {

  Text lastName = new Text();
  @Override
  public void reduce(Person key, Iterable<Text> values,
                     Context context)
      throws IOException, InterruptedException {
    lastName.set(key.getLastName());
    for (Text firstName : values) {
      context.write(lastName, firstName);
    }
  }
}
```

To see this sort in action, you can upload a small file with unordered names and test whether the secondary sort code produces output sorted by first name:

```
$ hadoop fs -put test-data/ch6/usernames.txt .

$ hadoop fs -cat usernames.txt
Smith John
Smith Anne
Smith Ken

$ hip hip.ch6.sort.secondary.SortMapReduce \
    --input usernames.txt --output output

$ hadoop fs -cat output/part*
Smith Anne
Smith John
Smith Ken
```

The output is sorted as expected.

◾ Summary

As you can see in this technique, it's nontrivial to use secondary sort. It requires you to write a custom partitioner, sorter, and grouper. If you're working with simple data types, consider using htuple (http://htuple.org/), an open source project I developed, which simplifies secondary sort in your jobs.

htuple exposes a Tuple class, which allows you to store one or more Java types and provides helper methods to make it easy for you to define which fields are used for partitioning, sorting, and grouping. The following code shows how htuple can be used to secondary sort on the first name, just like in the technique:

```
enum TupleFields {                        It's useful to create an
    LAST_NAME,                            enum for the fields being
    FIRST_NAME                            stored in the tuple.
}
                                                    Specify which tuple fields are
ShuffleUtils.configBuilder()                        used for partitioning, sorting,
            .useNewApi()                            and grouping in the job driver.
            .setPartitionerIndices(TupleFields.LAST_NAME)
            .setSortIndices(TupleFields.values())
            .setGroupIndices(TupleFields.LAST_NAME)
            .configure(conf);

...

public static class Map extends Mapper<LongWritable, Text,
                Tuple, Text> {

    @Override
    protected void map(LongWritable key, Text value, Context context)
        throws IOException, InterruptedException {

        String nameParts[] = line.split("\t");       Create a new Tuple
                                                     object and set the
        Tuple tuple = new Tuple();                   last and first names.
        tuple.set(TupleFields.LAST_NAME, nameParts[0]);
        tuple.set(TupleFields.FIRST_NAME, nameParts[1]);

        // emit the tuple and the original contents of the line
        context.write(outputKey, value);
    }
}
```

Next we'll look at how to sort outputs across multiple reducers.

6.2.2   *Total order sorting*

You'll find a number of situations where you'll want to have your job output in total sort order.[22] For example, if you want to extract the most popular URLs from a web graph, you'll have to order your graph by some measure of popularity, such as Page-Rank. Or if you want to display a table in your portal of the most active users on your site, you'll need the ability to sort them based on some criteria, such as the number of articles they wrote.

TECHNIQUE 65   **Sorting keys across multiple reducers**

You know that the MapReduce framework sorts map output keys prior to feeding them to reducers. But this sorting is only guaranteed within each reducer, and unless you specify a partitioner for your job, you'll be using the default MapReduce partitioner, Hash-Partitioner, which partitions using a hash of the map output keys. This ensures that all

---

[22] Total sort order is when the reducer records are sorted across all the reducers, not just within each reducer.

records with the same map output key go to the same reducer, but the HashPartitioner doesn't perform total sorting of the map output keys across all the reducers. Knowing this, you may be wondering how you could use MapReduce to sort keys across multiple reducers so that you can easily extract the top and bottom *N* records from your data.

■ **Problem**

You want a total ordering of keys in your job output, but without the overhead of having to run a single reducer.

■ **Solution**

This technique covers use of the TotalOrderPartitioner class, a partitioner that is bundled with Hadoop, to assist in sorting output across all reducers. The partitioner ensures that output sent to the reducers is totally ordered.

■ **Discussion**

Hadoop has a built-in partitioner called the TotalOrderPartitioner, which distributes keys to specific reducers based on a partition file. The partition file is a precomputed SequenceFile that contains *N* − 1 keys, where *N* is the number of reducers. The keys in the partition file are ordered by the map output key comparator, and as such, each key represents a logical range of keys. To determine which reducer should receive an output record, the TotalOrderPartitioner examines the output key, determines which range it falls into, and maps that range into a specific reducer.

Figure 6.18 shows the two parts of this technique. You need to create the partition file and then run your MapReduce job using the TotalOrderPartitioner.

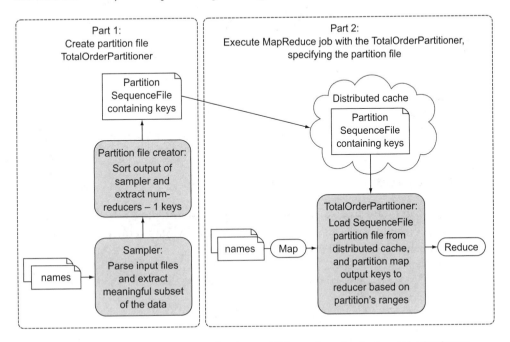

Figure 6.18   Using sampling and the TotalOrderPartitioner **to sort output across all reducers.**

First you'll use the InputSampler class, which samples the input files and creates the partition file. You can use one of two samplers: the RandomSampler class, which as the name suggests picks random records from the input, or the IntervalSampler class, which for every record includes the record in the sample. Once the samples have been extracted, they're sorted, and then $N-1$ keys are written to the partition file, where N is the number of reducers. The InputSampler isn't a MapReduce job; it reads records from the InputFormat and produces the partition within the process calling the code.

The following code shows the steps you need to execute prior to calling the Input-Sampler function:[23]

```
int numReducers = 2;
Path input = new Path(args[0]);
Path partitionFile = new Path(args[1]);

InputSampler.Sampler<Text, Text> sampler =
    new InputSampler.RandomSampler<Text,Text>
        (0.1,
         10000,
         10);

JobConf job = new JobConf();

job.setNumReduceTasks(numReducers);
job.setInputFormat(KeyValueTextInputFormat.class);
job.setMapOutputKeyClass(Text.class);
job.setMapOutputValueClass(Text.class);

TotalOrderPartitioner.setPartitionFile(job, partitionFile);
FileInputFormat.setInputPaths(job, input);

InputSampler.writePartitionFile(job, sampler);
```

The number of samples to extract from the input.

The maximum number of input splits that will be read to extract the samples.

Set the InputFormat for the job, which the InputSampler uses to retrieve records from the input.

Specify the location of the partition file.

The probability that a key will be picked from the input.

Set the number of reducers (which is used by the InputSampler when creating the partition file).

Specify the map output key and value classes, even if the InputFormat explicitly types them.

Set the job input files.

Run the InputSampler code to sample and create the partition file. This code uses all the items set in the JobConf object to perform this task.

Next up, you need to specify that you want to use the TotalOrderPartitioner as the partitioner for your job:

```
job.setPartitionerClass(TotalOrderPartitioner.class);
```

You don't want to do any processing in your MapReduce job, so you won't specify the map or reduce classes. This means the identity MapReduce classes will be used, so you're ready to run the code:

```
$ hadoop fs -put test-data/names.txt names.txt

$ hip hip.ch6.sort.total.TotalSortMapReduce \
    --input names.txt \
```

The input file containing the names to be sorted.

---

[23] GitHub source: https://github.com/alexholmes/hiped2/blob/master/src/main/java/hip/ch6/sort/total/TotalSortMapReduce.java.

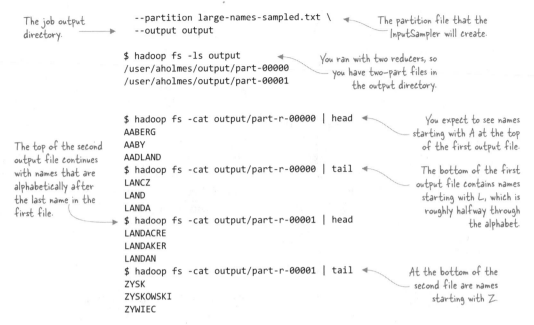

The job output directory.

```
  --partition large-names-sampled.txt \
  --output output
```

The partition file that the InputSampler will create.

```
$ hadoop fs -ls output
/user/aholmes/output/part-00000
/user/aholmes/output/part-00001
```

You ran with two reducers, so you have two-part files in the output directory.

```
$ hadoop fs -cat output/part-r-00000 | head
AABERG
AABY
AADLAND
$ hadoop fs -cat output/part-r-00000 | tail
LANCZ
LAND
LANDA
$ hadoop fs -cat output/part-r-00001 | head
LANDACRE
LANDAKER
LANDAN
$ hadoop fs -cat output/part-r-00001 | tail
ZYSK
ZYSKOWSKI
ZYWIEC
```

You expect to see names starting with A at the top of the first output file.

The bottom of the first output file contains names starting with L, which is roughly halfway through the alphabet.

The top of the second output file continues with names that are alphabetically after the last name in the first file.

At the bottom of the second file are names starting with Z.

You can see from the results of the MapReduce job that the map output keys are indeed sorted across all the output files.

■ Summary

This technique used the `InputSampler` to create the partition file, which is subsequently used by the `TotalOrderPartitioner` to partition map output keys.

You could also use MapReduce to generate the partition file. An efficient way of doing this would be to write a custom `InputFormat` class that performs the sampling and then output the keys to a single reducer, which in turn can create the partition file. This brings us to sampling, the last section of this chapter.

6.3 *Sampling*

Imagine you're working with a terabyte-scale dataset, and you have a MapReduce application you want to test with that dataset. Running your MapReduce application against the dataset may take hours, and constantly making code refinements and rerunning against the large dataset isn't an optimal workflow.

To solve this problem, you look to sampling, which is a statistical methodology for extracting a relevant subset of a population. In the context of MapReduce, sampling provides an opportunity to work with large datasets without the overhead of having to wait for the entire dataset to be read and processed. This greatly enhances your ability to quickly iterate when developing and debugging MapReduce code.

TECHNIQUE 66   **Writing a reservoir-sampling InputFormat**

You're developing a MapReduce job iteratively with a large dataset, and you need to do testing. Testing with the entire dataset takes a long time and impedes your ability to rapidly work with your code.

■ **Problem**

You want to work with a small subset of a large dataset during the development of a MapReduce job.

■ **Solution**

Write an input format that can wrap the actual input format used to read data. The input format that you'll write can be configured with the number of samples that should be extracted from the wrapped input format.

■ **Discussion**

In this technique you'll use reservoir sampling to choose samples. Reservoir sampling is a strategy that allows a single pass through a stream to randomly produce a sample.[24] As such, it's a perfect fit for MapReduce because input records are streamed from an input source. Figure 6.19 shows the algorithm for reservoir sampling.

Step 1:
Fill the reservoir until it is full.

Step 2:
Randomly replace a sample in the reservoir.

```
 1: Samples ← ∅
 2: i ← 0
 3: for all record ∈ largeDataSet do
 4:     if |Samples| ≠ requiredSamples then
 5:         Samples[i] = record
 6:     else
 7:         j ← random(1, i) {random number between 1 and i inclusive}
 8:         if j <= requiredSamples then
 9:             Samples[j] = record
10:     i ← i + 1
```

Figure 6.19 The reservoir-sampling algorithm allows one pass through a stream to randomly produce a sample.

The input split determination and record reading will be delegated to wrapped Input-Format and RecordReader classes. You'll write classes that provide the sampling functionality and then wrap the delegated InputFormat and RecordReader classes.[25] Figure 6.20 shows how the ReservoirSamplerRecordReader works.

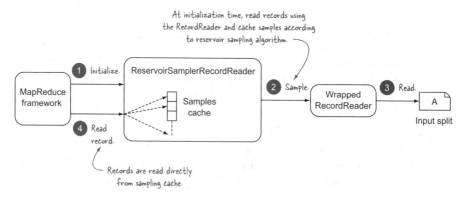

At initialization time, read records using the RecordReader and cache samples according to reservoir sampling algorithm.

Records are read directly from sampling cache.

Figure 6.20 The ReservoirSamplerRecordReader in action

---

[24] For more information on reservoir sampling, see the Wikipedia article at http://en.wikipedia.org/wiki/Reservoir_sampling.

[25] If you need a refresher on these classes, please review chapter 3 for more details.

The following code shows the ReservoirSamplerRecordReader:[26]

The RecordReader that you use to read records from the data source.

The number of record samples to extract from the data source.

An upper bound on the number of records read from the data source; this is to avoid having to read the entire data source.

Create the samples at initialization time.

When you've collected the minimum number of samples, use the reservoir algorithm to determine if you should update existing samples with the current record.

If you haven't collected the target number of samples, add the current record to your samples.

```java
public static class ReservoirSamplerRecordReader
  <K extends Writable, V extends Writable> extends RecordReader {

    private final RecordReader<K, V> rr;
    private final int numSamples;
    private final int maxRecords;

    private final ArrayList<K> keys;
    private final ArrayList<V> values;

    @Override
    public void initialize(InputSplit split,
                               TaskAttemptContext context)
        throws IOException, InterruptedException {
      rr.initialize(split, context);

      Random rand = new Random();
      for (int i = 0; i < maxRecords; i++) {
        if (!rr.nextKeyValue()) {
          break;
        }
        K key = rr.getCurrentKey();
        V val = rr.getCurrentValue();

        if (keys.size() < numSamples) {
          keys.add(WritableUtils.clone(key, conf));
          values.add(WritableUtils.clone(val, conf));
        } else {
          int r = rand.nextInt(i);
          if (r < numSamples) {
            keys.set(r, WritableUtils.clone(key, conf));
            values.set(r, WritableUtils.clone(val, conf));
          }
        }
      }
    }
  }
  ...
```

To use the ReservoirSamplerInputFormat class in your code, you'll use convenience methods to help set up the input format and other parameters, as shown in the following code:[27]

```java
ReservoirSamplerInputFormat.setInputFormat(job,
    TextInputFormat.class);
```

This is the only method that needs to be called; it sets the input format to read the records from the data source.

---

[26] GitHub source: https://github.com/alexholmes/hiped2/blob/master/src/main/java/hip/ch6/sampler/ReservoirSamplerInputFormat.java.

[27] GitHub source: https://github.com/alexholmes/hiped2/blob/master/src/main/java/hip/ch6/sampler/SamplerJob.java

Set the maximum number of records that will be read from each input split to create the samples.

Set the number of samples to be extracted. This number is either across all input splits or for each input split. The behavior is driven by the setUseSamplesNumberPerInputSplit method.

```
ReservoirSamplerInputFormat.setNumSamples(job, 10);
ReservoirSamplerInputFormat.setMaxRecordsToRead(job, 10000);
ReservoirSamplerInputFormat.
    setUseSamplesNumberPerInputSplit(job, true);
```

Determine whether the number of samples should be extracted per input split or across all input splits. If set to false (the default), the number of samples is divided by the number of input splits.

You can see the sampling input format in action by running an identity job against a large file containing names:

The input file has 88,799 lines.

```
$ wc -l test-data/names.txt
88799 test-data/names.txt
$ hadoop fs -put test-data/names.txt names.txt

$ hip hip.ch6.sampler.SamplerJob \
    --input names.txt --output output

$ hadoop fs -cat output/part* | wc -l
10
```

The sampling input format sampled ten lines, as per your job configuration.

You configured the ReservoirSamplerInputFormat to extract ten samples, and the output file contained that number of lines.

■ **Summary**

Sampling support in MapReduce code can be a useful development and testing feature when engineers are running code against production-scale datasets. That begs the question: what's the best approach for integrating sampling support into an existing codebase? One approach would be to add a configurable option that would toggle the use of the sampling input format, similar to the following code:

```
if(appConfig.isSampling()) {

  ReservoirSamplerInputFormat.setInputFormat(job,
    TextInputFormat.class);
  ...
} else {
  job.setInputFormatClass(TextInputFormat.class);
}
```

You can apply this sampling technique to any of the preceding sections as a way to work efficiently with large datasets.

6.4   *Chapter summary*

Joining and sorting are cumbersome tasks in MapReduce, and we spent this chapter discussing methods to optimize and facilitate their use. We looked at three different join strategies, two of which were on the map side, and one on the reduce side. The goal was to simplify joins in MapReduce, and I presented two frameworks that reduce the amount of user code required for joins.

We also covered sorting in MapReduce by examining how secondary sorts work and how you can sort all of the output across all the reducers. And we wrapped things up with a look at how you can sample data so that you can quickly iterate over smaller samples of your data.

We'll cover a number of performance patterns and tuning steps in chapter 8, which will result in faster join and sorting times. But before we get there, we'll look at some more advanced data structures and algorithms, such as graph processing and working with Bloom filters.

Utilizing data structures and algorithms at scale

7

This chapter covers

- Representing and using data structures such as graphs, HyperLogLog, and Bloom filters in MapReduce
- Applying algorithms such as PageRank and semi-joins to large amounts of data
- Learning how social network companies recommend making connections with people outside your network

---

In this chapter we'll look at how you can implement algorithms in MapReduce to work with internet-scale data. We'll focus on nontrivial data, which is commonly represented using graphs.

We'll also look at how you can use graphs to model connections between entities, such as relationships in a social network. We'll run through a number of useful algorithms that can be performed over graphs, such as shortest path and friends-of-friends (FoF), to help expand the interconnectedness of a network, and PageRank, which looks at how to determine the popularity of web pages.

You'll learn how to use Bloom filters, whose unique space-saving properties make them handy for solving distributed system problems in P2P (peer-to-peer) and distributed databases. We'll also create Bloom filters in MapReduce and then look at their usefulness for filtering.

You'll also learn about another approximate data structure called HyperLogLog, that provides approximate unique counts, which are invaluable in aggregation pipelines.

A chapter on scalable algorithms wouldn't be complete without mention of sorting and joining algorithms, which are covered in chapter 6.

Let's kick things off with a look at how you can model graphs in MapReduce.

7.1 Modeling data and solving problems with graphs

Graphs are mathematical constructs that represent an interconnected set of objects. They're used to represent data such as the hyperlink structure of the internet, social networks (where they represent relationships between users), and internet routing to determine optimal paths for forwarding packets.

A graph consists of a number of nodes (formally called *vertices*) and links (informally called *edges*) that connect nodes together. Figure 7.1 shows a graph with nodes and edges.

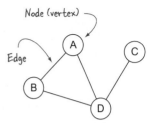

The edges can be directed (implying a one-way relationship) or undirected. For example, you would use a directed graph to model relationships between users in a social network, because relationships are not always bidirectional. Figure 7.2 shows examples of directed and undirected graphs.

Figure 7.1 A small graph with highlighted nodes and edges

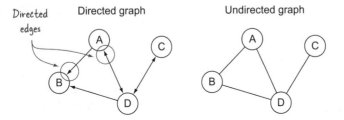

Figure 7.2 Directed and undirected graphs

Directed graphs, where the edges have a direction, can be cyclic or acyclic. In cyclic graphs, it's possible for a vertex to reach itself by traversing a sequence of edges. In an acyclic graph, it's not possible for a vertex to traverse a path to reach itself. Figure 7.3 shows examples of cyclic and acyclic graphs.

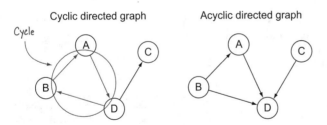

Figure 7.3 Cyclic and acyclic graphs

To start working with graphs, you'll need to be able to represent them in your code. So what are the common methods used to represent these graph structures?

7.1.1   Modeling graphs

Two common ways of representing graphs are with *adjacency matrices* and *adjacency lists.*

Adjacency matrix

With an adjacency matrix, you represent a graph as an N x N square matrix M, where N is the number of nodes and Mij represents an edge between nodes i and j.

Figure 7.4 shows a directed graph representing connections in a social graph. The arrows indicate one-way relationships between two people. The adjacency matrix shows how this graph would be represented.

	jim	ali	bob	dee
jim	0	0	0	0
ali	1	0	1	1
bob	1	1	0	0
dee	0	1	0	0

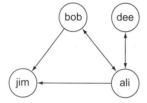

Figure 7.4   An adjacency matrix representation of a graph

The disadvantage of adjacency matrices are that they model both the existence and lack of a relationship, which makes them dense data structures requiring more space than adjacency lists.

Adjacency list

Adjacency lists are similar to adjacency matrices, except that they don't model the lack of relationships. Figure 7.5 shows how you'd represent a graph using an adjacency list.

	jim	ali	bob	dee
jim	0	0	0	0
ali	1	0	1	1
bob	1	1	0	0
dee	0	1	0	0

jim →
ali → jim, bob, dee
bob → jim, ali
dee → ali

Figure 7.5   An adjacency list representation of a graph

The advantage of the adjacency list is that it offers a sparse representation of the data, which is good because it requires less space. It also fits well when representing graphs in Map-Reduce because the key can represent a vertex, and the values are a list of vertices that denote a directed or undirected relationship node.

Next up we'll cover three graph algorithms, starting off with the shortest-path algorithm.

7.1.2   Shortest-path algorithm

The shortest-path algorithm is a common problem in graph theory, where the goal is to find the shortest route between two nodes. Figure 7.6

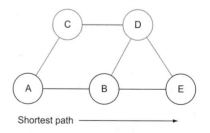

Figure 7.6   Example of shortest path between nodes A and E

shows an example of this algorithm on a graph where the edges don't have a weight, in which case the shortest path is the path with the smallest number of hops or intermediary nodes between the source and destination.

Applications of this algorithm include determining the shortest route between two addresses in traffic mapping software, routers computing the shortest path tree for each route, and social networks determining connections between users.

TECHNIQUE 67   Find the shortest distance between two users

Dijkstra's algorithm is a shortest-path algorithm commonly taught in undergraduate computer science courses. A basic implementation uses a sequential iterative process to traverse the entire graph from the starting node, as seen in the algorithm presented in figure 7.7.

The basic algorithm doesn't scale to graphs that exceed your memory sizes, and it's also sequential and not optimized for parallel processing.

■ **Problem**

You need to use MapReduce to find the shortest path between two people in a social graph.

■ **Solution**

Use an adjacency matrix to model a graph, and for each node, store the distance from the original node, as well as a backpointer to the original node. Use the mappers to

All nodes other than the starting node start with a distance of infinity, denoting the fact that they haven't been visited.

The start node's distance is set to zero.

```
 1: for all vertex v in V do
 2:     distance[v] ← ∞ {set distances to indicate they are unvisited}
 3: end for
 4: distance[source] ← 0 {the distance from source to itself is 0}
 5: unvisitednodes ← V {priority queue of unvisited nodes ordered by distance}
 6: while unvisitednodes ≠ ∅ do
 7:     node ← unvisitednodes.head {node with smallest distance}
 8:     for all adjacent nodes adjnode ∈ node.adjnodes do
 9:         if adjnode ∈ unvisitednodes then
10:             adjnodedistance' ← distance[node] + weight(node, adjnode)
11:             if adjnodedistance' < distance[adjnode] then
12:                 distance[adjnode] ← adjnodedistance'
13:             end if
14:         end if
15:     end for
16:     remove node from unvisitednodes
17: end while
```

Iterative process where all the unvisited nodes are iterated, and the distance from the start node is propagated through the graph by adding weights encountered when edges are traversed.

Figure 7.7 Pseudocode for Dijkstra's algorithm

propagate the distance to the original node, and the reducers to restore the state of the graph. Iterate until the target node has been reached.

■ Discussion

Figure 7.8 shows a small social network that you'll use for this technique. Your goal is to find the shortest path between Dee and Joe. There are four paths that you can take from Dee to Joe, but only one of them results in the fewest hops.

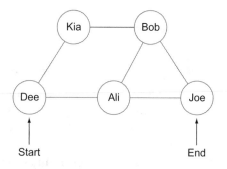

Figure 7.8   Social network used in this technique

You'll implement a parallel breadth-first search algorithm to find the shortest path between two users. Because you're operating on a social network, you don't need to care about weights on your edges. The pseudocode for the algorithm can be seen in figure 7.9.

Figure 7.10 shows the algorithm iterations in play with your social graph. Just like Dijkstra's algorithm, you'll start with all the node distances set to infinite and set the distance for the starting node, Dee, at zero. With each MapReduce pass, you'll determine nodes that don't have an infinite distance and propagate their distance values to their adjacent nodes. You'll continue this until you reach the end node.

You first need to create the starting point. This is done by reading in the social network (which is stored as an adjacency list) from the file and setting the initial distance values. Figure 7.11 shows the two file formats, the second being the format that's used iteratively in your MapReduce code.

Map(node-name, node)
```
1: emit(node-name, node) {to preserve node}
2: if node.distance ≠ ∞ then {process neighbors if the current node distance
   has been computed}
3:     neighbor-distance ← node.distance + 1
4:     for all adjacent nodes adjnode ∈ node.adjnodes do
5:         {output the adjacent node, the adjacent node's distance, and the
           path backpointer}
6:         emit (adjnode.name, [neighbor-distance, node.backpointer+node.name])
7:     end for
8: end if
```

Reduce(node-name, list-of-nodes)
```
1: node.distance ← ∞
2: node.backpointer ← null
3: for all reducer-node ∈ nodes do
4:     distance ← reducer-.distance
5:     backpointer ← reducer-.backpointer
6:     if distance < node.distance then
7:         node.distance ← distance
8:         node.backpointer ← backpointer
9:     end if
10: end for
11: emit(node-name, node)
```

Figure 7.9   Pseudocode for breadth-first parallel search on graph using MapReduce

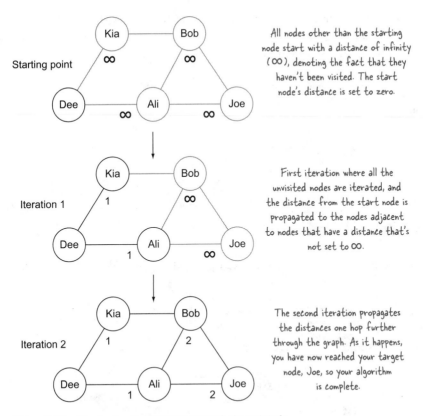

Starting point

All nodes other than the starting node start with a distance of infinity (∞), denoting the fact that they haven't been visited. The start node's distance is set to zero.

Iteration 1

First iteration where all the unvisited nodes are iterated, and the distance from the start node is propagated to the nodes adjacent to nodes that have a distance that's not set to ∞.

Iteration 2

The second iteration propagates the distances one hop further through the graph. As it happens, you have now reached your target node, Joe, so your algorithm is complete.

Figure 7.10   Shortest path iterations through the network

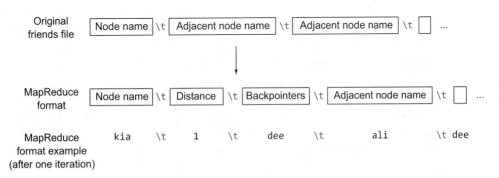

Original friends file

MapReduce format

MapReduce format example (after one iteration)

Figure 7.11   Original social network file format and MapReduce form optimized for algorithm

Your first step is to create the MapReduce form from the original file. The following listing shows the original input file and the MapReduce-ready form of the input file generated by the transformation code:

```
$ cat test-data/ch7/friends-short-path.txt        ◄──── The input data.
dee  kia  ali
ali  dee  bob  joe
joe  bob  ali
kia  bob  dee
bob  kia  ali  joe

$ hadoop fs -cat output/input.txt        ◄──
dee  0            kia  ali
ali  2147483647  dee  kia  bob  joe
joe  2147483647  bob  ali
kia  2147483647  ali  dee
bob  2147483647  ali  joe
```

The MapReduce-ready form of the input data, with the addition of a number that indicates the number of hops from the source node. The starting node is Dee, so she has a hop of 0. All other nodes use Integer.MAX_VALUE to indicate that they haven't been visited.

The code that generates the previous output is shown here:[1]

Set the default distance to the node to be infinite (which you represent with Integer.MAX_VALUE).

```
OutputStream os = fs.create(targetFile);
LineIterator iter = org.apache.commons.io.IOUtils
    .lineIterator(fs.open(file), "UTF8");
while (iter.hasNext()) {
    String line = iter.nextLine();

    String[] parts = StringUtils.split(line);
    int distance = Map.INFINITE;
    if (startNode.equals(parts[0])) {
        distance = 0;
    }
    IOUtils.write(parts[0] + '\t' +
      String.valueOf(distance) + "\t\t", os);
    IOUtils.write(StringUtils.join(parts, '\t',
      1, parts.length), os);
    IOUtils.write("\n", os);
}
```

Read each line from the original social network file.

If the current node is the starting node, set its distance to zero.

Write out the distance and an empty backpointer.

Write out the adjacent nodes (the friends).

The structure of the MapReduce data isn't changed across iterations of the algorithm; each job produces the same structure, which makes it easy to iterate, because the input format is the same as the output format.

Your map function will perform two major tasks. First, it outputs all the node data to preserve the original structure of the graph. If you didn't do this, you couldn't make this an interactive process, because the reducer wouldn't be able to reproduce the original graph structure for the next map phase. The second task of the map is to output that adjacent node with its distance and a backpointer if the node has a non-infinite distance number. The backpointer carries information about the nodes visited

---

[1] GitHub source: https://github.com/alexholmes/hiped2/blob/master/src/main/java/hip/ch7/shortestpath/Main.java.

from the starting node, so when you reach the end node, you know the exact path that was taken to get there. Here's the code for the map function:[2]

```
@Override
protected void map(Text key, Text value, Context context)
    throws IOException, InterruptedException {

    Node node = Node.fromMR(value.toString());

    context.write(key, value);

    if (node.isDistanceSet()) {
        int neighborDistance = node.getDistance() + 1;

        String backpointer = node.
            constructBackpointer(key.toString());
        String[] adjNodes = node.getAdjacentNodeNames();
        for (int i = 0; i < adjNodes.length; i++) {

            String neighbor = adjNodes[i];

            outKey.set(neighbor);

            Node adjacentNode = new Node()
                .setDistance(neighborDistance)
                .setBackpointer(backpointer);

            outValue.set(adjacentNode.toString());
            context.write(outKey, outValue);
        }
    }
}
```

Create a Node object from the inputs. The fromMR method splits the string and extracts the distance, backpointer, and adjacent nodes.

Preserve the graph structure.

Only output the neighbor details if you have a distance value set.

Calculate the distance for the adjacent nodes.

If the node has a backpointer, preserve it.

Calculate the backpointer, which is the existing node's backpointer with the node's name concatenated to the end.

Loop through all the adjacent nodes.

Output the adjacent node details.

When outputting the original input node, as well as the adjacent nodes and the distances to them, the format (not contents) of the map output value is identical to make it easier for your reducer to read the data. To do this, you use a Node class to model the notion of a node, its adjacent nodes, and the distance from the starting node. Its toString method generates a String form of this data, which is used as the map output key, as shown in the following listing.[3]

Listing 7.1 The Node class helps with serialization in MapReduce code

```
public class Node {
    private int distance = INFINITE;
    private String backpointer;
    private String[] adjacentNodeNames;

    public static int INFINITE = Integer.MAX_VALUE;
    public static final char fieldSeparator = '\t';
```

---

[2] GitHub source: https://github.com/alexholmes/hiped2/blob/master/src/main/java/hip/ch7/shortestpath/Map.java.

[3] GitHub source: https://github.com/alexholmes/hiped2/blob/master/src/main/java/hip/ch7/shortestpath/Node.java.

...

```
public String constructBackpointer(String name) {
  StringBuilder backpointer = new StringBuilder();
  if (StringUtils.trimToNull(getBackpointer()) != null) {
    backpointers.append(getBackpointer()).append(":");
  }
  backpointer.append(name);
  return backpointer.toString();
}

@Override
public String toString() {
  StringBuilder sb = new StringBuilder();
  sb.append(distance)
      .append(fieldSeparator)
      .append(backpointer);

  if (getAdjacentNodeNames() != null) {
    sb.append(fieldSeparator)
        .append(StringUtils
            .join(getAdjacentNodeNames(), fieldSeparator));
  }
  return sb.toString();
}

public static Node fromMR(String value) throws IOException {
  String[] parts = StringUtils.splitPreserveAllTokens(
      value, fieldSeparator);
  if (parts.length < 2) {
    throw new IOException(
        "Expected 2 or more parts but received " + parts.length);
  }
  Node node = new Node()
      .setDistance(Integer.valueOf(parts[0]))
      .setBackpointer(StringUtils.trimToNull(parts[1]));
  if (parts.length > 2) {
    node.setAdjacentNodeNames(Arrays.copyOfRange(parts, 2,
        parts.length));
  }
  return node;
}
```

The reducer is invoked for each node and is supplied a list of all the adjacent nodes and their shortest paths. It iterates through all the adjacent nodes and determines the current node's shortest path by selecting the adjacent node with the smallest, shortest path. The reducer then outputs the minimum distance, the backpointer, and the original adjacent nodes. The following listing shows this code.[4]

Listing 7.2   The reducer code for the shortest-path algorithm

```
public static enum PathCounter {
  TARGET_NODE_DISTANCE_COMPUTED,
  PATH
```

The counter enum you'll use to set the number of hops when you've reached the target node.

---

[4] GitHub source: https://github.com/alexholmes/hiped2/blob/master/src/main/java/hip/ch7/shortest-path/Reduce.java.

```
}

private Text outValue = new Text();
private String targetNode;

protected void setup(Context context
) throws IOException, InterruptedException {
  targetNode = context.getConfiguration().get(
     Main.TARGET_NODE);
}

public void reduce(Text key, Iterable<Text> values,
                   Context context)
   throws IOException, InterruptedException {

  int minDistance = Node.INFINITE;

  Node shortestAdjacentNode = null;
  Node originalNode = null;

  for (Text textValue : values) {

    Node node = Node.fromMR(textValue.toString());

    if(node.containsAdjacentNodes()) {
      // the original data
      //
      originalNode = node;
    }

    if(node.getDistance() < minDistance) {
      minDistance = node.getDistance();
      shortestAdjacentNode = node;
    }
  }

  if(shortestAdjacentNode != null) {
    originalNode.setDistance(minDistance);
    originalNode.setBackpointer(
      shortestAdjacentNode.getBackpointer());
  }

  outValue.set(originalNode.toString());

  context.write(key, outValue);

  if (minDistance != Node.INFINITE &&
      targetNode.equals(key.toString())) {
    Counter counter = context.getCounter(
        PathCounter.TARGET_NODE_DISTANCE_COMPUTED);
    counter.increment(minDistance);
    context.getCounter(PathCounter.PATH.toString(),
        shortestAdjacentNode.getBackpointer()).increment(1);
  }
}
```

Annotations:

Read the target node name from the configuration.

The initial minimum distance is infinite.

Convert the input value into a Node.

If the node represents the original node (with adjacent nodes), preserve it.

If the distance to this node from an adjacent node is less than the minimum distance, preserve it.

Store the minimum distance and backpointer from the adjacent node.

Write out the node.

If the current node is the target node and you have a valid distance value, you're done, and you indicate this by setting the distance and backpointer in MapReduce counters.

You're ready to run your code. You need to copy the input file into HDFS, and then kick off your MapReduce job, specifying the start node name (dee) and target node name (joe):

```
$ hadoop fs -put \
    test-data/ch7/friends-short-path.txt \
    friends-short-path.txt

$ hip hip.ch7.shortestpath.Main \
    --start dee \
    --end joe \
    --input friends-short-path.txt \
    --output output

=============================================
= Shortest path found, details as follows.
=
= Start node:  dee
= End node:    joe
= Hops:        2
= Path:        dee:ali
=============================================

$ hadoop fs -cat output/2/part*
ali  1  dee        dee  bob  joe
bob  2  dee:kia  kia  ali  joe
dee  0             kia  ali
joe  2  dee:ali  bob  ali
kia  1  dee        bob  dee
```

The output of your job shows that the minimum number of hops between Dee and Joe is 2, and that Ali was the connecting node.

■ **Summary**

This exercise showed how a shortest-path algorithm could be used to determine the minimum number of hops between two people in a social network. An algorithm related to the shortest-path algorithm, called *graph diameter estimation*, attempts to determine the average number of hops between nodes.[5] This has been used to support the notion of *six degrees of separation* in large social network graphs with millions of nodes.[6]

> **Inefficiencies of using MapReduce for iterative graph processing** Using MapReduce for graph processing is inefficient from an I/O perspective—each graph iteration is executed within a single MapReduce job. As a result, the entire graph structure must be written to HDFS (in triplicate, or whatever your HDFS replication setting is) in between jobs and then be read by the subsequent job. Graph algorithms that may require a large number of iterations (such as this shortest-path example) are best executed using Giraph, which is covered in section 7.1.4.

---

[5] See U. Kang et al., "HADI: Fast Diameter Estimation and Mining in Massive Graphs with Hadoop" (December 2008), http://reports-archive.adm.cs.cmu.edu/anon/ml2008/CMU-ML-08-117.pdf.

[6] See Lars Backstrom et al., "Four Degrees of Separation," http://arxiv.org/abs/1111.4570.

The shortest-path algorithm has multiple applications, but an arguably more useful and utilized algorithm in social networks is friends-of-friends (FoF).

7.1.3   *Friends-of-friends algorithm*

Social network sites such as LinkedIn and Facebook use the friends-of-friends (FoF) algorithm to help users broaden their networks.

TECHNIQUE 68   **Calculating FoFs**

The friends-of-friends algorithm suggests friends that a user may know but who aren't part of their immediate network. For this technique, we'll consider a FoF to be in the second degree of separation, as shown in figure 7.12.

The key ingredient to success with this approach is to order the FoFs by the number of common friends, which increases the chances that the user knows the FoF.

■ **Problem**

You want to implement the FoF algorithm in MapReduce.

■ **Solution**

Two MapReduce jobs are required to calculate the FoFs for each user in a social network. The first job calculates the common friends for each user, and the second job sorts the common friends by the number of connections to your friends. You can then recommend new friends by selecting the top FoFs based on this sorted list.

■ **Discussion**

You should first look at an example graph and understand what results you're looking for. Figure 7.13 shows a network of people with Jim, one of the users, highlighted. In this graph, Jim's FoFs are in bold circles, and the number of friends that the FoF and Jim have in common is also identified.

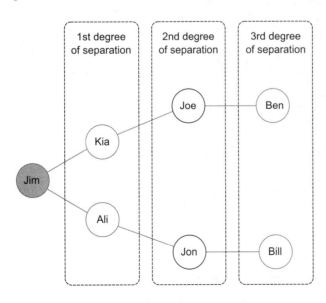

Figure 7.12   An example of FoF where Joe and Jon are considered FoFs to Jim

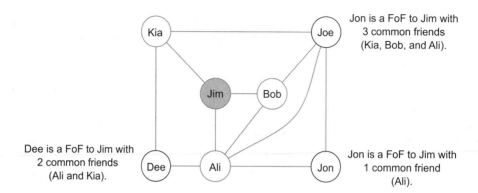

Figure 7.13   A graph representing Jim's FoFs

Your goal is to determine all the FoFs and order them by the number of friends in common. In this case, your expected results would have Joe as the first FoF recommendation, followed by Dee, and then Jon.

The text file that represents the social graph for this technique is shown here:

```
$ cat test-data/ch7/friends.txt
joe  jon  kia  bob  ali
kia  joe  jim  dee
dee  kia  ali
ali  dee  jim  bob  joe  jon
jon  joe  ali
bob  joe  ali  jim
jim  kia  bob  ali
```

This algorithm requires you to write two MapReduce jobs. The first job, the pseudo-code for which is shown in figure 7.14, calculates the FoFs and, for each FoF, counts the number of friends in common. The result of the job is a line for each FoF relationship, excluding people who are already friends.

Map(node-name, node)
1: **for all** *adjnode* ∈ *node.adjacency-list* **do**
2:    *emit(lexicographically-ordered-tuple(node-name, adjnode.name), 1)*
3:    **for all** *adj2node* ∈ *node.adjacency-list* **do**
4:       **if** the *tuple(adjnode.name, adj2node.name)* hasn't already been emitted **then**
5:          *emit(lexicographically-ordered-tuple(adjnode.name, adj2node.name), 2)*

Reduce(tuple(node1.name, node2.name), [i_1, i_2, ...])
1: *common-friends* ← 0
2: *already-friends* ← *false*
3: **for all** *i* ∈ *counts[i_1, i_2, ...]* **do**
4:    **if** *i* = 1 **then**
5:       *already-friends* ← *true*
6:    *common-friends* ← *common-friends* + 1
7: **if** *already-friends* ≠ *true* **then**
8:    *emit(tuple(node1.name, node2.name), common-friends)*

Figure 7.14   The first MapReduce job, which calculates the FoFs

The output when you execute this job against the graph in figure 7.13 is shown here:

```
ali  kia  3
bob  dee  1
bob  jon  2
bob  kia  2
dee  jim  2
dee  joe  2
dee  jon  1
jim  joe  3
jim  jon  1
jon  kia  1
```

The second job needs to produce output that lists FoFs in order of the number of common friends. Figure 7.15 shows the algorithm. You're using a secondary sort to order a user's FoFs in order of the number of common friends.

The output of executing this job against the output of the previous job can be seen here:

```
ali  kia:3
bob  kia:2,jon:2,dee:1
dee  jim:2,joe:2,jon:1,bob:1
jim  joe:3,dee:2,jon:1
joe  jim:3,dee:2
jon  bob:2,kia:1,dee:1,jim:1
kia  ali:3,bob:2,jon:1
```

Let's dive into the code. The following listing shows the first MapReduce job, which calculates the FoFs for each user.[7]

Map(tuple(node1.name, node2.name), common-friends)
  1: *emit(tuple(node1.name, common-friends), tuple(node2.name, common-friends))*
  2: *emit(tuple(node2.name, common-friends), tuple(node1.name, common-friends))*

Partitioner(tuple(node.name, common-friends))
  1: partition by *node.name*

Sort(tuple(node.name, common-friends))
  1: sort by *tuple(node.name, common-friends)*

Reduce(tuple(node.name, common-friends), [tuple₁, tuple₂, ...]
  1: *potential-friends ← ∅*
  2: **for all** *t ∈ tuples[tuple₁, tuple₂, ...]* **do**
  3:      *potential-friendsᵢ ← tuple(t.name, t.common-friends)*
  4: *emit(node.name, potential-friends)*

Figure 7.15   The second MapReduce job, which sorts the FoFs by the number of friends in common

---

[7] GitHub source: https://github.com/alexholmes/hiped2/blob/master/src/main/java/hip/ch7/friendsofa-friend/CalcMapReduce.java.

Listing 7.3 Mapper and reducer implementations for FoF calculation

```
public static class Map
    extends Mapper<Text, Text, TextPair, IntWritable> {

  private TextPair pair = new TextPair();
  private IntWritable one = new IntWritable(1);
  private IntWritable two = new IntWritable(2);

  @Override
  protected void map(Text key, Text value, Context context)
      throws IOException, InterruptedException {
    String[] friends = StringUtils.split(value.toString());
    for (int i = 0; i < friends.length; i++) {

      pair.set(key.toString(), friends[i]);
      context.write(pair, one);

      for (int j = i + 1; j < friends.length; j++) {
        pair.set(friends[i], friends[j]);
        context.write(pair, two);
      }
    }
  }
}

public static class Reduce
    extends Reducer<TextPair, IntWritable, TextPair, IntWritable> {

  private IntWritable friendsInCommon = new IntWritable();

  public void reduce(TextPair key, Iterable<IntWritable> values,
                     Context context)
      throws IOException, InterruptedException {

    int commonFriends = 0;
    boolean alreadyFriends = false;
    for (IntWritable hops : values) {
      if (hops.get() == 1) {
        alreadyFriends = true;
        break;
      }

      commonFriends++;
    }
    if (!alreadyFriends) {
      friendsInCommon.set(commonFriends);
      context.write(key, friendsInCommon);
    }
  }
}
```

Go through all the adjacent nodes in the graph (the user's friends).

For each friend, emit the fact that they're friends so that this relationship can be discarded in the reduce phase. The TextPair class alphabetically orders the two names so that for a given pair of users there'll be a single reducer key.

For each friend, go through the remaining friends and emit the fact that they're an FoF.

Ignore this relationship if the users are already friends.

Output the fact that they're FoFs, including a count of common friends. This also uses the TextPair class to alphabetically order the user names.

The job of the second MapReduce job in the following listing is to sort the FoFs so that you see FoFs with a higher number of mutual friends ahead of those that have a smaller number of mutual friends.[8]

---

[8] GitHub source: https://github.com/alexholmes/hiped2/blob/master/src/main/java/hip/ch7/friendsofa-friend/SortMapReduce.java.

Listing 7.4   Mapper and reducer implementations that sort FoFs

```
public static class Map
      extends Mapper<Text, Text, Person, Person> {

    private Person outputKey = new Person();
    private Person outputValue = new Person();

    @Override
    protected void map(Text key, Text value, Context context)
        throws IOException, InterruptedException {
      String[] parts = StringUtils.split(value.toString());
      String name = parts[0];
      int commonFriends = Integer.valueOf(parts[1]);

      outputKey.set(name, commonFriends);
      outputValue.set(key.toString(), commonFriends);
      context.write(outputKey, outputValue);

      outputValue.set(name, commonFriends);
      outputKey.set(key.toString(), commonFriends);
      context.write(outputKey, outputValue);
    }
}
```

Emit one half of the relationship.

Emit the other half of the relationship.

```
public static class Reduce
      extends Reducer<Person, Person, Text, Text> {

    private Text name = new Text();
    private Text potentialFriends = new Text();

    @Override
    public void reduce(Person key, Iterable<Person> values,
                       Context context)
        throws IOException, InterruptedException {

      StringBuilder sb = new StringBuilder();

      int count = 0;
      for (Person potentialFriend : values) {
        if(sb.length() > 0) {
          sb.append(",");
        }
        sb.append(potentialFriend.getName())
            .append(":")
            .append(potentialFriend.getCommonFriends());

        if (++count == 10) {
          break;
        }
      }

      name.set(key.getName());
      potentialFriends.set(sb.toString());
      context.write(name, potentialFriends);
    }
}
```

All the people in your list are sorted in order of number of common friends.

Only keep the top 10.

Emit the FoFs for the user.

I won't show the whole driver code, but to enable the secondary sort, I had to write a few extra classes as well as inform the job to use the classes for partitioning and sorting purposes: [9]

```
job.setPartitionerClass(PersonNamePartitioner.class);
job.setSortComparatorClass(PersonComparator.class);
job.setGroupingComparatorClass(PersonNameComparator.class);
```

For more details on how secondary sort works, look at chapter 6.

Copy the input file containing the friend relationships into HDFS, and then run the driver code to run your two MapReduce jobs. The last two arguments are the output directories for the two MapReduce jobs:

```
$ hadoop fs -put test-data/ch7/friends.txt .
$ hip hip.ch7.friendsofafriend.Main \
    --input friends.txt \
    --calc-output outputcalc \
    --sort-output outputsort
```

After running your code, you can look at the output in HDFS:

```
$ hadoop fs -cat outputsort/part*
ali   kia:3
bob   kia:2,jon:2,dee:1
dee   jim:2,joe:2,jon:1,bob:1
jim   joe:3,dee:2,jon:1
joe   jim:3,dee:2
jon   bob:2,kia:1,dee:1,jim:1
kia   ali:3,bob:2,jon:1
```

This output verifies what you saw with your own eyes in figure 7.13. Jim has three FoFs, and they're ordered by the number of common friends.

■ Summary

This approach can be used not only as a recommendation engine to help users grow their networks, but also for informational purposes when the user is browsing the social network's website. For example, when you view people in LinkedIn, you'll be shown the degrees of separation between you and the person being viewed. This approach can be used to precompute that information for two hops. To reproduce this for three hops (for example, to show friends-of-friends-of-friends) you'd need to introduce a third MapReduce job to compute the third hop from the output of the first job.

To simplify this approach, we used an undirected graph, which implies that user relationships are bidirectional. Most social networks don't have such a notion, and the algorithm would need some minor tweaks to model directed graphs.

---

[9] GitHub source: https://github.com/alexholmes/hiped2/blob/master/src/main/java/hip/ch7/friendsofafriend/Main.java.

This example required two MapReduce jobs to complete the algorithm, which means that the entire graph was written to HDFS between jobs. This isn't particularly inefficient given the number of jobs, but once the number of iterations over your graph data goes beyond two, it's probably time to start looking at more efficient ways of working with your graph data. You'll see this in the next technique, where Giraph will be used to calculate the popularity of web pages.

7.1.4   Using Giraph to calculate PageRank over a web graph

Using MapReduce for iterative graph processing introduces a number of inefficiencies, which are highlighted in figure 7.16.

This isn't something that should be of concern if your graph algorithm only requires one or two iterations, but beyond that the successive HDFS barriers between jobs will start to add up, especially with large graphs. At that point it's time to look at alternative methods for graph processing, such as Giraph.

This section presents an overview of Giraph and then applies it to calculate PageRank over a web graph. PageRank is a good fit for Giraph as it's an example of an iterative graph algorithm that can require many iterations before the graph converges.

AN INTRODUCTION TO GIRAPH

Giraph is an Apache project modeled after Google's Pregel, which describes a system for large-scale graph processing. Pregel was designed to reduce the inefficiencies of using MapReduce for graph processing and to provide a programming model that is vertex-centric.

To combat the disk and network barriers that exist in MapReduce, Giraph loads all the vertices into memory across a number of worker processes and keeps them in memory during the whole process. Each graph iteration is composed of the workers supplying inputs to the vertices that they manage, the vertices performing their processing,

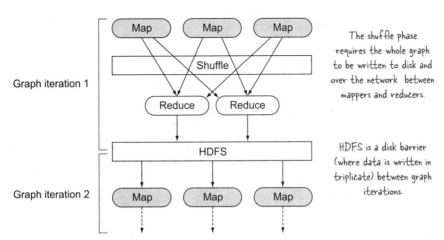

Figure 7.16   An iterative graph algorithm implemented using MapReduce

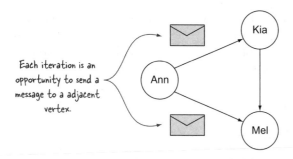

Each iteration is an opportunity to send a message to a adjacent vertex.

Figure 7.17   **Giraph message passing**

and the vertices then emitting messages that the framework routes to the appropriate adjacent vertices in the graph (as seen in figure 7.17).

Giraph uses bulk synchronous communication (BSP) to support workers' communication. BSP is essentially an iterative message-passing algorithm that uses a global synchronization barrier between successive iterations. Figure 7.18 shows Giraph workers each containing a number of vertices, and worker intercommunication and synchronization via the barrier.

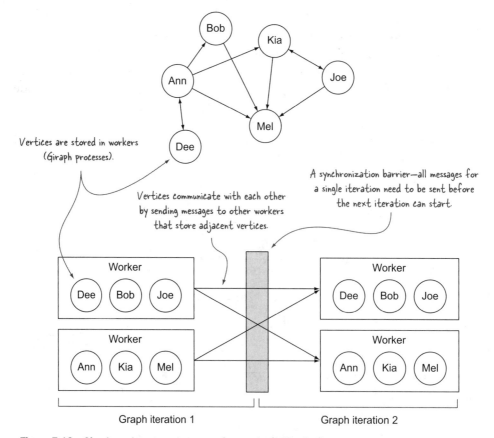

Vertices are stored in workers (Giraph processes).

Vertices communicate with each other by sending messages to other workers that store adjacent vertices.

A synchronization barrier—all messages for a single iteration need to be sent before the next iteration can start.

Graph iteration 1   Graph iteration 2

Figure 7.18   Giraph workers, message passing, and synchronization

Technique 69 will go further into the details, but before we dive in, let's take a quick look at how PageRank works.

A BRIEF OVERVIEW OF PAGERANK

PageRank is a formula introduced by the founders of Google during their Stanford years in 1998.[10] Their paper discusses an overall approach to crawling and indexing the web, and it includes, as part of that, a calculation that they titled *PageRank*, which gives a score to each web page indicating the page's importance. This wasn't the first paper to introduce a scoring mechanism for web pages,[11] but it was the first to weigh scores propagated to each outbound link based on the total number of outbound links.

Fundamentally, PageRank gives pages that have a large number of inbound links a higher score than pages that have a smaller number of inbound links. When evaluating the score for a page, PageRank uses the scores for all the inbound links to calculate a page's PageRank. But it penalizes individual inbound links that have a high number of outbound links by dividing that outbound link PageRank by the number of outbound links. Figure 7.19 presents a simple example of a web graph with three pages and their respective PageRank values.

Figure 7.20 shows the PageRank formula. In the formula, $|webGraph|$ is a count of all the pages in the graph, and d, set to 0.85, is a constant damping factor used in two parts. First, it denotes the probability of a random surfer reaching the page after clicking on many links (this is a constant equal to 0.15 divided by the total number of pages), and second, it dampens the effect of the inbound link PageRanks by 85%.

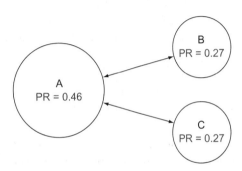

Figure 7.19 **PageRank values for a simple web graph**

$$PageRank(n) = \frac{1-d}{|webGraph|} + d \sum_{i \in InboundLinks(n)} \frac{PageRank(i)}{|i.outboundLinks|}$$

Figure 7.20 **The PageRank formula**

---

[10] See Sergey Brin and Lawrence Page, "The Anatomy of a Large-Scale Hypertextual Web Search Engine," http://infolab.stanford.edu/pub/papers/google.pdf.

[11] Before PageRank, the HITS link-analysis method was popular; see the "Hubs and Authorities" page of Christopher D. Manning, Prabhakar Raghavan, and Hinrich Schütze, *Introduction to Information Retrieval*, http://nlp.stanford.edu/IR-book/html/htmledition/hubs-and-authorities-1.html.

Calculate PageRank over a web graph

PageRank is a graph algorithm that typically requires multiple iterations, and as such doesn't lend itself to being implemented in MapReduce due to the disk barrier overhead discussed in this section's introduction. This technique looks at how you can use Giraph, which is well-suited to algorithms that require multiple iterations over large graphs, to implement PageRank.

■ **Problem**

You want to implement an iterative PageRank graph algorithm using Giraph.

■ **Solution**

PageRank can be implemented by iterating a MapReduce job until the graph has converged. The mappers are responsible for propagating node PageRank values to their adjacent nodes, and the reducers are responsible for calculating new PageRank values for each node, and for re-creating the original graph with the updated PageRank values.

■ **Discussion**

One of the advantages of PageRank is that it can be computed iteratively and applied locally. Every vertex starts with a seed value, which is 1 divided by the number of nodes, and with each iteration, each node propagates its value to all pages it links to. Each vertex in turn sums up all the inbound vertex values to compute a new seed value. This iterative process is repeated until such a time as convergence is reached.

Convergence is a measure of how much the seed values have changed since the last iteration. If the convergence value is below a certain threshold, it means that there's been minimal change and you can stop the iteration. It's also common to limit the number of iterations for large graphs where convergence takes too many iterations.

Figure 7.21 shows two iterations of PageRank against the simple graph you saw earlier in this chapter.

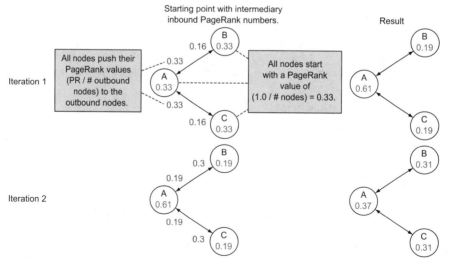

Figure 7.21   An example of PageRank iterations

$Map(node\text{-}name, node)$

1: $emit(node\text{-}name, node)$ {preserve the graph structure}
2: $outPageRank \leftarrow \dfrac{node.pageRank}{|node.adjacency\text{-}list|}$
3: **for all** $adjnode \in node.adjacency\text{-}list$ **do**
4:      $emit(adjnode.name, outPageRank)$

$Reduce(node\text{-}name, [node, inPageRank_1, inPageRank_2, ...])$

1: $sumInPageRanks \leftarrow 0$
2: $node \leftarrow null$
3: **for all** $i \in [node, inPageRank_1, inPageRank_2, ...]$ **do**
4:      **if** i isa $node$ **then**
5:            $node \leftarrow i$
6:      **else**
7:            $sumInPageRanks \leftarrow sumInPageRanks + i$
8: $m.pageRank \leftarrow sumInPageRanks$
9: $emit(node\text{-}name, node)$

Figure 7.22 PageRank decomposed into map and reduce phases

Figure 7.22 shows the PageRank algorithm expressed as map and reduce phases. The map phase is responsible for preserving the graph as well as emitting the PageRank value to all the outbound nodes. The reducer is responsible for recalculating the new PageRank value for each node and including it in the output of the original graph.

In this technique, you'll operate on the graph shown in figure 7.23. In this graph, all the nodes have both inbound and outbound edges.

Giraph supports various input and output data formats. For this technique we'll use `JsonLongDoubleFloatDouble-VertexInputFormat` as the input format; it requires vertices to be expressed numerically along with an associated weight

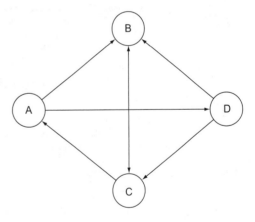

Figure 7.23 Sample web graph for this technique

that we won't use for this technique. We'll map vertex A to integer 0, B to 1, and so on, and for each vertex we'll identify the adjacent vertices. Each line in the data file represents a vertex and the directed edges to adjacent vertices:

```
[<vertex id>,<vertex value>,[[<dest vertex id>,<vertex weight>][...]]]
```

The following input file represents the graph in figure 7.23:

```
[0,0,[[1,0],[3,0]]]
[1,0,[[2,0]]]
[2,0,[[0,0],[1,0]]]
[3,0,[[1,0],[2,0]]]
```

Copy this data into a file called webgraph.txt and upload it to HDFS:

```
$ hadoop fs -put webgraph.txt .
```

Your next step is to write the Giraph vertex class. The nice thing about Giraph's model is that it's simple—it provides a vertex-based API where you need to implement the graph-processing logic for a single iteration on that vertex. The vertex class is responsible for processing incoming messages from adjacent vertices, using them to calculate the node's new PageRank value, and propagating the updated PageRank value (divided by the number of outbound edges) to the adjacent vertices, as shown in the following listing.[12]

Listing 7.5   The PageRank vertex

The compute method is supplied a sequence of PageRank values propagated from adjacent vertices.

A configurable that determines the number of graph iterations.

Only calculate the PageRank value after the first iteration.

Propagate the PageRank value to adjacent vertices if this iteration is less than the number of configured iterations.

Calculate the PageRank value and set it for the vertex.

Once you've reached the maximum number of iterations, indicate that this vertex no longer requires iterations.

```java
public class PageRankVertex extends Vertex<LongWritable, DoubleWritable,
    FloatWritable, DoubleWritable> {

    public static final String SUPERSTEP_COUNT =
        "pageRank.superstepCount";

    @Override
    public void compute(Iterable<DoubleWritable> messages) {
        if (getSuperstep() >= 1) {
            double sum = 0;
            for (DoubleWritable message : messages) {
                sum += message.get();
            }
            getValue().set((0.15f / getTotalNumVertices()) + 0.85f * sum);
        }

        if (getSuperstep() < getConf().getInt(SUPERSTEP_COUNT, 0)) {
            double propagated = getValue().get() / getNumEdges();
            sendMessageToAllEdges(new DoubleWritable(propagated));
        } else {
            voteToHalt();
        }
    }
}
```

> **Installing Giraph**   Giraph is a Java library and is bundled with the code distribution for this book. Therefore, it doesn't need to be installed for the examples in this technique to work. The Giraph website at http://giraph.apache.org/ contains download installation for releases if you wish to play with Giraph further.

If you push the web graph into HDFS and run your job, it will run for five iterations until the graph converges:

---

[12] GitHub source: https://github.com/alexholmes/hiped2/blob/master/src/main/java/hip/ch7/pagerank/giraph/PageRankVertex.java.

The JAR that contains the PageRank vertex class

The input file that models the graph

The output directory

```
$ hadoop org.apache.giraph.GiraphRunner \
    -Dgiraph.zkList=127.0.0.1:2181 \
    -libjars $HIP_HOME/hip-2.0.0.jar \
    hip.ch7.pagerank.giraph.PageRankVertex \
    -vif org.apache.giraph.io.formats.\
JsonLongDoubleFloatDoubleVertexInputFormat \
    -of org.apache.giraph.io.formats.IdWithValueTextOutputFormat \
    -vip webgraph.txt \
    -op output \
    -ca pageRank.superstepCount=10 \
    -w 1
```

The ZooKeeper port

The input format

The output format

The number of graph iterations

The number of workers

After the process has completed, you can look at the output in HDFS to see the Page-Rank values for each vertex:

```
$ hadoop fs -cat output/art*
0  0.15472094578266
2  0.28902904137380575
1  0.25893832306149106
3  0.10043738978626424
```

According to the output, node C (vertex 2) has the highest PageRank, followed by node B (vertex 1). Initially, this observation may be surprising, given that B has three inbound links and C has just two. But if you look at who's linking to C, you can see that node B, which also has a high PageRank value, only has one outbound link to C, so node C gets B's entire PageRank score in addition to its other inbound PageRank score from node D. Therefore, node C's PageRank will always be higher than B's.

■ **Summary**

When you compare the code you had to write for the MapReduce compared to the code for Giraph, it's clear that Giraph provides a simple and abstracted model that richly expresses graph concepts. Giraph's efficiency over that of MapReduce results in Giraph being a compelling solution for your graph-processing needs.

Giraph's ability to scale to large graphs is highlighted by a Facebook article discussing how Facebook used Giraph to process a graph with a trillion edges.[13] There are other graph technologies that you can evaluate for your needs:

- Faunus is a Hadoop-based open source project that supports HDFS and other data sources (http://thinkaurelius.github.io/faunus/).
- GraphX is an in-memory Spark-based project. GraphX is currently not supported by any of the commercial Hadoop vendors, although it will soon be included in Cloudera CDH 5.1 (https://amplab.cs.berkeley.edu/publication/graphx-grades/).
- GraphLab is a C++-based, distributed, graph-processing framework out of Carnegie Mellon University (http://graphlab.com/).

---

[13] Avery Ching, "Scaling Apache Giraph to a trillion edges," https://www.facebook.com/notes/facebook-engineering/scaling-apache-giraph-to-a-trillion-edges/10151617006153920.

Although you implemented the PageRank formula, it was made simple by the fact that your graph was well connected and that every node had outbound links. Pages with no outbound links are called *dangling pages*, and they pose a problem for the PageRank algorithm because they become *PageRank sinks*—their PageRank values can't be further propagated through the graph. This, in turn, causes convergence problems because graphs that aren't strongly connected aren't guaranteed to converge.

There are various approaches to solving this problem. You could remove the dangling nodes before your PageRank iterations and then add them back for a final PageRank iteration after the graph has converged. Or you could sum together the PageRank totals for all dangling pages and redistribute them across all the nodes in the graph. For a detailed examination of dealing with dangling pages as well as advanced PageRank practices, see *Google's PageRank and Beyond* by Amy N. Langville and Carl Dean Meyer (Princeton University Press, 2012).

This concludes the section on graphs. As you learned, graphs are useful mechanisms for representing people in a social network and pages in a web. You used these models to discover some useful information about your data, such as finding the shortest path between two points and what web pages are more popular than others.

This brings us to the subject of the next section, Bloom filters. Bloom filters are a different kind of data structure from graphs. Whereas graphs are used to represent entities and their relationships, Bloom filters are a mechanism for modeling sets and performing membership queries on their data, as you'll discover next.

7.2   *Bloom filters*

A Bloom filter is a data structure that offers a membership query mechanism where the answer to a lookup is one of two values: a definitive *no*, meaning that the item being looked up doesn't exist in the Bloom filter, or a *maybe*, meaning that there's a probability that the item exists. Bloom filters are popular due to their space efficiencies—representing the existence of *N* elements requires much less space than *N* positions in the data structure, which is why the membership query can yield false positive results. The amount of false positives in a Bloom filter can be tuned, which we'll discuss shortly.

Bloom filters are used in BigTable and HBase to remove the need to read blocks from disk to determine if they contain a key. They're also used in distributed network applications such as Squid to share cache details between multiple instances without having to replicate the whole cache or incur a network I/O hit in the case of cache misses.

The implementation of Bloom filters is simple. They use a bit array of size *m* bits, where initially each bit is set to 0. They also contain *k* hash functions, which are used to map elements to *k* locations in the bit array.

To add an element to a Bloom filter, it's hashed *k* times, and a modulo of the hashed value and the size of the bit array is used to map the hashed value to a specific bit array location. That bit in the bit array is then toggled to 1. Figure 7.24 shows three elements being added to a Bloom filter and their locations in the bit array.

To check the membership of an element in the Bloom filter, just like with the add operation, the element is hashed *k* times, and each hash key is used to index into the

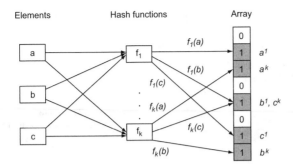

Figure 7.24 Adding elements to a Bloom filter

bit array. A true response to the membership query is only returned in cases where all *k* bit array locations are set to 1. Otherwise, the response to the query is false.

Figure 7.25 shows an example of a membership query where the item was previously added to the Bloom filter, and therefore all the bit array locations contained a 1. This is an example of a true positive membership result.

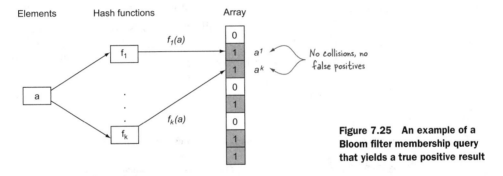

Figure 7.25 An example of a Bloom filter membership query that yields a true positive result

Figure 7.26 shows how you can get a false positive result for a membership query. The element being queried is *d*, which hadn't been added to the Bloom filter. As it happens, all *k* hashes for *d* are mapped to locations that are set to 1 by other elements. This is an example of collision in the Bloom filter, where the result is a false positive.

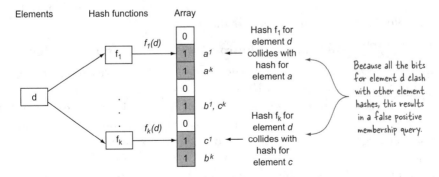

Figure 7.26 An example of a Bloom filter membership query that yields a false positive result

$$m = -\frac{n \ln p}{(\ln(2))^2}$$

m is the required number of bits in the bit array to achieve the desired false probability rate of p for n inserted elements

n is the number of elements inserted

p is the desired false positive rate (0.01 means 1%)

Figure 7.27 Equation to calculate the desired number of bits for a Bloom filter

The probability of false positives can be tuned based on two factors: m, the number of bits in the bit array, and k, the number of hash functions. Or expressed another way, if you have a desired false positive rate in mind and you know how many elements will be added to the Bloom filter, you can calculate the number of bits needed in the bit array with the equation in figure 7.27.

The equation shown in figure 7.28 assumes an optimal number of k hashes and that the hashes being produced are random over the range *{1..m}*.

$$k = \frac{m \ln(2)}{n}$$

Figure 7.28 Equation to calculate the optimal number of hashes

Put another way, if you want to add 1 million elements into a Bloom filter with a 1% false positive rate for your membership queries, you'll need 9,585,058 bits or 1.2 megabytes with seven hash functions. This is around 9.6 bits for each element.

Table 7.1 shows the calculated number of bits per element for various false positive rates.

Table 7.1 Number of bits required per element for different false positive rates

False positives	Bits required per element
2%	8.14
1%	9.58
0.1%	14.38

With all that theory in your head, you now need to turn your attention to the subject of how Bloom filters can be utilized in MapReduce.

TECHNIQUE 70   **Parallelized Bloom filter creation in MapReduce**

MapReduce is good for processing large amounts of data in parallel, so it's a good fit if you want to create a Bloom filter based on a large set of input data. For example, let's say you're a large, internet, social-media organization with hundreds of millions of users, and you want to create a Bloom filter for a subset of users that are within a certain age demographic. How would you do this in MapReduce?

■ **Problem**

You want to create a Bloom filter in MapReduce.

■ **Solution**

Write a MapReduce job to create and output a Bloom filter using Hadoop's built-in `BloomFilter` class. The mappers are responsible for creating intermediary Bloom filters, and the single reducer combines them together to output a combined Bloom filter.

■ **Discussion**

Figure 7.29 shows what this technique will do. You'll write a mapper, which will process user data and create a Bloom filter containing users in a certain age bracket. The mappers will emit their Bloom filters, and a single reducer will combine them together. The final result is a single Bloom filter stored in HDFS in Avro form.

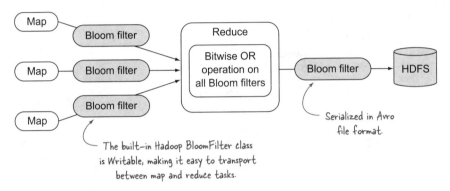

Figure 7.29   A MapReduce job to create a Bloom filter

Hadoop comes bundled with an implementation of a Bloom filter in the form of the `org.apache.hadoop.util.bloom.BloomFilter` class, illustrated in figure 7.30. Luckily, it's a

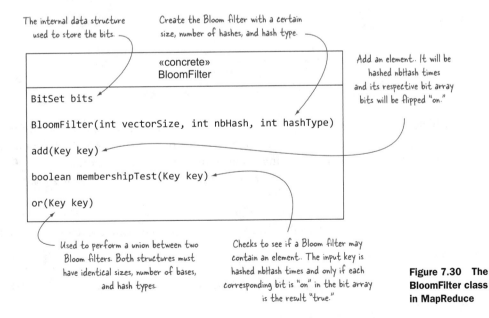

Figure 7.30   The BloomFilter class in MapReduce

Writable, which makes it easy to ship around in MapReduce. The Key class is used to represent an element, and it is also a Writable container for a byte array.

The constructor requires that you tell it what hashing function to use. There are two implementations you can choose from: Jenkins and Murmur. They're both faster than cryptographic hashers such as SHA-1 and they produce good distributions. Benchmarks indicate that Murmur has faster hashing times than Jenkins, so that's what we'll use here.

Let's press on with the code. Your map function will operate on your user information, which is a simple key/value pair, where the key is the user name, and the value is the user's age:[14]

Create the BloomFilter with 1,000 bits and 5 hash functions using the Murmur hash.

```java
public static class Map implements
    Mapper<Text, Text, NullWritable, BloomFilter> {
  private BloomFilter filter =
      new BloomFilter(1000, 5, Hash.MURMUR_HASH);
  OutputCollector<NullWritable, BloomFilter> collector;

  @Override
  public void configure(JobConf job) {
  }

  @Override
  public void map(Text key, Text value,
                  OutputCollector<NullWritable, BloomFilter> output,
                  Reporter reporter) throws IOException {

    int age = Integer.valueOf(value.toString());
    if (age > 30) {
      filter.add(new Key(key.toString().getBytes()));
    }
    collector = output;
  }

  @Override
  public void close() throws IOException {
    collector.collect(NullWritable.get(), filter);
  }
}
```

If the user's age is over 30, add the user name to the BloomFilter.

When the map function has executed over all the input data, output the BloomFilter to the reducer.

Why do you output the Bloom filter in the close method, and not output it for every record you process in the map method? You do this to cut down on the amount of traffic between the map and reduce phases; there's no reason to output a lot of data if you can pseudo-combine them yourself on the map side and emit a single BloomFilter per map.

Your reducer's job is to combine all the Bloom filters outputted by the mappers into a single Bloom filter. The unions are performed with the bitwise OR method

---

[14] GitHub source: https://github.com/alexholmes/hiped2/blob/master/src/main/java/hip/ch7/bloom/BloomFilterCreator.java.

exposed by the `BloomFilter` class. When performing a union, all the `BloomFilter` attributes, such as bit array size and number of hashes, must be identical:[15]

```
public static class Reduce implements
    Reducer<NullWritable, BloomFilter,
            AvroWrapper<GenericRecord>, NullWritable> {
  private BloomFilter filter =
    new BloomFilter(1000, 5, Hash.MURMUR_HASH);

  OutputCollector<AvroWrapper<GenericRecord>, NullWritable>
      collector;

  @Override
  public void reduce(NullWritable key, Iterator<BloomFilter> values,
                     OutputCollector<AvroWrapper<GenericRecord>,
                       NullWritable> output,
                     Reporter reporter) throws IOException {
    while (values.hasNext()) {
      BloomFilter bf = values.next();
      filter.or(bf);
    }
    collector = output;
  }

  @Override
  public void close() throws IOException {
    collector.collect(
        new AvroWrapper<GenericRecord>(
          AvroBytesRecord.toGenericRecord(filter)),
        NullWritable.get());
  }
}
```

Create an empty BloomFilter. It's important that all the constructor fields be identical to the ones you created in the mappers.

Extract the BloomFilter from the input.

Perform a union of the Bloom filters.

Write the Bloom filter in Avro form.

To try this out, upload your sample user file and kick off your job. When the job is complete, dump the contents of the Avro file to view the contents of your `BloomFilter`:

```
$ hadoop fs -put test-data/ch7/user-ages.txt .
$ hadoop fs -cat user-ages.txt
anne    23
joe     45
alison  32
mike    18
marie   54

$ hip hip.ch7.bloom.BloomFilterCreator \
    --input user-ages.txt \
    --output output

$ hip hip.ch7.bloom.BloomFilterDumper output/part-00000.avro
{96, 285, 292, 305, 315, 323, 399, 446, 666, 667, 670,
 703, 734, 749, 810}
```

[15] GitHub   source: https://github.com/alexholmes/hiped2/blob/master/src/main/java/hip/ch7/bloom/ BloomFilterCreator.java.

The `BloomFilterDumper` code unmarshals the `BloomFilter` from the Avro file and calls the `toString()` method, which in turn calls the `BitSet.toString()` method, which outputs the offset for each bit that is "on."

■ Summary

You used Avro as a serialization format for the Bloom filter. You could have just as easily emitted the `BloomFilter` object in your reducer, because it's a `Writable`.

You used a single reducer in this technique, which will scale well to jobs that use thousands of map tasks and `BloomFilters` whose bit array sizes are in the millions. If the time taken to execute the single reducer becomes too long, you can run with multiple reducers to parallelize the Bloom filter unions, and have a postprocessing step to combine them further into a single Bloom filter.

Another distributed method for creating a Bloom filter would be to view the set of reducers as the overall bit array, and perform the hashing and output the hashes in the map phase. The partitioner would then partition the output to the relevant reducer that manages that section of the bit array. Figure 7.31 illustrates this approach.

For code comprehensibility, you hardcoded the `BloomFilter` parameters in this technique; in reality, you'll want to either calculate them dynamically or move them into a configuration file.

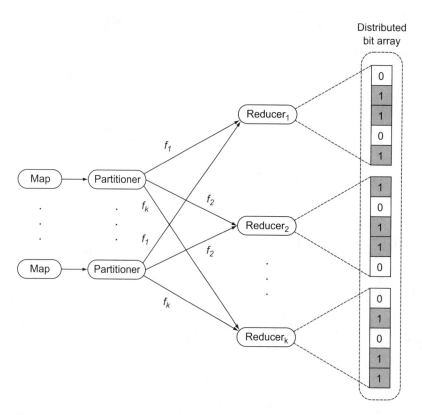

Figure 7.31   An alternate architecture for creating Bloom filters

This technique resulted in the creation of a `BloomFilter`. This `BloomFilter` could be pulled out of HDFS and used in another system, or it could be used directly in Hadoop, as shown in technique 61, where a Bloom filter was used as a way to filter data emitted from reducers in joins.

7.3 HyperLogLog

Imagine that you're building a web analytics system where one of the data points you're calculating is the number of unique users that have visited a URL. Your problem domain is web-scale, so you have hundreds of millions of users. A naive MapReduce implementation of aggregation would involve using a hashtable to store and calculate the unique users, but this could exhaust your JVM heap when dealing with a large number of users. A more sophisticated solution would use a secondary sort so that user IDs are sorted, and the grouping occurs at the URL level so that you can count unique users without any storage overhead.

These solutions work well when you have the ability to process the entire dataset at once. But if you have a more complex aggregation system where you create aggregations in time buckets and you need to combine buckets together, then you'd need to store the entire set of unique users for each URL in each time bucket, which would explode your data storage needs.

To combat this, you could use a probabilistic algorithm such as HyperLogLog, which has a significantly smaller memory footprint than a hashtable. The trade-off with these probabilistic data structures is accuracy, which you can tune. In some ways, HyperLogLog is similar to a Bloom filter, but the key difference is that HyperLogLog will estimate a count, whereas a Bloom filter only provides membership capabilities.

In this section you'll learn how HyperLogLog works and see how it can be used in MapReduce to efficiently calculate unique counts.

7.3.1 A brief introduction to HyperLogLog

HyperLogLog was first introduced in a 2007 paper to "estimate the number of distinct elements of very large data ensembles."[16] Potential applications include link-based spam detection on the web and data mining over large datasets.

HyperLogLog is a probabilistic cardinality estimator—it relaxes the constraint of exactly calculating the number of elements in a set and instead estimates the number of elements. Data structures that support exact set-cardinality calculations require storage that is proportional to the number of elements, which may not be optimal when working with large datasets. Probabilistic cardinality structures occupy less memory than their exact cardinality counterparts, and they're applicable in situations where the cardinality can be off by a few percentage points.

---

[16] Philippe Flajolet et al., "HyperLogLog: the analysis of a near-optimal cardinality estimation algorithm," http://algo.inria.fr/flajolet/Publications/FlFuGaMe07.pdf.

HyperLogLog can perform cardinality estimation for counts beyond 10^9 using 1.5 KB of memory with an error rate of 2%. HyperLogLog works by counting the maximum number of consecutive zeros in a hash and using probabilities to predict the cardinality of all the unique items. Figure 7.32 shows how a hashed value is represented in HyperLogLog. For additional details, refer to the HyperLogLog paper.

There are two parameters you'll need to tune when working with HyperLogLog:

- The number of buckets, usually expressed by a number, b, which is then used to determine the number of buckets by calculating 2^b. Therefore, each increment in b doubles the number of buckets. The lower bound on b is 4, and the upper bound varies by implementation.
- The number of bits used to represent the maximum number of consecutive zeros in a bucket.

As a result, the size of the HyperLogLog is calculated by 2^b * bits-per-bucket. In typical usage, b is 11 and the number of bits per bucket is 5, which results in 10,240 bits, or 1.25 KB.

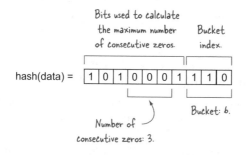

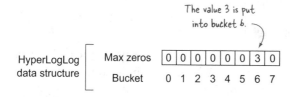

Figure 7.32 How HyperLogLog works

Using HyperLogLog to calculate unique counts

In this technique you'll see a simple example of HyperLogLog in action. The summary will present some details on how HyperLogLog can be incorporated into your MapReduce flows.

■ **Problem**

You're working with a large dataset and you want to calculate distinct counts. You are willing to accept a small percentage of error.

■ **Solution**

Use HyperLogLog.

■ **Discussion**

For this technique you'll use a HyperLogLog Java implementation from a GitHub project called java-hll (https://github.com/aggregateknowledge/java-hll). This code provides the basic HyperLogLog functions, in addition to useful functions that allow you to perform a union and intersect multiple logs together.

The following example shows a simple case where your data consists of an array of numbers, and Google's Guava library is used to create a hash for each number and add it to the HyperLogLog:[17]

```
                                                              The data over which you want
                                                               to calculate a distinct count.
Use Guava's 128-      HashFunction hasher = Hashing.murmur3_128();
bit Murmur hash
algorithm.            final Integer[] data = new Integer[]{1, 1, 2, 2, 3, 3, 4, 4, 5, 5};

                      final HLL hll = new HLL(
                          13,                           Number of buckets—must be
Number of bits per        5                             at least 4 and at most 30.
bucket—at least 1     );
and at most 8.
                      for (int item : data) {
                         final long hashedValue = hasher.newHasher()       Calculate the hash
                             .putInt(item)                                   of an item.
                             .hash()
                             .asLong();

Add the hashed        hll.addRaw(hashedValue);
value to the          }                                           Calculate the estimated
HyperLogLog.                                                        distinct count.
                      System.out.println("Distinct count = " + hll.cardinality());
```

Running this example yields the expected number of distinct items:

```
$ hip hip.ch7.hyperloglog.Example
Distinct count = 5
```

This code can be easily adapted into a Hadoop job to perform distinct counts over large datasets. For example, imagine that you're writing a MapReduce job to calculate

---

[17] GitHub source: https://github.com/alexholmes/hiped2/blob/master/src/main/java/hip/ch7/hyperloglog/Example.java.

the distinct number of users that visit each page on your website. In MapReduce, your mappers would output a URL and user ID as the key and value respectively, and your reducers would need to calculate the unique set of users for each web page. In this situation, you can use a HyperLogLog structure to efficiently calculate an approximate distinct count of users without the overhead that would be incurred by using a hash set.

■ **Summary**

The `hll` HyperLogLog implementation used in this example has a `toBytes` method that you can use to serialize the HyperLogLog, and it also has a `fromBytes` method for deserialization. This makes it relatively straightforward to use within a MapReduce flow and for persistence. Avro, for example, has a `bytes` field that you can use to write the `hll` byte form into your records. You could also write your own `Writable` if you're working with SequenceFiles.

If you're using Scalding or Summingbird, then Algebird has a HyperLogLog implementation that you can use—take a look at https://github.com/twitter/algebird for more details.

7.4   *Chapter summary*

Most of the algorithms laid out in this chapter are straightforward. What makes things interesting is how they're applied in MapReduce in ways that enable you to work efficiently with large datasets.

The two main data structures presented were graphs—good for modeling relationships—and Bloom filters, which excel at compact set membership. In the case of graphs, we looked at how you would use them to model social networks and web graphs, and we went through some algorithms such as FoF and PageRank to mine some interesting facts about your data.

In the case of Bloom filters, we looked at how to use MapReduce to create a Bloom filter in parallel, and then apply that Bloom filter to optimize a semi-join operation in MapReduce.

We've only scratched the surface in this chapter regarding how data can be modeled and processed. Algorithms related to sorting and joins are covered in other chapters. The next chapter covers techniques to diagnose and tune Hadoop to squeeze as much performance as you can out of your clusters.

8

Tuning, debugging, and testing

This chapter covers

- Measuring and tuning MapReduce execution times
- Debugging your applications
- Testing tips to improve the quality of your code

Imagine you've written a new piece of MapReduce code, and you're executing it on your shiny new cluster. You're surprised to learn that despite having a good-sized cluster, your job is running significantly longer than you expected. You've obviously hit a performance issue with your job, but how do you figure out where the problem lies?

This chapter starts out by reviewing common performance problems in MapReduce, such as the lack of data locality and running with too many mappers. This tuning section also examines some enhancements that you can make to your jobs to increase their efficiency by using binary comparators in the shuffle phase and using a compact data format to minimize parsing and data transfer times.

337

The second part of this chapter covers some tips that will help you debug your applications, including instructions on how to access YARN container startup scripts, and some suggestions on how to design your MapReduce jobs to aid future debugging efforts.

The final section looks at how to provide adequate unit testing for MapReduce code and examines some defensive coding techniques you can use to minimize badly behaving code. All the preparation and testing in the world can't guarantee that you won't encounter any problems, and in case you do, we'll look at how you can debug your job to figure out what went wrong.

> **Hadoop 2** The techniques in this chapter work with Hadoop 2. Due to incompatibilities across major Hadoop versions, some of these techniques won't work with earlier versions.

8.1   *Measure, measure, measure*

Before you can start performance tuning, you need to have the tools and processes in place to capture system metrics. These tools will help you gather and examine empirical data related to your application and determine whether or not you're suffering from a performance problem.

In this section we'll look at the tools and metrics that Hadoop provides, and we'll also touch on monitoring as an additional tool in your performance-tuning toolkit.

It's important to capture the CPU, memory, disk, and network utilization of your cluster. If possible, you should also capture MapReduce (or any other YARN application) statistics. Having historical and current metrics for your cluster will allow you to view anomalies in both hardware and software, and to correlate them against any other observations that may point to your work not proceeding at expected rates.

Ultimately, the goal is to ensure that you aren't over-utilizing or under-utilizing your hardware. If you're over-utilizing your hardware, your systems are likely spending a considerable amount of time competing for resources, be it CPU context-switching or memory page-swapping. Under-utilization of your cluster means you're not getting all that you can from your hardware.

Luckily there are a number of tools available to help you monitor your cluster, ranging from sar, the built-in Linux utility that collects and reports on system activity,[1] to more sophisticated tools such as Nagios and Ganglia. Nagios (http://www.nagios.org/) and Ganglia (http://ganglia.sourceforge.net/) are both open source projects designed to monitor your infrastructure, and Ganglia in particular provides a rich user interface with useful graphs, some of which can be seen in figure 8.1. Ganglia has the added advantage of being able to pull statistics from Hadoop.[2]

---

[1] This IBM article discusses using sar and gnuplot to generate system-activity graphs: David Tansley, "Using gnuplot to display data in your Web pages," http://www.ibm.com/developerworks/aix/library/au-gnuplot/index.html.

[2] The Hadoop wiki has basic instructions on Ganglia and Hadoop integration: GangliaMetrics, http://wiki.apache.org/hadoop/GangliaMetrics.

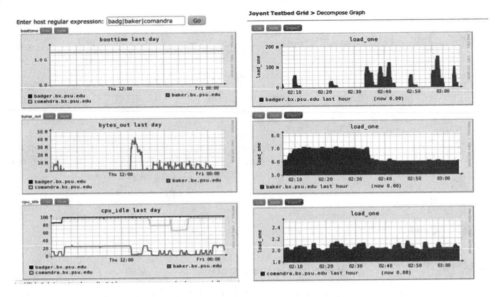

Figure 8.1 Ganglia screenshots showing CPU utilization for multiple hosts

If you're using a commercial Hadoop distribution, it was likely bundled with management user interfaces that include monitoring. If you're using the Apache Hadoop distribution, you should be using Apache Ambari, which simplifies provisioning, management, and monitoring of your cluster. Ambari uses Ganglia and Nagios behind the scenes.

With your monitoring tools in place, it's time to take a look at how to tune and optimize your MapReduce jobs.

8.2   Tuning MapReduce

In this section we'll cover common issues that impact the performance of MapReduce jobs and look at how you can address these issues. Along the way, I'll also point out some best practices to help you optimize your jobs.

We'll start by looking at some of the more common issues that hamper MapReduce job performance.

8.2.1   Common inefficiencies in MapReduce jobs

Before we delve into the techniques, let's take a high-level look at a MapReduce job and identify the various areas that can impact its performance. Take a look at figure 8.2.

The rest of this section on performance tuning covers the issues identified in figure 8.2. But before we start tuning, we need to look at how you can easily get access to job statistics, which will help you identify areas in need of tuning.

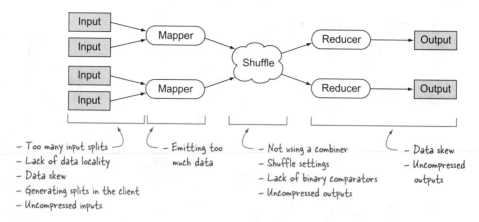

Figure 8.2   Inefficiencies that can occur in various parts of a MapReduce job

TECHNIQUE 72   Viewing job statistics

The first port of call when evaluating the performance of a MapReduce job is the metrics that Hadoop measures for your job. In this technique you'll learn how to access these metrics.

■ **Problem**

You want to access the metrics for a MapReduce job.

■ **Solution**

Use the JobHistory UI, the Hadoop CLI, or a custom utility.

■ **Discussion**

MapReduce collects various system and job counters for each job and persists them in HDFS. You can extract these statistics in two different ways:

- Use the JobHistory UI.
- Use the Hadoop command-line interface (CLI) to view job and task counters and other metrics from the job history.

> **Job-history retention**   The job history is kept around for one week by default. This can be altered by updating mapreduce.jobhistory.max-age-ms.

Let's examine both of these tools, starting with the JobHistory UI.

JobHistory

In Hadoop 2, JobHistory is a MapReduce-specific service that gathers metrics from completed MapReduce jobs and provides a user interface for viewing them.[3] Figure 8.3 shows how you can access the job statistics in the JobHistory UI.

This screen shows you the aggregated metrics for map tasks, reduce tasks, and across all the tasks. In addition, each metric allows you to drill down into all the tasks

---

[3] Chapter 2 contains details on how to access the JobHistory user interface.

After you click on a specific job in the main JobHistory UI, click on the Counters submenu to access the metrics.

Figure 8.3 Accessing job counters in the JobHistory UI

that reported that metric. Within each metric-specific screen, you can sort by the metric values to quickly identify tasks that exhibit unusually high or low metric values.

> **Metrics improvements in Hadoop 2** Hadoop 2 improved the job metrics by adding CPU, memory, and garbage collection statistics, so you can get a good sense of the system utilization of each process.

All is not lost if you can't access the JobHistory UI, as you can also access the data via the Hadoop CLI.

Accessing the job history with the CLI
The job history output is stored in the directory specified by the configurable `mapreduce`
`.jobhistory.done-dir`, the default location being /tmp/hadoop-yarn/staging/history/
done/ for Apache Hadoop.[4] Within this directory, jobs are partitioned by the job submission date. If you know your job ID, you can search for your directory:

```
$ hadoop fs -lsr /tmp/hadoop-yarn/staging/history/done/ \
  | grep job_1398974791337_0037
```

---

[4] Non-Apache Hadoop distributions may have a customized value for `mapreduce.jobhistory.done-dir`—for example, in CDH this directory is /user/history/done.

One of the files returned from this command should be a file with a .jhist suffix, which is the job history file. Use the fully qualified path of this file with the Hadoop `history` command to view your job history details:

```
$ hadoop job -history <history file>

Hadoop job: job_1398974791337_0037
======================================
User: aholmes
JobName: hip-2.0.0.jar
JobConf: hdfs://localhost:8020/tmp/hadoop-yarn/...
Submitted At: 11-May-2014 13:06:48
Launched At: 11-May-2014 13:07:07 (19sec)
Finished At: 11-May-2014 13:07:17 (10sec)
Status: SUCCEEDED
Counters:

|Group Name  |Counter name                      |Map Value |Reduce |Total |
------------------------------------------------------------------------------
|File System |FILE: Number of bytes read        |0         |288    |288
|File System |FILE: Number of bytes written     |242,236   |121,304 |363,540
|File System |FILE: Number of read operations   |0         |0      |0
|File System |FILE: Number of write operations  |0         |0      |0

...


Task Summary
==============================
Kind   Total Successful Failed Killed StartTime FinishTime

Setup   0 0 0 0
Map     2 2 0 0  11-May-2014 13:07:09  11-May-2014 13:07:13
Reduce  1 1 0 0  11-May-2014 13:07:15  11-May-2014 13:07:17
==============================


Analysis
=========

Time taken by best performing map task task_1398974791337_0037_m_000001:
  3sec
Average time taken by map tasks: 3sec
Worse performing map tasks:
TaskId          Timetaken
task_1398974791337_0037_m_000000 3sec
task_1398974791337_0037_m_000001 3sec
The last map task task_1398974791337_0037_m_000000 finished at
(relative to the Job launch time): 11-May-2014 13:07:13 (5sec)

Time taken by best performing shuffle task
task_1398974791337_0037_r_000000: 1sec
Average time taken by shuffle tasks: 1sec
Worse performing shuffle tasks:
TaskId          Timetaken
task_1398974791337_0037_r_000000 1sec
The last shuffle task task_1398974791337_0037_r_000000 finished at
```

```
(relative to the Job launch time): 11-May-2014 13:07:17 (9sec)

Time taken by best performing reduce task
task_1398974791337_0037_r_000000: 0sec
Average time taken by reduce tasks: 0sec
Worse performing reduce tasks:
TaskId        Timetaken
task_1398974791337_0037_r_000000 0sec
The last reduce task task_1398974791337_0037_r_000000 finished at
(relative to the Job launch time): 11-May-2014 13:07:17 (10sec)
=========
```

The previous output is only a small subset of the overall output produced by the command, and it's worth executing it yourself to see the full metrics it exposes. This output is useful in quickly evaluating metrics such as average- and worst-task execution times.

Both the JobHistory UI and the CLI can be used to identify a number of performance issues in your job. As we go through the techniques in this section, I'll highlight how the job history counters can be used to help identify issues.

Let's get things moving by looking at the optimizations that can be made on the map side.

8.2.2 Map optimizations

Optimizations in the map side of a MapReduce job are usually related to the input data and how it's being processed, or to your application code. Your mappers are responsible for reading the job inputs, so variables such as whether your input files are splittable, data locality, and the number of input splits all can have an impact on the performance of your job. Inefficiencies in your mapper code can also lead to longer-than-expected job execution times.

This section covers some of the data-related issues that your job could encounter. The application-specific issues are covered in section 8.2.6.

TECHNIQUE 73 **Data locality**

One of MapReduce's biggest performance traits is the notion of "pushing compute to the data," which means that map tasks are scheduled so that they read their inputs from local disk. Data locality isn't guaranteed, however, and your file formats and cluster utilization can impact data locality. In this technique you'll learn how to identify indications of lack of locality, and also learn about some solutions.

■ **Problem**

You want to detect whether you have map tasks that are reading inputs over the network.

■ **Solution**

Examine some key counters in the job history metadata.

■ **Discussion**

There are a number of counters in the job history that you should keep an eye on to make sure data locality is in play in your mappers. These are listed in table 8.1.

Table 8.1   Counters that can indicate if nonlocal reads are occurring

Counter name	JobHistory name	You may have nonlocal reads if ...
HDFS_BYTES_READ	HDFS: Number of bytes read	... this number is greater than the block size of the input file.
DATA_LOCAL_MAPS	Data-local map tasks	... any map tasks have this value set to 0.
RACK_LOCAL_MAPS	Rack-local map tasks	... any map tasks have this value set to 1.

There could be a number of causes for non-local reads:

- You're working with large files and a file format that can't be split, which means that mappers need to stream some of the blocks from other data nodes.
- The file format supports splitting, but you're using an input format that doesn't support splitting. An example of this is using LZOP to compress a text file and then using `TextInputFormat`, which doesn't know how to split the file.
- The YARN scheduler wasn't able to schedule the map container to a node. This can happen if your cluster is under load.

There are a few options you can consider to address the problems:

- When using an unsplittable file format, write files at or near the HDFS block size to minimize nonlocal reads.
- If you're using the capacity scheduler, set `yarn.scheduler.capacity.node-locality-delay` to introduce more delay in the scheduler and thus increase the chance that a map task is scheduled onto a data-local node.
- If you're using text files, switch to a compression codec that supports splitting, such as LZO or bzip2.

Next let's look at another data-related optimization that comes into play when you're working with large datasets.

TECHNIQUE 74   **Dealing with a large number of input splits**

Jobs with a large number of input splits are not optimal, because each input split is executed by a single mapper, and each mapper executes as a single process. The aggregate pressure on the scheduler and the cluster due to forking these processes results in slow job execution times. This technique examines some methods that can be used to reduce the number of input splits and still maintain data locality.

■ **Problem**

You want to optimize a job that runs with thousands of mappers.

■ **Solution**

Use the `CombineFileInputFormat` to combine multiple blocks that are run with fewer mappers.

■ **Discussion**

There are two primary issues that will cause a job to require a large number of mappers:

- Your input data consists of a large number of small files. The total size of all these files may be small, but MapReduce will spawn a mapper for each small file, so your job will spend more time launching processes than it will actually processing the input data.
- Your files aren't small (they're close to, or over, the HDFS block size), but your aggregate data size is large and spans thousands of blocks in HDFS. Each block is assigned to an individual mapper.

If your problem is related to small files, you should consider compacting these files together or using a container format such as Avro to store your files.

In either of the preceding situations, you can use the CombineFileInputFormat, which will combine multiple blocks into input splits to reduce the overall number of input splits. It does so by examining all the blocks that are occupied by the input files, mapping each block to the set of data nodes that stores it, and then combining blocks that exist on the same data node into a single input split to preserve data locality. There are two concrete implementations of this abstract class:

- CombineTextInputFormat works with text files and uses TextInputFormat as the underlying input format to process and emit records to the mappers.
- CombineSequenceFileInputFormat works with SequenceFiles.

Figure 8.4 compares the splits generated by TextInputFormat with those generated by CombineTextInputFormat.

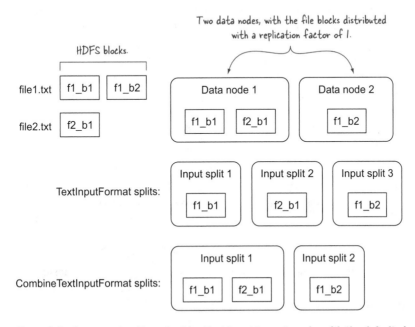

Figure 8.4   An example of how CombineTextInputFormat works with the default size settings

There are some configurables that allow you to tune how input splits are composed:

- `mapreduce.input.fileinputformat.split.minsize.per.node`—Specifies the minimum number of bytes that each input split should contain within a data node. The default value is `0`, meaning that there is no minimum size.
- `mapreduce.input.fileinputformat.split.minsize.per.rack`—Specifies the minimum number of bytes that each input split should contain within a single rack. The default value is `0`, meaning that there is no minimum size.
- `mapreduce.input.fileinputformat.split.maxsize`—Specifies the maximum size of an input split. The default value is `0`, meaning that there is no maximum size.

With the default settings, you'll end up with a maximum of one input split for each data node. Depending on the size of your cluster, this may hamper your parallelism, in which case you can play with `mapreduce.input.fileinputformat.split.maxsize` to allow more than one split for a node.

If the input files for a job are significantly smaller than the HDFS block size, it's likely that your cluster will spend more effort starting and stopping Java processes than it spends performing work. If you're suffering from this problem, you should consult chapter 4, where I explained various approaches you can take to working efficiently with small files.

TECHNIQUE 75   **Generating input splits in the cluster with YARN**

If the client that submits MapReduce jobs is not in a network that's local to your Hadoop cluster, then input split calculation can be expensive. In this technique you'll learn how to push the input split calculation to the MapReduce ApplicationMaster.

I Only on YARN   This technique only works with YARN.

■ **Problem**

Your client is remote and input split calculation is taking a long time.

■ **Solution**

Set `yarn.app.mapreduce.am.compute-splits-in-cluster` to `true`.

■ **Discussion**

By default, input splits are calculated in the MapReduce driver. When the input source is HDFS, then the input format needs to perform operations such as file listings and file status commands to retrieve block details. When working with a large number of input files, this can be slow, especially when there's network latency between the driver and the Hadoop cluster.

The solution is to set `yarn.app.mapreduce.am.compute-splits-in-cluster` to `true`, pushing the input split calculation to the MapReduce ApplicationMaster, which runs inside the Hadoop cluster. This minimizes the time taken to calculate input splits and thus reduces your overall job execution time.

EMITTING TOO MUCH DATA FROM YOUR MAPPERS

Outputting a lot of data from your mappers is to be avoided if possible, because all of that emitted data results in a lot of disk and network I/O as a result of the shuffle. You can use filters and projections in your mappers to cut down on the amount of data that you're working with, and spilling, in MapReduce. Pushdowns can further improve your data pipeline. Technique 55 contains examples of filters and pushdowns.

8.2.3 Shuffle optimizations

The shuffle in MapReduce is responsible for organizing and delivering your mapper outputs to your reducers. There are two parts to the shuffle: the map side and the reduce side. The map side is responsible for partitioning and sorting data for each reducer. The reduce side fetches data from each mapper and merges it before supplying it to the reducer.

As a result there are optimizations you can perform on both sides of the shuffle, including writing a combiner, which is covered in the first technique.

TECHNIQUE 76 Using the combiner

The combiner is a powerful mechanism that aggregates data in the map phase to cut down on data sent to the reducer. It's a map-side optimization, where your code is invoked with a number of map output values for the same output key.

■ **Problem**

You're filtering and projecting your data, but your shuffle and sort are still taking longer than you want. How can you cut down on them even further?

■ **Solution**

Define a combiner and use the `setCombinerClass` method to set it for your job.

■ **Discussion**

The combiner is invoked on the map side as part of writing map output data to disk in both the spill and merge phases, as shown in figure 8.5. To help with grouping values together to maximize the effectiveness of a combiner, use a sorting step in both phases prior to calling the combiner function.

Calling the `setCombinerClass` sets the combiner for a job, similar to how the map and reduce classes are set:

```
job.setCombinerClass(Combine.class);
```

Your combiner implementation must conform to the reducer specification. In this technique you'll write a simple combiner whose job is to remove duplicate map output

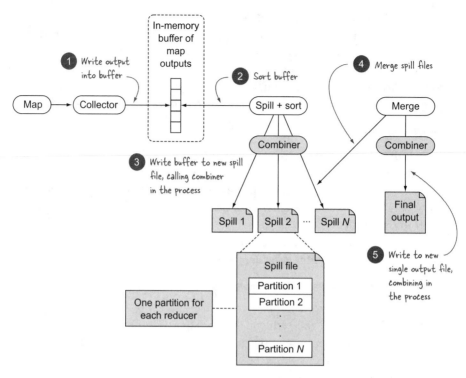

Figure 8.5   How the combiner is called in the context of the map task

records. As you iterate over the map output values, you'll only emit those that are contiguously unique:[5]

```
public static class Combine
    implements Reducer<Text, Text, Text, Text> {

  @Override
  public void reduce(Text key, Iterator<Text> values,
                  OutputCollector<Text,
                      Text> output,
                  Reporter reporter) throws IOException {

    Text prev = null;
    while (values.hasNext()) {
      Text t = values.next();

      if (!t.equals(prev)) {
        output.collect(key, t);
      }
      prev = ReflectionUtils.copy(job, t, prev);
    }
  }
}
```

Much like a reducer, the combiner will be called with multiple values for the same key in situations where a block of map outputs contains the same key.

You only output a key/value pair if you detect a new value.

The MapReduce framework reuses the iterator value objects supplied to combiners/reducers, so you need to clone the value to ensure it's not overwritten.

---

[5] GitHub source: https://github.com/alexholmes/hiped2/blob/master/src/main/java/hip/ch8/Combine-Job.java.

It's important that if you have a combiner, the function is distributive. In figure 8.5 you saw that the combiner will be called multiple times for the same input key, and there are no guarantees about how the output values will be organized when they're sent to the combiner (other than that they were paired with the combiner key). A distributive function is one where the end result is identical regardless of how inputs were combined.

■ **Summary**

The combiner is a powerful tool in your MapReduce toolkit, as it helps cut down on the amount of data transmitted over the network between mappers and reducers. Binary comparators are another tool that will improve the execution times of your MapReduce jobs, and we'll examine them next.

TECHNIQUE 77 **Blazingly fast sorting with binary comparators**

When MapReduce is sorting or merging, it uses the RawComparator for the map output key to compare keys. Built-in Writable classes (such as Text and IntWritable) have byte-level implementations that are fast because they don't require the byte form of the object to be unmarshaled to Object form for the comparison.

When writing your own Writable, it may be tempting to implement the Writable-Comparable interface, but this can lead to longer shuffle and sort phases because it requires Object unmarshaling from byte form for comparisons.

■ **Problem**

You have custom Writable implementations and you want to reduce the sort times for your jobs.

■ **Solution**

Write a byte-level comparator to ensure optimal comparisons during sorting.

■ **Discussion**

In MapReduce there are multiple stages where output keys are compared to each other when data is being sorted. To facilitate key sorting, all map output keys must implement the WritableComparable interface:

```
public interface WritableComparable<T>
  extends Writable, Comparable<T> {
}
```

In the PersonWritable you created in technique 64 (when implementing a secondary sort), your implementation was as follows: [6]

```
public class Person implements WritableComparable<Person> {

  private String firstName;
  private String lastName;
```

---

[6] GitHub source: https://github.com/alexholmes/hiped2/blob/master/src/main/java/hip/ch6/sort/secondary/Person.java.

```
@Override
public int compareTo(Person other) {
  int cmp = this.lastName.compareTo(other.lastName);
  if (cmp != 0) {
    return cmp;
  }
  return this.firstName.compareTo(other.firstName);
}
...
```

The trouble with this `Comparator` is that MapReduce stores your intermediary map output data in byte form, and every time it needs to sort your data it has to unmarshal it into `Writable` form to perform the comparison. This unmarshaling is expensive because it re-creates your objects for comparison purposes.

If you look at the built-in `Writables` in Hadoop, you'll see that not only do they extend the `WritableComparable` interface, but they also provide their own custom `Comparator` that extends the `WritableComparator` class. The following code presents a subsection of the `WritableComparator` class:

The bl field contains a byte array, part of which contains the WritableComparable in byte form. The sl field is the offset into the byte array where the WritableComparable object starts, and ll is the number of bytes that the WritableComparable occupies in the byte array.

The second batch of arguments pertain to the second object being compared.

```
public class WritableComparator implements RawComparator {

    public int compare(byte[] b1, int s1, int l1,
                       byte[] b2, int s2, int l2
                      ) {
        try {
            buffer.reset(b1, s1, l1);
            key1.readFields(buffer);

            buffer.reset(b2, s2, l2);
            key2.readFields(buffer);

        } catch (IOException e) {
            throw new RuntimeException(e);
        }

        return compare(key1, key2);
    }

    /** Compare two WritableComparables.
     *
     * <p> The default implementation uses the natural ordering,
     * calling {@link
     * Comparable#compareTo(Object)}. */
    @SuppressWarnings("unchecked")
    public int compare(WritableComparable a, WritableComparable b) {
        return a.compareTo(b);
    }
    ...
}
```

Unmarshal the first object into WritableComparable form. The class reuses the key1 instance so that it's not recreated.

Unmarshal the second object into WritableComparable form.

Call a function to compare the objects.

The default implementation uses the WritableComparable's compare function.

To write a byte-level `Comparator`, the `compare` method needs to be overridden. Let's look at how the `IntWritable` class implements this method:

```
public class IntWritable implements WritableComparable {

    public static class Comparator extends WritableComparator {
        public Comparator() {
            super(IntWritable.class);
        }

        public int compare(byte[] b1, int s1, int l1,
                            byte[] b2, int s2, int l2) {
            int thisValue = readInt(b1, s1);
            int thatValue = readInt(b2, s2);
            return (thisValue<thatValue ? -1 :
              (thisValue==thatValue ? 0 : 1));
        }
    }

    static {
        WritableComparator.define(IntWritable.class,
            new Comparator());
    }
}
```

Override the WritableComparator.compare method to provide an optimized version.

Use the WritableComparator's helper method to read the integer form of the first value.

Read the second value.

Register the WritableComparator. This tells MapReduce to use the WritableComparator implementation rather than the IntWritable's compareTo method for comparison.

The built-in `Writable` classes all provide `WritableComparator` implementations, which means you don't need to worry about optimizing the `Comparators` as long as your MapReduce job output keys use these built-in `Writables`. But if you have a custom `Writable` that you use as an output key, you'll ideally provide a `WritableComparator`. We'll now revisit your `Person` class and look at how you can do this.

In your `Person` class, you had two fields: the first and last names. Your implementation stored them as strings and used the `DataOutput`'s `writeUTF` method to write them out:

```
private String firstName;
private String lastName;

@Override
public void write(DataOutput out) throws IOException {
  out.writeUTF(lastName);
  out.writeUTF(firstName);
}
```

The first thing you need to understand is how your `Person` object is represented in byte form, based on the previous code. The `writeUTF` method writes two bytes containing the length of the string, followed by the byte form of the string. Figure 8.6 shows how this information is laid out in byte form.

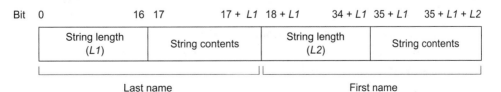

Bit   0   16 17   17 + *L1* 18 + *L1*   34 + *L1* 35 + *L1*   35 + *L1* + *L2*

| String length (*L1*) | String contents | String length (*L2*) | String contents |

Last name   First name

Figure 8.6 Byte layout of `Person`

You want natural ordering of your records that include both the last and first names, but you can't do this directly using the byte array because the string lengths are also encoded in the array. Instead, the Comparator needs to be smart enough to skip over the string lengths. The following code shows how to do this:[7]

Compare the last name.

Read the size of the last name from the first byte array.

Read the size of the UTF-8 string containing the last name from the first record.

Read the size of the UTF-8 string containing the last name from the second record.

If the last name isn't identical, return the result of the comparison.

Read the size of the last name from the second byte array.

Return the result of the comparison on the first name.

Use the WritableComparator.compareBytes method to perform a natural ordering of the UTF-8 binary data.

```java
@Override
public int compare(byte[] b1, int s1, int l1, byte[] b2, int s2,
                   int l2) {
  int lastNameResult = compare(b1, s1, b2, s2);

  if (lastNameResult != 0) {
    return lastNameResult;
  }
  int b1l1 = readUnsignedShort(b1, s1);
  int b2l1 = readUnsignedShort(b2, s2);

  return compare(b1, s1 + b1l1 + 2, b2, s2 + b2l1 + 2);
}
public static int compare(byte[] b1, int s1, byte[] b2, int s2) {
  int b1l1 = readUnsignedShort(b1, s1);
  int b2l1 = readUnsignedShort(b2, s2);

  return compareBytes(b1, s1 + 2, b1l1, b2, s2 + 2, b2l1);
}

public static int readUnsignedShort(byte[] b, int offset) {
  int ch1 = b[offset];
  int ch2 = b[offset + 1];
  return (ch1 << 8) + (ch2);
}
```

■ **Summary**

The writeUtf method is limited because it can only support strings that contain less than 65,536 characters. This is probably fine for the scenario where you're working with people's names, but if you need to work with a larger string, you should look at using Hadoop's Text class, which can support much larger strings. If you look at the Comparator inner class in the Text class, you'll see that its binary string comparator works in a fashion similar to the one discussed here. This approach could easily be extended to work with names represented with Text objects rather than Java String objects.

The next issue in performance tuning is how you can guard against the impact that data skews can have on your MapReduce jobs.

USING A RANGE PARTITIONER TO AVOID DATA SKEW

It's common for a handful of the reducers to be in the long tail when it comes to task execution time, due to the way that the default hash partitioner works. If this is

---

[7] GitHub source: https://github.com/alexholmes/hiped2/blob/master/src/main/java/hip/ch8/PersonBinaryComparator.java.

impacting your job, then take a look at technique 63 on handling skews generated by the hash partitioner.

TECHNIQUE 78 Tuning the shuffle internals

The shuffle phase involves fetching the map output data from the shuffle service and merging it in the background. The sort phase, which is another merge, will merge the files together into a smaller number of files.

■ **Problem**

You want to determine if a job runs slowly due to the shuffle and sort phases.

■ **Solution**

Use the JobHistory metadata to extract statistics related to the shuffle and sort execution times.

■ **Discussion**

We're going to look at three areas of the shuffle and for each identify areas that can be tuned for increased performance.

Tuning the map side

When a mapper emits output records, they're first stored in an in-memory buffer. After the buffer grows to a certain size, the data is spilled to a new file on disk. This process continues until the mapper has completed emitting all its output records. Figure 8.7 shows this process.

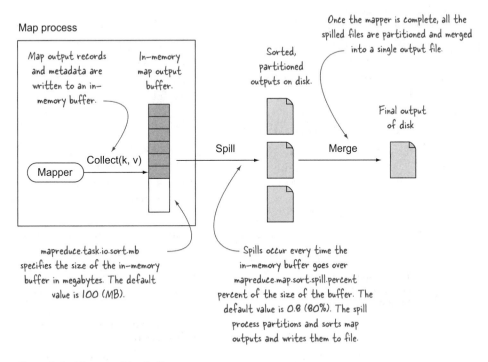

Figure 8.7   The map-side shuffle

The expensive part of the map-side shuffle is the I/O related to spilling and merging the spill files. The merge is expensive, as all the map outputs need to be read from the spill files and rewritten to the merged spill file.

An ideal mapper is able to fit all its output in the in-memory buffer, which means that only one spill file is required. Doing so negates the need to merge multiple spill files together. This isn't possible for all jobs, but if your mapper filters or projects the input data so that the input data can fit into memory, then it's worthwhile tuning `mapreduce.task.io.sort.mb` to be large enough to store the map outputs.

Examine the job counters shown in table 8.2 to understand and tune the shuffle characteristics of your job.

Table 8.2   Map shuffle counters

Counter	Description
MAP_OUTPUT_BYTES	Use the MAP_OUTPUT_BYTES counter for your map tasks to determine if it's possible to increase your `mapreduce.task.io.sort.mb` so that it can store all the map outputs.
SPILLED_RECORDS MAP_OUTPUT_RECORDS	Ideally these two values will be the same, which indicates that only one spill occurred.
FILE_BYTES_READ FILE_BYTES_WRITTEN	Compare these two counters with MAP_OUTPUT_BYTES to understand the additional reads and writes that are occurring as a result of the spilling and merging.

Tuning the reduce side

On the reduce side, the map outputs for the reducer are streamed from the auxiliary shuffle service that runs on each slave node. The map outputs are written into an in-memory buffer that is merged and written to disk once the buffer reaches a certain size. In the background, these spilled files are continuously merged into a smaller number of merged files. Once the fetchers have fetched all their outputs, there's a final round of merging, after which data from the merged files is streamed to the reducer. Figure 8.8 shows this process.

Much like with the map side, the goal of tuning the reduce-size shuffle is to attempt to fit all the map outputs into memory to avoid spilling to disk and merging spilled files. By default, records are always spilled to disk even if they can all fit in memory, so to enable a memory-to-memory merge that bypasses disk, set `mapreduce.reduce.merge.memtomem.enabled` to true.

The job counters in table 8.3 can be used to understand and tune the shuffle characteristics of your job.

Table 8.3   Map shuffle counters

Counter	Description
SPILLED_RECORDS	The number of records that are written to disk. If your goal is for map outputs to never touch disk, this value should be 0.
FILE_BYTES_READ FILE_BYTES_WRITTEN	These counters will give you an idea of how much data is being spilled and merged to disk.

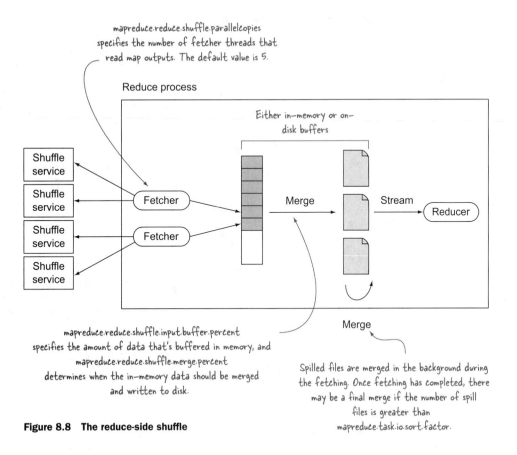

mapreduce.reduce.shuffle.parallelcopies
specifies the number of fetcher threads that
read map outputs. The default value is 5.

Reduce process

Either in–memory or on–
disk buffers

Shuffle service

Shuffle service

Fetcher

Merge

Stream

Reducer

Shuffle service

Fetcher

Shuffle service

Merge

mapreduce.reduce.shuffle.input.buffer.percent
specifies the amount of data that's buffered in memory, and
mapreduce.reduce.shuffle.merge.percent
determines when the in–memory data should be merged
and written to disk.

Spilled files are merged in the background during
the fetching. Once fetching has completed, there
may be a final merge if the number of spill
files is greater than
mapreduce.task.io.sort.factor.

Figure 8.8 The reduce-side shuffle

Shuffle settings

Table 8.4 shows the properties covered in this technique.

Table 8.4 Configurables to tune the shuffle

Name	Default value	Map side or reduce side?	Description
mapreduce.task.io.sort .mb	100 (MB)	Map	The total amount of buffer memory in megabytes to use when buffering map outputs. This should be approximately 70% of the map task's heap size.
mapreduce.map.sort .spill.percent	0.8 (80%)	Map	The soft limit in the serialization buffer. Once reached, a thread will begin to spill the contents to disk in the background. Note that collection will not block if this threshold is exceeded while a spill is already in progress, so spills may be larger than this threshold when it is set to less than 0.5.

Table 8.4 Configurables to tune the shuffle *(continued)*

Name	Default value	Map side or reduce side?	Description
`mapreduce.task.io.sort .factor`	10	Map and reduce	The number of streams to merge at once while sorting files. This determines the number of open file handles. Larger clusters with 1,000 or more nodes can bump this up to 100.
`mapreduce.reduce .shuffle.parallelcopies`	5	Reduce	The default number of parallel transfers run on the reduce side during the copy (shuffle) phase. Larger clusters with 1,000 or more nodes can bump this up to 20.
`mapreduce.reduce.shuffle .input.buffer.percent`	0.70	Reduce	The percentage of memory to be allocated from the maximum heap size to store map outputs during the shuffle.
`mapreduce.reduce.shuffle .merge.percent`	0.66	Reduce	The usage threshold at which an in-memory merge will be initiated, expressed as a percentage of the total memory allocated to storing in-memory map outputs, as defined by `mapreduce.reduce.shuffle.input .buffer.percent`.
`mapreduce.reduce.merge .memtomem.enabled`	false	Reduce	If all the map outputs for each reducer can be stored in memory, then set this property to `true`.

■ **Summary**

The simplest way to cut down on shuffle and sort times is to aggressively filter and project your data, use a combiner, and compress your map outputs. These approaches reduce the amount of data flowing between the map and reduce tasks and lessen the network and CPU/disk burden related to the shuffle and sort phases.

  If you've done all that, you can look at some of the tips outlined in this technique to determine if your job can be tuned so that the data being shuffled touches disk as little as possible.

8.2.4 *Reducer optimizations*

Much like map tasks, reduce tasks have their own unique problems that can affect performance. In this section we'll look at how common problems can affect the performance of reducer tasks.

TECHNIQUE 79 **Too few or too many reducers**

For the most part, parallelism on the map side is automatically set and is a function of your input files and the input format you're using. But on the reduce side you have total control over the number of reducers for your job, and if that number is too small or too large, you're potentially not getting the most value out of your cluster.

■ **Problem**

You want to determine if a job runs slowly due to the number of reducers.

■ **Solution**

The JobHistory UI can be used to inspect the number of reducers running for your job.

■ **Discussion**

Use the JobHistory UI to look at the number of reducers for your job and the number of input records for each reducer. You may be running with too few or too many reducers. Running with too few reducers means that you're not using the available parallelism of your cluster; running with too many reducers means the scheduler may have to stagger the reducer execution if there aren't enough resources to execute the reducers in parallel.

There are circumstances where you can't avoid running with a small number of reducers, such as when you're writing to an external resource (such as a database) that you don't want to overwhelm.

Another common anti-pattern in MapReduce is using a single reducer when you want job output to have total order and not be ordered within the scope of a reducer's output. This anti-pattern can be avoided with the TotalOrderPartitioner, which we looked at in technique 65.

DEALING WITH DATA SKEW

Data skew can be easily identified—it's manifested by a small percentage of your reduce tasks taking significantly longer to complete than the other tasks. This is usually due to one of two reasons—poor hash partitioning or high join-key cardinality when you're performing joins. Chapter 6 provides solutions to both problems in section 6.1.5.

8.2.5 *General tuning tips*

In this section we'll look at problems that can affect both map and reduce tasks.

COMPRESSION

Compression is an important part of optimizing Hadoop. You can gain substantial space and time savings by compressing both intermediary map outputs and job outputs. Compression is covered in detail in chapter 4.

USING A COMPACT DATA FORMAT

Much like compression, using space-efficient file formats such as Avro and Parquet results in a more compact representation of your data and yields improved marshaling and unmarshaling times compared to storing data as text. A large part of chapter 3 is dedicated to working with these file formats.

It should also be noted that text is an especially inefficient data format to work with—it's space-inefficient and computationally expensive to parse, and parsing data at scale can cost a surprising amount of time, especially if regular expressions are involved.

Even when the end result of your work in MapReduce is a nonbinary file format, it's good practice to store your intermediate data in binary form. For example, if you have a MapReduce pipeline involving a sequence of MapReduce jobs, you should consider using Avro or SequenceFiles to store your individual job outputs. The last job that produces the final results can use whatever output format is required for your use case, but intermediate jobs should use a binary output format to speed up the writing and reading parts of MapReduce.

TECHNIQUE 80   **Using stack dumps to discover unoptimized user code**

Imagine you're running a job and it's taking longer than you expect. You can often determine if this is due to inefficient code by taking several stack dumps and examining the output to see if the stacks are executing in the same location. This technique walks you through taking stack dumps of a running MapReduce job.

■ **Problem**

You want to determine if a job runs slowly due to inefficiencies in your code.

■ **Solution**

Determine the host and process ID of currently executing tasks, take a number of stack dumps, and examine them to narrow down bottlenecks in your code.

■ **Discussion**

If there's anything particularly inefficient in your code, chances are that you'll be able to discover what it is by taking some stack dumps of the task process. Figure 8.9 shows how to identify the task details so that you can take the stack dumps.

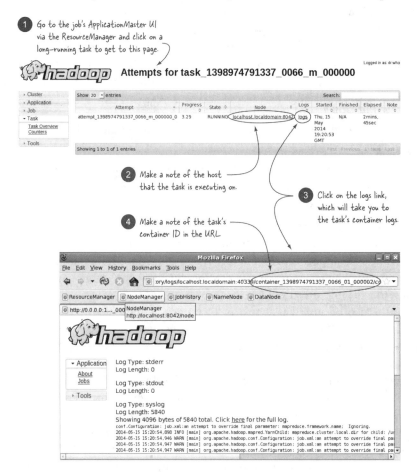

Figure 8.9   Determining the container ID and host for a MapReduce task

Now that you know the container ID and the host it's executing on, you can take stack dumps of the task process, as shown in figure 8.10.

■ **Summary**

The best approach to understanding what your code is spending time doing is to profile your code, or update your code to time how long you spend in each task. But using stack dumps is useful if you want to get a rough sense of whether this is an issue without having to change your code.

Stack dumps are a primitive, yet often effective, means of discovering where a Java process is spending its time, particularly if that process is CPU-bound. Clearly dumps are not as effective as using a profiler, which will more accurately pinpoint where time is being spent, but the advantage of stack dumps is that they can be performed on any running Java process. If you were to use a profiler, you'd need to reexecute the process with the required profiling JVM settings, which is a nuisance in MapReduce.

When taking stack dumps, it's useful to take multiple dumps with some pauses between successive dumps. This allows you to visually determine if the code execution stacks across multiple dumps are roughly in the same point. If this is the case, there's a good chance the code in the stack is what's causing the slowness.

⑤ ssh to the machine that the task is running on, and take a number of stack dumps.

The task's container ID.

```
$ ssh cdh
$ ps auxwww | grep container_1398974791337_0066_01_000002
0 S aholmes    8168 554284  ...
```

The process ID (PID) of the task...

... which you use to send a SIGKILL signal to the process, telling the JVM to perform a stack dump.

```
$ kill -s SIGQUIT 554284
$ kill -s SIGQUIT 554284
$ kill -s SIGQUIT 554284
```

Wait a few seconds between each execution of the kill.

⑥ View the contents of the task's output file and determine if time is being spent in a particular method call.

```
$ cd $yarn.nodemanager.log-dirs/application_139337_0066/container_1398974791337_0066_01_000002/
```

Location of container logs (view your yarn-site.xml to determine this location).   *Application ID*   *Container ID*

```
$ less stdout
```
View the contents of standard out, which will contain the three stack dumps.

Figure 8.10 Taking stack dumps and accessing the output

If your code isn't in the same location across the different stack dumps, this doesn't necessarily indicate that there aren't inefficiencies. In this case, the best approach is to profile your code or add some measurements in your code and rerun the job to get a more accurate breakdown of where time is being spent.

TECHNIQUE 81 Profiling your map and reduce tasks

Profiling standalone Java applications is straightforward and well supported by a large number of tools. In MapReduce, you're working in a distributed environment running multiple map and reduce tasks, so it's less clear how you would go about profiling your code.

■ **Problem**

You suspect that there are inefficiencies in your map and reduce code, and you need to identify where they exist.

■ **Solution**

Use HPROF in combination with a number of MapReduce job methods, such as `set-ProfileEnabled`, to profile your tasks.

■ **Discussion**

Hadoop has built-in support for the HPROF profiler, Oracle's Java profiler built into the JVM. To get started, you don't need to understand any HPROF settings—you can call `JobConf.setProfileEnabled(true)` and Hadoop will run HPROF with the following settings:

```
-agentlib:hprof=cpu=samples,heap=sites,force=n,

thread=y,verbose=n,file=%s
```

This will generate object allocation stack sizes that are too small to be useful, so instead you can programmatically set custom HPROF parameters:

```
job.setProfileEnabled(true);            ◀── Enable profiling.
job.setProfileParams(
    "-agentlib:hprof=depth=8,cpu=samples,heap=sites,force=n," +
    "thread=y,verbose=n,file=%s");
job.setProfileTaskRange(true, "0,1,5-10");   ◀──
job.setProfileTaskRange(false, "");

JobClient.runJob(job);
```

Specify the HPROF options. (annotation pointing to `job.setProfileParams`)

You don't want to profile any reduce tasks, because your example job uses the identity reducer. (annotation pointing to `job.setProfileTaskRange(false, "")`)

This method sets the range of tasks that will be profiled. The first flag is a Boolean that indicates whether the range is being specified for the map or reduce tasks. (annotation pointing to `job.setProfileTaskRange(true, "0,1,5-10")`)

The sample job profiled is quite simple. It parses a file containing IP addresses, extracts the first octet from the address, and emits it as the output value:[8]

```
public void map(LongWritable key, Text value,
                OutputCollector<LongWritable, Text> output,
                Reporter reporter) throws IOException {
```

---

[8] GitHub source: https://github.com/alexholmes/hiped2/blob/master/src/main/java/hip/ch8/SlowJob.java.

```
    String[] parts = value.toString().split("\\.");
    Text outputValue = new Text(parts[0]);
    output.collect(key, outputValue);
}
```

You can upload a large(ish) file of IP addresses and run your job against it, with the previous profiling options set:

```
$ hadoop fs -put test-data/ch8/large-ips.txt .

$ hip hip.ch8.SlowJob \
    --input large-ips.txt \
    --output output
```

The HPROF option you specified earlier via the setProfileParams method call will create a text file that can be easily parsed. The file is written to the container's log directory into a file titled profile.out. There are two ways of accessing this file: either through the JobHistory UI or by using your shell to ssh to the node that ran the task. The previous technique showed you how to determine the host and log directory for a task.

The profile.out file contains a number of stack traces, and at the bottom contains memory and CPU time accumulations, with references to stack traces that accounted for the accumulations. In the example you ran, look at the top two items, which accounted for the most CPU time, and correlate them with the code:

```
CPU SAMPLES BEGIN (total = 995) Sat Dec 24 18:26:15 2011
rank   self  accum    count trace method
   1  7.44%  7.44%       74 313153 java.lang.Object.<init>
   2  4.42% 11.86%       44 313156 java.lang.Object.<init>
   3  3.52% 15.38%       35 313176 java.lang.Object.<init>
   4  3.32% 18.69%       33 313132 java.util.regex.Pattern.compile
   5  2.81% 21.51%       28 313172 java.lang.Object.<init>
   6  2.61% 24.12%       26 313151 java.lang.Object.<init>
   7  2.61% 26.73%       26 313152 java.lang.Object.<init>
   8  2.51% 29.25%       25 313128 java.nio.HeapCharBuffer.<init>
```

The stack trace that had the most accumulated time has a trace ID of 313153. You can use this ID to search for the stack in the file.

```
TRACE 313153: (thread=200001)
java.lang.Object.<init>(Object.java:20)
java.lang.String.<init>(String.java:636)
java.lang.String.substring(String.java:1939)
java.lang.String.subSequence(String.java:1972)
java.util.regex.Pattern.split(Pattern.java:1002)
java.lang.String.split(String.java:2292)
java.lang.String.split(String.java:2334)
com.manning.hip.ch8.SlowJob$Map.map(SlowJob.java:23)
```

This is the stack trace for ID 313153. It looks like your String.split method is using a regular expression, which is slow.

The second-most utilized time in your task is in the constructor of the Text object, which has the overhead of creating a BinaryComparable. This is also something that you need to optimize.

```
TRACE 313156: (thread=200001)
java.lang.Object.<init>(Object.java:20)
org.apache.hadoop.io.BinaryComparable.<init>(BinaryComparable.java:25)
org.apache.hadoop.io.Text.<init>(Text.java:80)
com.manning.hip.ch8.SlowJob$Map.map(SlowJob.java:24)
```

The first issue identified is the use of the `String.split` method, which uses regular expressions to tokenize strings. Regular expressions are computationally expensive, especially when they're executed over millions of records, which is normal when working with data volumes typical with MapReduce. One solution is to replace the `String.split` method with any of the `StringUtils.split` methods in the Apache Commons Lang library, which doesn't use regular expressions.

To avoid the overhead associated with the `Text` class constructor, construct the instance once and call the `set` method repeatedly, which is much more efficient.

■ **Summary**

Running HPROF adds significant overhead to the execution of Java; it instruments Java classes to collect the profiling information as your code is executing. This isn't something you'll want to regularly run in production.

There's a simpler way to profile tasks by adding `-Xprof` to `mapred.child.java.opts` as recommended in Todd Lipcon's excellent presentation.[9]

In fact, the ideal way to profile your code is to isolate your map or reduce code in such a way that it can be executed outside of Hadoop using a profiler of your choice. Then you can focus on quickly iterating your profiling without worrying about Hadoop getting in your way.

This wraps up our look at some of the methods you can use to tune the performance of your jobs and to make your jobs as efficient as possible. Next up is a look at various mechanisms that can help you debug your applications.

8.3   *Debugging*

In this section we'll cover a number of topics that will help with your debugging efforts. We'll kick things off with a look at the task logs.

8.3.1   *Accessing container log output*

Accessing your task logs is the first step to figuring out what issues you're having with your jobs.

TECHNIQUE 82   **Examining task logs**

In this technique we'll look at ways to access task logs in the event that you have a problem job you want to debug.

■ **Problem**

Your job is failing or generating unexpected outputs, and you want to determine if the logs can help you figure out the problem.

■ **Solution**

Learn how to use the JobHistory or ApplicationMaster UI to view task logs. Alternatively, you can SSH to individual slave nodes and access the logs directly.

---

[9]   Todd Lipcon, "Optimizing MapReduce Job Performance," http://www.slideshare.net/cloudera/mr-perf.

■ **Discussion**

When a job fails, it's useful to look at the logs to see if they tell you anything about the failure. For MapReduce applications, each map and reduce task runs in its own container and has its own logs, so you need to identify the tasks that failed. The easiest way to do this is to use the JobHistory or ApplicationMaster UI, which in the task views provide links to the task logs.

You can also use the steps outlined in technique 80 for accessing stack dumps to directly access the logs on the slave node that executed a task.

YARN will automatically delete the log files after `yarn.nodemanager.log.retain-seconds` seconds if log aggregation isn't enabled, or `yarn.nodemanager.delete.debug-delay-sec` seconds if log aggregation is enabled.

If a container fails to start, you'll need to examine the NodeManager logs that executed the task. To do this, use the JobHistory or ApplicationMaster UI to determine which node executed your task, and then navigate to the NodeManager UI to examine its logs.

Often, when things start going wrong in your jobs, the task logs will contain details on the cause of the failure. Next we'll look at how you get at the command used to launch a map or reduce task, which is useful when you suspect there's an issue related to the environment.

8.3.2 Accessing container start scripts

This a useful technique in situations where you suspect there's an issue with the environment or startup arguments for a container. For example, sometimes the classpath ordering of JARs is significant, and issues with it can cause class-loading problems. Also, if a container has dependencies on native libraries, the JVM arguments can be used to debug issues with `java.library.path`.

TECHNIQUE 83 Figuring out the container startup command

The ability to examine the various arguments used to start a container can be helpful in debugging container-launching problems. For example, let's say you're trying to use a native Hadoop compression codec, but your MapReduce containers are failing, and the errors complain that the native compression libraries can't be loaded. In this case, review the JVM startup arguments to determine if all of the required settings exist for native compression to work.

■ **Problem**

You suspect that a container is failing due to missing arguments when a task is being launched, and you want to examine the container startup arguments.

■ **Solution**

Set the `yarn.nodemanager.delete.debug-delay-sec` YARN configuration parameter to stop Hadoop from cleaning up container metadata, and use this metadata to view the shell script used to launch the container.

■ **Discussion**

As the NodeManager prepares to launch a container, it creates a shell script that's subsequently executed to run the container. The problem is that YARN, by default, removes these scripts after a job has completed. During the execution of a long-running application, you'll have access to these scripts, but if the application is short-lived (which it may well be if you're debugging an issue that causes the containers to fail off the bat), you'll need to set `yarn.nodemanager.delete.debug-delay-sec` to `true`.

Figure 8.11 shows all of the steps required to gain access to the task shell script.

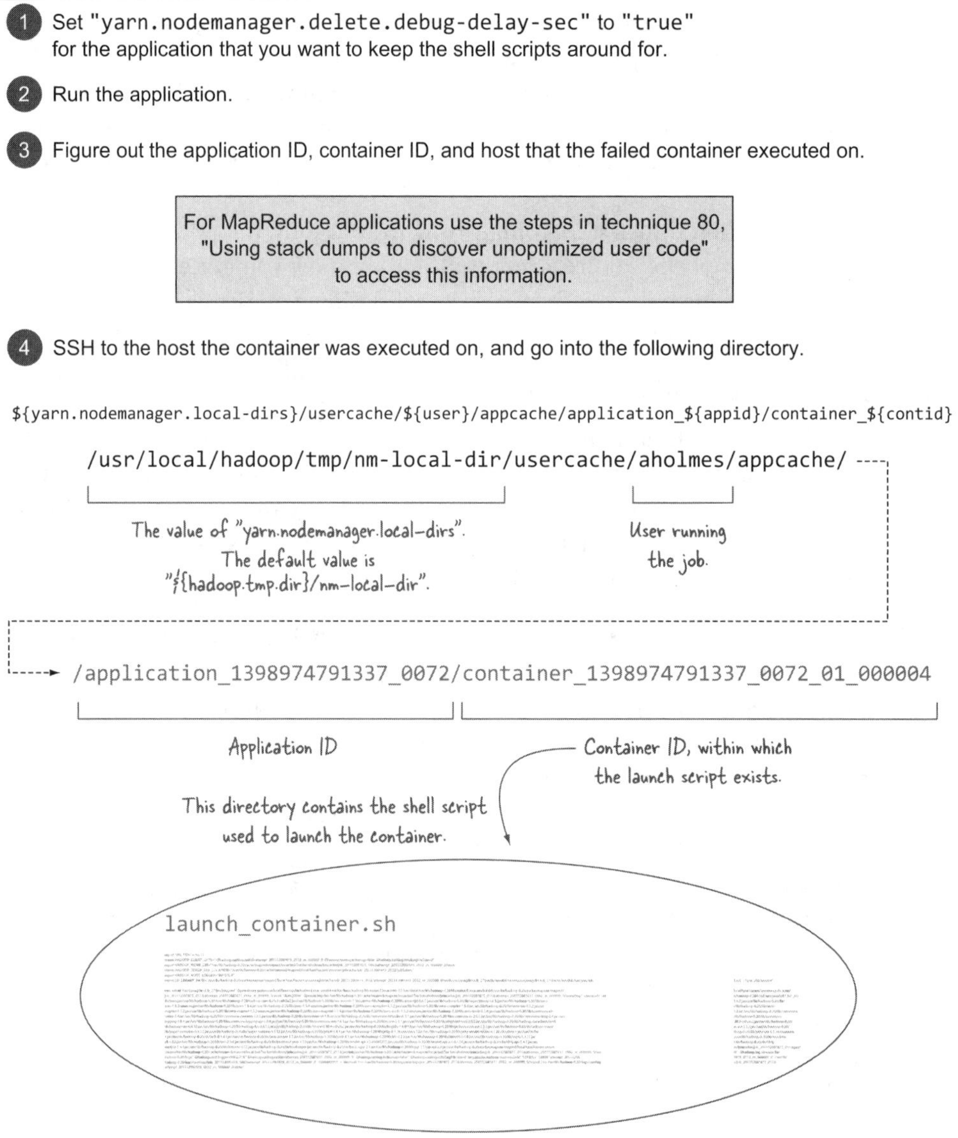

1 Set `"yarn.nodemanager.delete.debug-delay-sec"` to `"true"`
for the application that you want to keep the shell scripts around for.

2 Run the application.

3 Figure out the application ID, container ID, and host that the failed container executed on.

> For MapReduce applications use the steps in technique 80,
> "Using stack dumps to discover unoptimized user code"
> to access this information.

4 SSH to the host the container was executed on, and go into the following directory.

`${yarn.nodemanager.local-dirs}/usercache/${user}/appcache/application_${appid}/container_${contid}`

`/usr/local/hadoop/tmp/nm-local-dir/usercache/aholmes/appcache/ ----┐`

The value of "yarn.nodemanager.local-dirs".
The default value is
"${hadoop.tmp.dir}/nm-local-dir".

User running
the job.

`----▶ /application_1398974791337_0072/container_1398974791337_0072_01_000004`

Application ID

Container ID, within which
the launch script exists.

This directory contains the shell script
used to launch the container.

```
launch_container.sh
```

Figure 8.11 How to get to the launch_container.sh script

It's also useful to examine the logs of the NodeManager that attempted to launch the container, as they may contain container startup errors. Also double-check the container logs if they exist.

■ **Summary**

This technique is useful in situations where you want to be able to examine the arguments used to launch the container. If the data in the logs suggests that the problem with your job is with the inputs (which can be manifested by a parsing exception), you'll need to figure out what kind of input is causing the problem.

8.3.3 Debugging OutOfMemory errors

OutOfMemory (OOM) errors are common in Java applications that have memory leaks or are trying to store too much data in memory. These memory errors can be difficult to track down, because often you aren't provided enough information when a container exits.

TECHNIQUE 84 Force container JVMs to generate a heap dump

In this technique you'll see some useful JVM arguments that will cause Java to write a heap dump to disk when OOM errors occur.

■ **Problem**

Containers are failing with OutOfMemory errors.

■ **Solution**

Update the container JVM arguments to include `-XX:+HeapDumpOnOutOfMemoryError -XX:HeapDumpPath=<path>`, where `<path>` is a common directory across all your slave nodes.

■ **Discussion**

If you're running a MapReduce application, you can update `mapred.child.java.opts` with the preceding JVM arguments. For non-MapReduce applications, you'll need to figure out how to append these JVM startup arguments for the container exhibiting the OOM errors.

Once a container running with the preceding JVM arguments fails, you can load the generated dump file using jmap or your favorite profiling tool.

8.3.4 MapReduce coding guidelines for effective debugging

Debugging MapReduce code in production can be made a lot easier if you follow a handful of logging and exception-handling best practices.

TECHNIQUE 85 Augmenting MapReduce code for better debugging

Debugging a poorly written MapReduce job consumes a lot of time and can be challenging in production environments where access to cluster resources is limited.

■ **Problem**

You want to know the best practices to follow when writing MapReduce code.

■ **Solution**

Look at how counters and logs can be used to enhance your ability to effectively debug and handle problem jobs.

■ **Discussion**

Add the following features to your code:

- Include logs that capture data related to inputs and outputs to help isolate where problems exist.
- Catch exceptions and provide meaningful logging output to help track down problem data inputs and logic errors.
- Think about whether you want to rethrow or swallow exceptions in your code.
- Use counters and task statuses that can be utilized by driver code and humans alike to better understand what happened during the job execution.

In the following code, you'll see a number of the previously described principles applied.

Listing 8.1   A mapper job with some best practices applied to assist debugging

```
public static class Map
    extends Mapper<Text, Text, Text, Text> {
  protected Text outputValue = new Text();
  protected int failedRecords;
  public static enum Counters {
    FAILED_RECORDS
  }

  @Override
  protected void setup(Context context)
      throws IOException, InterruptedException {
    super.setup(context);
    log.info("Input split = {}", context.getInputSplit());
  }

  @Override
  protected void map(Text key, Text value, Context context)
      throws IOException, InterruptedException {

    if(log.isDebugEnabled()) {
      log.debug("Input K[{}],V[{}]", key, value);
    }

    try {
      String id = StringUtils.split(value.toString())[5];
      outputValue.set(id);
      if(log.isDebugEnabled()) {
        log.debug("Output K[{}],V[{}]", key, value);
      }
      context.write(key, outputValue);
    } catch(Exception t) {
      processError(context, t, key, value);
    }
  }
}
```

When the task starts, write the input split details to the log. This will tell you the input file for each specific task and the byte offset within that input file that was used to read map input records.

If the logger is in debug mode (which it should never be in production environments unless you're debugging a job), write out the input record key and value. You wouldn't want this to be a System.out or log.info because that would dramatically slow down your job. Enclose both the key and value with square brackets so you can easily identify leading and trailing whitespace. This will help isolate potential problems in your input data or InputFormat/RecordReader classes.

Log the map output key and value. This can be compared to reducer inputs to help determine if there's a serialization or partitioning problem between map and reduce tasks.

Catch any exceptions thrown in your code.

Write out the key and value to the logs. Enclose both
strings with square brackets so you can easily track
down leading or trailing whitespace.

```
protected void processError(Context c, Throwable t, Text k, Text v) {
    log.error("Caught exception processing key[" +
    k + "], value[" + v + "]", t);
    c.getCounter(Counters.FAILED_RECORDS).increment(1);
    c.setStatus("Records with failures = " +
    (++failedRecords));
}
}
```

Increment a counter
to signal that you hit
an error.

Set the task status to indicate you hit
an issue with a record, including a count
of the total number of failed records
this task encountered.

The reduce task should have similar debug log statements added to write out each
reduce input key and value and the output key and value. Doing so will help identify
any issues between the map and reduce sides, in your reduce code, or in the Output-
Format or RecordWriter.

> **Should exceptions be swallowed?** In the previous code example, you caught
> any exceptions in your code and then wrote the exception to the logs, along
> with as much contextual information as possible (such as the current key and
> value that the reducer was working on). The big question is whether you
> should rethrow the exception or swallow it.
>
> Rethrowing the exception is tempting because you'll immediately be aware of
> any issues in your MapReduce code. But if your code is running in produc-
> tion and fails every time it encounters a problem—such as some input data
> that's not handled correctly—the ops, dev, and QA teams will be spending
> quite a few cycles addressing each issue as it comes along.
>
> Writing code that swallows exceptions has its own problems—for example, what
> if you encounter an exception on all inputs to the job? If you write your code
> to swallow exceptions, the correct approach is to increment a counter (as in the
> code example), which the driver class should use after job completion to ensure
> that most of the input records within some tolerable threshold were successfully
> processed. If they weren't, the workflow being processed should probably be
> terminated and the appropriate alerts be sent to notify operations.
>
> Another approach is to not swallow exceptions and to configure record skip-
> ping with a call to setMapperMaxSkipRecords or setReducerMaxSkipGroups, indicat-
> ing the number of records that you can tolerate losing if an exception is
> thrown when they're processed. This is covered in more detail in *Hadoop in
> Action* by Chuck Lam (Manning, 2010).

You used counters to count the number of bad records you encountered, and the
ApplicationMaster or JobHistory UI can be used to view the counter values, as shown
in figure 8.12.

com.manning.hip.ch13.ArrayOutOfBoundsImprovedMapCounters	FAILED_RECORDS	10	0	10

Figure 8.12   Screenshot of a counter in the JobHistory counter page

Depending on how you executed the job, you'll see the counters dumped on standard out. If you look at the logs for your tasks, you'll also see some informative data related to the task:

```
Input split = hdfs://localhost/user/aholmes/users.txt:0+110
```

This tells you what file the task was working on, as well as the input split range.

```
Caught exception processing key[anne], value[22 NY]
```

Write out the key and value. Note that because you used square brackets to encapsulate your strings, any whitespace issues will be easily identified.

Because you also updated the task status in your code, you can use the Application-Master or JobHistory UI to easily identify the tasks that had failed records, as shown in figure 8.13.

Task	Complete	Status	Start Time	Finish Time	Errors	Counters
task_201112081615_0552_m_000000	100.00%	Records with failures = 10	18-Jan-2012 07:45:40	18-Jan-2012 07:45:42 (2sec)		7

Figure 8.13   JobTracker UI showing map task and status

■ Summary

We looked at a handful of simple yet useful coding guidelines for your MapReduce code. If they're applied and you hit a problem with your job in production, you'll be in a great position to quickly narrow down the root cause of the issue. If the issue is related to the input, your logs will contain details about how the input caused your processing logic to fail. If the issue is related to some logic error or errors in serialization or deserialization, you can enable debug-level logging and better understand where things are going awry.

8.4   *Testing MapReduce jobs*

In this section we'll look at the best methods for testing your MapReduce code, as well as design aspects to consider when writing MapReduce jobs to help in your testing efforts.

8.4.1   *Essential ingredients for effective unit testing*

It's important to make sure unit tests are easy to write and to ensure that they cover a good spectrum of positive and negative scenarios. Let's take a look at the impact that test-driven development, code design, and data have on writing effective unit tests.

TEST-DRIVEN DEVELOPMENT

When it comes to writing Java code, I'm a big proponent of test-driven development (TDD),[10] and with MapReduce things are no different. Test-driven development emphasizes writing unit tests ahead of writing the code, and it recently has gained in

---

[10] For an explanation of test-driven development, see the Wikipedia article: http://en.wikipedia.org/wiki/Test-driven_development.

importance as quick development turnaround times have become the norm rather than the exception. Applying test-driven development to MapReduce code is crucial, particularly when such code is part of a critical production application.

Writing unit tests prior to writing your code forces you to structure your code in a way that easily facilitates testing.

CODE DESIGN

When you write code, it's important to think about the best way to structure it so you can easily test it. Using concepts such as abstraction and dependency injection will go a long way toward reaching this goal.[11]

When you write MapReduce code, it's a good idea to abstract away the code doing the work, which means you can test that code in regular unit tests without having to think about how to work with Hadoop-specific constructs. This is true not only for your map and reduce functions, but also for your input formats, output formats, data serialization, and partitioner code.

Let's look at a simple example to better illustrate this point. The following code shows a reducer that calculates the mean for a stock:

```
public static class Reduce
    extends Reducer<Text, DoubleWritable, Text, DoubleWritable> {

  DoubleWritable outValue = new DoubleWritable();
  public void reduce(Text stockSymbol, Iterable<DoubleWritable> values,
                     Context context)
      throws IOException, InterruptedException {

    double total = 0;
    int instances = 0;
    for (DoubleWritable stockPrice : values) {
      total += stockPrice.get();
      instances++;
    }
    outValue.set(total / (double) instances);
    context.write(stockSymbol, outValue);
  }
}
```

This is a trivial example, but the way the code is structured means you can't easily test this in a regular unit test, because MapReduce has constructs such as Text, DoubleWritable, and the Context class that get in your way. If you were to structure the code to abstract away the work, you could easily test the code that's doing your work, as the following code shows:

```
public static class Reduce2
    extends Reducer<Text, DoubleWritable, Text, DoubleWritable> {

  SMA sma = new SMA();
```

---

[11] For an explanation of dependency injection, see the Wikipedia article: http://en.wikipedia.org/wiki/ Dependency_injection.

```
  DoubleWritable outValue = new DoubleWritable();
  public void reduce(Text key, Iterable<DoubleWritable> values,
                     Context context)
     throws IOException, InterruptedException {
    sma.reset();
    for (DoubleWritable stockPrice : values) {
      sma.add(stockPrice.get());
    }
    outValue.set(sma.calculate());
    context.write(key, outValue);
  }
}

public static class SMA {
  protected double total = 0;
  protected int instances = 0;

  public void add(double value) {
    total += value;
    instances ++;
  }

  public double calculate() {
    return total / (double) instances;
  }

  public void reset() {
    total = 0;
    instances = 0;
  }
}
```

With this improved code layout, you can now easily test the SMA class that's adding and calculating the simple moving average without the Hadoop code getting in your way.

IT'S THE DATA, STUPID

When you write unit tests, you try to discover how your code handles both positive and negative input data. In both cases, it's best if the data you're testing with is a representative sample from production.

Often, no matter how hard you try, issues in your code in production will arise from unexpected input data. It's important that when you do discover input data that causes a job to blow up, you not only fix the code to handle the unexpected data, but you also pull the data that caused the blowup and use it in a unit test to prove that the code can now correctly handle that data.

8.4.2 *MRUnit*

MRUnit is a test framework you can use to unit-test MapReduce code. It was developed by Cloudera (a vendor with its own Hadoop distribution) and it's currently an Apache project. It should be noted that MRUnit supports both the old (org.apache.hadoop .mapred) and new (org.apache.hadoop.mapreduce) MapReduce APIs.

Using MRUnit to unit-test MapReduce

In this technique we'll look at writing unit tests that use each of the four types of tests provided by MRUnit:

- `MapDriver` class—A map test that only tests a map function
- `ReduceDriver` class—A reduce test that only tests a reduce function
- `MapReduceDriver` class—A map and reduce test that tests both the map and reduce functions
- `TestPipelineMapReduceDriver` class—A pipeline test that allows a series of Map-Reduce functions to be exercised

■ **Problem**

You want to test map and reduce functions, as well as MapReduce pipelines.

■ **Solution**

Use MRUnit's `MapDriver`, `ReduceDriver`, `MapReduceDriver`, and `PipelineMapReduceDriver` classes as part of your unit tests to test your MapReduce code.

■ **Discussion**

MRUnit has four types of unit tests—we'll start with a look at the map tests.

Map tests

Let's kick things off by writing a test to exercise a map function. Before starting, let's look at what you need to supply to MRUnit to execute the test, and in the process learn about how MRUnit works behind the scenes.

Figure 8.14 shows the interactions of the unit test with MRUnit and how it in turn interacts with the mapper you're testing.

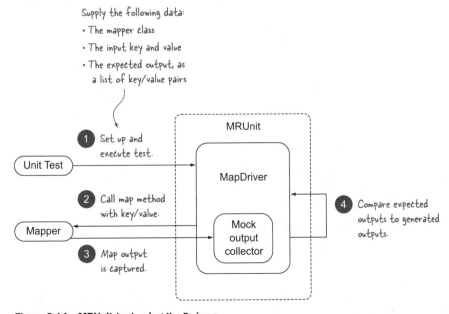

Figure 8.14 MRUnit test using MapDriver

The following code is a simple unit test of the (identity) mapper class in Hadoop:[12]

The MRUnit driver class you'll use in your test. This is the MapDriver, and as such you need to specify the key/value input and output types for the mapper you're testing.

Create the map class you're testing. Here you're using Hadoop's built-in IdentityMapper, which outputs the input data without any transformations.

The withInput method is used to specify an input key/value, which will be fed to the IdentityMapper.

Run the test. If a failure is encountered, it logs the discrepancy and throws an exception.

The withOutput method is used to specify the output key/value, which MRUnit will compare against the output generated by the mapper being tested.

```java
public class IdentityMapTest {

    private Mapper<Text, Text, Text, Text> mapper;
    private MapDriver<Text, Text, Text, Text> driver;

    @Before
    public void setUp() {
        mapper = new Mapper<Text, Text, Text, Text>();
        driver = new MapDriver<Text, Text, Text, Text>(mapper);
    }

    @Test
    public void testIdentityMapper() {
        driver.withInput(new Text("foo"), new Text("bar"))
            .withOutput(new Text("foo"), new Text("bars"))
            .runTest();
    }
}
```

MRUnit is not tied to any specific unit-testing framework, so if it finds an error, it logs the error and throws an exception. Let's see what would happen if your unit test had specified output that didn't match the output of the mapper, as in the following code:

```java
driver.withInput(new Text("foo"), new Text("bar"))
    .withOutput(new Text("foo"), new Text("bar2"))
    .runTest();
```

If you run this test, your test will fail, and you'll see the following log output:

```
ERROR Received unexpected output (foo, bar)
ERROR Missing expected output (foo, bar2) at position 0
```

> **MRUnit logging configuration** Because MRUnit uses the Apache Commons logging, which defaults to using log4j, you'll need to have a log4j.properties file in the classpath that's configured to write to standard out, similar to the following:
>
> ```
> log4j.rootLogger=WARN, stdout
> log4j.appender.stdout=org.apache.log4j.ConsoleAppender
> log4j.appender.stdout.layout=org.apache.log4j.PatternLayout
> log4j.appender.stdout.layout.ConversionPattern=
>     %-5p [%t][%d{ISO8601}] [%C.%M] - %m%n
> ```

One of the powerful features of JUnit and other test frameworks is that when tests fail, the failure message includes details on the cause of the failure. Unfortunately, MRUnit

---

[12] GitHub source: https://github.com/alexholmes/hiped2/blob/master/src/test/java/hip/ch8/mrunit/
IdentityMapTest.java.

logs and throws a nondescriptive exception, which means you need to dig through the test output to determine what failed.

What if you wanted to use the power of MRUnit, and also use the informative errors that JUnit provides when assertions fail? You could modify your code to do that and bypass MRUnit's testing code:

```
@Test
public void testIdentityMapper() throws IOException {
  List<Pair<Text, Text>> results = driver
      .withInput(new Text("foo"), new Text("bar"))
      .run();

  assertEquals(1, results.size());
  assertEquals(new Text("foo"), results.get(0).getFirst());
  assertEquals(new Text("bar"), results.get(0).getSecond());
}
```

The run method executes the map function and returns a list of all the output records emitted by the function. Also note that there was no need to call the withOutput method, because you'll do the validation yourself.

You assert the size and contents of the records.

With this approach, if there's a mismatch between the expected and actual outputs, you get a more meaningful error message, which report-generation tools can use to easily describe what failed in the test:

```
junit.framework.AssertionFailedError: expected:<bar2> but was:<bar>
```

To cut down on the inevitable copy-paste activities with this approach, I wrote a simple helper class to use JUnit asserts in combination with using the MRUnit driver.[13] Your JUnit test now looks like this:

```
@Test
public void testIdentityMapper() throws IOException {
  List<Pair<Text, Text>> results = driver
      .withInput(new Text("foo"), new Text("bar"))
      .withOutput(new Text("foo"), new Text("bar"))
      .run();

  MRUnitJUnitAsserts.assertOutputs(driver, results);
}
```

You call withOutput because the helper function can extract the outputs directly from the driver.

Call the helper function that uses JUnit asserts to test the contents of the expected output with the generated output.

This is much cleaner and removes any mistakes that might arise from the copy-paste anti-pattern.

Reduce tests

Now that we've looked at map function tests, let's look at reduce function tests. The MRUnit framework takes a similar approach for reduce testing. Figure 8.15 shows the interactions of your unit test with MRUnit, and how it in turn interacts with the reducer you're testing.

---

[13] GitHub source: https://github.com/alexholmes/hiped2/blob/master/src/test/java/hip/ch8/mrunit/
MRUnitJUnitAsserts.java

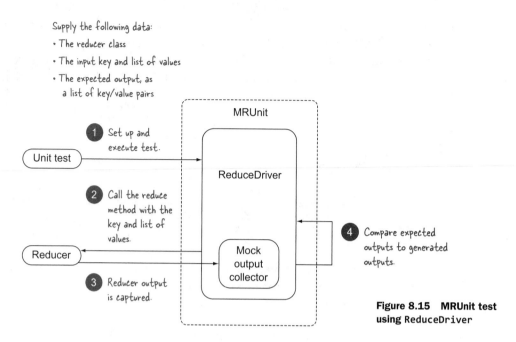

Supply the following data:
- The reducer class
- The input key and list of values
- The expected output, as a list of key/value pairs

Figure 8.15   MRUnit test using ReduceDriver

The following code is a simple unit test for testing the (identity) reducer class in Hadoop:[14]

```java
public class IdentityReduceTest {

    private Reducer<Text, Text, Text, Text> reducer;
    private ReduceDriver<Text, Text, Text, Text> driver;

    @Before
    public void setUp() {
        reducer = new Reducer<Text, Text, Text, Text>();
        driver = new ReduceDriver<Text, Text, Text, Text>(reducer);
    }

    @Test
    public void testIdentityMapper() throws IOException {
        List<Pair<Text, Text>> results = driver
            .withInput(new Text("foo"),
                Arrays.asList(new Text("bar1"), new Text("bar2")))
            .withOutput(new Text("foo"), new Text("bar1"))
            .withOutput(new Text("foo"), new Text("bar2"))
            .run();

        MRUnitJUnitAsserts.assertOutputs(driver, results);
    }
}
```

When testing the reducer, you specify a list of values that MRUnit sends to your reducer.

With the identity reducer you specified two value inputs, so you expect two outputs.

Add the expected output for the second value.

Use the helper class from the previous map section.

---

[14] GitHub source: https://github.com/alexholmes/hiped2/blob/master/src/test/java/hip/ch8/mrunit/IdentityReduceTest.java.

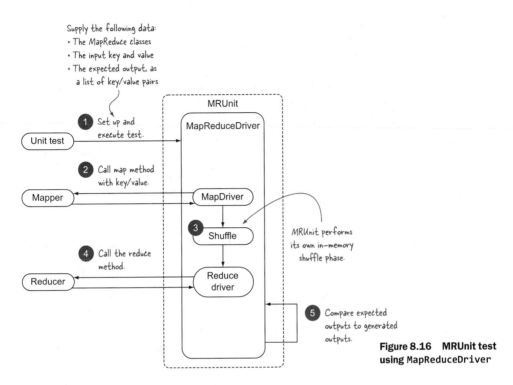

Supply the following data:
• The MapReduce classes
• The input key and value
• The expected output, as
  a list of key/value pairs

Figure 8.16   MRUnit test using `MapReduceDriver`

Now that we've completed our look at the individual map and reduce function tests, let's look at how you can test a map and reduce function together.

MapReduce tests

MRUnit also supports testing the map and reduce functions in the same test. You feed MRUnit the inputs, which in turn are supplied to the mapper. You also tell MRUnit what reducer outputs you expect.

Figure 8.16 shows the interactions of your unit test with MRUnit and how it in turn interacts with the mapper and reducer you're testing.

The following code is a simple unit test for testing the (identity) mapper and reducer classes in Hadoop:[15]

```
public class IdentityMapReduceTest {

    private Reducer<Text, Text, Text, Text> reducer;
    private Mapper<Text, Text, Text, Text> mapper;
    private MapReduceDriver<Text, Text, Text, Text, Text, Text> driver;

    @Before
    public void setUp() {
        mapper = new Mapper<Text, Text, Text, Text>();
        reducer = new Reducer<Text, Text, Text, Text>();
        driver =
```

With the MapReduce driver, you need to specify six types: the map input and output key/value types, as well as the reducer key/value output types.

---

[15] GitHub source: https://github.com/alexholmes/hiped2/blob/master/src/test/java/hip/ch8/mrunit/
IdentityMapReduceTest.java.

```
    new MapReduceDriver<Text, Text, Text, Text, Text, Text>(
    mapper, reducer);
}

@Test
public void testIdentityMapper() throws IOException {
  List<Pair<Text, Text>> results = driver
      .withInput(new Text("foo"), new Text("bar"))
      .withInput(new Text("foo2"), new Text("bar2"))
      .withOutput(new Text("foo"), new Text("bar"))
      .withOutput(new Text("foo2"), new Text("bar2"))
      .run();

  MRUnitJUnitAsserts.assertOutputs(driver, results);
}
}
```

Supply the map inputs. In contrast to the MapDriver and ReduceDriver, the MapReduceDriver supports multiple inputs.

Set the expected reducer outputs.

Now we'll look at the fourth and final type of test that MRUnit supports, pipeline tests, which are used to test multiple MapReduce jobs.

Pipeline tests

MRUnit supports testing a series of map and reduce functions—these are called *pipeline tests*. You feed MRUnit one or more MapReduce functions, the inputs to the first map function, and the expected outputs of the last reduce function.

Figure 8.17 shows the interactions of your unit test with the MRUnit pipeline driver.

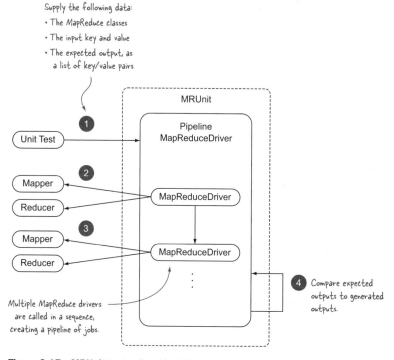

Figure 8.17   MRUnit test using `PipelineMapReduceDriver`

The following code is a unit test for testing a pipeline containing two sets of (identity) mapper and reducer classes in Hadoop:[16]

```
public class PipelineTest {

  private Mapper<Text, Text, Text, Text> mapper1;
  private Reducer<Text, Text, Text, Text> reducer1;
  private Mapper<Text, Text, Text, Text> mapper2;
  private Reducer<Text, Text, Text, Text> reducer2;

  private PipelineMapReduceDriver<Text, Text, Text, Text> driver;

  @Before
  public void setUp() {
    mapper1 = new IdentityMapper<Text, Text>();
    reducer1 = new IdentityReducer<Text, Text>();
    mapper2 = new IdentityMapper<Text, Text>();
    reducer2 = new IdentityReducer<Text, Text>();
    driver = new PipelineMapReduceDriver<Text, Text, Text, Text>();
    driver.addMapReduce(
      new Pair<Mapper, Reducer>(mapper1, reducer1));
    driver.addMapReduce(
      new Pair<Mapper, Reducer>(mapper2, reducer2));
  }

  @Test
  public void testIdentityMapper() throws IOException {
    List<Pair<Text, Text>> results = driver
        .withInput(new Text("foo"), new Text("bar"))
        .withInput(new Text("foo2"), new Text("bar2"))
        .withOutput(new Text("foo"), new Text("bar"))
        .withOutput(new Text("foo2"), new Text("bar2"))
        .run();

    MRUnitJUnitAsserts.assertOutputs(driver, results);
  }
}
```

Add the first map and reduce pair to the pipeline.

Add the second map and reduce pair to the pipeline.

As with the MapReduceDriver, the PipelineMapReduceDriver supports multiple input records.

Note that the `PipelineMapReduceDriver` is the only driver in MRUnit that doesn't come in both old and new MapReduce API versions, which is why the preceding code uses the old MapReduce API.

■ **Summary**

What type of test should you use for your code? Take a look at table 8.5 for some pointers.

Table 8.5 MRUnit tests and when to use them

Type of test	Works well in these situations
Map	You have a map-only job, and you want low-level unit tests where the framework takes care of testing the expected map outputs for your test map inputs.
Reduce	Your job has a lot of complexity in the reduce function, and you want to isolate your tests to only that function.

---

[16] GitHub source: https://github.com/alexholmes/hiped2/blob/master/src/test/java/hip/ch8/mrunit/PipelineTest.java.

Table 8.5   MRUnit tests and when to use them *(continued)*

Type of test	Works well in these situations
MapReduce	You want to test the combination of the map and reduce functions. These are higher-level unit tests.
Pipeline	You have a MapReduce pipeline where the input of each MapReduce job is the output from the previous job.

MRUnit has a few limitations, some of which we touched on in this technique:

- MRUnit isn't integrated with unit-test frameworks that provide rich error-reporting capabilities for quicker determination of errors.
- The pipeline tests only work with the old MapReduce API, so MapReduce code that uses the new MapReduce API can't be tested with the pipeline tests.
- There's no support for testing data serialization, or InputFormat, RecordReader, OutputFormat, or RecordWriter classes.

Notwithstanding these limitations, MRUnit is an excellent test framework that you can use to test at the granular level of individual map and reduce functions; MRUnit also can test a pipeline of MapReduce jobs. And because it skips the InputFormat and OutputFormat steps, your unit tests will execute quickly.

Next we'll look at how you can use the LocalJobRunner to test some MapReduce constructs that are ignored by MRUnit.

8.4.3   LocalJobRunner

In the last section we looked at MRUnit, a great, lightweight unit-test library. But what if you want to test not only your map and reduce functions, but also the InputFormat, RecordReader, OutputFormat, and RecordWriter code, as well as the data serialization between the map and reduce phases? This becomes important if you've written your own input and output format classes, because you want to make sure you're testing that code too.

Hadoop comes bundled with the LocalJobRunner class, which Hadoop and related projects (such as Pig and Avro) use to write and test their MapReduce code. LocalJob-Runner allows you to test all the aspects of a MapReduce job, including the reading and writing of data to and from the filesystem.

TECHNIQUE 87   **Heavyweight job testing with the LocalJobRunner**

Tools like MRUnit are useful for low-level unit tests, but how can you be sure that your code will play nicely with the whole Hadoop stack?

■ **Problem**

You want to test the whole Hadoop stack in your unit test.

■ **Solution**

Use the LocalJobRunner class in Hadoop to expand the coverage of your tests to include code related to processing job inputs and outputs.

■ **Discussion**

Using the LocalJobRunner makes your unit tests start to feel more like integration tests, because what you're doing is testing how your code works in combination with the whole MapReduce stack. This is great because you can use this to test not only your own MapReduce code, but also to test input and output formats, partitioners, and advanced sort mechanisms.

The code in the next listing shows an example of how you can use the LocalJobRunner in your unit tests.[17]

Listing 8.2 Using LocalJobRunner to test a MapReduce job

```
public class IdentityTest {

  @Test
  public void run() throws Exception {
    Path inputPath = new Path("/tmp/mrtest/input");
    Path outputPath = new Path("/tmp/mrtest/output");

    Configuration conf = new Configuration();

    conf.set("mapred.job.tracker", "local");
    conf.set("fs.default.name", "file:///");

    FileSystem fs = FileSystem.get(conf);
    if (fs.exists(outputPath)) {
      fs.delete(outputPath, true);
    }
    if (fs.exists(inputPath)) {
      fs.delete(inputPath, true);
    }
    fs.mkdirs(inputPath);

    String input = "foo\tbar";
    DataOutputStream file = fs.create(new Path(inputPath, "part-" + 0));
    file.writeBytes(input);
    file.close();

    Job job = runJob(conf, inputPath, outputPath);
    assertTrue(job.isSuccessful());

    List<String> lines =
        IOUtils.readLines(fs.open(new Path(outputPath, "part-r-00000")));

    assertEquals(1, lines.size());
    String[] parts = StringUtils.split(lines.get(0), "\t");
    assertEquals("foo", parts[0]);
    assertEquals("bar", parts[1]);
  }

  public Job runJob(Configuration conf, Path inputPath, Path outputPath)
```

Annotations:
- Force the filesystem to be local (which is the default).
- Force the use of the LocalJobRunner by setting mapred.job.tracker to local (which is the default).
- Retrieve the filesystem. By default this will be the local filesystem. The next few lines of code delete the input and output directories to remove any lingering data from other tests.
- Write the job inputs into a file.
- Assert that the job completed successfully.
- Run an identity MapReduce job.
- Read the job output from the filesystem.
- Verify the job output.

[17] GitHub source: https://github.com/alexholmes/hiped2/blob/master/src/test/java/hip/ch8/localjobrunner/IdentityTest.java.

```
        throws ClassNotFoundException, IOException, InterruptedException {
        Job job = new Job(conf);
        job.setInputFormatClass(KeyValueTextInputFormat.class);
        job.setMapOutputKeyClass(Text.class);
        FileInputFormat.setInputPaths(job, inputPath);
        FileOutputFormat.setOutputPath(job, outputPath);
        job.waitForCompletion(false);
        return job;
    }
}
```

Writing this test is more involved because you need to handle writing the inputs to the filesystem and reading them back out. That's a lot of boilerplate code to have to deal with for every test, and it's probably something that you'll want to factor out into a reusable helper class.

Here's an example of a utility class to do that; the following code shows how IdentityTest code can be condensed into a more manageable size:[18]

```
@Test
public void run() throws Exception {

    TextIOJobBuilder builder = new TextIOJobBuilder()      Set the job
        .addInput("foo", "bar")                               inputs.
        .addExpectedOutput("foo", "bar")    ◄──────── Set the expected job outputs.
        .writeInputs();        ◄──────
                                       Write the inputs
    Job job = runJob(           to the filesystem.
        builder.getConfig(),
        builder.getInputPath(),
        builder.getOutputPath());
                                        Delegate testing the
    assertTrue(job.isSuccessful());     expected results with
                                          the results to the
    builder.verifyResults();   ◄──────      utility class.
}
```

■ Summary

What are some of the limitations to be aware of when using LocalJobRunner?

- LocalJobRunner runs only a single reduce task, so you can't use it to test partitioners.

- As you saw, it's also more labor intensive; you need to read and write the input and output data to the filesystem.

- Jobs are also slow because much of the MapReduce stack is being exercised.

- It's tricky to use this approach to test input and output formats that aren't file-based.

The most comprehensive way of testing your code is covered next. It uses an in-memory cluster that can run multiple mappers and reducers.

---

[18] GitHub source: https://github.com/alexholmes/hiped2/blob/master/src/test/java/hip/ch8/localjobrunner/
IdentityWithBuilderTest.java.

8.4.4   *MiniMRYarnCluster*

All of the unit-testing techniques so far have had restrictions on which parts of a MapReduce job could be tested. The LocalJobRunner, for example, only runs with a single map and reduce task, so you can't simulate production jobs that run with multiple tasks. In this section you'll learn about a built-in mechanism in Hadoop that allows you to exercise your job against the full-stack Hadoop.

TECHNIQUE 88   **Using MiniMRYarnCluster to test your jobs**

The MiniMRYarnCluster class is included in the Hadoop testing code, and it supports test cases that require the complete Hadoop stack to be executed. This includes tests that need to test input and output format classes, including output committers, which can't be tested using MRUnit or LocalTestRunner. In this technique, you'll see how to use MiniMRYarnCluster.

▪ **Problem**

You want to execute your tests against an actual Hadoop cluster, giving you the additional assurance that your jobs work as expected.

▪ **Solution**

Use MiniMRYarnCluster and MiniDFSCluster, which allow you to launch in-memory YARN and HDFS clusters.

▪ **Discussion**

MiniMRYarnCluster and MiniDFSCluster are classes contained in Hadoop's testing code, and are used by various tests in Hadoop. They provide in-process YARN and HDFS clusters that give you the most realistic environment within which to test your code. These classes wrap the full-fledged YARN and HDFS processes, so you're actually running the complete Hadoop stack in your test process. Map and reduce containers are launched as processes external to the test process.

There's a useful wrapper class called ClusterMapReduceTestCase that encapsulates these classes and makes it easy to quickly write your unit tests. The following code shows a simple test case that tests the identity mapper and reducer:[19]

```
import com.google.common.collect.Lists;
import org.apache.commons.io.IOUtils;
import org.apache.hadoop.fs.FileUtil;
import org.apache.hadoop.fs.Path;
import org.apache.hadoop.io.Text;
import org.apache.hadoop.mapred.*;

import java.io.*;
import java.util.List;

public class IdentityMiniTest extends ClusterMapReduceTestCase {

    public void testIdentity() throws Exception {
```

Extend ClusterMapReduceTestCase to leverage the mini-cluster wrapping.

---

[19] GitHub source: https://github.com/alexholmes/hiped2/blob/master/src/test/java/hip/ch8/minimrcluster/ IdentityMiniTest.java.

```
JobConf conf = createJobConf();
```
Call a base class method to create the job configuration for the mini-clusters.

```
createInput();
```
Create the test input for the job.

```
conf.setNumReduceTasks(1);

conf.setInputFormat(KeyValueTextInputFormat.class);
conf.setMapOutputKeyClass(Text.class);
conf.setMapOutputValueClass(Text.class);
FileInputFormat.setInputPaths(conf, getInputDir());
FileOutputFormat.setOutputPath(conf, getOutputDir());
RunningJob runningJob = JobClient.runJob(conf);

assertTrue(runningJob.isSuccessful());

Path[] outputFiles = FileUtil.stat2Paths(
    getFileSystem().listStatus(getOutputDir(),
        new Utils.OutputFileUtils.OutputFilesFilter()));
```
Extract the job output files and verify there's just one (you ran with a single reducer).

```
assertEquals(1, outputFiles.length);

InputStream is = getFileSystem().open(outputFiles[0]);
List<String> lines = IOUtils.readLines(is);
assertEquals(1, lines.size());
assertEquals("foo\tbar", lines.get(0));
is.close();
}
```
Read the output file into a list and verify the expected output.

```
  private void createInput() throws Exception {
    OutputStream os = getFileSystem().create(new Path(getInputDir(),
        "text.txt"));
    Writer wr = new OutputStreamWriter(os);
    for(String inp : Lists.newArrayList("foo\tbar")) {
      wr.write(inp+"\n");
    }wr.close();
  }
}
```

■ Summary

The only disadvantage to using the mini-clusters is the overhead of running your tests—each test class that extends ClusterMapReduceTestCase will result in a cluster being brought up and down, and each test has a considerable amount of time overhead because the full Hadoop stack is being executed.

But using the mini-clusters will provide you with the greatest assurance that your code will work as you expect in production, and it's worth considering for jobs that are critical to your organization.

Therefore, the optimal way to test your code is to use MRUnit for simpler jobs that use built-in Hadoop input and output classes, and only use this technique for test cases where you want to test input and output classes and output committers.

8.4.5 *Integration and QA testing*

Using the TDD approach, you wrote some unit tests using the techniques in this section. You next wrote the MapReduce code and got it to the point where the unit tests were passing. Hooray! But before you break out the champagne, you still want assurance that the MapReduce code is working prior to running it in production. The last thing you want is your code to fail in production and have to debug it over there.

But why, you ask, would my job fail if all of my unit tests pass? Good question, and it could be due to a variety of factors:

- The data you used for your unit tests doesn't contain all of the data aberrations and variances of the data used in production.
- Volume or data skew issues could cause side effects in your code.
- Differences in Hadoop and other libraries result in behaviors different from those in your build environment.
- Hadoop and operating system configuration differences between your build host and production may cause problems.

Because of these factors, when you build integration or QA test environments, it's crucial to ensure that the Hadoop version and configurations mirror those of the production cluster. Different versions of Hadoop will behave differently, as will the same version of Hadoop configured in different ways. When you're testing changes in test environments, you'll want to ensure a smooth transition to production, so do as much as you can to make sure that the version and configuration are as close as possible to production.

After your MapReduce jobs are successfully running in integration and QA, you can push them into production, knowing there's a much higher probability that your jobs will work as expected.

This wraps up our look at testing MapReduce code. We looked at some TDD and design principles to help you write and test your Java code, and we also covered some unit-test libraries that make it easier to unit-test MapReduce code.

8.5 *Chapter summary*

This chapter only scratched the surface when it comes to tuning, debugging, and testing. We laid the groundwork for how to tune, profile, debug, and test your MapReduce code.

For performance tuning, it's important that you have the ability to collect and visualize the performance of your cluster and jobs. In this chapter we presented some of the more common issues that can impact the performance of your jobs.

If you're running any critical MapReduce code in production, it's crucial to at least follow the steps in the testing section of this chapter, where I showed you how to best design your code so it easily lends itself to basic unit-testing methodologies outside the scope of Hadoop. We also covered how the MapReduce-related parts of your code could be tested in both lightweight (MRUnit) and more heavyweight (LocalTestRunner) setups.

In part 4, we'll venture beyond the world of MapReduce and examine various systems that allow you to interact with your data using SQL. Most SQL systems have moved beyond MapReduce to use YARN, so our last chapter looks at how to write your own YARN applications.

Part 4

Beyond MapReduce

This part of the book is dedicated to examining languages, tools, and processes that make it easier to do your work with Hadoop.

Chapter 9 dives into Hive, a SQL-like domain-specific language that's one of the most accessible interfaces for working with data in Hadoop. Impala and Spark SQL are also shown as alternative SQL-processing systems on Hadoop; they provide some compelling features, such as increased performance over Hive and the ability to intermix SQL with Spark.

Chapter 10, the final chapter, shows you how to write a basic YARN application, and goes on to look at key features that will be important for your YARN applications.

SQL on Hadoop

This chapter covers

- Learning the Hadoop specifics of Hive, including user-defined functions and performance-tuning tips
- Learning about Impala and how you can write user-defined functions
- Embedding SQL in your Spark code to intertwine the two languages and play to their strengths

Let's say that it's nine o'clock in the morning and you've been asked to generate a report on the top 10 countries that generated visitor traffic over the last month. And it needs to be done by noon. Your log data is sitting in HDFS ready to be used. Are you going to break out your IDE and start writing Java MapReduce code? Not likely. This is where high-level languages such as Hive, Impala, and Spark come into play. With their SQL syntax, Hive and Impala allow you to write and start executing queries in the same time that it would take you to write your main method in Java.

The big advantage of Hive is that it no longer requires MapReduce to execute queries—as of Hive 0.13, Hive can use Tez, which is a general DAG-execution framework that doesn't impose the HDFS and disk barriers between successive steps as MapReduce does. Impala and Spark were also built from the ground up to not use MapReduce behind the scenes.

These tools are the easiest ways to quickly start working with data in Hadoop. Hive and Impala are essentially Hadoop data-warehousing tools that in some organizations (such as Facebook) have replaced traditional RDBMS-based data-warehouse tools. They owe much of their popularity to the fact that they expose a SQL interface, and as such are accessible to those who've had some exposure to SQL in the past.

We'll spend most of this chapter focusing on Hive, as it's currently the most adopted SQL-on-Hadoop tool out there. I'll also introduce Impala as an MPP database on Hadoop and a few features unique to Impala. Finally we'll cover Spark SQL, which allows you to use SQL inline with your Spark code, and it could create a whole new paradigm for programmers, analysts, and data scientists.

We'll start with Hive, which has been the mainstay of SQL-on-Hadoop.

9.1   Hive

Hive was originally an internal Facebook project that eventually tenured into a full-blown Apache project. It was created to simplify access to MapReduce by exposing a SQL-based language for data manipulation. The Hive architecture can be seen in figure 9.1.

In this chapter we'll look at practical examples of how you can use Hive to work with Apache web server logs. We'll look at different ways you can load and arrange data in Hive to optimize how you access that data. We'll also look at some advanced join mechanisms and other relational operations such as grouping and sorting. We'll kick things off with a brief introduction to Hive.

> **Learning more about Hive basics**   To fully understand Hive fundamentals, refer to Chuck Lam's *Hadoop in Action* (Manning, 2010). In this section we'll just skim through some Hive basics.

9.1.1   Hive basics

Let's quickly look at some Hive basics, including recent developments in its execution framework.

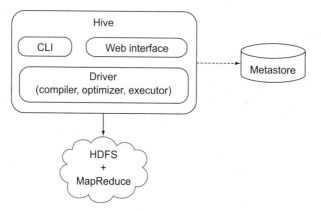

Figure 9.1   The Hive high-level architecture

INSTALLING HIVE

The appendix contains installation instructions for Hive. All the examples in this book were executed on Hive 0.13, and it's possible some older Hive versions don't support some of the features we'll use in this book.

THE HIVE METASTORE

Hive maintains metadata about Hive in a metastore, which is stored in a relational database. This metadata contains information about what tables exist, their columns, user privileges, and more.

By default, Hive uses Derby, an embedded Java relational database, to store the metastore. Because it's embedded, Derby can't be shared between users, and as such it can't be used in a multi-user environment where the metastore needs to be shared.

DATABASES, TABLES, PARTITIONS, AND STORAGE

Hive can support multiple databases, which can be used to avoid table-name collisions (two teams or users that have the same table name) and to allow separate databases for different users or products.

A Hive table is a logical concept that's physically composed of a number of files in HDFS. Tables can either be internal, where Hive organizes them inside a warehouse directory (controlled by the `hive.metastore.warehouse.dir` property with a default value of /user/hive/warehouse [in HDFS]), or they can be external, in which case Hive doesn't manage them. Internal tables are useful if you want Hive to manage the complete lifecycle of your data, including the deletion, whereas external tables are useful when the files are being used outside of Hive.

Tables can be partitioned, which is a physical arrangement of data, into distinct subdirectories for each unique partitioned key. Partitions can be static and dynamic, and we'll look at both cases in technique 92.

HIVE'S DATA MODEL

Hive supports the following data types:

- *Signed integers*—BIGINT (8 bytes), INT (4 bytes), SMALLINT (2 bytes), and TINYINT (1 byte)
- *Floating-point numbers*—FLOAT (single precision) and DOUBLE (double precision)
- *Booleans*—TRUE or FALSE
- *Strings*—Sequences of characters in specified character sets
- *Maps*—Associative arrays with collections of key/value pairs where keys are unique
- *Arrays*—Indexable lists, where all elements must be of the same type
- *Structs*—Complex types that contain elements

HIVE'S QUERY LANGUAGE

Hive's query language supports much of the SQL specification, along with Hive-specific extensions, some of which are covered in this section. The full list of statements supported in Hive can be viewed in the Hive Language Manual: https://cwiki.apache.org/confluence/display/Hive/LanguageManual.

TEZ

On Hadoop 1, Hive was limited to using MapReduce to execute most of the statements because MapReduce was the only processing engine supported on Hadoop. This wasn't ideal, as users coming to Hive from other SQL systems were used to highly interactive environments where queries are frequently completed in seconds. MapReduce was designed for high-throughput batch processing, so its startup overhead coupled with its limited processing capabilities resulted in very high-latency query executions.

With the Hive 0.13 release, Hive now uses Tez on YARN to execute its queries, and as a result, it's able to get closer to the interactive ideal for working with your data.[1] Tez is basically a generalized Directed Acyclic Graph (DAG) execution engine that doesn't impose any limits on how you compose your execution graph (as opposed to MapReduce) and that also allows you to keep data in-memory in between phases, reducing the disk and network I/O that MapReduce requires. You can read more about Tez at the following links:

- Hive on Tez: https://cwiki.apache.org/confluence/display/Hive/Hive+on+Tez
- Tez incubation Apache project page: http://incubator.apache.org/projects/tez.html

In the Hive 0.13 release, Tez isn't enabled by default, so you'll need to follow these instructions to get it up and running:

- Tez installation instructions: https://github.com/apache/incubator-tez/blob/branch-0.2.0/INSTALL.txt
- Configuring Hive to work on Tez: https://issues.apache.org/jira/browse/HIVE-6098

INTERACTIVE AND NON-INTERACTIVE HIVE

The Hive shell provides an interactive interface:

```
$ hive
hive> SHOW DATABASES;
OK
default
Time taken: 0.162 seconds
```

Hive in non-interactive mode lets you execute scripts containing Hive commands. The following example uses the -S option so that only the output of the Hive command is written to the console:

```
$ cat hive-script.ql
SHOW DATABASES;

$ hive -S -f hive-script.ql
default
```

---

[1] Carter Shanklin, "Benchmarking Apache Hive 13 for Enterprise Hadoop," http://hortonworks.com/blog/benchmarking-apache-hive-13-enterprise-hadoop/.

Another non-interactive feature is the -e option, which lets you supply a Hive command as an argument:

```
$ hive -S -e "SHOW DATABASES"
default
```

If you're debugging something in Hive and you want to see more detailed output on the console, you can use the following command to run Hive:

```
$ hive -hiveconf hive.root.logger=INFO,console
```

That concludes our brief introduction to Hive. Next we'll look at how you can use Hive to mine interesting data from your log files.

9.1.2 Reading and writing data

This section covers some of the basic data input and output mechanics in Hive. We'll ease into things with a brief look at working with text data before jumping into how you can work with Avro and Parquet data, which are becoming common ways to store data in Hadoop.

   This section also covers some additional data input and output scenarios, such as writing and appending to tables and exporting data out to your local filesystem. Once we've covered these basic functions, subsequent sections will cover more advanced topics such as writing UDFs and performance tuning tips.

TECHNIQUE 89 **Working with text files**

Imagine that you have a number of CSV or Apache log files that you want to load and analyze using Hive. After copying them into HDFS (if they're not already there), you'll need to create a Hive table before you can issue queries. If the result of your work is also large, you may want to write it into a new Hive table. This section covers these text I/O use cases in Hive.

■ **Problem**

You want to use Hive to load and analyze text files, and then save the results.

■ **Solution**

Use the RegexSerDe class, bundled with the contrib library in Hive, and define a regular expression that can be used to parse the contents of Apache log files. This technique also looks at how serialization and deserialization works in Hive, and how to write your own SerDe to work with log files.

■ **Discussion**

If you issue a CREATE TABLE command without any row/storage format options, Hive assumes the data is text-based using the default line and field delimiters shown in table 9.1.

   Because most of the text data that you'll work with will be structured in more standard ways, such as CSV, let's look at how you can work with CSV.

Table 9.1 Default text file delimiters

Default delimiter	Syntax example to change default delimiter	Description
\n	LINES TERMINATED BY '\n'	Record separator.
^A	FIELDS TERMINATED BY '\t'	Field separator. If you wanted to replace ^A with another non-readable character, you'd represent it in octal, e.g., '\001'.
^B	COLLECTION ITEMS TERMINATED BY ';'	An element separator for ARRAY, STRUCT, and MAP data types.
^C	MAP KEYS TERMINATED BY ':'	Used as a key/value separator in MAP data types.

First you'll need to copy the stocks CSV file included with the book's code into HDFS. Create a directory in HDFS and then copy the stocks file into the directory:[2]

```
$ hadoop fs -mkdir hive-stocks
$ hadoop fs -put test-data/stocks.txt hive-stocks
```

Now you can create an external Hive table over your stocks directory:

```
hive> CREATE EXTERNAL TABLE stocks (
  symbol STRING,
  date STRING,
  open FLOAT,
  high FLOAT,
  low FLOAT,
  close FLOAT,
  volume INT,
  adj_close FLOAT
)
ROW FORMAT DELIMITED FIELDS TERMINATED BY ','
LOCATION '/user/YOUR-USERNAME/hive-stocks';
```

> **Creating managed tables with the LOCATION keyword** When you create an external (unmanaged) table, Hive keeps the data in the directory specified by the LOCATION keyword intact. But if you were to execute the same CREATE command and drop the EXTERNAL keyword, the table would be a managed table, and Hive would move the contents of the LOCATION directory into /user/hive/warehouse/stocks, which may not be the behavior you expect.

Run a quick query to verify that things look good:

```
hive> SELECT symbol, count(*) FROM stocks GROUP BY symbol;
AAPL    10
CSCO    10
GOOG     5
MSFT    10
YHOO    10
```

---

[2] Hive doesn't allow you to create a table over a file; it must be a directory.

Sweet! What if you wanted to save the results into a new table and then show the schema of the new table?

```
hive> CREATE TABLE symbol_counts
ROW FORMAT DELIMITED FIELDS TERMINATED BY ','
LOCATION '/user/YOUR-USERNAME/symbol_counts'
AS SELECT symbol, count(*) FROM stocks GROUP BY symbol;

hive> describe symbol_counts;
symbol          string
```

> **Create-Table-As-Select (CTAS) and external tables** CAS statements like the preceding example don't allow you to specify that the table is EXTERNAL. But because the table that you're selecting from is already an external table, Hive ensures that the new table is also an external table.

If the target table already exists, you have two options—you can either overwrite the entire contents of the table, or you can append to the table:

```
hive> INSERT OVERWRITE TABLE stock_symbols
SELECT symbol, count(*) FROM stocks GROUP BY symbol;
```
The OVERWRITE keyword replaces the contents of the existing table with the results of the SELECT.

```
hive> INSERT INTO TABLE stock_symbols
SELECT symbol, count(*) FROM stocks GROUP BY symbol;
```
If the INTO keyword is used, the operation appends the results of the SELECT to the table.

You can view the raw table data using the Hadoop CLI:

```
$ hdfs -cat symbol_counts/*
AAPL,10
CSCO,10
GOOG,5
MSFT,10
YHOO,10
```

The great thing about Hive external tables is that you can write into them using any method (it doesn't have to be via a Hive command), and Hive will automatically pick up the additional data the next time you issue any Hive statements.

Tokenizing files with regular expressions

Let's make things more complicated and assume you want to work with log data. This data is in text form, but it can't be parsed using Hive's default deserialization. Instead, you need a way to specify a regular expression to parse your log data. Hive comes with a contrib RegexSerDe class that can tokenize your logs.

First, copy some log data into HDFS:

```
$ hadoop fs -mkdir log-data
$ hadoop fs -put test-data/ch9/hive-log.txt log-data/
```

Next, specify that you want to use a custom deserializer. The `RegexSerDe` is bundled with the Hive contrib JAR, so you'll need to add this JAR to Hive:

```
hive> ADD JAR <HIVE-HOME>/lib/hive-contrib-<version>.jar;

hive> CREATE EXTERNAL TABLE logs (
        host STRING,
        identity STRING,
        user STRING,
        time STRING,
        request STRING,
        status STRING,
        size STRING)
ROW FORMAT SERDE 'org.apache.hadoop.hive.contrib.serde2.RegexSerDe'
WITH SERDEPROPERTIES (
 "input.regex" =
    "([^ ]*) ([^ ]*) ([^ ]*) (-|\\[[^\\]]*\\])
    ([^ \"]*|\"[^\"]*\") (-|[0-9]*) (-|[0-9]*)",
 "output.format.string"="%1$s %2$s %3$s %4$s %5$s %6$s %7$s"
)
STORED AS TEXTFILE LOCATION '/user/YOUR-USERNAME/log-data/';
```

The regular expression used to match and extract groups that are mapped to the table columns. Also note that there's a single space separator where the regular expression is split across two lines.

Determines the order and formatting of the table when it's being written.

A quick test will tell you if the data is being correctly handled by the SerDe:

```
hive> SELECT host, request FROM logs LIMIT 10;

89.151.85.133     "GET /movie/127Hours HTTP/1.1"
212.76.137.2      "GET /movie/BlackSwan HTTP/1.1"
74.125.113.104    "GET /movie/TheFighter HTTP/1.1"
212.76.137.2      "GET /movie/Inception HTTP/1.1"
127.0.0.1         "GET /movie/TrueGrit HTTP/1.1"
10.0.12.1         "GET /movie/WintersBone HTTP/1.1"
```

If you're seeing nothing but NULL values in the output, it's probably because you have a missing space in your regular expression. Ensure that the regex in the CREATE statement looks like figure 9.2.

Hive's SerDe is a flexible mechanism that can be used to extend Hive to work with any file format, as long as an InputFormat exists that can work with that file format. For more details on SerDes, take a look at the Hive documentation at https://cwiki.apache.org/confluence/display/Hive/SerDe.

WORKING WITH AVRO AND PARQUET

Avro is an object model that simplifies working with your data, and Parquet is a columnar storage format that can efficiently support advanced query optimizations

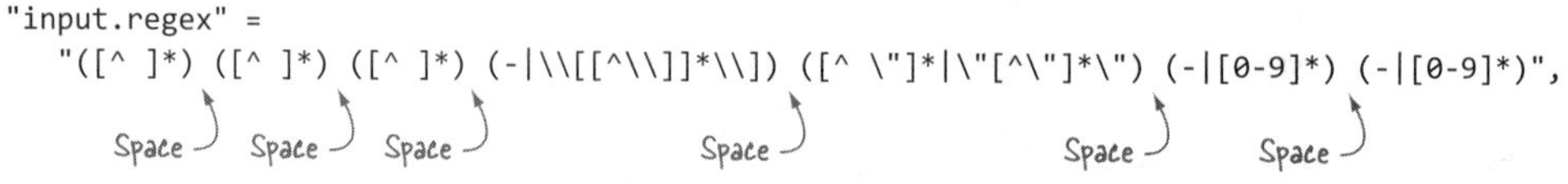

```
"input.regex" =
    "([^ ]*) ([^ ]*) ([^ ]*) (-|\\[[^\\]]*\\]) ([^ \"]*|\"[^\"]*\") (-|[0-9]*) (-|[0-9]*)",
```

Space Space Space Space Space Space

Figure 9.2 CREATE **table regex showing spaces**

such as predicate pushdowns. Combined, they're a compelling pair and could well become the canonical way that data is stored in Hadoop. We covered both Avro and Parquet in depth in chapter 3, which in technique 23 shows you how to use Avro and Parquet in Hive.

TECHNIQUE 90   **Exporting data to local disk**

Getting data out of Hive and Hadoop is an important function you'll need to be able to perform when you have data that you're ready to pull into your spreadsheets or other analytics software. This technique examines a few methods you can use to pull out your Hive data.

- **Problem**

You have data sitting in Hive that you want to pull out to your local filesystem.

- **Solution**

Use the standard Hadoop CLI tools or a Hive command to pull out your data.

- **Discussion**

If you want to pull out an entire Hive table to your local filesystem and the data format that Hive uses for your table is the same format that you want your data exported in, you can use the Hadoop CLI and run a `hadoop -get /user/hive/warehouse/...` command to pull down the table.

Hive comes with `EXPORT` (and corresponding `IMPORT`) commands that can be used to export Hive data and metadata into a directory in HDFS. This is useful for copying Hive tables between Hadoop clusters, but it doesn't help you much in getting data out to the local filesystem.

If you want to filter, project, and perform some aggregations on your data and then pull it out of Hive, you can use the `INSERT` command and specify that the results should be written to a local directory:

```
hive> INSERT OVERWRITE LOCAL DIRECTORY 'local-stocks' SELECT * FROM stocks;
```

This will create a directory on your local filesystem containing one or more files. If you view the files in an editor such as vi, you'll notice that Hive used the default field separator (^A) when writing the files. And if any of the columns you exported were complex types (such as `STRUCT` or `MAP`), then Hive will use JSON to encode these columns.

Luckily, newer versions of Hive (including 0.13) allow you to specify a custom delimiter when you export tables:

```
hive> INSERT OVERWRITE LOCAL DIRECTORY 'local-stocks'
ROW FORMAT DELIMITED FIELDS TERMINATED BY ','
SELECT * FROM stocks;
```

With Hive's reading and writing basics out of the way, let's take a look at more complex topics, such as user-defined functions.

### 9.1.3	*User-defined functions in Hive*

We've looked at how Hive reads and writes tables, so it's time to start doing something useful with your data. Since we want to cover more advanced techniques, we'll look at how you can write a custom Hive user-defined function (UDF) to geolocate your logs. UDFs are useful if you want to mix custom code inline with your Hive queries.

TECHNIQUE 91	**Writing UDFs**

This technique shows how you can write a Hive UDF and then use it in your Hive Query Language (HiveQL).

■ **Problem**

How do you write a custom function in Hive?

■ **Solution**

Extend the UDF class to implement your user-defined function and call it as a function in your HiveQL.

■ **Discussion**

You can geolocate the IP addresses from the logs table using the free geolocation database from MaxMind.

Download the free country geolocation database,[3] gunzip it, and copy the GeoIP.dat file to your /tmp/ directory. Next, use a UDF to geolocate the IP address from the log table that you created in technique 89:

> *Add the JAR containing your UDF so that it can be used in MapReduce.*

Add the geolocation data file into the distributed cache.

```
hive> ADD JAR <HIVE_HOME>/lib/hive-contrib-0.13.0.jar;
hive> ADD JAR <HIP_HOME>/hip-2.0.0.jar;
hive> ADD JAR <HIP_HOME>/lib/geoip-api-1.2.13.jar;
hive> ADD file /tmp/GeoIP.dat;
hive> CREATE temporary function country AS 'hip.ch9.hive.Geoloc';

hive> SELECT host, country(host, "GeoIP.dat") FROM logs;

89.151.85.133    GB
212.76.137.2     RU
74.125.113.104   US
212.76.137.2     RU
127.0.0.1        NULL
10.0.12.1        NULL
```

Define country as the alias for your geolocation UDF, and specify the class name.

Call your UDF, specifying the field on which it should operate (the host column from the logs table), and the filename of the geolocation data file, which is in the distributed cache.

When writing a UDF, there are two implementation options: either extend the UDF class or implement the GenericUDF class. The main differences between them are that the GenericUDF class can work with arguments that are complex types, so UDFs that extend GenericUDF are more efficient because the UDF class requires Hive to use reflection for discovery and invocation. Figure 9.3 shows the two Hive UDF classes, one of which you need to extend to implement your UDF.

---

[3] See MaxMind's "GeoIP Country Database Installation Instructions," http://dev.maxmind.com/geoip/legacy/install/country/.

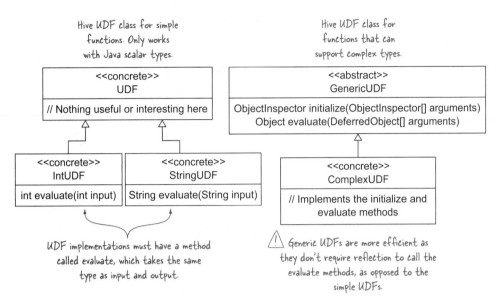

Hive UDF class for simple functions. Only works with Java scalar types.

Hive UDF class for functions that can support complex types.

UDF implementations must have a method called evaluate, which takes the same type as input and output.

⚠ Generic UDFs are more efficient as they don't require reflection to call the evaluate methods, as opposed to the simple UDFs.

Figure 9.3   Hive UDF class diagram

The following listing shows the geolocation UDF, which you'll implement using the GenericUDF class.[4]

Listing 9.1   The geolocation UDF

The Description annotation is used to provide usage information in the Hive shell (you'll see how this works following this code).

The geolocation lookup class.

Converters, which you'll use to convert the input types to the types you want to operate with.

Create a converter that you can use in the evaluate method to convert all the arguments (which in your case are the IP address and geolocation file) from their native types into Java Strings.

Specify that the return type for the UDF (in other words, the evaluate function) will be a Java String.

```java
@Description(
    name = "country",
    value = "_FUNC_(ip, geolocfile) - Returns the geolocated " +
    "country code for the IP"
)
public class GeolocUDF extends GenericUDF {
    private LookupService geoloc;
    private ObjectInspectorConverters.Converter[] converters;

    @Override
    public ObjectInspector initialize(ObjectInspector[] arguments) {
        converters =
            new ObjectInspectorConverters.Converter[arguments.length];
        for (int i = 0; i < arguments.length; i++) {
            converters[i] =
                ObjectInspectorConverters.getConverter(arguments[i],
                PrimitiveObjectInspectorFactory.javaStringObjectInspector);
        }

        return PrimitiveObjectInspectorFactory
            .getPrimitiveJavaObjectInspector(
```

---

[4]   GitHub source: https://github.com/alexholmes/hiped2/blob/master/src/main/java/hip/ch9/hive/ Geoloc.java.

```
                          PrimitiveObjectInspector.PrimitiveCategory.STRING);
           }

           @Override
           public Object evaluate(GenericUDF.DeferredObject[] arguments) {

               Text ip = (Text) converters[0].convert(arguments[0].get());
               Text filename = (Text) converters[1].convert(arguments[1].get());

               return lookup(ip, filename);
           }

           protected String lookup(Text ip, Text filename)
                                   throws HiveException {
               try {
                   if (geoloc == null) {
                       URL u = getClass().getClassLoader()
                       .getResource(filename.toString());
                       geoloc =
                           new LookupService(u.getFile(),
                                           LookupService.GEOIP_MEMORY_CACHE);
                   }

                   String countryCode =
                       geoloc.getCountry(ip.toString()).getCode();

                   if ("--".equals(countryCode)) {
                       return null;
                   }

                   return countryCode;
               } catch (IOException e) {
                   throw new HiveException("Caught IO exception", e);
               }
           }

           @Override
           public String getDisplayString(String[] children) {
               assert (children.length == 2);
               return "country(" + children[0] + ", " + children[1] + ")";
           }
       }
```

After retrieving the IP address and geolocation filename from the arguments, call a function to perform the geolocation.

Load the geolocation data file from the distributed cache.

Create an instance of the MaxMind Lookup class.

Perform the geolocation and extract the country code.

Return the country code.

Create a string that's used in situations such as exceptions to provide some context on how the UDF was being invoked.

The Description annotation can be viewed in the Hive shell with the describe function command:

```
hive> describe function country;
OK
country(ip, geolocfile) - Returns the geolocated country code
for the IP
```

■ Summary

Although the UDF we looked at operates on scalar data, Hive also has something called user-defined aggregate functions (UDAF), which allows more complex processing capabilities over aggregated data. You can see more about writing a UDAF on the

Hive wiki at the page titled "Hive Operators and User-Defined Functions (UDFs)" (https://cwiki.apache.org/confluence/display/Hive/LanguageManual+UDF).

Hive also has user-defined table functions (UDTFs), which operate on scalar data but can emit more than one output for each input. See the `GenericUDTF` class for more details.

Next we'll take a look at what you can do to optimize your workflows in Hive.

9.1.4 *Hive performance*

In this section, we'll examine some methods that you can use to optimize data management and processing in Hive. The tips presented here will help you ensure that as you scale out your data, the rest of Hive will keep up with your needs.

TECHNIQUE 92 Partitioning

Partitioning is a common technique employed by SQL systems to horizontally or vertically split data to speed up data access. With reduced overall volume of data in a partition, partitioned read operations have a lot less data to sift through, and as a result can execute much more rapidly.

This same principle applies equally well to Hive, and it becomes increasingly important as your data sizes grow. In this section you'll explore the two types of partitions in Hive: static partitions and dynamic partitions.

■ **Problem**

You want to arrange your Hive files so as to optimize queries against your data.

■ **Solution**

Use `PARTITIONED BY` to partition by columns that you typically use when querying your data.

■ **Discussion**

Imagine you're working with log data. A natural way to partition your logs would be by date, allowing you to perform queries on specific time periods without incurring the overhead of a full table scan (reading the entire contents of the table). Hive supports partitioned tables and gives you control of determining which columns are partitioned.

Hive supports two types of partitions: static partitions and dynamic partitions. They differ in the way you construct `INSERT` statements, as you'll discover in this technique.

Static partitioning

For the purpose of this technique, you'll work with a very simple log structure. The fields are IP address, year, month, day, and HTTP status code:

```
$ cat test-data/ch9/logs-partition.txt
127.0.0.1,2014,06,21,500
127.0.0.1,2014,06,21,400
127.0.0.1,2014,06,21,300
127.0.0.1,2014,06,22,200
127.0.0.1,2014,06,22,210
127.0.0.1,2014,06,23,100
```

Load them into HDFS and into an external table:

```
$ hadoop fs -mkdir logspartext
$ hadoop fs -put test-data/ch9/logs-partition.txt logspartext/

hive> CREATE EXTERNAL TABLE logs_ext (
  ip STRING,
  year INT,
  month INT,
  day INT,
  status INT
)
ROW FORMAT DELIMITED FIELDS TERMINATED BY ','
LOCATION '/user/YOUR-USERNAME/logspartext';
```

Now you can create a partitioned table, where the year, month, and day are partitions:

```
CREATE EXTERNAL TABLE IF NOT EXISTS logs_static (
  ip STRING,
  status INT)
PARTITIONED BY (year INT, month INT, day INT)
ROW FORMAT DELIMITED FIELDS TERMINATED BY '\t'
LOCATION '/user/YOUR-USERNAME/logs_static';
```

By default, Hive inserts follow a static partition method that requires all inserts to explicitly enumerate not only the partitions, but the column values for each partition. Therefore, an individual INSERT statement can only insert into one day's worth of partitions:

```
INSERT INTO TABLE logs_static
PARTITION (year = '2014', month = '06', day = '21')
SELECT ip, status FROM logs_ext WHERE year=2014 AND month=6 AND day=21;
```

Luckily Hive has a special data manipulation language (DML) statement that allows you to insert into multiple partitions in a single statement. The following code will insert all the sample data (spanning three days) into the three partitions:

```
FROM logs_ext se
INSERT INTO TABLE logs_static
PARTITION (year = '2014', month = '6', day = '21')
SELECT ip, status WHERE year=2014 AND month=6 AND day=21
INSERT INTO TABLE logs_static
PARTITION (year = '2014', month = '6', day = '22')
SELECT ip, status WHERE year=2014 AND month=6 AND day=22
INSERT INTO TABLE logs_static
PARTITION (year = '2014', month = '6', day = '23')
SELECT ip, status WHERE year=2014 AND month=6 AND day=23;
```

This approach has an additional advantage in that it will only make one pass over the logs_ext table to perform the inserts—the previous approach would have required N queries on the source table for N partitions.

> **Flexibility of single-pass static partitioned inserts** Hive doesn't limit either the
> destination tables or whether the query conditions need to align with the par-
> titions. Therefore, there's nothing stopping you from inserting into different
> tables and having overlapping rows in multiple partitions or tables.

One disadvantage of static partitions is that when you're inserting data, you must
explicitly specify the partition that's being inserted into. But you're not stuck with
static partitions as the only partitions supported in Hive. Hive has the notion of
dynamic partitions, which make life a little easier by not requiring you to specify the
partition when inserting data.

Dynamic partitioning
Dynamic partitions are smarter than static partitions, as they can automatically determine which partition a record needs to be written to when data is being inserted.

Let's create a whole new table to store some dynamic partitions. Notice how the
syntax to create a table that uses dynamic partitions is exactly the same as that for
static partitioned tables:

```
CREATE EXTERNAL TABLE IF NOT EXISTS logs_dyn (
  ip STRING,
  status INT)
PARTITIONED BY (year INT, month INT, day INT)
ROW FORMAT DELIMITED FIELDS TERMINATED BY '\t'
LOCATION '/user/YOUR-USERNAME/logs_dyn';
```

The differences only come into play at INSERT time:

Dynamic partitions need to be explicitly enabled via this configuration setting.

The INSERT statement doesn't require you to call out specific partitions.

```
hive> SET hive.exec.dynamic.partition=true;
hive> SET hive.exec.dynamic.partition.mode=nonstrict;

hive> INSERT INTO TABLE logs_dyn
      PARTITION (year, month, day)
      SELECT ip, status, year, month, day FROM logs_ext;
```

By default, Hive requires dynamic partition inserts to contain at least one static partition. This disables that requirement.

That's a lot better—you no longer need to explicitly tell Hive which partitions you're
inserting into. It'll dynamically figure this out.

Mixing dynamic and static partitions in the same table
Hive supports mixing both static and dynamic columns in a table. There's also nothing stopping you from transitioning from a static partition insert method to dynamically partitioned inserts.

Partition directory layout
Partitioned tables are laid out in HDFS differently from nonpartitioned tables. Each
partition value occupies a separate directory in Hive containing the partition column
name as well as its value.

These are the contents of HDFS after running the most recent INSERT:

```
logs_static/year=2014/month=6/day=21/000000_0
logs_static/year=2014/month=6/day=22/000000_0
logs_static/year=2014/month=6/day=23/000000_0
```

The "000000_0" are the files that contain the rows. There's only one per partitioned day due to the small dataset (running with a larger dataset with more than one task will result in multiple files).

Customizing partition directory names

As you just saw, left to its own devices, Hive will create partition directory names using the column=value format. What if you wanted to have more control over the directories? Instead of your partitioned directory looking like this,

```
logs_static/year=2014/month=6/day=27
```

what if you wanted it to look like this:

```
logs_static/2014/6/27
```

You can achieve this by giving Hive the complete path that should be used to store a partition:

```
ALTER TABLE logs_static
ADD PARTITION(year=2014, month=6, day=27)
LOCATION '/user/YOUR-USERNAME/logs_static/2014/6/27';
```

You can query the location of individual partitions with the DESCRIBE command:

```
hive> DESCRIBE EXTENDED logs_static
  PARTITION (year=2014, month=6, day=28);
...
location:hdfs://localhost:8020/user/YOUR-USERNAME/logs_static/2014/6/27
...
```

This can be a powerful tool, as Hive doesn't require that all the partitions for a table be on the same cluster or type of filesystem. Therefore, a Hive table could have a partition sitting in Hadoop cluster A, another sitting in cluster B, and a third in a cluster in Amazon S3. This opens up some powerful strategies for aging out data to other filesystems.

Querying partitions from Hive

Hive provides some commands to allow you to see the current partitions for a table:

```
hive> SHOW PARTITIONS logs_dyn;
year=2014/month=6/day=21
year=2014/month=6/day=22
year=2014/month=6/day=23
```

Bypassing Hive to load data into partitions

Let's say you had some data for a new partition (2014/6/24) that you wanted to manually copy into your partitioned Hive table using HDFS commands (or some other mechanism such as MapReduce).

Here's some sample data (note that the date parts are removed because Hive only retains these column details in the directory names):

```
$ cat test-data/ch9/logs-partition-supplemental.txt
127.0.0.1  500
127.0.0.1  600
```

Create a new partitioned directory and copy the file into it:

```
$ hdfs -mkdir logs_dyn/year=2014/month=6/day=24
$ hdfs -put test-data/ch9/logs-partition-supplemental.txt \
    logs_dyn/year=2014/month=6/day=24
```

Now go to your Hive shell and try to select the new data:

```
hive> SELECT * FROM logs_dyn
  WHERE year = 2014 AND month = 6 AND day = 24;
```

No results! This is because Hive doesn't yet know about the new partition. You can run a repair command so that Hive can examine HDFS to determine the current partitions:

```
hive> msck repair table logs_dyn;
Partitions not in metastore:     logs_dyn:year=2014/month=6/day=24
Repair: Added partition to metastore logs_dyn:year=2014/month=6/day=24
```

Now your SELECT will work:

```
hive> SELECT * FROM logs_dyn
  WHERE year = 2014 AND month = 6 AND day = 24;
127.0.0.1  500  2014  6  24
127.0.0.1  600  2014  6  24
```

Alternatively, you could explicitly inform Hive about the new partition:

```
ALTER TABLE logs_dyn
ADD PARTITION (year=2014, month=6, day=24);
```

■ Summary

Given the flexibility of dynamic partitions, in what situations would static partitions offer an advantage? One example is in cases where the data that you're inserting doesn't have any knowledge of the partitioned columns, but some other process does.

For example, suppose you have some log data that you want to insert, but for whatever reason the log data doesn't contain dates. In this case, you can craft a static partitioned insert as follows:

```
$ hive -hiveconf year=2014 -hiveconf month=6 -hiveconf day=28
hive> INSERT INTO TABLE logs_static
PARTITION (year=${hiveconf:year},
           month=${hiveconf:month},
           day=${hiveconf:day})
SELECT ip, status FROM logs_ext;
```

Let's next take a look at columnar data, which is another form of data partitioning that can provide dramatic query execution time improvements.

COLUMNAR DATA

Most data that we're used to working with is stored on disk in row-oriented order, meaning that all the columns for a row are contiguously located when stored at rest on persistent storage. CSV, SequenceFiles, and Avro are typically stored in rows.

Using a column-oriented storage format for saving your data can offer huge performance benefits, both from space and execution-time perspectives. Contiguously locating columnar data together allows storage formats to use sophisticated data-compression schemes such as run-length encoding, which can't be applied to row-oriented data. Furthermore, columnar data allows execution engines such as Hive, MapReduce, and Tez to push predicates and projections to the storage formats, allowing these storage formats to skip over data that doesn't match the pushdown criteria.

There are currently two hot options for columnar storage on Hive (and Hadoop): Optimized Row Columnar (ORC) and Parquet. They come out of Hortonworks and Cloudera/Twitter, respectively, and both offer very similar space- and time-saving optimizations. The only edge really comes out of the goal of Parquet to maximize compatibility in the Hadoop community, so at the time of writing, Parquet has greater support for the Hadoop ecosystem.

Chapter 3 has a section devoted to Parquet, and technique 23 includes instructions on how Parquet can be used with Hive.

TECHNIQUE 93 **Tuning Hive joins**

It's not uncommon to execute a join over some large datasets in Hive and wait hours for it to complete. In this technique we'll look at how joins can be optimized, much like we did for MapReduce in chapter 4.

■ **Problem**

Your Hive joins are running slower than expected, and you want to learn what options you have to speed them up.

■ **Solution**

Look at how you can optimize Hive joins with *repartition joins*, *replication joins*, and *semi-joins*.

■ **Discussion**

We'll cover three types of joins in Hive: the repartition join, which is the standard reduce-side join; the replication join, which is the map-side join; and the semi-join, which only cares about retaining data from one table.

Before we get started, let's create two tables to work with:

```
$ hadoop fs -mkdir stocks-mini
$ hadoop fs -put test-data/ch9/stocks-mini.txt stocks-mini
$ hadoop fs -mkdir symbol-names
$ hadoop fs -put test-data/ch9/symbol-names.txt symbol-names

hive> CREATE EXTERNAL TABLE stocks (
  symbol STRING,
  date STRING,
```

```
  open FLOAT
)
ROW FORMAT DELIMITED FIELDS TERMINATED BY ','
LOCATION '/user/YOUR-USERNAME/stocks-mini';

hive> CREATE EXTERNAL TABLE names (
  symbol STRING,
  name STRING
)
ROW FORMAT DELIMITED FIELDS TERMINATED BY ','
LOCATION '/user/YOUR-USERNAME/symbol-names';
```

You've created two tables. The stocks table contains just three columns—the stock symbol, the date, and the price. The names table contains the stock symbols and the company names:

```
hive> select * from stocks;
AAPL  2009-01-02  85.88
AAPL  2008-01-02  199.27
CSCO  2009-01-02  16.41
CSCO  2008-01-02  27.0
GOOG  2009-01-02  308.6
GOOG  2008-01-02  692.87
MSFT  2009-01-02  19.53
MSFT  2008-01-02  35.79
YHOO  2009-01-02  12.17
YHOO  2008-01-02  23.8

hive> select * from names;
AAPL  Apple
GOOG  Google
YHOO  Yahoo!
```

Join table ordering

As with any type of tuning, it's important to understand the internal workings of a system. When Hive executes a join, it needs to select which table is streamed and which table is cached. Hive picks the last table in the JOIN statement for streaming, so you should take care to ensure that this is the largest table.

Let's look at the example of our two tables. The stocks table, which includes daily quotes, will continue to grow over time, but the names table, which contains the stock symbol names, will be mostly static. Therefore, when these tables are joined, it's important that the larger table, stocks, comes last in the query:

```
SELECT stocks.symbol, date, open, name
FROM names
JOIN stocks ON (names.symbol = stocks.symbol);
```

You can also explicitly tell Hive which table it should stream:

```
SELECT /*+ STREAMTABLE(stocks) */ stocks.symbol, date, open, name
FROM names
JOIN stocks ON (names.symbol = stocks.symbol);
```

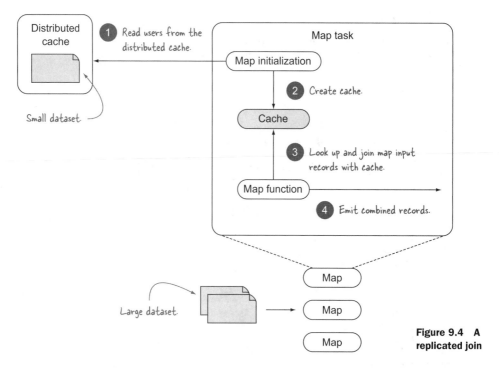

Figure 9.4   A replicated join

Map-side joins

A replicated join is a map-side join where a small table is cached in memory and the large table is streamed. You can see how it works in MapReduce in figure 9.4.

Map-side joins can be used to execute both inner and outer joins. The current recommendation is that you configure Hive to automatically attempt to convert joins into map-side joins:

```
hive> set hive.auto.convert.join = true;
hive> SET hive.auto.convert.join.noconditionaltask = true;
hvie> SET hive.auto.convert.join.noconditionaltask.size = 10000000;
```

The first two settings must be set to `true` to enable autoconversion of joins to map-side joins (in Hive 0.13 they're both enabled by default). The last setting is used by Hive to determine whether a join can be converted. Imagine you have *N* tables in your join. If the size of the smallest *N* − 1 tables on disk is less than `hive.auto.convert.join.noconditionaltask.size`, then the join is converted to a map-side join. Bear in mind that the check is rudimentary and only examines the size of the tables on disk, so factors such as compression and filters or projections don't come into the equation.

> **Map-join hint**   Older versions of Hive supported a hint that you could use to instruct Hive which table was the smallest and should be cached. Here's an example:

```
SELECT /*+ MAPJOIN(names) */ stocks.symbol, date, open, name
FROM names
JOIN stocks ON (names.symbol = stocks.symbol);
```

Recent versions of Hive ignore this hint (`hive.ignore.mapjoin.hint` is set to true by default) because it put the onus on the query author to determine the smaller table, which can lead to slow queries due to user error.

Sort-merge-bucket joins

Hive tables can be bucketed and sorted, which helps you to easily sample data, and it's also a useful join optimization as it enables sort-merge-bucket (SMB) joins. SMB joins require that all tables be sorted and bucketed, in which case joins are very efficient because they require a simple merge of the presorted tables.

The following example shows how you'd create a sorted and bucketed stocks table:

```
CREATE TABLE stocks_bucketed (
  symbol STRING,
  date STRING,
  open FLOAT
)
CLUSTERED BY(symbol) SORTED BY(symbol) INTO 32 BUCKETS;
```

Inserting into bucketed tables You can use regular INSERT statements to insert into bucketed tables, but you need to set the `hive.enforce.bucketing` property to true. This instructs Hive that it should look at the number of buckets in the table to determine the number of reducers that will be used when inserting into the table (the number of reducers must be equal to the number of buckets).

To enable SMB joins, you must set the following properties:

```
set hive.auto.convert.sortmerge.join=true;
set hive.optimize.bucketmapjoin = true;
set hive.optimize.bucketmapjoin.sortedmerge = true;
set hive.auto.convert.sortmerge.join.noconditionaltask=true;
```

In addition, you'll also need to ensure that the following conditions hold true:

- All tables being joined are bucketed and sorted on the join column.
- The number of buckets in each join table must be equal, or factors of one another.

Skew

Skew can lead to lengthy MapReduce execution times because a small number of reducers may receive a disproportionately large number of records for some join values. Hive, by default, doesn't attempt to do anything about this, but it can be configured to detect skew and optimize joins on skewed keys:

```
hive> SET hive.optimize.skewjoin = true;
hive> SET hive.skewjoin.key = 100000;
```

Sets the threshold beyond which a key is considered to be skewed.

Tell Hive to optimize joins where it sees skewed data.

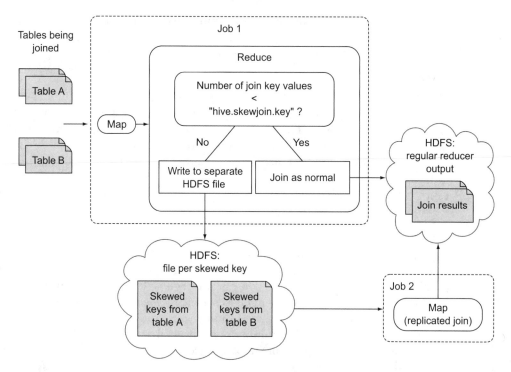

Figure 9.5   Hive skew optimization

So what happens when Hive detects skew? You can see the additional step that Hive adds in figure 9.5, where skewed keys are written to HDFS and processed in a separate MapReduce job.

It should be noted that this skew optimization only works with reduce-side repartition joins, not map-side replication joins.

Skewed tables

If you know ahead of time that there are particular keys with high skews, you can tell Hive about them when creating your table. If you do this, Hive will write out skewed keys into separate files that allow it to further optimize queries, and even to skip over the files if possible.

Imagine that you have two stocks (Apple and Google) that have a much larger number of records compared to the others—in this case you'd modify your CREATE TABLE statement with the keywords SKEWED BY, as follows:

```
CREATE TABLE stocks_skewed (
  symbol STRING,
  date STRING,
  open FLOAT
)
SKEWED BY (symbol) ON ('AAPL', 'GOOGL');
```

9.2 *Impala*

Impala is a low-latency, massively parallel query engine, modeled after Google's Dremel paper describing a scalable and interactive query system.[5] Impala was conceived and developed out of Cloudera, which realized that using MapReduce to execute SQL wasn't viable for a low-latency SQL environment.

Each daemon in Impala is designed to be self-sufficient, and a client can send a query to any Impala daemon. Impala does have some metadata services, but it can continue to function even when they're not working, as the daemon nodes talk directly to one another to execute queries. An overview of the Impala architecture can be seen in figure 9.6.

Impala allows you to query data in HDFS or HBase with a SQL syntax, so it supports access via ODBC. It uses the Hive metastore, so it can read existing Hive tables, and DDL statements executed via Impala are also reflected in Hive.

In this section I'll present some of the differences between Impala and Hive, and we'll also look at some basic examples of Impala in action, including how Hive UDFs can be used.

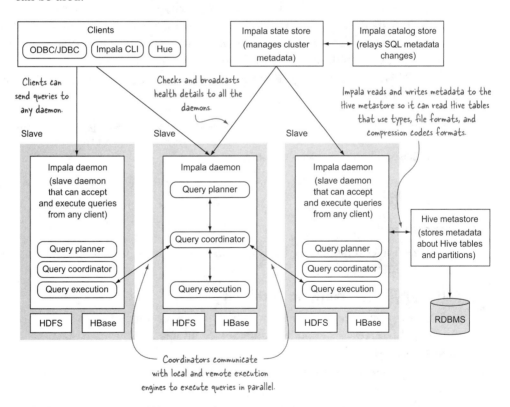

Figure 9.6 **The Impala architecture**

---

[5] Sergey Melnik et al., "Dremel: Interactive Analysis of Web-Scale Datasets," http://research.google.com/pubs/pub36632.html.

9.2.1 *Impala vs. Hive*

There are a handful of differences between Impala and Hive:

- Impala is designed from the ground up as a massively parallel query engine and doesn't need to translate SQL into another processing framework. Hive relies on MapReduce (or more recently Tez) to execute.
- Impala and Hive are both open source, but Impala is a curated project under Cloudera's control.
- Impala isn't fault-tolerant.
- Impala doesn't support complex types such as maps, arrays, and structs (including nested Avro data). You can basically only work with flat data.[6]
- There are various file formats and compression codec combinations that require you to use Hive to create and load tables. For example, you can't create or load data into an Avro table in Impala, and you can't load an LZO-compressed text file in Impala. For Avro you need to create the table in Hive before you can use it in Impala, and in both Avro and LZO-compressed text, you'll need to load your data into these tables using Hive before you can use them in Impala.
- Impala doesn't support Hive user-defined table-generating functions (UDTSs), although it does support Hive UDFs and UDAFs and can work with existing JARs that contain these UDFs without any changes to the JAR.
- There are certain aggregate functions and HiveQL statements that aren't supported in Impala.

> **Impala and Hive versions**   This list compares Hive 0.13 and Impala 1.3.1, both of which are current at the time of writing. It should be noted that the Impala 2 release will address some of these items.

Cloudera has a detailed list of the SQL differences between Impala and Hive: http://mng.bz/0c2F.

9.2.2 *Impala basics*

This section covers what are likely the two most popular data formats for Impala—text and Parquet.

TECHNIQUE 94   **Working with text**

Text is typically the first file format that you'll work with when exploring a new tool, and it also serves as a good learning tool for understanding the basics.

- **Problem**

You have data in text form that you want to work with in Impala.

- **Solution**

Impala's text support is identical to Hive's.

---

[6] Impala and Avro nested type support is planned for Impala 2.0: https://issues.cloudera.org/browse/IMPALA-345.

■ **Discussion**

Impala's basic query language is identical to Hive's. Let's kick things off by copying the stocks data into a directory in HDFS:

```
$ hadoop fs -mkdir hive-stocks
$ hadoop fs -put test-data/stocks.txt hive-stocks
```

Next you'll create an external table and run a simple aggregation over the data:

```
$ impala-shell

> CREATE EXTERNAL TABLE stocks (
  sym STRING,
  dt STRING,
  open FLOAT,
  high FLOAT,
  low FLOAT,
  close FLOAT,
  volume INT,
  adj_close FLOAT
)
ROW FORMAT DELIMITED FIELDS TERMINATED BY ','
LOCATION '/user/YOUR-USERNAME/hive-stocks';

> SELECT sym, min(close), max(close) FROM stocks GROUP BY sym;
+------+-------------------+-------------------+
| sym  | min(close)        | max(close)        |
+------+-------------------+-------------------+
| MSFT | 20.32999992370605 | 116.5599975585938 |
| AAPL | 14.80000019073486 | 194.8399963378906 |
| GOOG | 202.7100067138672 | 685.1900024414062 |
| CSCO | 13.64000034332275 | 108.0599975585938 |
| YHOO | 12.85000038146973 | 475               |
+------+-------------------+-------------------+
```

> **Using Hive tables in Impala** The example in technique 94 shows how to create a table called stocks in Impala. If you've already created the stocks table in Hive (as shown in technique 89), then rather than create the table in Impala, you should refresh Impala's metadata and then use that Hive table in Impala.
>
> After creating the table in Hive, issue the following statement in the Impala shell:
>
> ```
> > INVALIDATE METADATA stocks;
> ```
>
> At this point, you can issue queries against the stocks table inside the Impala shell.
>
> Alternatively, if you really want to create the table in Impala and you've already created the table in Hive, you'll need to issue a DROP TABLE command prior to issuing the CREATE TABLE command in Impala.

That's it! You'll notice that the syntax is exactly the same as in Hive. The one difference is that you can't use `symbol` and `date` as column names because they're reserved symbols in Impala (Hive doesn't have any such restrictions).

Let's take a look at working with a storage format that's a bit more interesting: Parquet.

TECHNIQUE 95 Working with Parquet

It's highly recommended that you use Parquet as your storage format for various space and time efficiencies (see chapter 3 for more details on Parquet's benefits). This technique looks at how you can create Parquet tables in Impala.

■ **Problem**

You need to save your data in Parquet format to speed up your queries and improve the compression of your data.

■ **Solution**

Use `STORED AS PARQUET` when creating tables.

■ **Discussion**

One way to get up and started quickly with Parquet is to create a new Parquet table based on an existing table (the existing table doesn't need to be a Parquet table). Here's an example:

```
CREATE TABLE stocks_parquet LIKE stocks STORED AS PARQUET;
```

Then you can use an `INSERT` statement to copy the contents from the old table into the new Parquet table:

```
INSERT OVERWRITE TABLE stocks_parquet SELECT * FROM stocks;
```

Now you can ditch your old table and start using your shiny new Parquet table!

```
> SHOW TABLE STATS stocks_parquet;
Query: show TABLE STATS stocks_parquet
+-------+--------+--------+---------+
| #Rows | #Files | Size   | Format  |
+-------+--------+--------+---------+
| -1    | 1      | 2.56KB | PARQUET |
+-------+--------+--------+---------+
```

Alternatively, you can create a new table from scratch:

```
CREATE TABLE stocks_parquet_internal (
   sym STRING,
   dt STRING,
   open DOUBLE,
   high DOUBLE,
   low DOUBLE,
   close DOUBLE,
   volume INT,
   adj_close DOUBLE
) STORED AS PARQUET;
```

One of the great things about Impala is that it allows the INSERT ... VALUES syntax, so you can easily get data into the table:[7]

```
INSERT INTO stocks_parquet_internal
VALUES ("YHOO","2000-01-03",442.9,477.0,429.5,475.0,38469600,118.7);
```

Parquet is a columnar storage format, so the fewer columns you select in your query, the faster your queries will execute. Selecting all the columns, as in the following example, can be considered an anti-pattern and should be avoided if possible:

```
SELECT * FROM stocks;
```

Next, let's look at how you can handle situations where the data in your tables is modified outside of Impala.

TECHNIQUE 96 Refreshing metadata

If you make table or data changes inside of Impala, that information is automatically propagated to all the other Impala daemons to ensure that any subsequent queries will pick up that new data. But Impala (as of the 1.3 release) doesn't handle cases where data is inserted into tables outside of Impala.

Impala is also sensitive to the block placement of files that are in a table—if the HDFS balancer runs and relocates a block to another node, you'll need to issue a refresh command to force Impala to reset the block locations cache.

In this technique you'll learn how to refresh a table in Impala so that it picks up the new data.

■ **Problem**

You've inserted data into a Hive table outside of Impala.

■ **Solution**

Use the REFRESH statement.

■ **Discussion**

Impala daemons cache Hive metadata, including information about tables and block locations. Therefore, if data has been loaded into a table outside of Impala, you'll need to use the REFRESH statement so that Impala can pull the latest metadata.

Let's look at an example of this in action; we'll work with the stocks table you created in technique 94. Let's add a new file into the external table's directory with a quote for a brand new stock symbol:

```
echo "TSLA,2014-06-25,236,236,236,236,38469600,236" \
| hadoop fs -put - hive-stocks/append.txt
```

---

[7] The use of INSERT ... VALUES isn't recommended for large data loads. Instead, it's more efficient to move files into your table's HDFS directory, use the LOAD DATA statement, or use INSERT INTO ... SELECT or CREATE TABLE AS SELECT ... statements. The first two options will move files into the table's HDFS directory, and the last two statements will load the data in parallel.

Bring up the Hive shell and you'll immediately be able to see the stock:

```
hive> select * from stocks where sym = "TSLA";
TSLA  2014-06-25  236.0  236.0  236.0  236.0  38469600  236.0
```

Run the same query in Impala and you won't see any results:

```
> select * from stocks where sym = "TSLA";

Returned 0 row(s) in 0.33s
```

A quick REFRESH will remedy the situation:

```
> REFRESH stocks;

> select * from stocks where sym = "TSLA";
+------+------------+------+------+-----+-------+----------+-----------+
| sym  | dt         | open | high | low | close | volume   | adj_close |
+------+------------+------+------+-----+-------+----------+-----------+
| TSLA | 2014-06-25 | 236  | 236  | 236 | 236   | 38469600 | 236       |
+------+------------+------+------+-----+-------+----------+-----------+
```

> **What's the difference between REFRESH and INVALIDATE METADATA?** In the "Using Hive tables in Impala" sidebar (see technique 94), you used the INVALIDATE METADATA command in Impala so that you could see a table that had been created in Hive. What's the difference between the two commands?
>
> The INVALIDATE METADATA command is more resource-intensive to execute, and it's required when you want to refresh Impala's state after creating, dropping, or altering a table using Hive. Once the table is visible in Impala, you should use the REFRESH command to update Impala's state if new data is loaded, inserted, or changed.

■ Summary

You don't need to use REFRESH when you use Impala to insert and load data because Impala has an internal mechanism by which it shares metadata changes. Therefore, REFRESH is really only needed when loading data via Hive or when you're externally manipulating files in HDFS.

9.2.3   *User-defined functions in Impala*

Impala supports native UDFs written in C++, which ostensibly provide improved performance over their Hive counterparts. Coverage of the native UDFs is out of scope for this book, but Cloudera has excellent online documentation that comprehensively covers native UDFs.[8] Impala also supports using Hive UDFs, which we'll explore in the next technique.

---

[8] For additional details on Impala UDFs, refer to the "User-Defined Functions" page on Cloudera's website at http://mng.bz/319i.

TECHNIQUE 97 Executing Hive UDFs in Impala

If you've been working with Hive for a while, it's likely that you've developed some UDFs that you regularly use in your queries. Luckily, Impala provides support for these Hive UDFs and allows you to use them without any change to the code or JARs.

■ **Problem**

You want to use custom or built-in Hive UDFs in Impala.

■ **Solution**

Create a function in Impala referencing the JAR containing the UDF.

■ **Discussion**

Impala requires that the JAR containing the UDF be in HDFS:

```
$ hadoop fs -put <PATH-TO-HIVE-LIB-DIR>/hive-exec.jar
```

Next, in the Impala shell you'll need to define a new function and point to the JAR location on HDFS and to the fully qualified class implementing the UDF.

For this technique, we'll use a UDF that's packaged with Hive and converts the input data into a hex form. The UDF class is UDFHex and the following example creates a function for that class and gives it a logical name of my_hex to make it easier to reference it in your SQL:

```
create function my_hex(string) returns string
location '/user/YOUR-USERNAME/hive-exec.jar'
symbol='org.apache.hadoop.hive.ql.udf.UDFHex';
```

At this point you can use the UDF—here's a simple example:

```
> select my_hex("hello");
+------------------------+
| default.my_hex('hello') |
+------------------------+
| 68656C6C6F             |
+------------------------+
```

■ **Summary**

What are the differences between using a Hive UDF in Hive versus using it in Impala?

- The query language syntax for defining the UDF is different.
- Impala requires you to define the argument types and the return type of the function. This means that even if the UDF is designed to work with any Hive type, the onus is on you to perform type conversion if the defined parameter type differs from the data type that you're operating on.
- Impala currently doesn't support complex types, so you can only return scalar types.
- Impala doesn't support user-defined table functions.

This brings us to the end of our coverage of Impala. For a more detailed look at Impala, see Richard L. Saltzer and Istvan Szegedi's book, *Impala in Action* (Manning, scheduled publication 2015).

Next let's take a look at how you can use SQL inline with Spark for what may turn out to be the ultimate extract, transform, and load (ETL) and analytical tool in your toolbox.

9.3   *Spark SQL*

New SQL-on-Hadoop projects seem to pop up every day, but few look as promising as Spark SQL. Many believe that Spark is the future for Hadoop processing due to its simple APIs and efficient and flexible execution models, and the introduction of Spark SQL in the Spark 1.0 release only furthers the Spark toolkit.

Apache Spark is a cluster-computing engine that's compatible with Hadoop. Its main selling points are enabling fast data processing by pinning datasets into memory across a cluster, and supporting a variety of ways for processing data, including Map-Reduce styles, iterative processing, and graph processing.

Spark came out of UC Berkeley and became an Apache project in 2014. It's generating a lot of momentum due to its expressive language and because it lets you get up and running quickly with its API, which is currently defined in Java, Scala, and Python. In fact, Apache Mahout, the machine-learning project that historically has implemented its parallelizable algorithms in MapReduce, has recently stated that all new distributed algorithms will be implemented using Spark.

Early in Spark's evolution, it used a system called Shark to provide a SQL interface to the Spark engine. More recently, in the Spark 1.0 release we were introduced to Spark SQL, which allows you to intermingle SQL with your Spark code. This promises a new Hadoop processing paradigm of intermixing SQL with non-SQL code.

> **What's the difference between Spark SQL and Shark?**   Shark was the first Spark system that provided SQL abilities in Spark. Shark uses Hive for query planning and Spark for query execution. Spark SQL, on the other hand, doesn't use the Hive query planner and instead uses its own planner (and execution) engine. The goal is to keep Shark as the Hive-compatible part of Spark, but there are plans to move to Spark SQL for query planning once Spark SQL has stabilized.[9]

In this section we'll look at how you can work with SQL in Spark and also look at its SQL-like APIs, which offer a fluent style to compose your queries in.

> **Production readiness of Spark SQL**   At the time of writing, Spark 1.0 has been released, which introduced Spark SQL for the first time. It is currently labeled as alpha quality and is being actively developed.[10] As a result, the code in this section may differ from the production-ready Spark SQL API.

Before we get started with Spark SQL, let's become familiar with Spark by looking at some simple Spark examples.

---

[9] The future of Shark is discussed by Michael Armbrust and Reynold Xin, "Spark SQL: Manipulating Structured Data Using Spark," http://mng.bz/9057.

[10] Michael Armbrust and Zongheng Yang, "Exciting Performance Improvements on the Horizon for Spark SQL," http://mng.bz/efqV.

9.3.1 Spark 101

Spark consists of a core set of APIs and an execution engine, on top of which exist other Spark systems that provide APIs and processing capabilities for specialized activities, such as designing stream-processing pipelines. The core Spark systems are shown in figure 9.7.

Any Spark system can work on an RDD generated by another system, allowing you to colocate your processing code.

Shark (SQL and Hive support)	Spark streaming (stream processing that uses the same language as batch)	MLlib (scalable machine learning)	GraphX (work with graphs and collections)

Spark (a generalized processing engine that supports distributed datasets)

Figure 9.7   Spark systems

The Spark components can be seen in figure 9.8. The Spark driver is responsible for communicating with a cluster manager to execute operations and the Spark executors handle the actual operation execution and data management.

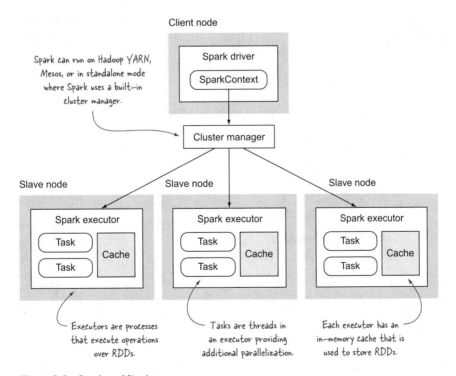

Figure 9.8   Spark architecture

Data in Spark is represented using RDDs (resilient distributed datasets), which are an abstraction over a collection of items. RDDs are distributed over a cluster so that each cluster node will store and manage a certain range of the items in an RDD. RDDs can be created from a number of sources, such as regular Scala collections or data from HDFS (synthesized via Hadoop input format classes). RDDs can be in-memory, on disk, or a mix of the two.[11]

The following example shows how an RDD can be created from a text file:

```
scala> val stocks = sc.textFile("stocks.txt")
stocks: org.apache.spark.rdd.RDD[String] = MappedRDD[122] at textFile
```

The Spark RDD class has various operations that you can perform on the RDD. RDD operations in Spark fall into two categories—transformations and actions:

- *Transformations* operate on an RDD to create a new RDD. Examples of transformation functions include map, flatMap, reduceByKey, and distinct.[12]
- *Actions* perform some activity over an RDD, after which they return results to the driver. For example, the collect function returns the entire RDD contents to the driver process, and the take function allows you to select the first *N* items in a dataset.[13]

Lazy transformations   Spark will lazily evaluate transformations, so you actually need to execute an action for Spark to execute your operations.

Let's take a look at an example of a Spark application that calculates the average stock price for each symbol. To run the example, you'll need to have Spark installed,[14] after which you can launch the shell:

Tokenize the CSV file and project the stock symbol and the price inside a Scala tuple.

Create an RDD from the stocks file.

Reduce the stocks using the symbols, and sum and calculate the averages.

```
$ ./bin/spark-shell  --master yarn-client
scala> val stocks = sc.textFile("stocks.txt")
scala> val pairs = stocks.map(_.split(",")).map(p =>
              (p(0), p(2).trim.toDouble))
scala> val counts = pairs.mapValues((_, 1)).reduceByKey((a, b) =>
      (a._1 + b._1, a._2 + b._2)).mapValues{ case (sum, count) =>
      (1.0 * sum)/count}
scala> counts.collect.foreach(println)
...
(MSFT,44.63100000000001)
(GOOG,417.47799999999995)
(AAPL,68.631)
(CSCO,31.148000000000003)
(YHOO,69.333)
```

Execute the collect action, which results in Spark executing the operations.

---

[11] More information on RDD caching and persistence can be found in the Spark Programming Guide at https://spark.apache.org/docs/latest/programming-guide.html#rdd-persistence.

[12] A more complete list of transformations is shown in the Spark Programming Guide at https://spark.apache.org/docs/latest/programming-guide.html#transformations.

[13] A more complete list of actions can be found in the Spark Programming Guide at https://spark.apache.org/docs/latest/programming-guide.html#actions.

[14] To install and configure Spark on YARN, follow the instructions on "Running Spark on YARN" at http://spark.apache.org/docs/latest/running-on-yarn.html.

This was a very brief introduction to Spark—the Spark online documentation is excellent and is worth exploring to learn more about Spark.[15] Let's now turn to an introduction to how Spark works with Hadoop.

9.3.2 Spark on Hadoop

Spark supports several cluster managers, one of them being YARN. In this mode, the Spark executors are YARN containers, and the Spark ApplicationMaster is responsible for managing the Spark executors and sending them commands. The Spark driver is either contained within the client process or inside the ApplicationMaster, depending on whether you're running in client mode or cluster mode:

- In *client mode* the driver resides inside the client, which means that executing a series of Spark tasks in this mode will be interrupted if the client process is terminated. This mode works well for the Spark shell, but it isn't suitable for use when Spark is being used in a non-interactive method.

- In *cluster mode* the driver executes in the ApplicationMaster and doesn't rely on the client to exist in order to execute tasks. This mode works best for cases where you have some existing Spark code that you wish to execute and that doesn't require any interaction from you.

Figure 9.9 shows the architecture of Spark running on YARN.

The default installation of Spark is set up for standalone mode, so you'll have to configure Spark to make it work with YARN.[16] The Spark scripts and tools don't change when you're running on YARN, so once you've configured Spark to use YARN, you can run the Spark shell just like you did in the previous example.

Now that you understand some Spark basics and how it works on YARN, let's look at how you can execute SQL using Spark.

9.3.3 SQL with Spark

This section covers Spark SQL, which is part of the core Spark system. Three areas of Spark SQL will be examined: executing SQL against your RDDs, using integrated query language features that provide a more expressive way to work with your data, and integrating HiveQL with Spark.

> **Stability of Spark SQL**   Spark SQL is currently labeled as alpha quality, so it's probably best not to use it in your production code until it's marked as production-ready.

---

[15] A great starting place for learning about Spark is the Spark Programming Guide, http://spark.apache.org/docs/latest/programming-guide.html.

[16] Follow the instructions at https://spark.apache.org/docs/latest/running-on-yarn.html to set up Spark to use YARN.

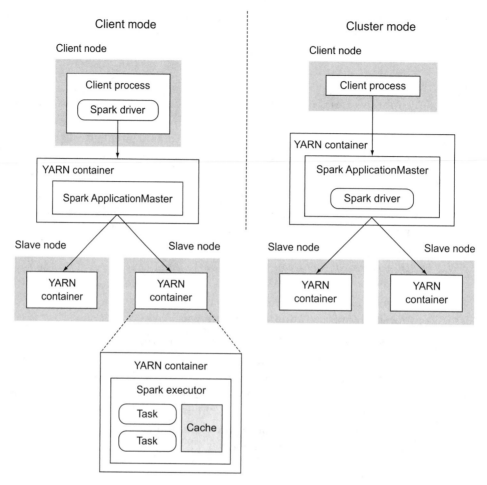

Figure 9.9   Spark running on YARN

Calculating stock averages with Spark SQL

In this technique you'll learn how to use Spark SQL to calculate the average price for each stock symbol.

■ **Problem**

You have a Spark processing pipeline, and expressing your functions would be simpler using SQL as opposed to the Spark APIs.

■ **Solution**

Register an RDD as a table and use the Spark sql function to execute SQL against the RDD.

■ **Discussion**

The first step in this technique is to define a class that will represent each record in your Spark table. In this example, you'll calculate the stock price averages, so all you need is a class with two fields to store the stock symbol and price:

```
scala> case class Stock(symbol: String, price: Double)
```

> **Why use Scala for Spark examples?** In this section we'll use Scala to show Spark examples. The Scala API, until recently, has been much more concise than Spark's Java API, although with the release of Spark 1.0, the Java support in Spark now uses lambdas to expose a less verbose API.

Next you need to register an RDD of these Stock objects as a table so that you can perform SQL operations on it. You can create a table from any Spark RDD. The following example shows how you can load the stocks data from HDFS and register it as a table:

Create a SQL context.

Create an RDD
of Stock objects
by loading the
stocks from a
text file,
tokenizing the
file, and creating
Stock instances.

```
scala> val sqlContext = new org.apache.spark.sql.SQLContext(sc)

scala> import sqlContext._                              Import the context to access
                                                        all the SQL functions.
scala> val stocks = sc.textFile("stocks.txt").map(_.split(",")).map(
          p => Stock(p(0), p(3).trim.toDouble))
scala> stocks.registerAsTable("stocks")          Register the RDD as
                                                 a table called stocks.
```

Now you're ready to issue queries against the stocks table. The following shows how you'd calculate the average price for each symbol:

```
scala> val stock_averages = sql(
          "SELECT symbol, AVG(price) FROM stocks GROUP BY symbol")

scala> stock_averages.collect().foreach(println)
[CSCO,31.564999999999998]
[GOOG,427.032]
[MSFT,45.281]
[AAPL,70.54599999999999]
[YHOO,73.29299999999999]
```

The sql function returns a SchemaRDD, which supports standard RDD operations. This is where the novel aspect of Spark SQL comes into play—mixing SQL and regular data processing paradigms together. You use SQL to create an RDD and you can then immediately turn around and execute your usual Spark transformations over that data.

In addition to supporting the standard Spark RDD operations, SchemaRDD also allows you to execute SQL-like functions such as where and join over the data, which is covered in the next technique.[17]

---

[17] Language-integrated queries that allow more natural language expression of queries can be seen at the Scala docs for the SchemaRDD class at http://spark.apache.org/docs/latest/api/scala/index.html#org.apache.spark.sql .SchemaRDD.

TECHNIQUE 99   Language-integrated queries

The previous technique demonstrated how you can execute SQL over your Spark data. Spark 1.0 also introduced a feature called language-integrated queries, which expose SQL constructs as functions, allowing you to craft code that's not only fluent but that expresses operations using natural language constructs. In this technique you'll see how to use these functions on your RDDs.

■ **Problem**

Although the Spark RDD functions are expressive, they don't yield code that is particularly human-readable.

■ **Solution**

Use Spark's language-integrated queries.

■ **Discussion**

Once again, let's try to calculate the average stock prices, this time using language-integrated queries. This example uses the groupBy function to calculate the average stock price:

Import aggregated functions.

Load stocks data from file and create a SchemaRDD.

```
scala> val sqlContext = new org.apache.spark.sql.SQLContext(sc)
scala> import sqlContext._
scala> import org.apache.spark.sql.catalyst.expressions._

scala> val stocks = sc.textFile("stocks.txt").map(_.split(",")).map(
         p => Stock(p(0), p(3).trim.toDouble)).toSchemaRDD

scala> val stocks_avg =
stocks.groupBy('symbol)(First('symbol) as
'symbol, Average('price) as 'avgPrice)
scala> stocks_avg.collect.foreach(println)
[CSCO,31.564999999999998]
[GOOG,427.032]
[MSFT,45.281]
[AAPL,70.54599999999999]
[YHOO,73.29299999999999]
```

View the resulting RDD.

Execute the groupBy function and specify that the grouping should occur on the symbol field and that the result should retain the stock name. The Average aggregate function is used over the grouped stock prices.

The preceding code leverages the Average and First aggregate functions—there are other aggregate functions such as Count, Min, and Max, among others.[18]

The next is more straightforward; it simply selects all the quotes for days where the value was over $100:

```
scala> stocks.where('price >= 100).collect.foreach(println)
[AAPL,200.26]
[AAPL,112.5]
...
```

The third option with Spark SQL is to use HiveQL, which is useful when you want to execute more complex SQL grammar.

---

[18] See the code at the following link for the complete list: https://github.com/apache/spark/blob/master/ sql/catalyst/src/main/scala/org/apache/spark/sql/catalyst/expressions/aggregates.scala.

TECHNIQUE 100	**Hive and Spark SQL**

You can also work with data in Hive tables in Spark. This technique examines how you can execute a query against a Hive table.

■ **Problem**

You want to work with Hive data in Spark.

■ **Solution**

Use Spark's `HiveContext` to issue HiveQL statements and work with the results in Spark.

■ **Discussion**

Earlier in this chapter you created a stocks table in Hive (in technique 89). Let's query that stocks table using HiveQL from within Spark and then perform some additional manipulations within Spark:

Execute a Hive query and load the results into a Spark SchemaRDD.

```
spark> val hiveContext = new org.apache.spark.sql.hive.HiveContext(sc)
spark> import hiveContext._
spark> import org.apache.spark.sql.catalyst.expressions._

spark> val stocks = hql("FROM stocks SELECT symbol, open")
```

A HiveContext instance must be created before you can issue HiveQL statements.

```
spark> stocks.take(3).foreach(println)
[AAPL,85.88]
[AAPL,199.27]
[CSCO,16.41]
```

Dump out the first three records in the RDD.

Convert the Row objects into tuples and perform the stock average calculation.

```
spark> val pairs = stocks.map{ case Row(symbol: String, open: Float) =>
                      (symbol, open) }.mapValues((_, 1)).reduceByKey((a, b) =>
        (a._1 + b._1, a._2 + b._2)).mapValues{ case (sum, count) =>
        (1.0 * sum)/count}
```

```
spark> counts.collect.foreach(println)
(MSFT,27.65999984741211)
(GOOG,500.7349853515625)
(AAPL,142.5749969482422)
(CSCO,21.704999923706055)
(YHOO,17.985000610351562)
```

Dump the contents of the resulting RDD.

You have access to the complete HiveQL grammar in Spark, as the commands that are wrapped inside the `hql` calls are sent directly to Hive. You can load tables, insert into tables, and perform any Hive command that's needed, all directly from Spark. Spark's Hive integration also includes support for using Hive UDFs, UDAFs, and UDTFs in your queries.

This completes our brief look at Spark SQL.

9.4 *Chapter summary*

SQL access to data in Hadoop is essential for organizations, as not all users who want to interact with data are programmers. SQL is often the lingua franca for not only data analysts but also for data scientists and nontechnical members of your organization.

In this chapter I introduced three tools that can be used to work with your data via SQL. Hive has been around the longest and is currently the most full-featured SQL engine you can use. Impala is worth a serious look if Hive is not providing a rapid enough level of interaction with your data. And finally, Spark SQL provides a glimpse into the future, where technical members of your organization such as programmers and data scientists can fuse together SQL and Scala to build complex and efficient processing pipelines.

This chapter covers

- Understanding key capabilities of a YARN application
- How to write a basic YARN application
- An examination of YARN frameworks and applications

Looking at the source code for any reasonably sized YARN application typically results in words like "complex" and "low-level" being thrown around. At its core, writing a YARN application isn't that complex, as you'll discover in this chapter. The complexity with YARN is typically introduced once you need to build more advanced features into your application, such as supporting secure Hadoop clusters or handling failure scenarios, which are complicated in distributed systems regardless of the framework. That being said, there are emerging frameworks that abstract away the YARN APIs and provide common features that you'll require.

In this chapter, you'll write a simple YARN application that will run a Linux command on a node in the cluster. Once you've run your application, you'll be introduced to some of the more advanced features that you may need in your YARN application. Finally, this chapter looks at some of the open source YARN abstractions and examine their features.

Before we get started, let's ease into YARN programming by looking at the building blocks of a YARN application.

10.1 Fundamentals of building a YARN application

This section provides a brief high-level overview of the YARN actors and the basic communication flows that you'll need to support in your YARN application.

10.1.1 Actors

There are five separate pieces of a YARN application that are either part of the YARN framework or components that you must create yourself (which I call the *user space*), all of which are shown in figure 10.1.

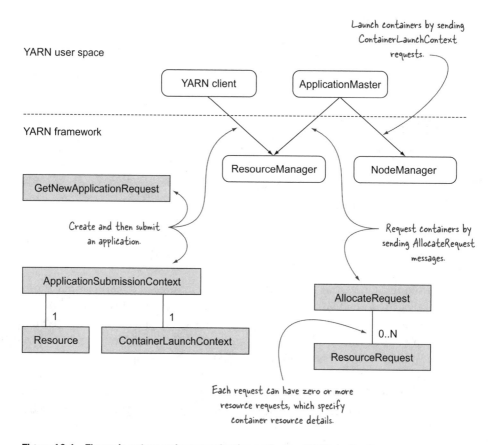

Figure 10.1   The main actors and communication paths in a YARN application

The actors in a YARN application and the YARN framework include

- *YARN client*—The YARN client, in the user space, is responsible for launching the YARN application. It sends createApplication and submitApplication requests to the ResourceManager and can also kill the application.
- *ResourceManager*—In the framework, a single cluster-wide ResourceManager is responsible for receiving container allocation requests and asynchronously notifying clients when resources become available for their containers.
- *ApplicationMaster*—The ApplicationMaster in the user space is the main coordinator for an application, and it works with the ResourceManager and Node-Managers to request and launch containers.
- *NodeManager*—In the framework, each node runs a NodeManager that's responsible for servicing client requests to launch and kill containers.
- *Container*—The container in the user space is an application-specific process that performs work on behalf of the application. A container could be a simple fork of an existing Linux process (such as the find command to find files), or an application-developed service such as a map or reduce task for MapReduce YARN applications.

The following sections discuss these actors and their role in your Yarn application.

10.1.2 *The mechanics of a YARN application*

When implementing a YARN application, there are a number of interactions that you need to support. Let's examine each interaction and what information is relayed between the components.

RESOURCE ALLOCATION

When the YARN client or the ApplicationMaster asks the ResourceManager for a new container, they indicate the resources that the container needs in a Resource object. In addition, the ApplicationMaster sends some more attributes in a ResourceRequest, as shown in figure 10.2.

The resourceName specifies the host and rack where the container should be executed, and it can be wildcarded with an asterisk to inform the ResourceManager that the container can be launched on any node in the cluster.

The ResourceManager responds to a resource request with a Container object that represents a single unit of execution (a process). The container includes an ID, a resourceName, and other attributes. Once the YARN client or ApplicationMaster receives this message from the ResourceManager, it can communicate with the Node-Manager to launch the container.

LAUNCHING A CONTAINER

Once a client receives the Container from the ResourceManager, it's ready to talk to the NodeManager associated with the container to launch the container. Figure 10.3 shows the information that the client sends to the NodeManager as part of the request.

<<org.apache.hadoop.yarn.api.records>> ResourceRequest	
`priority`	The priority assigned to a ResourceRequest or Application or Container.
`resourceName`	The resource name (e.g., host/rack) on which the allocation is desired.
`containers`	Number of containers.
`relaxLocality`	Should locality be loose (i.e., allow container allocation to fall through to another node on the local rack or any node in the cluster), or strict (i.e., hard constraint on resource allocation).

0..1

1

<<org.apache.hadoop.yarn.api.records>> Resource	
`vCores`	Number of virtual cores.
`memory`	Memory required.

Figure 10.2   Resource properties that can be requested for a container

<<org.apache.hadoop.yarn.api.records>> ContainerLaunchContext	
`localResources`	Resources required for the container to run (e.g., binary files, JARs, shared objects).
`environment`	Environment variables that should be set prior to launching the container process.
`commands`	The command used to launch the container.
`serviceData`	Identify data needed from any auxiliary services. For example, MRv2 uses the shuffle auxiliary service for MapReduce.
`tokens`	Security tokens needed by the container (required if security is enabled).
`acls`	Application ACLs.

Figure 10.3   Container request metadata

The NodeManager is responsible for downloading any local resources identified in the request (including items such as any libraries required by the application or files in the distributed cache) from HDFS. Once these files are downloaded, the NodeManager launches the container process.

With these YARN preliminaries out of the way, let's go ahead and start writing a YARN application.

10.2 Building a YARN application to collect cluster statistics

In this section you'll build a simple YARN application that will launch a single container to execute the vmstat Linux command. As you build this simple example, we'll focus on the plumbing needed to get a YARN application up and running. The next section covers the more advanced capabilities that you'll likely require in a full-blown YARN application.

Figure 10.4 shows the various components that you'll build in this section and their interactions with the YARN framework.

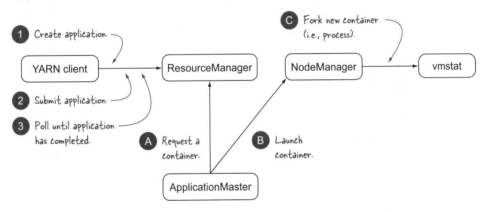

Figure 10.4   An overview of the YARN application that you'll build

Let's get started by building the YARN client.

TECHNIQUE 101   **A bare-bones YARN client**

The role of the YARN client is to negotiate with the ResourceManager for a YARN application instance to be created and launched. As part of this work, you'll need to inform the ResourceManager about the system resource requirements of your ApplicationMaster. Once the ApplicationMaster is up and running, the client can choose to monitor the status of the application.

This technique will show you how to write a client that performs the three steps illustrated in figure 10.5.

■ **Problem**

You're building a YARN application, so you need to write a client to launch your application.

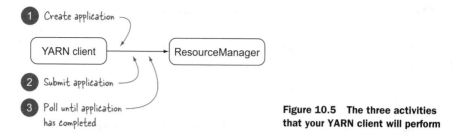

Figure 10.5   The three activities that your YARN client will perform

■ Solution

Use the YarnClient class to create and submit a YARN application.

■ Discussion

Let's walk through the code for each of the steps highlighted in figure 10.5, starting with creating a new YARN application.

Creating a YARN application

The first thing your YARN client needs to do is communicate with the Resource-Manager about its intent to start a new YARN application. The response from the ResourceManager is a unique application ID that's used to create the application and that's also supported by the YARN command line for queries such as retrieving logs.

The following code shows how you can get a handle to a YarnClient instance and use that to create the application:[1]

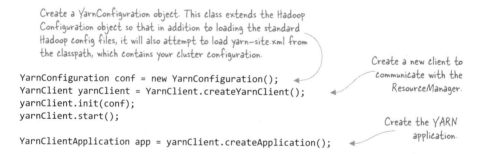

The createApplication method will call the ResourceManager, which will return a new application ID. In addition, the YarnClientApplication object contains information about the cluster, such as the resource capabilities that can be used to predetermine container resource properties.

The YarnClient class used in the preceding code contains a number of APIs that result in an RPC call to the ResourceManager. Some of these methods are shown in the following extract from the code:[2]

---

[1] GitHub source: https://github.com/alexholmes/hiped2/blob/master/src/main/java/hip/ch10/dstat/Client.java.

[2] Some queue and security APIs were omitted from the YarnClient class—refer to the YarnClient Javadocs for the complete API: http://hadoop.apache.org/docs/stable/api/org/apache/hadoop/yarn/client/api/YarnClient.html.

Create a new application, a precursor to submitting the application.

Tell the ResourceManager to launch the ApplicationMaster.

```
package org.apache.hadoop.yarn.client.api;

public abstract class YarnClient extends AbstractService {

    YarnClientApplication createApplication();

    ApplicationId submitApplication(ApplicationSubmissionContext ctx);

    void killApplication(ApplicationId applicationId);

    ApplicationReport getApplicationReport(ApplicationId appId);

    List<ApplicationReport> getApplications();

    YarnClusterMetrics getYarnClusterMetrics();

    List<NodeReport> getNodeReports(NodeState... states);

    ...
}
```

Fetch the current state of an application.

Kill an application.

Fetch all applications currently running in the cluster.

Retrieve the cluster metrics, which as of the Hadoop 2.2 release only return the number of NodeManagers.

Fetch a summary of each node in the cluster.

Creating an application in YARN doesn't actually do anything other than inform the ResourceManager of your intent to actually launch the application. The next step shows what you need to do to have the ResourceManager launch your ApplicationMaster.

Submitting a YARN application

Submitting the YARN application launches your ApplicationMaster in a new container in your YARN cluster. But there are several items you need to configure before you can submit the application, including the following:

- An application name
- The command to launch the ApplicationMaster, along with the classpath and environment settings
- Any JARs, configuration files, and other files that your application needs to perform its work
- The resource requirements for the ApplicationMaster (memory and CPU)
- Which scheduler queue to submit the application to and the application priority within the queue
- Security tokens

Let's look at the code required to get a basic Java-based ApplicationMaster up and running. We'll break this code up into two subsections: preparing the Container-LaunchContext object, and then specifying the resource requirements and submitting the application.

First up is the ContainerLaunchContext, which is where you specify the command to launch your ApplicationMaster, along with any other environmental details required for your application to execute:[3]

---

[3] GitHub source: https://github.com/alexholmes/hiped2/blob/master/src/main/java/hip/ch10/dstat/Client.java.

```
ContainerLaunchContext container =
    Records.newRecord(ContainerLaunchContext.class);
```

Specify the launch command and instruct the process to pipe standard output and error to the container's work directory.

```
String amLaunchCmd =
    String.format(
        "$JAVA_HOME/bin/java -Xmx256M %s 1>%s/stdout 2>%s/stderr",
        ApplicationMaster.class.getName(),
        ApplicationConstants.LOG_DIR_EXPANSION_VAR,
        ApplicationConstants.LOG_DIR_EXPANSION_VAR);

container.setCommands(Lists.newArrayList(amLaunchCmd));
```

Find the JAR that contains your code.

```
String jar = ClassUtil.findContainingJar(Client.class);
FileSystem fs = FileSystem.get(conf);
Path src = new Path(jar);
Path dest = new Path(fs.getHomeDirectory(), src.getName());
fs.copyFromLocalFile(src, dest);
```

Copy the JAR to HDFS.

```
FileStatus jarStat = FileSystem.get(conf).getFileStatus(dest);

LocalResource appMasterJar = Records.newRecord(LocalResource.class);
appMasterJar.setResource(ConverterUtils.getYarnUrlFromPath(dest));
appMasterJar.setSize(jarStat.getLen());
appMasterJar.setTimestamp(jarStat.getModificationTime());
appMasterJar.setType(LocalResourceType.FILE);
appMasterJar.setVisibility(LocalResourceVisibility.APPLICATION);
```

Create a LocalResource for the JAR and populate the HDFS URI for the JAR.

```
container.setLocalResources(
    ImmutableMap.of("AppMaster.jar",  appMasterJar));
```

Add the JAR as a local resource for the container.

```
Map<String, String> appMasterEnv = Maps.newHashMap();
for (String c : conf.getStrings(
    YarnConfiguration.YARN_APPLICATION_CLASSPATH,
    YarnConfiguration.DEFAULT_YARN_APPLICATION_CLASSPATH)) {
  Apps.addToEnvironment(appMasterEnv, Environment.CLASSPATH.name(),
      c.trim());
}
```

Add the YARN JARs to the classpath for the ApplicationMaster.

```
Apps.addToEnvironment(appMasterEnv,
    Environment.CLASSPATH.name(),
    Environment.PWD.$() + File.separator + "*");
container.setEnvironment(appMasterEnv);
```

Include the classpath as a variable to export to the container's environment.

The final steps are specifying the memory and CPU resources needed by the ApplicationMaster, followed by the application submission:[4]

Set the number of virtual cores.

Specify the amount of memory needed by the ApplicationMaster in megabytes.

```
Resource capability = Records.newRecord(Resource.class);
capability.setMemory(256);
capability.setVirtualCores(1);
```

Give your application a name.

```
// Finally, set-up ApplicationSubmissionContext for the application
ApplicationSubmissionContext appContext =
    app.getApplicationSubmissionContext();
appContext.setApplicationName("basic-dshell");
```

---

[4] GitHub source: https://github.com/alexholmes/hiped2/blob/master/src/main/java/hip/ch10/dstat/Client.java.

Set the memory
and CPU
properties.

Set the container properties
(specified in the previous code).

Specify which
scheduler queue
to submit the
container to.

```
appContext.setAMContainerSpec(container);
appContext.setResource(capability);
appContext.setQueue("default");

ApplicationId appId = appContext.getApplicationId();
yarnClient.submitApplication(appContext);
```

Tell the ResourceManager to
launch the ApplicationMaster.

All container requests sent to the ResourceManager are processed asynchronously, so just because submitApplication returns doesn't mean your ApplicationMaster is up and running. To figure out the state of your application, you'll need to poll the Resource-Manager for the application status, which will be covered next.

Waiting for the YARN application to complete

After submitting an application, you can poll the ResourceManager for information on the state of your ApplicationMaster. The result will contain details such as

- The state of your application
- The host the ApplicationMaster is running on, and an RPC port (if any) where it's listening for client requests (not applicable in our example)
- A tracking URL, if supported by the ApplicationMaster, which provides details on the progress of the application (again not supported in our example)
- General information such as the queue name and container start time

Your ApplicationMaster can be in any one of the states shown in figure 10.6 (the states are contained in the enum YarnApplicationState).

The following code performs the final step of your client, which is to regularly poll the ResourceManager until the ApplicationMaster has completed:[5]

Define the
terminal
ApplicationMaster
states.

Loop until the
ApplicationMaster
is in a terminal
state.

```
ApplicationReport report = yarnClient.getApplicationReport(appId);
YarnApplicationState state = report.getYarnApplicationState();

EnumSet<YarnApplicationState> terminalStates =
    EnumSet.of(YarnApplicationState.FINISHED,
        YarnApplicationState.KILLED,
        YarnApplicationState.FAILED);

while (!terminalStates.contains(state)) {
    TimeUnit.SECONDS.sleep(1);
    report = yarnClient.getApplicationReport(appId);
    state = report.getYarnApplicationState();
}
```

Fetch current state of
the application from
the ResourceManager.

Refetch the
application state.

---

[5] GitHub source: https://github.com/alexholmes/hiped2/blob/master/src/main/java/hip/ch10/dstat/ Client.java.

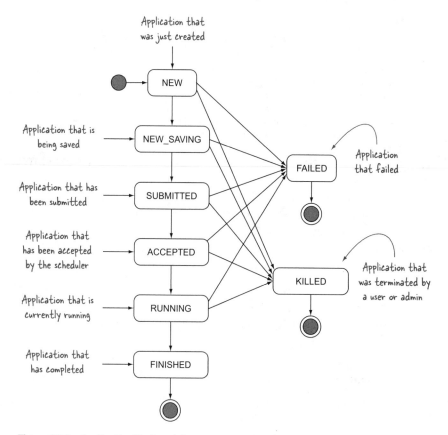

Figure 10.6   ApplicationMaster states

■ **Summary**

There are a number of more advanced client capabilities that weren't explored in this section, such as security. Section 10.3 discusses this and other features that you'll probably want to build into your client.

With your YARN client in place, it's time to turn to the second half of your YARN application—the ApplicationMaster.

TECHNIQUE 102   A bare-bones ApplicationMaster

The ApplicationMaster is the coordinator of the YARN application. It's responsible for asking the ResourceManager for containers and then launching the containers via the NodeManager. Figure 10.7 shows these interactions, which you'll explore in this technique.

■ **Problem**

You're building a YARN application and need to implement an ApplicationMaster.

■ **Solution**

Use the YARN ApplicationMaster APIs to coordinate your work via the Resource-Manager and NodeManager.

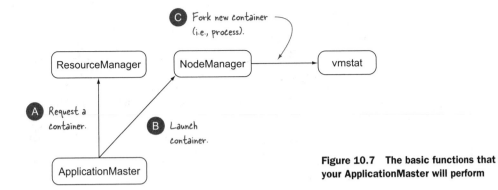

Figure 10.7   The basic functions that
your ApplicationMaster will perform

■ **Discussion**

As in the previous technique, we'll break down the actions that the ApplicationMaster
needs to perform.

Register with the ResourceManager

The first step is to register the ApplicationMaster with the ResourceManager. To do
so, you need to get a handle to an `AMRMClient` instance, which you'll use for all your
communication with the ResourceManager:[6]

```
Configuration conf = new YarnConfiguration();
```
Create a client to talk to the ResourceManager.

```
AMRMClient<ContainerRequest> client = AMRMClient.createAMRMClient();
client.init(conf);
client.start();
```
Register with the ResourceManager.

```
client.registerApplicationMaster("", 0, "");
```

Submit a container request and launch it when one is available

Next you'll need to specify all the containers that you want to request. In this simple
example, you'll request a single container, and you won't specify a specific host or rack
on which it'll run:[7]

Create a client to talk to the NodeManagers.

```
NMClient nmClient = NMClient.createNMClient();
nmClient.init(conf);
nmClient.start();
```

Specify the priority for the container.

```
Priority priority = Records.newRecord(Priority.class);
priority.setPriority(0);
```

Set the resource requirements for the container.

```
Resource capability = Records.newRecord(Resource.class);
capability.setMemory(128);
capability.setVirtualCores(1);
```

Create the request object that you'll send to the ResourceManager.

```
ContainerRequest containerAsk =
```

---

[6] GitHub   source: https://github.com/alexholmes/hiped2/blob/master/src/main/java/hip/ch10/dstat/
ApplicationMaster.java.

[7] GitHub   source: https://github.com/alexholmes/hiped2/blob/master/src/main/java/hip/ch10/dstat/
ApplicationMaster.java.

Send any pending client-side messages (such as the container request), and pull any messages from the ResourceManager.

```
    new ContainerRequest(capability, null, null, priority);
rmClient.addContainerRequest(containerAsk);

boolean allocatedContainer = false;
while (!allocatedContainer) {
  AllocateResponse response = rmClient.allocate(0);
    for (Container container : response.getAllocatedContainers()) {
      allocatedContainer = true;

      ContainerLaunchContext ctx =
          Records.newRecord(ContainerLaunchContext.class);
      ctx.setCommands(
          Collections.singletonList(
            String.format("%s 1>%s/stdout 2>%s/stderr",
              "/usr/bin/vmstat",
              ApplicationConstants.LOG_DIR_EXPANSION_VAR,
              ApplicationConstants.LOG_DIR_EXPANSION_VAR)
        ));
      nmClient.startContainer(container, ctx);
    }
    TimeUnit.SECONDS.sleep(1);
}
```

Loop until you have allocated and launched a container.

Loop through any containers that the ResourceManager allocated to you.

Create a request to launch your container via the NodeManager.

Specify your command and redirect the outputs to disk.

Tell the NodeManager to launch your container.

The `AMRMClient`'s allocate method performs a number of important functions:

- It acts as a heartbeat message to the ResourceManager. If the ResourceManager doesn't receive a heartbeat message after 10 minutes, it will consider the ApplicationMaster to be in a bad state and will kill the process. The default expiry value can be changed by setting `yarn.am.liveness-monitor.expiry-interval-ms`.
- It sends any container allocation requests that were added to the client.
- It receives zero or more allocated containers that resulted from container allocation requests.

The first time that allocate is called in this code, the container request will be sent to the ResourceManager. Because the ResourceManager handles container requests asynchronously, the response won't contain the allocated container. Instead, a subsequent invocation of allocate will return the allocated container.

Wait for the container to complete

At this point you've asked the ResourceManager for a container, received a container allocation from the ResourceManager, and communicated with a NodeManager to launch the container. Now you have to continue to call the allocate method and extract from the response any containers that completed:[8]

Call the allocate method, which also returns completed containers.

```
boolean completedContainer = false;
while (!completedContainer) {
  AllocateResponse response = rmClient.allocate(0);
    for (ContainerStatus s : response.getCompletedContainersStatuses()) {
```

Loop until you receive word that the container has completed.

---

[8] GitHub source: https://github.com/alexholmes/hiped2/blob/master/src/main/java/hip/ch10/dstat/ApplicationMaster.java.

```
                    completedContainer = true;
                }
                TimeUnit.SECONDS.sleep(1);
            }
    rmClient.unregisterApplicationMaster(
            FinalApplicationStatus.SUCCEEDED, "", "");
```

Unregister with the ResourceManager, and then exit the process.

If you received any completed containers, you're done (because you only launched one container).

■ Summary

In this technique you used the `AMRMClient` and `NMClient` classes to communicate with the ResourceManager and NodeManagers. These clients provide synchronous APIs to the YARN services. They have asynchronous counterparts (`AMRMClientAsync` and `NMClient-Async`) that encapsulate the heartbeat functionality and will call back into your code when messages are received from the ResourceManager. The async APIs may make it easier to reason about the interactions with the ResourceManager because the ResourceManager processes everything asynchronously.

There are a few more features that the ResourceManager and NodeManager expose to ApplicationMasters:[9]

Register the ApplicationMaster. This must be called before any other interaction.

Request containers for resources before calling allocate.

Remove previous container request. The previous container request may have already been sent to the ResourceManager, so the app must be prepared to receive an allocation for the previous request even after the remove request.

```
package org.apache.hadoop.yarn.client.api;

abstract class AMRMClient<T extends AMRMClient.ContainerRequest>
        extends AbstractService {

    RegisterApplicationMasterResponse
                registerApplicationMaster(String appHostName,
                                    int appHostPort,
                                    String appTrackingUrl);
    void unregisterApplicationMaster(FinalApplicationStatus appStatus,
                                    String appMessage,
                                    String appTrackingUrl);

    void addContainerRequest(T req);
    AllocateResponse allocate(float progressIndicator);
    void removeContainerRequest(T req);
    void releaseAssignedContainer(ContainerId containerId);

    Resource getAvailableResources();
    int getClusterNodeCount();

    ...
}
```

Unregister the ApplicationMaster. This must be called at the end.

Request additional containers and receive new container allocations.

Release containers assigned by the ResourceManager. If the app can't use the container or wants to give up the container, then it can release it. The app needs to make new requests for the released resource capability if it still needs it.

Get the current number of nodes in the cluster. A valid value is available after a call to allocate has been made.

Get the currently available resources in the cluster. A valid value is available after a call to allocate has been made.

---

9 The complete Javadocs for `AMRMClient` can be viewed at http://hadoop.apache.org/docs/stable/api/org/apache/hadoop/yarn/client/api/AMRMClient.html.

Similarly, the NMClient API exposes a handful of mechanisms that you can use to control and get metadata about your containers:[10]

```
package org.apache.hadoop.yarn.client.api;

abstract class NMClient extends AbstractService {

  Map<String, ByteBuffer> startContainer(Container container,
      ContainerLaunchContext containerLaunchContext);

  void stopContainer(ContainerId containerId, NodeId nodeId);

  ContainerStatus getContainerStatus(ContainerId containerId,
      NodeId nodeId);

  void cleanupRunningContainersOnStop(boolean enabled);
}
```

Start an allocated container.

Stop a started container.

Query the status of a container.

Set whether the containers that are started by this client and are still running should be stopped when the client stops. By default, this feature should be enabled.

At this point you've written the code for a complete YARN application! Next you'll execute your application on a cluster.

TECHNIQUE 103   **Running the application and accessing logs**

At this point you have a functional YARN application. In this section, you'll look at how to run the application and access its output.

■ **Problem**

You want to run your YARN application.

■ **Solution**

Use the regular Hadoop command line to launch it and view the container outputs.

■ **Discussion**

The hip script that you've been using to launch all the examples in this book also works for running the YARN application. Behind the scenes, hip calls the hadoop script to run the examples.

The following example shows the output of running the YARN application that was written in the last two techniques. It runs a vmstat Linux command in a single container:

```
$ hip --nolib hip.ch10.dstat.basic.Client
client.RMProxy: Connecting to ResourceManager at /0.0.0.0:8032
Submitting application application_1398974791337_0055
impl.YarnClientImpl: Submitted application
  application_1398974791337_0055 to ResourceManager at /0.0.0.0:8032
Application application_1398974791337_0055 finished with state FINISHED
```

---

[10] The complete Javadocs for NMClient are available at http://hadoop.apache.org/docs/stable/api/org/apache/hadoop/yarn/client/api/NMClient.html.

If you have log aggregation enabled (see technique 3 for more details), you can issue the following command to view the log output of both the ApplicationMaster and the vmstat container:

```
$ yarn logs -applicationId application_1398974791337_0055
client.RMProxy: Connecting to ResourceManager at /0.0.0.0:8032

Container: container_1398974791337_0055_01_000002          ◄          The output of the
=================================================                      vmstat container
LogType: stderr
LogLength: 0
Log Contents:

LogType: stdout
LogLength: 244
Log Contents:
procs -----------memory---------- -----io---- --system-- -----cpu------
 r  b   swpd   free  buff cache  bi   bo    in  cs us sy id wa st
 2  0  37600  57648 24988 479752  16  109   55  18  1  0 99  0  0


Container: container_1398974791337_0055_01_000001          ◄          The ApplicationMaster
=================================================                                  output
LogType: stderr
LogLength: 297
Log Contents:
client.RMProxy: Connecting to ResourceManager at /0.0.0.0:8030

LogType: stdout
LogLength: 603
Log Contents:
registerApplicationMaster: pending
registerApplicationMaster: complete
adding container ask:Capability[<memory:128, vCores:1>]Priority[0]
Launching container Container: [
  ContainerId: container_1398974791337_0055_01_000002,
  NodeId: localhost.localdomain:40339,
  NodeHttpAddress: localhost.localdomain:8042,
  Resource: <memory:1024, vCores:1>,
  Priority: 0, Token: Token ... ]
Completed container container_id {
  app_attempt_id { application_id {
    id: 55 cluster_timestamp: 1398974791337 }
    attemptId: 1 } id: 2 }
  state: C_COMPLETE diagnostics: ""
  exit_status: 0
```

The ApplicationMaster directed the container standard output to the stdout file, and you can see the output of the vmstat command in that file.

Accessing logs when containers fail to start

It's likely that during the development of your YARN application, either the ApplicationMaster or one of your containers will fail to launch due to missing resources or errors in the startup command. Depending on where the failure occurs, your container logs will have the error related to startup or you'll need to examine the NodeManager logs if the process failed to start outright.

Retaining localized and log directories

The yarn.nodemanager.delete.debug-delay-sec configuration property controls how long the localized and log directories for the application are kept around. The localized directory contains the command executed by the NodeManager to launch containers (both the ApplicationMaster and the application containers), as well as any JARs and other localized resources that were specified by the application for the container.

It's recommended that you set this property to a value that gives you enough time to diagnose failures. But don't set this value too high (say, in the order of days) as this could create pressure on your storage.

An alternative to hunting down ApplicationMaster startup problems is to run an unmanaged ApplicationMaster, which is covered in the next technique.

TECHNIQUE 104 **Debugging using an unmanaged application master**

Debugging a YARN ApplicationMaster is a challenge, as it's launched on a remote node and requires you to pull logs from that node to troubleshoot your code. ApplicationMasters that are launched by the ResourceManager in this way are called *managed* ApplicationMasters, as shown in figure 10.8.

YARN also supports the notion of an *unmanaged* ApplicationMaster, where the ApplicationMaster is launched on a local node, as seen in figure 10.9. Issues with an ApplicationMaster are easier to diagnose when it's running on the local host.

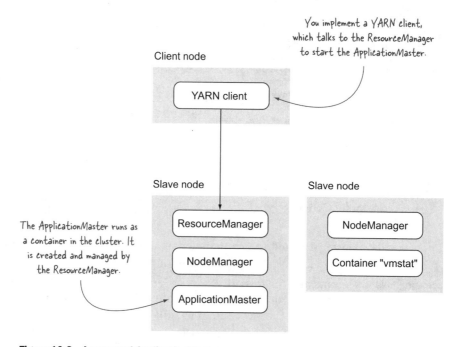

Figure 10.8   A managed ApplicationMaster

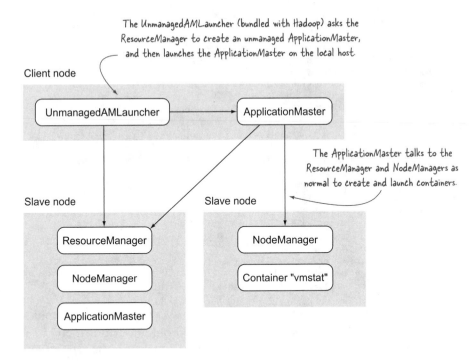

Figure 10.9 An unmanaged ApplicationMaster

In this section you'll discover how to run an unmanaged ApplicationMaster and learn how they can be used by projects.

■ **Problem**

You want to run a local instance of an ApplicationMaster.

■ **Solution**

Run an unmanaged ApplicationMaster.

■ **Discussion**

YARN comes bundled with an application called the UnmanagedAMLauncher, which launches an unmanaged ApplicationMaster. An unmanaged ApplicationMaster is one that is not launched by the ResourceManager. Instead, the UnmanagedAMLauncher liaises with the ResourceManager to create a new application, but instead of issuing a submit-Application call to the ResourceManager (as is the case with managed Application-Masters), the UnmanagedAMLauncher starts the process.

When using the UnmanagedAMLauncher, you don't have to define a YARN client, so all you need to provide are the details required to launch your ApplicationMaster. The following example shows how you can execute the ApplicationMaster that you wrote in the previous techniques:

```
$ hadoop jar $HADOOP_YARN_HOME/share/hadoop/yarn/
hadoop-yarn-applications-unmanaged-am-launcher-2.2.0.jar \        The classpath containing
    Client \                                                       your YARN application
    -classpath $HIP_HOME/hip-2.0.0.jar \    ◀
```

```
-cmd "java hip.ch10.dstat.ApplicationMaster"
```
The command to launch the ApplicationMaster

```
client.RMProxy: Connecting to ResourceManager at /0.0.0.0:8032
UnmanagedAMLauncher: Setting up application submission context for ASM
UnmanagedAMLauncher: Setting unmanaged AM
UnmanagedAMLauncher: Submitting application to ASM
impl.YarnClientImpl: Submitted application
   application_1398974791337_0065 to ResourceManager at /0.0.0.0:8032
UnmanagedAMLauncher: Got application report from ASM for, appId=65, ...
UnmanagedAMLauncher: Launching application with id:
   appattempt_1398974791337_0065_000001
client.RMProxy: Connecting to ResourceManager at /0.0.0.0:8030
registerApplicationMaster: pending
registerApplicationMaster: complete
adding container ask:Capability[<memory:128, vCores:1>]Priority[0]
Launching container Container:
  [ContainerId: container_1398974791337_0065_01_000001, ... ]
ContainerManagementProtocolProxy: Opening proxy : localhost:40339
Completed container ... exit_status: 0
UnmanagedAMLauncher: AM process exited with value: 0
UnmanagedAMLauncher: App ended with state: FINISHED
UnmanagedAMLauncher: Application has completed successfully.
```

The UnmanagedAMLauncher captures the ApplicationMaster's standard output and standard error and outputs them to its own standard output. This is useful in situations where your ApplicationMaster is failing to start, in which case the error will be seen in the output of the preceding command, as opposed to being tucked away in the logs of the NodeManager.

Figure 10.10 shows the interactions between the UnmanagedAMLauncher and the ResourceManager.

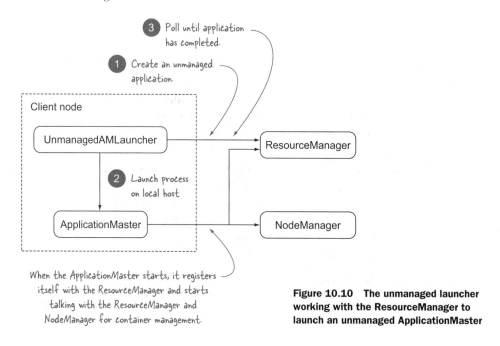

Figure 10.10   The unmanaged launcher working with the ResourceManager to launch an unmanaged ApplicationMaster

There's nothing stopping you from writing your own unmanaged ApplicationMaster launcher if the capabilities in UnmanagedAMLauncher are too limited. The following code shows the key step that the UnmanagedAMLauncher takes to tell the ResourceManager that the ApplicationMaster is unmanaged:

```
ApplicationSubmissionContext appContext = ...;

appContext.setUnmanagedAM(true);
```

Unmanaged ApplicationMasters are useful as they provide local access to an ApplicationMaster, which can ease your debugging and profiling efforts.

Next, let's look at some more advanced capabilities that you may want to support in your YARN applications.

10.3 *Additional YARN application capabilities*

So far in this chapter, we've looked at a bare-bones YARN application that launches a Linux command in a container. However, if you're developing a YARN application, it's likely that you'll need to support more sophisticated capabilities. This section highlights some features that you may need to support in your application.

10.3.1 *RPC between components*

If you have a long-running application, you may want to allow clients to communicate with the ApplicationMaster. Your ApplicationMaster may also need to be able to communicate with containers, and vice versa. An example could be a SQL-on-Hadoop application that allows clients to send queries to the ApplicationMaster, and whose ApplicationMaster then coordinates containers to perform the work.

YARN doesn't provide you with any plumbing here, so you need to pick an RPC protocol and supporting library. You have a few options:

- *Thrift or Avro*—Both of these provide an interface definition language (IDL) where you can define endpoints and messages, which are compiled into concrete client and service code that can be easily incorporated into your code. The advantages of these libraries are code generation and schema evolution, allowing your services to evolve over time.
- *Protocol Buffers*—Google didn't open source the RPC layer, so you'll need to roll your own. You can use REST over HTTP for your transport and easily implement it all using Jersey's annotations.
- *Hadoop's RPC*—Behind the scenes, this uses Protocol Buffers.

Because YARN doesn't support communication between your components, how can you know which hosts or ports your services are listening on?

10.3.2 Service discovery

YARN can schedule multiple containers on the same node, so hard-wiring the listening port for any service in your container or ApplicationMaster isn't ideal. Instead, you can pick one of the following strategies:

- If your ApplicationMaster has a built-in service, pass the launched containers the ApplicationMaster host and port details, and have containers call back to the ApplicationMaster with their port number.
- Use ZooKeeper as a service registry by having containers publish their host and port details to ZooKeeper, and have clients look up services in ZooKeeper. This is the strategy that Apache Twill, covered later in this chapter, employs.

Next up is a look at maintaining state in your application so that you can resume from a well-known state in the event of an application restart.

10.3.3 Checkpointing application progress

If your application is long-running and maintains and builds state during its execution, you may need to periodically persist that state so that in the event of a container restart, a container or ApplicationMaster can pick up where it left off. Containers can be killed for a variety of reasons, including making resources available for other users and applications. ApplicationMasters going down are typically the result of an error in your application logic, the node going down, or a cluster restart.

Two services you can use for checkpointing are HDFS and ZooKeeper. Apache Twill, an abstracted framework for writing YARN applications, uses ZooKeeper to checkpoint container and ApplicationMaster state.

One area to be aware of with checkpointing is handling split-brain situations.

10.3.4 Avoiding split-brain

It's possible that a networking problem will result in the ResourceManager believing that an ApplicationMaster is down and launching a new ApplicationMaster. This can lead to an undesired outcome if your application produces outputs or intermediary data in a way that's not idempotent.

This was a problem in the early MapReduce YARN application, where task- and job-level commits could be executed more than once, which was not ideal for commit actions that couldn't be repeatedly executed.[11] The solution was to introduce a delay in committing, and to use the ResourceManager heartbeat to verify that the Application-Master was still valid. Refer to the JIRA ticket for more details.

10.3.5 Long-running applications

Some YARN applications, such as Impala, are long-running, and as a result have requirements that differ from applications that are more transient in nature. If your

---

[11] See the JIRA ticket titled "MR AM can get in a split brain situation" at https://issues.apache.org/jira/browse/MAPREDUCE-4832.

application is also long-lived, you should be aware of the following points, some of which are currently being worked on in the community:

- Gang scheduling, which allows a large number of containers to be scheduled in a short period of time (YARN-624).
- Long-lived container support, allowing containers to indicate the fact that they're long-lived so that the scheduler can make better allocation and management decisions (YARN-1039).
- Anti-affinity settings, so that applications can specify that multiple containers aren't allocated on the same node (YARN-397).
- Renewal of delegation tokens when running on a secure Hadoop cluster. Kerberos tokens expire, and if they're not renewed, you won't be able to access services such as HDFS (YARN-941).

There's an umbrella JIRA ticket that contains more details: https://issues.apache.org/jira/browse/YARN-896.

Even though Impala is a YARN application, it uses unmanaged containers and its own gang-scheduling mechanism to work around some of the issues with long-running applications. As a result, Cloudera created a project called Llama (http://cloudera.github.io/llama/), which mediates resource management between Impala and YARN to provide these features. Llama may be worth evaluating for your needs.

10.3.6 Security

YARN applications running on secure Hadoop clusters need to pass tokens to the ResourceManager that will be passed on to your application. These tokens are required to access services such as HDFS. Twill, detailed in the next section, provides support for secure Hadoop clusters.

This concludes our overview of additional capabilities that you may need in your YARN applications. Next up is a look at YARN programming abstractions, some of which implement the capabilities discussed in this section.

10.4 YARN programming abstractions

YARN exposes a low-level API and has a steep learning curve, especially if you need to support many of the features that were outlined in the previous section. There are a number of abstractions on top of YARN that simplify the development of YARN applications and help you focus on implementing your application logic without worrying about the mechanics of YARN. Some of these frameworks, such as Twill, also support more advanced capabilities, such as shipping logs to the YARN client and service discovery via ZooKeeper.

In this section I'll provide a brief summary of three such abstractions: Apache Twill, Spring, and REEF.

10.4.1 *Twill*

Apache Twill (http://twill.incubator.apache.org/), formerly known as Weave, not only provides a rich and high-level programming abstraction, but also supports many features that you'll likely require in your YARN application, such as service discovery, log shipping, and resiliency to failure.

The following code shows an example YARN client written in Twill. You'll note that construction of the YarnTwillRunnerService requires a ZooKeeper connection URL, which is used to register the YARN application. Twill also supports shipping logs to the client (via Kafka), and here you're adding a log handler to write the container and ApplicationMaster logs to standard output:

```
YarnConfiguration config = new YarnConfiguration();

YarnTwillRunnerService runnerService = new YarnTwillRunnerService(
    new YarnConfiguration(),
    "127.0.0.1:2181/twill");
runnerService.startAndWait();

TwillController controller =
    runnerService.prepare(new DStats())
    .addLogHandler(new PrinterLogHandler(
        new PrintWriter(System.out)))
    .start();

final CountDownLatch stopLatch = new CountDownLatch(1);
controller.addListener(new ServiceListenerAdapter() {

    @Override
    public void terminated(Service.State from) {
        stopLatch.countDown();
    }

    @Override
    public void failed(Service.State from, Throwable failure) {
        stopLatch.countDown();
    }
}, Threads.SAME_THREAD_EXECUTOR);

stopLatch.await();
```

Create the client service and configure it with the ZooKeeper URL.

The controller is used to configure and manage a YARN application.

Specify the Runnable that will be executed in a container.

Write out the container logs to standard output.

Register a callback handler to capture failure and termination messages.

Twill's programming model uses well-known Java types such as Runnable to model container execution. The following code shows a container that launches the vmstat utility:

AbstractTwillRunnable extends Runnable and provides additional capabilities, such as receiving messages from the YARN client or ApplicationMaster.

```
public final class DStats extends AbstractTwillRunnable {

    @Override
    public void run() {
        try {
```

Implement the Runnable.run method, which is executed within a container.

```
Process process = new ProcessBuilder("vmstat")          ◄─── Launch a vmstat process.
    .redirectErrorStream(true).start();
BufferedReader reader = new BufferedReader(             ◄───     Capture and log the
    new InputStreamReader(process.getInputStream(),             vmstat standard output.
                    Charsets.US_ASCII));
  try {
    String line = reader.readLine();
    while (line != null) {
      LOG.info(line);
      line = reader.readLine();
    }
  } finally {
    reader.close();
  }
} catch (IOException e) {
  LOG.error("Fail to execute command ", e);
}
}
}
```

Figure 10.11 shows how Twill uses ZooKeeper and Kafka to support features such as log shipping and service discovery.

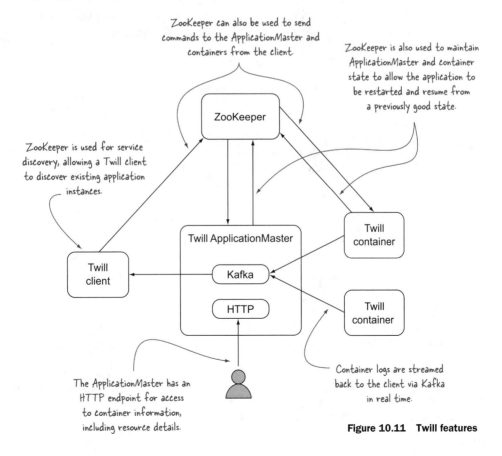

Figure 10.11   Twill features

You can get a detailed overview of Twill from Terence Yim's "Harnessing the Power of YARN with Apache Twill" (http://www.slideshare.net/TerenceYim1/twill-apache-con-2014?ref=). Yim also has a couple of blog entries on programming with Twill (formerly Weave).[12]

10.4.2 Spring

The 2.x release of Spring for Hadoop (http://projects.spring.io/spring-hadoop/) brings support for simplifying YARN development. It differs from Twill in that it's focused on abstracting the YARN API and not on providing application features; Twill, in contrast, offers log shipping and service discovers. But it's very possible that you may not want the added complexity that these features bring to Twill and instead want more control over your YARN application. If so, this may make Spring for Hadoop a better candidate.

Spring for Hadoop provides default implementations of a YARN client, ApplicationMaster, and container that can be overridden to provide application-specific functionality. You can actually write a YARN application without writing any code! The following example is from the Spring Hadoop samples, showing how you can configure a YARN application to run a remote command.[13] This first snippet shows the application context, and configures the HDFS, YARN, and application JARs:

```
<beans ...>

  <context:property-placeholder location="hadoop.properties"
                  system-properties-mode="OVERRIDE"/>

  <yarn:configuration>
    fs.defaultFS=${hd.fs}
    yarn.resourcemanager.address=${hd.rm}
    fs.hdfs.impl=org.apache.hadoop.hdfs.DistributedFileSystem
  </yarn:configuration>

  <yarn:localresources>
    <yarn:hdfs path="/app/simple-command/*.jar"/>
    <yarn:hdfs path="/lib/*.jar"/>
  </yarn:localresources>

  <yarn:environment>
    <yarn:classpath use-yarn-app-classpath="true"/>
  </yarn:environment>

  <util:properties id="arguments">
    <prop key="container-count">4</prop>
  </util:properties>
```

---

[12] Terence Yim, "Programming with Weave, Part I," http://blog.continuuity.com/post/66694376303/programming-with-weave-part-i; "Programming with Apache Twill, Part II," http://blog.continuuity.com/post/73969347586/programming-with-apache-twill-part-ii.

[13] "Spring Yarn Simple Command Example," https://github.com/spring-projects/spring-hadoop-samples/tree/master/yarn/yarn/simple-command.

```
    <yarn:client app-name="simple-command">
      <yarn:master-runner arguments="arguments"/>
    </yarn:client>
</beans>
```

The following code defines the ApplicationMaster properties and tells it to run the vmstat command:

```
<beans ...>

  <context:property-placeholder location="hadoop.properties"/>

  <bean id="taskScheduler" class="
org.springframework.scheduling.concurrent.ConcurrentTaskScheduler"/>
  <bean id="taskExecutor" class="
org.springframework.core.task.SyncTaskExecutor"/>

  <yarn:configuration>
    fs.defaultFS=${SHDP_HD_FS}
    yarn.resourcemanager.address=${SHDP_HD_RM}
    yarn.resourcemanager.scheduler.address=${SHDP_HD_SCHEDULER}
  </yarn:configuration>

  <yarn:localresources>
    <yarn:hdfs path="/app/simple-command/*.jar"/>
    <yarn:hdfs path="/lib/*.jar"/>
  </yarn:localresources>

  <yarn:environment>
    <yarn:classpath use-yarn-app-classpath="true" delimiter=":">
      ./*
    </yarn:classpath>
  </yarn:environment>

  <yarn:master>
    <yarn:container-allocator/>
    <yarn:container-command>
    <![CDATA[
    vmstat
    1><LOG_DIR>/Container.stdout
    2><LOG_DIR>/Container.stderr
    ]]>
    </yarn:container-command>
  </yarn:master>

</beans>
```

The samples also include a look at how you can extend the client, ApplicationMaster, and container.[14]

You can find some sample Spring for Hadoop applications on GitHub (https:// github.com/spring-projects/spring-hadoop-samples). There's also a wiki for the project: https://github.com/spring-projects/spring-hadoop/wiki.

---

[14] Example of extending the Spring YARN classes: "Spring Yarn Custom Application Master Service Example," https://github.com/spring-projects/spring-hadoop-samples/tree/master/yarn/yarn/custom-amservice.

10.4.3   *REEF*

REEF is a framework from Microsoft that simplifies scalable, fault-tolerant runtime environments for a range of computational models, including YARN and Mesos (www.reef-project.org/; https://github.com/Microsoft-CISL/REEF). REEF has some interesting capabilities, such as container reuse and data caching.

You can find a REEF tutorial on GitHub: https://github.com/Microsoft-CISL/REEF/wiki/How-to-download-and-compile-REEF.

10.4.4   *Picking a YARN API abstraction*

YARN abstractions are still in their early stages because YARN is a young technology. This section provided a brief overview of three abstractions that you could use to hide away some of the complexities of the YARN API. But which one should you pick for your application?

- *Apache Twill* looks the most promising, as it already encapsulates many of the features that you'll need in your application. It has picked best-of-breed technologies such as Kafka and ZooKeeper to support these features.
- *Spring for Hadoop* may be a better fit if you're developing a lightweight application and you don't want a dependency on Kafka or ZooKeeper.
- *REEF* may be useful if you have some complex application requirements, such as the need to run on multiple execution frameworks, or if you need to support more complex container choreographies and state sharing across containers.

10.5   *Chapter summary*

This chapter showed you how to write a simple YARN application and then introduced you to some of the more advanced capabilities that you may need in your YARN applications. It also looked at some YARN abstractions that make it easier to write your applications. You're now all set to go out and start writing the next big YARN application.

This concludes not only this chapter but the book as a whole! I hope you've enjoyed the journey and along the way have picked up some tips and tricks that you can employ in your Hadoop applications and environments. If you have any questions about items covered in this book, please head on over to Manning's forum dedicated to this book and post a question.[15]

---

[15] Manning forum for Hadoop in Practice: http://www.manning-sandbox.com/forum.jspa?forumID=901.

appendix
Installing
Hadoop and friends

This appendix contains instructions on how to install Hadoop and other tools that are used in the book.

Getting started quickly with Hadoop The quickest way to get up and running with Hadoop is to download a preinstalled virtual machine from one of the Hadoop vendors. Following is a list of the popular VMs:

- Cloudera Quickstart VM—http://www.cloudera.com/content/cloudera-content/ cloudera-docs/DemoVMs/Cloudera-QuickStart-VM/cloudera_quickstart_vm.html
- Hortonworks Sandbox—http://hortonworks.com/products/hortonworks-sandbox/
- MapR Sandbox for Hadoop—http://doc.mapr.com/display/MapR/MapR +Sandbox+for+Hadoop

A.1 Code for the book

Before we get to the instructions for installing Hadoop, let's get you set up with the code that accompanies this book. The code is hosted on GitHub at https:// github.com/alexholmes/hiped2. To get you up and running quickly, there are pre-packaged tarballs that don't require you to build the code—just install and go.

Downloading
First you'll need to download the most recent release of the code from https:// github.com/alexholmes/hiped2/releases.

Installing

The second step is to unpackage the tarball into a directory of your choosing. For example, the following untars the code into /usr/local, the same directory where you'll install Hadoop:

```
$ cd /usr/local
$ sudo tar -xzvf <download directory>/hip-<version>-package.tar.gz
```

Adding the home directory to your path

All the examples in the book assume that the home directory for the code is in your path. The methods for doing this differ by operating system and shell. If you're on Linux using Bash, then the following should work (use of the single quotes for the second command is required to avoid variable substitution):

```
$ echo "export HIP_HOME=/usr/local/hip-<version>" >> ~/.bash_profile
$ echo 'export PATH=${PATH}:${HIP_HOME}/bin' >> ~/.bash_profile
```

Running an example job

You can run the following commands to test your installation. This assumes that you have a running Hadoop setup (if you don't, please jump to section A.3):

```
# create two input files in HDFS
$ hadoop fs -mkdir -p hip/input
$ echo "cat sat mat" | hadoop fs -put - hip/input/1.txt
$ echo "dog lay mat" | hadoop fs -put - hip/input/2.txt

# run the inverted index example
$ hip hip.ch1.InvertedIndexJob --input hip/input --output hip/output

# examine the results in HDFS
$ hadoop fs -cat hip/output/part*
```

Downloading the sources and building

There are some techniques (such as Avro code generation) that require access to the full sources. First, check out the sources using git:

```
$ git clone git@github.com:alexholmes/hiped2.git
```

Set up your environment so that some techniques know where the source is installed:

```
$ echo "export HIP_SRC=<installation dir>/hiped2" >> ~/.bash_profile
```

You can build the project using Maven:

```
$ cd hiped2
$ mvn clean validate package
```

This generates a target/hip-<version>-package.tar.gz file, which is the same file that's uploaded to GitHub when releases are made.

A.2 Recommended Java versions

The Hadoop project keeps a list of recommended Java versions that have been proven to work well with Hadoop in production. For details, take a look at "Hadoop Java Versions" on the Hadoop Wiki at http://wiki.apache.org/hadoop/HadoopJavaVersions.

A.3 Hadoop

This section covers installing, configuring, and running the Apache distribution of Hadoop. Please refer to distribution-specific instructions if you're working with a different distribution of Hadoop.

Apache tarball installation

The following instructions are for users who want to install the tarball version of the vanilla Apache Hadoop distribution. This is a a pseudo-distributed setup and not for a multi-node cluster.[1]

First you'll need to download the tarball from the Apache downloads page at http://hadoop.apache.org/common/releases.html#Download and extract the tarball under /usr/local:

```
$ cd /usr/local
$ sudo tar -xzf <path-to-apache-tarball>

$ sudo ln -s hadoop-<version> hadoop

$ sudo chown -R <user>:<group> /usr/local/hadoop*
$ mkdir /usr/local/hadoop/tmp
```

> **Installation directory for users that don't have root privileges** If you don't have root permissions on your host, you can install Hadoop under a different directory and substitute instances of /usr/local in the following instructions with your directory name.

Configuration for pseudo-distributed mode for Hadoop 1 and earlier

The following instructions work for Hadoop version 1 and earlier. Skip to the next section if you're working with Hadoop 2.

Edit the file /usr/local/hadoop/conf/core-site.xml and make sure it looks like the following:

```
<?xml version="1.0"?>
<?xml-stylesheet type="text/xsl" href="configuration.xsl"?>

<configuration>

  <property>
    <name>hadoop.tmp.dir</name>
```

---

[1] Pseudo-distributed mode is when you have all the Hadoop components running on a single host.

```
    <value>/usr/local/hadoop/tmp</value>
  </property>

  <property>
    <name>fs.default.name</name>
    <value>hdfs://localhost:8020</value>
  </property>

</configuration>
```

Then edit the file /usr/local/hadoop/conf/hdfs-site.xml and make sure it looks like the following:

```
<?xml version="1.0"?>
<?xml-stylesheet type="text/xsl" href="configuration.xsl"?>

<configuration>
  <property>
    <name>dfs.replication</name>
    <value>1</value>
  </property>
  <property>
    <!-- specify this so that running 'hadoop namenode -format'
         formats the right dir -->
    <name>dfs.name.dir</name>
    <value>/usr/local/hadoop/cache/hadoop/dfs/name</value>
  </property>
</configuration>
```

Finally, edit the file /usr/local/hadoop/conf/mapred-site.xml and make sure it looks like the following (you may first need to copy mapred-site.xml.template to mapred-site.xml):

```
<?xml version="1.0"?>
<?xml-stylesheet type="text/xsl" href="configuration.xsl"?>

<configuration>
  <property>
    <name>mapred.job.tracker</name>
    <value>localhost:8021</value>
  </property>
</configuration>
```

Configuration for pseudo-distributed mode for Hadoop 2

The following instructions work for Hadoop 2. See the previous section if you're working with Hadoop version 1 and earlier.

Edit the file /usr/local/hadoop/etc/hadoop/core-site.xml and make sure it looks like the following:

```
<?xml version="1.0"?>
<?xml-stylesheet type="text/xsl" href="configuration.xsl"?>

<configuration>

  <property>
```

```
    <name>hadoop.tmp.dir</name>
    <value>/usr/local/hadoop/tmp</value>
  </property>

  <property>
    <name>fs.default.name</name>
    <value>hdfs://localhost:8020</value>
  </property>

</configuration>
```

Then edit the file /usr/local/hadoop/etc/hadoop/hdfs-site.xml and make sure it looks like the following:

```
<?xml version="1.0"?>
<?xml-stylesheet type="text/xsl" href="configuration.xsl"?>

<configuration>
  <property>
    <name>dfs.replication</name>
    <value>1</value>
  </property>
</configuration>
```

Next, edit the file /usr/local/hadoop/etc/hadoop/mapred-site.xml and make sure it looks like the following:

```
<?xml version="1.0"?>
<?xml-stylesheet type="text/xsl" href="configuration.xsl"?>

<configuration>
  <property>
    <name>mapreduce.framework.name</name>
    <value>yarn</value>
  </property>
</configuration>
```

Finally, edit the file /usr/local/hadoop/etc/hadoop/yarn-site.xml and make sure it looks like the following:

```
<?xml version="1.0"?>
<?xml-stylesheet type="text/xsl" href="configuration.xsl"?>

<configuration>
  <property>
    <name>yarn.nodemanager.aux-services</name>
    <value>mapreduce_shuffle</value>
    <description>Shuffle service that needs to be set for
                    Map Reduce to run.</description>
  </property>
  <property>
    <name>yarn.log-aggregation-enable</name>
    <value>true</value>
  </property>
  <property>
```

```
    <name>yarn.log-aggregation.retain-seconds</name>
    <value>2592000</value>
</property>
<property>
    <name>yarn.log.server.url</name>
    <value>http://0.0.0.0:19888/jobhistory/logs/</value>
</property>
<property>
    <name>yarn.nodemanager.delete.debug-delay-sec</name>
    <value>-1</value>
    <description>Amount of time in seconds to wait before
                deleting container resources.</description>
</property>
</configuration>
```

Set up SSH

Hadoop uses Secure Shell (SSH) to remotely launch processes such as the Data-Node and TaskTracker, even when everything is running on a single node in pseudo-distributed mode. If you don't already have an SSH key pair, create one with the following command:

```
$ ssh-keygen -b 2048 -t rsa
```

You'll need to copy the .ssh/id_rsa file to the authorized_keys file:

```
$ cp ~/.ssh/id_rsa.pub  ~/.ssh/authorized_keys
```

You'll also need an SSH agent running so that you aren't prompted to enter your password a bazillion times when starting and stopping Hadoop. Different operating systems have different ways of running an SSH agent, and there are details online for CentOS and other Red Hat derivatives[2] and for OS X.[3] Google is your friend if you're running on a different system.

To verify that the agent is running and has your keys loaded, try opening an SSH connection to the local system:

```
$ ssh 127.0.0.1
```

If you're prompted for a password, the agent's not running or doesn't have your keys loaded.

Java

You need a current version of Java (1.6 or newer) installed on your system. You'll need to ensure that the system path includes the binary directory of your Java installation. Alternatively, you can edit /usr/local/hadoop/conf/hadoop-env.sh, uncomment the JAVA_HOME line, and update the value with the location of your Java installation.

---

[2] See the Red Hat Deployment Guide section on "Configuring ssh-agent" at www.centos.org/docs/5/html/5.2/Deployment_Guide/s3-openssh-config-ssh-agent.html.

[3] See "Using SSH Agent With Mac OS X Leopard" at www-uxsup.csx.cam.ac.uk/~aia21/osx/leopard-ssh.html.

Environment settings

For convenience, it's recommended that you add the Hadoop binary directory to your path. The following code shows what you can add to the bottom of your Bash shell profile file in ~/.bash_profile (assuming you're running Bash):

```
HADOOP_HOME=/usr/local/hadoop
PATH=$PATH:$HADOOP_HOME/bin:$HADOOP_HOME/sbin
export PATH
```

Format HDFS

Next you need to format HDFS. The rest of the commands in this section assume that the Hadoop binary directory exists in your path, as per the preceding instructions. On Hadoop 1 and earlier, type

```
$ hadoop namenode -format
```

On Hadoop versions 2 and newer, type

```
$ hdfs namenode -format
```

After HDFS has been formatted, you're ready to start Hadoop.

Starting Hadoop 1 and earlier

A single command can be used to start Hadoop on versions 1 and earlier:

```
$ start-all.sh
```

After running the start script, use the jps Java utility to check that all the processes are running. You should see the following output (with the exception of the process IDs, which will be different):

```
$ jps
23836 JobTracker
23475 NameNode
23982 TaskTracker
23619 DataNode
24024 Jps
23756 SecondaryNameNode
```

If any of these processes aren't running, check the logs directory (/usr/local/hadoop/logs) to see why the processes didn't start correctly. Each of the preceding processes has two output files that can be identified by name and should be checked for errors.

The most common error is that the HDFS formatting step, which I showed earlier, was skipped.

Starting Hadoop 2

The following commands are required to start Hadoop version 2:

```
$ yarn-daemon.sh start resourcemanager
$ yarn-daemon.sh start nodemanager
$ hadoop-daemon.sh start namenode
$ hadoop-daemon.sh start datanode
$ mr-jobhistory-daemon.sh start historyserver
```

After running the start script, use the jps Java utility to check that all the processes are running. You should see the output that follows, although the ordering and process IDs will differ:

```
$ jps
32542 NameNode
1085  Jps
32131 ResourceManager
32613 DataNode
32358 NodeManager
1030  JobHistoryServer
```

If any of these processes aren't running, check the logs directory (/usr/local/ hadoop/logs) to see why the processes didn't start correctly. Each of the preceding processes has two output files that can be identified by name and should be checked for errors. The most common error is that the HDFS formatting step, which I showed earlier, was skipped.

Creating a home directory for your user on HDFS

Once Hadoop is up and running, the first thing you'll want to do is create a home directory for your user. If you're running on Hadoop 1, the command is

```
$ hadoop fs -mkdir /user/<your-linux-username>
```

On Hadoop 2, you'll run

```
$ hdfs dfs -mkdir -p /user/<your-linux-username>
```

Verifying the installation

The following commands can be used to test your Hadoop installation. The first two commands create a directory in HDFS and create a file in HDFS:

```
$ hadoop fs -mkdir /tmp
$ echo "the cat sat on the mat" | hadoop fs -put - /tmp/input.txt
```

Next you want to run a word-count MapReduce job. On Hadoop 1 and earlier, run the following:

```
$ hadoop jar /usr/local/hadoop/*-examples*.jar wordcount \
  /tmp/input.txt /tmp/output
```

On Hadoop 2, run the following:

```
$ hadoop jar /usr/local/hadoop/share/hadoop/mapreduce/*-examples*.jar \
  wordcount /tmp/input.txt /tmp/output
```

Examine and verify the MapReduce job outputs on HDFS (the outputs will differ based on the contents of the config files that you used for the job inputs):

```
$ hadoop fs -cat /tmp/output/part*
at    1
mat   1
on    1
sat   1
the   2
```

Stopping Hadoop 1

To stop Hadoop 1, use the following command:

```
$ stop-all.sh
```

Stopping Hadoop 2

To stop Hadoop 2, use the following commands:

```
$ mr-jobhistory-daemon.sh stop historyserver
$ hadoop-daemon.sh stop datanode
$ hadoop-daemon.sh stop namenode
$ yarn-daemon.sh stop nodemanager
$ yarn-daemon.sh stop resourcemanager
```

Just as with starting, the jps command can be used to verify that all the Hadoop processes have stopped.

Hadoop 1.x UI ports

There are a number of web applications in Hadoop. Table A.1 lists them, along with the ports they run on and their URLs (assuming they're running on the local host, as is the case if you have a pseudo-distributed installation running).

Table A.1 Hadoop 1.x web applications and ports

Component	Default port	Config parameter	Local URL
MapReduce JobTracker	50030	mapred.job.tracker.http.address	http://127.0.0.1:50030/
MapReduce TaskTracker	50060	mapred.task.tracker.http.address	http://127.0.0.1:50060/
HDFS NameNode	50070	dfs.http.address	http://127.0.0.1:50070/
HDFS DataNode	50075	dfs.datanode.http.address	http://127.0.0.1:50075/
HDFS Secondary-NameNode	50090	dfs.secondary.http.address	http://127.0.0.1:50090/
HDFS Backup and Checkpoint Node	50105	dfs.backup.http.address	http://127.0.0.1:50105/

Each of these URLs supports the following common paths:

- */logs*—This shows a listing of all the files under hadoop.log.dir. By default, this is under $HADOOP_HOME/logs on each Hadoop node.
- */logLevel*—This can be used to view and set the logging levels for Java packages.
- */metrics*—This shows JVM and component-level statistics. It's available in Hadoop 0.21 and newer (not in 1.0, 0.20.x, or earlier).
- */stacks*—This shows a stack dump of all the current Java threads in the daemon.

Hadoop 2.x UI ports

There are a number of web applications in Hadoop. Table A.2 lists them, including the ports that they run on and their URLs (assuming they're running on the local host, as is the case if you have a pseudo-distributed installation running).

Table A.2   Hadoop 2.x web applications and ports

Component	Default port	Config parameter	Local URL
YARN Resource-Manager	8088	`yarn.resourcemanager.webapp.address`	http://localhost:8088/cluster
YARN Node-Manager	8042	`yarn.nodemanager.webapp.address`	http://localhost:8042/node
MapReduce Job History	19888	`mapreduce.jobhistory.webapp.address`	http://localhost:19888/jobhistory
HDFS Name-Node	50070	`dfs.http.address`	http://127.0.0.1:50070/
HDFS DataNode	50075	`dfs.datanode.http.address`	http://127.0.0.1:50075/

A.4   Flume

Flume is a log collection and distribution system that can transport data across a large number of hosts into HDFS. It's an Apache project originally developed by Cloudera.

Chapter 5 contains a section on Flume and how it can be used.

Getting more information

Table A.3 lists some useful resources to help you become more familiar with Flume.

Table A.3   Useful resources

Resource	URL
Flume main page	http://flume.apache.org/
Flume user guide	http://flume.apache.org/FlumeUserGuide.html
Flume Getting Started guide	https://cwiki.apache.org/confluence/display/FLUME/Getting+Started

Installation on Apache Hadoop 1.x systems

Follow the Getting Started guide referenced in the resources.

Installation on Apache Hadoop 2.x systems

If you're trying to get Flume 1.4 to work with Hadoop 2, follow the Getting Started guide to install Flume. Next, you'll need to remove the protobuf and guava JARs from Flume's lib directory because they conflict with the versions bundled with Hadoop 2:

```
$ mv ${flume_bin}/lib/{protobuf-java-2.4.1.jar,guava-10.0.1.jar} ~/
```

A.5 Oozie

Oozie is an Apache project that started life inside Yahoo. It's a Hadoop workflow engine that manages data processing activities.

Getting more information

Table A.4 lists some useful resources to help you become more familiar with Oozie.

Table A.4   Useful resources

Resource	URL
Oozie project page	https://oozie.apache.org/
Oozie Quick Start	https://oozie.apache.org/docs/4.0.0/DG_QuickStart.html
Additional Oozie resources	https://oozie.apache.org/docs/4.0.0/index.html

Installation on Hadoop 1.x systems

Follow the Quick Start guide to install Oozie. The Oozie documentation has installation instructions.

If you're using Oozie 4.4.0 and targeting Hadoop 2.2.0, you'll need to run the following commands to patch your Maven files and perform the build:

```
cd oozie-4.0.0/
find . -name pom.xml | xargs sed -ri 's/(2.2.0\-SNAPSHOT)/2.2.0/'
mvn -DskipTests=true -P hadoop-2 clean package assembly:single
```

Installation on Hadoop 2.x systems

Unfortunately Oozie 4.0.0 doesn't play nicely with Hadoop 2. To get Oozie working with Hadoop, you'll first need to download the 4.0.0 tarball from the project page and then unpackage it. Next, run the following command to change the Hadoop version being targeted:

```
$ cd oozie-4.0.0/
$ find . -name pom.xml | xargs sed -ri 's/(2.2.0\-SNAPSHOT)/2.2.0/'
```

Now all you need to do is target the hadoop-2 profile in Maven:

```
$ mvn -DskipTests=true -P hadoop-2 clean package assembly:single
```

A.6   *Sqoop*

Sqoop is a tool for importing data from relational databases into Hadoop and vice versa. It can support any JDBC-compliant database, and it also has native connectors for efficient data transport to and from MySQL and PostgreSQL.

Chapter 5 contains details on how imports and exports can be performed with Sqoop.

Getting more information

Table A.5 lists some useful resources to help you become more familiar with Sqoop.

Table A.5   Useful resources

Resource	URL
Sqoop project page	http://sqoop.apache.org/
Sqoop User Guide	http://sqoop.apache.org/docs/1.4.4/SqoopUserGuide.html

Installation

Download the Sqoop tarball from the project page. Pick the version that matches with your Hadoop installation and explode the tarball. The following instructions assume that you're installing under /usr/local:

```
$ sudo tar -xzf \
    sqoop-<version>.bin.hadoop-<hadoop-version>.tar.gz \
    -C /usr/local/
$ ln -s /usr/local/sqoop-<version> /usr/local/sqoop
```

> **Sqoop 2**   This book currently covers Sqoop version 1. When selecting which tarball to download, please note that version 1.99.x and newer are the Sqoop 2 versions, so be sure to pick an older version.

If you're planning on using Sqoop with MySQL, you'll need to download the MySQL JDBC driver tarball from http://dev.mysql.com/downloads/connector/j/, explode it into a directory, and then copy the JAR file into the Sqoop lib directory:

```
$ tar -xzf mysql-connector-java-<version>.tar.gz
$ cd mysql-connector-java-<version>
$ sudo cp mysql-connector-java-<version>-bin.jar \
  /usr/local/sqoop/lib
```

To run Sqoop, there are a few environment variables that you may need to set. They're listed in table A.6.

The /usr/local/sqoop/bin directory contains the binaries for Sqoop. Chapter 5 contains a number of techniques that show how the binaries are used for imports and exports.

Table A.6 Sqoop environment variables

Environment variable	Description
JAVA_HOME	The directory where Java is installed. If you have the Sun JDK installed on Red Hat, this would be /usr/java/latest.
HADOOP_HOME	The directory of your Hadoop installation.
HIVE_HOME	Only required if you're planning on using Hive with Sqoop. Refers to the directory where Hive was installed.
HBASE_HOME	Only required if you're planning on using HBase with Sqoop. Refers to the directory where HBase was installed.

A.7 HBase

HBase is a real-time, key/value, distributed, column-based database modeled after Google's BigTable.

Getting more information

Table A.7 lists some useful resources to help you become more familiar with HBase.

Table A.7 Useful resources

Resource	URL
Apache HBase project page	http://hbase.apache.org/
Apache HBase Quick Start	http://hbase.apache.org/book/quickstart.html
Apache HBase Reference Guide	http://hbase.apache.org/book/book.html
Cloudera blog post on HBase Dos and Don'ts	http://blog.cloudera.com/blog/2011/04/hbase-dos-and-donts/

Installation

Follow the installation instructions in the Quick Start guide at https://hbase.apache.org/book/quickstart.html.

A.8 Kafka

Kafka is a publish/subscribe messaging system built by LinkedIn.

Getting more information

Table A.8 lists some useful resources to help you become more familiar with Kafka.

Table A.8 Useful resources

Resource	URL
Kafka project page	http://kafka.apache.org/
Kafka documentation	http://kafka.apache.org/documentation.html
Kafka Quick Start	http://kafka.apache.org/08/quickstart.html

Installation

Follow the installation instructions in the Quick Start guide.

A.9 Camus

Camus is a tool for importing data in Kafka into Hadoop.

Getting more information

Table A.9 lists some useful resources to help you become more familiar with Camus.

Table A.9 Useful resources

Resource	URL
Camus project page	https://github.com/linkedin/camus
Camus Overview	https://github.com/linkedin/camus/wiki/Camus-Overview

Installation on Hadoop 1

Download the code from the 0.8 branch in GitHub, and run the following command to build it:

```
$ mvn clean package
```

Installation on Hadoop 2

At the time of writing, the 0.8 version of Camus doesn't support Hadoop 2. You have a couple of options to get it working—if you're just experimenting with Camus, you can download a patched version of the code from my GitHub project. Alternatively, you can patch the Maven build files.

Using my patched GitHub project

Download my cloned and patched version of Camus from GitHub and build it just as you would the Hadoop 1 version:

```
$ wget https://github.com/alexholmes/camus/archive/camus-kafka-0.8.zip
$ unzip camus-kafka-0.8.zip
$ cd camus-camus-kafka-0.8
$ mvn clean package
```

Patching the Maven build files

If you want to patch the original Camus files, you can do that by taking a look at the patch I applied to my own clone: https://mng.bz/Q8GV.

A.10 Avro

Avro is a data serialization system that provides features such as compression, schema evolution, and code generation. It can be viewed as a more sophisticated version of a SequenceFile, with additional features such as schema evolution.

Chapter 3 contains details on how Avro can be used in MapReduce as well as with basic input/output streams.

Getting more information

Table A.10 lists some useful resources to help you become more familiar with Avro.

Table A.10 Useful resources

Resource	URL
Avro project page	http://avro.apache.org/
Avro issue tracking page	https://issues.apache.org/jira/browse/AVRO
Cloudera blog about Avro use	http://blog.cloudera.com/blog/2011/12/apache-avro-at-richrelevance/
CDH usage page for Avro	http://www.cloudera.com/content/cloudera-content/cloudera-docs/CDH5/5.0/CDH5-Installation-Guide/cdh5ig_avro_usage.html

Installation

Avro is a full-fledged Apache project, so you can download the binaries from the downloads link on the Apache project page.

A.11 Apache Thrift

Apache Thrift is essentially Facebook's version of Protocol Buffers. It offers very similar data-serialization and RPC capabilities. In this book, I use it with Elephant Bird to support Thrift in MapReduce. Elephant Bird currently works with Thrift version 0.7.

Getting more information

Thrift documentation is lacking, something which the project page attests to. Table A.11 lists some useful resources to help you become more familiar with Thrift.

Table A.11 Useful resources

Resource	URL
Thrift project page	http://thrift.apache.org/
Blog post with a Thrift tutorial	http://bit.ly/vXpZ0z

Building Thrift 0.7

To build Thrift, download the 0.7 tarball and extract the contents. You may need to install some Thrift dependencies:

```
$ sudo yum  install automake libtool flex bison pkgconfig gcc-c++ \
  boost-devel libevent-devel zlib-devel python-devel \
  ruby-devel php53.x86_64 php53-devel.x86_64 openssl-devel
```

Build and install the native and Java/Python libraries and binaries:

```
$ ./configure
$ make
$ make check
$ sudo make install
```

Build the Java library. This step requires Ant to be installed, instructions for which are available in the Apache Ant Manual at http://ant.apache.org/manual/index.html:

```
$ cd lib/java
$ ant
```

Copy the Java JAR into Hadoop's lib directory. The following instructions are for CDH:

```
# replace the following path with your actual
# Hadoop installation directory
#
# the following is the CDH Hadoop home dir
#
export HADOOP_HOME=/usr/lib/hadoop

$ cp lib/java/libthrift.jar $HADOOP_HOME/lib/
```

A.12   Protocol Buffers

Protocol Buffers is Google's data serialization and Remote Procedure Call (RPC) library, which is used extensively at Google. In this book, we'll use it in conjunction with Elephant Bird and Rhipe. Elephant Bird requires version 2.3.0 of Protocol Buffers (and won't work with any other version), and Rhipe only works with Protocol Buffers version 2.4.0 and newer.

Getting more information

Table A.12 lists some useful resources to help you become more familiar with Protocol Buffers.

Table A.12   Useful resources

Resource	URL
Protocol Buffers project page	http://code.google.com/p/protobuf/
Protocol Buffers Developer Guide	https://developers.google.com/protocol-buffers/docs/overview?csw=1
Protocol Buffers downloads page, containing a link for version 2.3.0 (required for use with Elephant Bird)	http://code.google.com/p/protobuf/downloads/list

Building Protocol Buffers

To build Protocol Buffers, download the 2.3 or 2.4 (2.3 for Elephant Bird and 2.4 for Rhipe) source tarball from http://code.google.com/p/protobuf/downloads and extract the contents.

You'll need a C++ compiler, which can be installed on 64-bit RHEL systems with the following command:

```
sudo yum install gcc-c++.x86_64
```

Build and install the native libraries and binaries:

```
$ cd protobuf-<version>/
$ ./configure
$ make
$ make check
$ sudo make install
```

Build the Java library:

```
$ cd java
$ mvn package install
```

Copy the Java JAR into Hadoop's lib directory. The following instructions are for CDH:

```
# replace the following path with your actual
# Hadoop installation directory
#
# the following is the CDH Hadoop home dir
#
export HADOOP_HOME=/usr/lib/hadoop

$ cp target/protobuf-java-2.3.0.jar $HADOOP_HOME/lib/
```

A.13 Snappy

Snappy is a native compression codec developed by Google that offers fast compression and decompression times. It can't be split (as opposed to LZOP compression). In the book's code examples, which don't require splittable compression, we'll use Snappy because of its time efficiency.

Snappy is integrated into the Apache distribution of Hadoop since versions 1.0.2 and 2.

Getting more information

Table A.13 lists some useful resources to help you become more familiar with Snappy.

Table A.13 Useful resources

Resource	URL
Google's Snappy project page	http://code.google.com/p/snappy/
Snappy integration with Hadoop	http://code.google.com/p/hadoop-snappy/

A.14   *LZOP*

LZOP is a compression codec that can be used to support splittable compression in MapReduce. Chapter 4 has a section dedicated to working with LZOP. In this section we'll cover how to build and set up your cluster to work with LZOP.

Getting more information

Table A.14 shows a useful resource to help you become more familiar with LZOP.

Table A.14   Useful resource

Resource	URL
Hadoop LZO project maintained by Twitter	https://github.com/twitter/hadoop-lzo

Building LZOP

The following steps walk you through the process of configuring LZOP compression. Before you do this, there are a few things to consider:

- It's highly recommended that you build the libraries on the same hardware that you have deployed in production.
- All of the installation and configuration steps will need to be performed on any client hosts that will be using LZOP, as well as all the DataNodes in your cluster.
- These steps are for Apache Hadoop distributions. Please refer to distribution-specific instructions if you're using a different distribution.

Twitter's LZO project page has instructions on how to download dependencies and build the project. Follow the Building and Configuring section on the project home page.

Configuring Hadoop

You need to configure Hadoop core to be aware of your new compression codecs. Add the following lines to your core-site.xml. Make sure you remove the newlines and spaces so that there are no whitespace characters between the commas:

```
<property>
  <name>mapred.compress.map.output</name>
  <value>true</value>
</property>
<property>
  <name>mapred.map.output.compression.codec</name>
  <value>com.hadoop.compression.lzo.LzoCodec</value>
</property>
<property>
  <name>io.compression.codecs</name>
  <value>org.apache.hadoop.io.compress.GzipCodec,
  org.apache.hadoop.io.compress.DefaultCodec,
  org.apache.hadoop.io.compress.BZip2Codec,
  com.hadoop.compression.lzo.LzoCodec,
  com.hadoop.compression.lzo.LzopCodec,
```

```
    org.apache.hadoop.io.compress.SnappyCodec</value>
  </property>
  <property>
    <name>io.compression.codec.lzo.class</name>
    <value>com.hadoop.compression.lzo.LzoCodec</value>
  </property>
```

The value for `io.compression.codecs` assumes that you have the Snappy compression codec already installed. If you don't, remove `org.apache.hadoop.io.compress.SnappyCodec` from the value.

A.15 Elephant Bird

Elephant Bird is a project that provides utilities for working with LZOP-compressed data. It also provides a container format that supports working with Protocol Buffers and Thrift in MapReduce.

Getting more information

Table A.15 shows a useful resource to help you become more familiar with Elephant Bird.

Table A.15 Useful resource

Resource	URL
Elephant Bird project page	https://github.com/kevinweil/elephant-bird

At the time of writing, the current version of Elephant Bird (4.4) doesn't work with Hadoop 2 due the use of an incompatible version of Protocol Buffers. To get Elephant Bird to work in this book, I had to build a version of the project from the trunk that works with Hadoop 2 (as will 4.5 when it is released).

A.16 Hive

Hive is a SQL interface on top of Hadoop.

Getting more information

Table A.16 lists some useful resources to help you become more familiar with Hive.

Table A.16 Useful resources

Resource	URL
Hive project page	http://hive.apache.org/
Getting Started	https://cwiki.apache.org/confluence/display/Hive/GettingStarted

Installation

Follow the installation instructions in Hive's Getting Started guide.

A.17 R

R is an open source tool for statistical programming and graphics.

Getting more information

Table A.17 lists some useful resources to help you become more familiar with R.

Table A.17   Useful resources

Resource	URL
R project page	http://www.r-project.org/
R function search engine	http://rseek.org/

Installation on Red Hat–based systems

Installing R from Yum makes things easy: it will figure out RPM dependencies and install them for you.

Go to http://www.r-project.org/, click on CRAN, select a download region that's close to you, select Red Hat, and pick the version and architecture appropriate for your system. Replace the URL in `baseurl` in the following code and execute the command to add the R mirror repo to your Yum configuration:

```
$ sudo -s
$ cat << EOF > /etc/yum.repos.d/r.repo
# R-Statistical Computing
[R]
name=R-Statistics
baseurl=http://cran.mirrors.hoobly.com/bin/linux/redhat/el5/x86_64/
enabled=1
gpgcheck=0
EOF
```

A simple Yum command can be used to install R on 64-bit systems:

```
$ sudo yum install R.x86_64
```

> **Perl-File-Copy-Recursive RPM**   On CentOS, the Yum install may fail, complaining about a missing dependency. In this case, you may need to manually install the perl-File-Copy-Recursive RPM (for CentOS you can get it from http://mng.bz/n4C2).

Installation on non–Red Hat systems

Go to http://www.r-project.org/, click on CRAN, select a download region that's close to you, and select the appropriate binaries for your system.

A.18 RHadoop

RHadoop is an open source tool developed by Revolution Analytics for integrating R with MapReduce.

Getting more information

Table A.18 lists some useful resources to help you become more familiar with RHadoop.

Table A.18 Useful resources

Resource	URL
RHadoop project page	https://github.com/RevolutionAnalytics/RHadoop/wiki
RHadoop downloads and prerequisites	https://github.com/RevolutionAnalytics/RHadoop/wiki/Downloads

rmr/rhdfs installation

Each node in your Hadoop cluster will require the following components:

- R (installation instructions are in section A.17).
- A number of RHadoop and dependency packages

RHadoop requires that you set environment variables to point to the Hadoop binary and the streaming JAR. It's best to stash this in your .bash_profile (or equivalent).

```
$ export HADOOP_CMD=/usr/local/hadoop/bin/hadoop
$ export HADOOP_STREAMING=${HADOOP_HOME}/share/hadoop/tools/lib/
hadoop-streaming-<version>.jar
```

We'll focus on the rmr and rhdfs RHadoop packages, which provide MapReduce and HDFS integration with R. Click on the rmr and rhdfs download links on https://github.com/RevolutionAnalytics/RHadoop/wiki/Downloads. Then execute the following commands:

```
$ sudo -s
yum install -y libcurl-devel java-1.7.0-openjdk-devel
$ export HADOOP_CMD=/usr/bin/hadoop
$ R CMD javareconf
$ R
> install.packages( c('rJava'),
    repos='http://cran.revolutionanalytics.com')
> install.packages( c('RJSONIO', 'itertools', 'digest', 'Rcpp','httr',
    'functional','devtools', 'reshape2', 'plyr', 'caTools'),
    repos='http://cran.revolutionanalytics.com')

$ R CMD INSTALL  /media/psf/Home/Downloads/rhdfs_1.0.8.tar.gz
$ R CMD INSTALL  /media/psf/Home/Downloads/rmr2_3.1.1.tar.gz
$ R CMD INSTALL rmr_<version>.tar.gz
$ R CMD INSTALL rhdfs_<version>.tar.gz
```

If you get an error installing rJava, you may need to set JAVA_HOME and reconfigure R prior to running the rJava installation:

```
$ sudo -s
$ export JAVA_HOME=/usr/java/latest
$ R CMD javareconf
$ R
> install.packages("rJava")
```

Test that the rmr package was installed correctly by running the following command—if no error messages are generated, this means you have successfully installed the RHadoop packages.

```
$ R
> library(rmr2)
```

A.19 *Mahout*

Mahout is a predictive analytics project that offers both in-JVM and MapReduce implementations for some of its algorithms.

Getting more information

Table A.19 lists some useful resources to help you become more familiar with Mahout.

Table A.19 Useful resources

Resource	URL
Mahout project page	http://mahout.apache.org/
Mahout downloads	https://cwiki.apache.org/confluence/display/MAHOUT/Downloads

Installation

Mahout should be installed on a node that has access to your Hadoop cluster. Mahout is a client-side library and doesn't need to be installed on your Hadoop cluster.

BUILDING A MAHOUT DISTRIBUTION

To get Mahout working with Hadoop 2, I had to check out the code, modify the build file, and then build a distribution. The first step is to check out the code:

```
$ git clone https://github.com/apache/mahout.git
$ cd mahout
```

Next you need to modify pom.xml and remove the following section from the file:

```
<plugin>
<inherited>true</inherited>
<groupId>org.apache.maven.plugins</groupId>
<artifactId>maven-gpg-plugin</artifactId>
<version>1.4</version>
```

```
<executions>
  <execution>
    <goals>
      <goal>sign</goal>
    </goals>
  </execution>
</executions>
</plugin>
```

Finally, build a distribution:

```
$ mvn -Dhadoop2.version=2.2.0 -DskipTests -Prelease
```

This will generate a tarball located at distribution/target/mahout-distribution-1.0-SNAPSHOT.tar.gz, which you can install using the instructions in the next section.

INSTALLING MAHOUT

Mahout is packaged as a tarball. The following instructions will work on most Linux operating systems.

If you're installing an official Mahout release, click on the "official release" links on the Mahout download page and select the current release. If Mahout 1 hasn't yet been released and you want to use Mahout with Hadoop 2, follow the instructions in the previous section to generate the tarball.

Install Mahout using the following instructions:

```
$ cd /usr/local
$ sudo tar -xzf <path-to-mahout-tarball>

$ sudo ln -s mahout-distribution-<version> mahout

$ sudo chown -R <user>:<group> /usr/local/mahout*
```

For convenience, it's worthwhile updating your ~/.bash_profile to export a MAHOUT_HOME environment variable to your installation directory. The following command shows how this can be performed on the command line (the same command can be copied into your bash profile file):

```
$ export MAHOUT_HOME=/usr/local/mahout
```

index

RELATED MANNING TITLES

Java 8 in Action
Lambdas, streams, and functional-style programming
by Raoul-Gabriel Urma, Mario Fusco,
  and Alan Mycroft

ISBN: 9781617291999
424 pages, $49.99
August 2014

Functional Programming in Scala
by Paul Chiusano and Rúnar Bjarnason

ISBN: 9781617290657
320 pages, $44.99
August 2014

The Joy of Clojure, Second Edition
by Michael Fogus and Chris Houser

ISBN: 9781617291418
520 pages, $49.99
May 2014

Solr in Action
by Trey Grainger and Timothy Potter

ISBN: 9781617291029
664 pages, $49.99
March 2014

For ordering information go to www.manning.com